MW00491207

Risk Analysis

third edition

Risk Analysis

A quantitative guide

David Vose

third edition

John Wiley & Sons, Ltd

Copyright © 2008   David Vose

Published by   John Wiley & Sons, Ltd, The Atrium, Southern Gate, Chichester,
West Sussex, PO19 8SQ, England

Telephone +44 (0)1243 779777

Email (for orders and customer service enquiries): cs-books@wiley.co.uk
Visit our Home Page on www.wileyeurope.com or www.wiley.com

Reprinted with corrections September 2009

Other Wiley Editorial Offices

John Wiley & Sons Inc., 111 River Street, Hoboken, NJ 07030, USA

Jossey-Bass, 989 Market Street, San Francisco, CA 94103-1741, USA

Wiley-VCH Verlag GmbH, Boschstr. 12, D-69469 Weinheim, Germany

John Wiley & Sons Australia Ltd, 42 McDougall Street, Milton, Queensland 4064, Australia

John Wiley & Sons (Asia) Pte Ltd, 2 Clementi Loop #02-01, Jin Xing Distripark, Singapore 129809

John Wiley & Sons Canada Ltd, 6045 Freemont Blvd, Mississauga, Ontario, Canada, L5R 4J3

Wiley also publishes its books in a variety of electronic formats. Some content that appears
in print may not be available in electronic books.

Library of Congress Cataloging-in-Publication Data

Vose, David.
  Risk analysis : a quantitative guide / David Vose. – 3rd ed.
    p. cm.
  Includes bibliographical references and index.
  ISBN 978-0-470-51284-5 (cloth : alk. paper)
  1. Monte Carlo method. 2. Risk assessment–Mathematical models. I.
Title.
  QA298.V67 2008
  658.4′0352 – dc22

                                2007041696

British Library Cataloguing in Publication Data

A catalogue record for this book is available from the British Library

ISBN: 978-0-470-51284-5 (hbk)

Typeset in 10/12pt Times by Laserwords Private Limited, Chennai, India

Dedicated to my children

Sophie
Sébastien
Iria

With Love

Contents

Preface   **xiii**

Part 1   Introduction   **1**

1   Why do a risk analysis?   **3**
   1.1   Moving on from "What If" Scenarios   3
   1.2   The Risk Analysis Process   5
   1.3   Risk Management Options   7
   1.4   Evaluating Risk Management Options   10
   1.5   Inefficiencies in Transferring Risks to Others   11
   1.6   Risk Registers   13

2   Planning a risk analysis   **21**
   2.1   Questions and Motives   21
   2.2   Determine the Assumptions that are Acceptable or Required   22
   2.3   Time and Timing   23
   2.4   You'll Need a Good Risk Analyst or Team   23

3   The quality of a risk analysis   **29**
   3.1   The Reasons Why a Risk Analysis can be Terrible   29
   3.2   Communicating the Quality of Data Used in a Risk Analysis   31
   3.3   Level of Criticality   34
   3.4   The Biggest Uncertainty in a Risk Analysis   35
   3.5   Iterate   36

4   Choice of model structure   **37**
   4.1   Software Tools and the Models they Build   37
   4.2   Calculation Methods   42
   4.3   Uncertainty and Variability   47
   4.4   How Monte Carlo Simulation Works   57
   4.5   Simulation Modelling   63

5   Understanding and using the results of a risk analysis   **67**
   5.1   Writing a Risk Analysis Report   67
   5.2   Explaining a Model's Assumptions   69

| | 5.3 | Graphical Presentation of a Model's Results | 70 |
| | 5.4 | Statistical Methods of Analysing Results | 91 |

Part 2   Introduction   **109**

6   **Probability mathematics and simulation**   **115**
	6.1	Probability Distribution Equations	115
	6.2	The Definition of "Probability"	118
	6.3	Probability Rules	119
	6.4	Statistical Measures	137

7   **Building and running a model**   **145**
	7.1	Model Design and Scope	145
	7.2	Building Models that are Easy to Check and Modify	146
	7.3	Building Models that are Efficient	147
	7.4	Most Common Modelling Errors	159

8   **Some basic random processes**   **167**
	8.1	Introduction	167
	8.2	The Binomial Process	167
	8.3	The Poisson Process	176
	8.4	The Hypergeometric Process	183
	8.5	Central Limit Theorem	188
	8.6	Renewal Processes	190
	8.7	Mixture Distributions	193
	8.8	Martingales	194
	8.9	Miscellaneous Examples	194

9   **Data and statistics**   **207**
	9.1	Classical Statistics	208
	9.2	Bayesian Inference	215
	9.3	The Bootstrap	246
	9.4	Maximum Entropy Principle	254
	9.5	Which Technique Should You Use?	255
	9.6	Adding uncertainty in Simple Linear Least-Squares Regression Analysis	256

10 **Fitting distributions to data**   **263**
	10.1	Analysing the Properties of the Observed Data	264
	10.2	Fitting a Non-Parametric Distribution to the Observed Data	269
	10.3	Fitting a First-Order Parametric Distribution to Observed Data	281
	10.4	Fitting a Second-Order Parametric Distribution to Observed Data	297

11 **Sums of random variables**   **301**
| | 11.1 | The Basic Problem | 301 |
| | 11.2 | Aggregate Distributions | 305 |

12 Forecasting with uncertainty   **321**
    12.1 The Properties of a Time Series Forecast   322
    12.2 Common Financial Time Series Models   327
    12.3 Autoregressive Models   335
    12.4 Markov Chain Models   339
    12.5 Birth and Death Models   343
    12.6 Time Series Projection of Events Occurring Randomly in Time   345
    12.7 Time Series Models with Leading Indicators   348
    12.8 Comparing Forecasting Fits for Different Models   351
    12.9 Long-Term Forecasting   352

13 Modelling correlation and dependencies   **353**
    13.1 Introduction   353
    13.2 Rank Order Correlation   356
    13.3 Copulas   367
    13.4 The Envelope Method   380
    13.5 Multiple Correlation Using a Look-Up Table   391

14 Eliciting from expert opinion   **393**
    14.1 Introduction   393
    14.2 Sources of Error in Subjective Estimation   394
    14.3 Modelling Techniques   401
    14.4 Calibrating Subject Matter Experts   412
    14.5 Conducting a Brainstorming Session   414
    14.6 Conducting the Interview   416

15 Testing and modelling causal relationships   **423**
    15.1 *Campylobacter* Example   424
    15.2 Types of Model to Analyse Data   426
    15.3 From Risk Factors to Causes   427
    15.4 Evaluating Evidence   429
    15.5 The Limits of Causal Arguments   429
    15.6 An Example of a Qualitative Causal Analysis   430
    15.7 Is Causal Analysis Essential?   434

16 Optimisation in risk analysis   **435**
    16.1 Introduction   435
    16.2 Optimisation Methods   436
    16.3 Risk Analysis Modelling and Optimisation   439
    16.4 Working Example: Optimal Allocation of Mineral Pots   444

17 Checking and validating a model   **451**
    17.1 Spreadsheet Model Errors   451
    17.2 Checking Model Behaviour   456
    17.3 Comparing Predictions Against Reality   460

18 Discounted cashflow modelling **461**
18.1 Useful Time Series Models of Sales and Market Size 463
18.2 Summing Random Variables 466
18.3 Summing Variable Margins on Variable Revenues 467
18.4 Financial Measures in Risk Analysis 469

19 Project risk analysis **473**
19.1 Cost Risk Analysis 474
19.2 Schedule Risk Analysis 478
19.3 Portfolios of risks 486
19.4 Cascading Risks 487

20 Insurance and finance risk analysis modelling **493**
20.1 Operational Risk Modelling 493
20.2 Credit Risk 494
20.3 Credit Ratings and Markov Chain Models 499
20.4 Other Areas of Financial Risk 503
20.5 Measures of Risk 503
20.6 Term Life Insurance 506
20.7 Accident Insurance 509
20.8 Modelling a Correlated Insurance Portfolio 511
20.9 Modelling Extremes 512
20.10 Premium Calculations 513

21 Microbial food safety risk assessment **517**
21.1 Growth and Attenuation Models 519
21.2 Dose–Response Models 527
21.3 Is Monte Carlo Simulation the Right Approach? 532
21.4 Some Model Simplifications 533

22 Animal import risk assessment **537**
22.1 Testing for an Infected Animal 539
22.2 Estimating True Prevalence in a Population 544
22.3 Importing Problems 553
22.4 Confidence of Detecting an Infected Group 556
22.5 Miscellaneous Animal Health and Food Safety Problems 559

I Guide for lecturers **567**

II About ModelRisk **569**

III A compendium of distributions **585**
III.1 Discrete and Continuous Distributions 585
III.2 Bounded and Unbounded Distributions 586
III.3 Parametric and Non-Parametric Distributions 587
III.4 Univariate and Multivariate Distributions 588

III.5   Lists of Applications and the Most Useful Distributions   588
III.6   How to Read Probability Distribution Equations   593
III.7   The Distributions   599
III.8   Introduction to Creating Your Own Distributions   696
III.9   Approximation of One Distribution with Another   703
III.10 Recursive Formulae for Discrete Distributions   710
III.11 A Visual Observation On The Behaviour Of Distributions   713

IV   Further reading   **715**

V   Vose Consulting   **721**

References   **725**

Index   **729**

Preface

I'll try to keep it short.

This third edition is an almost complete rewrite. I have thrown out anything from the second edition that was really of pure academic interest – but that wasn't very much, and I had a lot of new topics I wanted to include, so this edition is quite a bit bigger. I apologise if you had to pay postage.

There are two main reasons why there is so much material to add since 2000. The first is that our consultancy firm has grown considerably, and, with the extra staff and talent, we have had the privilege of working on more ambitious and varied projects. We have particularly expanded in the insurance and finance markets, so you will see that a lot of techniques from those areas, which have far wider applications, appear throughout this edition. We have had contracts where we were given carte blanche to think up new ideas, and that really got the creative juices flowing. I have also been involved in writing and editing various risk analysis guidelines that made me think more about the disconnect between what risk analysts produce and what risk managers need. This edition is split into two parts in an attempt to help remedy that problem.

The second reason is that we have built a really great software team, and the freedom to design our own tools has been a double espresso for our collective imagination. We now build a lot of bespoke risk analysis applications for clients and have our own commercial software products. It has been enormous fun starting off with a typical risk-based problem, researching techniques that would solve that problem if only they were easy to use and then working out how to make that happen. ModelRisk is the result, and we have a few others in the pipeline.

Some thank yous ...

I have imposed a lot on Veerle and our children to get this book done. V has spent plenty of evenings without me while I typed away in my office, but I think she suffered much more living with a guy who was perpetually distracted by what he was going to write next. Sophie and Sébastien have also missed out. Papa always seemed to be working instead of playing with them. Worse, perhaps, it didn't stop raining all summer in Belgium, and they had to forego a holiday in the sun so I could finish writing. I'll make it up to all three of you, I promise.

I have the luxury of having some really smart and motivated people working with me. I have leaned rather heavily on the partners and staff in our consultancy firm while I focused on this book, particularly on Huybert Groenendaal who has largely run the company in my "absence". He also wrote Appendix 5. Timour Koupeev heads our programming team and has been infinitely patient in converting my never-ending ideas for our ModelRisk software into reality. He also wrote Appendix 2. Murat Tomaev, our head programmer, has made it all work together. Getting new modules for me to look at always feels a little like Christmas.

My secretary, Jane Pooley, retired from the company this year. She was the first person with enough faith to risk working for me, and I couldn't have wished for a better start.

Wouter Smet and Michael van Hauwermeiren in our Belgian office have been a great support, going through the manuscript and models for this book. Michael wrote the enormous Appendix 3, which could be a book in its own right, and Wouter offered many suggestions for improving the English, which is embarrassing considering it's his third language.

Francisco Zagmutt wrote Chapter 16 while under pressure to finish his thesis for his *second* doctorate and being a full-time, jumping-on-airplanes, deadline-chasing senior consultant in our US office.

When Wiley sent me copies of the first edition, the first thing I did was go over to my parents' house and give them a copy. I did the same with the second edition, and the Japanese version too. They are all proudly displayed in the sitting room. I will be doing the same with this book. There's little that can beat knowing my parents are proud of me, as I am of them. Mum still plays tennis, rides and competes in target shooting. Dad is still a great golfer and neither ever seems to stop working on their house, unless they're off to a party. They are a constant reminder to make the most of life.

Paul Curtis copy-edited the manuscript with great diligence and diplomacy. I'd love to know how he spotted inconsistencies and repetitions in parts of the text that were a hundred or more pages apart. Any remaining errors are all my fault.

Finally, have you ever watched those TV programmes where some guy with a long beard is teaching you how to paint in thirty minutes? I did once. He didn't have a landscape in front of him, so he just started painting what he felt like: a lake, then some hills, the sky, trees. He built up his painting, and after about 20 minutes I thought – yes, that's finished. Then he added reflections, some snow, a bush or two in the foreground. Each time I thought – yes, *now* it's finished. That's the problem with writing a book (or software) – there's always something more to add or change or rewrite. So I have rather exceeded my deadline, and certainly the page estimate, and my thanks go to my editor at Wiley, Emma Cooper, for her gentle pushing, encouragement and flexibility.

Part 1

Introduction

The first part of this book is focused on helping those who have to make decisions in the face of risk. The second part of the book focuses on modelling techniques and has all the mathematics. The purpose of Part 1 is to help a manager understand what a risk analysis is and how it can help in decision-making. I offer some thoughts on how to build a risk analysis team, how to evaluate the quality of the analysis and how to ask the right questions so you get the most useful answers.

This section should also be of use to analysts because they need to understand the managers' viewpoint and work towards the same goal.

Chapter 1

Why do a risk analysis?

In business and government one faces having to make decisions all the time where the outcome is uncertain. Understanding the uncertainty can help us make a much better decision. Imagine that you are a national healthcare provider considering which of two vaccines to purchase. The two vaccines have the same reported level of efficacy (67%), but further study reveals that there is a difference in confidence attached to these two performance measures: one is twice as uncertain as the other (see Figure 1.1).

All else being equal, the healthcare provider would purchase the vaccine with the smallest uncertainty about its performance (vaccine A). Replace vaccine with investment and efficacy with profit and we have a problem in business, for which the answer is the same – pick the investment with the smallest uncertainty, all else being equal (investment A). The principal problem is determining that uncertainty, which is the central focus of this book.

We can think of two forms of uncertainty that we have to deal with in risk analysis. The first is a general sense that the quantity we are trying to estimate has some uncertainty attached to it. This is usually described by a distribution like the ones in Figure 1.1. Then we have risk events, which are random events that may or may not occur and for which there is some impact of interest to us. We can distinguish between two types of event:

- A *risk* is a random event that may possibly occur and, if it did occur, would have a *negative* impact on the goals of the organisation. Thus, a risk is composed of three elements: the scenario; its probability of occurrence; and the size of its impact if it did occur (either a fixed value or a distribution).

- An *opportunity* is also a random event that may possibly occur but, if it did occur, would have a *positive* impact on the goals of the organisation. Thus, an opportunity is composed of the same three elements as a risk.

A risk and an opportunity can be considered the opposite sides of the same coin. It is usually easiest to consider a potential event to be a *risk* if it would have a negative impact and its probability is less than 50%, and, if the risk has a probability in excess of 50%, to include it in a base plan and then consider the *opportunity* of it not occurring.

1.1 Moving on from "What If" Scenarios

Single-point or deterministic modelling involves using a single "best-guess" estimate of each variable within a model to determine the model's outcome(s). Sensitivities are then performed on the model to determine how much that outcome might in reality vary from the model outcome. This is achieved by selecting various combinations for each input variable. These various combinations of possible values

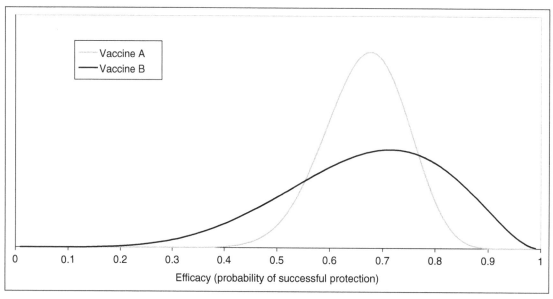

Legend:
- Vaccine A
- Vaccine B

Efficacy (probability of successful protection)

0   0.1   0.2   0.3   0.4   0.5   0.6   0.7   0.8   0.9   1

Figure 1.1 Efficacy comparison for two vaccines: the vertical axis represents how confident we are about the true level of efficacy. I've omitted the scale to avoid some confusion at this stage (see Section III.1.2).

around the "best guess" are commonly known as "what if" scenarios. The model is often also "stressed" by putting in values that represent worst-case scenarios.

Consider a simple problem that is just the sum of five cost items. We can use the three points, minimum, best guess and maximum, as values to use in a "what if" analysis. Since there are five cost items and three values per item, there are $3^5 = 243$ possible "what if" combinations we could produce. Clearly, this is too large a set of scenarios to have any practical use. This process suffers from two other important drawbacks: only three values are being used for each variable, where they could, in fact, take any number of values; and no recognition is being given to the fact that the best-guess value is much more likely to occur than the minimum and maximum values. We can stress the model by adding up the minimum costs to find the best-case scenario, and add up the maximum costs to get the worst-case scenario, but in doing so the range is usually unrealistically large and offers no real insight. The exception is when the worst-case scenario is still acceptable.

Quantitative risk analysis (QRA) using Monte Carlo simulation (the dominant modelling technique in this book) is similar to "what if" scenarios in that it generates a number of possible scenarios. However, it goes one step further by effectively accounting for every possible value that each variable could take *and* weighting each possible scenario by the probability of its occurrence. QRA achieves this by modelling each variable within a model by a probability distribution. The structure of a QRA model is *usually* (there are some important exceptions) very similar to a deterministic model, with all the multiplications, additions, etc., that link the variables together, except that each variable is represented by a probability distribution function instead of a single value. The objective of a QRA is to calculate the combined impact of the uncertainty[1] in the model's parameters in order to determine an uncertainty distribution of the possible model outcomes.

---

[1] I discuss the exact meaning of "uncertainty", randomness, etc., in Chapter 4.

1.2 The Risk Analysis Process

Figure 1.2 shows a typical flow of activities in a risk analysis, leading from problem formulation to decision. This section and those that follow provide more detail on each activity.

1.2.1 Identifying the risks

Risk identification is the first step in a complete risk analysis, given that the objectives of the decision-maker have been well defined. There are a number of techniques used to help formalise the identification of risks. This part of a formal risk analysis will often prove to be the most informative and constructive element of the whole process, improving company culture by encouraging greater team effort and reducing blame, and should be executed with care. The organisations participating in a formal risk analysis should take pains to create an open and blameless environment in which expressions of concern and doubt can be openly given.

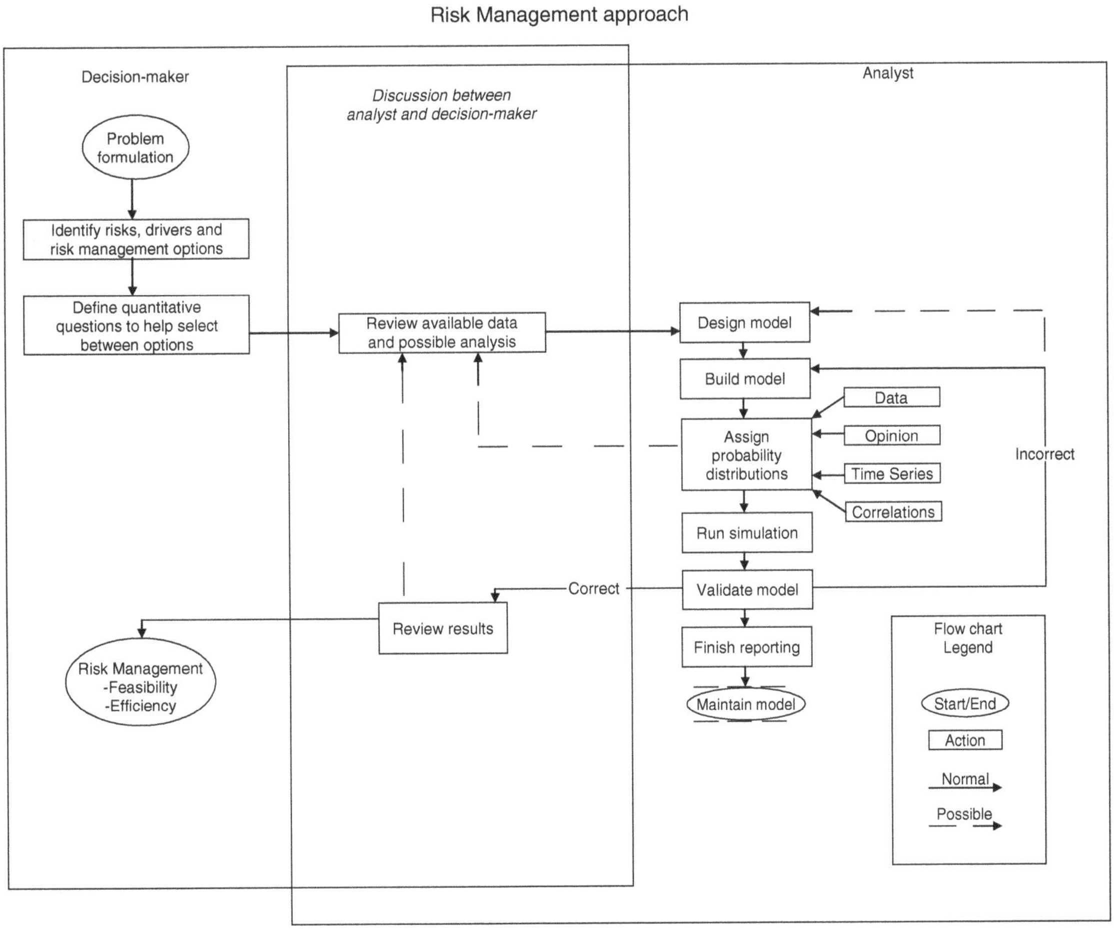

Risk Management approach

Figure 1.2   The risk analysis process.

Prompt lists

Prompt lists provide a set of categories of risk that are pertinent to the type of project under consideration or the type of risk being considered by an organisation. The lists are used to help people think about and identify risks. Sometimes different types of list are used together to improve further the chance of identifying all of the important risks that may occur. For example, in analysing the risks to some project, one prompt list might look at various aspects of the project (e.g. legal, commercial, technical, etc.) or types of task involved in the project (design, construction, testing). A project plan and a work breakdown structure, with all of the major tasks defined, are natural prompt lists. In analysing the reliability of some manufacturing plant, a list of different types of failure (mechanical, electrical, electronic, human, etc.) or a list of the machines or processes involved could be used. One could also cross-check with a plan of the site or a flow diagram of the manufacturing process. Check lists can be used at the same time: these are a series of questions one asks as a result of experience of previous problems or opportune events.

A prompt list will never be exhaustive but acts as a focus of attention in the identification of risks. Whether a risk falls into one category or another is not important, only that the risk is identified. The following list provides an example of a fairly general project prompt list. There will often be a number of subsections for each category:

- administration;
- project acceptance;
- commercial;
- communication;
- environmental;
- financial;
- knowledge and information;
- legal;
- management;
- partner;
- political;
- quality;
- resources;
- strategic;
- subcontractor;
- technical.

The identified risks can then be stored in a risk register described in Section 1.6.

1.2.2 Modelling the risk problem and making appropriate decisions

This book is concerned with the modelling of identified risks and how to make decisions from those models. In this book I try not to offer too many modelling rules. Instead, I have focused on techniques that I hope readers will be able to put together as necessary to produce a good model of their problem. However, there are a few basic principles that are worth adhering to. Morgan and Henrion (1990) offer the following excellent "ten commandments" in relation to quantitative risk and policy analysis:

1. Do your homework with literature, experts and users.
2. Let the problem drive the analysis.
3. Make the analysis as simple as possible, but no simpler.
4. Identify all significant assumptions.
5. Be explicit about decision criteria and policy strategies.
6. Be explicit about uncertainties.
7. Perform systematic sensitivity and uncertainty analysis.
8. Iteratively refine the problem statement and the analysis.
9. Document clearly and completely.
10. Expose to peer review.

The responses to correctly identified and evaluated risks are many, but generally fall into the following categories:

- Increase (the project plan may be overly cautious).
- Do nothing (because it would cost too much or there is nothing that can be done).
- Collect more data (to better understand the risk).
- Add a contingency (extra amount to budget, deadline, etc., to allow for possibility of risk).
- Reduce (e.g. build in redundancy, take a less risky approach).
- Share (e.g. with partner, contractor, providing they can reasonably handle the impact).
- Transfer (e.g. insure, back-to-back contract).
- Eliminate (e.g. do it another way).
- Cancel project.

This list can be helpful in thinking of possible responses to identified risks. It should be borne in mind that these risk responses might in turn carry *secondary risks*. *Fall-back plans* should be developed to deal with risks that are identified and not eliminated. If done well in advance, they can help the organisation react efficiently, calmly and in unison in a situation where blame and havoc might normally reign.

1.3 Risk Management Options

The purpose of risk analysis is to help managers better understand the risks (and opportunities) they face and to evaluate the options available for their control. In general, risk management options can be divided into several groups.

Acceptance (Do nothing)

Nothing is done to control the risk or one's exposure to that risk. Appropriate for risks where the cost of control is out of proportion with the risk. It is usually appropriate for low-probability, low-impact risks and opportunities, of which one normally has a vast list, but you may be missing some high-value risk mitigation or avoidance options, especially where they control several risks at once. If the chosen response is *acceptance*, some considerable thought should be given to risk *contingency planning*.

Increase

You may find that you are already spending considerable resources to manage a risk that is excessive compared with the level of protection that it affords you. In such cases, it is logical to reduce the level of protection and allocate the resources to manage other risks, thereby achieving a superior overall risk efficiency. Examples are:

- remove a costly safety regulation for nuclear power plants that affects a risk that would otherwise still be miniscule;
- cease the requirement to test all slaughtered cows for BSE and use saved money for hospital upgrades.

   It may be logical but nonetheless politically unacceptable. There are not too many politicians or CEOs who want to explain to the public that they've just authorised less caution in handling a risk.

Get more information

A risk analysis can describe the level of uncertainty there is about the decision problem (here we use uncertainty as distinct from inherent randomness). Uncertainty can often be reduced by acquiring more information (whereas randomness cannot). Thus, a decision-maker can determine that there is too much uncertainty to make a robust decision and request that more information be collected. Using a risk analysis model, the risk analyst can advise the least-cost method of collecting extra data that would be needed to achieve the required level of precision. Value-of-information arguments (see Section 5.4.5) can be used to assess how much, if any, extra information should be collected.

Avoidance (Elimination)

This involves changing a method of operation, a project plan, an investment strategy, etc., so that the identified risk is no longer relevant. Avoidance is usually employed for high-probability, high-impact type risks. Examples are:

- use a tried and tested technology instead of the new one that was originally envisaged;
- change the country location of a factory to avoid political instability;
- scrap the project altogether.

   Note that there may be a very real chance of introducing new (and perhaps much more important) risks by changing your plans.

Reduction (Mitigation)

Reduction involves a range of techniques, which may be used together, to reduce the probability of the risk, its impact or both. Examples are:

- build in redundancy (standby equipment, back-up computer at different location);
- perform more quality tests or inspections;
- provide better training to personnel;
- spread risk over several areas (portfolio effect).

   Reduction strategies are used for any level of risk where the remaining risk is not of very high severity (very high probability and impact) and where the benefits (amount by which risk is reduced) outweigh the reduction costs.

Contingency planning

These are plans devised to optimise the response to risks should they occur. They can be used in conjunction with acceptance and reduction strategies. A contingency plan should identify individuals who take responsibility for monitoring the occurrence of the risk, and/or identified risk drivers for changes in the risk's probability or possible impact. The plan should identify what to do, who should do it and in which order, the window of opportunity, etc. Examples are:

- have a trained firefighting team on site;
- have a prepared press release;
- have a visible phone list (or email distribution list) of whom to contact if the risk occurs;
- reduce police and emergency service leave during a strike;
- fit lifeboats on ships.

Risk reserve

Management's response to an identified risk is to add some reserve (buffer) to cover the risk should it occur. Appropriate for small to medium impact risks. Examples are:

- allocate extra funds to a project;
- allocate extra time to complete a project;
- have cash reserves;
- have extra stock in shops for a holiday weekend;
- stockpile medical and food supplies.

Insurance

Essentially, this is a risk reduction strategy, but it is so common that it is worth mentioning separately. If an insurance company has done its numbers correctly, in a competitive market you will pay a little above the expected cost of the risk (i.e. probability $*$ expected impact should the risk occur). In general, we therefore insure for risks that have an impact outside our comfort zone (i.e. where we value the risk higher than its expected value). Alternatively, you may feel that your exposure is higher than the average policy purchaser, in which case insurance may be under your expected cost and therefore extremely attractive.

Risk transfer

This involves manipulating the problem so that the risk is transferred from one party to another. A common method of transferring risk is through contracts, where some form of penalty is included into a contractor's performance. The idea is appealing and used often but can be very inefficient. Examples are:

- penalty clause for running over agreed schedule;
- performance guarantee of product;
- lease a maintained building from the builder instead of purchasing;
- purchase an advertising campaign from some media body or advertising agency with payment contingent on some agreed measure of success.

You can also consider transferring risks to you, where there is some advantage to relieving another party of a risk. For example, if you can guarantee a second party against some small risk resultant from an activity you wish to take that provides you with much greater benefit than the other party's risk, the second party may remove its objection to your proposed activity.

1.4 Evaluating Risk Management Options

The manager evaluating the possible options for dealing with a defined risk issue needs to consider many things:

- Is the risk assessment of sufficient quality to be relied upon?
- How sensitive is the ranking of each option to model uncertainties?
- What are the benefits relative to the costs associated with each risk management option?
- Are there any secondary risks associated with a chosen risk management option?
- How practical will it be to execute the risk management option?
- Is the risk assessment of sufficient quality to be relied upon? (See Chapter 3.)
- How sensitive is the ranking of each option to model uncertainties?

On this last point, we almost always would like to have better data, or greater certainty about the form of the problem: we would like the distribution of what will happen in the future to be as narrow as possible. However, a decision-maker cannot wait indefinitely for better data and, from a decision-analytic point of view, may quickly reach the point where the best option has been determined and no

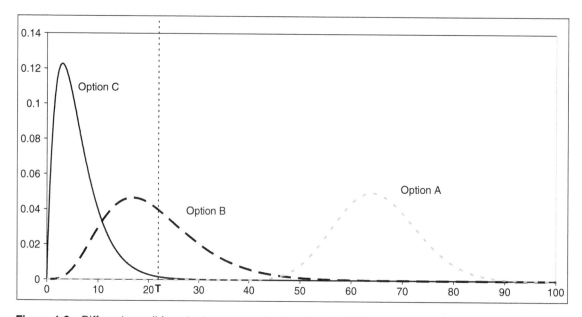

Figure 1.3 Different possible outputs compared with a threshold T.

further data (or perhaps only a very dramatic change in knowledge of the problem) will make another option preferable. This concept is known as decision sensitivity. For example, in Figure 1.3 the decision-maker considers any output below a threshold T (shown with a dashed line) to be perfectly acceptable (perhaps this is a regulatory threshold or a budget). The decision-maker would consider option A to be completely unacceptable and option C to be perfectly fine, and would only need more information about option B to be sure whether it was acceptable or not, in spite of all three having considerable uncertainty.

1.5 Inefficiencies in Transferring Risks to Others

A common method of managing risks is to force or persuade another party to accept the risk on your behalf. For example, an oil company could require that a subcontractor welding a pipeline accept the costs to the oil company resulting from any delays they incur or any poor workmanship. The welding company will, in all likelihood, be far smaller than the oil company, so possible penalty payments would be catastrophic. The welding company will therefore value the risk as very high and will require a premium greatly in excess of the expected value of the risk. On the other hand, the oil company may be able to absorb the risk impact relatively easily, so would not value the risk as highly. The difference in the utility of these two companies is shown in Figures 1.4 to 1.7, which demonstrate that the oil company will pay an excessive amount to eliminate the risk.

A far more realistic approach to sharing risks is through a partnership arrangement. A list of risks that may impact on various parties involved in the project is drawn up, and for each risk one then asks:

- How big is the risk?
- What are the risk drivers?
- Who is in control of the risk drivers? Who has the experience to control them?
- Who could absorb the risk impacts?
- How can we work together to manage the risks?

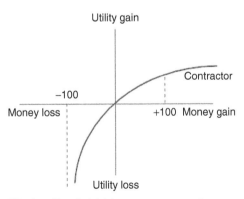

Figure 1.4 The contractor's utility function is highly concave over the money gain/loss range in question. That means, for example, that the contractor would value a loss of 100 units of money (e.g. $100 000) as a vastly larger loss in absolute utility terms than a gain of $100 000 might be.

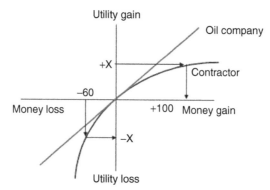

Figure 1.5 Over that same money gain/loss range, the oil company has an almost exactly linear utility function. The contractor, required to take on a risk with an expected value of −$60 000, would value this as − X utiles. To compensate, the contractor would have to charge an additional amount well in excess of $100 000. The oil company, on the other hand, would value −$60 000 in rough balance with +$60 000, so will be paying considerably in excess of its valuation of the risk to transfer it to the contractor.

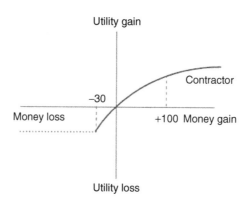

Figure 1.6 Imagine the risk has a 10 % probability of occurring, and its impact would be −$300 000, to give an expected value of −$30 000. If $300 000 is the total capital value of the contractor, it won't much matter to the contractor whether the risk impact is $300 000 or $3 000 000 – they still go bust. This is shown by the shortened utility curve and the horizontal dashed line for the contractor.

- What arrangement would efficiently allocate the risk impacts and rewards for good risk management?
- Can we insure, etc., to share risks with outsiders?

The more one can allocate ownership of risks, and opportunities, to those who control them the better – up to the point where the owner could not reasonably bear the risk impact where others can. Answering the questions above will help you construct a contractual arrangement that is risk efficient, workable and tolerable to all parties.

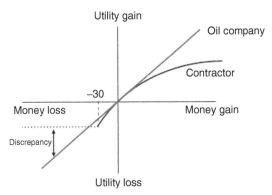

Figure 1.7 In this situation, the contractor now values any risk with an impact that exceeds its capital value at a level that is less than the oil company (shown as "Discrepancy"). It may mean that the contractor can offer a more competitive bid than another, larger contractor who would feel the full risk impact, but the oil company will not have covered the risk it had hoped to transfer, and so again will be paying more than it should to offload the risk. Of course, one way to avoid this problem is to require evidence from the contractor that they have the necessary insurance or capital base to cover the risk they are being asked to absorb.

1.6 Risk Registers

A risk register is a document or database that lists each risk pertaining to a project or organisation, along with a variety of information that is useful for the management of those risks. The risks listed in a risk register will have come from some collective exercise to identify risks. The following items are essential in any risk register entry:

- date the register was last modified;
- name of risk;
- description of what the risk is;
- description of why it would occur;
- description of factors that would increase or decrease its probability of occurrence or size of impact (risk drivers);
- semi-quantitative estimates of its probability and potential impact;
- $P-I$ scores;
- name of owner of the risk (the person who will assume responsibility for monitoring the risk and effecting any risk reduction strategies that have been agreed);
- details of risk reduction strategies that it is agreed will be taken (i.e. strategy that will reduce the impact on the project should the risk event occur and/or the probability of its occurrence);
- reduced impact and/or probability of the risk, given the above agreed risk reduction strategies have been taken;

- ranking of risk by scores of the reduced $P-I$;
- cross-referencing the risk event to identification numbers of tasks in a project plan or areas of operation or regulation where the risk may impact;
- description of secondary risks that may arise as a result of adopting the risk reduction strategies;
- action window – the period during which risk reduction strategies must be put in place.

The following items may also be useful to include:

- description of other optional risk reduction strategies;
- ranking of risks by the possible effectiveness of further risk mitigation [effectiveness = (total decrease in risk)/(cost of risk mitigation action)];
- fall-back plan in the event the risk event still occurs;
- name of the person who first identified the risk;
- date the risk was first identified;
- date the risk was removed from the list of active risks (if appropriate).

A risk register should include a description of the scale used in the semi-quantitative analysis, as explained in the section on $P-I$ scores. A risk register should also have a summary that lists the top risks (ten is a fairly usual number but will vary according to the project or overview level). The "top" risks are those that have the highest combination of probability and impact (i.e. severity), after the reducing effects of any agreed risk reduction strategies have been included. Risk registers lend themselves perfectly to being stored in a networked database. In this way, risks from each project or regulatory body's concerns, for example, can be added to a common database. Then, a project manager can access that database to look at all risks to his or her project. The finance director, lawyer, etc., can look at all the risks from any project being managed by their departments and the chief executive can look at the major risks to the organisation as a whole. What is more, head office has an easy means for assessing the threat posed by a risk that may impact on several projects or areas at the same time. "Dashboard" software can bring the outputs of a risk register into appropriate focus for the decision-makers.

1.6.1 $P-I$ tables

The risk identification stage attempts to identify all risks threatening the achievement of the project's or organisation's goals. It is clearly important, however, that attention is focused on those risks that pose the greatest threat.

Defining qualitative risk descriptions

A qualitative assessment of the probability P of a risk event (a possible event that would produce a negative impact on the project or organisation) and the impact(s) it would produce, I, can be made by assigning descriptions to the magnitudes of these probabilities and impacts. The assessor is asked to describe the probability and impact of each risk, selecting from a predetermined set of phrases such as: nil, very low, low, medium, high and very high. A range of values is assigned to each phrase in order to maintain consistency between the estimates of each risk. An example of the value range that might be given to each phrase in a risk register for a particular project is shown in Table 1.1.

Note that in Table 1.1 the value ranges are not evenly spaced. Ideally there is a multiple difference between each range (in this case roughly 3). If the same multiple is applied for probability and impact

Table 1.1 An example of the value ranges that could be associated with qualitative descriptions of the probabilities and impacts of a risk on a project.

Category	Probability (%)	Delay (days)	Cost ($k)	Quality
Very high	10–50	>100	>1000	Failure to meet acceptance criteria
High	5–10	30–100	30–100	Failure to meet > 1 important specification
Medium	2–5	10–30	100–300	Failure to meet an important specification
Low	1–2	2–10	20–100	Failure to meet > 1 minor specification
Very low	<1	<2	<20	Failure to meet a minor specification

Table 1.2 An example of the descriptions that could be associated with impacts of a risk on a corporation.

Category	Description
Catastrophic	Jeopardises the existence of the company
Major	No longer possible to achieve business objectives
Moderate	Reduced ability to achieve business objectives
Minor	Some business disruptions but little effect on business objectives
Insignificant	No impact on business strategy objectives

scales, we can more easily determine severity scores as described below. The value ranges can be selected to match the size of the project. Alternatively, they can be matched to the effect the risks would have on the organisation as a whole. The drawback in making the definition of each phrase specific to a project is that it becomes very difficult to perform a combined analysis of the risks from all projects in which the organisation is involved. From a corporate perspective one can describe how a risk affects the health of a company, as shown in Table 1.2.

Visualising a portfolio of risks

A $P-I$ table offers a quick way to visualise the relative importance of all identified risks that pertain to a project (or organisation). Table 1.3 illustrates an example. All risks are plotted on the one table, allowing easy identification of the most threatening risks as well as providing a general picture of the overall riskiness of the project. Risk numbers 13, 2, 12 and 15 are the most threatening in this example.

The impact of a project risk that is most commonly considered is a delay in the scheduled completion of the project. However, an analysis may also consider the increased cost of the project resulting from

Table 1.3 Example of a $P-1$ table for schedule delay.

Impact	Profit impact for identified risks				
		V Low	Low	Med	High	V High
V High			6			13,2
High					15	12
Med		5		5	1	
Low						
V Low		11	7	3		
		V Low	Low	Med	High	V High
		Probability				

Table 1.4 *P–I* table for a specific risk.

	V High				
	High				*T*
	Med				$
	Low				
	V Low		*Q*		
		V Low	Low	Med	High	V High

Impact for Risk # 15 — Impact / Probability

each risk. It might further consider other, less numerically definable impacts on the project, for example: the quality of the final product; the goodwill that could be lost; sociological impacts; political damage; or strategic importance of the project to the organisation. A *P–I* table can be constructed for each type of impact, enabling the decision-maker to gain a more rounded understanding of a project's riskiness.

P–I tables can be constructed for the various types of impact of each single risk. Table 1.4 illustrates an example where the impacts of schedule delay, *T*, cost, $, and product quality, *Q*, are shown for a specific risk. The probability of each impact may not be the same. In this example, the probability of the risk event occurring is high, and hence the probability of schedule delay and cost impacts are high, but it is considered that, even if this risk event does occur, the probability of a quality impact is still low. In other words, there is a fairly small probability of a quality impact even when the risk event does occur.

Ranking risks

P–I scores can be used to rank the identified risks. A scaling factor, or weighting, is assigned to each phrase used to describe each type of impact. Table 1.5 provides an example of the type of scaling factors that could be associated with each phrase/impact type combination.

In this type of scoring system, the higher the score, the greater is the risk. A base measure of risk is probability * impact. The categorising system in Table 1.1 is on a log scale, so, to make Table 1.5 consistent, we can define the severity of a risk with a single type of impact as

$$S = P + I$$

which leaves the severity on a log scale too. If a risk has k possible types of impact (quality, delay, cost, reputation, environmental, etc.), perhaps with different probabilities for each impact type, we can

Table 1.5 An example of the scores that could be associated with descriptive risk categories to produce a severity score.

Category	Score
Very high	5
High	4
Medium	3
Low	2
Very low	1

Table 1.6   Segregation of risks into levels of severity.

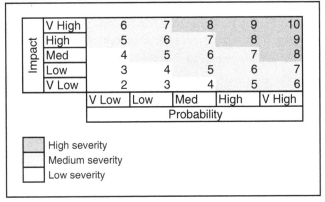

		V Low	Low	Med	High	V High
Impact	V High	6	7	8	9	10
	High	5	6	7	8	9
	Med	4	5	6	7	8
	Low	3	4	5	6	7
	V Low	2	3	4	5	6
		V Low	Low	Med	High	V High
				Probability		

☐ High severity
☐ Medium severity
☐ Low severity

still combine them into one score as follows:

$$S = \log 10 \left[\sum_{i=1}^{k} 10^{P_i + I_i} \right]$$

The severity scores are then used to determine the most important risks, enabling the management to focus resources on reducing or eliminating risks from the project in a rational and efficient manner. A drawback to this approach of ranking risks is that the process is quite dependent on the granularity of the scaling factors that are assigned to each phrase describing the risk impacts. If we have better information on probability or impact than the scoring system would allow, we can assign a more accurate (non-integer) score.

In the scoring regime of Table 1.5, for example, a high severe risk could be defined as having a score higher than 7, and a low risk as having a score lower than 5. Given the crude scaling used, risks with a severity of 7 may require further investigation to determine whether they should be categorised as high severity. Table 1.6 shows how this segregates the risks shown in a $P-I$ table into the three regions.

$P-I$ scores for a project provide a consistent measure of risk that can be used to define metrics and perform trend analyses. For example, the distribution of severity scores for a project gives an indication of the overall "amount" of risk exposure. More complex metrics can be derived using severity scores, allowing risk exposure to be normalised and compared with a baseline status. These permit trends in risk exposure to be identified and monitored, giving valuable information to those responsible for controlling the project.

Efficient risk management with severity scores

Efficient risk management seeks to achieve the maximum reduction in risk for a given amount of investment (of people, time, money, restriction of liberty, etc.). Thus, we need to evaluate in some sense the ratio (reduction in risk)/(investment to achieve reduction). If you use the log scale for severity described here, this would equate to calculating

$$\text{Efficiency} = \left(\sum_i 10^{S_{\text{new}}(i)} - \sum_i 10^{S_{\text{old}}(i)} \right) \Big/ \text{investment}$$

The risk management options that provide the greatest efficiency should logically be preferred, all else being equal.

Inherent risks are the risk estimates before accounting for any mitigation efforts. They can be plotted against a guiding risk response framework where the $P-I$ table is split, covered by overlapping areas of avoid, control, transfer and accept, as shown in Figure 1.8:

- "Avoid" applies where an organisation would be accepting a high-probability, high-impact risk without any compensating benefits.
- "Control" applies usually to high-probability, low-impact risks, normally associated with repetitive actions, and therefore usually managed through better internal processes.
- "Transfer" applies to low-probability, high-impact risks usually managed through insurance or other means of transferring the risk to parties better capable of absorbing the impact.
- "Accept" applies to the remaining low-probability, low-impact risks for which it may not be effective to focus on too much.

Figure 1.9 plots residual risks after any implemented risk mitigation strategies and tracks the progress in managing the residual risks compared with the previous year using arrows. Grey letters represent the status of the risk last year if it is different. A dashed arrow pointing out of the graph means that the risk

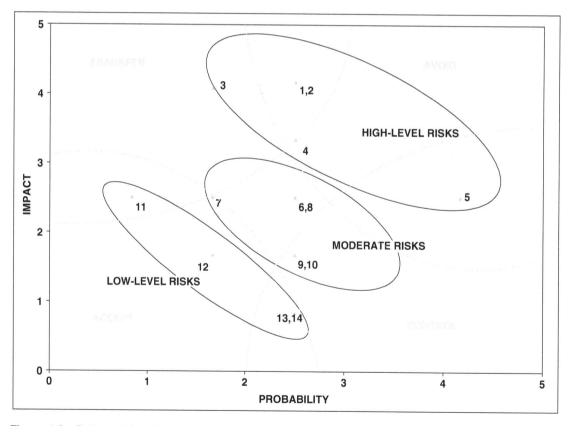

Figure 1.8 *P–I* graph for inherent risks.

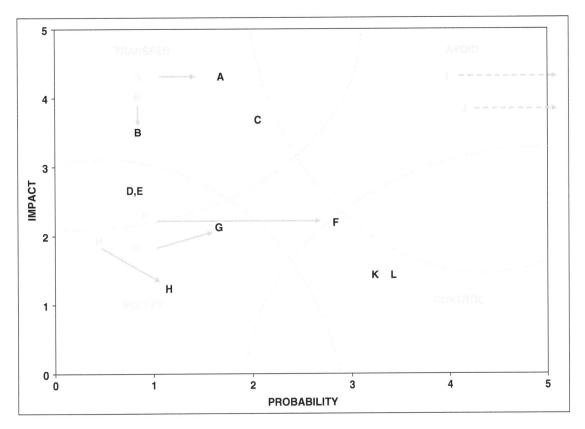

Figure 1.9 *P–I* graph for residual risks.

has been avoided. An enhancement to the residual risk graph that you might like to add is to plot each risk as a circle whose radius reflects how comfortable you are in dealing with the residual risk – for example, perhaps you have handled the occurrence of similar risks before and minimised their impact through good management, or perhaps they got out of hand. A small circle represents risks that one is comfortable managing, and a large circle represents the opposite, so the less manageable risks stand out in the plot.

Chapter 2

Planning a risk analysis

In order to plan a risk analysis properly, you'll need to answer a few questions:

- What do you want to know and why?
- What assumptions are acceptable?
- What is the timing?
- Who is going to do the risk analysis?

I'll go through each of these in turn.

2.1 Questions and Motives

The purpose of a risk analysis is to provide information to help make better decisions in an uncertain world. A decision-maker has to work with the risk analyst precisely to define the questions that need answering. You should consider a number of things:

1. *Rank the questions that need answering from "critical" down to "interesting".* Often a single model cannot answer all questions, or has to be built in a complicated way to answer several questions, so a common recognition of the extra effort needed to answer each question going down the list helps determine a cut-off point.

2. *Discuss with the risk analyst the form of the answer.* For example, if you want to know how much extra revenue might be made by buying rather than leasing a vessel, you'll need to specify a currency, whether this should be as a percentage or in actual currency and whether you want just the mean (which can make the modelling a *lot* easier) or a graph of the distribution. Explain what statistics you need and to what accuracy (e.g. asking for the 95th percentile to the nearest $1000), as this will help the risk analyst save time or figure out that an unusual approach might be needed to get the required accuracy.

3. *Explain what arguments will be based on these outputs.* I am of the view that this is a key breakdown area because a decision-maker might ask for specific outputs and then put them together into an argument that is probabilistically incorrect. Much embarrassment and frustration all round. It is better to explain the arguments (e.g. comparing with the distribution of another potential project's extra revenue) that would be put forward and find out if the risk analyst agrees that this is technically correct before you get started.

4. *Explain whether the risk analysis has to sit within a framework.* This could be a formal framework, like a regulatory requirement or a company policy, or it could be informal, like building up a portfolio of risk analyses that can be compared on the same footing (for example, we are helping a

large chemical manufacturer to build up a combined toxicological, environmental, etc., risk analysis database for their treasure chest of compounds). It will help the risk analyst ensure the maximum level of compatibility – e.g. that the same base assumptions are used between risk analyses.

5. *Explain the target audience.* We write reports on all our risk analyses, of course, but sometimes there can be several versions: the executive summary; the main report; and the technical report with all the formulae and guides for testing. Often, others will want to run the model and change parameters, so we make a model version that minimises the ability to mess up the mathematics, and write the code to allow the most flexibility. These days we usually put a VBA user interface on the front to make life easier and perhaps add a reporting facility to compare results. We might add a help file too. Clients will also sometimes ask us to prepare a PowerPoint presentation. Knowing the knowledge level and focus of each target audience, and knowing what types of reporting will be needed at the offset, saves a lot of time.

6. *Discuss any possible hostile reactions.* The results of a risk analysis will not always be popular, and when people dislike the answers they start attacking the model (or, if you're unlucky, the modeller). Assumptions are the primary Achilles' heel, as we can argue forever about whether assumptions are right. I talk about getting buy-in for assumptions in Section 5.2. Statistical analysis of data is also rather draining – it usually involves a couple of very technical people with opposing arguments about the appropriateness of a statistical procedure that nobody else understands. The decision to include and exclude certain datasets can also create a lot of tension. The arguments can be minimised, or at least convincingly dismissed, if people likely to be hostile are brought into the analysis process early, or an external expert is asked to give an independent review.

7. *Figure out a timeline.* Decision-makers have something of a habit of setting unrealistic deadlines. When these deadlines pass, nothing very dramatic usually happens, as the deadlines are some artificial internal confection. Our consultants deal with deadlines all the time, of course, but we openly discuss whether a deadline is really that important because, if we have to meet a tight deadline (and that happens), the quality of the risk analysis may be lower than would have been achievable with more time. The decision-maker has to be honest about time limits and decide whether it is worth postponing things for a bit.

8. *Figure out the priority level.* The risk analyst might have other work to juggle too. The project might be of high importance and justify pulling off other resources to help with the analysis or instructing others in the organisation to set aside time to provide good quality input.

9. *Decide on how regularly the decision-maker and risk analyst will meet.* Things change and the risk analysis may have to be modified, so find that out sooner rather than later.

2.2 Determine the Assumptions that are Acceptable or Required

If a risk analysis is to sit within a certain framework, discussed above, it may well have to comply with a set of common assumptions to allow meaningful comparisons between the results of different analyses. Sometimes it is better not to revise some assumptions for a new analysis because it makes it impossible to compare. You can often see a similar problem with historic data, e.g. calculating crime or unemployment statistics. It seems that the basis for these statistics keeps changing, making it impossible to know whether the problem is getting better or worse.

In a corporate environment there will be certain base assumptions used for things like interest and exchange rates, production capacity and energy price. The same assumptions should be used in all models. In a risk analysis world these should be probabilistic forecasts, but they are nonetheless often fixed-point values. Oil companies, for example, have the challenging job of figuring out what the oil price might be in the future. They can get it very wrong so often take a low price for planning purposes, e.g. $16 a barrel, which in 2007 might seem rather unlikely for the future. The risk analyst working hard on getting everything else really precise could find such an assumption irritating, but it allows consistency between analyses where oil price forecast uncertainty could be so large as to mask the differences between investment opportunities.

Some assumptions we make are conservative, meaning that, if, for example, we need a certain percentile of the output to be above X before we accept the risk as acceptable, then a conservative assumption will bias the output to lower values. Thus, if the output still gives numbers that say the risk is acceptable, we know we are on pretty safe ground. Conservative assumptions are most useful as a sensitivity tool to demonstrate that one has not taken an unacceptable risk, but they are to be avoided whenever possible because they run counter to the principle of risk analysis which is to give an unbiased report of uncertainty.

2.3 Time and Timing

We get a lot of requests to help "risk" a model. The potential client has spent a few months working on a problem, building up a cashflow model, etc., and the decision-makers decide the week before the board meeting that they really should have a risk analysis done.

If done properly, risk analysis is an integral part of the planning of a project, not an add-on at the end. One of the prime reasons for doing risk analyses is to identify risks and risk management strategies so the decision-makers can decide how the risks can be managed, which could well involve a revision of the project plan. That can save a lot of time and money on a project. If risk analysis is added on at the end, you lose all that potential benefit.

The data collection efforts required to produce a fixed-value model of a project are little different from the efforts required for a risk analysis, so adding a risk analysis on at the end is inefficient and delays a project, as the risk analyst has to go back over previous work.

We advocate that a risk analyst write the report as the model develops. This helps keep a track of what one is doing and makes it easier to meet the report submission deadline at the end. I also like to write down my thinking because it helps me spot any mistakes early.

Finally, try to allow the risk analyst enough time to check the model for errors and get it reviewed. Chapter 16 offers some advice on model validation.

2.4 You'll Need a Good Risk Analyst or Team

If the risk analysis is a one-off and the outcome is important to you, I recommend you hire in a consultant risk analyst. Well I would say that, of course, but it does make a lot of sense. Consultants are expensive on a daily basis, but, certainly at Vose Consulting, we are far faster (my guess is over 10 times faster than a novice) – we know what we're doing and we know how to communicate and organise effectively. Please don't get a bright person within your organisation, install some risk analysis software on their computer and tell them to get on with the job. It will end in tears.

The publishers of risk analysis software (Crystal Ball, @RISK, Analytica, Risk+, PERTmaster, etc.) have made risk analysis modelling very easy to implement from a software viewpoint. The courses they teach show you how to drive the software and reinforce the notion that risk analysis modelling is pretty easy (Vose Consulting courses generally assume you have already attended a software familiarisation course). In a lot of cases, risk analysis is in fact pretty easy, as long as you avoid some common basic errors discussed in Section 7.4. However, it can also become quite tricky too, for sometimes subtle reasons, and you should have someone who understands risk analysis well enough to be able to recognise and handle the trickier models. Knowing how to use Excel won't make you an accountant (but it's a good first step), and learning how to use risk analysis software won't make you a risk analyst (but it's also a good first step).

There are still very few tertiary courses in risk analysis, and these courses tend to be highly focused in particular areas (financial modelling, environmental risk assessment, etc.). I don't know of any tertiary courses that aim to produce professional risk analysts who can work across many disciplines. There are very few people who could say they are qualified to be a risk analyst. This makes it pretty tough to know where to search and to be sure you have found someone who will have the knowledge to analyse your risks properly. It seems that industry-specific risk analysts also have little awareness of the narrowness of their knowledge: a little while ago we advertised for two highly qualified actuarial and financial risk analysts with several years experience and received a large number of applications from people who were risk analysts in toxicology, microbial, environmental and project areas with almost no overlap in required skill sets.

2.4.1 Qualities of a risk analyst

I often get asked by companies and government agencies what sort of person they should look for to fill a position as a risk analyst. In my view, candidates should have the following characteristics:

- *Creative thinkers*. Risk analysis is about problem-solving. This is at the top of my list and is the rarest quality.
- *Confident*. We often have to come up with original solutions. I've seen too many pieces of work that have followed some previously published method because it is "safer". We also have to present to senior decision-makers and maybe defend our work in front of hostile stakeholders or a court.
- *Modest*. Too many risk analyses fail to meet their requirements because of a risk analyst who thought she/he could do it without help or consultation.
- *Thick-skinned*. Risk analysts bring together a lot of disparate information and ideas, sometimes conflicting, sometimes controversial, and we produce outputs that are not always what people want to see, so we have to be prepared for a fair amount of enthusiastic criticism.
- *Communicators*. We have to listen to a lot of people and present ideas that are new and sometimes difficult to understand.
- *Pragmatic*. Our models could always be better with more time, data and resources, but decision-makers have deadlines.
- *Able to conceptualise*. There are a lot of tools at our disposal that are developed in various fields of risk, so the risk analyst needs to read widely and be able to extrapolate an idea from one application to another.
- *Curious*. Risk analysts need to keep learning.
- *Good at mathematics*. Take a look at Part 2 of this book to get a feel for the level. It will depend on the area: project risk requires more intuition and perseverance but less mathematics, insurance

and finance require intuition and high mathematical skills, food safety requires medium levels of everything.

- *A feel for numbers*. It is one thing to be good at mathematics, but we also have to have an idea of where the numbers should lie because it (a) helps us check the work and (b) allows us to know where we can take shortcuts.
- *Finishers*. Some people are great at coming up with ideas, but lose interest when it comes to implementing them. Risk analysts have to get the job done.
- *Cynical*. We have to maintain a healthy cynicism about published work and about how good our subject matter experts are.
- *Pedantic*. When developing probability models, one needs to be very precise about exactly what each variable represents.
- *Careful*. It is easy to make mistakes.
- *Social*. We have to work in teams.
- *Neutral*. Our job is to produce an objective risk analysis. A project manager is not usually ideal to perform the project risk analysis because it may reflect on his/her ability to manage and plan. A scientist is not ideal if she/he has a pet theory that could slant the approach taken.

It's a demanding list and indicates, I think, that risk analysis should be performed by people of high skill levels who are fairly senior and in a respected position within a company or agency. It is also rather unlikely that you will find all these qualities in the one person: the best risk analysis units with which we work are composed of a number of individuals with complementary skills and strengths.

2.4.2 Suitable education

I interviewed a statistics student a couple of months back. This person was just finishing a PhD and had top grades throughout from a very reputable school. I asked a pretty simple question about estimating a prevalence and got a vague answer about how this person would perform the appropriate test and report the confidence interval, but the student couldn't tell me what that test might be (this is a really basic Statistics 101-type question). I offered some numbers and asked what the bounds might roughly be, but the interviewee had absolutely no idea. With each question it became very clear that this person had been taught a lot of theory but had no feel for how to use it, and no sense of numbers. We didn't hire.

I interviewed another person who had written a very sophisticated traffic model using discrete event simulation (which we use a fair bit) that was helping decide how to manage boat traffic. The model predicted that putting in traffic lights on the narrow part of some waterway would produce a horrendous number of crashes at the traffic light queues, easily outweighing the crashes avoided by letting vessels pass each other in the narrow part of the waterway. Conclusion: no traffic lights. That seemed strange to me and, after some thought, the interviewee explained it was probably because the model used a probability of crashing that was inversely proportional to the distance between the vessels, and vessels in a queue are very close, so the model generated lots of crashes. But they are also barely moving, I pointed out, so the probability of a collision will be lower at a given distance for vessels at the lights than for vessels passing each other at speed, and any contact between waiting vessels would have a negligible effect. The modeller responded that the probability could be changed. We didn't hire that person either because the modeller had never stepped back and asked "does this make sense?".

I interviewed a student who was just finishing a Masters degree and was writing up a thesis on applying probability models from physics to financial markets. This person explained that studying had become rather dull because it was always about learning what others had done, but the thesis was a different story because there was a chance to think for oneself and come up with something new. The student was very enthusiastic, had great mathematics and could really explain to me what the thesis was about. We hired and I have no regrets.

A prospective hire for a risk analysis position will need some sort of quantitative background. I think the best candidates tend to have a background that combines attempting to model the real world with using the results to make decisions. In these areas, approximations and the tools of approximation are embraced as necessary and useful, and there is a clear purpose to modelling that goes beyond the academic exercise of producing the model itself. Applied physics, engineering, applied statistics and operations research are all very suitable. Applied physics is the most appealing of all of them (I may be biased, I studied physics as an undergraduate) because in physics we hypothesise how the world might work, describe the theory with mathematics, make predictions and figure out an experiment that will *challenge* the theory, perform the experiment, collect and analyse data and conclude whether our theory was supported. Learning this basic thinking is extraordinarily valuable: risk analysis follows much of the same process, uses many of the same modelling and statistical techniques, makes approximations and should critically review scientific data when relevant. Most published papers describe studies that were designed to show supportive evidence for someone's theory.

Pure mathematics and classical statistics are not that great: pure mathematics is too abstract; we find that pure statistics teaching is very constrained, and encourages formulaic thinking and reaching for a computer rather than a pen and paper. The schools also don't seem to emphasise communication skills very much. It's a shame because the statistician has so much of the basic knowledge requirements. Bayesian statistics is somewhat better – it does not have such a problem with subjective estimates, its techniques are more conducive to risk analysis and it's a newer field, so the teaching is somewhat less staid. Don't be swayed by a six-sigma black belt qualification – the ideas behind Six Sigma certainly have merit, but the technical knowledge gained to get a black belt is quite basic and the production-line teaching seems to be at the expense of in-depth understanding and creativity. The main things you will need to look out for are a track record of independent thinking, strong communication skills and some reasonable grasp of probability modelling. The more advanced techniques can be learned from courses and books.

2.4.3 Our team

I thought it might be helpful to give you a brief description of how we organise our teams. If your organisation is large enough to need 10 or more people in a risk analysis team, you might get some ideas from how we operate.

Vose Consulting has quite a mixture of people, roughly split into three groups, and we seem to have hired organically to match people's skills and characters to the roles of these groups. I love to learn, teach, develop new talent and dream up new ideas, so my team is made up of conceptual thinkers with great mathematics, computing and researching skills. They are young and very intelligent, but are too young for us to put them into the most stressful jobs, so part of my role is to give them challenging work and the confidence to meet consulting deadlines by solving their problems with them. My office is the nursery for Huybert's team to which they can migrate once they have more experience. Huybert is an ironman triathlon competitor with boundless energy. His consulting group fly around everywhere solving problems, writing reports and meeting deadlines. They are real finishers and my team provide as much technical support as they need (though they are no slouches, we have four quantitative PhDs and nobody with less than a Masters degree in that team). Timour is a very methodical, deep thinker.

Unlike me, he tends not to say anything unless he has something to say. His programming group writes our commercial software like ModelRisk, requiring a long-term development view, but he has a couple of people who write bespoke software for our clients meeting strict deadlines too.

When we get a consulting enquiry, the partners will discuss whether we have the time and knowledge to do the job, who it would involve and who would lead it. Then the prospective lead is invited to talk with us and the client about the project and then takes over. The lead consultant has to agree to do the project, his/her name and contact details are put on the MOU and he/she remains in charge and responsible to the client throughout the project. A partner will monitor progress, or a partner could be the lead consultant. The lead consultant can ask anyone within the company for advice, for manpower assistance, to review models and reports, to write bespoke software for the client, to be available for a call with the client, etc. I like this approach because it means we spread around the satisfaction of a job well done, it encourages responsibility and creativity, it emphasises a flat company structure and we all get to know what others in the company can do, and because the poor performance in a project would be the company's failure, not one individual's.

I read Ricardo Semler's book *Maverick* a few months ago and loved it for showing me that much of what we practise in our small company can work in a company as large as Semco. Semco also works in groups that mix around depending on the project and has a flat hierarchy. We give our staff a lot of responsibility, so we also assume that they are responsible: we give them considerable freedom over their working hours and practices, we expect them to keep expenses at a sensible level, but don't set daily rates, etc. Staff choose their own computers, can buy a printer, etc., without having to get approval. The only thing we have no flexibility on is honesty.

Chapter 3

The quality of a risk analysis

We've seen a fair number of quantitative risk analyses that are terrible. They might also have been very expensive, taken a long time to complete and used up valuable human resources. In fact, I'll stick my neck out and say the more complex and expensive a quantitative risk analysis is, the more likely it is to be terrible. Worst of all, the people making decisions on the results of these analyses have little if any idea of how bad they are. These are rather attention-grabbing sentences, but this chapter is small and I would really like you not to skip over it: it could save you a lot of heartache.

In our company we do a lot of reviews of models for decision-makers. We'd love to be able to say "it's great, trust the results" a lot more often than we do, and I want to spend this short chapter explaining what, in our experience, goes wrong and what you can do about it. First of all, to give some motivation for this chapter, I want to show you some of the results of a survey we ran a couple of years ago in a well-developed science-based area of risk analysis (Figure 3.1). The question appears in the title of each pane. Which results do you find most worrying?

3.1 The Reasons Why a Risk Analysis can be Terrible

From Figure 3.1 I think you'll see that there really needs to be more communication between decision-makers and their risk analysts and a greater attempt to work as a team. I see the risk analyst as an important avenue of communication between those "on the ground" who understand the problem at hand and hold the data and those who make decisions. The risk analyst needs to understand the context of the decision question and have the flexibility to be able to find the method of analysis that gives the most useful information. I've heard too many risk analysts complain that they get told to produce a quantitative model by the boss, but have to make the numbers up because the data aren't there. Now doesn't that seem silly? I'm sure the decision-maker would be none too happy to know the numbers are all made up, but the risk analyst is often not given access to the decision-makers to let them know. On the other hand, in some business and regulatory environments they are trying to follow a rule that says a quantitative risk analysis needs to be completed – the box needs ticking.

Regulations and guidelines can be a real impediment to creative thinking. I've been in plenty of committees gathered to write risk analysis guidelines, and I've done my best to reverse the tendency to be formulaic. My argument is that in 19 years we have never done the same risk analysis twice: every one has its individual peculiarities. Yet the tendency seems to be the reverse: I trained over a hundred consultants in one of the big four management consultancy firms in business risk modelling techniques, and they decided that, to ensure that they could maintain consistency, they would keep it simple and essentially fill in a template of three-point estimates with some correlation. I can see their point – if every risk analyst developed a fancy and highly individual model it would be impossible to ensure any quality standard. The problem is, of course, that the standard they will maintain is very low. Risk analysis should not be a packaged commodity but a voyage of reasoned thinking leading to the best possible decision at the time.

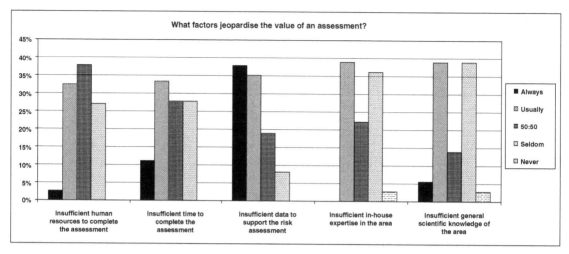

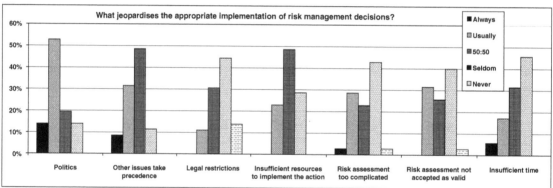

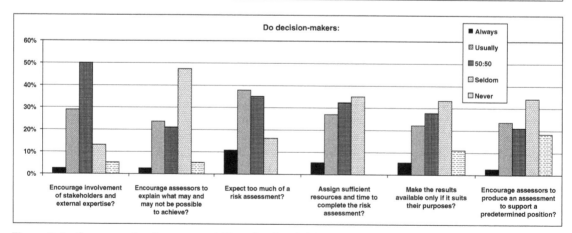

Figure 3.1 Some results of a survey of 39 professional risk analysts working in a scientific field where risk analysis is well developed and applied very frequently.

I think it is usually pretty easy to see early on in the risk analysis process that a quantitative risk analysis will be of little value. There are several key areas where it can fall down:

1. It can't answer all the key questions.
2. There are going to be a lot of assumptions.
3. There is going to be one or more show-stopping assumption.
4. There aren't enough good data or experts.

We can get around **1** sometimes by doing different risk analyses for different questions, but that can be problematic when each risk analysis has a different set of fundamental assumptions – how do we compare their results?

For **2** we need to have some way of expressing whether a lot of little assumptions compound to make a very vulnerable analysis: if you have 20 assumptions (and 20 is quite a small number), all pretty good ones – e.g. we think there's a 90 % chance they are correct, but the analysis is only useful if all the assumptions are correct, then we only have a $0.9^{20} = 12\%$ chance that the assumption set is correct. Of course, if this were the real problem we wouldn't bother writing models. In reality, in the business world particularly, we deal with assumptions that are good enough because the answers we get are close enough. In some more scientific areas, like human health, we have to deal with assumptions such as: compound X is present; compound X is toxic; people are exposed to compound X; the exposure is sufficient to cause harm; and treatment is ineffective. The sequence then produces the theoretical human harm we might want to protect against, but if any one of those assumptions is wrong there is no human health threat to worry about.

If **3** occurs we have a pretty good indication that we don't know enough to produce a decent risk analysis model, but maybe we can produce two or three crude models under different possible assumptions and see whether we come to the same conclusion anyway.

Area **4** is the least predictable because the risk analyst doing a preliminary scoping can be reassured that the relevant data are available, but then finds out they are not available either because the data turn out to be clearly wrong (we see this a lot), the data aren't what was thought, there is a delay past the deadline in the data becoming available or the data are dirty and need so much rework that it becomes impractical to analyse them within the decision timeframe.

There is a lot of emphasis placed on transparency in a risk analysis, which usually manifests itself in a large report describing the model, all the data and sources, the assumptions, etc., and then finishes with some of the graphical and numerical outputs described in Chapter 5. I've seen reports of 100 or 200 pages that seem far from transparent to me – who really has the time or inclination to read such a document? The executive summary tends to focus on the decision question and numerical results, and places little emphasis on the robustness of the study.

3.2 Communicating the Quality of Data Used in a Risk Analysis

Elsewhere in this book you will find lots of techniques for describing the numerical accuracy that a model can provide given the data that are available. These analyses are at the heart of a quantitative risk analysis and give us distributions, percentiles, sensitivity plots, etc.

In this section I want to discuss how we can communicate any impact on the robustness of a model owing to the assumptions behind using data or settling on a model scope and structure. Elsewhere in this book I encourage the risk analyst to write down each assumption that is made in developing equations

Table 3.1 Pedigree matrix for parameter strength (adapted from Boone *et al.*, 2007).

Score	Proxy	Empirical	Method	Validation
4	Exact measure of the desired quantity (e.g. geographically representative)	Large sample, direct measurements, recent data, controlled experiments	Best available practice in well-established discipline (accredited method for sampling / diagnostic test)	Compared with independent measurements of the same variable over long domain, rigorous correction of errors
3	Good fit or measure	Small sample, direct measurements, less recent data, uncontrolled experiments, low non-response rate	Reliable and common method. Best practice in immature discipline	↑
2	Well correlated but not the same thing	Several expert estimates in general agreement	Acceptable method but limited consensus on reliability	↑
1	Weak correlation (very large geographical differences)	One expert opinion, rule-of-thumb estimate	Preliminary methods with unknown reliability	Weak very indirect validation
0	Not clearly connected	Crude speculation	No discernible rigour	No validation

and performing statistical analyses. We get participants to do the same in the training courses we teach as they solve simple class exercises, and there is a general surprise at how many assumptions are implicit in even the simplest type of equation. It becomes rather onerous to write all these assumptions down, but it is even more difficult to convert the conceptual assumptions underpinning our probability models into something that a reader rather less familiar with probability modelling might understand.

The NUSAP (Numeral Unit Spread Assessment Pedigree) method (Funtowicz and Ravetz, 1990) is a notational system that communicates the level of uncertainty for data in scientific analysis used for policy making. The idea is to use a number of experts in the field to score independently the data under different categories. The system is well established as being useful in toxicological risk assessment. I will describe here a generalisation of the idea. It's key attractions are that it is easy to implement and can be summarised into consistent pictorial representations. In Table 3.1 I have used the categorisation descriptions of data from van der Sluijs, Risbey and Ravetz (2005), which are: *proxy* – reflecting how close data being used are to ideal; *empirical* – reflecting the quantity and quality of the data; *method* – reflecting where the method used to collect the data lies between careful and well established and haphazard; and *validation* – reflecting whether the acquired data have been matched to real-world experience (e.g. does an effect observed in a laboratory actually occur in the wider world).

Each dataset is scored in turn by each expert. The average of all scores is calculated and then divided by the maximum attainable score of 4. For example:

	Proxy	Empirical	Method	Validation
Expert A	3	2	4	3
Expert B	3	2	4	3
Expert C	2	1	3	4

gives an average score of 2.833. Dividing by the maximum score of 4 gives 0.708. An additional level of sophistication is to allow the experts to weight their level of expertise for the particular variable in

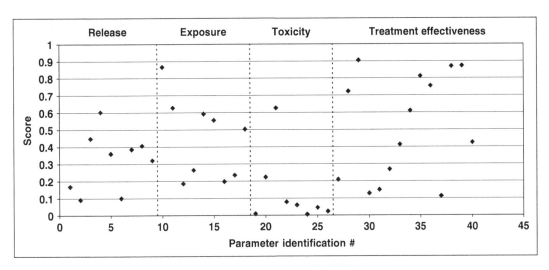

Figure 3.2   Plot of average scores for datasets in a toxicological risk assessment.

question (e.g. 0.3 for low, 0.6 for medium and 1.0 for high, as well as allowing experts to select not to make any comment when it is outside their competence), in which case one calculates a weighted average score. One can then plot these scores together and segregate them by different parts of the analysis if desired, which gives an overview of the robustness of data used in the analysis (Figure 3.2).

Scores can be generally categorised as follows:

$$<0.2 \qquad \text{weak}$$
$$0.2{-}0.4 \qquad \text{moderate}$$
$$>0.4{-}0.8 \qquad \text{high}$$
$$>0.8 \qquad \text{excellent}$$

So, for example, Figure 3.2 shows that the toxicity part of the analysis appears to be the weakest, with several datasets in the weak category.

We can summarise the scores for each dataset using a kite diagram to give a visual "traffic light", green indicating that the parameter support is excellent, red indicating that it is weak and one or two levels of orange representing gradations between these extremes. Figure 3.3 gives an example: one works from the centre-point, marking on the axes the weighted fraction of all the experts considering the parameter support to be "excellent", then adds the weighted fraction considering the support to be "high", etc. These points are then joined to make the different colour zones – from green in the centre for "excellent", through yellow and orange, to red in the last category: a kite will be green if all experts agree the parameter support is excellent and red for weak. Plotting these kite diagrams together can give a strong visual representation: a sea of green should give great confidence, a sea of red says the risk analysis is extremely weak. In practice, we'll end up with a big mix of colours, but over time one can get a sense of what colour mix is typical, when an analysis is comparatively weak or strong and when it can be relied upon for your field.

The only real impediment to using the system above is that you need to develop a database software tool. Some organisations have developed their own in-house products that are effective but somewhat limited in their ability for reviewing, sorting and tracking. Our software developers have it on their "to do" list to make a tool that can be used across an organisation, where one can track the current status

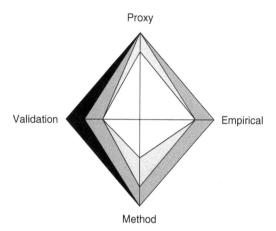

Figure 3.3 A kite diagram summarising the level of data support the experts believe that a model parameter will have: red (dark) in the outer band = weak; green (light) in the inner band = excellent.

of a risk analysis, drill down to see the reasons for the vulnerability of a parameter, etc., so you might like to visit www.vosesoftware.com and see if we've got anywhere yet.

3.3 Level of Criticality

The categorisation system of Section 3.2 helps determine whether a parameter is well supported, but it can still misrepresent the robustness of the risk analysis. For example, we might have done a food safety microbial risk analysis involving 10 parameters – nine enjoy high or excellent support, and one is suffering weak support. If that weakly supported parameter is defining the dose–response relationship (the probability a random individual will experience an adverse health effect given the number of pathogenic organisms ingested), then the whole risk analysis is jeopardised because the dose–response is the link between all the exposure pathways and the amount of pathogen involved (often a big model) and the size of human health impact that results. It is therefore rather useful to separate the kite diagrams and other analyses into different categories for the level of dependence the analysis has on each parameter: critical, important or small, for example.

A more sophisticated version for separating the level of dependence is statistically to analyse the degree of effect each parameter has on the numerical result; for example, one might look at the difference in the mean of the model output when the parameter distribution is replaced by its 95th and 5th percentile. Taking that range and multiplying by (1 − the support score), giving 0 for excellent and 1 for terrible, gives one a sense of the level of vulnerability of the output numbers. However, this method suffers other problems. Imagine that we are performing a risk analysis on an emerging bacterium for which we have absolutely no dose–response data, so we use a dataset for a surrogate bacterium that we *think* will have a very similar effect (e.g. because it produces a similar toxin). We might have large amounts of excellent data for the surrogate bacterium and may therefore have little uncertainty about the dose–response model, so using the 5th and 95th percentiles of the uncertainty about that dose–response model will result in a small change in the output and multiplying that by (1 − the support score) will under-represent the real uncertainty. A second problem is that we often estimate two or more model parameters from the same dataset; for example, a dose–response model often has two or three parameters that are fitted to data. Each parameter might be quite uncertain, but the dose–response curve can be nonetheless quite stable, so this numerical analysis needs to look at the combined effect of the uncertain parameters as a single entity, which requires a fair bit of number juggling.

3.4 The Biggest Uncertainty in a Risk Analysis

The techniques discussed above have focused on the vulnerability of the results of a risk analysis to the parameters of a model. When we are asked to review or audit a risk analysis, the client is often surprised that our first step is not to look at the model mathematics and supporting statistical analyses, but to consider what the decision questions are, whether there were a number of assumptions, whether it would be possible to do the analysis a different (usually simpler, but sometimes more complex and precise) way and whether this other way would give the same answers, and to see if there are any means for comparing predictions against reality. What we are trying to do is see whether the structure and scope of the analysis are correct. The biggest uncertainty in a risk analysis is whether we started off analysing the right thing and in the right way.

Finding the answer is very often not amenable to any numerical technique because we will not have any alternative to compare against. If we do, it might nonetheless take a great deal of effort to put together an alternative risk analysis model, and a model audit is usually too late in the process to be able to start again. A much better idea, in my view, is to get a sense at the *beginning* of a risk analysis of how confident we should be that the analysis will be scoped sufficiently broadly, or how confident we are that the world is adequately represented by our model. Needless to say, we can also start rather confident that our approach will be quite adequate and then, once having delved into the details of the problem, find out we were quite mistaken, so it is important to keep revisiting our view of the appropriateness of the model.

We encourage clients, particularly in the scientific areas of risk in which we work, to instigate a solid brainstorming session of experts and decision-makers whenever it has been decided that a risk analysis is to be undertaken, or maybe is just under consideration. The focus is to discuss the form and scope of the potential risk analysis. The experts first of all need to think about the decision questions, discuss with decision-makers any possible alternatives or supplements to those questions and then consider how they can be answered and what the outputs should look like (e.g. only the mean is required, or some high percentile). Each approach will have a set of assumptions that need to be thought through carefully: What would the effect be if the assumptions are wrong? If we use a conservative assumption and estimate a risk that is too high, are we back to where we started? We need to think about data requirements too: Is the quality likely to be good and are the data easily attainable? We also need to think about software. I was once asked to review a 2 year, $3 million model written entirely in interacting C++ modules – nobody else had been able to figure it out (I couldn't either).

When the brainstorming is over, I recommend that you pass around a questionnaire to each expert and ask those attending independently to answer a questionnaire something like this:

> *We discussed three risk analysis approaches (description A, description B, description C). Please indicate your level of confidence (0 = none, 1 = slight, 2 = good, 3 = excellent, −1 = no opinion) to the following:*

1. What is your confidence that method A, B or C will be sufficiently flexible and comprehensive to answer any foreseeable questions from the management about this risk?

2. What is your confidence that method A, B or C is based on assumptions that are correct?

3. What is your confidence for method A, B or C that the necessary data will be available within the required timeframe and budget?

4. What is your confidence that the method A, B or C analysis will be completed in time?

5. What is your confidence that there will be strong support for method A, B or C among reviewing peers?

6. What is your confidence that there will be strong support for method A, B or C among stakeholders?

Asking each brainstorming participant independently will help you attain a balanced view, particularly if the chairperson of that meeting has enforced the discipline of requiring participants not to express their view on the above questions during the meeting (it won't be completely possible, but you are trying to make sure that nobody will be influenced into giving a desired answer). Asking people independently rather than trying to achieve consensus during the meeting will also help remove the overconfidence that often appears when people make a group decision.

3.5 Iterate

Things change. The political landscape in which the decision is to be made can become more hostile or accepting to some assumptions, data can prove better or worse than we initially thought, new data turn up, new questions suddenly become important, the timeframe or budget can change, a risk analysis consultant sees an early model and shows you a simpler way, etc.

So it makes sense to go back from time to time over the types of assumption analysis I discussed in Sections 3.2 and 3.3 and to remain open to taking a different approach, even to making as dramatic a change as going from a quantitative to a qualitative risk analysis. That means you (analysts and decision-makers alike) should also be a little guarded in making premature promises so you have some space to adapt. In our consultancy contracts, for example, a client will usually commission us to do a quantitative risk analysis and tell us about the data they have. We'll probably have had a little look at the data too. We prefer to structure our proposal into stages. In the first stage we go over the decision problem, review any constraints (time, money, political, etc.), take a first decent look at the available data and figure out possible ways of getting to the answer. Then we produce a report describing how we want to tackle the problem and why. At that stage the client can stop the work, continue with us, do it themselves or maybe hire someone else if they wish. It may take a little longer (usually a day or two), but everyone's expectations are kept realistic, we aren't cornered into doing a risk analysis that we know is inappropriate and clients don't waste their time or money. As consultants, we are in the somewhat privileged position of turning down work that we know would be terrible. A risk analyst employed by a company or government department may not have that luxury. If you, the reader, are a risk analyst in the awkward position of being made to produce terrible risk analyses, perhaps you should show your boss this chapter, or maybe check to see if we have any vacancies.

Chapter 4

Choice of model structure

There is a tendency to settle on the form that a risk analysis model will take too early on in the risk analysis process. In part that will be because of a limited knowledge of the available options, but also because people tend not to take a step back and ask themselves what the purpose of the analysis is, and also how it might evolve over time. In this chapter I give a short guide to various types of model used in risk analysis.

4.1 Software Tools and the Models they Build

4.1.1 Spreadsheets

Spreadsheets, and by that I mean Excel these days, are the most natural and the first choice for most people because it is perceived that relatively little additional knowledge is required to produce a risk analysis model. Products like @RISK, Crystal Ball, ModelRisk and many other contenders for their shared crown have made adding uncertainty into a spreadsheet as simple as clicking a few buttons. You can run a simulation and look at the distribution results in a few seconds and a few more button clicks. Monte Carlo simulation software tools for Excel have focused very much on the graphical interfaces to make risk analysis modelling easy: combine that with the ability to track formulae across spreadsheets, imbed graphs and format sheets in many ways, and with VBA and data importing capabilities, and we can see why Excel is so popular. I have even seen a whole trading floor run on Excel using VBA, and not a single recognisable spreadsheet appeared on any dealer's screen.

But Excel has its limitations. ModelRisk overcomes many of them for high-level financial and insurance modelling, and I have used its features in this book a fair bit to help explain some modelling concepts. However, there are many types of problem for which Excel is not suitable. Project cost and schedule risk analysis can be done in spreadsheets at a crude level, which I cover in Chapter 19, and a crude level is often enough for large-scale risk analysis, as we are rarely interested in the minutia that can be built into a project planning model (like you might make with Primevera or Microsoft Project). However, a risk register is better constructed in an electronic database with various levels of access. The problem with building a project plan in a spreadsheet is that expanding the model into greater detail becomes mechanically very awkward, while it is a simple matter in project planning software.

In other areas, risk analysis models with spreadsheets have a number of limitations:

1. They scale very badly, meaning that spreadsheets can become really huge when one has a lot of data, or when one is performing repetitive calculations that could be succinctly written in another language (e.g. a looping formula), although one can get round this to some degree with Visual Basic. Our company reviews many risk models built in spreadsheets, and they can be vast, often unnecessarily so because there are shortcuts to achieving the same result if one knows a bit of

probability mathematics. The next version of Excel will handle even bigger sheets, so I predict this problem will only get worse.

2. They are limited to the two dimensions of a grid, three at a push if one uses sheets as a third dimension; if you have a multidimensional problem you should really think hard before deciding on a spreadsheet. There are a lot of other modelling environments one could use: C++ is highly flexible, but opaque to anyone who is not a C++ programmer. Matlab and, to a lesser extent, Mathematica and Maple are highly sophisticated mathematical modelling software with very powerful built-in modelling capabilities that will handle many dimensions and can also perform simulations.

3. They are really slow. Running a simulation in Excel will take hundreds or more times longer than specialised tools. That's a problem if you have a huge model, or if you need to achieve a high level of precision (i.e. require many iterations).

4. Simulation models built in spreadsheets calculate in one direction, meaning that, if one acquires new data that can be matched to a forecast in the model, the data cannot be integrated into the model to update the estimates of parameters on which the model was based and therefore produce a more accurate forecast. The simulation software WinBUGS can do this, and I give a number of examples through this book.

5. Spreadsheets cannot easily handle modelling dynamic systems. There are a number of flexible and user-friendly tools like Simul8 which give very good approximations to continuously varying stochastic systems with many interacting components. I give an example later in this chapter. Attempting to achieve the same in Excel is not worth the pain.

There are other types of model that one can build, and software that will let you do so easily, which I describe below.

4.1.2 Influence diagrams

Influence diagrams are quite popular – they essentially replicate the mathematics you can build in a spreadsheet, but the modelling environment is quite different (Figure 4.1 is a simple example). Analytica® is the most popular influence diagram tool. Variables (called nodes) are represented as graphical objects (circles, squares, etc.) and are connected together with arrows (called arcs) which show the direction of interaction between these variables. The visual result is a network that shows the

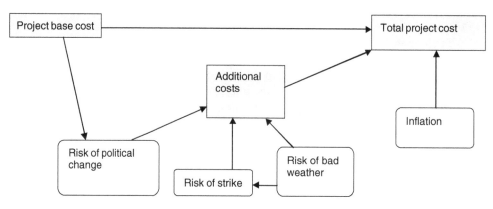

Figure 4.1 Example of a simple influence diagram.

viewer which variables affect which, but you can imagine that such a diagram quickly becomes overly complex, so one builds submodels. Click on a model object and it opens another view to show a lower level of interaction. Personally, I don't like them much because the mathematics and data behind the model are hard to get to, but others love them. They are certainly very visual.

4.1.3 Event trees

Event trees offer a way to describe a sequence of probabilistic events, together with their probabilities and impacts. They are perhaps the most useful of all the methods for depicting a probabilistic sequence, because they are very intuitive, the mathematics to combine the probabilities is simple and the diagram helps ensure the necessary discipline. Event trees are built out of nodes (boxes) and arcs (arrows) (Figure 4.2).

The tree starts from the left with a node (in the diagram below, "Select animal" to denote the random selection of an animal from some population), and arrows to the right indicate possible outcomes (here, whether the animal is infected with some particular disease agent, or not) and their probabilities (p, which would be the prevalence of infected animals in the population, and $(1 - p)$ respectively). Branching out from these boxes are arrows to the next probability event (the testing of an animal for the disease), and attached to these arrows are the conditional probabilities of the next level of event occurring. The conditional nature of the probabilities in an event tree is extremely important to underline. In this example:

$$Se = P(\text{test positive for disease } given \text{ the animal is infected})$$

$$Sp = P(\text{test negative for disease } given \text{ the animal is not infected})$$

Thus, following the rules of conditional probability algebra, we can say, for example:

$$P(\text{animal is infected and tests positive}) = p^*Se$$

$$P(\text{animal is infected and tests negative}) = p^*(1 - Se)$$

$$P(\text{animal tests positive}) = p^*Se + (1 - p)^*(1 - Sp)$$

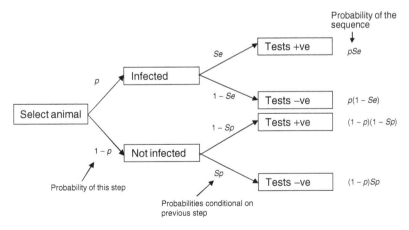

Figure 4.2 Example of a simple event tree.

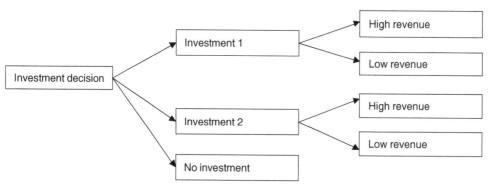

Figure 4.3   Example of a simple decision tree. The decision options are to make either of two investments or do nothing with associated revenues as a result. More involved decision trees would include two or more sequential decisions depending on how well the investment went.

Event trees are very useful for building up your probability thinking, although they will get quite complex rather quickly. We use them a great deal to help understand and communicate a problem.

4.1.4 Decision trees

Decision trees are like event trees but add possible decision options (Figure 4.3). They have a role in risk analysis, and in fields like petroleum exploration they are very popular. They sketch the possible decisions that one might make and the outcomes that might result. Decision tree software (which can also produce event trees) can calculate the best option to take under the assumption of some user-defined utility function. Again, personally I am not a big fan of decision trees in actual model writing. I find that it is difficult for decision-makers to be comfortable with defining a utility curve, so I don't have much use for the analytical component of decision tree software, but they are helpful for communicating the logic of a problem.

4.1.5 Fault trees

Fault trees start from the reverse approach to an event tree. An event tree looks forward from a starting point and considers the possible future outcomes. A fault tree starts with the outcome and looks at the ways it could have arisen. A fault tree is therefore constructed from the right with the outcome, moves to the left with the possible immediate events that could have made that outcome arise, continues backwards with the possible events that could have made the first set of events arise, etc.

Fault trees are very useful for focusing attention on what might go wrong and why. They have been used in reliability engineering for a long time, but also have applications in areas like terrorism. For example, one might start with the risk of deliberate contamination of a city's drinking water supply and then consider routes that the terrorist could use (pipeline, treatment plant, reservoir, etc.) and the probabilities of being able to do that given the security in place.

4.1.6 Discrete event simulation

Discrete event simulation (DES) differs from Monte Carlo simulation mainly in that it models the evolution of a (usually stochastic) system over time. It does this by allowing the user to define equations for each element in the model for how it changes, moves and interacts with other elements. Then it steps the system through small time increments and keeps track of where all elements are at any time (e.g. parts in a manufacturing system, passengers in an airport or ships in a harbour). More sophisticated tools can increase the clock steps when nothing is happening, then decrease again to get a more accurate approximation to the continuous behaviour it is modelling.

We have used DES for a variety of clients, one of which was a shipping firm that regularly received LNG-ships at its site on a narrow shared waterway. The client wanted to investigate the impact of constructing an alternative berthing system designed to reduce the impact of their activities on other shipping movements, and the model evaluated the benefits of such a system. Within the DES model, movements of the client's and any other relevant shipping traffic were simulated, taking into account restrictions of movements by certain rules and regulations and evaluating the costs of delays. The stand-alone model, as well as documentation and training, was provided to the client and helped them to persuade the other shipping operators and the Federal Energy Regulatory Commission (FERC) of the effectiveness of their plan.

Figure 4.4 shows a screen shot of the model (it looks better in colour). Going from left to right, we can see that currently there is one ship in the upper harbour, four in the inner harbour, none at the city front and one in the outer harbour. In the client's berth, two ships are unloading with 1330 and 2430 units of materials still on board. In the upper right-hand corner the number of ships entering the shared waterway is visible, including the number of ships that are currently in a queue (three and two ships of a particular type). Finally, the lower right-hand corner shows the current waterway conditions, which dictate some of the rules such as "only ships of a certain draft can enter or exit the waterway given a particular current, tide, wind speed and visibility".

DES allows us to model extremely complicated systems in a simple way by defining how the elements interact and then letting the model simulate what might happen. It is used a great deal to model, for example, manufacturing processes, the spread of epidemics, all sorts of complex queuing systems, traffic

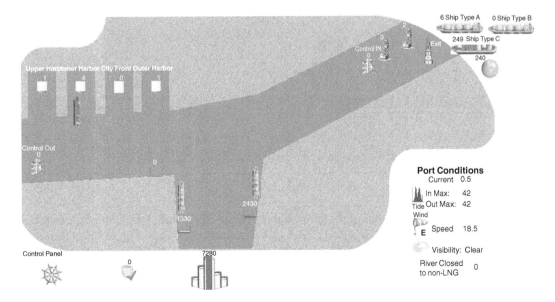

Figure 4.4 Example of a DES model.

flows and crowd behaviour to design emergency exits. The beauty of a visual interface is that anyone who knows the system can check whether it behaves as expected, which makes it a great communication and validation tool.

4.2 Calculation Methods

Given a certain probability model that we wish to evaluate, there are several methods that we could use to produce the required answer, which I describe below.

4.2.1 Calculating moments

This method uses some probability laws that are discussed later in this book. In particular it uses the following rules:

1. The mean of the sum of two distributions is equal to the sum of their means, i.e. $\overline{(a+b)} = \overline{a} + \overline{b}$ and $\overline{(a-b)} = \overline{a} - \overline{b}$.
2. The mean of the product of two distributions is equal to the product of their means, i.e. $\overline{(a \cdot b)} = \overline{a} \cdot \overline{b}$.
3. The variance of the sum of two independent distributions is equal to the sum of their variances, i.e. $V(a+b) = V(a) + V(b)$ and $V(a-b) = V(a) + V(b)$.
4. $V(na) = n^2 V(a), \overline{na} = n\overline{a}$, where n is some constant.

The moments calculation method replaces each uncertain variable with its mean and variance and then uses the above rules to estimate the mean and variance of the model's outcome.

So, for example, three variables a, b and c have the following means and variances:

$$
\begin{array}{lll}
a & \text{Mean} = 70 & \text{Variance} = 14 \\
b & \text{Mean} = 16 & \text{Variance} = 2 \\
c & \text{Mean} = 12 & \text{Variance} = 4
\end{array}
$$

If the problem is to calculate $2a + b - c$, the result can be estimated as follows:

$$\text{Mean} = (2 * 70) + 16 - 12 = 144$$

$$\text{Variance} = (2^2 * 14) + 2 + 4 = 62$$

These two values are then used to construct a normal distribution of the outcome:

$$\text{Result} = \text{Normal}(144, \sqrt{62})$$

where $\sqrt{62}$ is the standard deviation of the distribution which is the square root of the variance.

This method is useful in certain situations, like the summation of a large number of potential risks and in the determination of aggregate distributions (Section 11.2). It does have some fairly severe limitations – it cannot easily cope with divisions, exponents, power functions, branching, etc. In short, this technique becomes very difficult to execute for all but the most simple models that *also* reasonably obey its set of assumptions.

4.2.2 Exact algebraic solutions

Each probability distribution has associated with it a probability distribution function that mathematically describes its shape. Algebraic methods have been developed for determining the probability distribution functions of some combinations of variables, so for simple models one may be able to find an equation directly that describes the output distribution. For example, it is quite simple to calculate the probability distribution function of the sum of two independent distributions (the following maths might not make sense until you've read Chapter 6).

Let X be the first distribution with density $f(x)$ and cumulative distribution function $F_X(x)$, and let Y be the second distribution with density $g(x)$. Then the cumulative distribution function of the sum of X and Y, F_{X+Y}, is given by

$$F_{X+Y}(a) = \int_{-\infty}^{\infty} F_X(a - y)g(y) \, dy \qquad (4.1)$$

The sum of two independent distributions is sometimes known as the *convolution* of the distributions. By differentiating this equation, we obtain the density function of $X + Y$:

$$f_{X+Y}(a) = \int_{-\infty}^{\infty} f(a - y)g(y) \, dy \qquad (4.2)$$

So, for example, we can determine the distribution of the sum of two independent Uniform(0, 1) distributions. The probability distribution functions $f(x)$ and $g(x)$ are both 1 for $0 \le x \le 1$, and zero otherwise. From Equation (4.2) we get

$$f_{X+Y}(a) = \int_{0}^{1} f(a - y) \, dy$$

For $0 \le a \le 1$, this yields

$$f_{X+Y}(a) = \int_{0}^{a} dy$$

which gives $f_{X+Y}(a) = a$.

For $1 \le a \le 2$, this yields

$$f_{X+Y}(a) = 2 - a$$

which is a Triangle(0, 1, 2) distribution.

Thus, if our risk analysis model was just the sum of several simple distributions, we could use these equations repeatedly to determine the exact output distribution. There are a number of advantages to this approach, for example: the answer is exact; one can immediately see the effect of changing a parameter value; and one can use differential calculus to explore the sensitivity of the output to the model parameters.

A variation of the same approach is to recognise the relationship between certain distributions. For example:

$$\text{Normal}(a, b) + \text{Normal}(c, d) = \text{Normal}(a + b, \text{SQRT}(b^2 + d^2))$$

$$\text{Binomial}(\text{Poisson}(a), p) = \text{Poisson}(a * p)$$

$$\text{Binomial}(n, p) + \text{Binomial}(m, p) = \text{Binomial}(n + m, p)$$

$$\text{Binomial}(n, p) = n - \text{Binomial}(n, 1 - p)$$

$$\text{Beta}(a, b) = 1 - \text{Beta}(b, a)$$

$$\text{NegBin}(s, p) + \text{NegBin}(t, p) = \text{NegBin}(s + t, p)$$

$$\text{Poisson}(a) + \text{Poisson}(b) = \text{Poisson}(a + b)$$

$$\text{Gamma}(a, b) + \text{Gamma}(d, b) = \text{Gamma}(a + d, b)$$

$$\text{Gamma}(1 + \text{Geometric}(p), b) = \text{Gamma}(1, b/p)$$

There are plenty of such relationships, and many are described in Appendix III, but nonetheless the distributions used in a risk analysis model don't usually allow such simple manipulation and the exact algebraic technique becomes hugely complex and often intractable very quickly, so it cannot usually be considered as a practical solution.

4.2.3 Numerical approximations

Some fast Fourier transform and recursive techniques have been developed for directly, and very accurately, determining the aggregate distribution of a random number of independent random variables. A lot of focus has been paid to this particular problem because it is central to the actuarial need to determine the aggregate claim payout an insurance company will face. However, the same generic problem occurs in banking and other areas. I describe these techniques in Section 11.2.2. There are other numerical techniques that can solve certain types of problem, particularly via numerical integration. ModelRisk, for example, provides the function VoseIntegrate which will perform a very accurate numerical integration. Consider a function that relates the probability of illness, $P_{\text{ill}}(D)$, to the number of virus particles ingested, D, as follows:

$$P_{\text{ill}}(D) = 1 - \left(1 + \frac{D}{1472}\right)^{-0.00032}$$

If we believed that the number of virus particles followed a Lognormal(100,10) distribution, we could calculate the probability of illness as follows:

$$= \text{VoseIntegrate}("(1 - (1 + \#/1472)^\wedge - 0.00032) * \text{VoseLognormalProb}(\#, 100, 10, 0)", 1, 1000)$$

where the VoseIntegrate function interprets "#" to be the variable to integrate over and the integration is done between 1 and 1000. The answer is 2.10217E-05 – a value that we could only determine with accuracy using Monte Carlo simulation by running a large number of iterations.

4.2.4 Monte carlo simulation

This technique involves the random sampling of each probability distribution within the model to produce hundreds or even thousands of scenarios (also called iterations or trials). Each probability distribution is sampled in a manner that reproduces the distribution's shape. The distribution of the values calculated for the model outcome therefore reflects the probability of the values that could occur. Monte Carlo simulation offers many advantages over the other techniques presented above:

- The distributions of the model's variables do not have to be approximated in any way.
- Correlation and other interdependencies can be modelled.
- The level of mathematics required to perform a Monte Carlo simulation is quite basic.
- The computer does all of the work required in determining the outcome distribution.
- Software is commercially available to automate the tasks involved in the simulation.
- Complex mathematics can be included (e.g. power functions, logs, IF statements, etc.) with no extra difficulty.
- Monte Carlo simulation is widely recognised as a valid technique, so its results are more likely to be accepted.
- The behaviour of the model can be investigated with great ease.
- Changes to the model can be made very quickly and the results compared with previous models.

Monte Carlo simulation is often criticised as being an approximate technique. However, in theory at least, any required level of precision can be achieved by simply increasing the number of iterations in a simulation. The limitations are in the number of random numbers that can be produced from a random number generating algorithm and, more commonly, the time a computer needs to generate the iterations. For a great many problems, these limitations are irrelevant or can be avoided by structuring the model into sections.

The value of Monte Carlo simulation can be demonstrated by considering the cost model problem of Figure 4.5. Triangular distributions represent uncertainty variables in the model. There are many other, very intuitive, distributions in common use (Figure 4.6 gives some examples) that require little or no probability knowledge to understand. The cumulative distribution of the results is shown in Figure 4.7, along with the distribution of the values that are generated from running a "what if" scenario analysis using three values as discussed at the beginning of this chapter. The figure shows that the Monte Carlo outcome does not have anywhere near as wide a range as the "what if" analysis. This is because the "what if" analysis effectively gives equal probability weighting to all scenarios, including where all costs turned out to be their maximum and all costs turned out to be their minimum. Let us allow, for a minute, the maximum to mean the value that only has a 1 % chance of being exceeded (say). The probability that all five costs could be at their maximum at the same time would equal $(0.01)^5$ or $1:10\,000\,000\,000$: not a realistic outcome! Monte Carlo simulation therefore provides results that are also far more realistic than those that are produced by simple "what if" scenarios.

Total construction costs

	Minimum	Best guess	Maximum
Excavation	£ 30 500	£ 33 200	£ 37 800
Foundations	£ 23 500	£ 27 200	£ 31 100
Structure	£ 172 000	£ 178 000	£ 189 000
Roofing	£ 56 200	£ 58 500	£ 63 700
Services and finishes	£ 29 600	£ 37 200	£ 43 600

Figure 4.5 Construction project cost model.

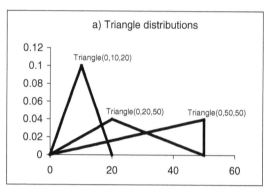

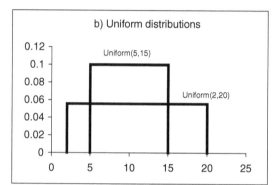

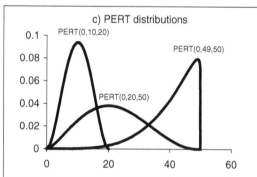

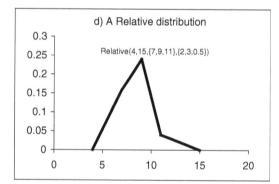

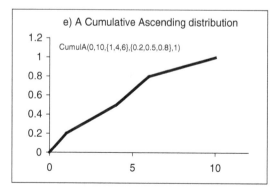

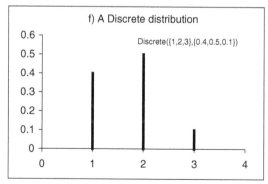

Figure 4.6 Examples of intuitive and simple probability distributions.

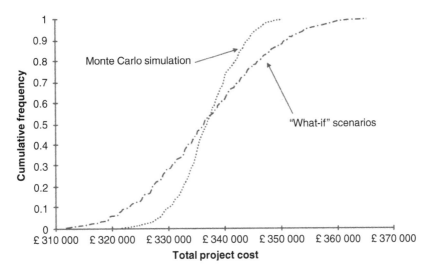

Figure 4.7   Comparison of distributions of results from "what if" and risk analyses.

4.3 Uncertainty and Variability

"Variability is a phenomenon in the physical world to be measured, analysed and where appropriate explained. By contrast, uncertainty is an aspect of knowledge".

Sir David Cox

There are two components of our inability to be able precisely to predict what the future holds: these are *variability* and *uncertainty*. This is a difficult subject, not least because of the words that we risk analysts have available to describe the various concepts and how these words have been used rather carelessly. Bearing this in mind, a good start will be to define the meaning of various keywords. I have used the now fairly standard meanings for uncertainty and variability, but might be considered to be deviating a little from the common path in my explanation of the units of uncertainty and variability. The reader should bear in mind the comments I'll make about the different meanings that various disciplines assign to certain words. As long as the reader manages to keep the concepts clear, it should be an easy enough task to work out what another author means even if some of the terminology is different.

Variability

Variability is the effect of chance and is a function of the system. It is not reducible through either study or further measurement, but may be reduced by changing the physical system. Variability has been described as "aleatory uncertainty", "stochastic variability" and "interindividual variability".

Tossing a coin a number of times provides us with a simple illustration of variability. If I toss the coin once, I will have a head (H) or tail (T), each with a probability of 50 % if one presumes a fair coin. If I toss the coin twice, I have four possible outcomes {HH, HT, TH, TT}, each with a probability of 25 % because of the coin's symmetry. We cannot predict with certainty what the tosses of a coin will produce because of the inherent randomness of the coin toss.

The variation among a population provides us with another simple example. If I randomly select people off the street and note some physical characteristic, like their height, weight, sex, whether they wear glasses, etc., the result will be a random variable with a probability distribution that matches the frequency distribution of the population from which I am sampling. So, for example, if 52 % of the population are female, a randomly sampled person will be female with a probability of 52 %.

In the nineteenth century a rather depressing philosophical school of thought, usually attributed to the mathematician Marquis Pierre-Simon de Laplace, became popular, which proposed that there was no such thing as variability, only uncertainty, i.e. that there is no randomness in the world and an omniscient being or machine, a "Laplace machine", could predict any future event. This was the foundation of the physics of the day, Newtonian physics, and even Albert Einstein believed in determinism of the physical world, saying the often quoted "Der Herr Gott wurfelt nicht" – "God does not play dice".

Heisenberg's uncertainty principle, one of the foundations of modern physics and, in particular, quantum mechanics, shows us that this is not true at the molecular level, and therefore subtly at any greater scale. In essence, it states that, the more one characteristic of a particle is constrained (for example, its location in space), the more random another characteristic becomes (if the first characteristic is location, the second will be its velocity). Einstein tried to prove that it is our *knowledge* of one characteristic that we are losing as we gain knowledge of another characteristic, rather than any characteristic being a random variable, but he has subsequently been proven wrong both theoretically and experimentally. Quantum mechanics has so far proved itself to be very accurate in predicting experimental outcomes at the molecular level where the predictable random effects are most easily observed, so we have a lot of empirical evidence to support the theory. Philosophically, the idea that everything is predetermined (i.e. the world is deterministic) is very difficult to accept too, as it deprives us humans of free will. The non-existence of free will would in turn mean that we are not responsible for our actions – we are reduced to complicated machines and it is meaningless to be either praised or punished for our deeds and misdeeds, which of course is contrary to the principles of any civilisation or religion. Thus, if one accepts the existence of free will, one must also accept an element of randomness in all things that humans affect. Popper (1988) offers a fuller discussion of the subject.

Sometimes systems are too complex for us to understand properly. For example, stock markets produce varying stock prices all the time that appear random. Nobody knows all the factors that influence a stock price over time – it is essentially infinitely complex and we accept that this is best modelled as a random process.

Uncertainty

Uncertainty is the *assessor's* lack of knowledge (level of ignorance) about the parameters that characterise the physical system that is being modelled. It is sometimes reducible through further measurement or study, or by consulting more experts. Uncertainty has also been called "fundamental uncertainty", "epistemic uncertainty" and "degree of belief". Uncertainty is by definition subjective, as it is a function of the assessor, but there are techniques available to allow one to be "objectively subjective". This essentially amounts to a logical assessment of the information contained in available data about model parameters without including any prior, non-quantitative information. The result is an uncertainty analysis that any logical person should agree with, given the available information.

Total uncertainty

Total uncertainty is the combination of uncertainty and variability. These two components act together to erode our ability to be able to predict what the future holds. Uncertainty and variability are philosophically very different, and it is now quite common for them to be kept separate in risk analysis modelling. Common mistakes are failure to include uncertainty in the model, or modelling variability in some parts of the model as if it were uncertainty. The former will provide an overconfident (i.e. insufficiently spread) model output, while the latter can grossly overinflate the total uncertainty.

Unfortunately, as you will have gathered, the term "uncertainty" has been applied to both the meaning described above and total uncertainty, which has left the risk analyst with some problems of terminology. Colleagues have suggested the word "indeterminability" to describe total uncertainty (perhaps a bit of a mouthful, but still the best suggestion I've heard so far). There has been a rather protracted argument between traditional (frequentist) and Bayesian statisticians over the meaning of words like probability, frequency, confidence, etc. Rather than go through their various interpretations here, I will simply present you with how I use these words. I have found my terminology helps clarify my thoughts and those of my clients and course participants very well. I hope they will do the same for you.

Probability

Probability is a numerical measurement of the likelihood of an outcome of some stochastic process. It is thus one of the two components, along with the values of the possible outcomes, that describe the *variability* of a system. The concept of probability can be developed neatly from two different approaches. The frequentist approach asks us to imagine repeating the physical process an extremely large number of times (trials) and then to look at the fraction of times that the outcome of interest occurs. That fraction is asymptotically (meaning as we approach an infinite number of trials) equal to the probability of that particular outcome for that physical process. So, for example, the frequentist would imagine that we toss a coin a very large number of times. The fraction of the tosses that comes up heads is approximately the true probability of a single toss producing a head, and, the more tosses we do, the closer the fraction becomes to the true probability. So, for a fair coin we should see the number of heads stabilise at around 50 % of the trials as the number of trials gets truly huge. The philosophical problem with this approach is that one usually does not have the opportunity to repeat the scenario a very large number of times.

The physicist or engineer, on the other hand, could look at the coin, measure it, spin it, bounce lasers off its surface, etc., until one could declare that, owing to symmetry, the coin must logically have a 50 % probability of falling on either surface (for a fair coin, or some other value for an unbalanced coin as the measurements dictated).

Probability is used to define a probability distribution, which describes the range of values the variable may take, together with the probability (likelihood) that the variable will take any specific value.

Degree of uncertainty

In this context, "degree of uncertainty" is our measure of how much we believe something to be true. It is one of the two components, along with the plausible values of the parameter, that describe the uncertainty we may have about the parameter of the physical system ("the state of nature", if you like) to be modelled. We can thus use the degree of uncertainty to define an uncertainty distribution, which describes the range of values within which we believe the parameter lies, as well as the level of confidence we have about the parameter being any particular value, or lying within any particular range. A distribution of confidence looks exactly the same as a distribution of probability, and this can lead, all to easily, to confusion between the two quantities.

Frequency

Frequency is the number of times a particular characteristic appears in a population. Relative frequency is the fraction of times the characteristic appears in the population. So, in a population of 1000 people,

22 of whom have blue eyes, the frequency of blue eyes is 22 and the relative frequency is 0.022 or 2.2 %. Frequency, by the definition used here, must relate to a known population size.

4.3.1 Some illustrations of uncertainty and variability

Let us look at a couple of examples to clarify the meaning of uncertainty and variability. Since variability is the more fundamental concept, we'll deal with it first. If I toss a fair coin, there is a 50 % chance that each toss will come up heads (let's call this a "success"). The result of each toss is independent of the results of any previous tosses, and it turns out that the probability distribution of the number of heads in n tosses of a fair coin is described by a Binomial(n, 50 %) distribution, which will be explained in detail in Section 8.2. Figure 4.8 illustrates this binomial distribution for $n = 1$, 2, 5 and 10. This is a distribution of variability because I am not a machine, so I am not perfectly repetitive, and the system (the number of times the coin spins, the air resistance and movement, the angle at which it hits the ground, the topology of the ground, etc.) is too complicated for me to attempt to influence the outcome, and the tosses are therefore random.

These binomial distributions are distributions of variability and reflect the randomness inherent in the tossing of a coin (our stochastic system). We are assuming that there is no uncertainty here, as we are assuming the coin to be fair and we are defining the number of tosses; in other words, we are assuming the parameters of the system to be exactly known. The vertical axis of Figure 4.8 gives the probability of each result, and, naturally, these probabilities add up to 1. In general, probability distributions or distributions of variability are simple to understand. They give me some comfort that

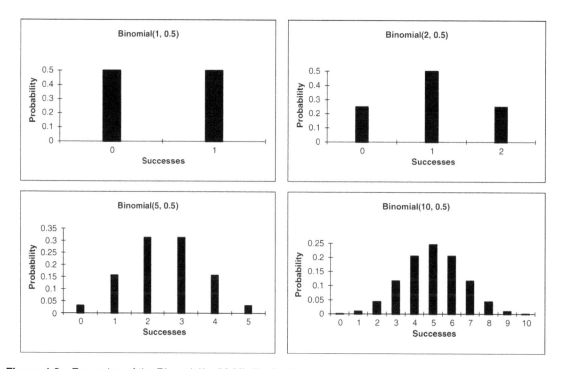

Figure 4.8 Examples of the Binomial(n, 50 %) distribution.

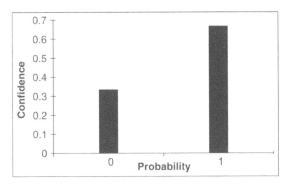

Figure 4.9 Confidence distributions for the ball in the box being black: 0 = No, 1 = Yes. The left panel is confidence before any ball is revealed; the right panel is confidence after seeing a blue ball removed from the sack.

randomness (variability) really does exist in the world: if we take a group of 100 people[1] and ask them to toss a coin 10 times, the resulting distribution of the number of heads will closely follow a Binomial(10, 50 %).

Now, let's look at a distribution of uncertainty. Imagine I have a sack of 10 balls, six of which are black and the remaining four of which are blue, and I know these figures. Now imagine that, out of my sight, a ball is randomly selected from the sack and placed in an opaque box. I am asked the question: "What is the probability that the ball in the box is black?", and I could quickly answer 6/10 or 60 %. Now, another ball is removed from the sack and shown to me: it is blue. I am asked: "Now what is the probability that the ball in the box is black?", and, as there are now a total of nine balls I have not seen, six of which I know are black, I could answer 6/9 or 66.66 %. But that is strange, because it is difficult to believe that the *probability* of the ball in the box being black has changed from events that occurred *after* its selection. The problem lies in my use of the term "probability" which is inconsistent with the definition I have given above. When the ball has been placed in the box, the deed is done, so the ball in the box *is* black (i.e. the probability is 1) or it is *not* (i.e. the probability is 0). I don't know the truth but could collect information (i.e. look in the box or look in the sack) to find out what the true value is. Before any ball was revealed to me, I should have said that I was 60 % confident that the probability was 1, and therefore 40 % confident that the probability was 0. This is an uncertainty distribution of the true probability. Now, when the blue ball was revealed to me from the sack I had extra information and would therefore change my uncertainty distribution to show a 66.66 % confidence that the ball in the box was black (i.e. that the probability was 1). These two confidence distributions are shown in Figure 4.9. Note that the distributions of Figure 4.9 are pure uncertainty distributions. The x axis is probability but may only take a value of 0 and 1, and a system with a probability of 0 (or 1) has no variability: its outcome is deterministic.

4.3.2 Separating uncertainty and variability in a risk analysis model

Uncertainty and variability are described by distributions that, to all intents and purposes, look and behave exactly the same. One might therefore reasonably conclude that they can be used together in the same Monte Carlo model: some distributions reflecting the uncertainty about certain parameters in

---

[1] I don't recommend the experiment. I've done this a couple of times with a big lecture group sitting in a large banked auditorium. The coins went everywhere.

the model, the other distributions reflecting the inherent stochastic nature of the system. We could then run a simulation on such a model which would randomly sample from all the distributions and our output would therefore take account of all uncertainty and variability. Unfortunately, this does not work out *completely*. The resultant single distribution is equivalent to our "best-guess" distribution of the composite of the two components. Technically, it is difficult to interpret, as the vertical scale represents neither uncertainty nor variability, and we have lost some information in knowing what component of the resultant distribution is due to the inherent randomness (variability) of the system, and what component is due to our ignorance of that system. It is therefore useful to know how to keep these two components separate in an analysis if necessary.

Why separate uncertainty and variability?

Keeping uncertainty and variability separate in a risk analysis model is mathematically more correct. Mixing the two together, i.e. by simulating them together, produces a reasonable estimate of the level of total uncertainty under most conditions. Figure 4.10 shows a Binomial(10, p) distribution, where p is uncertain with distribution Beta(10, 10). The spaghetti-looking graph represents a number of possible true binomial distributions, shown in cumulative form, and the bold line shows the result one gets from simulating the binomial and beta distributions together. The combined model may be wrong, but it covers the possible range very well. But consider doing the same with just one binomial trial, e.g. Binomial(1, Beta(10,10)). The result is either a 1 or a 0, each occurring in about 50 % of the simulation run, the same result as we would have had by modelling Binomial(1, 50 %). The output has lost the information that p is uncertain.

Mixing uncertainty and variability means, of course, that we cannot see how much of the total uncertainty comes from variability and how much from uncertainty, and that information is useful. If we know that a large part of the total uncertainty is due to uncertainty (as in the example of Figure 4.11), then we know that collecting further information, thereby reducing uncertainty, would enable us to improve our estimate of the future. On the other hand, if the total uncertainty is nearly all due to variability (as in the example of Figure 4.12), we know that it is a waste of time to collect more

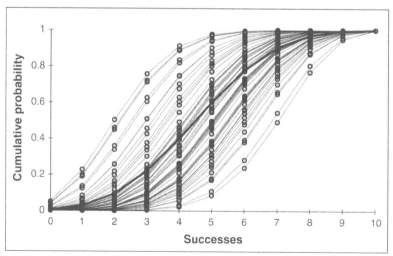

Figure 4.10   300 Binomial(10, p) distributions resulting from random samples of p from a Beta(10, 10) distribution.

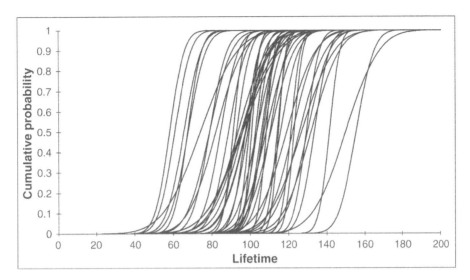

Figure 4.11 Example of second-order risk analysis model output with uncertainty dominating variability.

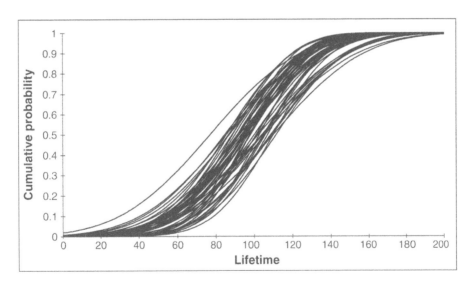

Figure 4.12 Example of second-order risk analysis model output with variability dominating uncertainty.

information and the only way to reduce the total uncertainty would be to change the physical system. In general, the separation of uncertainty and variability allows us to understand what steps can be taken to reduce the total uncertainty of our model, and allows us to gauge the value of more information or of some potential change we can make to the system.

A much larger problem than mixing uncertainty and variability distributions together can occur when a variability distribution is used as if it were an uncertainty distribution. Separating uncertainty and variability very deliberately gives us the discipline and understanding to avoid the much larger errors that this mistake will produce. Consider the following problem.

A group of 10 jurors is randomly picked from a population for some court case. In this population, 50 % are female, 0.2 % have severe visual disability and 1.1 % are Native American. The defence would like to have at least one member on the jury who is female and either Native American or visually disabled or both. What is the probability that there will be at least one such juror in the selection? This is a pure variability problem, as all the parameters are considered well known and the answer is quite easy to calculate, assuming independence between the characteristics. The probability that a person is not Native American and not visually disabled is $(100\% - 1.1\%) * (100\% - 0.2\%) = 98.7022\%$. The probability that a person is either Native American or visually disabled or both is $(100\% - 98.7022\%) = 1.2978\%$. Thus, the probability that a person is either Native American or visually disabled or both *and* female is $(50\% * 1.2978\%) = 0.6489\%$. The probability that *none* of the potential jurors is either Native American or visually disabled or both and female is then $(100\% - 0.6489\%)^{10} = 93.697\%$, and so, finally, the probability that at least one potential juror is either Native American or visually disabled or both and female is $(100\% - 93.697\%) = 6.303\%$.

Now let's compare this calculation with the spreadsheet of Figure 4.13 and the result it produces in Figure 4.14. In this model, the number of females in the jury has been simulated, but the rest of the calculation has been explicitly calculated. The output thus has a distribution that is meaningless since it should be a single figure. The reason for this is that the model both calculated and simulated variability. We are treating the number of females as if it were an uncertain parameter rather than a variable.

Now, having said how useful it is to separate uncertainty and variability, we must take a step back and ask whether the effort is worth the extra information that can be gained. In truth, if we run simulations that combine uncertainty and variability in the same simulation, we can get a good idea of their contribution to total uncertainty by running the model twice: the first time sampling from all distributions, and the second time setting all the uncertainty distributions to their mean value. The difference in spread is a reasonable description of the contribution of uncertainty to total uncertainty. Writing a model where uncertainty and variability are kept separate, as described in the next section,

	A	B	C	D	E
1					
2		Female	50%		
3		Visually impaired	0.20%		
4		Native American	1.10%		
5		Potential jurors	10		
6					
7		No. female jurors	9		
8		Probability neither NA or VI	98.7022%		
9		Probability all females are neither NA nor VI	0.889081		
10		Probability at least one female is either NA or VI or both	11.092%		
11					
12		Formulae table			
13		C2:C5	Input values		
14		C7	=Binomial(C5,C2)		
15		C8	=(1-C3)*(1-C4)		
16		C9	=C8^C7		
17		C10 (output)	=1-C9		
18					

Figure 4.13   Example of model that incorrectly mixes uncertainty and variability.

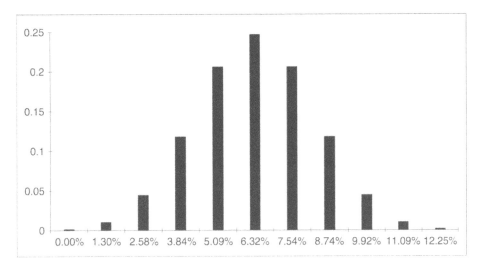

Figure 4.14 Result of the model of Figure 4.13.

can be very time consuming and cumbersome, so we must keep an eye out for the value of such an exercise.

4.3.3 Structuring a Monte Carlo model to separate uncertainty and variability

The core structure of a risk analysis model is the variability of the stochastic system. Once this variability model has been constructed, the uncertainty about parameters in that variability model can be overlaid. A risk analysis model that separates uncertainty and variability is described as *second order*. A variability model comes in two forms: explicit calculation and simulation. In a variability model with explicit calculation, the probability of each possible outcome is explicitly calculated. So, for example, if one were calculating the number of heads in 10 tosses of a coin, the explicit calculation model would take the

	A	B	C	D	E	F	G
1							
2		*n*	10		*x*	*f (x)*	
3		*p*	0.5		0	0.0009766	
4					1	0.0097656	
5		Mean		5	2	0.0439453	
6		Standard deviation	1.58114		3	0.1171875	
12					9	0.0097656	
13					10	0.0009766	
14							
15			Formulae table				
16		E3:E13	1,2,3,...				
17		F3:F13	=BINOMDIST(E3,n,p,0)				
18		D5	=SUMPRODUCT(E3:E13,F3:F13)				
19		D6	=SQRT(SUMPRODUCT((E3:E13-D5)^2,F3:F13))				
20							

Figure 4.15 Model calculating the outcome of 10 tosses of a coin.

form of the spreadsheet in Figure 4.15. Here, we have used the Excel function BINOMDIST($x, n, p,$ *cumulative*) which returns the probability of x successes in n trials with a binomial probability of success p. The *cumulative* parameter requires either a TRUE (or 1) or a FALSE (or 0): using TRUE, the function returns the cumulative probability $F(x)$, using FALSE the function returns the probability mass $f(x)$. Plotting columns E and F together in an $x-y$ scatter plot produces the binomial distribution which can be the output of the model. Statistical results, like the mean and standard deviation shown in the spreadsheet model, can also be determined explicitly as needed. The formulae calculating the mean and standard deviation use an Excel array function SUMPRODUCT which multiplies terms in the two arrays pair by pair and then sums these pair products. In an explicitly calculated model like this it is a simple matter to include uncertainty about any parameters of the model. For example, if we are not confident that the coin was truly fair but instead wish to describe our estimate of the probability of heads as a Beta(12, 11) distribution (see Section 8.2.3 for explanation of the beta distribution in this context), we can simply enter the beta distribution in place of the 0.5 value in cell C3 and simulate for the cells in column F containing the outputs.

The separation of uncertainty and variability is simple and clear when using a model that explicitly calculates the variability, as we use formulae for the variability and simulation for the uncertainty. But what do we do if the model is set up to simulate the variability? Figure 4.16 shows the same coin tossing problem, but now we are simulating the number of heads using a Binomial(n, p) function in @RISK. Admittedly, it seems rather unnecessary here to simulate such a simple problem, but in many circumstances it is extremely unwieldy, if not impossible, to use explicit calculation models, and simulation is the only feasible approach. Since we are using the random sampling of simulation to model the variability, it is no longer available to us to model uncertainty. Let us imagine that we put a possible value for the binomial probability p into the model and run a simulation. The result is the binomial distribution that would be the correct model of variability if that value of p were correct. Now, we believe that p could actually be quite a different value – our confidence about the true value of p is described by a Beta(12, 11) distribution – so we would really like to take repeated samples from the beta distribution, run a simulation for each sample and plot all the binomial distributions together to give us a true picture. This sounds immensely tedious, but @RISK provides a RiskSimtable function that will automate the process. Crystal Ball also provides a similar facility in its Pro version that allows one to nominate uncertainty and variability distributions within a model separately and then completely automates the process.

We proceed by taking (say 50) Latin hypercube samples from the beta distribution, then import them back into the spreadsheet model. We then use a RiskSimtable function to reference the list of values.

	A	B	C	D	E	F	G
1							
2		Probability heads	63.40%	50 samples		Beta values	
3		Probability simtable	42.60%	taken from C2		42.60%	
4						54.28%	
5		Number of heads	5			43.40%	
6						41.37%	
50			Formulae table			32.46%	
51		C2	=Beta(12,11)			38.31%	
52		C3	=RiskSimtable(F3:F52)			46.08%	
53		C5	=Binomial(10,C3)				
54							

Figure 4.16 A simulation version of the model of Figure 4.15.

The RiskSimtable function returns the first value in the list, but when we instruct @RISK to run 50 simulations, each of say 500 iterations, the RiskSimtable function will go through the list, using one value at a time for each simulation. Note that the number of simulations is set to equal the number of samples we have from the beta uncertainty distribution. The binomial distribution is then linked to the RiskSimtable function and named as an output. We now run the 50 simulations and produce 50 different possible binomial distributions which can be plotted together and analysed in much the same way as an explicit calculation output. Of course, there are an infinite number of possible binomial distributions, but, by using Latin hypercube sampling (see Section 4.4.3 for an explanation of the value of Latin hypercube sampling), we are ensuring that we get a good representation of the uncertainty with a few simulations.

In spite of the automation provided by the RiskSimtable function in @RISK or the facilities of Crystal Ball Pro and the speed of modern computers, the simulations can take some time. However, in most non-trivial models that time is easily balanced by the reduction in complexity of the model itself and therefore the time it takes to construct, as well as the more intuitive manner in which the models can be constructed which greatly helps avoiding errors.

The ModelRisk software makes uncertainty analysis much easier, as all its fitting functions offer the option of either returning best fitting parameters (or distributions, time series, etc., based on best fitting parameters), which is more common practice, *or* including the statistical uncertainty about those parameters, which is more correct.

4.4 How Monte Carlo Simulation Works

This section looks at the technical aspects of how Monte Carlo risk analysis software generates random samples for the input distributions of a model. The difference between Monte Carlo and Latin hypercube sampling is explained. An illustration of the improvement in reliability and efficiency of Latin hypercube sampling over Monte Carlo is also presented. The use of a random number generator seed is explained, and the reader is shown how it is possible to generate probability distributions of one's own design. Finally, a brief introduction is given into the methods used by risk analysis software to produce rank order correlation of input variables.

4.4.1 Random sampling from input distributions

Consider the distribution of an uncertain input variable x. The cumulative distribution function $F(x)$, defined in Chapter 6.1.1, gives the probability P that the variable X will be less than or equal to x, i.e.

$$F(x) = P(X \leq x)$$

$F(x)$ obviously ranges from 0 to 1. Now, we can look at this equation in the reverse direction: what is the value of $F(x)$ for a given value of x? This inverse function $G(F(x))$ is written as

$$G(F(x)) = x$$

It is this concept of the inverse function $G(F(x))$ that is used in the generation of random samples from each distribution in a risk analysis model. Figure 4.17 provides a graphical representation of the relationship between $F(x)$ and $G(F(x))$.

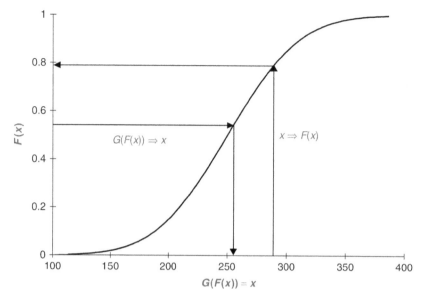

Figure 4.17 The relationship between x, $F(x)$ and $G(F(x))$.

To generate a random sample for a probability distribution, a random number r is generated between 0 and 1. This value is then fed into the equation to determine the value to be generated for the distribution:

$$G(r) = x$$

The random number r is generated from a Uniform(0, 1) distribution to provide equal opportunity of an x value being generated in any percentile range. The inverse function concept is employed in a number of sampling methods, discussed in the following sections. In practice, for some types of probability distribution it is not possible to determine an equation for $G(F(x))$, in which case numerical solving techniques can be employed.

ModelRisk uses the inversion method for all of its 70+ families of univariate distributions and allows the user to control how the distribution is sampled via its "U-parameter". For example:

$$\text{VoseNormal(mu, sigma, } U)$$

where mu and sigma are the mean and standard deviation of the normal distribution;

$$\text{VoseNormal(mu, sigma, 0.9)}$$

returns the 90th percentile of the distribution;

$$\text{VoseNormal(mu, sigma)}$$

or

$$\text{VoseNormal(mu, sigma, RiskUniform(0, 1))}$$

for @RISK users or

$$VoseNormal(mu, sigma, CB.Uniform(0, 1))$$

for Crystal Ball users, etc., returns random samples from the distribution that are controlled by Model-Risk, @RISK or Crystal Ball respectively. The inversion method also allows us to make use of copulas to correlate variables, as explained in Section 13.3.

4.4.2 Monte Carlo sampling

Monte Carlo sampling uses the above sampling method exactly as described. It is the least sophisticated of the sampling methods discussed here, but is the oldest and best known. Monte Carlo sampling got its name as the code word for work that von Neumann and Ulam were doing during World War II on the Manhattan Project at Los Alamos for the atom bomb, where it was used to integrate otherwise intractable mathematical functions (Rubinstein, 1981). However, one of the earliest examples of the use of the Monte Carlo method was in the famous Buffon's needle problem where needles were physically thrown randomly onto a gridded field to estimate the value of π. At the beginning of the twentieth century the Monte Carlo method was also used to examine the Boltzmann equation, and in 1908 the famous statistician Student (W. S. Gossett) used the Monte Carlo method for estimating the correlation coefficient in his t-distribution.

Monte Carlo sampling satisfies the purist's desire for an unadulterated random sampling method. It is useful if one is trying to get a model to imitate a random sampling from a population or for doing statistical experiments. However, the randomness of its sampling means that it will over- and undersample from various parts of the distribution and cannot be relied upon to replicate the input distribution's shape unless a very large number of iterations are performed.

For nearly all risk analysis modelling, the pure randomness of Monte Carlo sampling is not really relevant. We are almost always far more concerned that the model will reproduce the distributions that we have determined for its inputs. Otherwise, what would be the point of expending so much effort on getting these distributions right? Latin hypercube sampling addresses this issue by providing a sampling method that *appears* random but that also guarantees to reproduce the input distribution with much greater efficiency than Monte Carlo sampling.

4.4.3 Latin Hypercube sampling

Latin hypercube sampling, or LHS, is an option that is now available for most risk analysis simulation software programs. It uses a technique known as "stratified sampling without replacement" (Iman, Davenport and Zeigler, 1980) and proceeds as follows:

- The probability distribution is split into n intervals of equal probability, where n is the number of iterations that are to be performed on the model. Figure 4.18 illustrates an example of the stratification that is produced for 20 iterations of a normal distribution. The bands can be seen to get progressively wider towards the tails as the probability density drops away.

- In the first iteration, one of these intervals is selected using a random number.

- A second random number is then generated to determine where, within that interval, $F(x)$ should lie. In practice, the second half of the first random number can be used for this purpose, reducing simulation time.

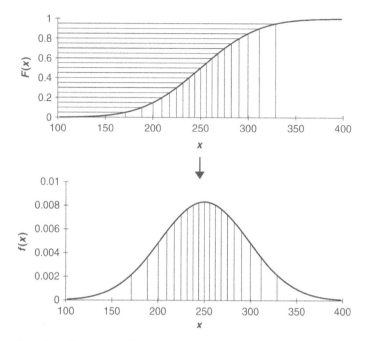

Figure 4.18 Example of the effect of stratification in Latin hypercube sampling.

- $x = G(F(x))$ is calculated for that value of $F(x)$.
- The process is repeated for the second iteration, but the interval used in the first iteration is marked as having already been used and therefore will not be selected again.
- This process is repeated for all of the iterations. Since the number of iterations n is also the number of intervals, each interval will only have been sampled once and the distribution will have been reproduced with predictable uniformity over the $F(x)$ range.

The improvement offered by LHS over Monte Carlo can be easily demonstrated. Figure 4.19 compares the results obtained by sampling from a Triangle(0, 10, 20) distribution with LHS and Monte Carlo sampling. The top panels of Figure 4.19 show histograms of the triangular distribution after one simulation of 300 iterations. The LHS clearly reproduces the distribution much better. The middle panels of Figure 4.19 show an example of the convergence of the two sampling techniques to the true values of the distribution's mean and standard deviation. In the Monte Carlo test, the distribution was sampled 50 times, then another 50 to make 100, then another 100 to make 200, and so on to give simulations of 50, 100, 200, 300, 500, 1000 and 5000 iterations. In the LHS test, seven different simulations were run for the seven different numbers of iterations. The difference between the approaches was taken because the LHS has a "memory" and the Monte Carlo sampling does not. A "memory" is where the sampling algorithm takes account of from where it has already sampled in the distribution. From these two panels, one can get the feel for the consistency provided by LHS. The bottom two panels provide a more general picture. To produce these diagrams, the triangular distribution was sampled in seven separate simulations again with the following number of iterations: 50, 100, 200, 300, 500, 1000 and 5000 for both LHS and Monte Carlo sampling. This was repeated 100 times and the mean and standard deviation of the results were noted. The standard deviations of these statistics were calculated to give a feel for

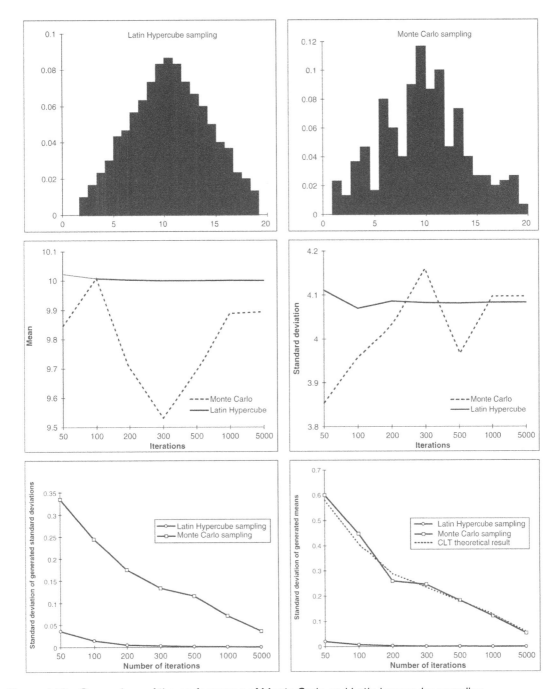

Figure 4.19   Comparison of the performance of Monte Carlo and Latin hypercube sampling.

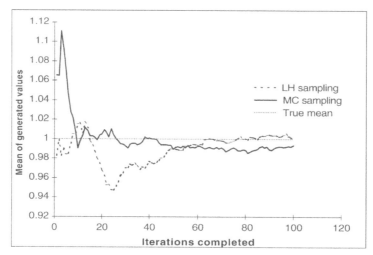

Figure 4.20 Example comparison of the convergence of the mean for Monte Carlo and Latin hypercube distributions.

how much the results might naturally vary from one simulation to another. LHS consistently produces values for the distribution's statistics that are nearer to the theoretical values of the input distribution than Monte Carlo sampling. In fact, one can see that the spread in results using just 100 LHS samples is smaller than the spread using 5000 MC samples!

The benefit of LHS is eroded if one does not complete the number of iterations nominated at the beginning, i.e. if one halts the program in mid-simulation. Figure 4.20 illustrates an example where a Normal(1, 0.1) distribution is simulated for 100 iterations with both Monte Carlo sampling and LHS. The mean of the values generated has roughly the same degree of variance from the true mean of 1 until the number of iterations completed gets close to the prescribed 100, when LHS pulls more sharply in to the desired value.

4.4.4 Other sampling methods

There are a couple of other sampling methods, and I mention them here for completeness, although they do not appear very often and are not offered by the standard risk analysis packages. *Mid-point LHS* is a version of standard LHS where the mid-point of each interval is used for the sampling. In other words, the data points (x_i) generated from a distribution using n iterations will be at the $(i - 0.5)/n$ percentiles. Mid-point LHS will produce even more precise and predictable values for the output statistics than LHS, and in most situations it would be very useful. However, there are the odd occasions where its equidistancing between the $F(x)$ values causes interference effects that would not be observed in standard LHS.

In certain problems, one might only be concerned with the extreme tail of the distribution of possible outcomes. In such cases, even a very large number of iterations may fail to produce *many* sufficient values in the extreme tail of the output for an accurate representation of the area of interest. It can then be useful to employ *importance sampling* (Clark, 1961) which artificially raises the probability of sampling from the ranges within the input distributions that would cause the extreme values of interest in the output. The accentuated tail of the output distribution is rescaled back to its correct probability density at the end of the simulation, but there is now good detail in the tail. In Section 4.5.1 we will look at another method of simulation that ensures that one can get sufficient detail in the modelling of rare events.

Sobol numbers are non-random sequences of numbers that progressively fill in the Latin hypercube space. The advantage they offer is that one can keep adding more iterations and they keep filling gaps previously left. Contrast that with LHS for which we need to define the number of iterations at the beginning of the simulation and, once it is complete, we have to start again – we can't build on the sampling already done.

4.4.5 Random number generator seeds

There are many algorithms that have been developed to generate a series of random numbers between 0 and 1 with equal probability density for all possible values. There are plenty of reviews you can find online. The best general-purpose algorithm is currently widely held to be the Mersenne twister. These algorithms will start with a value between 0 and 1, and all subsequent random numbers that are generated will rely on this initial *seed value*. This can be very useful. Most decent risk analysis packages now offer the option to select a seed value. I personally do this as a matter of course, setting the seed to 1 (because I can remember it!). Providing the model is not changed, and that includes the position of the distributions in a spreadsheet model and therefore the order in which they are sampled, the same simulation results can be exactly repeated. More importantly, one or more distributions can be changed within the model and a second simulation run to look at the effect these changes have on the model's outputs. It is then certain that any observed change in the result is due to changes in the model and not a result of the randomness of the sampling.

4.5 Simulation Modelling

My *cardinal rule of risk analysis modelling* is: "Every iteration of a risk analysis model must be a scenario that could physically occur". If the modeller follows this "cardinal rule", he or she has a much better chance of producing a model that is both accurate and realistic and will avoid most of the problems I so frequently encounter when reviewing a client's work. Section 7.4 discusses the most common risk modelling errors.

A second very useful rule is: "Simulate when you can't calculate". In other words, don't simulate when it is possible and not too onerous to determine exactly the answer directly through normal mathematics. There are several reasons for this: simulation provides an approximate answer and mathematics can give an exact answer; simulation will often not be able to provide the entire distribution, especially at the low probability tails; mathematical equations can be updated instantaneously in light of a change in the value of a parameter; and techniques like partial differentiation that can be applied to mathematical equations provide methods to optimise decisions much more easily than simulation. In spite of all these benefits, algebraic solutions can be excessively time consuming or intractable for all but the simplest problems. For those who are not particularly mathematically inclined or trained, simulation provides an efficient and intuitive approach to modelling risky issues.

4.5.1 Rare events

It is often tempting in a risk analysis model to include very unlikely events that would have a very large impact should they occur; for example, including the risk of a large earthquake in a cost model of a Sydney construction project. True, the large earthquake could happen and the effect would be devastating, but there is generally little to be gained from including the rare event in an overview model.

The expected impact of a rare event is determined by two factors: the probability that it will occur and, if it did occur, the distribution of possible impact it would have. For example, we may determine that there is about a 1:50 000 chance of a very large earthquake during the construction of a skyscraper. However, if there were an earthquake, it would inflict anything between a few hundred pounds damage and a few million.

In general, the distribution of the impact of a rare event is far more straightforward to determine than the probability that the rare event will occur in the first place. We often can be no more precise about the probability than to within one or two orders of magnitude (i.e. to within a factor of 10–100). It is usually this determination of the *probability* of the event that provides a stumbling block for the analyst.

One method to determine the probability is to look at past frequencies and assume that they will represent the future. This may be of use if we are able to collect a sufficiently large and reliable dataset. Earthquake data in the New World, for example, only extends for 200 or 300 years and could give us, at its smallest, a one in 200 year probability.

Another method, commonly used in fields like nuclear power reliability, is to break the problem down into components. For an explosion to occur in a nuclear power station (excluding human error), a potential hazard would have to occur and a string of safety devices would all have to fail together. The probability of an explosion is the product of the probability of the initial conditions necessary for an explosion and the probabilities of each safety device failing. This method has also been applied in epidemiology where agricultural authorities have sought to determine the risk of introduction of an exotic disease. These analyses typically attempt to map out the various routes through which contaminated animals or animal products can enter the country and then infect the country's livestock. In some cases, the structure of the problem is relatively simple and the probabilities can be reasonably calculated; for example, the risk of introducing a disease through importing semen straws or embryos. In this case the volume is easily estimated, its source determinable and regulations can be imposed to minimise the risk.

In other cases, the structure of the problem is extremely complex and a sensible analysis may be impossible except to place an upper limit on the probability; for example, the risk of introducing disease into native fish by importing salmon. There are so many paths through which a fish in a stream or fish farm could be exposed to imported contaminated salmon, ranging from a seagull picking up a scrap from a dump and dropping it in a stream right in front of a fish to a saboteur deliberately buying some salmon and feeding it to fish in a farm. It is clearly impossible to cover all of the scenarios that might exist, or even to calculate the probability of each individual scenario. In such cases, it makes more sense to set an upper bound to the probability that infection occurs.

It is very common for people to include rare events in a risk analysis model that is primarily concerned with the general uncertainty of the problem, but provides little extra insight. For example, we might construct a model to estimate how long it will take to develop a software application for a client: designing, coding, testing, etc. The model would be broken down into key tasks and probabilistic estimates made for the duration of each task. We would then run a simulation to find the total effect of all these uncertainties. We would not include in such an analysis the effect of a plane crashing into the office or the project manager quitting. We might recognise these risks and hold back-up files at a separate location or make the project manager sign a tight contract, but we would gain no greater understanding of our project's chance of meeting the deadline by incorporating such risks into our model.

4.5.2 Model uncertainty

Model building is subjective. The analyst has to decide the way he will build a necessarily simple model to attempt to represent a frequently very complicated reality. One needs to make decisions about which bits can be left out as insignificant, perhaps without a great deal of data to back up the decision. We also have to reason which type of stochastic process is actually operating. In truth, we rarely have a purely binomial, Poisson or any other theoretical stochastic process occurring in nature. However, we can often convince ourselves that the degree of deviation from the simplified model we chose to use is not terribly significant. It is important in any model to consider how it could fail to represent the real world. In any mathematical abstraction we are making certain assumptions, and it is important to run through these assumptions, both the explicit assumptions that are easy to identify and the implicit assumptions that one may easily fail to spot. For example, using a Poisson process to model frequencies of epidemics may seem quite reasonable, as they could be considered to occur randomly in time. However, the individuals in one epidemic can be the source of the next epidemic, in which case the events are not independent. Seasonality of epidemics means that the Poisson intensity varies with month, which can be catered for once it is recognised, but if there are other random elements affecting the Poisson intensity then it may be more appropriate to model the epidemics as a mixture process.

Sometimes one may have two possible models (for example, two equations relating bacteria growth rates to time and ambient temperature, or two equations for the lifetime of a device), both of which seem plausible. In my view, these represent subjective uncertainty that should be included in the model, just as other uncertain parameters have distributions assigned to them. So, for example, if I have two plausible growth models, I might use a discrete distribution to use one or the other randomly during each iteration of the model.

There is no easy solution to the problems of model uncertainty. It is essential to identify the simplifications and assumptions one is making when presenting the model and its results, in order for the reader to have an appropriate level of confidence in the model. Arguments and counterarguments can be presented for the factors that would bring about a failure of the model. Analysts can be nervous about pointing out these assumptions, but practical decision-makers will understand that any model has assumptions and they would rather be aware of them than not. In any case, I think it is always much better for me to be the person who points out the potential weaknesses of my models first. One can also often analyse the effects of changing the model assumptions, which gives the reader some feel for the reliability of the model's results.

Chapter 5

Understanding and using the results of a risk analysis

A risk analysis model, however carefully crafted, is of no value unless its results are understandable, useful, believable and tailored to the problem in hand. This chapter looks at various techniques to help the analyst achieve these goals.

Section 5.1 gives a brief overview of the points that should be borne in mind in the preparation of a risk analysis report. Section 5.2 looks at how to present the assumptions of the model in a succinct and comprehensible way. The results of a risk analysis model are far more likely to be accepted by decision-makers if they understand the model and accept its assumptions.

Section 5.3 illustrates a number of graphical presentations that can be employed to demonstrate a model's results and offers guidance for their most appropriate use. Finally, Section 5.4 looks at a variety of statistical analyses that can be performed on the output data of a risk analysis.

In addition to writing comprehensive risk analysis reports, I have found it particularly helpful to my clients to run short courses for senior management that explain:

- how to manage a risk assessment (time and resources required, typical sequence of activities, etc.);
- how to ensure that a risk assessment is being performed properly;
- what a risk assessment can and cannot do;
- what outputs one can ask for;
- how to interpret, present and communicate a risk assessment and its results.

This type of training eases the introduction of risk analysis into an organisation. We see many organisations where the engineers, analysts, scientists, etc., have embraced risk analysis, trained themselves and acquired the right tools and then fail to push the extra knowledge up the decision chain because the decision-makers remain unfamiliar and perhaps intimidated by all this new "risk analysis stuff". If you are intending to present the results of a risk analysis to an unknown audience, consider assuming that the audience knows nothing about risk analysis modelling and explain some basic concepts (like Monte Carlo simulation) at the beginning of the presentation.

5.1 Writing a Risk Analysis Report

Complex models, probability distributions and statistics often leave the reader of a risk analysis report confused (and probably bored). The reader may have little understanding of the methods employed in risk analysis or of how to interpret, and make decisions from, its results. In this environment it is essential that a risk analysis report guide the reader through the assumptions, results and conclusions (if any) in a manner that is transparently clear but neither esoteric nor oversimplistic.

The model's assumptions should always be presented in the report, even if only in a very shorthand form. I have found that a report puts across its message to the reader much more effectively if these model assumptions are put to the back of the report, the front being reserved for the model's results, an assessment of its robustness (see Chapter 3) and any conclusions. We tend to write reports with the following components (depending on the situation):

- summary;
- introduction to problem;
- decision questions addressed and those not addressed;
- discussion of available data and relation to model choice;
- major model assumptions and the impact on the results if incorrect;
- critique of model, comment on validation;
- presentation of results;
- discussion of possible options for improvement, extra data that would change the model or its results, additional work that could be done;
- discussion of modelling strategy;
- decision question(s);
- available data;
- methods of addressing decision questions with available information;
- assumptions inherent in different modelling options;
- explanation of choice of model;
- discussion of model used;
- overview of model structure, how the sections relate together;
- discussion of each section (data, mathematics, assumptions, partial results);
- results (graphical and statistical analyses);
- model validation;
- references and datasets;
- technical appendices;
- explanation of unusual equation derivations;
- guide on how to interpret and use statistical and graphical outputs.

The results of the model must be presented in a form that clearly answers the questions that the analyst sets out to answer. It sounds rather obvious, but I have seen many reports that have failed in this respect for several reasons:

- The report relied purely on statistics. Graphs help the reader enormously to get a "feel" for the uncertainty that the model is demonstrating.
- The key question is never answered. The reader is left instead to make the last logical step. For example, a distribution of a project's estimated cost is produced but no guidance is offered for determining a budget, risk contingency or margin.
- The graphs and statistics use values to five, six or more significant figures. This is an unnatural way for most readers to think of values and impairs their ability to use the results.

- The report is filled with volumes of meaningless statistics. Risk analysis software programs, like @RISK and Crystal Ball, automatically generate very comprehensive statistics reports. However, most of the statistics they produce will be of no relevance to any one particular model. The analyst should pare down any statistics report to those few statistics that are germane to the problem being modelled.

- The graphs are not properly labelled! Arrows and notes on a graph can be particularly useful.

In summary:

1. Tailor the report to the audience and the problem.
2. Keep statistics to a minimum.
3. Use graphs wherever appropriate.
4. Always include an explanation of the model's assumptions.

5.2 Explaining a Model's Assumptions

We recommend that you are very explicit about your assumptions, and make a summary of them in a prominent place in the report, rather than just have them scattered through the report in the explanation of each model component.

A risk analysis model will often have a fairly complex structure, and the analyst needs to find ways of explaining the model that can quickly be checked. The first step is usually to draw up a schematic diagram of the structure of the model. The type of schematic diagram will obviously depend on the problem being modelled: GANTT charts, site plans with phases, work breakdown structure, flow diagrams, event trees, etc. – any pictorial representation that conveys the required information.

The next step is to show the key quantitative assumptions that are made for the model's variables.

Distribution parameters

Using the parameters of a distribution to explain how a model variable has been characterised will often be the most informative when explaining a model's logic. We tend to use tables of formulae for more technical models where there are a lot of parametric distributions and probability equations, because the logic is apparent from the relationship between a distribution's parameters and other variables. For non-parametric distributions, which are generally used to model expert opinion, or to represent a dataset, a thumbnail sketch helps the reader most. Influence diagram plots (Figure 5.1 illustrates a simple example) are excellent for showing the flow of the logic and interrelationships between model components, but not the mathematics underlying the links.

Graphical illustrations of quantitative assumptions are particularly useful when non-parametric distributions have been used. For example, a sketch of a VoseRelative (Custom in Crystal Ball, General in @RISK), a VoseHistogram or a VoseCumulA distribution will be a lot more informative than noting its parameters values. Sketches are also very good when you want to explain partial model results. For example, summary plots are useful for demonstrating the numbers that come out of what might be a quite complex time series model. Scatter plots are useful for giving an overview of what might be a very complicated correlation structure between two or more variables.

Figure 5.2 illustrates a simple format for an assumptions report. Crystal Ball offers a report-writing feature that will do most of this automatically. There will usually be a wealth of data behind these key quantitative assumptions and the formulae that have been used to link them. Explanations of the

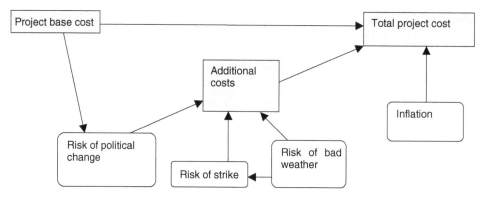

Figure 5.1 Example of a schematic diagram of a model's structure.

data and how they translate into the quantitative assumptions can be relegated to an appendix of a risk analysis report, if they are to be included at all.

5.3 Graphical Presentation of a Model's Results

There are two forms in which a model's results can be presented: graphs and numbers. Graphs have the advantage of providing a quick, intuitive way to understand what is usually a fairly complex, number-intensive set of information. Numbers, on the other hand, give us the raw data and statistics from which we can make quantitative decisions. This section looks at graphical presentations of results, and the following section reviews statistical methods of reporting. The reader is strongly encouraged to use graphs wherever it is useful to do so, and to avoid intensive use of statistics.

5.3.1 Histogram plots

The histogram, or relative frequency, plot is the most commonly used in risk analysis. It is produced by grouping the data generated for a model's output into a number of bars or classes. The number of values in any class is its frequency. The frequency divided by the total number of values gives an approximate probability that the output variable will lie in that class's range. We can easily recognise common distributions such as triangular, normal, uniform, etc., and we can see whether a variable is skewed. Figure 5.3 shows the result of a simulation of 500 iterations, plotted into a 20-bar histogram.

The most common mistake in interpreting a histogram is to read off the y-scale value as the probability of the x value occurring. In fact, the probability of any x value, given the output is continuous (and most are), is infinitely small. If the model's output is discrete, the histogram *will* show the probability of each allowable x value, providing the class width is less than the distance between each allowable x value. The number of classes used in a histogram plot will determine the scale of the y axis. Clearly, the wider the bar width, the more chance there will be that values will fall within it. So, for example, by doubling the number of histogram bars, the probability scale will approximately halve.

Monte Carlo add-ins generally offer two options for scaling the vertical axis: density and relative frequency plots, shown in Figures 5.4 and 5.5.

In plotting a histogram, the number of bars should be chosen to balance between a lack of detail (too few bars) and overwhelming random noise (too many bars). When the result of a risk analysis model

KEY UNCERTAIN ASSUMPTIONS

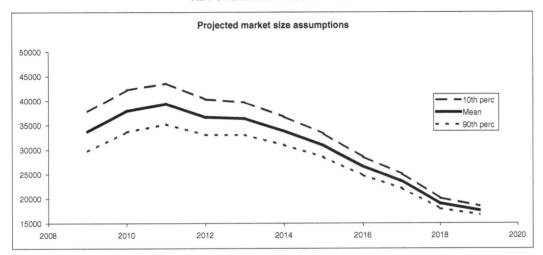

Year	2009	2010	2011	2012	2013	2014	2015	2016	2017	2018	2019
10th perc	37859	42237	43575	40322	39736	36725	33312	28507	25064	20085	18460
Mean	33803	37949	39399	36690	36388	33848	30902	26617	23556	19002	17581
90th perc	29747	33661	35223	33058	33040	30971	28492	24727	22048	17919	16702

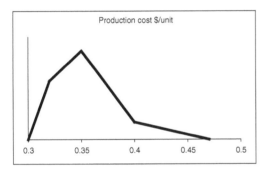

Distribution parameters used for key quantities			
Variable	Min	Mode	Max
Labour rate $/day	51	52	55.5
Advertising budget $k/year	17.2	20.3	24.1
Admin costs $k/year	173	176	181
Transient market share	0.13	0.17	0.19
Commission rate	0.14	0.145	0.18
Factory rental $k/year	172	174	181

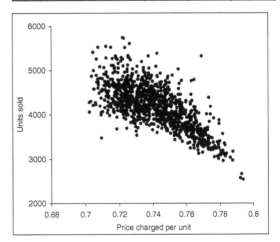

Figure 5.2   Example of an assumptions report for a risk analysis.

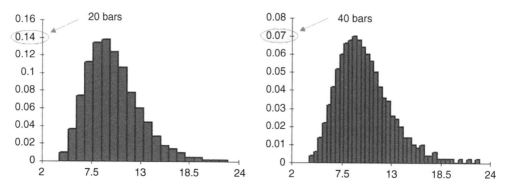

Figure 5.3   Doubling the number of bars on average halves the probability height for a bar.

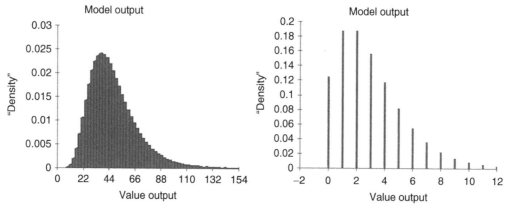

Figure 5.4   Histogram "density" plot. The vertical scale is calculated so that the sum of the histogram bar areas equals unity. This is only appropriate for continuous outputs (left). Simulation software won't recognise if an output is discrete (right), so treats the generated output data in the same way as a continuous output. The result is a plot where the probability values make no intuitive sense – in the right-hand plot the probabilities appear to add up to more than 1. To be able to tell the probability of the output being equal to 4, for example, we first need to know the width of the histogram bar.

is a discrete distribution, it is usually advisable to set the number of histogram bars to the maximum possible, as this will reveal the discrete nature of the output unless the output distribution takes a large number of discrete values.

Some risk analysis software programs offer the facility to smooth out a histogram plot. I don't recommend this approach because: (a) it suggests greater accuracy than actually exists; (b) it fits a spline curve that will accentuate (unnecessarily) any peaks and troughs; and (c) if the scale remains the same, the area does not integrate to equal 1 unless the original bandwidths were one x-axis unit wide.

The histogram plot is an excellent way of illustrating the distribution of a variable, but is of little value for determining quantitative information about that variability, which is where the cumulative frequency plot takes over.

Several histogram plots can be overlaid on each other if the histograms are not filled in. This allows one to make a visual comparison, for example, between two decision options one may be considering. The same type of graph can also be used to represent the results of a second-order risk analysis model

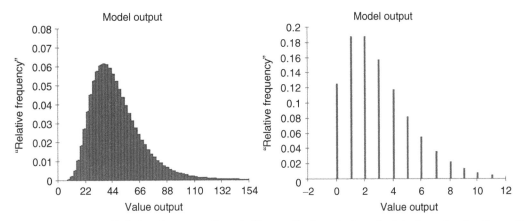

Figure 5.5 Histogram "relative frequency" plot. The vertical scale is calculated as the fraction of the generated values that fall into each histogram bar's range. Thus, the sum of the bar heights equals unity. Relative frequency is only appropriate for discrete variables (right), where the histogram heights now sum to unity. For continuous variables (left), the area under the curve no longer sums to unity.

where the uncertainty and variability have been separated, in which case each distribution curve would represent the system variability given a random sample from the uncertainty distribution of the model.

5.3.2 The cumulative frequency plot

The cumulative frequency plot has two forms: ascending and descending, shown in Figure 5.6. The ascending cumulative frequency plot is the most commonly used of the two and shows the probability of being less than or equal to the x-axis value. The descending cumulative frequency plot, on the other hand, shows the probability of being greater than or equal to the x-axis value. From now on, we shall assume use of the *ascending* plot. Note that the mean of the distribution is sometimes marked on the curve, in this case using a black square.

The cumulative frequency distribution of an output can be plotted directly from the generated data as follows:

1. Rank the data in ascending order.

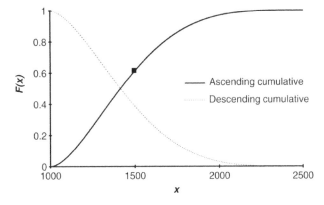

Figure 5.6 Ascending and descending cumulative frequency plots.

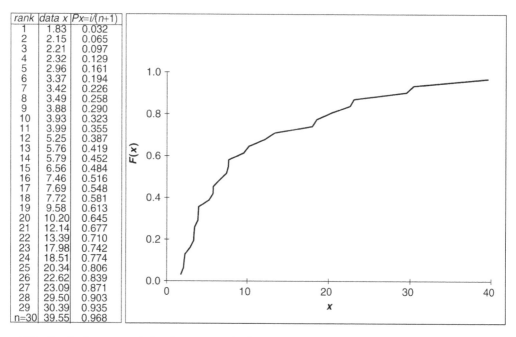

rank	data x	Px=i/(n+1)
1	1.83	0.032
2	2.15	0.065
3	2.21	0.097
4	2.32	0.129
5	2.96	0.161
6	3.37	0.194
7	3.42	0.226
8	3.49	0.258
9	3.88	0.290
10	3.93	0.323
11	3.99	0.355
12	5.25	0.387
13	5.76	0.419
14	5.79	0.452
15	6.56	0.484
16	7.46	0.516
17	7.69	0.548
18	7.72	0.581
19	9.58	0.613
20	10.20	0.645
21	12.14	0.677
22	13.39	0.710
23	17.98	0.742
24	18.51	0.774
25	20.34	0.806
26	22.62	0.839
27	23.09	0.871
28	29.50	0.903
29	30.39	0.935
n=30	39.55	0.968

Figure 5.7 Producing a cumulative frequency plot from generated data points.

2. Next to each value, calculate its cumulative percentile $P_x = i/(n + 1)$, where i is the rank of that data value and n is the total number of generated values. $i/(n + 1)$ is used because it is the best estimate of the theoretical cumulative distribution function of the output that the data are attempting to reproduce.

3. Plot the data (x axis) against the $i/(n + 1)$ values (y axis). Figure 5.7 illustrates an example.

A total of 200–300 iterations are usually quite sufficient to plot a smooth curve. The above technique is very useful if one wishes to avoid using the standard format that Monte Carlo software offer and if one wishes to plot two or more cumulative frequency plots together.

The cumulative frequency plot is very useful for reading off quantitative information about the distribution of the variable. One can read off the probability of exceeding any value; for example, the probability of going over budget, failing to meet a deadline or of achieving a positive NPV (net present value).

One can also find the probability of lying between any two x-axis values: it is simply the difference between their cumulative probabilities. From Figure 5.8 we can see that the probability of lying between 1000 and 2000 is 89 % − 48 % = 41 %.

The cumulative frequency plot is often used in project planning to determine contract bid prices and project budgets, as shown in Figure 5.9. The budget is set as the expected (mean) value of the variable determined from the statistics report. A risk contingency is then added to the budget to bring it up to a cumulative percentile that is comfortable for the organisation. The risk contingency is typically the amount available to project managers to spend without recourse to their board. The (budget + contingency) value is set to match a cumulative probability that the board of directors is happy to plan for: in this case 85 %. A more controlling board might set the sum at the 80th percentile or lower.

The margin is then added to the (budget + contingency) to determine a bid price or project budget. The project cost might still possibly exceed the bid price and the company would then make a loss. Conversely, they would hope, by careful management of the project, to avoid using all of the risk

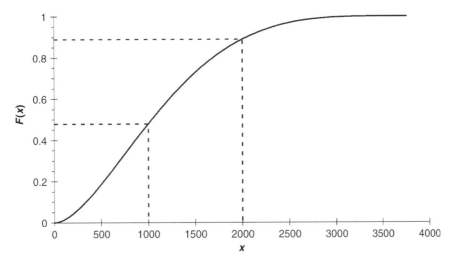

Figure 5.8 Using the cumulative frequency plot to determine the probability of being between two values.

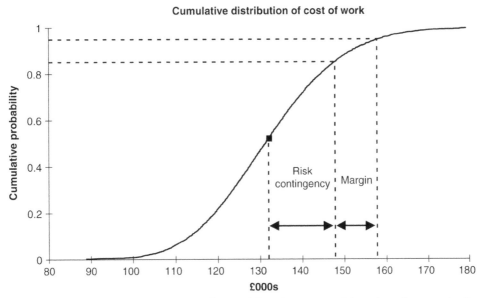

Figure 5.9 Using the cumulative frequency plot to determine appropriate values for a project's budget, contingency and margin.

contingency and actually increase their margin. The x axis of a cumulative distribution of project cost or duration can be thought of roughly as listing risks in decreasing order of importance. The easiest risks to manage, i.e. those that should be removed with good project management, are the first to erode the total cost or duration. So a target set at the 80th percentile, sometimes called the 20 % risk level, is roughly equivalent to removing the identified, easily managed risks. Then there are those risks that will be removed with a lot of hard work, good management and some luck, which brings us down to the

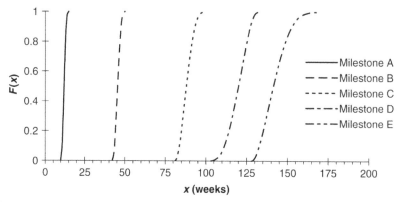

Figure 5.10   Overlaying of the cumulative frequency plots of several project milestones illustrates any increase in uncertainty with time.

50th percentile, or so. To reduce the actual cost or duration to somewhere around the 20th percentile will usually require very hard work, good management and a *lot* of luck.

It is sometimes useful to overlay cumulative frequency plots together. One reason to do this is to get a visual picture of stochastic dominance, described in Section 5.4.5. Another reason is to visualise the increase (or perhaps decrease) in uncertainty as a project progresses. Figure 5.10 illustrates an example for a project with five milestones. The time until completion of a milestone becomes progressively more uncertain the further from the start the milestone is. Furthermore, the results of a second-order risk analysis can be plotted as a number of overlying cumulative distributions, each curve representing a distribution of variability for a particular random sample from the uncertainty distributions of the model.

5.3.3 Second-order cumulative probability plot

A second-order cdf is the best presentation of an output probability distribution when you run a second-order Monte Carlo simulation. The second-order cdf is composed of many lines, each of which represents

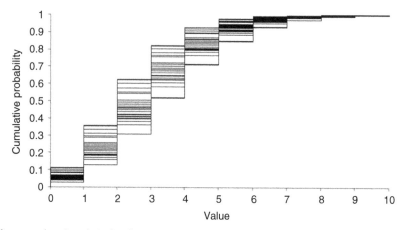

Figure 5.11   A second-order plot of a discrete random variable. The step nature of the plot makes it difficult to read.

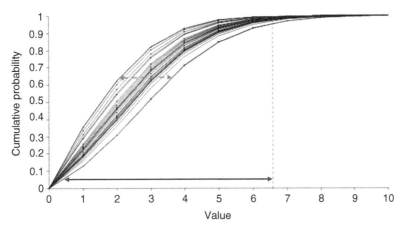

Figure 5.12 Another second-order plot of a discrete variable, where the probabilities are marked with small points and joined by straight lines. The connection between the probability estimates is now clear, and the uncertainty and randomness components can now be compared: at its widest the uncertainty contributes a spread of about two units (dashed horizontal line), while the randomness ranges over some eight units (filled horizontal line), so the inability to predict this variable is more driven by its randomness than by our uncertainty in the model parameters.

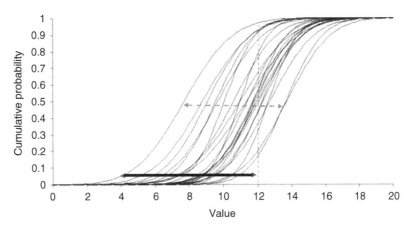

Figure 5.13 A second-order plot of a continuous variable where our inability to predict its value is equally driven by uncertainty (dashed horizontal line) about the model parameters as by the randomness of the system (filled horizontal line). This is a useful plot for decision-makers because it tells them potentially how much more sure one would be of the predicted value if more information could be collected, and thus the uncertainty reduced.

a distribution of possible variability or probability generated by picking a single value from each uncertainty distribution in the model (Figures 5.11 to 5.13).

5.3.4 Overlaying of cdf plots

Several cumulative distribution plots can be overlaid together (Figure 5.14). The plots are easier to read if the curves are formatted into line plots rather than area plots.

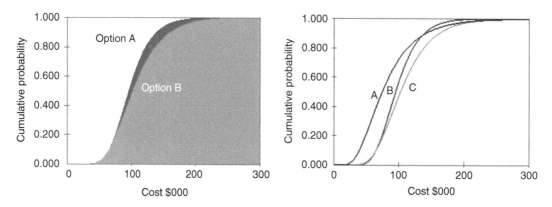

Figure 5.14 Several cumulative distribution plots overlaid together.

The overlaying of cumulative plots like this is an intuitive and easy way of comparing probabilities, and is the basis of stochastic dominance tests. It is not very useful, however, for comparing the location, spread and shape of two or more distributions, for which overlying density plots are much better.

We recommend that a complementary cumulative distribution plot be given alongside the histogram (density) plot to provide the maximum information.

5.3.5 Plotting a variable with discrete and continuous elements

If a risk event does not occur, we could say it has zero impact, but if it occurs it will have an uncertain impact. For example: a fire may have a 20 % chance of occurring and, if it does, will incur $Lognormal(120 000, 30 000). We could model this as

$$= \text{VoseBernoulli}(20 \%) * \text{VoseLognormal}(120\,000, 30\,000)$$

or better still

$$= \text{VoseRiskEvent}(20 \%, \text{VoseLognormalObject}(120\,000, 30\,000))$$

Running a simulation with this variable as an output, we would get the uninformative, relative frequency histogram plot (shown with different numbers of bars) in Figure 5.15.

There really is no useful way to show such a distribution as a histogram, because the spike at zero (in this case) requires a relative frequency scale, while the continuous component requires a continuous scale. A cumulative distribution, however, would produce the plot in Figure 5.16, which is meaningful.

5.3.6 Relationship between cdf and density (histogram) plots

For a continuous variable, the gradient of a cdf plot is equal to the probability density at that value. That means that, the steeper the slope of a cdf, the higher a relative frequency (histogram) plot would look at that point (Figure 5.17).

The disadvantage of a cdf is that one cannot readily determine the central location or shape of the distribution. We cannot even easily recognise common distributions such as triangular, normal and uniform without practice in cdf form. Looking at the plots in Figure 5.18, you will readily identify the distribution form from the left panels, but not so easily from the right panels.

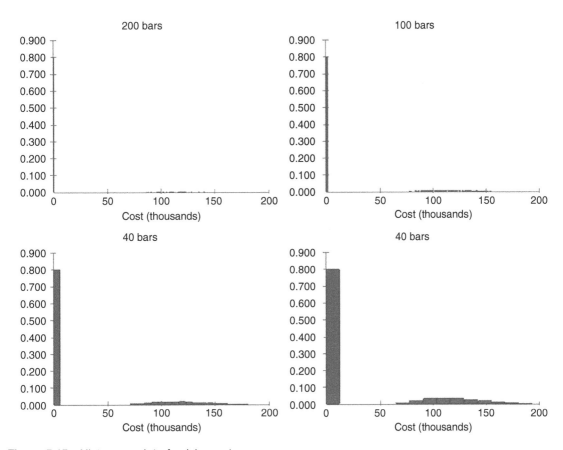

Figure 5.15   Histogram plot of a risk event.

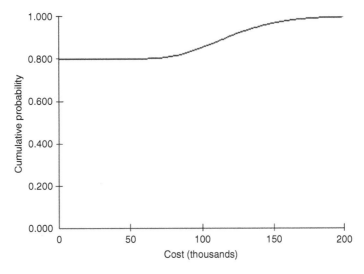

Figure 5.16   Cumulative distribution of a risk event.

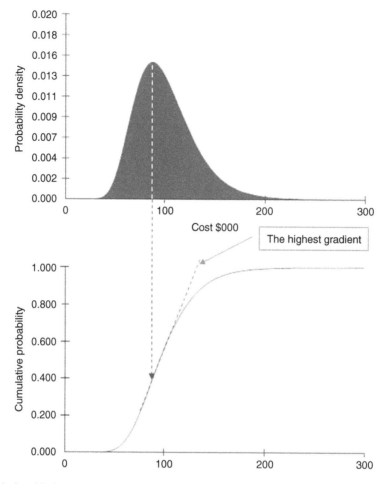

Figure 5.17 Relationship between density and cumulative probability curves.

For a discrete distribution, the cdf increases in steps equal to the probability of the x value occurring (Figure 5.19).

5.3.7 Crude sensitivity analysis and tornado charts

Most Monte Carlo add-ins can perform a crude sensitivity analysis that is often used to identify the key input variables, as a precursor to performing a tornado chart or similar, more advanced, analysis on these key variables. It achieves this by performing one of two statistical analyses on data that have been generated from input distributions and data calculated for the selected output. Built into this operation are two important assumptions:

1. All the tested input parameters have either a purely positive or negative statistical correlation with the output.
2. Each uncertain variable is modelled with a single distribution.

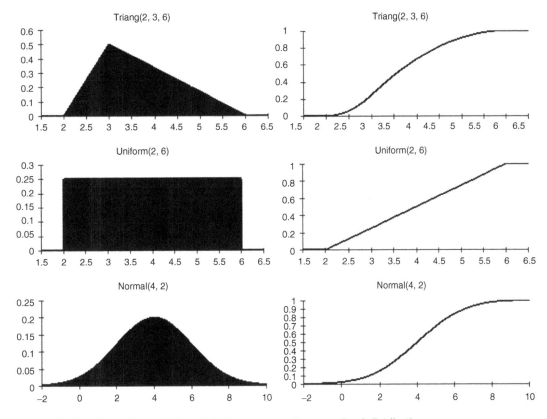

Figure 5.18   Density and cumulative plots for some easily recognised distributions.

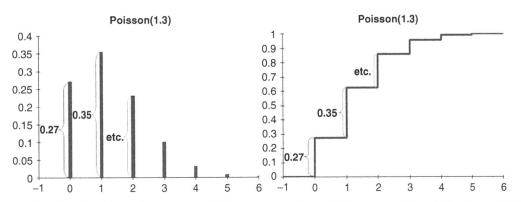

Figure 5.19   Relationship between probability mass and cumulative probability plots for a discrete distribution.

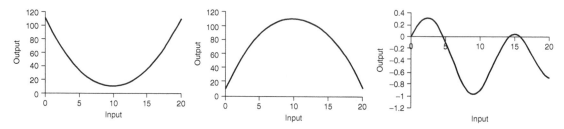

Figure 5.20   Example input–output relationships for which crude sensitivity analysis is inappropriate.

Assumption 1 is rarely invalid, but would be incorrect if the output value were at a maximum or minimum for an input value somewhere in the middle of its range (see, for example, Figure 5.20).

Assumption 2 is very often incorrect. For example, the impact of a risk event might be modelled as

$$= \text{Bernoulli}(20\%) * \text{Triangle}(10, 20, 50)$$

or

$$= \text{Binomial}(1, 20\%) * \text{Triangle}(10, 20, 50)$$

Monte Carlo software will generate the Bernoulli (or equivalently, the binomial) and triangular distributions independently. Performing the standard sensitivity analysis will evaluate the effect of the Bernoulli and the triangular distributions separately, so the measured effect on the output will be divided between these two distributions. ModelRisk gets round this by providing the function VoseRiskEvent, for example:

$$= \text{VoseRiskEvent}(20\%, \text{VoseTriangleObject}(10, 20, 50))$$

The function constructs a single distribution so only one Uniform(0, 1) variate is being used to drive the sampling of the risk impact. If you use @RISK, you can write

$$= \text{VoseRiskEvent}(20\%, \text{VoseTriangleObject}(10, 20, 50), \text{RiskUniform}(0, 1))$$

and @RISK will then drive the sampling for that risk event so the @RISK built-in sensitivity analysis will now work correctly.

Similarly, if you were an insurance company you might be interested in the impact on your corporate cashflow of the aggregate claims distribution for some particular policy. ModelRisk offers a number of aggregate distribution functions that internally calculate the aggregation of claim size and frequency distributions. So, for example, one can write

$$= \text{VoseAggregatePanjer}(\text{VosePoissonObject}(5500), \text{VoseLognormalObject}(2350, 1285),,, U)$$

which will return the aggregate cost of Poisson(5500) claims each drawn independently from a Lognormal(2350, 1285) distribution, and the generated aggregate cost value will be controlled by the U variate. ModelRisk has many such tools for simulating from constructed distributions to help you perform a correct sensitivity analysis.

Assumption 2 also means that this method of sensitivity analysis is invalid for a variable that is modelled over a series of cells, like a time series of exchange rates or sales volumes. The automated analysis will evaluate the sensitivity of the output to each distribution within the time series separately. You can still evaluate the sensitivity of a time series by running two simulations: one with all the distributions simulating random values, the other with the distributions of the time series locked to their expected value. If the distributions vary significantly, the variable time series is important.

Two statistical analyses

Tornado charts for two different methods of sensitivity analysis are in common use. Both methods plot the variable against a statistic that takes values from −1 (the output is wholly dependent on this input, but when the input is large, the output is small), through 0 (no influence) to +1 (the output is wholly dependent on this input, and when the input is large, the output is also large):

- Stepwise least-squares regression between collected input distribution values and the selected output values. The assumption here is that there is a relationship between each input I and the output O (when all other inputs are held constant) of the form $O = I * m + c$, where m and c are constants. That assumption is correct for additive and subtractive models, and will give very accurate results in those circumstances, but is otherwise less reliable and somewhat unpredictable. The r-squared statistic is then used as the measure of sensitivity in a tornado chart.

- Rank order correlation. This analysis replaces each collected value by its rank among other values generated for that input or output, and then calculates the Spearman's rank order correlation coefficient r between each input and the output. Since this is a non-parametric analysis, it is considerably more robust than the regression analysis option where there are complex relationships between the inputs and output.

Tornado charts are used to show the influence an input distribution has on the change in value of the output (Figure 5.21). They are also useful to check that the model is behaving as you expect. Each input distribution is represented by a bar, and the horizontal range the bars cover give some measure of the input distribution's influence on the selected model output. Their main use is as a quick overview to identify the most influential input model parameters. Once these parameters are determined, other sensitivity analysis methods like spider plots and scatter plots are more effective.

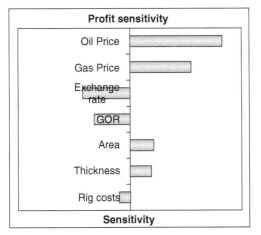
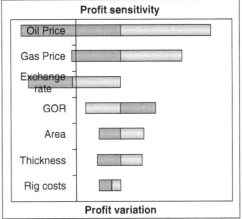

Figure 5.21 Examples of tornado charts.

The left-hand plot of Figure 5.21 is the crudest type of sensitivity analysis, where some statistical measure of the statistical correlation is calculated between the input and output values. The logic is that, the higher the degree of correlation between the input and output variables, the more the input variable is affecting the output. The degree of correlation can be calculated using either rank order correlation or stepwise least-squares regression. My preference is to use rank order correlation because it makes no assumption about the form of relationship between the input and the output, beyond the assumption that the direction of the relationship is the same across the entire input parameter's range. Least-squares regression, on the other hand, assumes that there would be a *straight-line* relationship between the input and the output variables. If the model is a sum of costs or task durations, or some other purely additive model, this assumption is fine. However, divisions and power functions in a model will strongly violate such an assumption. Be careful with this simple type of sensitivity because input–output relationships that strongly deviate from a continuously increasing or decreasing trend can be completely missed. The x-axis scale is a correlation statistic so is not very intuitive because it does not relate to the impact on the output in terms of the output's units. Moreover, rank order correlation can be deceptive. Consider the following simple model:

$$A = \text{Normal}(100, 10)$$

$$B = \text{Normal}(A, 0.1)$$

$$C = \text{Normal}(1, 3)$$

$$D(\text{output}) = A + B + C$$

Running a simulation model gives the following levels of correlation:

Variable	Regression coefficient	Rank order correlation
A	0.495	0.988
B	0.495	0.988
C	0.148	0.139

Clearly from the model structure we can see that variable A is actually driving most of the output uncertainty. If we set the standard deviation of each variable to zero in turn and compare the drop in standard deviation of the output (a good measure of variation in this case because we are just adding normal distributions), then

$$A : \text{drops output standard deviation by } 85.1562\,\%$$

$$B : \text{drops output standard deviation by } 0.0004\,\%$$

$$C : \text{drops output standard deviation by } 1.1037\,\%$$

which tells an entirely different story from the regression and correlation statistics. The reason for this is that variable B is being driven by A, so the influence of A is being divided essentially equally between A and B. A proper regression analysis would require us to build in the direction of influence from A to B, and then the influence of B would come out as insignificant, but to do so we would have to specify that relationship – a very difficult thing to do in a complex spreadsheet model.

The right-hand plot of Figure 5.21 is a little more robust and is typically created by fixing an input distribution to a low value (say its 5th percentile), running a simulation, recording the output mean and then repeating the process with a medium value (say the 50th percentile) and a high value (say the 95th percentile) of the input distribution: these output means define the extremes of the bars. This type of plot is a cut-down version of a spider plot. It is a little more robust, and the x-axis scale is in units of the output so is more intuitive.

At low levels of correlation you will often see a variable with correlations of the opposite sign to what you would expect. This is particularly so for rank order correlation. It just means that the level of correlation is so low that a spurious correlation of generated values will occur. For presentation purposes, it will obviously be better to remove these bars.

It is standard practice to plot the variables from the top down in decreasing size of correlation. If there are positive and negative correlations, the result looks a bit like a tornado, hence the name. It is sensible, of course, to limit the number of variables that are shown on the plot. I usually limit the plot to those variables that have a correlation of at least a quarter of the maximum observed correlation, or at least down to the first correlation that has the opposite sign to what one would logically have expected. This usually means that below such levels of correlation the relationships are statistically insignificant, although of course one can make a mistake in reasoning the sense of a correlation.

The tornado chart is useful for identifying the key variables and uncertain parameters that are driving the result of the model. It makes sense that, if the uncertainty of these key parameters can be reduced through improved knowledge, or the variability of the problem can be reduced by changing the system, the total uncertainty of the problem will be reduced too. The tornado chart is therefore very useful for planning any strategy for the reduction of total uncertainty. The key model components can often be made more certain by:

- Collecting more information on the parameter if it has some level of uncertainty.
- Determining strategies to reduce the effect of the variability of the model component. For a project schedule, this might be altering the project plan to take the task off the critical path. For a project cost, this might be offloading the uncertainty via a fixed-price subcontract. For a model of the reliability of a system, this might be increasing the scheduled number of checks or installing some parallel redundancy.

The rank order correlation between the model components and its output can be easily calculated if the uncertainty and variability components are all simulated together, because the simulation software will have all the values generated for the input distributions and the output together in the one database. It may sometimes be useful to show in a tornado chart that certain model components are uncertain and others are variable by using, for example, white bars for uncertainty and black bars for variability.

5.3.8 More advanced sensitivity analysis with spider plots

To construct a spider plot we proceed as follows:

- Before starting, set the number of iterations to a fairly low value (e.g. 300).
- Determine the input distributions to analyse (performing a crude sensitivity analysis will guide you).

- Determine the cumulative probabilities you wish to test (we generally use 1%, 5%, 25%, 50%, 75%, 95%, 99%).
- Determine the output statistic you wish to measure (mean, a particular percentile, etc.).

Then:

- Select an input distribution.
- Replace the distribution with one of the percentiles you specified.
- Run a simulation and record the statistic of the output.
- Select the next cumulative percentile and run another simulation.
- Repeat until all percentiles have been run for this input, then put back the distribution and move on to the next selected input.

Once all inputs have been treated this way, we can produce the spider plot shown in Figure 5.22.

This type of plot usually has several horizontal lines for variables that have almost no influence on the output. It makes the graph a lot clearer to delete these (Figure 5.23).

Now we can very clearly see how the output mean is influenced by each input. The vertical range produced by the oil price line shows the range of expected profits there would be if the oil price were fixed somewhere between the minimum and maximum (a range of $180 million). The next largest range is for the gas price ($110 million), etc. The analysis helps us understand the degree of sensitivity in terms decision-makers understand as opposed to correlation or regression coefficients. The plot will also allow us to see variables that have unusual relationships, e.g. a variable that has no influence except at its extremes, or some sort of U-shaped relationship that would be missed in a correlation analysis.

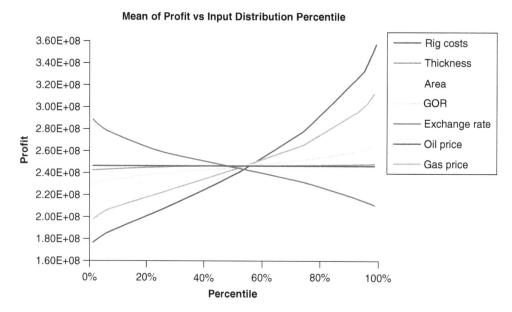

Figure 5.22   Spider plot example.

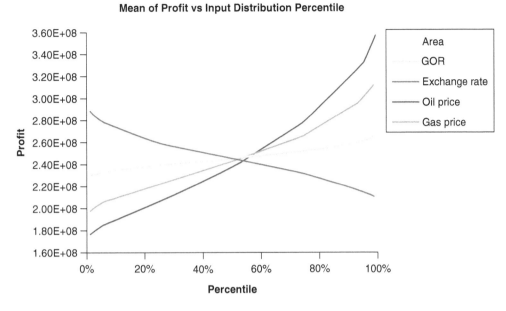

Figure 5.23 Spider plot example with inconsequential variables removed.

5.3.9 More advanced sensitivity analysis with scatter plots

By plotting the generated values for an input against the output corresponding values for each model iteration in a scatter plot one can get perhaps the best understanding of the effect of the input on the output value. Plotting generated values for two outputs is also commonly done; for example, plotting a project's duration against its total cost. Scatter plots are easy to produce by exporting the simulation data at the end of a simulation into Excel.

It takes a little effort to generate these scatter plots, so we recommend that you perform a rough sensitivity analysis to help you determine which of a model's input distributions are most affecting the output first.

Figure 5.24 shows 3000 points, which is enough to get across any relationship but not too many to block out central areas if you use small circular markers. The chart tells the story that the model predicts increasing advertising expenditure will increase sales – up to a point. Since this is an Excel plot we can add a few useful refinements. For example, we could show scenarios above and below a certain advertising budget (Figure 5.25).

We could also perform some statistical analysis of the two subsets, like a regression analysis (Figure 5.26 shows how in an Excel chart).

The equations of the fitted lines show that you are getting about 3 times more return for your advertising dollar below $150k than above (0.0348/0.0132 ≈ 2.6). It is also possible, though mindbogglingly tedious, to plot scatter plot matrices in Excel to show the interrelationship of several variables. Much better is to export the generated values to a statistical package like SPSS. At the time of writing (2007), planned versions of @RISK and Crystal Ball will also do this.

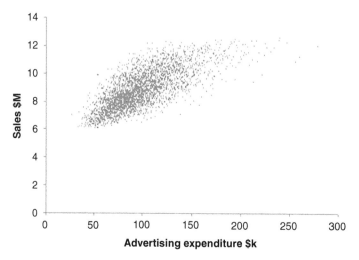

Figure 5.24 Example scatter plot.

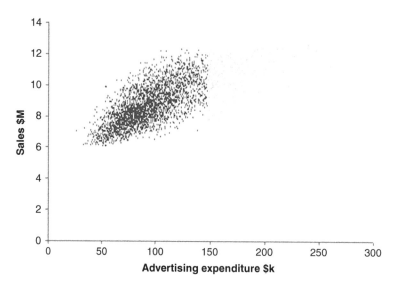

Figure 5.25 Scatter plot separating scenarios where expenditure was above or below $150k.

5.3.10 Trend plots

If a model includes a time series forecast or other type of trend, it is useful to be able to picture the general behaviour of the trend. A trend or summary plot provides this information. Figure 5.27 illustrates an example using the mean and 5th, 20th, 80th and 95th percentiles. Trend plots can be plotted using cumulative percentiles as shown here, or with the mean $\pm$ one and two standard deviations, etc. I recommend that you avoid using standard deviations, unless they are of particular interest for some technical reason, because a spread of, say, one standard deviation around the mean will encompass a

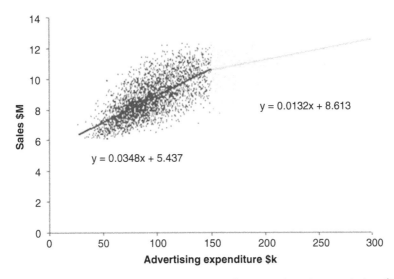

Figure 5.26   Scatter plot with separate regression analysis for scenarios above or below $150k.

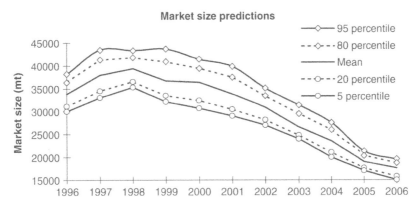

Figure 5.27   A trend or summary plot.

varying percentage of the distribution depending on its form. That means that there is no consistent probability interpretation attached to mean $\pm k$ standard deviations.

The trend plot is useful for reviewing a trending model to ensure that seasonality and any other patterns are being reproduced. One can also see at a glance whether nonsensical values are being produced; a forecasting series can be fairly tricky to model, as described in Chapter 12, so this is a nice reality check.

An alternative to the trend plot above is a Tukey or box plot (Figure 5.28).

A Tukey plot is more commonly used to represent variations between datasets, but it does have the possibility of including more information than trend plots. A word of caution: the minimum and maximum generated values from a simulation can vary enormously between simulations with different random number seeds, which means they are not usually values to be relied upon. Plotting the maximum value of an inflation model going out 15 years, for example, might produce a very large value if you ran it for many iterations and dominate the graph scaling.

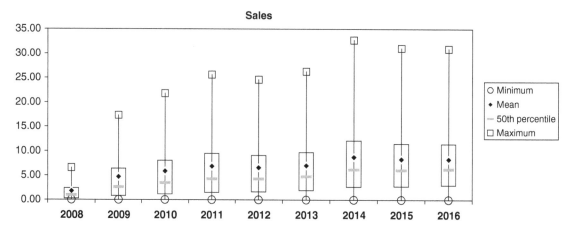

Figure 5.28 A Tukey or box plot. Box contains 25–75 percentile range.

5.3.11 Risk–return plots

Risk–return (or cost-benefit) plots are one way graphically to compare several decision options on the same plot. The expected return in some appropriate measure is plotted on the vertical axis versus the expected cost in some measure on the horizontal axis (Figure 5.29).

The plot should be tailored to the decision question, and it may be useful to plot two or more such plots to show different aspects.

Examples of measures of return (benefit) are as follows:

- the probability of making a profit;
- the income or expected return;
- the number of animals that could be imported for a given level of risk (if one were looking at various border control options for disease control, say);
- the number of extra votes that would be gained in an election campaign;
- the time that would be saved;
- the reduction in the number of complaints received by a utility company;
- the extra life expectancy of a kidney transplant patient.

Examples of measures of risk (cost) are as follows:

- the amount of capital invested;
- the probability of exceeding a schedule deadline;
- the probability of financial loss;
- the conditional mean loss;
- the standard deviation or variance of profit or cashflow;
- the probability of introduction of a disease;
- the semi-standard deviation of loss;

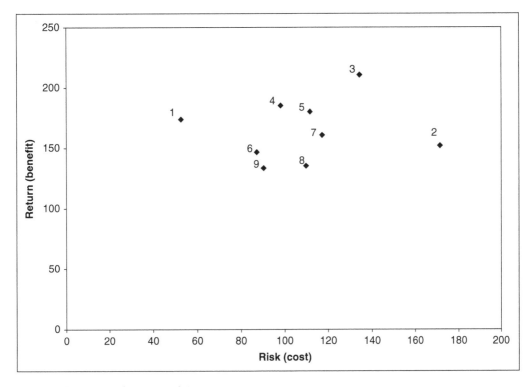

Figure 5.29   Example risk–return plot.

- the number of employees that would be made redundant;
- the increased number of fatalities;
- the level of chemical emission into the environment.

5.4 Statistical Methods of Analysing Results

Monte Carlo add-ins offer a number of statistical descriptions to help analyse and compare results. There are also a number of other statistical measures that you may find useful. I have categorised the statistical measures into three groups:

1. Measures of location – where the distribution is "centered".
2. Measures of spread – how broad the distribution is.
3. Measures of shape – how lopsided or peaked the distribution is.

In general, at Vose Consulting we use very few statistical measures in writing our reports. The following statistics are easy to understand and, for nearly any problem, communicate all the information one needs to get across:

- ***the mean*** which tells you where the distribution is located and has some important properties for comparing and combining risks;

- *cumulative percentiles* which give the probability statements that decision-makers need (like the probability of being above or below X or below X or between X and Y);
- *relative measures of spread*: normalised standard deviation (occasionally) for comparing the level of uncertainty of different options relative to their size (i.e. as a dimensionless measure) where the outputs are roughly normal, and normalised interpercentile range (more commonly) for the same purpose where the outputs being compared are not all normal.

5.4.1 Measures of location

There are essentially three measures of central tendency (i.e. measures of the central location of a distribution) that are commonly provided in statistics reports: the mode, the median and the mean. These are described below, along with the conditional mean, which the reader may find more useful in certain circumstances.

Mode

The mode is the output value that is most likely to occur (Figure 5.30).

For a discrete output, this is the value with the greatest observed frequency. For a continuous distribution output, the mode is determined by the point at which the gradient of the cumulative distribution of the model output generated values is at its maximum.

The estimate of the mode is quite imprecise if a risk analysis output is continuous or if it is discrete and the two (or more) most likely values have similar probabilities (Figure 5.31). In fact the mode is of no practical value in the assessment of most risk analysis results, and, as it is difficult to determine precisely, it should generally be ignored.

Median x_{50}

The median is the value above and below which the model output has generated equal numbers of data, i.e. the 50th percentile. This is simply another cumulative percentile and, in most cases, has no particular benefits over any other percentile.

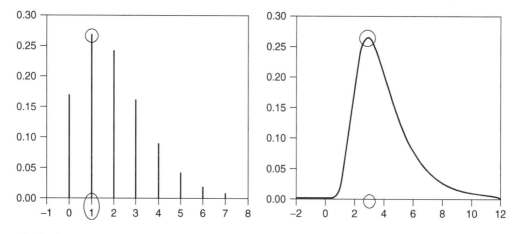

Figure 5.30 Locations of the mode for a discrete and a continuous distribution.

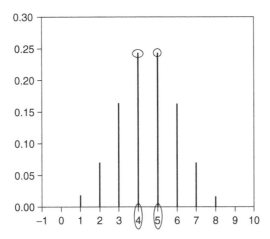

Figure 5.31   A discrete distribution with two modes, or no mode, depending on how you look at it.

Mean $\bar{x}$

This is the average of all the generated output values. It has less immediate intuitive appeal than the mode or median but it does have far more value. One can think of the mean of the output distribution as the x-axis point of balance of the histogram plot of the distribution. The mean is also known as the *expected value*, although I don't recommend the term as it implies for most people the most likely value. Sometimes also known as the first moment about the origin, it is the most useful statistic in risk analysis. The mean of a dataset $\{x_i\}$ is often given the notation $\bar{x}$. It is particularly useful for the following two reasons:

$$\overline{(a+b)} = \bar{a} + \bar{b} \text{ and therefore } \overline{(a-b)} = \bar{a} - \bar{b}$$

$$\overline{(a \cdot b)} = \bar{a} \cdot \bar{b}$$

where a and b are two stochastic variables. In other words: (1) the mean of the sum is the sum of their means; (2) the mean of their product is the product of their means. These two results are very useful if one wishes to combine risk analysis results or look at the difference between them.

Conditional mean

The conditional mean is used when one is only interested in the expected outcome of a portion of the output distribution; for example, the expected loss that would occur should the project fail to make a profit. The conditional mean is found by calculating the average of only those data points that fall into the scenario in question. In the example of expected loss, it would be found by taking the average of all the profit output's data points that were negative.

The conditional mean is sometimes accompanied with the probability of the output falling within the required range. In the loss example, it would be the probability of producing a negative profit.

Relative positions of the mode, median and mean

For any unimodal (single-mode) distribution that is positively skewed (i.e. has a longer right tail than left tail), the mode, median and mean fall in that order (Figure 5.32).

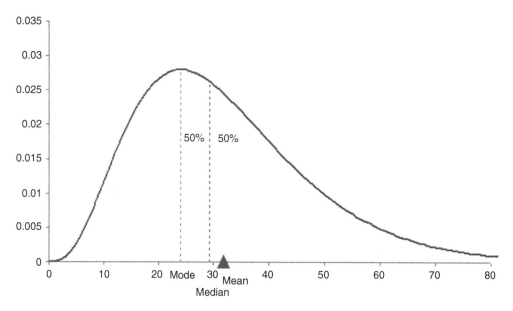

Figure 5.32 Relative positions of the mode, median and mean of a univariate distribution.

If the distribution has a longer left tail than right, the order is reversed. Of course, if the distribution is symmetric and unimodal, like the normal or Student distributions, the mode, median and mean will be equal.

5.4.2 Measures of spread

The three measures of spread commonly provided in statistics reports are the standard deviation σ, the variance V and the range. There are several other measures of spread, discussed below, that the reader may also find useful under certain circumstances.

Variance V

Variance is calculated on generated values as follows:

$$V = \frac{\sum_{i=1}^{n} (x_i - \overline{x})^2}{n-1}$$

i.e. it is essentially the average of the squared distance of all generated values from their mean. The larger the variance, the greater is the spread. The variance is called the second moment (because of its square term) about the mean and has units that are the square of the variable. So, if the output is in £, the variance is measured in £^{2}, making it difficult to have any intuitive feel for the statistic.

Since the distance between the mean and each generated value is squared, the variance is far more sensitive to the data points that make up the tails of the distribution. For example, a data point that was three units from the mean would contribute 9 times as much ($3^2 = 9$) to the variance as a data point that was only one unit from the mean ($1^2 = 1$). The variance is useful if one wishes to determine the spread of the sum of several *uncorrelated* variables X, Y as it follows these rules:

$$V(X + Y) = V(X) + V(Y)$$

$$V(X - Y) = V(X) + V(Y)$$

$$V(nX) = n^2 V(X), \text{ where } n \text{ is some constant}$$

$$V\left(\sum_i X_i\right) = \sum_i V(X_i)$$

These formulae also provide us with a guideline of how uniformly to disaggregate an additive model so that each component provides a roughly equal contribution to the total output uncertainty. If the model sums a number of variables, the contribution of each variable to the output uncertainty will be approximately equal if each variable has about the same variance.

Standard deviation s

Standard deviation is calculated as the square root of the variance. In other words:

$$s = \sqrt{\frac{\sum_{i=1}^{n} (x_i - \bar{x})^2}{n - 1}}$$

It has the advantage over the variance that it is in the same units as the output to which it refers. However, it is still summing the squares of the distances of each generated value from the mean and is therefore far more sensitive to outlying data points that make up the tails of the distribution than to those that are close to the mean.

The standard deviation is frequently used in connection with the normal distribution. Results in risk analysis are often quoted using the output's mean and standard deviation, implicitly assuming that the output is normally distributed, and therefore:

- the range $\bar{x} - s$ to $\bar{x} + s$ contains 68 % or so of the distribution;
- the range $\bar{x} - 2s$ to $\bar{x} + 2s$ contains 95 % or so of the distribution.

Some care should be exercised here. The distribution of a risk analysis output is often quite skewed and these assumptions do not then follow at all. However, Tchebysheff's rule provides some weak interpretation of the fraction of a distribution contained within k standard deviations.

Range

The range of an output is the difference between the maximum and minimum generated values. In most cases this is not a very useful measure as it is obviously only sensitive to the two extreme values (which are, after all, randomly generated and could often take a wide range of legitimate values for any particular model).

Mean deviation (MD)

The mean deviation is calculated as

$$MD = \frac{\sum\limits_{i=1}^{n} |x_i - \overline{x}|}{n - 1}$$

i.e. the average of the absolute differences between the data points and their mean. This can be thought of as the expected distance that the variable will actually be from the mean. The mean deviation offers two potential advantages over the other measures of spread: it has the same units as the output and gives equal weighting to all generated data points.

Semi-variance V_s and Semi-standard deviation s_s

Variance and standard deviation are often used as measures of risk in the financial sector because they represent uncertainty. However, in a distribution of cashflow, a large positive tail (equivalent to the chance of a large income) is not really a "risk", although this tail will contribute to, and often dominate, the value of the calculated standard deviation and variance.

The semi-standard deviation and semi-variance compensate for this problem by considering only those generated values below (or above, as required) a threshold, the threshold delineating those scenarios that represent a "risk" and therefore should be included from those that are not a risk and therefore should be excluded (Figure 5.33).

The semi-variance and semi-standard deviation are

$$V_s = \frac{\sum\limits_{i=1}^{k} (x_i - x_0)^2}{k} \quad \text{and} \quad s_s = \sqrt{V_s}$$

where x_0 is the specified threshold value and $x_1, \ldots, x_k$ are all of the data points that are either above or below x_0, as required.

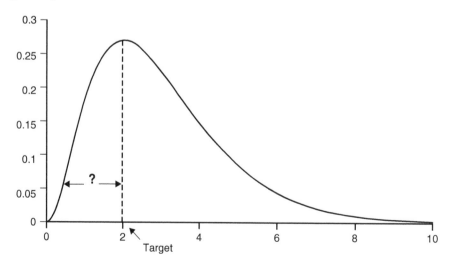

Figure 5.33 The semi-standard deviation concept.

Normalised standard deviation s_n

This is the standard deviation divided by the mean, i.e.

$$s_n = \frac{s}{\bar{x}}$$

It achieves two purposes:

1. The standard deviation is given as a fraction of its mean. Using this statistic allows the spread of the distribution of a variable with a large mean and correspondingly large standard deviation to be compared more appropriately with the spread of the distribution of another variable with a smaller mean and a correspondingly smaller standard deviation.
2. The standard deviation is now independent of its units. So, for example, the relative variability of the EUR:HKD and USD:GBP exchange rates can be compared.

The normalised interpercentile range works in the same way:

$$= (x_B - x_A)/x_{50}, \text{ where } x_B > x_A \text{ are percentiles like } x_{95} \text{ and } x_{05} \text{ respectively}$$

Interpercentile range

The interpercentile range of an output is calculated as the difference between two percentiles, for example:

- $x_{95} - x_{05}$, to give the central 90 % range;
- x_{90} − minimum, to give the lower 90 % range;
- $x_{90} - x_{10}$, to give the central 80 % range.

The interpercentile range is a stablemeasure of spread (unless one of the percentiles is the minimum or maximum), meaning that the value is quickly obtained for relatively few iterations of a model. It also has the great advantage of having a consistent interpretation between distributions.

One potential problem you should be aware of is with applying an interpercentile range calculation to a discrete distribution, particularly when there are only a few important values, as shown in Figure 5.34.

In this example, several key cumulative percentiles fall on the same values, so of course several different interpercentile ranges take the same values. In addition, the interpercentile range becomes very sensitive to the percentile chosen. In the plot above, for example:

$$x_{95} - x_{05} = 4 - 1 = 3$$

but

$$x_{96} - x_{04} = 5 - 0 = 5$$

5.4.3 Measures of shape

Skewness S

This is the degree to which the distribution is "lopsided". A positive skewness means a longer right tail; a negative skewness means a longer left tail; zero skewness means the distribution is symmetric about its mean (Figure 5.35).

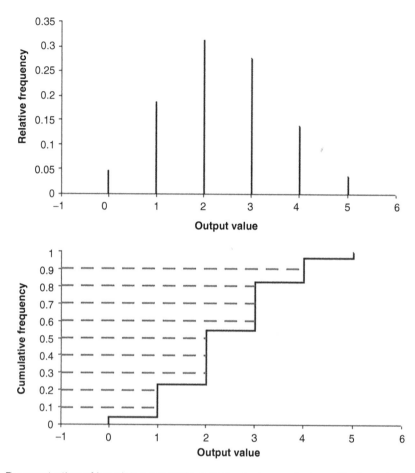

Figure 5.34 Demonstration of how interpercentile ranges can be confusing with discrete distributions.

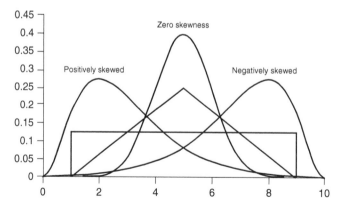

Figure 5.35 Skewness examples.

The skewness S is calculated as

$$S = \frac{\dfrac{1}{(n-1)} \displaystyle\sum_{i=1}^{n} (x_i - \bar{x})^3}{s^3}$$

The σ^3 factor is put in to make the skewness a pure number, i.e. it has no units of measurement. Skewness is also known as the third moment about the mean and is even more sensitive to the data points in the tails of a distribution than the variance or standard deviation because of the cubed term. It may be useful to note, for comparative purposes, that an exponential distribution has a skewness of 2.0, an extreme value distribution has a skewness of 1.14, a triangular distribution has a skewness of between 0.562 and 0, and the skewness of a lognormal distribution goes from zero to infinity as its mean approaches 0. Skewness has little practical purpose for most risk analysis work, although it is sometimes used in conjunction with kurtosis (see below) to test whether the output distribution is approximately normal. High skewness values from a simulation run are really quite unstable – if your simulation gives a skewness value of 100, say, think of it as "really big" rather than taking its value as being usable.

Another measure of skewness, though rarely used, is the percentile skewness, S_p, calculated as

$$S_p = \frac{(90 \text{ percentile} - 50 \text{ percentile})}{(50 \text{ percentile} - 10 \text{ percentile})}$$

It has the advantage over the standard skewness of being quite stable because it is not affected by the values of the extreme data points. However, its scaling is different to standard skewness: if $0 < S_p < 1$ the distribution is negatively skewed; if $S_p = 1$ the distribution is symmetric; if $S_p > 1$ the distribution is positively skewed.

Kurtosis K

Kurtosis is a measure of the peakedness of a distribution. Like skewness statistics, it is not of much use in general risk analysis. Kurtosis is calculated as

$$K = \frac{\dfrac{1}{(n-1)} \displaystyle\sum_{i=1}^{n} (x_i - \bar{x})^4}{s^4}$$

In a similar manner to skewness, the σ^4 factor is put in to make the kurtosis a pure number. Kurtosis is often known as the fourth moment about the mean and is even more sensitive to the values of the data points in the tails of the distribution than the standard skewness statistic. Stable values for the kurtosis of a risk analysis result therefore require many more iterations than for other statistics. High kurtosis values from a simulation run are very unstable – if your simulation gives a kurtosis in the hundreds or thousands, say, it means there is a big spike in the output and the simulation kurtosis is very dependent on whether that spike was appropriately sampled, so for such large values just think of it as "really big".

Kurtosis is sometimes used in conjunction with the skewness statistics to determine whether an output is approximately normally distributed. A normal distribution has a kurtosis of 3, so any output that looks symmetric and bell-shaped and has a zero skewness and a kurtosis of 3 can probably be considered normal.

A uniform distribution has a kurtosis of 1.8, a triangular distribution has a kurtosis of 2.387, the kurtosis of a lognormal distribution goes from 3.0 to infinity as its mean approaches 0 and an exponential distribution has a kurtosis of 9.0. The kurtosis statistic is sometimes (in Excel, for example) calculated as

$$K = \frac{\frac{1}{(n-1)} \sum_{i=1}^{n} (x_i - \overline{x})^4}{s^4} - 3$$

called the excess skewness, which can cause confusion, so be careful what statistic your software is reporting.

5.4.4 Percentiles

Cumulative percentiles

These are values below which the specified percentage of the generated data for an output fall. Standard notation is x_P, where P is the cumulative percentage, e.g. $x_{0.75}$ is the value that 75 % of the generated data were less than or equal to.

The cumulative percentiles can be plotted together to form the cumulative frequency plot, the use of which has been explained above.

Differences between cumulative percentiles are often used as a measure of the variable's range, e.g. $x_{0.95} - x_{0.05}$ would include the middle 90 % of the possible output values and $x_{0.80} - x_{0.20}$ would include the middle 60 % of the possible values of the output; $x_{0.25}$, $x_{0.50}$ and $x_{0.75}$ are sometimes referred to as the *quartiles*.

Relative percentiles

The relative percentiles are the fractions of the output data points that fall into each bar range of a histogram plot. They are of little use in most risk analyses and are dependent upon the number of bars that are used to plot the histogram.

Relative percentiles can be used to replicate the output distribution for inclusion in another risk analysis model. For example, cashflow models may have been produced for a number of subsidiaries of a large company. If an analyst wants to combine these uncertain cashflows into an aggregate model, he would want distributions of the cashflow from each subsidiary. This is achieved by using histogram distributions to model each subsidiary's cashflow and taking the required parameters (minimum, maximum, relative percentiles) from the statistics report. Providing the cashflow distributions are independent, they can then be summed in another model.

5.4.5 Stochastic dominance tests

Stochastic dominance tests are a statistical means of determining the superiority of one distribution over another. There are several types (or degrees) of stochastic dominance. We have never found any particular use for any but the first- and second-order tests described here. It would be a very rare problem where the distributions of two options can be selected for no better reason than a very marginal ordering provided by a statistical test. In the real world there are usually far more persuasive reasons to select one option over another: option A would expose us to a greater chance of losing money than B; or a greater maximum loss; or would cost more to implement; we feel more comfortable with option A because we've done something similar before; option B will make us more strategically placed for the future; option B is based on an analysis with fewer assumptions; etc.

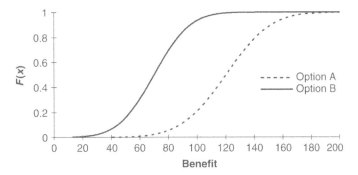

Figure 5.36   First-order stochastic dominance: $F_A < F_B$, so option A dominates option B.

First-order stochastic dominance

Consider options A and B having the distribution functions $F_A(x)$ and $F_B(x)$, where it is desirable to maximise the value of x.

If $F_A(x) \leq F_B(x)$ for all x, then option A dominates option B. That amounts to saying that the cdf of option A is to the right of that of option B in an ascending plot. This is shown graphically in Figure 5.36. Option A has a smaller probability than option B of being less than or equal to each x value, so it is the better option (unless $F_A(x) = F_B(x)$ everywhere). First-order stochastic dominance is intuitive and makes virtually no assumptions about the decision-maker's utility function, only that it is continuous and monotonically increasing with increasing x.

Second-order stochastic dominance

If

$$D(z) = \int_{min}^{z} (F_B(x) - F_A(x))\mathrm{d}x \geq 0$$

for all z, then option A dominates option B. Figure 5.37 illustrates how this looks graphically. Figure 5.38 illustrates a situation when second-order stochastic dominance does not hold.

Second-order stochastic dominance makes the additional assumption that the decision-maker has a risk averse utility function over the entire range of x. This assumption is not very restrictive and can almost always be assumed to apply. In most fields of risk analysis (finance being an obvious exception) it will not be necessary to resort to second-degree (or higher) dominance tests since the decision-maker should be able to find other, more important, differences between the available options.

Stochastic dominance is great in principle but tends to be rather onerous to apply in practice, particularly if one is comparing several possible options. ModelRisk has the facility to compare as many options as you wish. First of all one simulates, say, 5000 iterations of the outcome of each possible option and imports these into contiguous columns in a spreadsheet. These are then fed into the ModelRisk interface, as shown in Figure 5.39.

Selecting an output location allows you to insert the stochastic dominance matrix as an array function (VoseDominance), which will show all the dominance combinations and update if the simulation output arrays are altered.

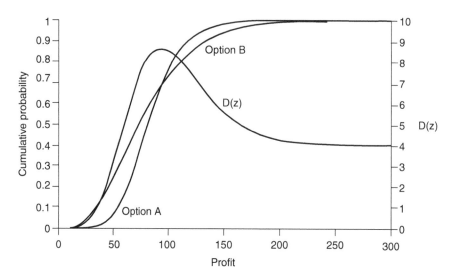

Figure 5.37 Second-order stochastic dominance: option A dominates option B because $D(z)$ is always >0.

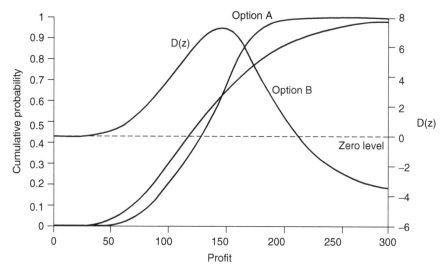

Figure 5.38 Second-order stochastic dominance: option A does not dominate option B because $D(z)$ is not always >0.

5.4.6 Value-of-information methods

Value-of-information (VOI) methods determine the worth of acquiring extra information to help the decision-maker. From a decision analysis perspective, acquiring extra information is only useful if it has a significant probability of changing the decision-maker's currently preferred strategy. The penalty of acquiring more information is usually valued as the cost of that extra information, and sometimes also the delay incurred in waiting for the information.

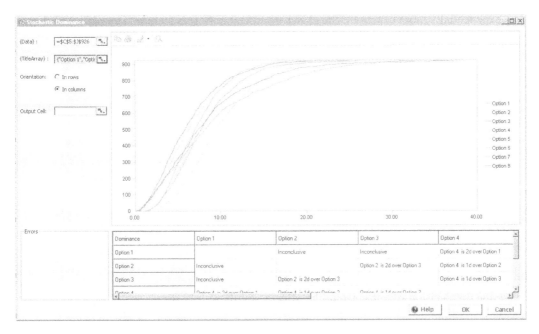

Figure 5.39   ModelRisk interface to determine stochastic dominance.

VOI techniques are based on analysing the revised estimates of model inputs that come with extra data, together with the costs of acquiring the extra data and a decision rule that can be converted into a mathematical formula to analyse whether the decision would alter. The ideas are well developed (Clemen and Reilly (2001) and Morgan and Henrion (1990), for example, explain VOI concepts in some detail), but the probability algebra can be somewhat complex, and simulation is more flexible and a lot easier for most VOI calculations.

The usual starting point of a VOI analysis is to consider the value of perfect information (VOPI), i.e. answering the question "What would be the benefit, in terms we are focusing on (usually money, but it could be lives saved, etc.), of being able to know some parameter(s) perfectly?". If perfect knowledge would not change a decision, the extra information is worthless, and, if it does change a decision, then the value of the extra knowledge is the difference in expected net benefit between the new selected option and that previously favoured. VOPI is a useful limiting tool, because it tells us the maximum value that any data may have in better evaluating the input parameter of concern. If the information costs more than that maximum value, we know not to pursue it any further.

After a VOPI check, one then looks at the value of imperfect information (VOII). Usually, the collection of more data will decrease, not eliminate, uncertainty about an input parameter, so VOII focuses on whether the decrease in uncertainty is worth the cost of collecting extra information. In fact, if new data are inconsistent with previous data or beliefs that were used to estimate the parameter, new data may even increase the uncertainty.

If the data being used are n random observations (e.g. survey or experimental results), the uncertainty about the value of a parameter has a width (roughly) proportional to $1/\text{SQRT}(n)$. So, if you already have n observations and would like to halve the uncertainty, you will need a total of $4n$ observations (an increase of $3n$). If you want to decrease uncertainty by a factor of 10, you will need a total of $100n$ observations (an increase of $99n$). In other words a decrease in uncertainty about a parameter value becomes exponentially more expensive the closer the uncertainty gets to zero. Thus, if a VOPI analysis shows that it is economically justified to collect more information before making a decision, there will certainly be a point in the data collection where the cost of collecting data will outweigh their benefit.

VOPI analysis method

- Consider the range of possible values for the parameter(s) for which you could collect more information.
- Determine whether there are possible values for these parameters that, if known, would make the decision-maker select a different option from the one currently deemed to be best.
- Calculated the extra value (e.g. expected profit) that the more informed decision would give. This is the VOPI.

VOII analysis method

Start with a prior belief about a parameter (or parameters), based on data or opinion.

- Model what observations might be made with new data using the prior belief.
- Determine the decision rule that would be affected by these new data.
- Calculate any improvement in the decision capability given the new data; the measure of improvement requires some valuation and comparison of possible outcomes, which is usually taken to be expected monetary or utility value, although this is rather restrictive.
- Determine whether any improvement in the decision capability exceeds the cost of the extra information.

VOI example

Your company wants to develop a new cosmetic but there is some concern that people will have a minor adverse skin reaction to the product. The cost of development of the product to market is $1.8 million. The revenue NPV (including the cost of development) if the product is of the required quality is $3.7 million.

Cosmetic regulations state that you will have to withdraw the product if 2 % or more of consumers have an adverse reaction to your product. You have already performed some preliminary trials on 200 random people selected from the target demographic, at a cost/person of $500. Three of those people had an adverse reaction to the product.

Management decide the product will only be developed if they can be 85 % confident that the product will affect less than the required 2 % of the population. Decision question: Should we test more people or just abandon the product development now? If we should test more people, then how many more?

Having observed three affected people out of 200, our prior belief about p can be modelled as Beta$(3 + 1, 200 - 3 + 1) = $ Beta$(4, 198)$, which gives a 57.24 % confidence that 2 % or less of the target demographic will be affected (calculated as VoseBetaProb(2 %, 4, 198, 1) or BETADIST(2 %, 4, 198)).

Thus, the current level of information means that management would not pursue development of the product, with no resultant cost or revenue, i.e. a net revenue of $0. However, the beta distribution shows that it is quite possible that p is less than 2 %, and we could be losing a good opportunity by quitting now. If this were known for sure, the company would get a profit of $3.7 million, so the VOPI $= 3.7 million $* 57.24 \% + 0 million $* 42.76 \% = 2.12 million, and each test only costs $500; it is certainly possible that more information could be worth the expense.

VOII analysis

The model in Figure 5.40 performs the VOII steps described above. The parameter of concern is the fraction of people (prevalence), p, in the target demographic (women 18–65) who would have an adverse reaction, with a prior uncertainty described by Beta(4, 198), cell C12.

The people in the study are randomly sampled from this demographic, so if we test m extra people (cell C22) we can assume the number of people who would be adversely affected, s, would follow a Binomial(m, p) distribution (cell C24).

The revised estimate for p would then become Beta($4 + s$, $198 + (m − s)$). The confidence we then have that p is $<2\%$ is given by VoseBetaProb(2%, $4 + s$, $198 + (m − s)$, 1), cell C27. If this confidence exceeds 85%, management would take the decision to develop the product (cells C31:C32).

The model simulates different possible values of p from the prior. It models various possible numbers of extra tests, m, and simulates the extra data generated (s out of m), then evaluates the expected return of the resultant decision. Of course, although one may have reached the required confidence for p, the true value for p doesn't change and a bad decision may still be taken. The value of information is calculated for each iteration, and the mean function is used to calculate the expected value of information.

Note that for this example the question being posed is how many more people to test in one go. A more optimal strategy would be to test a smaller number, review the results and perform a VOII analysis. This iterative process will either achieve the required confidence at a smaller test cost or lead one to abandon further testing because one is fairly sure that the required performance will not be achieved.

It might at first seem that we are getting something for nothing here. After all, we don't actually know anything more until we perform the extra tests. However, the decision that would be made would depend on the results of those extra tests, and those results depend on what the true value of p actually

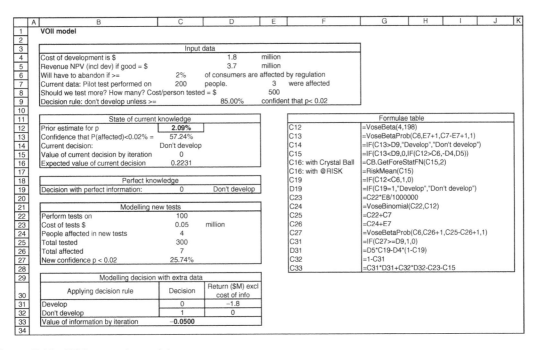

Figure 5.40 VOII example model.

is. Thus, the analysis is based on our prior for p (i.e. what we know to date about p) and the decision rule. When the model generates a scenario, it selects a value from the prior for p. It is saying: "Let's imagine that this is the true value for p". If that value is <2 %, we should develop the product of course, but we'll never know the value of p (until we have launched the product and have enough customer history to know its value). However, extra tests will get us closer to knowing its true value,

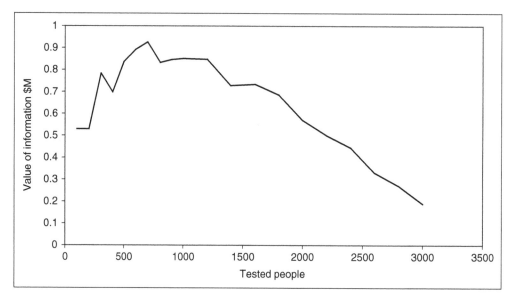

Figure 5.41 VOI example model results.

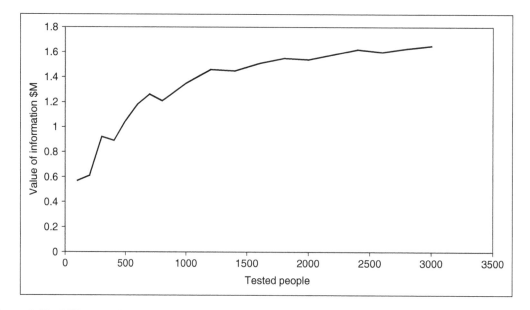

Figure 5.42 VOI example model results where tests have no cost.

and so we end up taking less of a gamble. When the model picks a small value for p, it will probably generate a small number of affected people in our new tests, and our interpretation of this small number as meaning p is small will often be correct. The danger is that a high p value could by chance result in an unrepresentatively small fraction of m being affected, which will be misinterpreted as a small p and lead management to make the wrong decision. However, as m gets bigger, so that risk diminishes. The balance that needs to be made is that the tests cost money. The model simulates 20 scenarios where m is varied between 100 and 3000, with the results shown in Figure 5.41.

It tells us that the optimal strategy, i.e. the strategy with the greatest expected VOII, is to perform about another 700 tests. The sawtooth effect in these plots occurs because of the discrete nature of the extra number affected that one would observe in the new data. Note that, if the tests had no cost, the graph above would look very different (Figure 5.42). Now it is continually worth collecting more information (providing it is actually feasible to do) because there is no penalty to be paid in running more tests (except perhaps time, which is not included as part of this problem). In this case the value of information asymptotically approaches the VOPI($= \$2.12$ million) as the number of people tested approaches infinity.

Part 2

Introduction

Part 2 constitutes the bulk of this book and covers a wide range of risk analysis modelling techniques that are in general use. I have again almost exclusively used Microsoft Excel as the modelling environment because it is ubiquitous and makes it easy to show the principles of a model with printouts of the spreadsheet.

I have also used Vose Consulting's ModelRisk add-in to Excel (see Appendix II), but I have done my best to avoid making this book a glorified advertisement for a software tool. The reality is that you will need some specialist software to do risk analysis. Using ModelRisk gives me the opportunity to explain the thinking behind risk analysis modelling without the message getting lost in very long calculations or wrestling with the mechanical limitations of modelling in spreadsheets. Some of the simpler functions in ModelRisk are available in other risk analysis software tools, and Excel has some statistical functions (although they are of dubious quality). When I have used more complex functions in ModelRisk (like copulas or time series, for example), I have tried to give you enough information for you to do it yourself. Of course, we'd love you to buy ModelRisk – there is a lot more in the software than I have used in this book (Appendix II gives some highlights and explains how ModelRisk interacts with other risk analysis spreadsheet add-ins), it has a lot of very nice user-interfaces and its routines can be called from C++ and VBA. We offer an extended demo period for ModelRisk on the inside back-cover of this book, together with files for the models created for this book that you can play around with.

Notation used in the spreadsheet models

I have given printouts of spreadsheet models throughout this book. The models were produced in Microsoft Excel version 2003 and ModelRisk version 2.0 which complies with the standard Excel rules for cell formulae. The equations easily translate to @RISK, Crystal Ball and other Monte Carlo simulation packages where they have similar functions. In each spreadsheet, I have given a formulae table so that the reader can follow and reproduce the model, for example:

	A	B	C	D	E	F	G	H
1		Mean	Stdev	Variable				
2		10	3	8.605037			*Formulae table*	
3		8	2	1.054596		D2:D8	=VoseLognormal(B2,C2)	
4		7	5	0.429087		D10 (output)	=SUM(D2:D8)	
5		9	3	0.167958		D11 (output)	=STDEV(D2:D8)	
6		6	4	1.361706				
7		5	2	2.27072				
8		2	1	1.643187				
9								
10			Sum	15.53229				
11			Stdev	2.90451				
12								

Here you'll see an entry for cells D2:D8 as $=$ VoseLognormal(B2, C2). Where I have given one formula for a range of cells, it refers to the first cell of the range, and the formulae for other cells in the range are those that would appear by copying that formula over, for example by using the Excel Autofill facility. The formulae in the other cells in the range will vary according to their different position. So, for example, copying the formula above into the other cells would give:

$$D3 : = VoseLognormal(B3, C3)$$

$$D4 : = VoseLognormal(B4, C4)$$

$$D5 : = VoseLognormal(B5, C5)$$

etc.

If the formula had included a fixed reference using the "$" symbol in Excel notation, e.g. $=$ VoseLognormal(B$2, C2), it would have copied down as

$$D3 : = VoseLognormal(B\$2, C3)$$

$$D4 : = VoseLognormal(B\$2, C4)$$

$$D5 : = VoseLognormal(B\$2, C5)$$

etc.

The VoseLognormal function generates random samples from a lognormal distribution, a very common distribution that features pretty much in all Monte Carlo simulation add-ins to Excel. So, for example, VoseLognormal(2,3) could be replaced as follows:

$$@RISK = RiskLognorm(2, 3)$$

$$Crystal Ball = CB.Lognormal(2, 3)$$

There are maybe a dozen other, less common, Monte Carlo add-ins with varying levels of sophistication, and they all follow the same principle, but be careful to ensure that they parameterise a distribution in the same way.

Excel allows you to input a function as an array, meaning that one function covers several cells. Array formulae in Excel are inputted by highlighting a range of cells, typing the formula and then CTRL-SHIFT-Enter together. The function then appears within curly brackets in the formula bar. Array functions are used rather extensively with ModelRisk. For example:

	A	B	C	D	E	F	G
1		Value	Shuffled				
2		1	3			*Formulae table*	
3		2	5		C2:C8	{=VoseShuffle(B2:B8)}	
4		3	2				
5		4	6				
6		5	4				
7		6	1				
8		7	7				
9							

The VoseShuffle function simply randomises the order of the values listed in its parameter array. You'll see how I display the formula within curly brackets because the VoseShuffle covers that whole range with one function, which is how it appears when you see it in Excel's formula bar.

Note also that all functions with a name all in upper-case letters are always native Excel functions, which is how they appear in the spreadsheet. Functions of the form VoseXxxx belong to ModelRisk.

Types of function in ModelRisk

ModelRisk has several types of function that apply to a probability distribution. I'll use the normal distribution as an example.

VoseNormal(2, 3) generates random values from a normal distribution with mean $= 2$ and standard deviation $= 3$. An optional third parameter (we call it the "U-parameter") is the quantile of the distribution; for example, VoseNormal(2, 3, 0.9) returns the 90th percentile of the distribution. The U-parameter must obviously lie on [0, 1]. The main use of the U-parameter is to control how random samples are generated from the distribution. For example:

$$\text{VoseNormal}(2, 3, \text{RiskUniform}(0, 1))$$

or

$$\text{VoseNormal}(2, 3, \text{CB.Uniform}(0, 1))$$

or

$$\text{VoseNormal}(2, 3, \text{RAND}())$$

will generate random values from the normal distribution using the random number generators of @RISK, Crystal Ball or Excel respectively to control the sampling.

The second type of function calculates probabilities for each distribution featured in ModelRisk. For example, VoseNormalProb(0.7, 2, 3, FALSE) returns the probability density function of the normal distribution evaluated at $x = 0.7$, as would VoseNormalProb(0.7, 2, 3, **0**) or VoseNormalProb(0.7, 2, 3), since the last parameter is assumed FALSE if omitted. VoseNormalProb(0.7, 2, 3, **TRUE**) or VoseNormalProb(0.7, 2, 3, **1**) returns the cumulative distribution function of the normal distribution evaluated at $x = 0.7$. To this degree, these functions are analogous to Excel's NORMDIST function, e.g.

$$\text{VoseNormalProb}(x, m, s, 0) = \text{NORMDIST}(x, m, s, 0)$$

$$\text{VoseNormalProb}(x, m, s, 1) = \text{NORMDIST}(x, m, s, 1)$$

However, the probability calculation functions can take an array of x values and then return the joint probability. For example, VoseNormalProb({0.1, 0.2, 0.3}, 2, 3, 0) = VoseNormalProb(0.1, 2, 3, 0) $*$ VoseNormalProb(0.2, 2, 3, 0) $*$ VoseNormalProb(0.3, 2, 3, 0). There are two advantages to this feature: we don't need a vast array of functions to calculate the joint probability for a large dataset, and the functions are far faster and more accurate than multiplying a long array because, depending on the distribution, there will be a lot of calculations that can be simplified. Joint probabilities can quickly tend to very small values, beyond the range that Excel can handle, so ModelRisk offers log base 10 versions of these functions too, for example:

$$\text{VoseNormalProb10}(\{0.1, 0.2, 0.3\}, 2, 3, 0)$$

$$= \text{LOG10}(\text{VoseNormalProb}(\{0.1, 0.2, 0.3\}, 2, 3, 0))$$

These functions allow us to develop very efficient log likelihood models, for example, which we can then optimise to fit to data (see Chapter 10).

Finally, ModelRisk offers what we call object functions, for example VoseNormalObject(2, 3). If you type =VoseNormalObject(2, 3) into a cell, it returns the string "VoseNormalObject(2, 3)". In many types of risk analysis calculation we want to do more with a distribution than simply take a random sample or calculate a probability. For example, we might want to determine its moments (mean, variance, etc.). The following model does this for a Gamma(3, 7) distribution in two different ways:

	A	B	C	D	E	F	G	H
1								
2		alpha	3					
3		beta	7		Object	VoseGamma($C$2,$C$3)		
4								
5		Mean	21		Mean	21		
6		Variance	147		Variance	147		
7		Skewness	1.154701		Skewness	1.15470054		
8		Kurtosis	5		Kurtosis	5		
9								
10			*Formulae table*					
11		{B5:C8}	{=VoseMoments(VoseGammaObject(C2,C3))}					
12		F3	=VoseGammaObject(C2,C3)					
13		E5:F8	{=VoseMoments(F3)}					
14								

The VoseMoments array function returns the first four moments of a distribution and takes as its input parameter the distribution type and parameter values. There are many other situations in which we want to manipulate distributions as objects, for example:

$$= \text{VoseAggregateMC}(\text{VosePoisson}(50), \text{VoseLognormalObject}(10, 5))$$

This function uses a hybrid Monte Carlo approach to add n Lognormal(10, 5) distributions together, where n is itself a Poisson(50) random variable. Note that the lognormal distribution is defined as an object here because we are using the distribution many times, taking on average 50 independent samples from the distribution for each execution of the function. However, the Poisson distribution is not an object because for one execution of the function it simply draws a single random sample. Objects can be imbedded into other objects too. For example:

$$\text{VoseSpliceObject}(\text{VoseGammaObject}(3, 0.8), \text{VosePareto2Object}(4, 6, \text{VoseShift}(1.5)), 3)$$

is the object for a distribution constructed by splicing a gamma distribution (left) and a shifted Pareto2 distribution (right) together at $x = 3$. Allowing objects to exist alone in cells (e.g. cell F3 in the above figure) allows us to create very transparent and efficient models.

Mathematical notation

There are some mathematical notations listed below that the reader will come across in a few parts of the text. I have tried to keep the algebra to a minimum and the reader should not worry unduly about this list. There is nothing in this book that really extends beyond the level of mathematics that one learns in a quantitative undergraduate course.

x is the label generally given to the value of a variable

θ is the label generally given to an uncertain parameter

$\displaystyle\int_a^b f(x)\mathrm{d}x$ means the integral between a and b of the function $f(x)$

$\displaystyle\sum_{i=1}^n x_i$ means the sum of all x_i values, where i is between 1 and n, i.e. $x_1 + x_2 + \cdots + x_n$

$\displaystyle\prod_{i=1}^n x_i$ means the product of all x_i values, where $i = 1$ to n, i.e. $x_1.x_2.\ldots.x_n$

$\dfrac{\mathrm{d}}{\mathrm{d}x}f(x)$ means the differential of $f(x)$ with respect to x

$\dfrac{\partial}{\partial x}f(x,y)$ means the partial derivative of a function of x and y, $f(x,y)$, with respect to x

$\approx$ means "is approximately equal to"

$\leq, \geq$ mean "is less than or equal to" and "is greater than or equal to"

$\ll, \gg$ mean "is much less than" and "is much greater than"

$x!$ means "x-factorial", $= 1*2*3*\cdots*x$ or $\displaystyle\prod_{i=1}^x i$

$\exp[x]$ or e^x means "exponential x" $= 2.7182818\ldots^x$

$\ln[x]$ means the natural logarithm of x, so $\ln[\exp[x]] = x$

$\overline{x}$ means the average of all x values

$|x|$ means "modulus x", the absolute value of x

$\Gamma(x)$ is the gamma function evaluated at x : $\Gamma(x) = \displaystyle\int_0^\infty e^{-u}u^{x-1}\,\mathrm{d}u$

$B(x,y)$ is the beta function evaluated at (x,y) : $\displaystyle\int_0^1 t^{x-1}(1-t)^{y-1}\,\mathrm{d}t = \dfrac{\Gamma(x)\Gamma(y)}{\Gamma(x+y)}$

Other special functions are explained in the text where they appear. For those readers with some background in probability modelling, you might not be used to the notation I use for stating that a variable follows some distribution. For example, I write:

$$X = \mathrm{Normal}(100, 10)$$

whereas the reader might be used to

$$X \sim \mathrm{Normal}(100, 10)$$

I use the "=" notation because it is easier to write formulae that combine variables and it reflects how one uses Excel. For example, where I might write

$$X = \mathrm{Normal}(100, 10) + \mathrm{Gamma}(2, 3)$$

using the other notation, we would need to write

$$Y \sim \text{Normal}(100, 10)$$

$$Z \sim \text{Gamma}(2, 3)$$

$$X = Y + Z$$

which gets to be rather tedious.

   This chapter is set out in sections, each of which solves a number of problems in a particular area. I hope that the problem-solving approach will complement the theory discussed earlier in the book. References are made to where the theory used in the problems is more fully discussed. The solution to each problem finishes with the symbol ♦.

Chapter 6

Probability mathematics and simulation

This chapter explores some very basic theories of probability and statistics that are essential for risk analysis modelling and that we need to understand before moving on. In my experience, ignorance of these fundamentals is a prime cause of the logical failure of a model. Risk analysis software is often sold on the merits of removing the need for any in-depth statistical theory. Although this is quite true with respect to using the software, it is often not the case when it comes to producing a logical model.

In this chapter we begin by looking at the concepts that are used in the mathematics of probability distributions. Then we define some basic statistics in common use. We look at a few probability concepts that are essential to understand if one is to be assured of producing logical models. This chapter is designed to offer a reference of statistical and probability concepts: the application of these principles is left to the appropriate chapters later in the book.

For most people (myself included), probability theory and statistics were not their favourite subjects at college. I would, however, encourage those readers who find themselves equipped with limited endurance for statistical theory to get at least as far as the end of Section 6.4.4 before moving on.

6.1 Probability Distribution Equations

6.1.1 Cumulative distribution function (cdf)

The (cumulative) distribution function, or *probability distribution function*, $F(x)$, is the mathematical equation that describes the probability that a variable X is less than or equal to x, i.e.

$$F(x) = P(X \leq x) \quad \text{for all } x$$

where $P(X \leq x)$ means the probability of the event $X \leq x$.

A cumulative distribution function has the following properties:

1. $F(x)$ is always non-decreasing, i.e. $\dfrac{\mathrm{d}}{\mathrm{d}x} F(x) \geq 0$.

2. $F(x) = 0$ at $x = -\infty$;
   $F(x) = 1$ at $x = \infty$.

6.1.2 Probability mass function (pmf)

If a random variable X is discrete, i.e. it may take any of a specific set of n values x_i, $i = 1, \ldots, n$, then

$$P(X = x_i) = p(x_i)$$

$p(x)$ is called the *probability mass function*.

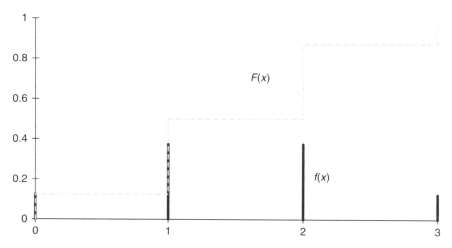

Figure 6.1 Distribution of the possible number of heads in three tosses of a coin.

Note that

$$\sum_{i=1}^{n} p(x_i) = 1$$

and

$$F(x_k) = \sum_{i=1}^{k} p(x_i) \qquad (6.1)$$

For example, if a coin is tossed 3 times, the number of observed heads is discrete. The possible values of x_i are shown in Figure 6.1 against their probability mass function $f(x)$ and probability distribution function $F(x)$. In this book, I will often show a discrete variable's probability mass function by joining together the probability masses with straight lines and marking each allowed value with a point. Vertical histograms are usually more appropriate representations of discrete variables, but, by using the points-and-lines type of graph, one can show several discrete distributions together in the same plot.

6.1.3 Probability density function (pdf)

If a random variable X is continuous, i.e. it may take any value within a defined range (or sometimes ranges), the probability of X having any precise value within that range is vanishingly small because we are allocating a probability of 1 between an infinite number of values. In other words, there is no probability mass associated with any specific allowable value of X. Instead, we define a probability density function $f(x)$ as

$$f(x) = \frac{\mathrm{d}}{\mathrm{d}x} F(x) \qquad (6.2)$$

i.e. $f(x)$ is the rate of change (the gradient) of the cumulative distribution function. Since $F(x)$ is always non-decreasing, $f(x)$ is always non-negative.

So, for a continuous distribution we cannot define the probability of observing any exact value. However, we can determine the probability of x lying between any two exact values (a, b):

$$P(a \leq x \leq b) = F(b) - F(a) \text{ where } b > a \tag{6.3}$$

Example 1.6

Consider a continuous variable that takes a Rayleigh(1) distribution. Its cumulative distribution function is given by

$$F(x) = 0 \quad x < 0$$

$$F(x) = 1 - e^{-x^2/2} \quad x > 0$$

and its probability density function is given by

$$f(x) = 0 \quad x < 0$$

$$f(x) = xe^{-x^2/2} \quad x > 0$$

The probability that the variable will be between 1 and 2 is given by

$$p(1 < x < 2) = F(2) - F(1) = (1 - e^{-2}) - (1 - e^{-0.5}) \approx 47.12\%$$

$F(x)$ and $f(x)$ for this example are shown in Figure 6.2. In this book, we will show a continuous variable's probability density function with a smooth curve, as illustrated. A square sometimes plotted in

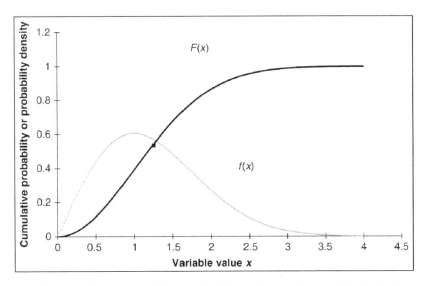

Figure 6.2   Probability density and cumulative probability plots for a Rayleigh(1) distribution.

the middle of this curve represents the position of the mean of the distribution. Providing the distribution is unimodal, if this point is higher than the 50 percentile, the distribution will be right skewed, and if lower than the 50 percentile it will be left skewed. ♦

6.2 The Definition of "Probability"

Probability is a numerical measurement of the likelihood of an outcome of some random process. Randomness is the effect of chance and is a fundamental property of the system, even if we cannot directly measure it. It is not reducible through either study or further measurement, but may be reduced by changing the physical system. Randomness has been described as "aleatory uncertainty" and "stochastic variability". The concept of probability can be developed neatly from two different approaches:

Frequentist definition

The frequentist approach asks us to imagine repeating the physical process an extremely large number of times (trials) and then to look at the fraction of times that the outcome of interest occurs. That fraction is asymptotically (meaning as we approach an infinite number of trials) equal to the probability of that particular outcome for that physical process. So, for example, the frequentist would imagine that we toss a coin a very large number of times. The fraction of the tosses that come up heads is approximately the true probability of a single toss producing a head, and the more tosses we do the closer the fraction becomes to the true probability. So, for a fair coin, we should see the number of heads stabilise at around 50 % of the trials as the number of trials gets truly huge. The philosophical problem with this approach is that one usually does not have the opportunity to repeat the scenario a very large number of times. How do we match this approach with, for example, the probability of it raining tomorrow, or you having a car crash?

Axiomatic definition

The physicist or engineer, on the other hand, could look at the coin, measure it, spin it, bounce lasers off its surface, etc., until one could declare that, owing to symmetry, the coin must logically have a 50 % probability of falling on either surface (for a fair coin, or some other value for an unbalanced coin, as the measurements dictated). Determining probabilities on the basis of deductive reasoning has a far broader application than the frequency approach because it does not require us to imagine being able to repeat the same physical process infinitely.

A third, subjective, definition

In this context, "probability" would be our measure of how much we believe something to be true. I'll use the term "confidence" instead of probability to make the separation between belief and real-world probability clear. A distribution of confidence looks exactly the same as a distribution of probability and must follow the same rules of complementation, addition, etc., which easily lead to mixing up of the two ideas. Uncertainty is the assessor's lack of knowledge (level of ignorance) about the parameters that characterise the physical system that is being modelled. It is sometimes reducible through further measurement or study. Uncertainty has also been called "fundamental uncertainty", "epistemic uncertainty" and "degree of belief".

6.3 Probability Rules

There are four important probability theorems for risk analysis, the meaning and use of which are discussed in this section:

- strong law of large numbers (also called Tchebysheff's inequality[1]);
- binomial theorem;
- Bayes' theorem;
- central limit theorem (CLT).

I will also describe a number of mathematical techniques useful in risk analysis and referenced elsewhere:

- Taylor series;
- Tchebysheff's rule (theorem);
- Markov inequality;
- least-squares linear regression;
- rank order correlation coefficient.

We'll begin with some basics on conditional probability, using Venn diagrams to help visualise the thinking.

6.3.1 Venn diagrams

Venn diagrams are introduced here to help visualise some basic rules of probability. In a Venn diagram the squared area, denoted by ε, contains all possible events, and we assign it an area equal to 1. The circles represent specific events. Probabilities are represented by the ratios of areas. For example, the probability of event A in Figure 6.3 is the ratio of area A to the total area ε:

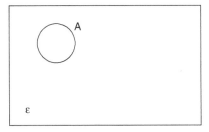

Figure 6.3   Venn diagram for a single event A.

Mutually exclusive events

Figure 6.4 gives an example of a Venn diagram where two events (A and B) are identified. The events are mutually exclusive, meaning that they cannot occur together, and therefore the circles do not overlap.

---

[1]   After the Russian mathematician Pafnuti Tchebysheff (1821–1894). Other transliterations of his name are Tchebycheff, Chebyshev and Tchebichef.

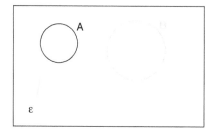

Figure 6.4   Venn diagram for two mutually exclusive events.

The areas of the circles are denoted by A and B, and the probability of the occurrence of events A and B are denoted by $P(A)$ and $P(B)$:

$$P(A) = A/\varepsilon$$

$$P(B) = B/\varepsilon$$

You can think of a Venn diagram as an archery target. Imagine that you are firing an arrow at the target and that you have an equal chance of landing anywhere within the target area, but will definitely hit it somewhere. The circles on the target represent each possible event, so if your arrow lands in circle A, it represents event A happening. In Figure 6.4 you cannot fire an arrow that will land in both A and B at the same time, so events A and B cannot occur at the same time:

$$P(A \cap B) = 0$$

The probability of either event occurring is then just the sum of the probabilities of each event, because we just need to add the A and B areas together:

$$P(A \cup B) = P(A) + P(B)$$

Events that are not mutually exclusive

In Figure 6.5, A and B are not mutually exclusive: they can occur together, represented by the overlap in the Venn diagram. The figure shows the four different areas that are now produced. It can be seen from these areas that

$$P(A \cup B) = P(A) + P(B) - P(A \cap B)$$

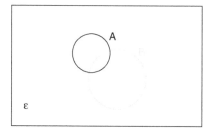

Figure 6.5   Venn diagram for two events that are not mutually exclusive.

We know from basic probability rules that

$$P(A \cap B) = P(A).P(B) \text{ if A and B are independent}$$

or

$$P(A \cap B) = P(A).P(B|A) \text{ if A and B are not independent}$$

How is that represented in the Venn diagram?

A and B are independent

$A \cap B$ is the area of overlap between the two circles. If A and B are independent, the probability of $A \cap B$ is $P(A)P(B)$.

Written in terms of areas, this would be

$$\frac{A \cap B}{\varepsilon} = \frac{A}{\varepsilon} * \frac{B}{\varepsilon}$$

$$\frac{A \cap B}{A} = \frac{B}{\varepsilon} = P(B)$$

In other words, the ratio between the overlap area and area A must be equal to $P(B)$. Similarly, the ratio between the overlap area and area B must be equal to $P(A)$.

A and B are dependent

$$P(A \cap B) = P(A).P(B|A)$$

Written in terms of areas, this would be

$$\frac{A \cap B}{\varepsilon} = \frac{A}{\varepsilon} * P(B|A)$$

$$\frac{A \cap B}{A} = P(B|A)$$

In other words, the ratio between the overlap area and area A must be equal to $P(B|A)$.

More complex example

A Venn diagram is a great way of getting across the complex interactions between probability events, providing you are released from making the areas actually correspond to the required probabilities (because that gets very tedious). The example in Figure 6.6 is difficult to describe mathematically, but simple in a Venn diagram.

6.3.2 The strong law of large numbers

The strong law of large numbers is the principle upon which Monte Carlo simulation is built. In layman's terms, it says that the larger the sample size (i.e. the greater the number of iterations), the closer their distribution (i.e. the risk analysis output) will be to the theoretical distribution (i.e. the exact distribution of the model's output if it could be mathematically derived).

This law is intuitively rather obvious, and many textbooks on probability theory reproduce a proof. It is sufficient for our needs just to say that the above law can be proven.

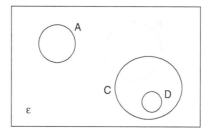

Figure 6.6 More complex Venn diagram example.

6.3.3 Central limit theorem

The central limit theorem (CLT) is one of the most important theorem for risk analysis modelling. It says that the mean $\bar{x}$ of a set of n variables (where n is large), drawn independently from the same distribution $f(x)$, will be normally distributed:

$$\bar{x} = \text{Normal}(\mu, \sigma/\sqrt{n}) \tag{6.4}$$

where μ and σ are the mean and standard deviation of the $f(x)$ distribution from which the n samples are drawn.

Example 6.2

If we had 40 variables, each following a Uniform(1, 3) distribution (with mean $= 2$ and standard deviation $= 1/\sqrt{3}$), the average of these variables would (approximately) have the following distribution:

$$\bar{x} = \text{Normal}\left(2, \frac{1}{\sqrt{3}\sqrt{40}}\right) = \text{Normal}\left(2, \frac{1}{\sqrt{120}}\right)$$

i.e. $\bar{x}$ is approximately normally distributed with mean $= 2$ and standard deviation $= 1/\sqrt{120}$. ♦

Exercise 6.1: Create a variety of Monte Carlo models, averaging n distributions of the same type with the same parameter values, and see what the resultant distribution looks like. Try different values for n, e.g. $n = 2, 5, 20, 50$ and 100, and different distribution types, e.g. triangular, normal, uniform and exponential. For what values of n are these average distributions close to normal? For the triangular distribution, does this value of n vary depending on where the most likely parameter's value lies relative to the minimum and maximum parameter values?

It follows, by multiplying both sides of Equation (6.4) by n, that the sum, Σ, of n variables drawn independently from the same distribution is given by

$$\Sigma = n\bar{x} = \text{Normal}(n\mu, \sqrt{n}\sigma) \tag{6.5}$$

Example 6.3

The sum Σ of 40 Uniform(1, 3) independent variables will have (approximately) the following distribution:

$$\Sigma = \text{Normal}\left(40 * 2, \sqrt{40} * \frac{1}{\sqrt{3}}\right) = \text{Normal}\left(80, \sqrt{\frac{40}{3}}\right) \blacklozenge$$

Remarkably, this theorem also applies to the sum (or average) of a large number of independent variables that have *different* probability distribution types, in that their sum will be approximately normally distributed providing no variable dominates the uncertainty of the sum.

The theorem can also be applied where a large number of positive variables are being *multiplied* together. Consider a set of X_i, $i = 1, \ldots, n$, variables that are being independently sampled from the same distribution. Then their product, Π, is given by

$$\Pi = \prod_{i=1}^{n} X_i$$

Taking the natural log of both sides:

$$\ln \Pi = \sum_{i=1}^{n} \ln X_i$$

Since each variable X_i has the same distribution, the variables ($\ln X_i$) must also have the same distribution, and thus, from the central limit theorem, $\ln \Pi$ is normally distributed. Now, a variable is *lognormally* distributed if its natural log is normally distributed, i.e. Π is lognormally distributed.

In fact, this application of the central limit theorem still *approximately* holds for the product of a large number of independent positive variables that have different distribution functions. There are a lot of situations where this seems to apply. For example, the volume of recoverable oil reserves within a field is approximately lognormally distributed since they are the product of a number of independent(ish) variables, i.e. reserve area, average thickness, porosity, gas/oil ratio, (1-water saturation), etc.

Most risk analysis models are a combination of adding (subtracting) and multiplying variables together. It should come as no surprise, therefore, that, from the above discussions, most risk analysis results seem to be somewhere between normally and lognormally distributed. A lognormal distribution also looks like a normal distribution when its mean is much larger than its standard deviation, so a risk analysis model result even more frequently looks approximately normal. This particularly applies to project and financial risk analyses where one is looking at cost or time to completion or the value of a series of cashflows.

It is important to note from the results of this theorem that the distribution of the average of a set of variables depends on the number of variables that are being averaged, as well as the uncertainty of each variable. It may be tempting, at times, to seek an expert's estimate of the distribution of the average of a number of variables; for example, the average time it will take to lay a kilometre of road, or the average weight of the fleece of a particular breed of sheep. The reader can now see that it will be a difficult task for experts to provide a distribution of an average measure: they will have to know the number of variables for which the estimate is the average *and* then apply the central limit theorem – which is no easy task to do in one's head. It is much better to estimate the distribution of the individual items and do the central limit theorem calculations oneself.

Many parametric distributions can be thought of as the sum of a number of other identical distributions. In general, if the mean is much larger than the standard deviation for these summary distributions, they can be approximated by a normal distribution. The central limit theorem is then useful for determining the parameters of the normal distribution approximation. Section III.9 discusses many of the useful approximations of one distribution for another.

6.3.4 Binomial theorem

The binomial theorem says that for some values a and b and a positive integer n

$$(a + b)^n = \sum_{x=0}^{n} \binom{n}{x} a^x b^{n-x}$$

The binomial coefficient, $\binom{n}{x}$, also sometimes written as nCx, is read as "n choose X" and is calculated as

$$\binom{n}{x} = \frac{n!}{x!(n-x)!} \tag{6.6}$$

where the exclamation mark denotes factorial, so $4! = 1 * 2 * 3 * 4$, for example. The binomial coefficient calculates the number of different ways one can order n articles where x of those articles are of one type and therefore indistinguishable from one another and the remaining $(n - x)$ are of another type, again each being indistinguishable from another. The Excel function COMBIN calculates the binomial coefficient.

The arguments underpinning this equation go as follows. There are $n!$ ways of ordering n articles, as there are n choices for the first article, then $(n - 1)$ choices for the second, $(n - 2)$ choices for the third, etc., until we are left with just the one choice for the last article. Thus, there are $n * (n - 1) * (n - 2) * \ldots * 1 = n!$ different ways of ordering these articles. Now, suppose that x of these articles were identical: we would not be able to differentiate between two orderings where we simply swapped the positions of two of these articles. Repeating the logic above, there are $x!$ different orderings that would all appear the same to us, so we would only recognise $1/x!$ of the possible orderings and the number of orderings would now be $n!/x!$ Now, suppose that the remaining $(n - x)$ articles are also identical but differentiable from the x articles. Then we could only distinguish $1/(n - x)!$ of the remaining possible orderings, and thus the total number of different combinations is given by

$$\frac{n!}{x!(n-x)!}$$

A useful way of quickly calculating the binomial coefficients for small n is given by Pascal's triangle (Figure 6.7). The outside of the triangle is filled with 1s, and each value inside the triangle is calculated

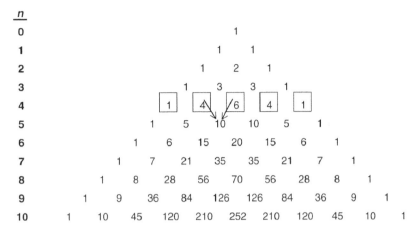

Figure 6.7 Pascal's triangle.

as the sum of the two values immediately above it. Row n then represents the binomial coefficient for n, which also appears as the second value in each row. So, for example,

$$\binom{4}{0} = 1, \quad \binom{4}{1} = 4, \quad \binom{4}{2} = 6, \quad \binom{4}{3} = 4 \text{ and } \binom{4}{4} = 1$$

as highlighted in the figure. Note that the binomial coefficients are symmetric so that

$$\binom{n}{x} = \binom{n}{n-x}$$

This makes sense, as, if we swap x for $(n-x)$ in Equation (6.6), we arrive back at the same formula. If we replace a with probability p, and b with probability $(1-p)$, the equation becomes

$$(p + (1-p))^n = \sum_{x=0}^{n} \binom{n}{x} p^x (1-p)^{n-x} = 1$$

The summed component

$$\binom{n}{x} p^x (1-p)^{n-x}$$

is the binomial probability mass function for x successes in n trials where each trial has a probability p of success. In a binomial process, all successes are considered identical and interchangeable, as are all failures.

Properties of the binomial coefficient

$$\binom{n}{n-x} = \binom{n}{x}$$

$$\binom{n+1}{x} = \binom{n}{x} + \binom{n}{x-1}$$

$$\binom{n}{0} = \binom{n}{n} = 1$$

$$\binom{a+b}{n} = \sum_{i=0}^{n} \binom{a}{i} \binom{b}{n-i}$$

The last identity is known as Vandermonde's theorem (A. T. Vandermonde, 1735–1796).

Calculating x! for large x

$x!$ is very laborious to calculate for high values of x. For example, $100! = 9.3326E+157$ and Excel's FACT(x) cannot calculate values higher than $170!$ The probability mass functions of many discrete probability distributions contain factorials, and we therefore often want to work out factorials for values larger than 170. Algorithms for generating distributions get around any calculation restriction by using approximations, for example the following equation, known as the *Stirling*[2] *formula*, can be used instead to get a very close approximation:

$$n! \sim \sqrt{2\pi n} \left(\frac{n}{e}\right)^n$$

where $\sim$ is read "asymptotically equal" and means that the right-hand side approaches the left-hand side as n approaches infinity.

However, if you are attempting to calculate a probability exactly, you can still use the Excel function GAMMALN():

$$\mathrm{Log}[x!] = \mathrm{GAMMALN}(x+1)$$

This may allow you to manipulate multiplications of factorials, etc., by adding them in log space. But, be warned, this formula will not return *exactly* the same answer as FACT(), for example

$$\mathrm{FACT}(170) = 7.2574156153E+306$$

$$\mathrm{EXP}(\mathrm{GAMMALN}(171)) = 7.2574156148E+306$$

and, while it is possible to get values for GAMMALN(x) where $x > 171$, Excel will return an error if you attempt to calculate the corresponding EXP(GAMMALN(x)).

6.3.5 Bayes' theorem

Bayes' theorem[3] is a logical extension of the conditional probability arguments we looked at in the Venn diagram section. We saw that

$$P(A|B) = \frac{P(A \cap B)}{P(B)} \quad \text{and} \quad P(B|A) = \frac{P(B \cap A)}{P(A)}$$

---

[2] James Stirling (1692–1770) – Scots mathematician.
[3] Rev. Thomas Bayes (1702–1761) – English philosopher. A short biography and a reprint of his original paper describing Bayes' theorem appear in Press (1989).

As $P(A \cap B) = P(B \cap A)$,

$$P(A \cap B) = P(B).P(A|B) = P(B \cap A)$$

and hence

$$P(A|B) = \frac{P(A)P(B|A)}{P(B)}$$

which is Bayes' theorem, and, in general,

$$P(A_i|B) = \frac{P(B|A_i) \cdot P(B)}{\sum\limits_{j=1}^{n} P(B|A_j)P(B)}$$

The following example illustrates the use of this equation. Many more are given in the section on Bayesian inference.

Example 6.4

Three machines A, B and C produce 20%, 45% and 35% respectively of a factory's wheel nuts output; 2%, 1% and 3% respectively of these machines outputs are defective:

(a) What is the probability that any wheel nut randomly selected from the factory's stock will be defective? Let X be the event where the wheel nut is defective, and A, B and C be the events where the selected wheel nut comes from machines A, B and C respectively:

$$P(X) = P(A) \cdot P(X|A) + P(B) \cdot P(X|B) + P(C) \cdot P(X|C)$$

$$= (0.2) \cdot (0.02) + (0.45) \cdot (0.01) + (0.35) \cdot (0.03)$$

$$= 0.019$$

(b) What is the probability that a randomly selected wheel nut will have come from machine A if it is defective?

From Bayes' theorem

$$P(A|X) = \frac{P(A).P(X|A)}{P(A) \cdot P(X|A) + P(B) \cdot P(X|B) + P(C) \cdot P(X|C)}$$

$$= \frac{(0.2) \cdot (0.02)}{(0.2) \cdot (0.02) + (0.45) \cdot (0.01) + (0.35) \cdot (0.03)} \approx 0.211$$

In other words, in Bayes' Theorem we divide the probability of the required path (the probability that it came from machine A and was defective) by the probability of all possible paths (the probability that it came from any machine and was defective). ♦

Example 6.5

We wish to know the probability that an animal will be infected (I), given that it passes (Pa) a specific veterinary check, i.e. $P(I|Pa)$.

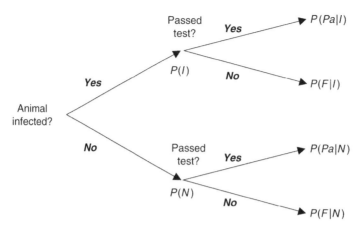

Figure 6.8   Event tree for Example 6.5.

The problem can be visualised by an event tree diagram (Figure 6.8). First of all, the animal will be infected (I) or not infected (N). Secondly, the animal will either pass (Pa) or fail (F) the test.

From Bayes' theorem

$$P(I|Pa) = \frac{P(Pa|I)P(I)}{P(Pa|I)P(I) + P(Pa|N)P(N)}$$

In veterinary terminology

$P(I) = \text{prevalence } p$ and thus $P(N) = (1 - p)$
$P(F|I) = \text{the sensitivity of the test } Se$ and thus $P(Pa|I) = (1 - Se)$
$P(Pa|N) = \text{the specificity of the test } Sp$

Putting these elements into Bayes' theorem,

$$P(I|Pa) = \frac{(1 - Se)p}{(1 - Se)p + Sp(1 - p)} \; \blacklozenge$$

6.3.6 Taylor series

The Taylor series is a formula that determines a polynomial approximation in x of some mathematical function $f(x)$ centred at some value x_0:

$$f(x) = \sum_{m=0}^{\infty} \frac{f^{(m)}(x_0)}{m!}(x - x_0)^m$$

where $f^{(m)}$ represents the mth derivative with respect to x of the function f.

In the special case where $x_0 = 0$, the series is known as the Maclaurin series of $f(x)$:

$$f(0) = \sum_{m=0}^{\infty} \frac{f^{(m)}(0)}{m!} x^m$$

The Taylor and Maclaurin series expansions are also used to provide polynomial approximations to probability distribution functions.

6.3.7 Tchebysheff's rule

If a dataset has mean $\bar{x}$ and standard deviation s, we are used to saying that 68 % of the data will lie between $(\bar{x} - s)$ and $(\bar{x} + s)$, 95 % lie between $(\bar{x} - 2s)$ and $(\bar{x} + 2s)$, etc. However, that is only true when the data follow a normal distribution. The same applies to a probability distribution. So, when the data, or probability distribution, are not normally distributed, how can we interpret the standard deviation?

Tchebysheff's rule applies to any probability distribution or dataset. It states:

> *"For any number k greater than 1, at least $(1 - 1/k^2)$ of the measurements will fall within k standard deviations of the mean".*

Substituting $k = 1$, Tchebysheff's rule says that at least 0 % of the data or probability distribution lies within one standard deviation of the mean. Well, we already knew that! However, substitute $k = 2$ tells us that at least 75 % of the data or distribution lie within two standard deviations of the mean. That is useful information because it applies to all distributions.

This is a fairly conservative rule in that, if we know the distribution type, we can specify a much higher percentage (e.g. 95 % for two standard deviations for a normal distribution, compared with 75 % with Tchebysheff's rule), but it is certainly helpful in interpreting the standard deviation of a dataset or probability distribution that is grossly non-normally distributed.

From Figure 6.9 you can see that, for any k, knowing the distribution type allows you to specify a much higher fraction of the distribution to be contained in the range mean $\pm k$ standard deviations.

The bimodal distribution tested was as shown in Figure 6.10.

6.3.8 Markov inequality

The Markov inequality gives some indication of the range of a distribution, in a similar way to Tchebysheff's rule. It states that for a *non-negative* random variable X with mean μ

$$P(X \geq k) \leq \frac{\mu}{k}$$

for any constant k greater than μ.

So, for example, for a random variable with mean 6, the probability of being greater than 20 is less than or equal to $6/20 = 30 \%$.

Of course, being very general like Tchebysheff's rule, it makes a rather conservative statement. For most distributions, the probability is much smaller than m/k (see Table 6.1 for some examples).

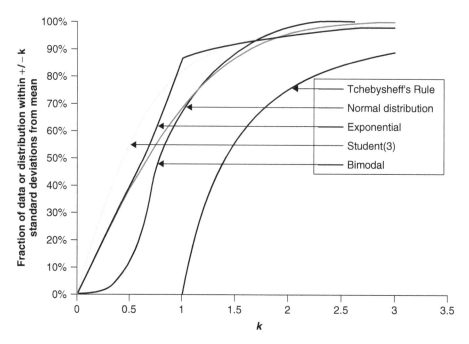

Figure 6.9 Comparison of Tchebysheff's rule with the results of a few distributions.

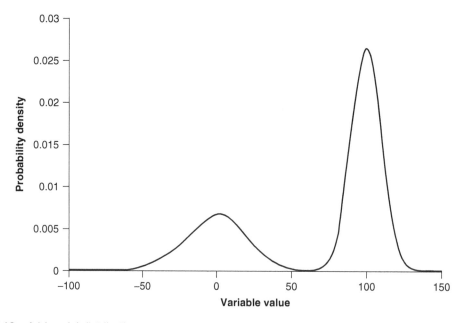

Figure 6.10 A bimodal distribution.

Table 6.1 Markov's rule for different distributions.

Distribution with $\mu = 6$	$P(X \geq 20)$
Exponential(6)	3.6 %
ChiSq(6)	0.3 %
Gamma(2, 3)	1 %
Inverse Gaussian(6, λ)	Max. of 6.9 %
Lognormal(6, σ)	Max. of 6.0 %
Pareto(θ, 6($\theta - 1$)/θ)	Max. of 3.21 %

6.3.9 Least-squares linear regression

The purpose of least-squares linear regression is to represent the relationship between one or more independent variables x_1, x_2 and a variable y that is dependent upon them in the following form:

$$y_i = \beta_0 + \beta_1 x_{1i} + \beta_2 x_{2i} + \ldots \varepsilon_i$$

where x_{ji} is the ith observed value of the independent variable x_j, y_i is the ith observed value of the dependent variable y, ε_i is the error term or residual (i.e. the difference between the observed y values and that predicted by the model), β_j is the regression slope for the variable x_j and β_0 is the y-axis intercept.

Simple least-squares linear regression assumes that there is only one independent variable x. If we assume that the error terms are normally distributed, the equation reduces to

$$y_i = \text{Normal}(m * x_i + c, s)$$

where m is the slope of the line and c is the y-axis intercept and s is the standard deviation of the variation of y about this line.

Simple least-squares linear regression is a very standard statistical analysis technique, particularly when one has little or no idea of the relationship between the x and y variables. It is probably particularly common because the analysis mathematics are simple (because of the normality assumption), rather than it being a very common rule for the relationship between variables. LSR makes four important assumptions (Figure 6.11):

1. Individual y values are independent.
2. For each x_i there are an infinite number of possible values of y, which are normally distributed.
3. The distribution of y given a value of x has equal standard deviation for all x values and is centred about the least-squares regression line.
4. The means of the distribution of y at each x value can be connected by a straight line $y = mx + c$.

Assumptions behind least-squares regression analysis

Statisticians often make transformations of the data (e.g. Log(Y), $\sqrt{X}$) to force a linear relationship. That greatly extends the applicability of the regression model, but one must be particularly careful that the errors are reasonably normal, and one runs an enormous risk in using the regression equations of making predictions outside the range of observations.

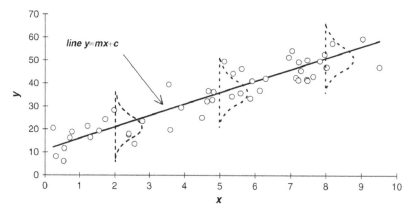

Figure 6.11 An illustration of the concepts of least-squares regression.

Estimation of parameters

The simple least-squares regression model determines the straight line that minimises the sum of the square of the e_i errors. It can be shown that this occurs when

$$m = \frac{\sum\limits_{i=1}^{n} (x_i - \bar{x})(y_i - \bar{y})}{\sum\limits_{i=1}^{n} (x_i - \bar{x})^2}$$

$$c = \bar{y} - m.\bar{x}$$

where $\bar{x}$, $\bar{y}$ are the mean of the observed x and y data and n is the number of data pairs (x_i, y_i).

The fraction of the total variation in the dependent variable that is explained by the independent variable is known as the coefficient of determination R^2, which is calculated as

$$R^2 = 1 - \frac{SSE}{TSS}$$

where the sum of squares errors, SSE, is given by

$$SSE = \sum_{i=1}^{n} (y_i - \hat{y}_i)^2$$

and the total sum of squares, TSS, is given by

$$TSS = \sum_{i=1}^{n} (y_i - \bar{y})^2$$

and where $\hat{y}_i$ are the predicted y values at each x_i:

$$\hat{y}_i = mx_i + c$$

For simple least-squares regression (i.e. only one independent variable), the square root of R^2 is equivalent to the simple correlation coefficient r:

$$r = \sqrt{R}$$

Correlation coefficient r may alternatively be calculated as

$$r = \frac{\left(\sum\limits_{i=1}^{n} (x_i - \overline{x})\right)\left(\sum\limits_{i=1}^{n} (y_i - \overline{y})\right)}{\sqrt{\left(\sum\limits_{i=1}^{n} (x_i - \overline{x})^2\right)\left(\sum\limits_{i=1}^{n} (y_i - \overline{y})^2\right)}}$$

Coefficient r provides a quantitative measure of the linear relationship between x and y. It ranges from -1 to $+1$: a value of $r = -1$ or $+1$ indicates a perfect linear fit, and $r = 0$ indicates no linear relationship exists at all. As

$$\sum_{i=1}^{n} (y_i - \hat{y}_i)^2$$

(the sum of squared errors between the observed and predicted y values) tends to zero, so r^2 tends to 1 and therefore r tends to -1 or $+1$, its sign depending on whether m is negative or positive respectively.

The value of r is used to determine the statistical significance of the fitted line, by first calculating the test statistic t as

$$t = r.\sqrt{\frac{n-2}{1-r^2}}$$

The t-statistic follows a t-distribution with $(n-2)$ degrees of freedom (provided the linear regression assumptions of normally distributed variation of y about the regression line hold) which is used to determine whether the fit should be rejected or not at the required level of confidence.

The standard error of the y estimate, S_{yx}, is calculated as

$$S_{yx} = \sqrt{\frac{\sum\limits_{i=1}^{n} (y_i - \hat{y}_i)^2}{(n-2)}}$$

This is equivalent to the standard deviation of the error terms ε_i. These errors reflect the true variability of the dependent variable y from the least-squares regression line. The denominator $(n-2)$ is used, instead of the $(n-1)$ we have seen before for sample standard deviation calculations, because two values m and c have been estimated from the data to determine the equation values, and we have therefore lost two degrees of freedom instead of the one degree of freedom usually lost in determining the mean.

The equations of the regression line equation and the S_{yx} statistic can be used together to produce a stochastic model of the relationship between X and Y, as follows:

$$Y = \text{Normal}(m * X + c, S_{yx})$$

Some caution is needed in using such a model. The regression model is intended to work within the range of the independent variable X for which there have been observations. Using the model outside this range can produce very significant errors if the relationship between x and y deviates from this linear relationship. This is also purely a model of variability, i.e. we are assuming that the linear relationship is correct and that the parameters are known. We should also include our uncertainty about the parameters, and perhaps about whether the linear relationship is even appropriate.

Example 6.6

Consider the dataset in Table 6.2 which shows the result of a survey of 30 people. They were asked to provide details of their monthly net income $\{x_i\}$ and the amount they spent on food each month $\{y_i\}$.
The values of m, c, r and S_{yx} were calculated using the Excel functions:

$$m = \text{SLOPE}(\{y_i\}, \{x_i\}) = 0.1356$$

$$c = \text{INTERCEPT}(\{y_i\}, \{x_i\}) = 167.8$$

$$r^2 = \text{RSQ}(\{y_i\}, \{x_i\}) = 0.8831$$

$$S_{yx} = \text{STEYX}(\{y_i\}, \{x_i\}) = 54.86$$

The line $\hat{y}_i = mx_i + c$ is plotted against the data points in Figure 6.12. ♦

Table 6.2 Data for Example 6.6.

Net monthly income x	Monthly food expenditure Y	Least-squares regression estimate y'	Error terms ε
505	268	236.07	31.93
517	243	237.70	5.30
523	202	238.51	−36.51
608	281	250.05	30.95
609	301	250.19	50.81
805	251	276.79	−25.79
974	248	299.73	−51.73
1095	187	316.15	−129.15
1110	331	318.19	12.81
1139	291	322.13	−31.13
1352	464	351.04	112.96
1453	402	364.75	37.25
1461	423	365.83	57.17
1543	265	376.96	−111.96
1581	415	382.12	32.88
1656	384	392.30	−8.30
1748	413	404.79	8.21
1760	448	406.42	41.58
1811	470	413.34	56.66
1944	448	431.39	16.61
1998	443	438.72	4.28
2054	418	446.33	−28.33
2158	422	460.44	−38.44
2229	428	470.08	−42.08
2319	417	482.30	−65.30
2371	529	489.35	39.65
2637	574	525.46	48.54
2843	511	553.42	−42.42
2889	514	559.67	−45.67
3096	657	587.76	69.24

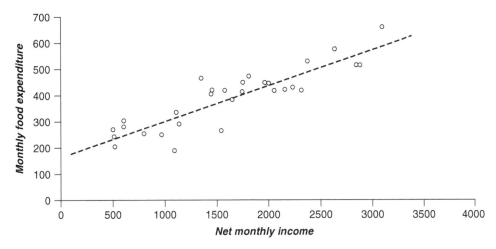

Figure 6.12   The line $\hat{y}_i = mx_i + c$ plotted against the data points from Table 6.2.

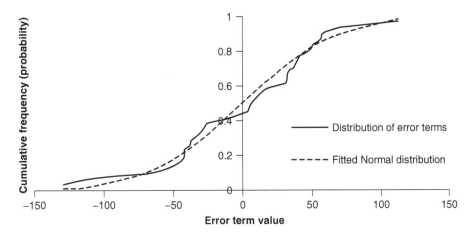

Figure 6.13   Distribution of the error terms.

The error terms $\varepsilon_i = y_i - \hat{y}_i$ are shown in Figure 6.13.

A distribution fit of these ε_i values shows that they are approximately normally distributed. A test of significance of r also shows that, for 28 degrees of freedom $(n - 2)$, there is only about a 5×10^{-11} chance that such a high value of r could have been observed from purely random data. We would therefore feel confident in modelling the relationship between any net monthly income value N (between the values 505 and 1581) and monthly expenditure on food F using

$$F = \text{Normal}(0.1356 * N + 167.8, 54.86)$$

Uncertainty about least-squares regression parameters

The parameters m, c and S_{yx} for the least-squares regression represent the best estimate of the variability model where we are assuming some stochastically linear relationship between x and y. However, since we will have only a limited number of observations (i.e. $\{x, y\}$ pairs), we do not have perfect knowledge of the stochastic system and there is therefore some uncertainty about the regression parameters. The t-test tells us whether the linear relationship might exist at some level of confidence. More useful, however, from a risk analysis perspective is that we can readily determine distributions of uncertainty about these parameters using the bootstrap.

6.3.10 Rank order correlation coefficient

Spearman's rank order correlation coefficient ρ is a non-parametric statistic for quantifying the correlation relationship between two variables. Non-parametric means that the correlation statistic is not affected by the type of mathematical relationship between the variables, unlike linear least-squares regression analysis, for example, which requires the relationship to be described by a straight line with normally distributed variation of the dependent variable about that line.

Calculating the rank order correlation analysis proceeds as follows. Replace the n observed values for the two variables X and Y by their ranking: the largest value for each variable has a rank of 1, the smallest a rank of n, or vice versa. The Excel function RANK() can do this, but it is inaccurate where there are ties, i.e. where two or more observations have the same value. In such cases, one should assign to each of the same-valued observations the average of the ranks they would have had if they had been infinitesimally different from the value they take.

The Spearman rank order correlation coefficient ρ is calculated as

$$\rho = 1 - \frac{6. \sum (u_i - v_i)^2}{n(n^2 - 1)}$$

where u_i and v_i are the ranks of the ith pair of the X and Y variables. This is, in fact, a shortcut formula: it is not exact when there are tied measurements, but still works well when there are not too many ties relative to the size of n. The exact formula is

$$\rho = \frac{SS_{uv}}{\sqrt{SS_{uu}SS_{vv}}}$$

where

$$SS_{uv} = \sum_{i=1}^{n} (u_i - \bar{u})(v_i - \bar{v})$$

$$SS_{uu} = \sum_{i=1}^{n} (u_i - \bar{u})^2$$

$$SS_{vv} = \sum_{i=1}^{n} (v_i - \bar{v})^2$$

and where u_i and v_i are the ranks of the ith observation in samples 1 and 2 respectively. This calculation does not require that one identify which variable is dependent and which is independent: the calculation for r is symmetric, so X and Y could swap places with no effect on the value of r. The value of r varies from -1 to 1 in the same way as the least-squares regression coefficient r. A value of r close to

-1 and 1 means that the variables are highly negatively and positively correlated respectively. A value of r close to zero means that there is no correlation between the variables. Just as with least-squares regression, it is important to determine whether the degree of correlation given by the value of r is real or a spurious result brought about by the effects of randomness. The value of r can be tested for statistical significance by constructing a test statistic t in the same way as we have seen for least-squares regression:

$$t = \rho \sqrt{\frac{n-2}{1-\rho^2}}$$

which approximates to a t-distribution with $(n-2)$ degrees of freedom.

6.4 Statistical Measures

We now consider some statistical measures that can be derived for a random variable with a distribution of known probability density functions $f(x)$ or probability mass functions $p(x)$.

6.4.1 Measures of central tendency

The Mean μ

The mean, also known as the *expected value* or *average*, is given by

$$\mu = \sum_{i=1}^{n} x_i \, p_i \text{ for discrete variables} \tag{6.7}$$

$$\mu = \int_{-\infty}^{\infty} x f(x) \, dx \text{ for continuous variables} \tag{6.8}$$

The mean is known as *the first moment about zero*. It can be considered to be the centre of gravity of the distribution. If one were to cut out the probability density function drawn on a piece of card, the mean would be the value at which the distribution balanced.

Example 6.7

The mean of the Uniform(1, 3) distribution is therefore calculated as follows:

$$\mu = \int_{1}^{3} \frac{1}{2} x \, dx = \left[\frac{x^2}{4} \right]_{1}^{3} = \frac{9-1}{4} = 2 \; \blacklozenge$$

The mean has the following properties:

$$\overline{(X+Y)} = \overline{X} + \overline{Y}, \overline{(X-Y)} = \overline{X} - \overline{Y} \text{ and } \overline{(X*Y)} = \overline{X} * \overline{Y}$$

where X and Y are positive, uncorrelated random variables.

The mode

The mode is the x value with the greatest probability $p(x)$ for a discrete distribution, or the greatest probability density $f(x)$ for a continuous distribution. The mode is not uniquely defined for a discrete distribution with two or more values that have the equal highest probability. For example, a distribution of the number of heads in three tosses of a coin gives equal probability ($\frac{3}{8}$) to both one and two heads. The mode may also not be uniquely defined if a distribution is multimodal (i.e. it has two or more peaks).

The median $x_{0.5}$

The median is the value where the variable has a 50 % probability of exceeding, i.e.

$$F(x_{0.5}) = 0.5$$

An interesting property of unimodal probability distributions relates the relative positions of the mean, mode and median. If the distribution is right (positively) skewed, these three measures of central tendency are positioned from left to right: mode, median and mean (see Figure 6.14). Conversely, a unimodal left (negatively) skewed distribution has them in the reverse order. For a unimodal, symmetric distribution, the mode, median and mean are all equal.

6.4.2 Measures of spread

Variance V

The variance is a measure of how much the distribution is spread from the mean:

$$V = E[(x - \mu)^2] = E(x^2) - \mu^2 \tag{6.9}$$

where $E[]$ denotes the expected value (mean) of whatever is in the brackets, so

$$V = \int_{-\infty}^{\infty} (x - \mu)^2 \cdot f(x) \cdot dx \tag{6.10}$$

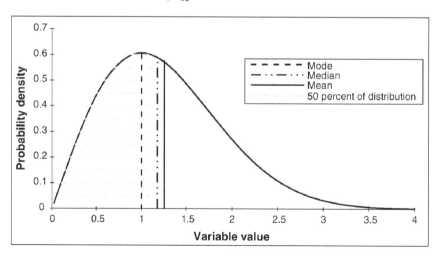

Figure 6.14   Relative positions of the mode, median and mean of a right-skewed unimodal distribution.

Thus, the variance sums up the squared distance from the mean of all possible values of x, weighted by the probability of x occurring. The variance is known as *the second moment about the mean*. It has units that are the square of the units of x. So, if x is cows in a random field, V has units of cows^2. This limits the intuitive value of the variance.

Standard deviation σ

The standard deviation is the positive square root of the variance, i.e. $\sigma = \sqrt{V}$. Thus, if the variance has units of cows^2, the standard deviation has units of cows, the same as the variable x. The standard deviation is therefore more popularly used to express a measure of spread.

Example 6.8

The variance V of the Uniform(1, 3) distribution is calculated as follows:

$$V = E(x^2) - \mu^2 \quad \mu = 2 \text{from before}$$

$$E(x^2) = \int \frac{1}{2} x^2 \, dx = \left[\frac{x^3}{6} \right]_1^3 = \frac{27-1}{6} = \frac{26}{6}$$

and therefore

$$V = \frac{26}{6} - 2^2 = \frac{1}{3}$$

and the standard deviation σ is therefore

$$\sigma = \sqrt{V} = \frac{1}{\sqrt{3}} \blacklozenge$$

Variance and standard deviation have the following properties, where a is some constant and X and X_i are random variables:

1. $V(X) \geq 0$ and $\sigma(X) \geq 0$.
2. $V(aX) = a^2 V(X)$ and $\sigma(aX) = a\sigma(X)$.
3. $V\left(\sum_{i=1}^n X_i\right) = \sum_{i=1}^n V(X_i)$, providing the X_i are uncorrelated.

6.4.3 Mean, standard deviation and the normal distribution

For a normal distribution *only*, the areas bounded 1, 2 and 3 standard deviations either side of the mean contain approximately 68.27, 95.45 and 99.73 % of the distribution, as shown in Figure 6.15. Since a lot of distributions look similar to a normal distribution under certain conditions, people often think of 70 % of a distribution being reasonably contained within one standard deviation either side of the mean, but this rule of thumb must be used with care. If it is applied to a distribution that is significantly non-normal, like an exponential distribution, the error can be quite large (the range $\mu \pm \sigma$ contains 87 % of an exponential distribution, for example).

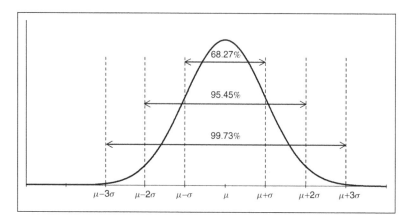

Figure 6.15 Some probability areas of the normal distribution.

Example 6.9

Panes of bullet-proof glass manufactured at a factory have a mean thickness over a pane that is normally distributed, with a mean of 25 mm and a variance of 0.04 mm². If 10 panes are purchased, what is the probability that all the panes will have a mean thickness between 24.8 and 25.4 mm?

The distribution of the mean thickness of a randomly selected pane is Normal(25, 0.2) mm, since the variance is the square of the standard deviation; 24.8 mm is one standard deviation below the mean, 25.4 mm is two standard deviations above the mean. The probability p that a pane lies between 24.8 and 25.4 mm is then half the probability of lying ± one standard deviation from the mean plus half the probability of lying ± two standard deviations from the mean, i.e. $p \approx (68.27\% + 95.45\%)/2 = 81.86\%$. The probability that all panes will have a mean thickness between 24.8 and 25.4 mm, provided that they are independent of each other, is therefore $\approx (81.86\%)^{10} = 13.51\%$. ◆

6.4.4 Measures of shape

The mean and variance are called the first moment about zero and the second moment about the mean. The third and fourth moments about the mean, called skewness and kurtosis respectively, are also occasionally used in risk analysis.

Skewness S

The skewness statistic is calculated from the following formulae:
  Discrete variable:

$$S = \frac{\sum_{i=1}^{n} (x_i - \mu)^3 p_i}{\sigma^3} \tag{6.11}$$

Continuous variable:

$$S = \frac{\int_{min}^{max} (x - \mu)^3 f(x) \, dx}{\sigma^3} \tag{6.12}$$

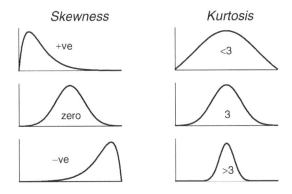

Figure 6.16 Examples of skewness and kurtosis.

This is often called the *standardised skewness*, as it is divided by σ^3 to give a unitless statistic. The skewness statistic refers to the *lopsidedness* of the distribution (see left-hand panel of Figure 6.16). If a distribution has a negative skewness (sometimes described as left skewed), it has a longer tail to the left than to the right. A positively skewed distribution (right skewed) has a longer tail to the right, and zero-skewed distributions are usually symmetric.

Kurtosis K

The kurtosis statistic is calculated from the following formulae:
   Discrete variable:

$$K = \frac{\sum\limits_{i=1}^{n} (x_i - \mu)^4 p_i}{\sigma^4} \tag{6.13}$$

Continuous variable:

$$K = \frac{\int_{\min}^{\max} (x - \mu)^4 f(x)\, dx}{\sigma^4} \tag{6.14}$$

This is often called the *standardised kurtosis*, since it is divided by σ^4, again to give a unitless statistic. The kurtosis statistic refers to the *peakedness* of the distribution (see right-hand panel of Figure 6.16) – the higher the kurtosis, the more peaked is the distribution. A normal distribution has a kurtosis of 3, so kurtosis values for a distribution are often compared with 3. For example, if a distribution has a kurtosis below 3 it is flatter than a normal distribution. Table 6.3 gives some examples of skewness and kurtosis for common distributions.

6.4.5 Raw and central moments

There are three sets of moments that are used in probability modelling to describe a distribution of a random variable x with density function $f(x)$. The first set are called raw moments μ'_k. The kth raw moment is defined as

$$\mu'_k = E\left[x^k\right] = \int_{\min}^{\max} x^k f(x)\, dx$$

Table 6.3 Skewness and kurtosis.

Distribution	Skewness	Kurtosis
Binomial	$-\infty$ to ∞	1 to ∞
ChiSq	0 to 2.828	3 to 15
Exponential	2	9
Lognormal	0 to ∞	3 to ∞
Normal	0	3
Poisson	0 to ∞	3 to ∞
Triangular	-0.562 to 0.562	2.4
Uniform	0	1.8

where $k = 1, 2, 3, \ldots$, or, for discrete variables with probability mass $p(x)$, as

$$\mu'_k = E\left[x^k\right] = \sum_{min}^{max} x^k p(x)$$

Then we have the *central moments*, m_k, defined as

$$\mu_k = E\left[x - \mu)^k\right] = \int_{min}^{max} (x - \mu)^k f(x)\, dx, \quad k = 2, 3, \ldots$$

where $\mu = \mu'_1$ is the mean of the distribution. Finally, we have the *normalised moments*:

$$\text{Mean} = \mu$$

$$\text{Variance} = \mu_2$$

$$\text{Skewness} = \frac{\mu_3}{(\text{variance})^{3/2}}$$

$$\text{Kurtosis} = \frac{\mu_4}{(\text{variance})^2}$$

The *normalised* moments are what appear most often in this book because they allow us to compare distributions most easily. One can translate between raw and central moments as follows:

From raw moments to central moments:

$$\mu_1 = \mu'_1$$

$$\mu_2 = \mu'_2 - \mu^2$$

$$\mu_3 = \mu'_3 - 3\mu'_2\mu + 2\mu^3$$

$$\mu_4 = \mu'_4 - 4\mu'_3\mu + 6\mu'_2\mu^2 - 3\mu^4$$

From central moments to raw moments:

$$\mu'_1 = \mu_1$$

$$\mu'_2 = \mu_2 + \mu^2$$

$$\mu_3' = \mu_3 + 3\mu_2\mu + \mu^3$$

$$\mu_4' = \mu_4 + 4\mu_3\mu + 6\mu_2\mu^2 + \mu^4$$

You might wonder why we don't always use normalised moments and avoid any confusion. Central moments don't actually have much use in risk analysis – they are more of an intermediary calculation step, but raw moments are very useful. First of all the equations are simpler and therefore sometimes easier to calculate than central moments, and we can then convert them to central moments using the equations above. Secondly, they allow us to determine the moments of some combinations of random variables. For example, consider a variable Y that has probability p of taking a value from variable A and a probability $(1 - p)$ of taking a value from variable B:

$$\mu_{k,Y}' = E\left[px_A^k + (1 - p)x_B^k\right] = p\mu_{k,A}' + (1 - p)\mu_{k,B}'$$

You may also come across something called a *moment generating function*. This is a function $M_X(t)$ specific to each distribution and defined as

$$M_X(t) = \int_{-\infty}^{\infty} e^{tx} f(x)\,\mathrm{d}x = 1 + t\mu_1' + \frac{t^2}{2!}\mu_2' + \cdots$$

where t is a dummy variable. This leads to the relationship with raw moments:

$$E[X^k] = \left.\frac{\mathrm{d}^k M_X(t)}{\mathrm{d}t^k}\right|_{t=0}$$

For example, the Normal(m, s) distribution has $M_X(t) = \exp\left[\mu t + \frac{\sigma^2 t^2}{2}\right]$ from which we get

$$\left.\frac{\mathrm{d}^1 M_X(t)}{\mathrm{d}t^1}\right|_{t=0} = \mu, \quad \left.\frac{\mathrm{d}^2 M_X(t)}{\mathrm{d}t^2}\right|_{t=0} = \mu^2 + \sigma^2$$

$$\left.\frac{\mathrm{d}^3 M_X(t)}{\mathrm{d}t^3}\right|_{t=0} = 3\mu\sigma^2 + \mu^3, \quad \left.\frac{\mathrm{d}^4 M_X(t)}{\mathrm{d}t^4}\right|_{t=0} = \mu^4 + 6\mu^2\sigma^2 + 3\sigma^4$$

The great thing about moment generating functions is that we can use them with the sums of random variables. For example, if $Y = rA + sB$, where A and B are random variables and r and s are constants, then

$$M_Y(k) = M_A(rk)M_B(sk)$$

Note that, for a few distributions, not all moments are defined. The calculation of the moments of the Cauchy distribution, for example, is the difference between two integrals that give infinite values. More commonly, a few distributions don't have defined moments unless their parameters exceed a certain value. Appendix III lists these distributions and the restrictions.

Chapter 7

Building and running a model

In this chapter I give a few tips on how to build a risk analysis model and techniques for making it run faster – very useful if your model is either very large or needs to be run for many iterations. I also explain the most common errors people make in their modelling.

7.1 Model Design and Scope

Risk analysis is about supporting decisions by answering questions about risk. We attempt to provide qualitative and, where time and knowledge permit, quantitative information to decision-makers that is pertinent to their questions. Inevitably, decision-makers must deal with other factors that may not be quantified in a risk analysis, which can be frustrating for a risk analyst when they see their work being "ignored". Don't let it frustrate you: the best risk analysts remain professionally neutral to the decisions that are made from their work. Our job is to make sure that we have represented the current knowledge and how that affects the variables on which decisions are made. Remaining neutral also relieves you of being frustrated by lack of available data or adequate opinion – you just have to work with what you have.

The first step to designing a good model is to put yourself in the position of the decision-maker by understanding how the information you might provide connects to the questions they are asking. A decision-maker often does not appreciate all that comes with asking a question in a certain way, and may not initially have worked out all the possible options for handling the risk (or opportunity).

When you believe that you properly understand the risk question or questions that need(s) answering, it is time to brainstorm with colleagues, stakeholders and the managers about how you might put an analysis together that satisfies the managers' needs. Effort put into this stage pays back tenfold: everyone is clear on the purpose of your analysis; the participants will be more cooperative in providing information and estimates; and you can discuss the feasibility of any risk analysis approach. Consider going through the quality check methods I described in Chapter 3. I recommend you think of mapping out your ideas with Venn diagrams and event trees. Then look at the data (and perhaps expertise for subjective estimates) you believe are available to populate the model. If there are data gaps (there usually are), consider whether you will be able to get the necessary data to fill the gaps, and quickly enough to be able to produce an analysis within the decision-maker's timeframe. If the answer is "no", look for other ways to produce an analysis that will meet the decision-maker's needs, or perhaps a subset of those needs. But, whatever you do, don't embark on a risk analysis where you know that data gaps will remain and your decision-maker will be left with no useful support. Some scientists argue that risk analysis can also be for research purposes – to determine where the data gaps lie. We see the value in that determination, of course, but, if that is your purpose, state it clearly and don't leave any expectation from the managers that will be unfulfilled.

7.2 Building Models that are Easy to Check and Modify

The better a model is explained and the better it is laid out, the easier it is to check. Model building is an iterative process, which means that you should construct your model to make it easy to add, remove and modify elements. A few basic rules will help you do this:

- Dedicate one sheet of the workbook to recording the history of changes to the model since conception, with emphasis on changes since the previous version.

- Document the model logic, data sources, etc., *during* the model build. It may seem tedious, especially for the parts you end up discarding, but writing down what you do as you go along ensures the documentation does get done (otherwise we move on to the next problem, the model remains a black box to others, etc.) and also gives you a great self-check on your approach.

- Avoid really long formulae if possible unless it is a formula you use very often. It might be rather satisfying to condense some complex logic into a single cell, but it will be very hard for someone else to figure out what you did.

- Avoid writing macros that rely on model elements being at specific locations in the workbook or in other files. Add *plenty* of annotations to macros. Don't put model parameter values in the macro code. Give each macro and input parameter a sensible name.

- Avoid being geeky – I'm reviewing a spreadsheet model right now written 10 years ago by a guy who is no longer around. It is almost completely written in macros, with almost no annotation, but worst of all is that he wrote the model to allow it automatically to expand to accommodate more assets, though there was no such requirement. He created dozens of macros to do simple things like search a table that would normally be done with a VLOOKUP or OFFSET function, and placing everything in macros linked to other macros, etc., means one cannot use Excel's audit tools like Trace Precedents. It also takes maybe a 100 times longer to run than it should.

- Break down a complex section into its constituent parts. This may best be done in a separate area of the model and the result placed into a summary area. Hit the F9 key (or whatever will generate another scenario) to see that the constituent parts are all working well. Often, in developing ModelRisk functions, we have built spreadsheet models to replicate the logic and have found that doing so can give us ideas for improvements too.

- Use a single formula for an array (e.g. column) so that only one cell need be changed and the formula copied across the rest of the array.

- Keep linking between sheets to a minimum. For example, if you need to do a calculation on a dataset residing in one sheet, do it in that sheet, then link the calculation to wherever it needs to be used. This saves huge formulae that are difficult to follow, like: =VoseCumulA('Capital required' !G25,'Capital required' !G26,'Capital required' !G28:G106,'Capital required' !H28:H106).

- Create conditional formatting and alerts that tell you when impossible or irrelevant values occur in the model. ModelRisk functions have a lot of imbedded checks so that, for example, VoseNormal(0, −1) will return the text "Error: sigma must be >= 0" rather than Excel's rather unhelpful #VALUE! approach. If you write macros, include similarly meaningful error messages.

- Use the Data/Validation tool in Excel to format cells so that another user cannot input inappropriate values into the model – for example, they cannot input a non-integer value for an integer variable.

- Use the Excel Tools/Protection/Protect_Sheet function together with the Tools/Protection/Allow_ Users_to_Edit_Ranges function to ensure other users can only modify input parameters (not calculation cells).

- In general, keep the number of unique formulae as small as possible – we often write columns containing the same formulae repeatedly with just the references changing. If you do need to write a different formula in certain cells of an array (usually the beginning or end), consider giving them a different format (we tend to use a grey background).

- Colour-code the model elements: we use blue for input data and red for outputs.

- Make good use of range naming. To give a name to a cell or range of contiguous cells, select the cells, click in the name box and type the name you want to use. So, for example, cell A1 might contain the value 22. Giving it the label "Peter" means that typing "=Peter" anywhere else in the sheet will return the value 22. For a lot of probability distributions there are standard conventions for naming the parameters of your model. For example, =VoseHypergeo(n, D, M) and VoseGamma(alpha, beta). So, if you have just one or two of these distributions in your model, using these names (e.g. alpha1, alpha2, etc., for each gamma distribution) actually makes it easier to write the formulae too. Note that a cell or range may have several names, and a cell in a range may have a separate name from the range's name. Don't follow my lead here because, for the purposes of writing models you can read in a book, I've rarely used range names.

7.3 Building Models that are Efficient

A model is most efficient when:

1. It takes the least time to run.
2. It takes the least effort to maintain and requires the least amount of assumptions.
3. It has a small file size (memory and speed issues).
4. It supports the most decision options (see Chapters 3 and 4).

7.3.1 Least time to run

Microsoft are making efforts to speed up Excel, but it has a very heavy visual interface that really can slow things down. I'll look at a few tips for making Excel run faster first, then for making your simulation software run faster and then for making a model that gets the answer faster. Finally, I'll give you some ideas on how to determine whether you can stop the model because you've run enough iterations.

Making Excel run faster

- Excel scans for calculations through worksheets in alphabetical order of the worksheet name, and starts at cell A1 in each sheet, scans the row and drops down to the next row. Then it dances around for all the links to other cells until it finds the cells it has to calculate first. It can therefore speed things up if you give names to each sheet that reflect their sequence (e.g. start each sheet with "1. Assumptions", "2. Market projection", "3.... " etc.), and keep the calculations within a sheet flowing down and across.

- Avoid array functions as they are slow to calculate, although faster than an equivalent VBA function.
- Use megaformulae (with the above caution) as they run about twice as fast as intermediary calculations, and 10 times as fast as VBA calculations.
- Custom Excel functions run more slowly than built-in functions but speed up model building and model reliability. Be careful with custom functions because they are hard to check through. There are a number of vendors, particularly in the finance field, who sell function libraries.
- Avoid links to external files.
- Keep the simulation model in one workbook.

Making your simulation software run faster

- Turn off the Update Display feature if your Monte Carlo add-in has that ability. It makes an enormous difference if there are imbedded graphs.
- Use Multiple CPUs if your simulation software offers this. It can make a big difference.
- Avoid the VoseCumulA(), VoseDiscrete(), VoseDUniform(), VoseRelative() and VoseHistogram() distributions (or other product's equivalents) with large arrays if possible, as they take much longer to generate values than other distributions.
- Latin hypercube sampling gets to the stable output quicker than Monte Carlo sampling, but the effect gets increasingly quickly lost the more significant distributions there are in the model, particularly if the model is not just adding and/or subtracting distributions. The sampling methods take the same time to run, however, so it makes sense to use Latin hypercube sampling for simulation runs.
- Run bootstrap analyses and Bayesian distribution calculations in a separate spreadsheet when you are estimating uncorrelated parameters, fit the results using your simulation software's fitting tool and, if the fit is good, use just the fitted distributions in your simulation model. This does have the disadvantage, however, of being more laborious to maintain when more data become available.
- If you write VBA macros, consider whether they need to be declared as volatile.

Getting the answer faster

As a general rule, it is much better to be able to create a probability model that calculates, rather than simulates, the required probability or probability distribution. Calculation is preferable because the model answer is updated immediately if a parameter value changes (rather than requiring a re-simulation of the model), and more importantly within this context it is far more efficient.

For example, let's imagine that a machine has 2000 bolts, each of which could shear off within a certain timeframe with a 0.02 % probability. We'll also say that, if a bolt shears off, there is a 0.3 % probability that it will cause some serious injury. What is the probability that at least one injury will occur within the timeframe? How many injuries could there be?

The pure simulation way would be to model the number of bolt shears

$$\text{Shears} = \text{VoseBinomial}(2000, 0.02\,\%)$$

and then model the number of injuries

$$\text{Injuries} = \text{VoseBinomial}(\text{Shears}, 0.3\,\%)$$

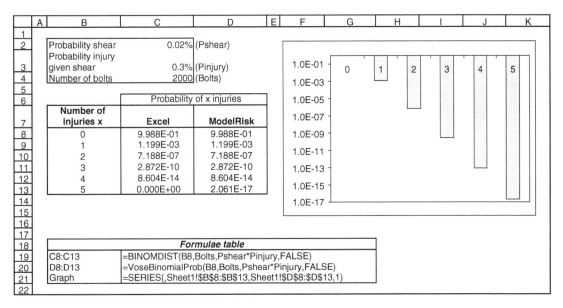

Figure 7.1   Example model determining a risk analysis outcome by calculation.

Or we could recognise that each bolt has a $0.02\% * 0.3\%$ chance of causing injury, so

$$\text{Injuries} = \text{VoseBinomial}(\text{Bolts}, 0.02\% * 0.3\%)$$

Run a simulation enough iterations and the fraction of the iterations where Injuries > 0 is the required probability, and collecting the simulated values gives us the required distribution. However, on average we should see $2000 * 0.02\% * 0.3\% = 0.0012$ injuries (that's 1 in 833), so your simulation will generate about 830 zeros for every non-zero value; for us to get an accurate description of the result (e.g. have 1000 or so non-zero values), we would have to run the model a long time. A better approach is to calculate the probabilities and construct the required distribution as in the model shown in Figure 7.1.

I have used Excel's BINOMDIST function to calculate the probability of each number of injuries x. You can see the probability of non-zero values is pretty small, hence the need for the y axis in the chart to be shown in log scale. The beauty of this method is that any change to the parameters immediately produces a new output. I have also shown the same calculation with ModelRisk's VoseBinomialProb function, which does the same thing because the probability that $x = 5$ is not actually zero (obviously) as BINOMDIST would have us believe – Excel's statistical functions aren't very good.

Of course, most of the risk analysis problems we face are not as simple as the example above, but we can nonetheless often find shortcuts. For example, imagine that we believe that the maximum daily wave height around a particular offshore rig follows a Rayleigh(7.45) metres. The deck height (distance from water at rest to underside of lower deck structure) is 32 metres, and the damage that will be caused as a fraction f of the value of the rig is a function of the wave height x above the deck level following the equation

$$f = \left[1 + \left(\frac{x}{1.6} \right)^{-0.91} \right]^{-0.82}$$

	A	B	C	D	E	F	G	H	I
1			Deck height		32 metres				
2			Rayleigh parameter		7.45				
3									
4		**a) Pure simulation**							
5			Max wave height (m)	Loss (fraction)					
6		Day 1	1.598661825	0					
7		Day 2	12.34919201	0					
369		Day 364	6.245851047	0					
370		Day 365	19.18746778	0					
371		Expected damage over year (mean=output)		0					
372									
373		**b) Simulation and calculation**							
374		P(wave > deck)		9.85635E-05					
375		Size of wave given > Deck		37.76709587					
376		Resultant damage (fractions)		0.800691151					
377		Expected damage over year (mean=output)		0.028805402					
378									
379		**c) Calculation only**							
380		Expected fractional loss per day		0.0000471					
381		Expected fractional loss over the year (output)		0.017205699					
382									
383			***Formulae table***						
384			a) Pure simulation						
385		C6:C370	=VoseRayleigh($D$2)						
386		D6:D371	=IF(C6>$D$1,(1+((C6-$D$1)/1.6)^-0.91)^-0.82,0)						
387		D371 o/p=mean	=SUM(D6:D370)						
388			b) Simulation and calculation						
389		D374	=1-VoseRayleighProb($D$1,$D$2,1)						
390		D375	=VoseRayleigh($D$2,,VoseXBounds($D$1,))						
391		D376	=(1+((D375-$D$1)/1.6)^-0.91)^-0.82						
392		D377 o/p=mean	=365*D374*D376						
393			c) Calculation only						
394		D380	=VoseIntegrate("VoseRayleighProb(#,D2,0)*(1+((#-D1)/1.6)^-0.91)^-0.82",D1,200,10)						
395		D381 o/p	=D380*365						
396									

Figure 7.2 Offshore platform damage model showing three methods to estimate expected damage as a fraction of rig value.

We would like to know the expected damage cost per year as a fraction of the rig value (this is a typical question, among others, that insurers need answered).

We could determine this by (a) pure simulation, (b) a combination of calculation and simulation or (c) pure calculation as shown in the model of Figure 7.2.

The simulation model is simple enough: the maximum wave height is simulated for each and then the resultant damage is simulated by writing an IF statement for when the wave height exceeds the deck height. The model has the advantage of being easy to follow, but the probability of damage is low, so it needs to run a long time. You also need an accurate algorithm for simulating a Rayleigh distribution.

The simulation and calculation model calculates the probability that a wave will exceed the deck height in cell D374 (about one in 10 000). ModelRisk has equivalent probability functions for all its distributions, whereas other Monte Carlo add-ins tend to focus only on generating random numbers, but Appendix III gives the relevant formulae so you can replicate this. Cell D375 generates a Rayleigh(7.45) distribution truncated to have a minimum equal to the deck height, i.e. we are only simulating those waves that would cause any damage. I've used the ModelRisk generating function but @RISK, Crystal Ball and some other simulation tools offer distribution truncation. Cell D376 then calculates the damage fraction for the generated wave height. Finally, cell D377 multiplies the probability that a wave will exceed the deck height by the damage it would then do and 365 for the days in the year. Running a simulation and taking the mean (=RiskMean(D377) in @RISK, =CB.GetForeStatFN(D377, 2) in Crystal Ball) will give us the required answer. This version of the model is still pretty easy to understand but has 1/365 of the simulation load and only simulates the 1 in 10 000 scenario where a wave hits the deck, so it achieves the same accuracy for about 1/3 650 000th of the iterations as the first model.

The third model performs the integral

$$\int_{D}^{\infty} f(x) \left[1 + \left(\frac{x - D}{1.6} \right)^{-0.91} \right]^{-0.82} dx$$

in Cell D380 where $f(x)$ is the Rayleigh(7.45) density function and D is the deck height. This is summing up the damage fraction for each possible wave height x weighted by x's probability of occurrence. The VoseIntegrate function in ModelRisk performs one-dimensional integration on the variable "#" using a sophisticated error minimisation algorithm that gives very accurate answers with short computation time (it took about 0.01 seconds in this model, for example). Mathematical software like Mathematica and Maple will also perform such integrals. The advantage of this approach is that the results are instantaneous and very accurate (to 15 significant figures!), but the downside is that you need to know what you are doing in probability modelling (plus you need a fancier tool such as ModelRisk, Maple, etc). ModelRisk helps out with the explanation and checking by displaying a plot of the function and the integrated area when you click the *Vf* (View Function) icon. Note that for numerical integration you have to pick a high value for the upper integration limit in place of infinity, but a quick look at the Rayleigh(7.45) shows that its probability of being above 200 is so small that it's outside a computer's floating point ability to display it anyway.

In summary, calculation is fast and more accurate (true, with simulation you can improve accuracy by running the model longer, but there's a limit) and simulation is slow. On the other hand, simulation is easier to understand and check than calculation. I often use the phrase "calculate when you can, simulate when you can't", and when you "can't" is as much a function of the expertise level of the reviewers as it is of the modeller. If you really would like to use a calculation method, or want to have a mixed calculation–simulation model, but worry about getting it right, consider writing both versions in parallel and checking they produce the same answers for a range of different parameter values.

7.3.2 Least effort to maintain

The biggest problem in maintaining a spreadsheet model is usually updating data, so make sure that you keep the data in predictable areas (colour-coding the tabs of each sheet is a nice way). Also, avoid Excel's data analysis features that dump the results of a data analysis as fixed values into a sheet. I think this is dreadful programming. Software like @RISK and Crystal Ball, which fit distributions to data, can be "hot-linked" to a dataset, which is a much better method than just exporting the fitted parameters if you think the dataset may be altered at some point. ModelRisk has a huge range of "hot-linking" fit functions that will return fitted parameters or random numbers for copulas, time series and distributions. You can sometimes replicate the same idea quite easily. For example, to fit a normal distribution one need only determine the mean and standard deviation of the dataset if the data are random samples, so using Excel's AVERAGE and STDEV functions on the dataset will automatically update a distribution fit. Sometimes you need to run Solver, e.g. to use maximum likelihood methods to fit to a gamma distribution, so make a macro with a button that will perform that operation (see, for example, Figure 7.3).

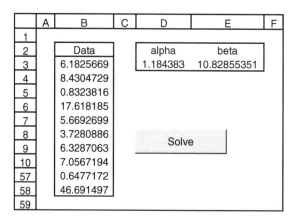

Figure 7.3 Spreadsheet with automation to run Solver.

The button runs the following macro which asks the user for the data array, runs Solver by creating a temporary file with the likelihood calculation and finally asks the user where to place the results (cells D3:E3 in this case):

```
Private Sub CommandButton1_Click()

On Error Resume Next

Dim DataRange As Excel.Range

Dim n As Long, Mean As Double, Var As Double

' -------------- Selecting input data --------------
1 Set DataRange = Application.InputBox("Select one-dimensional input data array", "Data",
    Selection.Address, , , , , 8)
If DataRange Is Nothing Then Exit Sub
n = DataRange.Cells.Count

' ----------------- Error messages -----------------
If n < 2 Then MsgBox "Please enter at least two data values": GoTo 1
If DataRange.Columns.Count > 1 And DataRange.Rows.Count > 1 Then MsgBox "Selected data is
    not one-dimensional": GoTo 1
If Application.WorksheetFunction.Min(DataRange.Value) <= 0 Then MsgBox "Input data must
    be non-negative": GoTo 1

Sheets.Add Sheets(1) ' adding a temporary sheet

' --- pasting input data into the temporary sheet ----
If DataRange.Columns.Count > 1 Then
    Sheets(1).Range("A1:A" & n).Value =
    Application.WorksheetFunction.Transpose(DataRange.Value)
Else
    Sheets(1).Range("A1:A" & n).Value = DataRange.Value
End If
```

```
Mean = Application.WorksheetFunction.Average(Sheets(1).Range("A1:A" & n)) ' calculating
    mean of data
Var = Application.WorksheetFunction.Var(Sheets(1).Range("A1:A" & n)) ' calculating
    variance of data

Alpha = Mean ^ 2 / Var ' Best guess estimate for Alpha
Beta = Var / Mean ' Best guess estimate for Beta

' ------ setting initial values for the Solver -------
Sheets(1).Range("D1").Value = Alpha
Sheets(1).Range("E1").Value = Beta

' -------- setting the LogLikelihood function --------
Sheets(1).Range("B1:B" & n).Formula = "=LOG10(GAMMADIST(A1,$D$1,$E$1,0))"

' ---------- setting the objective function ----------
Sheets(1).Range("G1").Formula = "=SUM(B1:B" & n & ")"

' -------------- Launching the Solver ---------------
SOLVER.Auto_open

    SOLVER.SolverReset
    SOLVER.SolverOk SetCell:=Sheets(1).Range("G1"), MaxMinVal:=1,
    ByChange:=Sheets(1).Range("D1:E1")
    SolverAdd CellRef:="$D$1", Relation:=3, FormulaText:="0.000000000000001"
    SolverAdd CellRef:="$E$1", Relation:=3, FormulaText:="0.000000000000001"
    SOLVER.SolverSolve UserFinish:=True
    SOLVER.SolverFinish KeepFinal:=1

SOLVER.SolverReset

' ------------- Remembering output values ------------
Alpha = Sheets(1).Range("D1").Value
Beta = Sheets(1).Range("E1").Value

' ----------- Deleting the temporary sheet -----------
Application.DisplayAlerts = False
Sheets(1).Delete
Application.DisplayAlerts = True

' ------------- Selecting output location ------------
2 Set DataRange = Application.InputBox("Select 2x1 output location", "Output",
    Selection.Address, , , , , 8)
If DataRange Is Nothing Then Exit Sub
n = DataRange.Cells.Count
If n < 2 Then MsgBox "Enter at least two data values": GoTo 2

' ---- Pasting outputs into the selected range -------
DataRange.Cells(1, 1) = Alpha
If DataRange.Columns.Count = 2 Then DataRange(1, 2) = Beta Else DataRange(2, 1) = Beta

End Sub
```

A minimum limit is placed on alpha and beta 0.000000000000001 to avoid errors and LOG10(...) is used around the GAMMADIST(...) functions because a LogLikelihood will behave less dramatically and let Solver find the solution more reliably. The moments-based estimate for alpha (=DataMean^2/ DataVariance) and beta (=DataVariance/DataMean) are used as starter values for Solver so it will find the answer more quickly. If a user needs to perform some operations prior to running a model, then write a description of what needs doing and why. These days, we attach a help file with the model, and this allows us to imbed little videos which is very helpful, but at the least try to imbed or couple the model to a pdf file with screen captures of each step.

In my experience, the other main reason a model can be hard to maintain is that it is complex and uses many different sources of data that go out of date. When you plan out a risk analysis (Chapters 3 and 4) for a model that will be used periodically, or that could take a long time to complete, consider whether there is a simpler model that will give answers that are pretty close in decision terms to the more complex model being planned. If the difference in accuracy is small, it may be balanced by the greater applicability that comes with updating the inputs more frequently.

7.3.3 Smallest file size

- Megaformulae reduce the file size considerably.

- Maintaining large datasets in your model will increase the file size. It is better to do the analysis outside the spreadsheet and copy across the results.

- Sometimes large datasets or calculation arrays are used to construct distributions (e.g. fitting first- or second-order non-parametric distributions to data, constructing Bayesian posterior distributions and bootstrap analysis). Replacing these calculations with a fitted distribution can have a marked effect on model size and speed.

- ModelRisk has been designed to maximise speed and minimise memory requirements. It has a large number of functions that will perform complex calculations in a single cell or small array. You might also be able to achieve some of the same effect in your models with VBA code, particularly if you need to perform iterative loops.

7.3.4 How many iterations of a model to run

You will often see risk analysis reports, or papers in journals, that show the results and tell you that this was based on 10 000 (or whatever) Latin hypercube (or whatever) iterations of the model. I suppose that may sometimes be useful to know, but not often. The author is usually trying to communicate that the model was run long enough for the results to be stable. The problem is that, for one model trying to determine a mean, 500 iterations may be good enough; for another trying to determine a 99.9th percentile, 100 000 iterations might be needed. It also depends on how sensitive the decision question is to the output's accuracy. A frequent question that pops up in our courses is "how many iterations do I need to run", and you can see there is no absolute answer to that. A short answer, burdened with many caveats, is "no less than 300" if you are interested in the entire output distribution. At 300 iterations you start to get a reasonably well-defined cumulative distribution, so you can approximately read off the 50th and 85th percentiles, for example, and the mean is pretty well determined for most output distributions. At the same time, if you export the generated values from two or more random variables in your model to produce scatter plots, 300 is really the minimum you need to get any sense of the patterns that they produce (i.e. their joint distribution). We usually have our models set to run 3000 iterations as a default (but obviously increase that figure if a particularly high level of accuracy is warranted), because we plot a great deal of scatter plots from generated data, and this is about the right number of points before

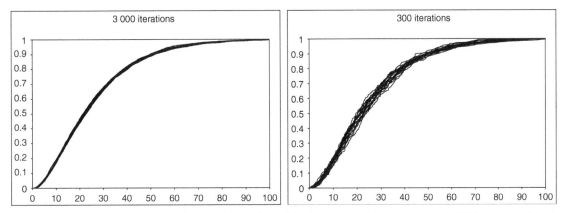

Figure 7.4 Comparison of cumulative distribution plots for 20 model runs each of 3000 and 300 Monte Carlo iterations for a well-behaved output (i.e. a nice smooth curve).

the scatter plot gets clogged up, and certainly enough for all the percentiles and statistics to be well specified.

Figure 7.4 shows what type of variation you would typically get for a cumulative distribution between runs of 300 iterations and of 3000 iterations. Since most models include an element of guesswork in the choice of model, distributions or parameter values to use, one should not usually be too concerned about exact precision in the Monte Carlo results, but you'll see that 300 iterations is probably the least level of accuracy you might find acceptable.

Figure 7.5 shows the same input and output plotted together as a scatter plot for 300 and 3000 iterations. We find scatter plots to be a great, intuitive presentation of how, among others, the input variability influences the output value. You'll see that the pattern is just about visible for 300 iterations, and just starting to get clogged up at 3000 iterations (of course, if you run more than 3000 iterations, you can plot a sample of just 3000 of them to keep the scatter plot clear). If the pattern were simpler, the left-hand panel of 300 iterations would of course be clearer.

In general, you'll have two opposing pressures:

- Too few iterations and you get inaccurate outputs, graphs (particularly histogram plots) that look "scruffy".

- Too many iterations and it takes a long time to simulate, and it may take even longer to plot graphs, export and analyse data, etc., afterwards. Export the data into Excel and you may also come upon row limitations, and limitations on the number of points that can plotted in a chart.

There will usually be one or more statistics in which you are interested from your model outputs, so it would be quite natural to wish to have sufficient iterations to ensure a certain level of accuracy. Typically, that accuracy can be described in the following way: "I need the statistic Z to be accurate to within $\pm d$ with confidence a".

I will show you how you can determine the number of iterations you need to run to get some specified level of accuracy for the most common statistics: the mean and cumulative probabilities. The example models let you monitor the level of accuracy in real time. Note that all models assume that you are using Monte Carlo sampling. This will therefore somewhat overestimate the number of iterations you'll need if you are using Latin hypercube sampling (which we recommend, in general). That said, in practice,

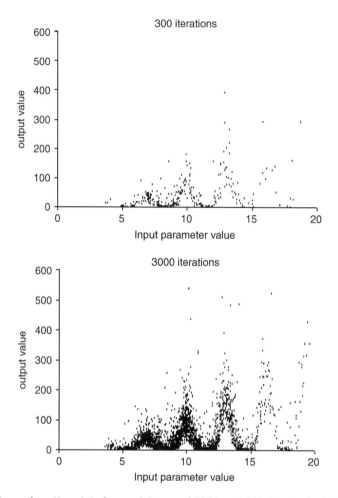

Figure 7.5 Comparison of scatter plots for model runs of 3000 and 300 Monte Carlo iterations.

Latin hypercube sampling will only offer useful improvement when a model is linear, or when there are very few distributions in the model.

Iterations to run to get sufficient accuracy for the mean

Monte Carlo simulation estimates the true mean μ of the output distribution by summing all of the generated values x_i and dividing by the number of iterations n:

$$\hat{\mu} = \frac{1}{n} \sum_{i=1}^{n} x_i$$

If Monte Carlo sampling is used, each x_i is an iid (independent identically distributed random variable). Central limit theorem then says that the distribution of the estimate of the true mean is (asymptotically)

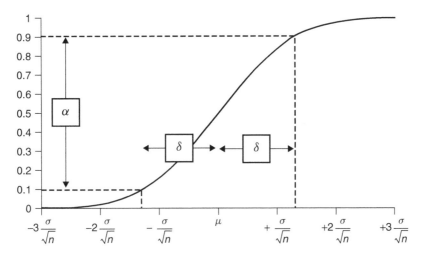

Figure 7.6 Cumulative distribution plot for the normal distribution of Equation (7.1).

given by

$$\hat{\mu} = \text{Normal}\left(\mu, \frac{\sigma}{\sqrt{n}}\right)$$

where σ is the true standard deviation of the model's output.

Using a statistical principle called the pivotal method, we can rearrange this equation to make it an equation for μ:

$$\mu = \text{Normal}\left(\hat{\mu}, \frac{\sigma}{\sqrt{n}}\right) \tag{7.1}$$

Figure 7.6 shows the cumulative form of the normal distribution for Equation (7.1). Specifying the level of confidence we require for our mean estimate translates into a relationship between δ, σ and n. More formally, this relationship is

$$\delta = \frac{\sigma}{\sqrt{n}} \Phi^{-1}\left(\frac{1+\alpha}{2}\right) \tag{7.2}$$

where $\Phi^{-1}(\cdot)$ is the inverse of the normal cumulative distribution function. Rearranging Equation (7.2) and recognising that we want to have at least this accuracy gives a minimum value for n:

$$n > \left(\frac{\Phi^{-1}\left(\frac{1+\alpha}{2}\right)\sigma}{\delta}\right)^2$$

We have one problem left: we don't know the true output standard deviation σ. It turns out that we can estimate this perfectly well for our purposes by taking the standard deviation of the first few

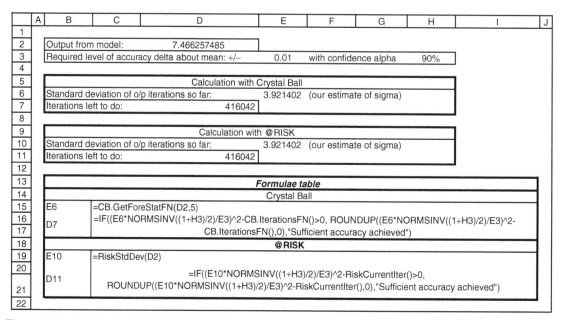

Figure 7.7 Models in @RISK and Crystal Ball to monitor whether the simulation mean has reached a required accuracy.

(say 50) iterations. The model in Figure 7.7 shows how you can do this continuously, using Excel's function NORMSINV to return values for $\Phi^{-1}(\cdot)$.

If you name cell D7 or D11 as an output, together with any other model outputs you are actually interested in, and select the "Pause on Error in Outputs" option in your host Monte Carlo add-in, it will automatically stop simulating when the required accuracy is achieved because the cell returns the "Sufficient accuracy achieved" text instead of a number.

Iterations to run to get sufficient accuracy for the cumulative probability F(x) associated with a particular value x

Percentiles closer to the 50th percentile of an output distribution will reach a stable value relatively far quicker than percentiles towards the tails. On the other hand, we are often most interested in what is going on in the tails because that is where the risks and opportunities lie. For example, Basel II and credit rating agencies often require that the 99.9th percentile or greater be accurately determined. The following technique shows you how you can ensure that you have the required level of accuracy for the percentile associated with a particular value.

Your Monte Carlo add-in will estimate the cumulative percentile $F(x)$ of the output distribution associated with a value x by determining what fraction of the iterations fell at or below x. Imagine that x is actually the 80th percentile of the true output distribution. Then, for Monte Carlo simulation, the generated value in each iteration independently has an 80 % probability of falling below x: it is a binomial process with probability $p = 80\%$. Thus, if so far we have had n iterations and s have fallen at or below x, the distribution $\text{Beta}(s + 1, n - s + 1)$ describes the uncertainty associated with the true cumulative percentile we should associate with x (see Section 8.2.3).

When we are estimating the percentile close to the median of the distribution, or when we are performing a large number of iterations, s and n will both be large, and we can use a normal approximation to the beta distribution:

$$\text{Beta}(s + 1, n - s + 1) \approx \text{Normal}\left(\hat{P}, \sqrt{\frac{\hat{P}(1 - \hat{P})}{n}}\right) \tag{7.3}$$

where $\hat{P} = \frac{s}{n}$ is the best-guess estimate for $F(x)$. Thus, we can produce a relationship similar to that in Equation (7.2) for determining the number of iterations to get the required precision for the output mean:

$$\delta = \sqrt{\frac{\hat{P}(1 - \hat{P})}{n}} \Phi^{-1}\left(\frac{1 + \alpha}{2}\right) \tag{7.4}$$

Rearranging Equation (7.4) and recognising that we want to have at least this accuracy gives a minimum value for n:

$$n > \hat{P}(1 - \hat{P})\left(\frac{\Phi^{-1}\left(\frac{1+\alpha}{2}\right)}{\delta}\right)^2$$

A model can now be written in a very similar fashion to Figure 7.7.

7.4 Most Common Modelling Errors

This section describes, and provides examples for, the three most common mistakes we come across in auditing risk models, even at the more elementary level. These mistakes probably constitute around 90 % of the errors we see. I strongly recommend studying them, and going through the examples thoroughly:

- *Common error 1.* Calculating means instead of simulating scenarios.
- *Common error 2.* Representing an uncertain variable more than once in a model.
- *Common error 3.* Manipulating probability distributions as if they were fixed numbers.

Common error 1: calculating means instead of simulating scenarios

When we first start thinking about risk, it is quite natural to want to convert the impact of a risk to a single number. For example, we might consider that there is a 20 % chance of losing a contract, which would result in a loss of income of $100 000. Put together, a person might reason that to be a risk of some $20 000 (i.e. 20 % * $100 000). This $20 000 figure is known as the "expected value" of the variable. It is the probability weighted average of all possible outcomes. So, the two outcomes are $100 000 with 20 % probability and $0 with 80 % probability:

$$\text{Mean risk(expected value)} = 0.2 * \$100\,000 + 0.8 * \$0 = \$20\,000$$

Calculating the expected values of risks might also seem a reasonable and simple method for comparing risks. For example, in Table 7.1, risks A to J are ranked in descending order of expected cost:

Table 7.1 A list of probabilities and impacts for 10 risks.

Risk	Probability	Impact if occurs $000	Expected impact $000
A	0.25	400	100
B	0.3	200	60
C	0.1	500	50
D	0.05	800	40
E	0.1	300	30
F	0.3	90	27
G	0.2	120	24
H	0.3	60	18
I	0.01	1000	10
J	0.001	8000	8
Total expected impact			**367**

If a loss of $500 000 or more would ruin your company, you may well rank the risks differently: risks C, D, I and, to a lesser extent, J pose a survival threat on your company. Note also that you may value the impact of risk D as no more severe than that of risk C because, if either of them occur, your company has gone bust.

On the other hand, if risk A occurs, giving you a loss of $400k, you are precariously close to ruin: it would just take any of the risks except F and H to occur (unless they both occurred) and you've gone bust. Looking at the sum of the expected values gives you no appreciation of how close you are to ruin. Figure 7.8 plots the distribution of possible outcomes for this set of risks.

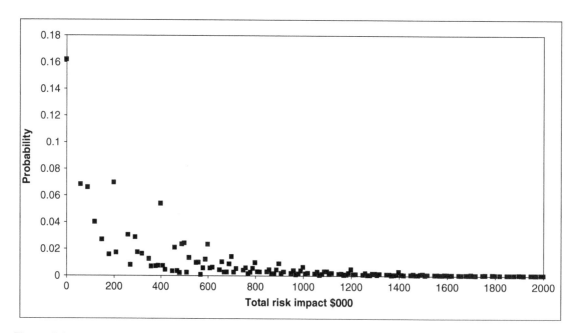

Figure 7.8 Probability distribution of total impact from risks A to J.

From a risk analysis point of view, by representing the impact of a risk by its expected value, we have removed the uncertainty (i.e. we can't see the breadth of different outcomes), which is a fundamental reason for doing risk analysis in the first place. That said, you might think that people running Monte Carlo simulations would be more attuned to describing risks with distributions rather than single values, but this is nonetheless one of the most common errors.

Another, slightly more disguised example of the same error is when the impact is uncertain. For example, let's imagine that there will be an election this year and that two parties are running: the Socialist Democrats Party and the Democratic Socialists Party. The SDP are currently in power and have vowed to keep the corporate tax rate at 17 % if they win the election. Political analysts reckon they have about a 65 % chance of staying in power. The DSP promise to lower the corporate tax rate by 1–4 %, most probably 3 %. We might chose to express next year's corporate tax rate as

$$\text{Rate} = 0.35 * \text{VosePERT}(13\%, 14\%, 16\%) + 0.65 * 17\%$$

Checking the formula by simulating, we'd get a probability distribution that could give us some comfort that we've assigned uncertainty properly to this parameter. However, a correct model would have drawn a value of 17 % with a probability of 0.65 and a random value from the PERT distribution with a probability of 0.35.

Common error 2: representing an uncertain variable more than once in a model

When we develop a large spreadsheet model, perhaps with several linked sheets in the same file, it is often convenient to have some parameter values that are used in several sheets appearing in each of those sheets. This makes it quicker to write formulae and trace back precedents in a formula. Even in a deterministic model (i.e. a model where there are only best-guess values, not distributions) it is important that there is only one place in the model where the parameter value can be changed (at Vose Consulting we use the convention that all changeable input parameter values or distributions are labelled blue). There are two reasons: firstly it is easier to update the model with new parameter values, and secondly it avoids the potential mistake of only changing the parameter values in some of the cells in which it appears, forgetting the others, and thereby having a model that is internally inconsistent. For example, a model could have a parameter "Cargo (mt)" in sheet 1 with a value of 10 000 and a value of 12 000 in sheet 2.

It becomes even more important to maintain this discipline when we create a Monte Carlo model if that parameter is modelled with a distribution. Although each cell in the model might carry the same probability distribution, left unchecked each distribution will generate different values for the parameter in the same iteration, thus rendering the generated scenario impossible.

If it really is important to you to have the probability distribution formula in each cell where the parameter is featured (perhaps because you wish to see what distribution equation was used without having to switch to the source sheet), you can make use of the U-parameter in ModelRisk's simulation functions to ensure that the same value is being generated in each place:

$$\text{Cell A1} := \text{VoseNormal}(100, 10, \text{Random1})$$

$$\text{Cell A2} := \text{VoseNormal}(100, 10, \text{Random1})$$

where Random1 is a Uniform(0, 1) distribution placed somewhere in the model. You can achieve the same thing using a 100 % rank order correlation in @RISK or Crystal Ball, for example, but this will only work when the simulation is running because rank order correlation generates a set of values before a simulation run and orders them; when you look at the model stepping through some scenarios, they won't match.

The error described so far is where the formula for the distribution of a random variable is featured in more than one cell of a spreadsheet model. These errors are quite easy to spot. Another form of the same error is where two or more distributions incorporate the same random variable in some way. For example, consider the following problem.

A company is considering restructuring its operations with the inevitable layoffs, and wishes to analyse how much it would save in the process. Looking at just the office space component, a consultant estimates that, if the company were to make the maximum number of redundancies and outsource some of its operations, it would save $PERT(1.1, 1.3, 1.6)M of office space costs. On the other hand, just making the redundancies in the accounting section and outsourcing that activity, it could save $PERT(0.4, 0.5, 0.9)M of office space costs.

It would be quite natural, at first sight, to put these two distributions into a model and run a simulation to determine the savings for the two redundancy options. On their own, each cost saving distribution would be valid. We might also decide to calculate in a spreadsheet cell the difference between the two savings, and here we would potentially be making a big mistake. Why? Well, what if there is an uncertain component that is common to both office cost savings? For example, what if inside these cost distributions there is the cost of getting out of a current lease contract, uncertain because negotiations would need to take place. The problem is that, by sampling from these two distributions independently, we are not recognising the common element, which is a problem if that common element is not a fixed value, because it induces some level of correlation.

The takeaway message from this example is: consider whether two or more uncertain parameters in your models share in some way a common element. If they do, you will need to separate out that common element and thereby allow it to appear just once in your model.

Common error 3: manipulating probability distributions like we do with fixed numbers

At school we learn things like

$$1 + 3 = 4 \text{ so } 4 - 1 = 3$$
$$3 * 2 = 6 \text{ so } 6/3 = 2$$

Later, when we take algebra, we learn

$$A + B = C \text{ therefore } C - A = B$$
$$D * E = F \text{ therefore } F/D = E$$

The problem is that these trusted rules do not apply so universally when manipulating random variables. This section explains how and when these simple algebraic rules no longer work, and shows you how to identify them in your model and how to make the appropriate corrections.

An example

Most deterministic spreadsheet models consist of linked formulae that contain nothing more complicated than simple operations like +, −, * and /. When we decide to start adding uncertainty to the values of the components in the model, it seems natural enough simply to replace a fixed value with a probability distribution describing our uncertainty. So, for example, the simple model for a company offering some credit service:

Money borrowed by a client M :	€10 000
Number of clients n :	6500
Interest rate per annum r :	7.5 %
Yearly revenue:	$M * n * r = €4\ 875\ 000$

The model can now be "risked":

Money borrowed by a client M :	Lognormal(€10 000, €4000)
Number of clients n :	PERT(6638, 6500, 8200)
Interest rate per annum r :	7.5 %
Yearly revenue:	$M * n * r$

The best-guess estimates of the money borrowed by a client and for the number of clients have been replaced by distributions, but the model is otherwise unchanged. This model is probably very wrong. The error is most easily seen by watching random values being generated on screen. Look at the values that are being used for the entire client base and compare with where these values sit on the Lognormal(10 000, 4000) distribution.

For example, the Lognormal(10 000, 4000) distribution has 10 % of its probability below £5 670. Thus, in 10 % of its iterations it will generate a value below this figure, and that value will be used for *all* customers. The lognormal distribution undoubtedly reflects the variability that is expected between customers (perhaps, for example, it was fit to a relevant dataset of amounts individual customers have previously borrowed). The probability that two randomly selected customers will borrow less than £5 670 is $10\% * 10\% = 1\%$. The probability that all (say) 6500 customers borrow less than £5 670 if the amounts they borrow are independent is 10^{-6500}, i.e. effectively impossible, yet our model gives it a 10 % probability.

In order to model this problem correctly, we need to consider what are the sources of uncertainty about the amount a customer borrowed. If the source is specific to each individual client, then the amounts can be considered independent and the techniques of Chapter 11 should be applied. If there is some systematic influence (like the state of the economy, recent bad press for companies offering credit, etc.), it will have to be separated out from the individual, independent component.

Let's look at another example. The sum of two independent Uniform(0, 1) distributions is ... what do you think? The answer often surprises people. It is hard to imagine a simpler problem, yet when we canvass a class we get quite a range of answers. Perhaps a Uniform(0, 2)? That's the most common response. Or something looking a little normal? The answer is a Triangle(0, 1, 2), so we could write

$$U(0, 1) + U(0, 1) = T(0, 1, 2)$$

The first message in this example is that it is difficult for a person not very well versed in risk analysis modelling to be able to predict well the results of even the most trivial model. Of course, that makes it very hard to check the model and be comfortable about its results.

On to the next question we often pose our class:

$$T(0, 1, 2) - U(0, 1) =?$$

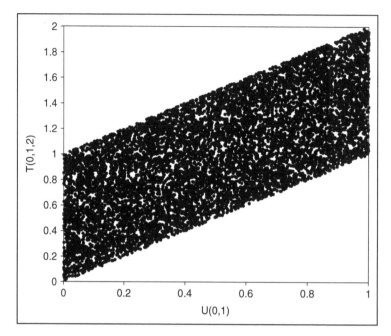

Figure 7.9 A plot of random samples of C against A, where $A = U(0, 1)$, $B = U(0, 1)$ and $C = A + B$.

Now wise to the trickiness of the question, most class participants are pretty sure that their first guess (i.e. $= U(0, 1)$) is wrong but don't have anything else to suggest. The answer is a symmetric distribution that looks a little normal, stretching from -1 to 2 with peak at 0.5. But why isn't it U(0, 1)? An easy way to visualise this is to run a simulation adding two Uniform(0, 1) distributions and plotting the generated values from one uniform distribution together with the calculated sum of them both. You get a scatter plot that looks like that in Figure 7.9.

The line $y = x$ shows the lowest value for the triangular distribution C for any given value of the uniform distribution A, and the line $y = 1 + x$ is the highest value, which makes intuitive sense. The uniform vertical distribution of points between these two lines is the effect of the second Uniform(0, 1) distribution B. Also note that all the generated values lie uniformly (but randomly) between these two lines. This actually is quite helpful in visualising why the sum of two Uniform(0, 1) distributions is a Triangle(0, 1, 2) by projecting all the dots onto the y axis. Can you extend this graph to work out graphically what $U(0, 1) + U(0, 3)$ would look like?

The point of the graph is to show you that there is a strong dependency pattern between these two distributions (a uniform and the triangle sum), which would need to be taken into account if one wished to extract back out the two uniform distributions from each other. For example, the formulae below do just that:

$$A := \text{VoseTriangle}(0, 1, 2)$$

$$B := \text{VoseUniform}(\text{IF}(A < 1, 0, A - 1), \text{IF}(A > 1, 1, A))$$

$$C := A - B$$

Try to follow the logic for the formula for B from the graph. B will generate a Uniform(0, 1) distribution with the right dependency relationship with A to leave C a Uniform(0, 1) distribution too. To recap, the problem is that we have three variables linked together as follows:

$$A + B = C$$

We know the distributions for A and C. How do we find B and how do we simulate A, B and C all together? The simple example above using two uniform distributions allows us to simulate A, B and C all together, but only because we assumed A and B were independent and the problem was *very* simple. In general, we cannot correctly determine B, so we need either to construct a model that avoids having to perform such a calculation or admit that we have insufficient information to specify B.

Chapter 8

Some basic random processes

8.1 Introduction

If you want to get the most out of the risk analysis and statistical modelling tools that are available, you really need to understand the conceptual thinking behind random processes and the equations and distributions that result, and be able to identify where these random processes occur in the real world. In this chapter we look at the binomial, Poisson and hypergeometric processes first because they share a common basis, and a very great deal of risk analysis problems can be tackled with a good knowledge of just these three processes. I've added the central limit theorem here too because it explains a lot about the behaviour of distributions. We'll look at the theory and assumptions behind each process, and the distributions that are used in their modelling. This approach provides us with an excellent opportunity to become very familiar with a number of important distributions, and to see the relationships between them, even between the distributions of the different random processes. Then we'll look at some extensions to these processes that greatly increase their range of applications. Finally, we look at a number of problems.

There are a number of other random processes discussed in this book relating to the sums of random variables (Chapter 11), time series modelling (Chapter 12) and correlated variables (Chapter 13). Chapter 9 on statistics relies heavily on an understanding of the random processes described here.

8.2 The Binomial Process

A binomial process is a random counting system where there are n independent identical trials, each one of which has the same probability of success p, which produces s successes from those n trials (where $0 \leq s \leq n$ and $n > 0$ obviously). There are thus three quantities $\{n, p, s\}$ that between them completely describe a binomial process. Associated with each of these three quantities are three distributions that describe the uncertainty about or variability of these quantities. The three distributions require knowledge of two quantities in order to use these distributions to estimate the third.

The simplest example of a binomial process is the toss of a coin. If we define "heads" as a success, each toss has the same probability of success p (0.5 for a fair coin). Then, for a given number of trials n (tosses of a coin), the number of successes will be s (the number of "heads"). Each trial can be thought of as a random variable that returns either a 1 with probability p or a 0 with probability $(1 - p)$. Such a trial is often known as a *Bernoulli trial*, and the probability $(1 - p)$ is often given the label q.

8.2.1 Number of successes in *n* trials

We start our exploration of the binomial process by looking at the probability of a certain number of successes s for a given number of trials n and probability of success p. Imagine we have one toss of

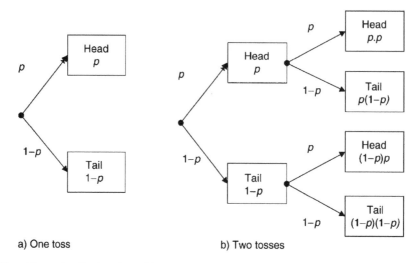

Figure 8.1 Event trees for the tossing of (a) one coin and (b) two coins.

a coin. The two outcomes are "heads" (H) with probability p and "tails" (T) with probability $(1 - p)$, as shown in the event tree of Figure 8.1(a). If we have two tosses of a coin there are four possible outcomes, as shown in Figure 8.1(b), namely HH, HT, TH and TT, where HT means "heads" followed by "tails", etc. These outcomes have probabilities p^2, $p(1 - p)$, $(1 - p)p$ and $(1 - p)^2$ respectively. If we are tossing a fair coin (i.e. $p = 0.5$), then each of the four outcomes has the same probability of 0.25. Now, the binomial process considers each success to be identical and therefore does not differentiate between the two events HT and TH: they are both just one success in two trials. The probability of one success in two trials is then just $2p(1 - p)$ or, for a fair coin, $= 0.5$. The two in this equation is the number of different paths that result in one success in two trials. Now imagine that we toss a coin 3 times. The eight outcomes are: HHH, HHT, HTH, HTT, THH, THT, TTH and TTT. Thus, one event produces three "heads", three events produce two "heads", three events produce one "head" and one event produces no "heads" for three coin tosses. In general, the number of ways that we can get s successes from n trials can be calculated directly using the binomial coefficient $_nC_s$, which is given by

$$_nC_s = \binom{n}{s} = \frac{n!}{s!(n - s)!}$$

We can check this is right by choosing $n = 3$ (remembering that $0! = 1$), then

$$\binom{3}{0} = \frac{3!}{0!(3)!} = 1$$

$$\binom{3}{1} = \frac{3!}{1!(2)!} = 3$$

$$\binom{3}{2} = \frac{3!}{2!(1)!} = 3$$

$$\binom{3}{3} = \frac{3!}{3!(0)!} = 1$$

which match the number of combinations we have already calculated. Each of the ways of getting s successes in n trials has the same probability, namely $p^s(1 - p)^{n-s}$, so the probability of observing x successes in n trial is given by

$$p_{\text{Bin}}(x) = \binom{n}{x} p^x(1 - p)^{n-x}$$

which is the probability mass function of the Binomial(n, p) distribution. In other words, the number of successes s one will observe in n trials, where each trial has the same probability of success, is given by

$$s = \text{Binomial}(n, p)$$

Figure 8.2 shows this distribution for four different combinations of n and p. The binomial distribution was first derived by Bernoulli (1713).

8.2.2 Number of trials needed to achieve s successes

We have seen how the binomial distribution allows us to model the number of successes that will occur in n trials where we know the probability of success p. Sometimes, we know how many successes we wish to have, we know the probability p and we would like to know the number of trials that we will have to complete in order to achieve the s successes, assuming we stop once the sth success has

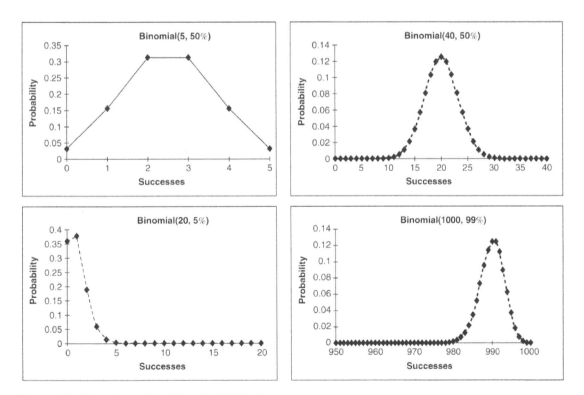

Figure 8.2   Examples of the binomial distribution.

occurred. In this case, n is the random variable. Now that we have the binomial distribution, we can readily determine the distribution for n. Let x be the total number of failures. The total number of trials we will execute is then $(s + x)$, and by the $(s + x - 1)$th trial we must have observed $(s - 1)$ successes and x failures (since the very last trial is, by assumption, a success). The probability of $(s - 1)$ successes in $(s + x - 1)$ trials is given immediately by the binomial distribution as

$$\binom{s + x - 1}{s - 1} p^{s-1}(1 - p)^x$$

The probability of this being followed by a success is the same equation multiplied by p, i.e.

$$p(x) = \binom{s + x - 1}{s - 1} p^s (1 - p)^x$$

which is the probability mass function of the negative binomial distribution NegBin(s, p). In other words, the NegBin(s, p) distribution returns the number of failures one will have before observing s successes. The total number of trials n is thus given by

$$n = s + \text{NegBin}(s, p)$$

Figure 8.3 shows various negative binomial distributions. If $s = 1$, then the distribution (known as the geometric distribution) is very right skewed and $p(0) = p$, i.e. the probability that there will be zero failures equals p, the probability that the first trial is a success. We can also see that, as s gets larger, the distribution looks more like a normal distribution. In fact, it is common to approximate the negative

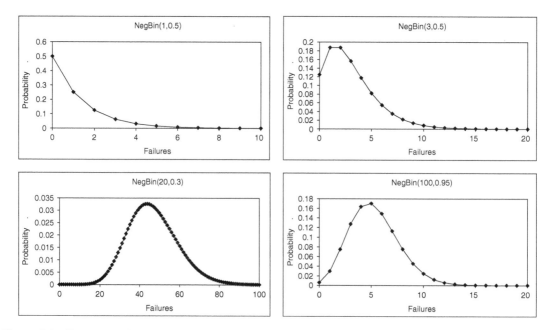

Figure 8.3 Examples of the negative binomial distribution.

binomial distribution with a normal distribution under certain circumstances where s is large, in order to avoid calculating the large factorials for $p(x)$ above. A negative binomial distribution shifting k values along the domain is sometimes called a *binomial waiting time* distribution, or a *Pascal* distribution.

8.2.3 Estimate of probability of success p

These results for the binomial and negative binomial distributions are both modelling variability: that is to say, they are returning probability distributions of possible future outcomes. At times, however, we are looking back at the results of a binomial process and wish to determine one of the parameters. For example, we may have observed n trials of which s were successes, and from that information we would like to estimate p. This binomial probability is a fundamental property of the stochastic system and can never be observed, but we can become progressively more certain about its true value by collecting data. As we shall see in Section 9.2.2, we can readily quantify our uncertainty about the true value of p by using a beta distribution. In brief, if we have no prior information about p, or do not wish to assume any prior information about p, then it is quite natural to use a uniform prior for p, and, through Bayes' theorem, we have the equation

$$f(x) = \frac{x^s (1 - x)^{n-s}}{\int_0^1 t^s (1 - t)^{n-s} dt}$$

which is just the Beta$(s + 1, n - s + 1)$ distribution, so

$$p = \text{Beta}(s + 1, n - s + 1)$$

The beta distribution can also be used in the event that we have an informed opinion about the value of p prior to collecting data. In such cases, providing we can reasonably model our prior opinion about p with a beta distribution of the form Beta(a, b), the posterior turns out to be a Beta$(a + s, b + n - s)$ distribution because the beta distribution is conjugate to the binomial distribution (see Section III.7.1). Figure 8.4 illustrates a number of beta distributions.

8.2.4 Estimate of the number of trials n that were completed

Consider the situation where we have observed s successes and know the probability of success p, but would like to know how many trials were actually done to have observed those successes. We wish to estimate a value that is fixed, so we require a distribution that represents our *uncertainty* about what the true value is. There are two possible situations: we either know that the trials stopped on the sth success or we do not. If we know that the trials stopped on the sth success, we can model our uncertainty about the true value of n as

$$n = \text{NegBin}(s, p) + s$$

If, on the other hand, we do not know that the last trial was a success (though it could have been), then our uncertainty about n is modelled as

$$n = \text{NegBin}(s + 1, p) + s$$

Both of these formulae result from a Bayesian analysis with uniform priors for n. We will now derive these two results using standard Bayesian inference. The reader unfamiliar with this technique should refer to Section 9.2. Let x be the number of failures that were carried out before the sth success. We

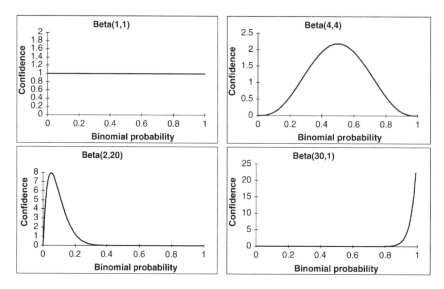

Figure 8.4 Examples of the beta distribution.

will use a uniform prior for x, i.e. $p(x) = c$, and, from the binomial distribution, the likelihood function is the probability that at the $(s + x - 1)$th trial there had been $(s - 1)$ successes *and* then the $(s + x)$th trial was a success, which is just the negative binomial probability mass function:

$$l(X|x) = \binom{s + x - 1}{s - 1} p^s (1 - p)^x$$

As we are using a uniform prior, and the equation for $l(X|x)$ comes directly from a distribution, so it must sum to unity, we can dispense with the formality of normalising the posterior distribution to 1 and observe

$$p(x) = \binom{s + x - 1}{s - 1} p^s (1 - p)^x$$

i.e. that $x = \text{NegBin}(s, p)$.

In the second case, we do not know that the last trial was a success, only that, in however many trials were completed, there were just s successes. We have the same uniform prior for the number of failures, but our likelihood function is just the binomial probability mass function, i.e.

$$l(X|x) = \binom{s + x}{s} p^s (1 - p)^x$$

As this does not have the form of a probability mass function of a distribution, we need to complete the Bayesian analysis, so

$$p(x) = \frac{\binom{s + x}{s} p^s (1 - p)^x}{\sum_{i=0}^{\infty} \binom{s + i}{s} p^s (1 - p)^i} \tag{8.1}$$

The sum in the denominator equals $1/p$. This can be easily seen by substituting $s = a - 1$, which gives

$$\binom{s+i}{s} p^s (1-p)^i = \binom{a+i-1}{a-1} p^{a-1}(1-p)^i \tag{8.2}$$

If the exponent for p were equal to a instead of $(a - 1)$, we would have the probability mass function of the negative binomial distribution, which would then sum to unity, so our denominator must sum to $1/p$.

The posterior distribution from Equation (8.1) then reduces to

$$p(x) = \binom{s+x}{s} p^{s+1}(1-p)^x$$

which is just a NegBin$(s + 1, p)$ distribution.

8.2.5 Summary of results for the binomial process

The results are shown in Table 8.1.

Table 8.1   Distributions of the binomial process.

Quantity	Formula	Notes
Number of successes	$s = \text{Binomial}(n, p)$	
Probability of success	$p = \text{Beta}(s + 1, n - s + 1)$	Assuming a uniform prior
	$= \text{Beta}(a + s, b + n - s)$	Assuming a Beta(a, b) prior
Number of trials	$n = s + \text{NegBin}(s, p)$	When the last trial is a success
	$= s + \text{NegBin}(s + 1, p)$	When the last trial is not known to be a success

8.2.6 The beta–binomial process

An extension of the binomial process is to consider the probability p to be a random variable. A natural candidate to model this variability is the Beta(α, β) distribution because it lies on $[0, 1]$ and can take a lot of shapes so it offers a great deal of flexibility.

The beta–binomial distribution models the number of successes:

$$s = \text{Binomial}(n, \text{Beta}(\alpha, \beta)) = \text{BetaBinomial}(n, \alpha, \beta)$$

The beta-negative binomial models the number of failures that will occur to achieve s successes:

$$n - s = \text{NegBin}(s, \text{Beta}(\alpha, \beta)) = \text{BetaNegBin}(s, \alpha, \beta)$$

Both distributions are included in ModelRisk.

It is important to remember that in the beta–binomial process the same value of p is applied to *all* the binomial trials, meaning that, if p is randomly 0.4 (say) for one trial, it is 0.4 for all the others too. If p were randomly varying between each trial, we would have each trial being an *independent* Bernoulli(Beta(α, β))), but since a Bernoulli distribution can only be 0 or 1, this condenses to a set of independent Bernoulli $\left(\frac{\alpha}{\alpha+\beta}\right)$ trials, where $\frac{\alpha}{\alpha+\beta}$ is the mean of the beta distribution, and a collection of n such trials would therefore be just a Binomial$\left(n, \frac{\alpha}{\alpha+\beta}\right)$.

8.2.7 The multinomial process

Whereas in the *bi*nomial process there are only two possible outcomes of a trial (0 or 1, yes or no, male or female, etc.), the *multi*nomial process allows for multiple outcomes. The list of possible outcomes must be exhaustive, meaning a trial cannot result in something that isn't listed as an outcome. For example, if we throw a die there are six possible mutually exclusive (they can't happen at the same time) and exhaustive (one must occur) outcomes.

There are three distributions associated with the multinomial process:

Multinomial$(n, \{p_1 \ldots p_k\})$ which describes the number of successes in n trials that fall into each of the k categories. It's joint probability mass function parallels the binomial equation

$$P(\{x_1 \ldots x_k\}) = \frac{n!}{\prod\limits_{i=1}^{k} x_i!} \prod\limits_{i=1}^{k} p_i^{s_i} \tag{8.3}$$

You can think of a multinomial distribution as a recursive sequence of nested binomial distributions where the trials and probability of success are modified through the sequence:

$$s_1 = \text{Binomial}(n, p_1)$$
$$s_2 = \text{Binomial}(n - s_1, p_2/(1 - p_1))$$
$$s_3 = \text{Binomial}(n - s_1 - s_2, p_3/(1 - p_1 - p_2))$$
$$\ldots$$

For example, imagine that a person being treated in hospital has three possible outcomes: {cured, not cured and deceased} with probabilities {0.6, 0.3, 0.1}. Assuming their outcomes are independent, we can model the outcome for 100 patients as follows:

$$Cured = \text{Binomial}(100, 0.6)$$
$$NotCured = \text{Binomial}(100 - Cured, 0.3/(0.3 + 0.1))$$
$$Deceased = \text{Binomial}(100 - Cured - NotCured, 0.1/0.1)$$
$$= \text{Binomial}(100 - Cured - NotCured, 1)$$
$$= 100 - Cured - NotCured$$

The model in Figure 8.5 shows this calculation in a spreadsheet, together with the ModelRisk distribution VoseMultinomial which achieves the same result but in a single array function.

Negative Multinomial$(\{s_1 \ldots s_k\}, \{p_1 \ldots p_k\})$ is the extension to the negative binomial distribution and describes the number of extra trials (we can't really say "failures" any more because there are several outcomes, not two in the binomial case where we could designate success or failure) there will be to observe $\{s_1 \ldots s_k\}$ successes. There are two versions of this question: "How many extra trials will there

	A	B	C	D	E	F	G	H	I	J	K
1											
2		Trials n:	100								
3											
4		Outcome	**A**	**B**	**C**	**D**	**E**	**F**		Total check	
5		P(outcome)	0.2	0.3	0.15	0.25	0.06	0.04		1	
6		Nested	28	30	12	16	7	7		100	
7		Multinomial	18	30	15	27	5	5		100	
8											
9					*Formulae table*						
10		C6 (output)	=VoseBinomial(C2,C5)								
11		D6:H6 (output)	=VoseBinomial($C$2-SUM($C$6:C6),D5/(1-SUM($C$5:C5)))								
12		{C7:H7} (alt output)	{=VoseMultinomial(C2,C5:H5)}								
13											

Figure 8.5 Model for the multinomial process.

	A	B	C	D	E	F	G	H	I
1									
2		Outcome	**A**	**B**	**C**	**D**	**E**	**F**	
3		P(outcome)	0.2	0.3	0.15	0.25	0.06	0.04	
4		Required successes	12	23	17	5	11	2	
5		Negative Multinomial 2	22	16	0	39	2	8	
6									
7		Negative Multinomial 1	126		Negative Multinomial 1 sum			87	
8									
9					*Formulae table*				
10		{C5:H5} (output)	{=VoseNegMultinomial2(C4:H4,C3:H3)}						
11		C7	=VoseNegMultinomial(C4:H4,C3:H3)						
12		H7	=SUM(C5:H5)						
13									

Figure 8.6 Model for the negative multinomial process.

be in total?", which has a univariate answer, and "How many extra trials will there be in each success category beyond the number required?", which has a multivariate answer. The probability mass function is quite complicated for both, but the modelling is pretty easy to see in the spreadsheet in Figure 8.6.

Note in this model that there will always be one zero (in row 5 in this random scenario) and that C7 and H7 will return the same distributions.

Dirichlet($\{a_1 \ldots a_k\}$) is the multivariate equivalent of the beta distribution which can be seen from its joint density function:

$$f(x_1, \ldots, x_k) = \frac{\Gamma\left(\sum_{i=1}^{k} \alpha_i\right)}{\prod_{i=1}^{k} \Gamma(\alpha_i)} \prod_{i=1}^{k} x_i^{\alpha_i - 1} \tag{8.4}$$

where $0 \leq x_i \leq 1$ (a probability lies on [0, 1]), $\sum_{i=1}^{k} x_i = 1$ (the probabilities must sum to 1) and $\alpha_i > 1$.

We can use the Dirichlet distribution to model the uncertainty about the set of probabilities $\{p_1 \ldots p_k\}$ of a multinomial process. There is a neat relationship with gamma distributions that we can use to simulate a Dirichlet distribution which is shown in the above model (Figure 8.7), together with the VoseDirichlet function. In this example, a clinical trial of some face cream has been performed with 300 randomly selected people to ascertain the level of allergic reactions, with the following outcomes: 227 – no effect; 41 – mild itching; 27 – significant discomfort; and 5 – lots of pain and regret. The Dirichlet($\{s_1 + 1 \ldots s_k + 1\}$) will return the joint uncertain estimate of the probability that another random person (a consumer) would experience each effect.

	A	B	C	D	E	F	G	H	I
1									
2		Outcome	**None**	**Itching**	**Discomfort**	**Pain and Regret**		Total check	
3		Number observed	227	41	27	5		300	
4		Estimated probability	0.744	0.155	0.079	0.022		1	
5		Gamma distributions	218.452	47.004	25.907	5.697		297.060	
6		Alternative method	0.735	0.158	0.087	0.019		1	
7									
8			*Formulae table*						
9		{C4:F4} (output)	{=VoseDirichlet(C3:F3+1)}						
10		C5:F5	=VoseGamma(C3+1,1)						
11		H3:H6	=SUM(C3:F3)						
12		C6:F6 (alt output)	=C5/$H$5						
13									

Figure 8.7 Model for the Dirichlet distribution.

8.3 The Poisson Process

In the binomial process there are n discrete opportunities for an event (a "success") to occur. In the Poisson process there is a continuous and constant opportunity for an event to occur. For example, lightning strikes might be considered to occur as a Poisson process during a storm. That would mean that, in any small time interval during the storm, there is a certain probability that a lightning strike will occur. In the case of lightning strikes, the continuum of opportunity is time. However, there are other types of exposure. The occurrence of discontinuities in the continuous manufacture of wire could be considered to be a Poisson process where the measure of exposure is, for example, kilometres or tonnes of wire produced. If Giardia cysts were randomly distributed in a lake, the consumption of cysts by campers drinking the water would be a Poisson process, where the measure of exposure would be the amount of water consumed. Typographic errors in a book might be Poisson distributed, in which case the measure of exposure could be inches of text, although one could just as easily consider the errors to be binomially distributed with $n =$ the number of characters in the book.

In a Poisson process, unlike the binomial, as there is a continuum of opportunity for an event to occur we can theoretically have anything between zero and an infinite number of events within a specific amount of opportunity, and there is a probability of the event occurring no matter how small a unit of exposure we might consider. In practice, few physical systems will exactly conform to such a set of assumptions, but many systems nevertheless are very well approximated by a Poisson process. In the

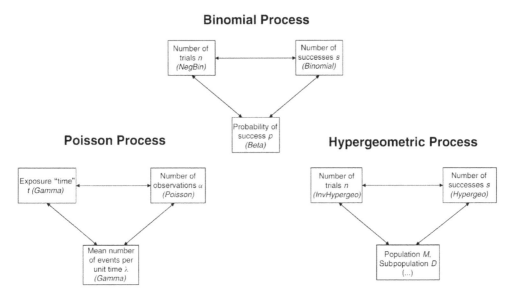

Figure 8.8 Comparison of the distributions of the binomial, Poisson and hypergeometric processes.

Giardia cyst example above, assuming a Poisson process would theoretically mean that we could have any number of cysts in a volume of water, no matter how small we made that volume. Obviously, this assumption breaks down when we consider a volume of liquid around the size of a cyst, or smaller, but this is almost never a restriction in practice.

The distributions describing the Poisson and binomial processes are strongly related to each other, as shown in Figure 8.8. In a binomial process, the key descriptive parameter is p, the probability of occurrence of an event, which is the same for all trials, so the trials are independent of each other. The key descriptive parameter for the Poisson process is λ, the mean number of events that will occur per unit of exposure, which is also considered to be constant over the total amount of exposure t. That means that there is a constant probability per second, for example, of an event occurring, whether or not an event has just occurred, has not occurred for an unexpectedly long time, etc. Such a process is called "memoryless", and both the binomial and Poisson processes can be so described.

Like p for a binomial process, λ is a property of the physical system. For static systems (stochastic processes), p and λ are not variables, but we still need distributions to express the state of our knowledge (uncertainty) about their values.

In a Poisson process, we consider, with the number of events that may occur in a period t, the amount of "time" one will have to wait to observe α events, and λ, the average number of events that could occur, known as the Poisson intensity. This section will now show how the Poisson distribution, which describes the number of events α that may occur in a period of exposure t, can be derived from the binomial distribution as p tends to zero and n tends to infinity. We will then look at how to determine the variability distribution of the time t one will need to wait before observing α events, which also turns out to be the distribution of uncertainty of the time one must have waited before having observed α events. Finally, we will discuss how to determine our state of knowledge (uncertainty) about λ given a set of observed events α in a period t.

8.3.1 Deriving the Poisson distribution from the binomial

Consider a binomial process where the number of trials tends to infinity, and the probability of success at the same time tends to zero, with the constraint that the mean of the binomial distribution $= np$ remains finitely large. The probability mass function of the binomial distribution can be altered closely to model the number of successes that will occur under such conditions, as follows:

$$p(X = x) = {}_nC_x \ px(1 - p)^{n-x}$$

Using $\lambda t = np$,

$$p(X = x) = \frac{n!}{x!(n - x)!} \left(\frac{\lambda t}{n}\right)^x \left(1 - \frac{\lambda t}{n}\right)^{n-x}$$

$$= \frac{n(n - 1) \cdots (n - x + 1)}{n^x} \frac{(\lambda t)^x}{x!} \frac{(1 - \lambda t/n)^n}{(1 - \lambda t/n)^x}$$

For n large and p small,

$$\left(1 - \frac{\lambda t}{n}\right)^n \approx e^{-\lambda t}, \quad \frac{n(n - 1) \cdots (n - x + 1)}{n^x} \approx 1, \quad \left(1 - \frac{\lambda t}{n}\right)^x \approx 1$$

which simplifies the equation to

$$p(X = x) \approx \frac{e^{-\lambda t} (\lambda t)^x}{x!}$$

This is the probability mass function for the Poisson(λt) distribution, i.e.

Number of events α in time $t = $ Poisson(λt)

when the average number of events that will occur in a unit interval of exposure is known to be λ. We can see how this interpretation fits in with the derivation from the binomial distribution. Imagine that a young lady decides to buy a pair of very high platform shoes that are in fashion. After some practice she gets used to the shoes, but there remains a smallish probability (say 1 in 50) that she will fall over with each step she takes. She decides to go for a short walk, say 100 metres. If we say that each step measures 1 metre, then we can model the number of falls she will have on her walk as either Binomial(100, 2 %) or Poisson($100 * 0.02$) = Poisson(2). Figure 8.9 plots these two distributions together and shows how closely the binomial distribution is approximated by the Poisson distribution in such limiting cases.

The Poisson distribution is often mistakenly considered to be only a distribution of rare events. It is certainly used in this sense to approximate a binomial distribution, but has far more importance than that. Where there is a continuum of exposure to an event, the measure of exposure can be split up into smaller and smaller divisions, until the probability of the event occurring in each division has become extremely small, while there are also an enormous number of divisions. For example, I could stand on a street corner during rush hour, looking for red cars to pass by. For the duration of the rush hour, one could consider that the frequency of cars going by is quite constant, and that the red cars in the traffic are randomly distributed among the city's traffic. Then the number of red cars passing by will

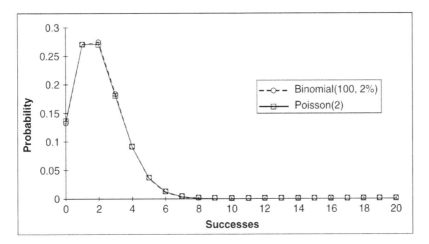

Figure 8.9 Comparison of the Binomial(100, 0.02) and Poisson(2) distributions.

be Poisson distributed. If, on average, 0.6 red cars passed by per minute, I could model the number of cars passing by: in the next 10 seconds as Poisson(0.1); in the next hour as Poisson(36), etc. I could divide up the time I stand on the street corner into such tiny elements (for example 1/100th of a second) that the probability of a red car passing by within a particular 1/100th of a second would be extremely small. The probability would be so small that the chance of two cars going by within that period would be absolutely negligible. In such circumstances, we can consider each of these small elements of time to be independent Bernoulli trials. Similarly, the number of raindrops falling on my head each second during a shower would also be Poisson distributed.

8.3.2 "Time" to wait to observe α events

The Poisson process assumes that there is a constant probability that an event will occur per increment of time. If we consider a small element of time Δt, then the probability an event will occur in that element of time is $k\Delta t$, where k is some constant. Now let $P(t)$ be the probability that the event will not have occurred by time t. The probability that an event occurs the first time during the small interval Δt after time t is then $k\Delta t P(t)$. This is also equal to $P(t) - P(t + \Delta t)$ and we have

$$\left[\frac{P(t + \Delta t) - P(t)}{P(t)} \right] = -k\Delta t$$

Making Δt infinitesimally small, this becomes the differential equation

$$\frac{\mathrm{d}P(t)}{P(t)} = -k\mathrm{d}t$$

Integration gives

$$\ln[P(t)] = -kt$$

$$P(t) = \exp[-kt]$$

If we define $F(t)$ as the probability that the event will occur before time t (i.e. the cumulative distribution function for t), we then have

$$F(t) = 1 - \exp[-kt]$$

which is the cumulative distribution function for an exponential distribution Expon($1/k$) with mean $1/k$. Thus, $1/k$ is the mean time between occurrences of events or, equivalently, k is the mean number of events per unit time, which is the Poisson parameter λ. The parameter $1/\lambda$, the mean time between occurrences of events, is given the notation β.

We have thus shown that the time until occurrence of the first event for a Poisson distribution is given by

$$t_1 = \text{Expon}(\beta)$$

where $\beta = 1/\lambda$. It can also be shown (although the maths is too laborious to repeat here) that the time until α events have occurred is given by a gamma distribution:

$$t_\alpha = \text{Gamma}(\alpha, \beta)$$

The Expon(β) distribution is therefore simply a special case of the gamma distribution, namely

$$\text{Gamma}(1, \beta) = \text{Expon}(\beta)$$

It is interesting to check the idea that a Poisson process is "memoryless". The probability that the first event will occur at time x, given it has not yet occurred by time t ($x > t$), is given by

$$f(x|x > t) = \frac{f(x)}{1 - F(t)} = \frac{1}{\beta}\exp\left[-\frac{(x - t)}{\beta}\right]$$

which is another exponential distribution. Thus, although the event may not have occurred after time t, the remaining time until it will occur has the same probability distribution as it had at any prior point in time.

8.3.3 Estimate of the mean number of events per period (Poisson intensity) λ

Like the binomial probability p, the mean events per period λ is a fundamental property of the stochastic system in question. It can never be observed and it can never be exactly known. However, we can become progressively more certain about its value as more data are collected. Bayesian inference, see Section 9.2, provides us with a means of quantifying the state of our knowledge as we accumulate data.

Assuming an uninformed prior $\pi(\lambda) = 1/\lambda$ (see Section 9.2.2) and the Poisson likelihood function for observing α events in period t:

$$l(\alpha|\lambda,\ t) = \frac{e^{-\lambda t}(\lambda t)^\alpha}{\alpha!} \propto e^{-\lambda t}(\lambda)^\alpha$$

since we can ignore terms that don't involve λ, and we then get the posterior distribution

$$p(\lambda|\alpha) \propto e^{-\lambda t}\lambda^{\alpha-1}$$

which is a gamma(α, $1/t$) distribution. The gamma distribution can also be used to describe our uncertainty about λ if we start off with an informed opinion and then observe α events in time t. From Table 9.1, if we can reasonably describe our prior belief with a Gamma(a, b) distribution, the posterior is given by a Gamma($a + \alpha$, $b/(1 + bt)$) distribution.

The choice of $\pi(\lambda) = 1/\lambda$ (which is equivalent to a Gamma($1/z$, z) distribution, where z is *extremely* large) as an uninformed prior is an uncomfortable one for many. This prior makes mathematical sense in that it is transformation invariant and therefore would give the same answer whether one performed an analysis from the point of view of λ or $\beta = 1/\lambda$ or even changed the unit of exposure relating to λ. On the other hand, a plot of this prior doesn't really seem "uninformed" since it is so peaked at zero. However, the shape of the posterior gamma distribution becomes progressively less sensitive to the prior distribution as data are collected. We can get a feel for the importance of the prior with the following train of thought:

(i) A $\pi(\lambda) = 1/\lambda$ prior is equivalent to Gamma($1/z$, z), where z approaches infinity. You can prove this by looking at the gamma probability distribution function and setting α to zero and β to infinity.

(ii) A flat prior (the opposite extreme to the $\pi(\lambda) = 1/\lambda$ prior) would be equivalent to a Gamma(1, z), where z approaches infinity, i.e. an infinitely drawn out exponential distribution.

(iii) We have seen that, for a Gamma(a, b) prior, the resultant posterior is Gamma($a + \alpha$, $b/(1 + bt)$), which means that the posterior for (i) would be Gamma(α, $1/t$), and the posterior for (ii) would be Gamma($\alpha + 1$, $1/t$).

(iv) Thus, the sensitivity of the gamma distribution to the prior amounts to whether ($\alpha + 1$) is approximately the same as α. Moreover, Gamma(α, β) is the sum of α independent Exponential(β) distributions, so one can think of the choice of priors as being whether we add one extra exponential distribution or not to the α exponential distributions from the data. Thus, if α were 100, for example, the distribution would be roughly 1 % influenced by the prior and 99 % influenced by the data.

8.3.4 Estimate of the elapsed period *t*

We can estimate the period t that has elapsed if we know λ and the number of events α that have occurred in time t. The maths turns out to be exactly the same as the estimate for λ in the previous section. The reader may like to verify that, by using a prior of $\pi(t) = 1/t$, we obtain a posterior distribution $t = $ Gamma(α, $1/\lambda$), which is the same result we would obtain if we were trying to predict forward (i.e. determine a distribution of variability of) the time required to observe α events given $\lambda = 1/\beta$. Also, if we can reasonably describe our prior belief with a Gamma(a, b) distribution, the posterior is given by a Gamma($a + \alpha$, $b/(1 + b\lambda)$) distribution.

8.3.5 Summary of results for the Poisson process

The results are shown in Table 8.2.

8.3.6 The multivariate Poisson process

The properties of the Poisson process make extending to a multivariate situation very easy. Imagine that we have three categories of car accident: (a) no injury; (b) one or more persons injured but no fatalities;

Table 8.2 Distributions of the Poisson process.

Quantity	Formula	Notes
Number of events	$\alpha = \text{Poisson}(\lambda t)$	
Mean number of events per unit exposure	$\lambda = \text{Gamma}(\alpha, 1/t)$ $= \text{Gamma}(a + \alpha, b/(1 + bt))$	Assuming uninformed prior Assuming Gamma(a, b) prior
Time until observation of first event	$t_1 = \text{Expon}(1/\lambda) = \text{Gamma}(1, 1/\lambda)$	
Time until observation of first α events	$t_\alpha = \text{Gamma}(\alpha, 1/\lambda)$	
Time that has elapsed for α events	$t_\alpha = \text{Gamma}(\alpha, 1/\lambda)$ $= \text{Gamma}(a + \alpha, b/(1 + b\lambda))$	Assuming uninformed prior Assuming Gamma(a, b) prior

(c) one or more persons killed. We'll assume that the accidents occur independently and follow a Poisson process with expected occurrences λ_a, λ_b and λ_c per year. The number that will occur in the next T years (assuming that the rates won't change over time) is Poisson$(T * (\lambda_a + \lambda_b + \lambda_c))$. The probability that the next accident is of type (a) is

$$P(\text{a}) = \frac{\lambda_\text{a}}{\lambda_\text{a} + \lambda_\text{b} + \lambda_\text{c}}$$

The time until the next a accident is

$$\text{Gamma}\left(\alpha, \frac{1}{\lambda_\text{a} + \lambda_\text{b} + \lambda_\text{c}}\right)$$

and the uncertainty about the true values of each λ can be estimated separately as described in Sections 8.3.3 and 9.1.5.

8.3.7 Modifying λ in a Poisson process

The Poisson model assumes that λ will be constant over the time in which we are counting. That can be a tenuous assumption. Hurricanes, disease outbreaks, suicides, etc., occur more frequently at certain times of the year; car accidents, robberies and high-street brawls occur more frequently at certain times of the day (and sometimes year too). In fact it turns out that, if λ has a consistent (even if unknown) seasonal variation, we can often get round the problem. Imagine that boat accidents occur in each month i at a rate $\lambda_i, i = 1, \ldots, 12$. The number occurring in each future month i will be $a_i = \text{Poisson}(\lambda_i)$, and the total over the year will be $\sum_{i=1}^{12} \text{Poisson}(\lambda_i)$. From the identity Poisson(a) + Poisson(b) = Poisson$(a + b)$, this equation can be rewritten Poisson $\left(\sum_{i=1}^{12} \lambda_i\right)$, i.e. the boat accidents occurring in a year also follow a Poisson process. Thus, as long as we ensure that we analyse data over a complete number of seasonal periods (a whole number of years in this case) and predict for a whole number of seasonal periods, we can ignore the fact that λ changes seasonally. That is immensely useful. If I've observed that historically there have been an average of 23 outbreaks per year of campylobacteriosis in a city (an outbreak is defined in epidemiology as an event unconnected to others, so we can think of them as occurring randomly in time and independently), then I can model the number of outbreaks next year as

Poisson(23) without worrying that most of those will occur over the summer months. I can also compare year-on-year data on outbreaks using Poisson mathematics. What I cannot do, of course, is say that July will have Poisson(23/12) outbreaks.

I used to live in a rural area of the South of France. As winter approached, the first time there was black ice on the roads in the morning you would see cars buried in hedges, woods and fields along the roadside. The more intense the sudden cold snap, the more cars you would see. Some years there weren't so many, others it was mayhem. Clearly in situations like this the expected rate of accidents is a random variable. The most common way to model that random variation is to multiply λ by a Gamma$\left(\frac{1}{h}, h\right)$ distribution. This gamma has a mean of 1 and a standard deviation of h, giving a Poisson rate of Gamma$\left(\frac{1}{h}, \lambda h\right)$. The idea therefore is that the gamma distribution is just adding a coefficient of variation of h to λ. It turns out that the combination of these two distributions is a Pólya$\left(\frac{1}{h}, \lambda h\right)$ or, if $\frac{1}{h}$ is an integer, simplifies to a NegBin$\left(\frac{1}{h}, \frac{1}{1+\lambda h}\right)$. The result is convenient because it means we can use the Pólya or NegBin distributions to model this Poisson(λ) $\hat{\lambda}$ Gamma(α, β) mixture. Along the way, we can also see that the Pólya and NegBin distributions have a greater coefficient of variation than the Poisson. Often you will see in statistics that researchers call the data "overdispersed" when they want to fit a Poisson distribution because the data have a variance greater than their mean (they would be equal for a Poisson distribution), and the statisticians then turn to a NegBin (although they would be better off with a Pólya but it is less well known).

The Gamma distribution is useful because we have an extra parameter h to play with and can therefore match, for example, the mean and variance (or any two other statistics) to data. However, at times that is not enough, and we might need more control to match, for example, the skewness too. Instead of modelling λ in the form Gamma(a, b), we can add a positive shift so we get Poisson(Gamma(a, b) $+ c$), which turns out to be a Delaporte(a, b, c) distribution.

8.4 The Hypergeometric Process

The hypergeometric process occurs when one is sampling randomly without replacement from some population, and where one is counting the number in that sample that have some particular characteristic. This is a very common type of scenario. For example, population surveys, herd testing and lotto are all hypergeometric processes. In many situations the population is very large in comparison with the sample, and we can assume that, if a sample were put back into the population, the probability is very small that it would be picked again. In that case, each sample would have the same probability of picking an individual with a particular characteristic: in other words, this becomes a binomial process. When the population is not very large compared with the sample (a good rule is that the population is less than 10 times the size of the sample), we cannot make a binomial approximation to the hypergeometric. This section discusses the distributions associated with the hypergeometric process.

8.4.1 Number in a sample with a particular characteristic

Consider a group of M individual items, D of which have a certain characteristic. Randomly picking n items from this group *without replacement*, where each of the M items has the same probability of being selected, is a hypergeometric process. For example, imagine I have a bag of seven balls, three of which are red, the other four of which are blue. What is the probability that I will select two red balls from the bag if I randomly pick three balls out without replacement?

First of all, we note that the probability of the second ball picked being red depends on the colour of the first picked ball. If the first ball was red (with probability $\frac{3}{7}$), there are only two red balls left of the six balls remaining. The probability of the second ball being red, given the first ball was red, is therefore $\frac{2}{6} = \frac{1}{3}$. However, each ball remaining in the bag has the same probability of being picked, which means that each event resulting in x red balls being selected in total has the same probability. We thus need only consider the different *combinations* of events that are possible. There are, from the discussion in Section 6.3.4, $\binom{7}{3} = 35$ different possible ways that one can select three items from seven. There are $\binom{3}{2} = 3$ ways to select two red balls from the three in the bag, and there are $\binom{4}{1} = 4$ ways to select one blue ball from the four in the bag. Thus, out of the 35 ways we could have picked three balls from the group of seven, only $\binom{3}{2}\binom{4}{1} = 3 * 4 = 12$ of those ways would give us two red balls. Thus, the probability of selecting two red balls is $12/35 = 34.29 \%$.

In general, for a population size M of which D have the characteristic of interest, in selecting a sample of size n from that population at random without replacement, the probability of observing x with the characteristic of interest is given by

$$p(x) = \frac{\binom{D}{x}\binom{M - D}{n - x}}{\binom{M}{n}}, 0 \leq x \leq n, \; x \leq D, \; n \leq M \tag{8.5}$$

which is the probability mass function of the *hypergeometric distribution* Hypergeo(n, D, M). Just in case you are curious, the hypergeometric distribution gets its name because its probabilities are successive terms in a gaussian hypergeometric series.

Binomial approximation to the hypergeometric

If we replaced each item one at a time back into the population when taking our sample of size n, the probability of each individual item having the characteristic of interest is D/M and the number of times we sampled from D is then given by a Binomial($n, D/M$). More usefully, if M is very large compared with n, the chance of picking the same item more than once if one were to replace the item after each selection would be very small. Thus, for large M (usually $n < 0.1M$ is quoted as being a satisfactory condition) there will be little difference in our sampling result whether we sample with or without replacement, and we can approximate a Hypergeo(n, D, M) with a Binomial($n, D/M$), which is much easier to calculate.

Multivariate hypergeometric distribution

The hypergeometric distribution can be extended to situations where there are more than two types of item in the population (i.e. more than D of one type and $(M - D)$ of another). The probability of getting s_1 from D_1, s_2 from D_2, etc., all in the sample n is given by

$$p(s_1, s_2, \ldots, s_k) = \frac{\binom{D_1}{s_1}\binom{D_2}{s_2} \cdots \binom{D_k}{s_k}}{\binom{M}{n}}$$

where $\sum_{i=1}^{k} s_i = n, \; \sum_{i=1}^{k} D_i = M, \; D_i \geq s_i \geq 0, \; M > D_i > 0.$

8.4.2 Number of samples to get a specific *s*

Consider the situation where we are sampling without replacement from a population M with D items with the characteristic of interest until we have s items with the required characteristic. The distribution of the number of failures we will have before the sth success can be easily calculated in the same manner as we developed for the negative binomial distribution in Section 8.2.2. The probability of observing $(s - 1)$ successes in $(x + s - 1)$ trials (i.e. x failures) is given by direct application of the hypergeometric distribution:

$$p(x, s - 1) = \frac{\binom{D}{s - 1} \binom{M - D}{x}}{\binom{M}{x + s - 1}}$$

The probability p of then observing a success in the next trial (the $(s + x)$th trial) is simply the number of D items remaining ($= D - (s - 1)$) divided by the size of the population remaining ($= M - (s + x - 1)$):

$$p = \frac{D - s + 1}{M - x - s + 1}$$

and the probability of having exactly x failures up to the sth success, where trials are stopped at the sth success, is then the product of these two probabilities:

$$p(x) = \frac{\binom{D}{s - 1} \binom{M - D}{x} (D - s + 1)}{\binom{M}{x + s - 1} (M - x - s + 1)}$$

This is the probability mass function for the *inverse hypergeometric* distribution InvHypergeo(s, D, M) and is analogous to the negative binomial distribution for the binomial process and the gamma distribution for the Poisson process. So

$$n = s + \text{InvHypergeo}(s, D, M)$$

For a population M that is large compared with s, the inverse hypergeometric distribution approximates the negative binomial

$$\text{InvHypergeo}(s, D, M) \approx \text{NegBin}(s, D/M)$$

and if the probability D/M is very small

$$\text{InvHypergeo}(s, D, M) \approx \text{Gamma}(s, M/D)$$

Figure 8.10 shows some examples of the inverse hypergeometric distribution. An inverse hypergeometric distribution shifted k units along the domain is sometimes called a *negative hypergeometric* distribution. ModelRisk offers the InvHypergeo(s, D, M) distribution, and the negative hypergeometric can be achieved by writing VoseInvHypergeo(s, D, M, VoseShift(k)).

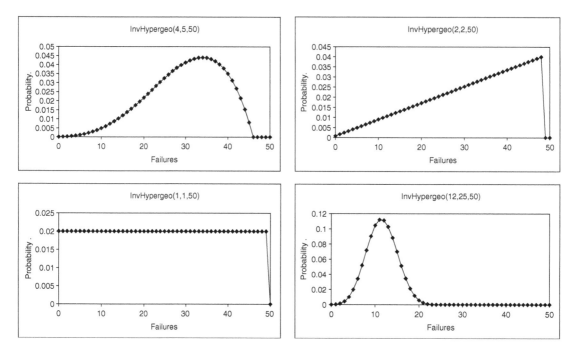

Figure 8.10 Examples of the inverse hypergeometric distribution.

8.4.3 Number of samples to have observed a specific *s*

The inverse hypergeometric distribution was derived above as a distribution of variability in predicting the number of failures one will have before the *s*th success. However, it can equally be derived as a distribution of uncertainty about the number of failures $x = n - s$ one must have had if one knows s, M, D using Bayes' theorem and a uniform (i.e. uninformed) prior on x. So

$$n = s + \text{InvHypergeo}(s, D, M)$$

In the case where you do *not* know that the trials had stopped with the *s*th success, we can still apply Bayes' theorem with a uniform prior for x and a likelihood function given by a hypergeometric probability:

$$l(x|s) = \frac{\binom{D}{s}\binom{M-D}{x}}{\binom{M}{x+s}} \propto \frac{\binom{M-D}{x}}{\binom{M}{x+s}}$$

which, with a uniform prior, is also the posterior distribution. Substituting $n - s$ for x yields

$$f(n) \propto \frac{n!(M-n)!}{(n-s)!(M-D-n+s)!} \tag{8.6}$$

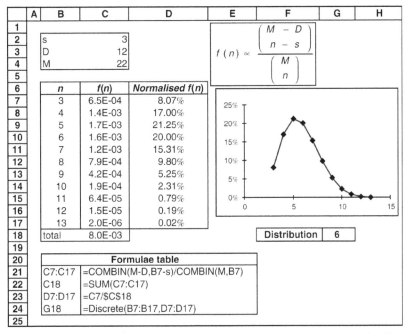

Figure 8.11 A Bayesian inference model with hypergeometric uncertainty. Note that the discrete distribution could have been used with columns B and C, removing the necessity to normalise the distribution.

Equation (8.6) has dropped out all the terms that are not a function of n and so can be normalised out of the equation. The uncertainty distribution for n doesn't equate to a standard distribution, so it needs to be manually normalised. However, it is easier just to work with Equation (8.6) and normalise in the spreadsheet. Figure 8.11 shows an example of such a calculation where the final distribution is in cell G18. Note that, if one uses a discrete distribution as shown in this spreadsheet, it is actually unnecessary to normalise the probabilities, since software like @RISK, Crystal Ball and ModelRisk automatically normalises them to sum to unity.

8.4.4 Estimate of population and subpopulation sizes

The size of D and M are fundamental properties of the stochastic system, like p for a binomial process and λ for a Poisson process. Distributions of our uncertainty about the value of these parameters can be determined from Bayesian inference, given a certain sample size taken from the population M, of which s belonged to the subpopulation D. The hypergeometric probability of s successes in n samples from a population M of which D have the characteristic of interest is given by Equation (8.5) as

$$p(s) = \frac{\begin{pmatrix} D \\ s \end{pmatrix} \begin{pmatrix} M - D \\ n - s \end{pmatrix}}{\begin{pmatrix} M \\ n \end{pmatrix}} \, 0 \le s \le n, \ s \le D, \ n \le M$$

So, with a uniform prior, we get the following posterior equations for D and M:

$$p(D) \propto \frac{\binom{D}{s}\binom{M-D}{n-s}}{\binom{M}{n}} \propto \frac{D!(M-D)!}{(D-s)!(M-D-n+s)!}$$

$$p(M) \propto \frac{\binom{D}{s}\binom{M-D}{n-s}}{\binom{M}{n}} \propto \frac{(M-D)!(M-n)!}{(M-D-n+s)!M!}$$

These formulae do not equate to standard distributions and need to be normalised in the same way as discussed for Equation (8.6).

8.4.5 Summary of results for the hypergeometric process

The results are shown in Table 8.3.

Table 8.3 Distributions of the hypergeometric process.

Quantity	Formula	Notes
Number of subpopulation in the sample	$s = \text{Hypergeo}(n, D, M)$	
Number of samples to observe s from the subpopulation	$n = s + \text{InvHyp}(s, D, M)$	
Number of samples there were to have observed s from the subpopulation	$n = s + \text{InvHyp}(s, D, M)$	Where the last sample *is* known to have been from the subpopulation
Number of samples n there were before having observed s from the subpopulation	$f(n) \propto \frac{n!(M-n)!}{(n-s)!(M-D-n+s)!}$	Where the last sample is *not* known to have been from the subpopulation. This uncertainty distribution needs to be normalised
Size of subpopulation D	$f(D) \propto \frac{D!(M-D)!}{(D-s)!(M-D-n+s)!}$	This uncertainty distribution needs to be normalised
Size of population M	$f(M) \propto \frac{(M-D)!(M-n)!}{M!(M-D-n+s)!}$	This uncertainty distribution needs to be normalised

8.5 Central Limit Theorem

The central limit theorem (CLT) is an asymptotic result of summing probability distributions. It turns out to be very useful for obtaining sums of individuals (e.g. sums of animal weights, yields, scraps). It also explains why so many distributions sometimes look like normal distributions. We won't look at the derivation, just see some examples and its use.

The sum Σ of n independent random variables X_i (where n is large), all of which have the same distribution, will asymptotically *approach* a normal distribution with known mean and standard deviation:

$$\sum_{i=1}^{n} X_i \approx \text{Normal}(n\mu, \sqrt{n}\sigma) \tag{8.7}$$

where μ and σ are the mean and standard deviation of the distribution from which the n samples are drawn.

8.5.1 Examples

Imagine that the distribution of the weight (read "mass" if you want to be technical) of random nails produced by some company has a mean of 27.4 g and a standard deviation 1.3 g. What will be the weight of a box of 100 nails? The answer, assuming that the nail weight distribution isn't really skewed, is the following normal distribution:

$$= \text{Normal}(100 * 27.4, \text{SQRT}(100) * 1.3)\text{g}$$

$$= \text{VoseNormal}(2740, 13)\text{g}$$

This CLT result turns out to be very important in risk analysis. Many distributions are the sum of a number of identical random variables, and so, as that sum gets larger, the distribution tends to look like a normal distribution. For example: Gamma(α, β) is the sum of α independent Expon(β) distributions, so, as α gets larger, the gamma distribution looks progressively more like a normal distribution. An exponential distribution has mean and variance of β, so we have

$$\text{Gamma}(\alpha, \beta) \to \text{Normal}(\alpha\beta, \alpha\sqrt{\beta}) \text{ as } n \to \infty$$

Other examples are discussed in the section on approximating one distribution with another.

How large does n have to be for the sum to be distributed normally?

Distribution of individual	Sufficient n
Uniform	12 (try it: an old way of generating normal distributions)
Symmetric triangular	6 (because U(a, b) + U(a, b) = T$(2a, a + b, 2b)$)
Normal	1!
Fairly skewed	30+ (e.g. 30 lots of Poisson(2) = Poisson(60))
Exponential	50+ (check with Gamma(a, b) = sum of a Exponential(b)s)

8.5.2 Other related results

The average of a large number of independent, identical distributions

Dividing both sides of Equation (8.7) by n, the average x of n variables drawn independently from the same distribution is given by

$$\bar{x} = \frac{\sum_{i=1}^{n} X_i}{n} \approx \frac{\text{Normal}(n\mu, \sqrt{n}\sigma)}{n} = \text{Normal}\left(\mu, \frac{\sigma}{\sqrt{n}}\right) \tag{8.8}$$

Note that the result of Equation (8.8) is correct because both the mean and standard deviation of the normal distribution are in the same units as the variable itself. However, be warned that for most distributions one cannot simply divide by n the distribution parameters of a variable X to get the distribution of X/n.

The product of a large number of independent, identical distributions

CLT can also be applied where a large number of identical random variables are being multiplied together. Let P be the product of a large number of random variables $X_i, i = 1, \ldots, n$, i.e.

$$\Pi = \prod_{i=1}^{n} X_i$$

Taking logs of both sides, we get

$$\ln[\Pi] = \sum_{i=1}^{n} \ln[X_i]$$

The right-hand side is the sum of a large number of random variables and will therefore tend to a normal distribution. Thus, from the definition of a lognormal distribution, P will be asymptotically lognormally distributed.

A neat result from this is that, if all X_i are lognormally distributed, their product will also be lognormally distributed.

Is CLT the reason the normal distribution is so popular?

Many stochastic variables are neatly described as the sum or product, or a mixture, of a number of random variables. A very loose form of CLT says that, if you add up a large number n of different random variables, and if none of those variables dominates the resultant distribution spread, the sum will eventually look normal as n gets bigger. The same applies to multiplying (positive) different random variables and the lognormal distribution. In fact, a lognormal distribution will also look very similar to a normal distribution if its mean is much larger than its standard deviation (see Figure 8.12), so perhaps it should not be too surprising that so many variables in nature seem to be somewhere between lognormally and normally distributed.

8.6 Renewal Processes

In a Poisson process, the times between successive events are described by independent identical exponential distributions. In a renewal process, like a Poisson process, the times between successive events are independent and identical, but they can take any distribution. The Poisson process is thus a particular case of a renewal process. The mathematics of the distributions of the number of events in a period (equivalent to the Poisson distribution for the Poisson process) and the time to wait to observe x events

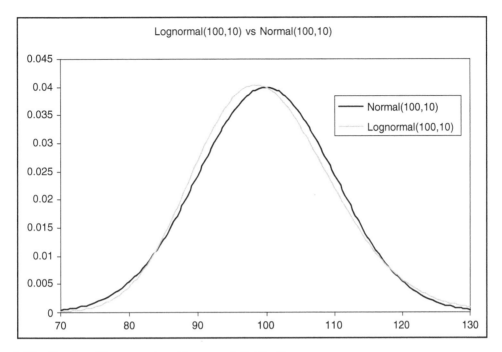

Figure 8.12 Graphs of the normal and lognormal distribution.

(equivalent to the gamma distribution in the Poisson process) can be quite complicated, depending on the distribution of time between events. However, Monte Carlo simulation lets us bypass the mathematics to arrive at both of these distributions, as we will see in the following examples.

Example 8.1 Number of events in a specific period

It is known that a certain type of light bulb has a lifetime that is Weibull(1.3, 4020) hours distributed. (a) If I have one light bulb working at all times, replacing each failed light bulb immediately with another, how many light bulbs will have failed in 10 000 hours? (b) If I have 10 light bulbs going at all times, how many will fail in 1000 hours? (c) If I had one light bulb going constantly, and I had 10 light bulbs to use, how long would it take before the last light bulb failed?

(a) Figure 8.13 shows a model to provide the solution to this question. Note that it takes account of the possibility of 0 failures.

(b) Figure 8.14 shows a model to provide the solution to this question. Figure 8.15 compares the results for this question and part (a). Note that they are significantly different. Had the time between events been exponentially distributed, the results would have been exactly the same.

(c) The answer is simply the sum of 10 independent Weibull(1.3, 4020) distributions. ◆

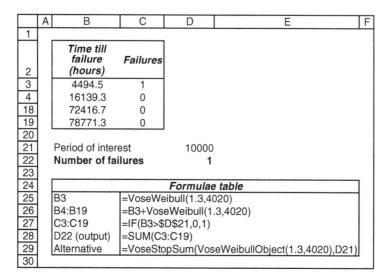

	A	B	C	D	E	F
1						
2		Time till failure (hours)	Failures			
3		4494.5	1			
4		16139.3	0			
18		72416.7	0			
19		78771.3	0			
20						
21		Period of interest		10000		
22		**Number of failures**		**1**		
23						
24				*Formulae table*		
25		B3	=VoseWeibull(1.3,4020)			
26		B4:B19	=B3+VoseWeibull(1.3,4020)			
27		C3:C19	=IF(B3>$D$21,0,1)			
28		D22 (output)	=SUM(C3:C19)			
29		Alternative	=VoseStopSum(VoseWeibullObject(1.3,4020),D21)			
30						

Figure 8.13   Model solution to Example 8.1(a).

	B	C	E	F	H	I	K	L	N	O
2	Time till failure (hours)	Failures	Time till failure (hours)	Failures	Time till failure (hours)	Failures	Time till failure (hours)	Failures	Time till failure (hours)	Failures
3	8560.8	0	1025.5	0	2734.5	0	4714.3	0	5488.5	0
4	8724.7	0	1894.2	0	3666.0	0	6159.8	0	14595.0	0
18	67130.4	0	69131.3	0	81390.4	0	43589.5	0	76693.1	0
19	68644.5	0	75706.3	0	82431.2	0	47222.3	0	81471.4	0
21	Time till failure (hours)	Failures	Time till failure (hours)	Failures	Time till failure (hours)	Failures	Time till failure (hours)	Failures	Time till failure (hours)	Failures
22	11102.1	0	352.1	1	4105.7	0	211.9	1	2011.3	0
23	11285.4	0	904.2	1	17911.3	0	391.1	1	3705.2	0
37	59256.1	0	38672.3	0	61940.7	0	69658.0	0	62324.3	0
38	66475.1	0	40089.5	0	71997.9	0	71679.4	0	69154.5	0

	B	C								
41	Period of interest	1000								
42	**Number of failures**	**4**								

44		*Formulae table*
45	B3, E3, etc.	=VoseWeibull(1.3,4020)
46	B4:B19, E4:E19, etc.	=B3+VoseWeibull(1.3,4020)
47	C4:C19, F4:F19, etc.	=IF(B3>$E$41,0,1)
48	E42 (output)	=SUM(C3:C19,F3:F19,I3:I19,L3:L19,O3:O19,C22:C38,F22:F38,I22:I38,L22:L38,O22:O38)

Figure 8.14   Model solution to Example 8.1(b).

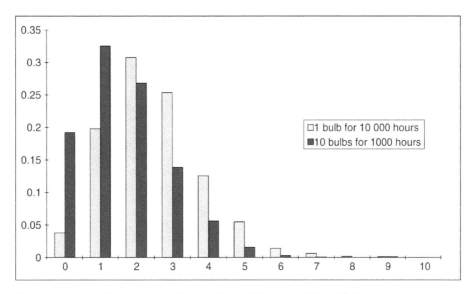

Figure 8.15   Comparison of results from the models of Figures 8.13 and 8.14.

8.7 Mixture Distributions

Sometimes a stochastic process can be a combination of two or more separate processes. For example, car accidents at some particular place and time could be considered to be a Poisson variable, but the mean number of accidents per unit time λ may be a variable too, as we have seen in Section 8.3.7.

A mixture distribution can be written symbolically as follows:

$$F_A \widehat{\Theta} F_B$$

where F_A represents the base distribution and F_B represents the mixing distribution, i.e. the distribution of Θ. So, for example, we might have

$$\text{Poisson}(\lambda) \; \hat{\lambda} \; \text{Gamma}(\alpha, \beta)$$

which reads as "a gamma mixture of Poisson distributions".

There are a number of commonly used mixture distributions. For example

$$\text{Binomial}(n, \; p) \; \hat{p} \; \text{Beta}(\alpha, \; \beta)$$

which is the Beta$-$Binomial(n, α, β) distribution, and

$$\text{Poisson}(\lambda) \; \widehat{\lambda/\Phi} \; \text{Beta}(\alpha, \; \beta)$$

where the Poisson distribution has parameter $\lambda = \phi \cdot p$, and $p = \text{Beta}(\alpha, \beta)$. [Though also used in biology, this should not be confused with the beta$-$Poisson dose$-$response model.]

The cumulative distribution function for a mixture distribution with parameters θ_i is given by

$$E[F(X|\theta_1, \theta_2, \ldots, \theta_m)]$$

where the expectation is with respect to the parameters that are random variables. Thus, the functional form of mixture distributions can quickly become extremely complicated or even intractable. However, Monte Carlo simulation allows us very simply to include mixture distributions in our model, providing the Monte Carlo software being used (for example, @RISK, Crystal Ball, ModelRisk) generates samples for each iteration in the correct logical sequence. So, for example, a Beta–Binomial(n, α, β) distribution is easily generated by writing =Binomial$(n, \text{Beta}(\alpha, \beta))$. In each iteration, the software generates a value first from the beta distribution, then creates the appropriate binomial distribution using this value of p and finally samples from that binomial distribution.

8.8 Martingales

A martingale is a stochastic process with sequential variables $X_i (i = 1, 2, \ldots)$, where the expected value of each variable is the same and independent of previous observations. Written more formally

$$E[X_{n+1}] = E[X_{n+1}|X_1, \ldots, X_n] = E[X_n]$$

Thus, a martingale is any stochastic process with a constant mean. The theory was originally developed to demonstrate the fairness of gambling games, i.e. to show that the expected winnings of each turn of a game were constant; for example, to show that remembering the cards that had already been played in previous hands of a card game wouldn't impact upon your expected winnings. [Next time a friend says to you "21 hasn't come up in the lottery numbers for ages, so it must show soon", you can tell him or her "Not true, I'm afraid, it's a martingale" – they'll be sure finally to understand]. However, the theory has proven to be of considerable value in many real-world problems.

A martingale gets its name from the gambling "system" of doubling your bet on each loss of an even odds bet (e.g. betting Red or Impaire at the roulette wheel) until you have a win. It works too – well, in theory anyway. You must have a huge bankroll, and the casino must have no bet limit. It gives low returns for high risk, so as risk analysis consultants we would advise you to invest in (gamble on) the stock market instead.

8.9 Miscellaneous Examples

I have given below a few example problems for different random processes discussed in this chapter to give you some practice.

8.9.1 Binomial process problems

In addition to the problems below, the reader will find the binomial process appearing in the following examples distributed through this book: examples in Sections 4.3.1, 4.3.2 and 5.4.6 and Examples 22.2 to 22.6, 22.8 and 22.10, as well as many places in Chapter 9.

Example 8.2 Wine sampling

Two wine experts are each asked to guess the year of 20 different wines. Expert A guesses 11 correctly, while expert B guesses 14 correctly. How confident can we be that expert B is really better at this exercise than expert A?

If we allow that the guess of the year for each wine tasted is independent of every other guess, we can assume this to be a binomial process. We are thus interested in whether the probability of one expert guessing correctly is greater than the other's. We can model our uncertainty about the true probability of success for expert A as Beta(12, 10) and for expert B as Beta(15, 7). The model in Figure 8.16 then randomly samples from the two distributions and cell C5 returns a 1 if the distribution for expert B has a greater value than the distribution for expert A. We run a simulation on this cell, and the mean result equals the percentage of time that the distribution for expert B generated a higher value than for expert A, and thus represents our confidence that expert B is indeed better at this exercise. In this case, we are 83 % confident. ♦

Example 8.3 Run of luck

If I toss a coin 10 times, what is the distribution of the maximum number of heads I will get in a row? The solution is provided in the spreadsheet model of Figure 8.17. ♦

Example 8.4 Multiple-choice exam

A multiple-choice exam gives three options for each of 50 questions. One student scores 21 out of 50. (a) What is the probability that the student would have achieved this score or higher without knowing anything about the subject? (b) Estimate how many questions to which the student actually knew the answer.

(a)   The student has a 1/3 probability of getting any answer right without knowing anything, and his or her possible score would then follow a Binomial(50, 1/3) distribution. The probability that the student would have achieved 21/50 or higher is then $= 1 - \text{BINOMDIST}(20, 50, 1/3, 1)$, i.e. (1 – the probability of achieving 20 or lower).

	A	B	C	D
1				
2			Probability of correct answer	
3		Expert A	51.40%	
4		Expert B	75.88%	
5		B is better?	1	
6				
7		**Formulae table**		
8		C3	=Beta(12,10)	
9		C4	=Beta(15, 7)	
10		C5 (output)	=IF(C4>C3,1,0)	
11				

Figure 8.16   Model for Example 8.2.

	A	B	C	D	E
1					
2			Result	Logic	
3		Toss 1	0	0	
4		Toss 2	1	1	
5		Toss 3	1	2	
6		Toss 4	1	3	
7		Toss 5	0	0	
8		Toss 6	1	1	
9		Toss 7	0	0	
10		Toss 8	1	1	
11		Toss 9	0	0	
12		Toss 10	0	0	
13					
14		**Max heads in a row**		**3**	
15					
16			**Formulae table**		
17		C3:C12	=Binomial(1,0.5)		
18		D3	=IF(C3=1,1,0)		
19		D4:D12	=IF(C4=1,D3+1,0)		
20		D14 (output)	=MAX(D3:D12)		
21					

Figure 8.17   Model for Example 8.3.

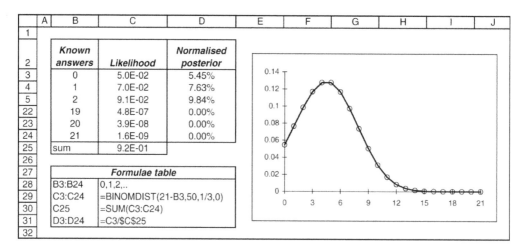

	A	B	C	D	E	F	G	H	I	J
1										
2		*Known answers*	*Likelihood*	*Normalised posterior*						
3		0	5.0E-02	5.45%						
4		1	7.0E-02	7.63%						
5		2	9.1E-02	9.84%						
22		19	4.8E-07	0.00%						
23		20	3.9E-08	0.00%						
24		21	1.6E-09	0.00%						
25		sum	9.2E-01							
26										
27			*Formulae table*							
28		B3:B24	0,1,2,..							
29		C3:C24	=BINOMDIST(21-B3,50,1/3,0)							
30		C25	=SUM(C3:C24)							
31		D3:D24	=C3/$C$25							
32										

Figure 8.18   Model for Example 8.4(b).

(b)   This is a Bayesian problem. Figure 8.18 illustrates a spreadsheet model of the Bayesian inference with a flat prior and a binomial likelihood function. The imbedded graph is the posterior distribution of our belief about how many questions the student actually knew.   ◆

8.9.2 Poisson process problems

In addition to the problems below, the reader will find the Poisson process appearing in the following examples distributed through this book: examples in Sections 9.2.2 and 9.3.2 and Examples 9.6, 9.11, 22.12, 22.14 and 22.16.

Example 8.5 Insurance problem

My company insures aeroplanes. They crash at a rate of 0.23 crashes per month. Each crash costs $Lognormal(120, 52) million. (a) What is the distribution of cost to the company for the next 5 years? (b) What is the distribution of the value of the liability if I discount it at the risk-free rate of 5 %?

The solution to part (a) is provided in the spreadsheet model of Figure 8.19, which uses the VLOOKUP Excel function. Part (b) requires that one know the time at which each accident occurred, using exponential distributions. The solution is shown in Figure 8.20. ◆

Example 8.6 Rainwater barrel problem

It is a monsoon and rain is falling at a rate of 270 drops per second per square metre. The rain drops each contain 1 millilitre of water. If I have a drum standing in the rain, measuring 1 metre high and 0.3 metres radius, how long will it be before the drum is full?

The solution is provided in the spreadsheet model of Figure 8.21. ◆

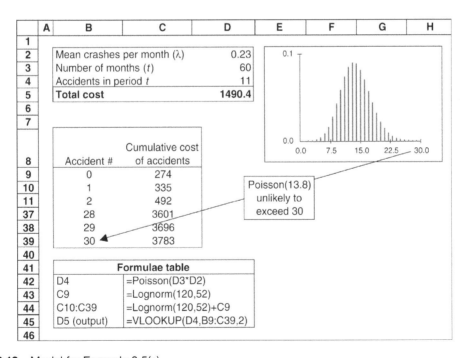

Figure 8.19 Model for Example 8.5(a).

	A	B	C	D	E
1					
2		Mean crashes per month (λ)		0.23	
3		Number of months (t)		60	
4		Risk free interest rate		5%	
5		**Total cost ($M)**		**1244.9**	
6					
7					
8		Time of accident (months)	Cost of accidents ($M)	Discounted cost ($M)	
9		5.105	158	154.69	
10		7.270	115	111.85	
11		13.338	63	59.93	
37		102.497	0	0.00	
38		105.567	0	0.00	
39		113.070	0	0.00	
40					
41			**Formulae table**		
42		B9	=Expon(1/$D$2)		
43		B10:B39	=Expon(1/$D$2)+B9		
44		C9:C39	=IF(B9>$D$3,0,Lognorm(120,52))		
45		D9:D39	=C9/((1+$D$4)^(B9/12))		
46		D5 (output)	=SUM(D9:D39)		
47					

Figure 8.20   Model for Example 8.5(b).

	A	B	C	D	E
1					
2			Drum height (m)	1	
3			Drum radius (m)	0.3	
4			Drum volume (m^3)	0.283	
5			Drops falling per second into barrel	76.341	
6			Number of raindrops needed to fill barrel	282744	
7			Time to wait to fill barrel (seconds)	3714.0	
8			Time to wait (hours)	1.032	
9					
10			**Formulae table**		
11		D4	=PI()*D3^2*D2		
12		D5	=PI()*D3^2*270		
13		D6	=ROUNDUP(D4/0.000001,0)		
14		D7	=Gamma(D6,1/D5)		
15		D8 (output)	=D7/3600		
16					

Figure 8.21   Model for Example 8.6.

Example 8.7   Equipment reliability

A piece of electronic equipment is composed of six components A to F. They have the mean time between failures shown in Table 8.4. The components are in serial and parallel configuration as shown in Figure 8.22. What is the probability that the machine will fail within 250 hours?

Table 8.4 Mean time
between failures of electronic
equipment components.

Component	MTBF (hours)
A	332
B	459
C	412
D	188
E	299
F	1234

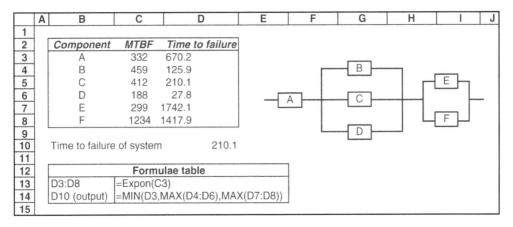

Figure 8.22 Model for Example 8.7.

We first assume that the components will fail with a constant probability per unit time, i.e. that their times to failure will be exponentially distributed, which is a reasonable assumption implied by the MTBF figure. The problem belongs to reliability engineering. Components in series make the machine fail if any of the components in series fail. For parallel components, all components in parallel must fail before the machine fails. Thus, from Figure 8.22 the machine will fail if A fails, or B, C and D all fail, or E and F both fail. Figure 8.22 also shows the spreadsheet modelling the time to failure. Running a simulation with 10 000 iterations on cell D10 gives an output distribution of which 63.5 % of the trials were less than 250 hours. ◆

8.9.3 Hypergeometric process problems

In addition to the problems below, the reader will find the hypergeometric process appearing in the following examples distributed through this book: examples in Sections 22.4.2 and 22.4.4, as well as Examples 9.2, 9.3, 22.4, 22.6 and 22.8.

Example 8.8 Equal selection

I am to pick out at random 10 names from each of two bags. The first bag contains the names of 15 men and 22 women. The second bag contains the names of 12 men and 15 women. (a) What is the probability that I will have the same proportion of men in the two selections? (b) How many times would I have to sample from these bags before I did have the same proportion?

(a)   The solution can be worked out mathematically or by simulation. Figure 8.23 provides the mathematical calculation and Figure 8.24 provides a simulation model, where the required probability is the mean of the output result.

A	B	C	D	E	F
1					
2		Bag 1	Bag 2		
3	n (sample size)	10	10		
4	D (men)	15	12		
5	M (men & women)	37	27		
6					
7			Probability		
8	Men in sample	Bag 1	Bag 2	Both	
9	0	0.19%	0.04%	0.00%	
10	1	2.14%	0.71%	0.02%	
11	2	9.64%	5.03%	0.49%	
12	3	22.28%	16.78%	3.74%	
13	4	29.24%	29.37%	8.59%	
14	5	22.70%	28.19%	6.40%	
15	6	10.51%	14.95%	1.57%	
16	7	2.84%	4.27%	0.12%	
17	8	0.43%	0.62%	0.00%	
18	9	0.03%	0.04%	0.00%	
19	10	0.00%	0.00%	0.00%	
20	**Total probability of same in each bag**			**20.93%**	
21					
22		Formulae table			
23	C9:D19	=HYPGEOMDIST($B9,C$3,C$4,C$5)			
24	E9:E19	=C9*D9			
25	E20 (output)	=SUM(E9:E19)			
26					

Figure 8.23   Mathematical model for Example 8.8.

A	B	C	D	E
1				
2		Bag 1	Bag 2	
3	n (sample size)	10	10	
4	D (men)	15	12	
5	M (men & women)	37	27	
6				
7	Number of men from bag	4	4	
8	**Probability flag**	1		
9				
10		Formulae table		
11	C7:D7	=Hypergeo(C3,C4,C5)		
12	C8 (output - p=o/p mean)	=IF(C7=D7,1,0)		
13				

Figure 8.24   Simulation model for Example 8.8.

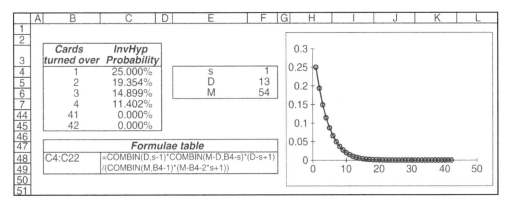

Figure 8.25   Model for Example 8.9.

(b)   Each trial is independent of every other, so the number of trials before one success $= 1 + \text{NegBin}$
   $(1, p) = 1 + \text{Geometric}(p)$, where p is the probability calculated from part (a). ◆

Example 8.9 Playing cards

How many cards in a well-shuffled pack, complete with jokers, do I need to turn over to see a heart?

There are 54 $(= M)$ cards, of which 13 $(= D)$ are hearts, and I am looking for $s = 1$ heart. The number of cards I must turn over is given by the formula $1 + \text{InvHyp}(1, 13, 54)$, which is the distribution shown in Figure 8.25. ◆

Example 8.10 Faulty tyres

A tyre manufacturer has accidentally mixed up four tyres from a faulty batch with 20 other good tyres. Testing a tyre for the fault ruins it. If each tyre cost \$75, and if the tyres are tested one at a time until the four faulty tyres are found, how much will this mistake cost?

The solution is provided in the spreadsheet model of Figure 8.26. ◆

8.9.4 Renewal and mixed process problems

In addition to the problems below, Examples 12.8 and 12.9 also deal with renewal and mixed process problems.

Example 8.11 Batteries

A certain brand of batteries lasts Weibull(2,27) hours in my CD player, which takes two batteries at a time. I have a pack of 10 batteries. For how long can I run my CD player, given that I replace all batteries when one has run down?

The solution is provided in the spreadsheet model of Figure 8.27. ◆

Example 8.12 Queuing at a bank (Visual Basic modelling with Monte Carlo simulation)

A post office has one counter that it recognises is insufficient for its customer volume. It is considering putting in another counter and wishes to model the effect on the maximum number in a queue at any one time. They are open from 9 a.m. to 5 p.m. each working day. Past data show that, when the doors

	A	B	C	D	E	F	G
1							
2							
3		*Possible* *tested tyres*	*InvHyp* *Probability*				
4		0	0.014%				
5		1	0.055%		s	4	
6		2	0.137%		D	4	
7		3	0.273%		M	22	
8		4	0.478%				
20		16	13.247%				
21		17	15.584%		Tyres actually tested	21	
22		18	18.182%		Total cost	1575	
23							
24			*Formulae table*				
25		C4:C22	=COMBIN(D,s-1)*COMBIN(M-D,B4)*(D-s+1)				
26			/(COMBIN(M,B4+s-1)*(M-B4-s+1))				
27		F21	=D+Discrete(B4:B22,C4:C22)				
28		F22 (output)	=F21*75				
29							

Figure 8.26   Model for Example 8.10.

	A	B	C	D	E	F
1						
2			Battery 1	Battery 2	Hours of play	
3		Set 1	44.75	32.23	32.23	
4		Set 2	17.00	1.82	1.82	
5		Set 3	13.93	3.06	3.06	
6		Set 4	35.32	45.50	35.32	
7		Set 5	51.05	15.93	15.93	
8				Total	88.36	
9						
10			Formulae table			
11		C3:D7	=Weibull(2,27)			
12		E3:E7	=MIN(C3:D3)			
13		E8 (output)	=SUM(E3:E7)			
14						

Figure 8.27   Model for Example 8.11.

open at 9 a.m., the number of people waiting to come in will be as shown in Table 8.5. People arrive throughout the day at a constant rate of one every 12 minutes. The amount of time it takes to serve each person is Lognormal(29, 23) minutes. What is the maximum queue size in a day?

This problem requires that one simulate a day, monitor the maximum queue size during the day and then repeat the simulation. One thus builds up a distribution of the maximum number in a queue. The solution provided in Figures 8.28 and 8.29 and in the following program runs a looping Visual Basic macro called "Main Program" at each iteration of the model. This is an advanced technique and, although this problem is very simple, one can see how it can be greatly extended. For example, one could change the rate of arrival of the customers to be a function of the time of day; one could add

Table 8.5 Historic data
on the number of people
waiting at the start of the
business day.

People	Probability
0	0.6
1	0.2
2	0.1
3	0.05
4	0.035
5	0.015

	A	B	C	D	E	F	G
1							
2		*Inputs*					
3		Average interarrival time (mins)	12				
4		Serving time mean	29				
5		Serving time stdev	23				
6							
7		*Model*					
8		People in queue	12				
9		Time of day (minutes from 00:00:00)	1037.92				
10			Customer	Arrive time	Serving time	Finish time	
11		Latest customer at counter 1	0	997.24	40.68	1037.92	
12		Latest customer at counter 2	0	1006.16	36.58	1042.74	
13							
14		*Outputs*					
15		Total customers served	35				
16		Maximum number in queue	18				
17							
18		Formulae table					
19		C8:C9, C11:E12, C15:C16	Values updated by macro				
20		F11:F12	=E11 + D11				
21							

Figure 8.28 Sheet "model" for the model for Example 8.12.

more counters, and one could monitor other statistical parameters aside from the maximum queue size, like the maximum amount of time any one person waits or the amount of free time the people working behind the counter have. ◆

Visual Basic macro for Example 8.12

```
'Set model variables
Dim modelWS As Object
Dim variableWS As Object
Sub Main_Program()
Set modelWS = Workbooks("queue_model_test.xls").Worksheets("model")
Set variableWS = Workbooks("queue_model_test.xls").Worksheets("variables")
'Reset the model with the starting values
  modelWS.Range("c9").Value = 9 * 60
```

	A	B	C	D
1	Label	Random Variable		
2	Counter serving time (min)	7.86		
3				
4	Customers arriving while serving	2		
5				
6	Wait time for next customer	57.03		
7				
8	People waiting at 9:00 a.m.	0		
9				
10	Time in last step	31.76		
11				
12		Formulae table		
13	B2	=Lognorm(Model!$C$4,Model!$C$5)		
14	B4	=IF(B10=0,0,Poisson(B10/Model!C3))		
15	B6	=Expon(Model!C3)		
16	B8	=Discrete({0,1,2,3,4,5},{0.6,0.2,0.1,0.05,0.035,0.015})		
17	B10	Value updated by macro		
18				

Figure 8.29 Sheet "variables" for the model for Example 8.12.

```
  modelWS.Range("C15,C11:E12").Value = 0
  modelWS.Range("c8") = variableWS.Range("b8").Value
  Application.Calculate
  modelWS.Range("c16") = modelWS.Range("c8").Value
'Start serving customers
  Serve_First_Customer
  Serve_Next_Customer
End Sub
Sub Serve_First_Customer()
'Serve at counter 1 if 0 ppl in queue
If modelWS.Range("c8") = 0 Then
  modelWS.Range("c9") = modelWS.Range("c9").Value + variableWS.
    Range("b6").Value
  modelWS.Range("c8") = 1
  Application.Calculate
  'MsgBox ~wait 1"
  Routine_A
End If
'Serve at counter 1 if 1 person in queue
If modelWS.Range("c8") = 1 Then
  Routine_A
End If
'Serve at counter 1 and 2 if 2 or more ppl in queue
If modelWS.Range("c8") > = 2 Then
  Routine_A
  Routine_B
End If
End Sub
Sub Serve_Next_Customer()
'Calculate the new time of day
variableWS.Range("b10") = Evaluate(" = Max(Model!C9,Min(model!F11,model!F12))- Model!C9")
modelWS.Range("c8") = modelWS.Range("c8").Value + variableWS.Range("B4"). Value
'Calculate the maximum number of people left in queue
```

```
modelWS.Range("C16") = Evaluate(" = max(model!c16,model!c8)")
Application.Calculate
modelWS.Range("c9") = modelWS.Range("c9").Value + variableWS.Range("B10"). Value
Application.Calculate
'MsgBox  wait 3"
'Check how many ppl are in queue
If modelWS.Range("c8") = 0 Then
  modelWS.Range("c9") = modelWS.Range("c9").Value + variableWS.
    Range("b6").Value
  modelWS.Range("c8") = 1
End If
  Application.Calculate
If modelWS.Range("c9") > 1020 Then Exit Sub
If modelWS.Range("f11") < = modelWS.Range("f12") Then
  Routine_A
Else
  Routine_B
End If
  Application.Calculate
  Serve_Next_Customer
End Sub
'Next customer for counter 1
Sub Routine_A()
  modelWS.Range("c11") = 1
  modelWS.Range("D11") = modelWS.Range("c9").Value
  Application.Calculate
  modelWS.Range("e11") = variableWS.Range("B2").Value
  modelWS.Range("c15") = modelWS.Range("c15").Value + 1
  modelWS.Range("c8") = modelWS.Range("c8").Value - 1
  modelWS.Range("C11") = 0
  Application.Calculate
End Sub
'Next customer for counter 2
Sub Routine_B()
  modelWS.Range("c12") = 1
  modelWS.Range("d12") = modelWS.Range("c9").Value
  Application.Calculate
  modelWS.Range("e12") = variableWS.Range("B2").Value
  modelWS.Range("c15") = modelWS.Range("c15") + 1
  modelWS.Range("c8") = modelWS.Range("c8") - 1
  modelWS.Range("C12") = 0
  Application.Calculate
End Sub
```

Chapter 9

Data and statistics

Statistics is the discipline of fitting probability models to data. In this chapter I go through a number of basic statistical techniques from the simple z-tests and t-tests of the classical statistics world, through the basic ideas behind Bayesian statistics and looking at the application of simulation in statistics – the bootstrap for classical statistics and Markov chain Monte Carlo modelling for Bayesian statistics. If you have some statistics training you may think my approach is rather inconsistent, as I have no problems with using Bayesian and classical methods in the same model in spite of the philosophical inconsistencies between them. That's because classical statistics is still the most readily accepted type of statistical analysis – so a model using these methods is less contentious among certain audiences, but on the other hand Bayesian statistics can solve more problems. Moreover, Bayesian statistics is more consistent with risk analysis modelling because we need to simulate uncertainty about model parameters so that we can see how that uncertainty propagates through a model to affect our ability to predict the outputs of interest, not just quote confidence intervals.

There are a few key messages I would like you to take away from this chapter. The first is that statistics is subjective: the choice of model that we are fitting to our data is a highly subjective decision. Even the most established statistical tests, like the z-test, t-test, F-test, chi-square test and regression models, have at their heart the (subjective) assumption that the underlying variable is normally distributed – which is very rarely the truth. These tests are really old – a hundred years old – and came to be used so much because one could restructure a number of basic problems into a form of one of these tests and look up the confidence values in published tables. We don't use tables anymore – well, we shouldn't anyway – they aren't very accurate and even basic software like Excel can give you the answers directly. It's rather strange, then, that statistics books often still publish such tables.

The second key message is that statistics does not need to be a black box. With a little understanding of probability models, it can become quite intuitive.

The third is that there is ample room in statistics for creative thinking. If you have access to simulation methods, you are freed from having to find the right "test" for your particular problem. Most real-world problems are too complex for standardised statistical testing.

The fourth is that statistics is intimately related to probability modelling. You won't understand statistics until you've understood probability theory, so learn that first.

And lastly, statistics can be really quite a lot of fun as well as very informative. It's rare that a person coming to one of our courses is excited about the statistics part, and I can't blame them, but I like to think that they change their mind by the end. I studied mathematics and physics at undergraduate level and came away with really no useful appreciation of statistics, just a solid understanding of how astonishingly boring it was, because statistics was taught to me as a set of rules and equations, and any explanation of "Why?" was far beyond what we could hope to understand (at the same time we were learning about general relativity theory, quantum electrodynamics, etc.).

At the beginning of this book, I discussed the importance of being able to distinguish between uncertainty (or epistemic uncertainty) and variability (or stochastic uncertainty). This chapter lays out a number of techniques that enable one quantitatively to describe the uncertainty (epistemic uncertainty) associated with the parameters of a model. Uncertainty is a function of the risk analyst, inasmuch as it is the description of the state of knowledge the risk analyst's clients have about particular parameters within his or her model.

A quantitative risk analysis model is structured around modelling the variability (randomness) of the world. However, we have imperfect knowledge of the parameters that define that model, so we must estimate their values from data, and, because we have only finite amounts of data, there will remain some uncertainty that we have to layer over our probability model. This chapter is concerned with determining the distributions of uncertainty for these parameters.

I will assume that the analyst has somehow accumulated a set of data $X = \{x_1, x_2, \ldots, x_n\}$ of n data points that has been obtained in some manner as to be considered a random sample from a random process. The purpose of this chapter will be to determine the level of uncertainty, given these available data, associated with some parameter or parameters of the probability model.

It will be useful here to set out some simple terminology:

- The estimate of some statistical parameter of the parent distribution with true (but unknown) value, say β, is denoted by a hat, e.g. $\hat{\beta}$.

- The sample mean of the dataset X is denoted by $\bar{x}$, i.e. $\bar{x} = \dfrac{1}{n} \sum_{i=1}^{n} x_i$.

- The (unbiased) sample standard deviation of the dataset X is denoted by s, i.e.

$$s = \sqrt{\frac{\sum_{i=1}^{n} (x_i - \bar{x})^2}{n - 1}}.$$

- The true mean and standard deviation of the population distribution are denoted by μ and σ respectively.

9.1 Classical Statistics

The classical statistics techniques we all know (or at least remember we were once taught) are the z-test, t-test and chi-square test. They allow us to estimate the mean and variance of a random variable for which we have some randomly sampled data, as well as a number of other problems. I'm going to offer some fairly simple ways of understanding these statistical tests, but I first want to explain why the "tests" aren't much good to us as risk analysts in their standard form. Let's take a typical t-test result: it will say something like the true mean $= 9.63$ with a 95% confidence interval of [9.32, 9.94], meaning that we are 95% sure that the true mean lies between 9.32 and 9.94. It doesn't mean that there is a 95% probability that it will lie within these values – it either does or does not, what we are describing is how well *we* (the data holders, i.e. it is subjective) know the mean value. In risk analysis I may have several such parameters in my model. Let's say we have just three such parameters A, B and C estimated from different datasets and each with its best estimate and 95% confidence bound. Let the model be $A^*B^\wedge(1/C)$. How can I combine these numbers to make an estimate of the uncertainty of my calculation? The answer is I can't. However, if I could convert the estimates to distributions I could perform a Monte Carlo simulation and get the answer at any confidence interval, or any percentile the decision-maker wishes. Thus, we have to convert these classical tests to distributions of uncertainty.

The classical statistics tests above are based on two basic statistical principles:

1. *The pivotal method*. This requires that I rearrange an equation so that the parameter being estimated is separated from any random variable.

2. *A sufficient statistic*. This means a sample statistic calculated from the data that contains all the information in the data that is related to estimating the parameter.

I'll use these ideas to explain the tests above and how they can be converted to uncertainty distributions.

9.1.1 The z-test

The z-test allows us to determine the best estimate and confidence interval for the mean of a normally distributed population *where we happen to know the standard deviation of that population*. That would be quite an unusual situation since the mean is usually more fundamental than the standard deviation, but does occur sometimes; for example, when we take repeated measures of some quantity (like the length of a room, the weight of a beam). In this situation the random variable is not the length of the room, etc., but the results we will get. Look at the manual of a scientific measuring instrument and it should tell you the accuracy (e.g. ± 1 mm). Sadly, the manufacturers don't usually tell us how to interpret these values – will the measurement lie within 1 mm of the true value 68 % (1 standard deviation), 95 % (two standard deviations), etc., of the time? If the instrument manual were to say the measurement error has a standard deviation of 1 mm, we could apply the z-test.

Let's say we are measuring some fixed quantity and that we take n such measurements. The sample mean is given by the formula

$$\overline{x} = \frac{1}{n} \sum_{i=1}^{n} x_i$$

Here $\overline{x}$ is the sufficient statistic. If the errors are normally distributed with mean μ and standard deviation σ we have

$$\overline{x} = \frac{1}{n} \sum_{i=1}^{n} \mathrm{N}(\mu, \sigma) = \frac{1}{n} \mathrm{N}(n\mu, \sigma\sqrt{n}) = \mathrm{N}(0, 1)\frac{\sigma}{\sqrt{n}} + \mu$$

Note how we have managed to rearrange the equation to place the random element Normal(0,1) apart from the parameter we are trying to estimate. Now, thanks to the pivotal method, we can rearrange to make μ the focus:

$$\mu = \mathrm{N}(0, 1)\frac{\sigma}{\sqrt{n}} + \overline{x} = \mathrm{N}\left(\overline{x}, \frac{\sigma}{\sqrt{n}}\right) \tag{9.1}$$

In the z-test we would have specified a confidence interval, say 95 %, and then looked up the "z-score" values for a Normal(0,1) distribution that would correspond to 2.5 % and 97.5 % (i.e. centrally positioned values with 95 % between them) which are -1.95996 and $+1.95996$ respectively.[1] Then we'd write

$$\mu_{\mathrm{L}} = -1.95996\frac{\sigma}{\sqrt{n}} + \overline{x}$$

$$\mu_{\mathrm{H}} = 1.95996\frac{\sigma}{\sqrt{n}} + \overline{x}$$

---

[1] You can get these values with ModelRisk using VoseNormal(0, 1, 0.025) and VoseNormal(0, 1, 0.975) or in Excel with = NORMSINV(0.025) and = NORMSINV(0.975).

to get the lower and upper bounds respectively. In a risk analysis simulation we just use

$$\mu = \text{VoseNormal}\left(\bar{x}, \frac{\sigma}{\sqrt{n}}\right)$$

9.1.2 The chi-square test

The chi-square (χ^2) test allows us to determine the best estimate and confidence interval for the standard deviation of a normally distributed population. There are two situations: we either know the mean μ or we don't. Knowing the mean seems like an unusual scenario but happens, for example, when we are calibrating a measuring device against some known standard. In this case, the formula for the sample variance is given by

$$V_s = \frac{1}{n}\sum_{i=1}^{n}(x_i - \mu)^2$$

The sample variance in this case is the sufficient statistic for the population variance. Rewriting to get a pivotal quantity, we have

$$V_s = \frac{\sigma^2}{n}\sum_{i=1}^{n}N(0, 1)^2$$

However, the sum of n unit normal distributions squared is the definition of a chi-square distribution. Rearranging, we get

$$\sigma^2 = \frac{nV_s}{\chi^2(n)} \tag{9.2}$$

A $\chi^2(n)$ distribution has mean n, so this formula is simply multiplying the sample variance by a random variable with mean 1. The chi-square test finds, say, the 2.5 an 97.5 percentiles[2] and inserts them into the above equation. For example, these percentiles for 10 degrees of freedom are 3.247 and 20.483. Since we are dividing by the chi-square random variable, the upper estimate corresponds to the lower chi-square value, and vice versa:

$$\sigma_L^2 = \frac{nV_s}{20.483}$$

$$\sigma_H^2 = \frac{nV_s}{3.247}$$

In risk analysis modelling we would instead simulate values for σ using Equation 9.2:

$$\sigma = \sqrt{\frac{nV_s}{\text{VoseChiSq}(n)}}$$

---

[2] In ModelRisk use VoseChiSq(n, 0.005) and VoseChiSq(n, 0.975), and in Excel use CHIINV(0.975, n) and CHIINV(0.025, n) respectively.

Now let's consider what happens when we don't know the population mean, in which case statistical convention says that we use a slightly different formula for the sample variance measure:

$$V_s = \frac{1}{n-1} \sum_{i=1}^{n} (x_i - \bar{x})^2$$

However, for a normal distribution it turns out that

$$\sum_{i=1}^{n} (x_i - \bar{x})^2 = \sum_{i=1}^{n-1} (x_i - \mu)^2 = \sigma^2 \sum_{i=1}^{n-1} N(0,1)^2 = \sigma^2 \chi^2(n-1)$$

Rearranging, we get

$$\sigma^2 = \sqrt{\frac{(n-1)V_s}{\text{VoseChiSq}(n-1)}} \tag{9.3}$$

9.1.3 The *t*-test

The *t*-test allows us to determine the best estimate and confidence interval for the mean of a normally distributed population where we don't know its standard deviation. From Equation 9.1 we had the result

$$\mu = N(0,1)\frac{\sigma}{\sqrt{n}} + \bar{x}$$

when the population variance was known, and from Equation 9.2 we had the estimate for the variance when the mean is unknown:

$$\sigma^2 = \frac{(n-1)V_s}{\chi^2(n-1)}$$

Substitute for σ and we get

$$\mu = N(0,1)\sqrt{\frac{(n-1)}{\chi^2(n-1)}\frac{V_s}{n}} + \bar{x}$$

The definition of a Student(ν) distribution is a normal distribution with mean 0 and variance following a random variable $\nu/\text{ChiSq}(\nu)$, so we have

$$\mu = N(0,1)\sqrt{\frac{(n-1)}{\chi^2(n-1)}\frac{V_s}{n}} + \bar{x}$$

$$= N\left(0, \sqrt{\frac{(n-1)}{\chi^2(n-1)}}\right)\frac{V_s}{n} + \bar{x}$$

$$= \text{VoseStudent}(n-1)\frac{V_s}{n} + \bar{x} \tag{9.4}$$

Knowing that the Student t-distribution is just a unit normal distribution with some randomness about the variance explains why a Student distribution has longer tails than a normal. The Student(ν) distribution has variance $\nu/(\nu - 2)$, $\nu > 2$, so at $\nu = 3$ the variance is 3 and rapidly decreases, so that by $\nu = 30$ it is only 1.07 (a standard deviation of 1.035) and for $\nu = 50$ a standard deviation of 1.02. The practical implication is that, when you have, say, 50 data points, there is only a 2 % difference in the confidence interval range whether you use a t-test (Equation 9.4) or approximate with a z-test (Equation 9.1), using the sample variance in place of σ^2.

9.1.4 Estimating a binomial probability or a proportion

In many problems we need to determine a binomial probability (e.g. the probability of a flood in a certain week of the year) or a proportion (e.g. the proportion of components that are made to a certain tolerance). In estimating both, we collect data. Each measurement point is a random variable that has a probability p of having the characteristic of interest. If all measurements are independent, and we assign a value to the measurement of 1 when the measurement has the characteristic of interest and 0 when it does not, the measurements can be thought of as a set of Bernoulli trials. Letting P be the random variable of the proportion of n of this set of trials $\{X_i\}$ that have the characteristic of interest, it will take a distribution given by

$$\hat{p} = \frac{\text{Binomial}(n, p)}{n} \tag{9.5}$$

We observe a proportion of the n trials that have the characteristic of interest $\hat{p}$, our one observation from the random variable P which is also our MLE (see later) and unbiased estimate for p. Switching around Equation (9.5), we can get an uncertainty distribution for the true value of p:

$$p = \frac{\text{Binomial}(n, \hat{p})}{n} \tag{9.6}$$

We shall see later how this exactly equates to the non-parametric and parametric bootstrap estimates of a binomial probability. Equation (9.6) is a bit awkward since it will allow only $(n + 1)$ discrete values for p, i.e. $\{0, 1/n, 2/n, \ldots, (n - 1)/n, 1\}$, whereas our uncertainty about p should really take into account all values between zero and 1. However, a Binomial$(n, \hat{p})$ has a mean and standard deviation given by

$$\mu = n\hat{p}$$

$$\sigma = \sqrt{n\hat{p}(1 - \hat{p})}$$

and, from the central limit theorem, as n gets large the proportion of observations P will tend to a normal distribution, in which case Equation (9.6) can be rewritten as

$$p \approx \text{Normal}(0,1) * \sqrt{\frac{\hat{p}(1 - \hat{p})}{n}} + \hat{p} \tag{9.7}$$

Equation (9.6) gives us what is known as the "exact binomial confidence interval", which is an awful name in my view because it actually gives us bounds for which we have *at least* the required confidence that the true value of p lies within. We never use this method. Another classical statistics method is to construct a cumulative uncertainty distribution, which is far more useful. We start by saying that, if

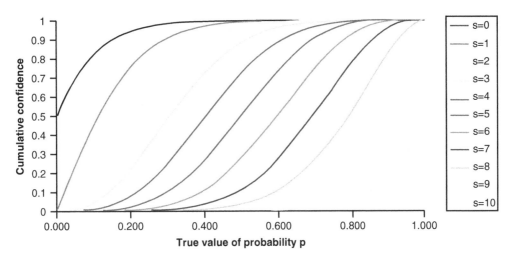

Figure 9.1   Cumulative distributions of estimate of p for $n = 10$ trials and varying number of successes s.

we've observed s successes in n trials, the confidence that the true value of the probability is less than some value x is given by

$$P(Y > s; n, x) + 0.5 * P(Y = s; n, x)$$

where $Y = \text{Binomial}(n, x)$. In Excel we would write

$$= 1 - \text{BINOMDIST}(s, n, x, 1) + 0.5 * \text{BINOMDIST}(s, n, x, 0)$$

By varying the value x from 0 to 1, we can construct the cumulative confidence. For example, Figure 9.1 shows examples with $n = 10$.

This is an interesting method. Look at the scenario for $s = 0$: the cumulative distribution starts with a value of 50 % at $p = 0$, so it is saying that, with no successes observed, we have 50 % confidence that there is no binomial process at all – trials can't become successes, and the remaining 50 % confidence is distributed over $p = (0, 1)$. The reverse logic applies where $s = n$. In ModelRisk we have a function VoseBinomialP(s, n, ProcessExists, U), where you input the successes s and trials n and, in the situation where $s = 0$ or n, you have the option to specify whether you know that the probability lies within $(0, 1)$ (ProcessExists = TRUE). The U-parameter also allows you to specify a cumulative percentile – if omitted, the function simulates random values of what the value p might be. So, for example:

VoseBinomialP(10, 20, TRUE, 0.99) = VoseBinomialP(10, 20, FALSE, 0.99) = 0.74605

VoseBinomialP(0, 20, TRUE, 0.99) = 0.02522 (it assumes that p cannot be zero)

VoseBinomialP(0, 20, FALSE, 0.4) = 0 (it allows that p could be zero)

9.1.5 Estimating a Poisson intensity

In a Poisson process, countable events occur randomly in time or space – like earthquakes, financial crashes, car crashes, epidemics and customer arrivals. We need to estimate the base rate λ at which these events occur. So, for example, a city of 500 000 people may have had α murders last year: perhaps that was unluckily high, or luckily low. We'd like to know the degree of accuracy that we can place around the statement "The risk is α murders per year". Following a classical statistics approach similar to section 9.1.4, we could write

$$\hat{\lambda} = \frac{\text{Poisson}(\alpha)}{1}$$

where 1 refers to the single year of counting.

We could recognise that a Poisson(α) distribution has mean and variance $= \alpha$ and looks normal when α is large:

$$\hat{\lambda} \approx \frac{\text{Normal}(\alpha, \sqrt{\alpha})}{1}$$

The method suffers the same problems as the binomial: if we haven't yet observed any murders this year, the formulae don't work. A classical statistics alternative is again to construct the cumulative confidence distribution using

$$= 1 - \text{POISSON}(\alpha, 1, 1) + 0.5 * \text{POISSON}(\alpha, 1, 0)$$

Figure 9.2 shows some examples of the cumulative distribution that can be constructed from this formula. In ModelRisk there is a function VosePoissonLambda(α, t, ProcessExists, U) where you input the counts α and the time over which they have been observed t, and in the situation where $\alpha = 0$ you have the option to specify whether you know that the intensity is non-zero (ProcessExists = TRUE). The U-parameter also allows you to specify a cumulative percentile – if omitted, the function simulates random values of what the value λ might be. So, for example:

$$\text{VosePoissonLambda}(2, 3, \text{TRUE}, 0.2) = \text{VosePoissonLambda}(2, 3, \text{FALSE}, 0.4)$$

$$= 0.36634$$

$$\text{VosePoissonLambda}(0, 3, \text{TRUE}, 0.2) = 0.203324 \text{ (it assumes that } \lambda \text{ cannot be zero)}$$

$$\text{VoseBinomialP}(0, 20, \text{FALSE}, 0.2) = 0 \text{ (it allows that } \lambda \text{ could be zero)}$$

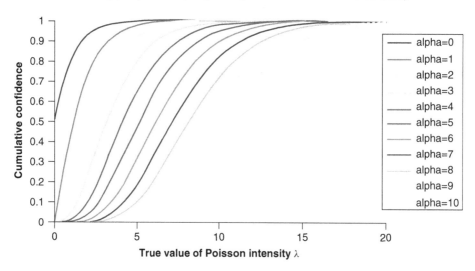

Figure 9.2 Cumulative distributions of estimate of λ for varying number of observations α.

9.2 Bayesian Inference

The Bayesian approach to statistics has enjoyed something of a renaissance over the latter half of the twentieth century, but there still remains a schism among the scientific community over the Bayesian position. Many scientists, and particularly many classically trained statisticians, believe that science should be objective and therefore dislike any methodology that is based on subjectivism. There are, of course, a host of counterarguments. Experimental design is subjective to begin with; classical statistics are limited in that they make certain assumptions (normally distributed errors or populations, for example) and scientists have to use their judgement in deciding whether such an assumption is sufficiently well met; moreover, at the end of a statistical analysis one is often asked to accept or reject a hypothesis by picking (quite subjectively) a level of significance (p values).

For the risk analyst, subjectivism is a fact of life. Each model one builds is only an approximation of the real world. Decisions about the structure and acceptable accuracy of the risk analyst's model are very subjective. Added to all this, the risk analyst must very often rely on subjective estimates for many model inputs, frequently without *any* data to back them up.

Bayesian inference is an extremely powerful technique, based on Bayes' theorem (sometimes called Bayes' formula), for using data to improve one's estimate of a parameter. There are essentially three steps involved: (1) determining a prior estimate of the parameter in the form of a confidence distribution; (2) finding an appropriate likelihood function for the observed data; (3) calculating the posterior (i.e. revised) estimate of the parameter by multiplying the prior distribution and the likelihood function, then normalising so that the result is a true distribution of confidence (i.e. the area under the curve equals 1).

The first part of this section introduces the concept and provides some simple examples. The second part explains how to determine prior distributions. The third part looks more closely at likelihood functions, and the fourth part explains how normalising of the posterior distribution is carried out.

9.2.1 Introduction

Bayesian inference is based on Bayes' theorem (Section 6.3.5), the logic of which was first proposed in Bayes (1763). Bayes' theorem states that

$$P(A_i|B) = \frac{P(B|A_i)P(A_i)}{\sum_{j=1}^{n} P(B|A_j)P(A_j)}$$

We will change the notation of that formula for the purpose of explaining Bayesian inference to a notation often used in the Bayesian world:

$$f(\theta|\boldsymbol{x}) = \frac{\pi(\theta)l(\boldsymbol{x}|\theta)}{\int \pi(\theta)l(\boldsymbol{x}|\theta)\,d\theta} \tag{9.8}$$

Bayesian inference mathematically describes the learning process. We start off with an opinion, however vague, and then modify our opinion when presented with evidence. The components of Equation (9.8) are:

- $\pi(\theta)$ – the "prior distribution". $\pi(\theta)$ is the density function of our prior belief about the parameter value θ before we have observed the data x. In other words, $\pi(\theta)$ is not a *probability* distribution of θ but rather an uncertainty distribution: it is an adequate representation of the state of our *knowledge* about θ before the data $\boldsymbol{x}$ were observed.

- $l(\boldsymbol{x}|\theta)$ – the "likelihood function". $l(\boldsymbol{x}|\theta)$ is the calculated probability of randomly observing the data $\boldsymbol{x}$ for a given value of θ. The *shape* of the likelihood function embodies the amount of *information* contained in the data. If the information it contains is small, the likelihood function will be broadly distributed, whereas if the information it contains is large, the likelihood function will be very focused around some particular value of the parameter. However, if the shape of the likelihood function corresponds strongly to the prior distribution, the amount of *extra* information the likelihood function embodies is relatively small and the posterior distribution will not differ greatly from the prior. In other words, one would not have learned very much from the data. On the other hand, if the shape of the likelihood function is very different from the prior we will have learned a lot from the data.

- $f(\theta|\boldsymbol{x})$ – the "posterior distribution". $f(\theta|\boldsymbol{x})$ is the description of our state of knowledge of θ after we have observed the data $\boldsymbol{x}$ and given our opinion of the value of θ before $\boldsymbol{x}$ was observed.

The denominator in Equation (9.8) simply normalises the posterior distribution to have a total area equal to 1. Since the denominator is simply a scalar value and not a function of θ, one can rewrite Equation (9.8) in a form that is generally more convenient:

$$f(\theta|\boldsymbol{x}) \propto \pi(\theta)l(\boldsymbol{x}|\theta) \tag{9.9}$$

The $\propto$ symbol means "is proportional to", so this equation shows that the value of the posterior distribution density function, evaluated at some value of θ, is proportional to the product of the prior distribution density function at that value of θ and the likelihood of observing the dataset $\boldsymbol{x}$ if that value of θ were the parameter's true value. It is interesting to observe that Bayesian inference is thus not interested in absolute values of the prior and likelihood function, but only their shapes. In writing equations of the form of Equation(9.9), we are taking as read that one will eventually have to normalise the distribution.

Bayesian inference seems to confuse a lot of people rather quickly. I have found that the easiest way to understand it, and to explain it, is through examples.

Example 9.1

I have three "loonies" (Canadian one dollar coins – they have a loon on the tail face) in my pocket. Two of them are regular coins, but the third is a weighted coin that has a 70 % chance of landing heads up. I cannot tell the coins apart on inspection. I take a coin out of my pocket at random and toss it – it lands heads up. What is the probability that the coin is the weighted coin?

Let's start by noting that the probability, as I have defined the term probability in Chapter 6.2, that the coin is the weighted one is either 0 or 1: it either is *not* the weighted coin or it *is*. The problem should really be phrased "What confidence do I have that the tossed coin is weighted?", as I am only dealing with the state of my knowledge. When I took the coin out of my pocket but before I had tossed it, I would have said I was $\frac{1}{3}$ confident that the coin in my hand was weighted, and $\frac{2}{3}$ confident it was not weighted. My prior distribution $\pi(\theta)$ for the state of the coin would thus look like Figure 9.3, i.e. a discrete distribution with two allowed values {not weighted, weighted} with confidences $\{\frac{2}{3}, \frac{1}{3}\}$ respectively.

Now I toss the coin and it lands heads up. If the coin were fair, it would have a probability of $\frac{1}{2}$ of landing that way. My confidence that I took out a *fair* coin from my pocket and then tossed a head (call it scenario A) is therefore proportional to my prior belief multiplied by the likelihood, i.e. $\frac{2}{3} * \frac{1}{2} = \frac{1}{3}$. On the other hand, I am also $\frac{1}{3}$ confident that the coin could have been weighted, and then it would

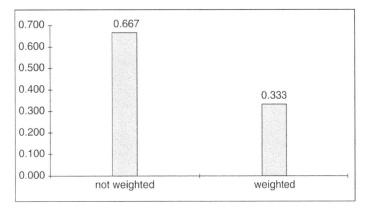

Figure 9.3 Prior distribution for the weighted coin example: a Discrete $(\{0, 1\}, \{\frac{2}{3}, \frac{1}{3}\})$.

have had a probability of $\frac{7}{10}$ of landing that way. My confidence that I took out the weighted coin from my pocket and then tossed a head (call it scenario B) is therefore proportional to $\frac{1}{3} * \frac{7}{10} = \frac{7}{30}$.

The two values 1/2 and 7/10 used for the probability of observing a head were conditional on the type of coin that was being tossed. These two values represent, in this problem, the likelihood function. We will look at some more general likelihood functions in the following examples.

Now, we know that one of scenarios A and B must have actually occurred since we did observe a head. We must therefore normalise my confidence for these two scenarios so that they add up to 1, i.e.

$$P(A) = \frac{1/3}{1/3 + 7/30} = \frac{10}{17}$$

$$P(B) = \frac{7/30}{1/3 + 7/30} = \frac{7}{17}$$

This normalising is the purpose of the denominator in Equation (9.8).

I am now 10/17 confident that the coin is fair and 7/17 confident that it is weighted: I still think it more likely I tossed a fair coin than a weighted coin. Let us imagine that we toss the coin again and observe another head. How would this affect my confidence distribution of the state of the coin? Well, the posterior confidence of selecting a fair coin and observing two heads (scenario C) is proportional to $\frac{2}{3} * \frac{1}{2} * \frac{1}{2} = \frac{1}{6}$. The posterior confidence of selecting the weighted coin and observing two heads (scenario D) is proportional to $1/3 * 7/10 * 7/10 = 49/300$. Normalising these two, we get

$$P(C) = \frac{1/6}{1/6 + 49/300} = \frac{50}{99}$$

$$P(D) = \frac{49/300}{1/6 + 49/300} = \frac{49}{99}$$

Now I am roughly equally confident about whether I had tossed a fair or a weighted coin. Figure 9.4 depicts posterior distributions for the above example, plus the posterior distributions for a few more tosses of a coin where each toss resulted in a head. One can see that, as the amount of observations (data) we have grows, our prior belief gets swamped by what the data say is really possible, i.e. by the information contained in the data. ♦

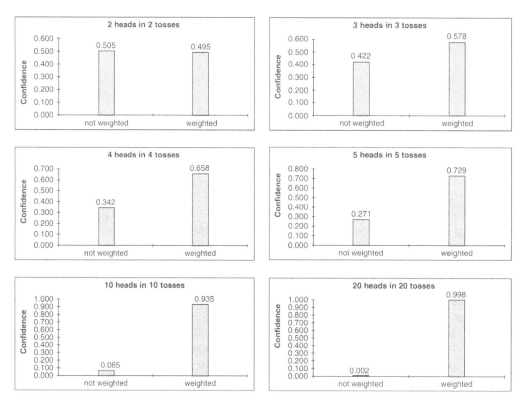

Figure 9.4 Posterior distributions for the coin tossing example with increasing numbers of heads.

Example 9.2

A game warden on a tropical island would like to know how many tigers she has on her island. It is a big island with dense jungle and she has a limited budget, so she can't search every inch of the island methodically. Besides, she wants to disturb the tigers and the other fauna as little as possible. She arranges for a capture–recapture survey to be carried out as follows.

Hidden traps are laid at random points on the island. The traps are furnished with transmitters that signal a catch, and each captured tiger is retrieved immediately. When 20 tigers have been caught, the traps are removed. Each of these 20 tigers are carefully sedated and marked with an ear tag, then all are released together back to the positions where they were originally caught. Some short time later, hidden traps are laid again, but at different points on the island, until 30 tigers have been caught and the number of tagged tigers is recorded. Captured tigers are held in captivity until the 30th tiger has been caught.

The game warden tries the experiment, and seven of the 30 tigers captured in the second set of traps are tagged. How many tigers are there on the island?

The warden has gone to some lengths to specify the experiment precisely. This is so that we will be able to assume within reasonable accuracy that the experiment is taking a hypergeometric sample from the tiger population (Section 8.4). A hypergeometric sample assumes that an individual with the characteristic of interest (in this case, a tagged tiger) has the same probability of being sampled as any individual that does not have that characteristic (i.e. the untagged tigers). The reader may enjoy thinking through what assumptions are being made in this analysis and where the experimental design has attempted to minimise any deviation from a true hypergeometric sampling.

We will use the usual notation for a hypergeometric process:

- n – the sample size, = 30.
- D – the number of individuals in the population of interest (tagged tigers) = 20.
- M – the population (the number of tigers in the jungle). In the Bayesian inference terminology, this is given the symbol θ as it is the parameter we are attempting to estimate.
- x – the number of individuals in the sample that have the characteristic of interest = 7.

We could get a best guess for M by noting that the most likely scenario would be for us to see tagged tigers in the sample in the same proportion as they occur in the population. In other words

$$\frac{x}{n} \approx \frac{D}{M}, \text{ i.e. } \frac{7}{30} \approx \frac{20}{M}, \text{ which gives } \hat{M} \approx 85 \text{ to } 86$$

but this does not take account of the uncertainty that occurs owing to the random sampling involved in the experiment. Let us imagine that before the experiment was started the warden and her staff believed that the number of tigers was equally likely to be any one value as any other. In other words, they knew absolutely nothing about the number of tigers in the jungle, and their prior distribution is thus a discrete uniform distribution over all non-negative integers. This is rather unlikely, of course, but we will discuss better prior distributions in Section 9.2.2.

The likelihood function is given by the probability mass function of the hypergeometric distribution, i.e.

$$l(X|\theta) = \frac{\binom{D}{x}\binom{M-D}{n-x}}{\binom{M}{n}} = \frac{\binom{20}{7}\binom{\theta-20}{23}}{\binom{\theta}{30}}, \quad \theta \geq 43$$

$$l(X|\theta) = 0, \qquad\qquad\qquad\qquad\qquad \text{otherwise}$$

The likelihood function is 0 for values of θ below 43, as the experiment tells us that there must be at least 43 tigers: 20 that were tagged plus the $(30 - 7)$ that were caught in the recapture part of the experiment and were not tagged.

The *probability mass function* (Section 6.1.2) applies to a discrete distribution and equals the probability that exactly x events will occur. Excel provides a convenient function HYPGEOMDIST(x, n, D, M) that will calculate the hypergeometric distribution mass function automatically, but generates errors instead of zero when $\theta < 43$ so I have used the equivalent ModelRisk function. Figure 9.5 illustrates a spreadsheet where a discrete uniform prior, with values of θ running from 0 to 150, is multiplied by the likelihood function above to arrive at a posterior distribution. We know that the total confidence must add up to 1, which is done in column F to produce the normalised posterior distribution. The shape of this posterior distribution is shown in Figure 9.6 by plotting column B against column F from the spreadsheet. The graph peaks at a value of 85, as we would expect, but it appears cut off at the right tail, which shows that we should also look at values of θ larger than 150. The analysis is repeated for values of θ up to 300, and this more complete posterior distribution is plotted in Figure 9.7. This second plot represents a good model of the state of the warden's knowledge about the number of tigers on the island. Don't forget that this is a distribution of belief and is not a true probability distribution since there *is* an exact number of tigers on the island.

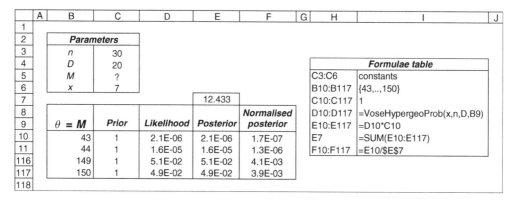

Figure 9.5 Bayesian inference model for the tiger capture–release–recapture problem.

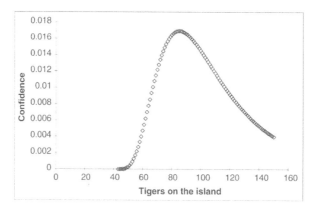

Figure 9.6 First pass at a posterior distribution for the tagged tiger problem.

In this example, we had to adjust our range of tested values of θ in light of the posterior distribution. It is quite common to review the set of tested values of θ, either expanding the prior's range or modelling some part of the prior's range in more detail when the posterior distribution is concentrated around a small range. It is entirely appropriate to expand the range of the prior as long as we would have been happy to have extended our prior to the new range before seeing the data. However, it would not be appropriate if we had a much more informed prior belief that gave an absolute range for the uncertain parameter outside of which we are now considering stepping. This would not be right because we would be revising our prior belief in light of the data: putting the cart before the horse, if you like. However, if the likelihood function is concentrated very much at one end of the range of the prior, it may well be worth reviewing whether the prior distribution or the likelihood function is appropriate, since the analysis could be suggesting that the true value of the parameter lies outside the preconceived range of the prior.

Continuing with our tigers on an island, let us imagine that the warden is unsatisfied with the level of uncertainty that remains about the number of tigers, which, from 50 to 250, is rather large. She decides to wait a short while and then capture another 30 tigers. The experiment is completed, and this time t tagged tigers are captured. Assuming that a tagged tiger still has the same probability of being captured as an untagged tiger, what is her uncertainty distribution now for the number of tigers on the island?

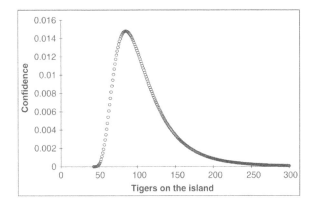

Figure 9.7 Improved posterior distribution for the tagged tiger problem.

This is simply a replication of the first problem, except that we no longer use a discrete uniform distribution as her prior. Instead, the distribution of Figure 9.7 represents the state of her knowledge prior to doing this second experiment, and the likelihood function is now given by the Excel function HYPGEOMDIST(t, 30, 20, θ), equivalently VoseHypergeoProb(t, 30, 20, θ, 0). The six panels of Figure 9.8 show what the warden's posterior distribution would have been if the second experiment had trapped $t = 1$, 3, 5, 7, 10 and 15 tagged tigers instead. These posteriors are plotted together with the prior of Figure 9.7 and the likelihood functions, normalised to sum to 1 for ease of comparison.

You might initially imagine that performing another experiment would make you *more* confident about the actual number of tigers on the island, but the graphs of Figure 9.8 show that this is not necessarily so. In the top two panels the posterior distribution is now more spread than the prior because the data contradict the prior (the prior and likelihood peak at very different values of θ). In the middle left panel, the likelihood disagrees moderately with the prior, but the extra information in the data compensates for this, leaving us with about the same level of uncertainty but with a posterior distribution that is to the right of the prior.

The middle right panel represents the scenario where the second experiment has the same results as the first. You'll see that the prior and likelihood overlay on each other because the prior of the first experiment was uniform and therefore the posterior shape was only influenced by the likelihood function. Since both experiments produced the same result, our confidence is improved and remains centred around the best guess of 85.

In the bottom two panels, the likelihood functions disagree with the priors, yet the posterior distributions have a narrower uncertainty. This is because the likelihood function is placing emphasis on the left tail of the possible range of values for θ, which is bounded at $\theta = 43$. ♦

In summary, the graphs of Figure 9.8 show that the amount of information contained in data is dependent on two things: (1) the manner in which the data were collected (i.e. the level of randomness inherent in the collection), which is described by the likelihood function, and (2) the state of our knowledge prior to observing the data and the degree to which it compares with the likelihood function. If the data tell us what we are already fairly sure of, there is little information contained in the data *for us* (though the data would contain much more information for those more ignorant of the parameter). On the other hand, if the data contradict what we already know, our uncertainty may either decrease or increase, depending on the circumstances.

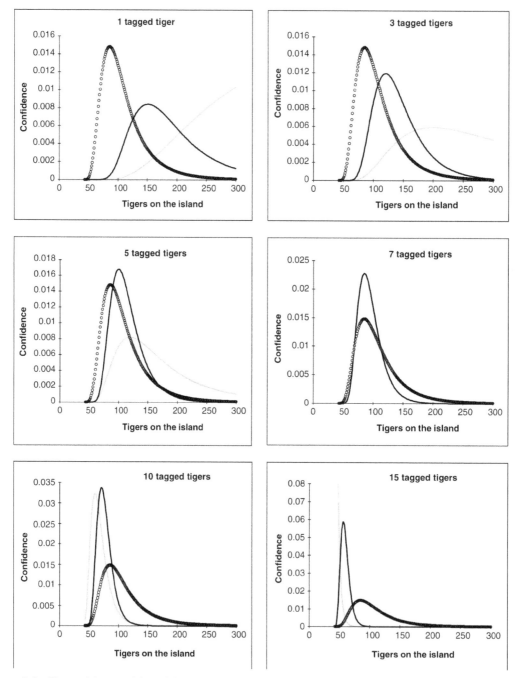

Figure 9.8 Tagged tiger problem: (a), (b), (c), (d), (e) and (f) show prior distributions, likelihood functions and posterior distributions if the second experiment had trapped 1, 3, 5, 7, 10 and 15 tigers tagged respectively (prior distribution shown as empty circles, likelihood function as grey lines and posterior distributions as black lines).

Example 9.3

Twenty people are randomly picked off a city street in France. Whether they are male or female is noted on 20 identical pieces of paper, put into a hat and the hat is brought to me. I have not seen these 20 people. I take out five pieces of paper from the hat and read them – three are female. I am then asked to estimate the number of females in the original group of 20.

I can express my estimate as a confidence distribution of the possible values. I might argue that, prior to reading the five names, I had no knowledge of the number of people who would be female and so would assign a discrete uniform prior from 0 to 20. However, it would be better to argue that roughly 50 % of people are female and so a much better prior distribution would be a Binomial(20, 0.5). This is equivalent to a Duniform prior, followed by a Binomial(20, 0.5) likelihood for the number of females that would be randomly selected from a population in a sample of 20.

The likelihood function relating to sampling five people from the population is again hypergeometric, except in this problem we know the total population (i.e. $M = 20$), we know the sample size ($n = 5$) and we know the number observed in the sample with the required property ($x = 3$), but we don't know the number of females D, which we denote by θ as it is the parameter to be estimated. Figure 9.9 illustrates the spreadsheet model for this problem, using the binomial distribution prior. This spreadsheet has made use of ModelRisk's VoseBinomialProb($x, n, p, cumulative$), equivalently the Excel function BINOMDIST($x, n, p, cumulative$), which returns a probability evaluated at x for a Binomial(n, p) distribution. The *cumulative* parameter in the function toggles the function to return a probability mass (cumulative $= 0$ or FALSE) or a cumulative probability (cumulative $= 1$ or TRUE). The IF statement in Cells C8:C28 is unnecessary because the VoseHypergeoProb function will return a zero, but necessary to avoid errors if you use Excel's HYPGEOMDIST function in its place.

Figure 9.10 shows the resultant posterior distribution, together with the likelihood function and the prior. Here we can see that the prior is very strong and the amount of information imbedded in the likelihood function is small, so the posterior distribution is quite close to the prior. The posterior distribution is a sort of compromise between the prior and likelihood function, in that it finds a distribution that agrees as much as possible with both. Hence, the peak of the posterior distribution now lies somewhere between the peaks of the prior and likelihood function. The effect of the likelihood function is small

	A	B	C	D	E	F	G	H	I	J
1										
2		*Parameters*								
3		n	5					C3:C4	Constants	
4		x	3						*Formulae table*	
5								C3:C4	Constants	
6						Normalised		B8:B28	{0,1,...,19,20}	
7		θ	Prior	Likelihood	Posterior	posterior		C8:C28	=VoseBinomialProb(B8,20,0.5,0)	
8		0	9.5E-07	0	0	0		D8:D28	=IF(OR(B8<x,B8>20-(n-x))	
9		1	1.9E-05	0	0	0			,0,VoseHypergeoProb(x,n,B8,20))	
10		2	1.8E-04	0	0	0		E8:E28	=C8*D8	
11		3	1.1E-03	8.8E-03	9.5E-06	3.1E-05		E29	=SUM(E8:E28)	
12		4	4.6E-03	3.1E-02	1.4E-04	4.6E-04		F8:F28	=E8/$E$29	
25		17	1.1E-03	1.3E-01	1.4E-04	4.6E-04				
26		18	1.8E-04	5.3E-02	9.5E-06	3.1E-05				
27		19	1.9E-05	0	0	0				
28		20	9.5E-07	0	0	0				
29					0.3125					
30										

Figure 9.9 Bayesian inference model for the number of "females in a hat" problem.

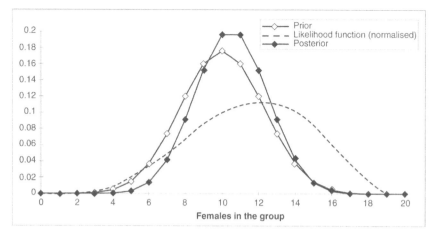

Figure 9.10 Prior distribution, likelihood function and posterior distribution for the model of Figure 9.9 using a Binomial(20, 0.5) prior.

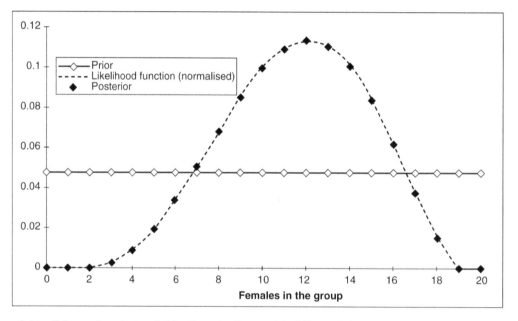

Figure 9.11 Prior and posterior distributions for the model of Figure 9.8 with a Duniform(0, ..., 20) prior.

because the sample is small (a sample of 5) and because it does not disagree with the prior (the prior has a maximum at $\theta = 10$, and this value of θ also produces one of the highest likelihood function values).

For comparison, Figure 9.11 shows the prior and posterior distributions if one had used a discrete uniform prior. Since the prior is flat in this case, it contributes nothing to the posterior's shape and the likelihood function becomes the posterior distribution. ◆

Hyperparameters

I assumed in Example 9.3 that the prevalence of females in France is 50%. However, knowing that females on average live longer than males, this figure will be a slight underestimate. Perhaps I should have used a value of 51% or 52%. In Bayesian inference, I can include uncertainty about one or more of the parameters in the analysis. For example, I could model p with a PERT(50%, 51%, 52%). Uncertain parameters are called hyperparameters. In the algebraic form of a Bayesian inference calculation, I then integrate out this nuisance parameter which in reality can be a bit tricky to carry out. Let's look again at the Bayesian inference calculation in the spreadsheet of Figure 9.9. If I have uncertainty about the prevalence of females p, I should assign a distribution to its value, in which case there would then be uncertainty about the posterior distribution. I cannot have an uncertainty about my uncertainty: it doesn't make sense. This is why we must integrate out (i.e. aggregate) the effect of uncertainty about p on the posterior distribution. We can do this very easily using Monte Carlo simulation, instead of the more onerous algebraic integration. We simply include a distribution for p in our model, nominate the entire array for the posterior distribution as an output and simulate. The set of means of the generated values for each cell in the array constitutes the final posterior distribution.

Simulating a Bayesian inference calculation

We could have done the same Bayesian inference analysis for Example 9.3 by simulation. Figure 9.12 illustrates a spreadsheet model that performs the Bayesian inference, together with a plot of the model result. In cell C3, a Binomial(20, 0.5) distribution represents the prior. It is randomly generating possible

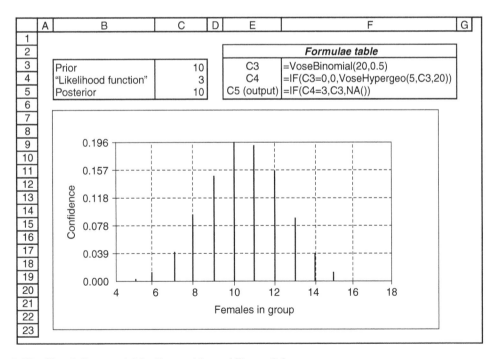

Figure 9.12 Simulation model for the problem of Figure 9.9.

scenarios of the number of "females" in the hat. In cell C4 a sample of five people is modelled using a Hypergeo(5, D, 20), where D is the result from the binomial distribution. The IF statement here is unnecessary because VoseHypergeo supports $D = 0$ but, for example, @RISK's RiskHypergeo(5,0,20) returns an error. This represents one-half of the likelihood function logic. Finally, in cell C5, the generated value from the binomial distribution in cell C3 is accepted (and therefore stored in memory) if the hypergeometric distribution produces a 3 – the number of females observed in the experiment. This is equivalent to the second half of the likelihood function logic. By running a large number of iterations, a large number of generated values from the binomial will be accepted. The proportion of times that a particular value from the binomial distribution will be accepted equates to the hypergeometric probability that three females would be subsequently observed in a random sample of five from the group. I ran this model for 100 000 iterations, and 31 343 values were accepted, which equates to about 31 % of the iterations. The technique is interesting but does have limited applications, since, for more complex problems or those with larger numbers, the technique becomes very inefficient as the percentage of iterations that are accepted becomes very small indeed. It is also difficult to use where the parameter being estimated is continuous rather than discrete, in which case one is forced to use a logic that accepts the generated prior value if the generated result lies within some range of the observed result. However, to combat this inefficiency, one can alter the prior distribution to generate values that the experimental results have shown to be possible. For example, in this problem, there must be between three and 18 females in the group of 20, whereas the Binomial(20, 0.5) is generating values between 0 and 20. Furthermore, one could run several passes, cutting down the prior with each pass to home in on only those values that are feasible. One can also get more detail in the tails by multiplying up the mass of some values x, y, z (for example, in the tails of the prior) by some factor, then dividing the heights of the posterior tail at x, y and z by that factor.

While this technique consumes a lot of simulation time, the models are very simple to construct and one can also consider multiple parameter priors.

Let us look again at the choice of priors for this problem, i.e. either a Duniform({0, ..., 20}) or a Binomial(20, 50 %). One might consider that the Duniform distribution is less informed (i.e. says less) than the binomial distribution. However, we can turn the Duniform distribution around and ask what that would have said about our prior belief of the probability p of a person randomly selected from the French population being female. We can show that a uniform assumption for p translates to a Duniform distribution of females in a group, as follows.

Let s_n be the number of successes in n Bernoulli trials where θ is the unknown probability of success of a trial. Then the probability that $s_n = r, r = \{0, 1, 2, \ldots, n\}$, is given by the *de Finetti theorem*:

$$P(s_n = r) = \int_0^1 \binom{n}{r} \theta^r (1 - \theta)^{n-r} f(\theta)\, \mathrm{d}\theta$$

where $f(\theta)$ is the probability density function for the uncertainty distribution for θ. The formula simply calculates, for any value of r, the binomial probability

$$\binom{n}{r} \theta^r (1 - \theta)^{n-r}$$

of observing r successes, integrated over the uncertainty distribution for the binomial probability θ. If we use a Uniform(0, 1) distribution to describe our uncertainty about θ, then $f(\theta) = 1$:

$$P(s_n = r) = \binom{n}{r} \int_0^1 \theta^r (1 - \theta)^{n-r}\, \mathrm{d}\theta$$

The integral is a beta function and, for integer values of r and n, we have the standard identity

$$\int_0^1 \theta^r (1 - \theta)^{n-r} \, d\theta = \frac{(n - r)!r!}{(n + 1)!}$$

Thus,

$$P(s_n = r) = \binom{n}{r} \frac{(n - r)!r!}{(n + 1)!} = \frac{n!}{r!(n - r)!} \frac{(n - r)!r!}{(n + 1)!} = \frac{1}{n + 1}$$

So each of the $n + 1$ possible values $\{0, 1, 2, \ldots, n\}$ has the same likelihood of $1/(n + 1)$. In other words, using a Duniform prior for the number of females in a group equates to saying that we are equally confident that the true probability of an individual from the population being female is any value between 0 and 1.

Example 9.4

A magician has three cups turned over on his table. Under one of the cups you see him put a pea. With much ceremony, he changes the cups around in a dazzling swirl. He then offers you a bet to pick which cup the pea is under. You pick one. He then shows you under one of the other cups – empty. The magician asks you whether you would like to swap your choice for the third, untouched cup. What is your answer? Note that the magician knows which cup has the pea and would not turn it over.

In this problem, until the magician turns over a cup, we are equally sure about which cup has the pea so our prior confidence assigns equal weighting to the three cups. We now need to calculate the probability of what was observed if the pea had been under each of the cups in turn. We can label the three cups as A for the cup I chose, B for the cup the magician chose and C for the remaining cup.

Let's start with the easy cup, B. What is the probability that the magician would turn over cup B if he knew the pea was under cup B? Answer: 0, because he would have spoiled the trick.

Next, look at the untouched cup, C. What is the probability that the magician would turn over cup B if he knew the pea was under cup C? Answer: 1, since he had no choice as I had already picked A, and C contained the pea.

Now look at my cup, A. What is the probability that the magician would turn over cup B if he knew the pea was under cup A? Answer: 1/2, since he could have chosen to turn over either B or C.

Thus, from Bayes' theorem,

$$P(A|X) = \frac{P(A)P(X|A)}{P(A)P(X|A) + P(B)P(X|B) + P(C)P(X|C)}, \text{etc.}$$

where $P(A) = P(B) = P(C) = \frac{1}{3}$ are the confidences we assign to the three cups before observing the data X (i.e. the magician turning over cup B) and $P(X|A) = 0.5$, $P(X|B) = 0$ and $P(X|C) = 1$.

Thus,

$$P(A|X) = \tfrac{1}{3}, \quad P(B|X) = 0 \quad \text{and } P(C|X) = \tfrac{2}{3}$$

So, after having made our choice of cup and then watching the magician turn over one of the other two cups, we should *always* change our mind and pick the third cup as we should now be twice as confident that the untouched cup will contain the pea as the one we originally chose. The result is a little hard for many people to believe in: the obstinate among us would like to stick to our original choice, and it does not seem that the probability can really have changed for the cup we chose to contain the pea. Indeed, the probability has not changed after the magician's selection: it remains either 0 or 1, depending on whether we picked the right cup. What has changed is our confidence (the state of our knowledge) about whether that probability is 1. Originally, we had a 1/3 confidence that the pea was under our cup, and that has not changed. There is another way to think of the same problem: we had 1/3 confidence in our original choice of cup, and 2/3 in the other choices, and we also knew that one of those other cups did not contain the pea, so the 2/3 migrated to the remaining cup that was not turned over. This exercise is known as the Monte Hall problem – Wikipedia has a nice explanatory page, and www.stat.sc.edu/~west/javahtml/LetsMakeaDeal.html has a nice simulation applet to test out the answer. ♦

Exercise 9.1:   Try repeating this problem where there are (a) four cups and one pea, and (b) five cups and two peas. Each time you get to select a cup, and each time the magician turns one of the others over.

9.2.2 Prior distributions

As we have seen above, the prior distributions are the description of one's state of knowledge about the parameter in question prior to observation of the data. Determination of the prior distribution is the primary focus for criticism of Bayesian inference, and one needs to be quite sure of the effects of choosing one particular prior over another. This section describes three different types of prior distribution: the uninformed prior; the conjugate prior and the subjective prior. We will look at the practical reasons for selecting each type and arguments for and against each selection.

An argument presented by frequentist statisticians (i.e. those who use only traditional statistical techniques) is that the Bayesian inference methodology is subjective. A frequentist might argue that, because we use prior distributions, representing the state of one's belief prior to accumulation of data, Bayesian inference may easily produce quite different results from one practitioner to the next because they can choose quite different priors. This is, of course, true – in principle. It is both one of the strengths and certainly an Achilles' heel of the technique. On the one hand, it is very useful in a statistical technique to be able to include one's prior experience and knowledge of the parameter, even if that is not available in a pure data form. On the other hand, one party could argue that the resultant posterior distribution produced by another party was incorrect. The solution to this dilemma is, in principle, fairly simple. If the purpose of the Bayesian inference is to make internal decisions within your organisation, you are very much at liberty to use any experience you have available to determine your prior. On the other hand, if the result of your analysis is likely to be challenged by a party with a conflicting agenda to your own, you may be better off choosing an "uninformed" prior, i.e. one that is neutral in that it provides no extra information. All that said, in the event that one has accumulated a reasonable dataset, the controversy regarding selection of priors disappears as the prior is overwhelmed by the information contained in the data.

It is important to specify a prior with a sufficiently large range to cover all possible true values for the parameter, as we have seen in Figure 9.6. Failure to specify a wide enough prior will curtail the posterior distribution, although this will nearly always be apparent when plotting the posterior distribution and a correction can be made. The only time it may not be apparent that the prior range is inadequate is when the likelihood function has more than one peak, in which case one might have extended the range of the prior to show the first peak but no further.

Uninformed priors

An uninformed prior has a distribution that would be considered to add no information to the Bayesian inference, except to specify the possible range of the parameter in question. For example, a Uniform(0, 1) distribution could be considered an uninformed prior when estimating a binomial probability because it states that, prior to collection of any data, we consider every possible value for the true probability to be as likely as every other. An uninformed prior is often desirable in the development of public policy to demonstrate impartiality. Laplace (1812), who also independently stated Bayes' theorem (Laplace, 1774) 11 years after Bayes' essay was published (he apparently had not seen Bayes' essay), proposed that public policy priors should assume all allowable values to have equal likelihood (i.e. uniform or Duniform distributions).

At first glance, then, it might seem that uninformed priors will just be uniform distributions running across the entire range of possible values for the parameter. That this is not true can be easily demonstrated from the following example. Consider the task of estimating the true mean number of events per unit exposure λ of a Poisson process. We have observed a certain number of events within a certain period, which we can use to give us a likelihood function very easily (see Example 9.6). It might seem reasonable to assign a Uniform(0, z) prior to λ, where z is some large number. However, we could just as easily have parameterised the problem in terms of β, the mean exposure between events. Since $\beta = 1/\lambda$, we can quickly check what a Uniform(0, z) prior for λ would look like as a prior for β by running a simulation on the formula: $= 1/\text{Uniform}(0, z)$. Figure 9.13 shows the result of such a simulation. It is alarmingly far from being uninformed with respect to β! Of course, the reverse equally applies: if we had performed a Bayesian inference on β with a uniform prior, the prior for λ would be just as far from being uninformed. The probability density function for the prior distribution of a parameter must be known in order to perform a Bayesian inference calculation. However, one can often choose between a number of different parameterisations that would equally well describe the same

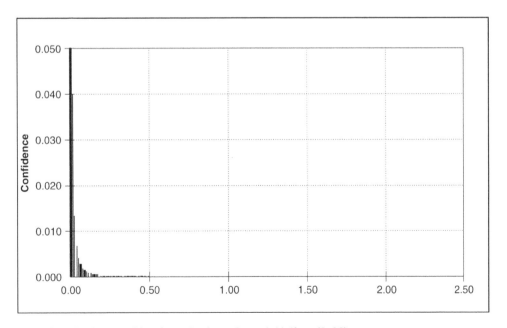

Figure 9.13   Distribution resulting from the formula: $= 1/\text{Uniform}(0, 20)$.

stochastic process. For example, one could describe a Poisson process by λ, the mean number of events per unit exposure, by β, the mean exposure between events as above, or by $P(x > 0)$, the probability of at least one event in a unit of exposure.

The Jacobian transformation lets us calculate the prior distribution for a Bayesian inference problem after reparameterising. If x is the original parameter with probability density function $f(x)$ and cumulative distribution function $F(x)$, and γ is the new parameter with probability density function $f(\gamma)$ and cumulative distribution function $F(\gamma)$ related to x by some function such that x and γ increase monotonically, then we can equate changes $dF(\gamma)$ and $dF(x)$ together, i.e.

$$|f(\gamma)\,d\gamma| = |f(x)\,dx|$$

Rearranging a little, we get

$$f(\gamma) = \left|\frac{\partial x}{\partial \gamma}\right| f(x)$$

where $\left|\dfrac{\partial x}{\partial \gamma}\right|$ is known as the Jacobian.

So, for example, if $x = \text{Uniform}(0, c)$ and $\gamma = 1/x$,

$$p(x) = 1/c$$

$$\gamma = 1/x \text{ so } x = 1/\gamma$$

$$\frac{\partial x}{\partial \gamma} = -1/\gamma^2 \text{ so the Jacobian is } \left|\frac{\partial x}{\partial \gamma}\right| = 1/\gamma^2$$

which gives the distribution for γ : $p(\gamma) = \dfrac{1}{c\gamma^2}$.

Two advanced exercises for those who like algebra:

Exercise 9.2: Suppose we model $p = U(0, 1)$. What is the density function for $Q = 1 - (1 - p)^n$?

Exercise 9.3: Suppose we want to model $P(0) = \exp(-\lambda) = U(0, 1)$. What is the density function for λ?

There is no all-embracing solution to the problem of setting uninformed priors that don't become "informed" under some reparameterising of the problem. However, one useful method is to use a prior such that $\log_{10}(\theta)$ is $\text{Uniform}(-z, z)$ distributed, which, using Jacobian transformation, can be shown to give the prior density $\pi(\theta) \propto 1/\theta$, for a parameter that can take any positive real value. We could just as easily use natural logs, i.e. $\log_e(\theta) = \text{Uniform}(-y, y)$, but in practice it is easier to set the value z because our minds think quite naturally in powers of 10. Using this prior, we get $\log_{10}(1/\theta) = -\log_{10}(\theta) = -\text{Uniform}(-z, z) = \text{Uniform}(-z, z)$. In other words, $1/\theta$ is distributed the same as θ: in mathematical terminology, the prior distribution is transformation invariant. Now, if

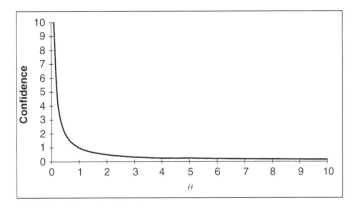

Figure 9.14   Prior distribution $\pi(\theta) = 1/\theta$.

$\log_{10}(\theta)$ is Uniform$(-z, z)$ distributed, then θ is distributed as $10^{\text{Uniform}(-z,z)}$. Figure 9.14 shows a graph of $\pi(\theta) = 1/\theta$. You probably wouldn't describe that distribution as very uninformed, but it is arguably the best one can do for this particular problem. It is worth remembering too that, if there is a reasonable amount of data available, the likelihood function $l(X|\theta)$ will overpower the prior $\pi(\theta) = 1/\theta$, and then the shape of the prior becomes unimportant. This will occur much more quickly if the likelihood function is a maximum in a region of θ where the prior is flatter: anywhere from 3 or 4 onwards in Figure 9.14, for example.

Another requirement might be to ensure that the prior distribution remains invariant under some rescaling. For example, the *location* parameter of a distribution should have the same effective prior under the linear shifting transformation $\gamma = \theta - a$, where a is some constant. This is achieved if we select a uniform prior for θ, i.e. $\pi(\theta) = $ constant. Similarly, a *scale* parameter should have a prior that is invariant under a change of units, i.e. $\gamma = k\theta$, where k is some constant. In other words, we require that the parameter be invariant under a linear transformation which, from the discussion in the previous paragraph, is achieved if we select the prior $\log(\theta) = $ uniform (i.e. $\pi(\theta) \propto 1/\theta$) on the real line, since $\log(\gamma) = \log(k\theta) = \log(k) + \log(\theta)$, which is still uniformly distributed.

Parametric distribution often has either or both a location parameter and a scale parameter. If more than one parameter is unknown and one is attempting to estimate these parameters, it is common practice to assume independence between the two parameters in the prior: the logic is that an assumption of independence is more uninformed than an assumption of any specific degree of dependence. The joint prior for a scale parameter and a location parameter is then simply the product of the two priors. So, for example, the prior for the mean of a normal distribution is $\pi(\mu) \propto 1$, as μ is a location parameter; the prior for the standard deviation of the normal distribution is $\pi(\sigma) \propto 1/\sigma$, as σ is a scale parameter, and their joint prior is given by the product of the two priors, i.e. $\pi(\mu, \sigma) \propto 1/\sigma$. The use of joint priors is discussed more fully in Chapter 10 where we will be fitting distributions to data.

Jeffreys prior

The Jeffreys prior, described in Jeffreys (1961), provides an easily computed prior that is invariant under any one-to-one transformation and therefore determines one version of what could be described as an uninformed prior. The idea is that one finds a likelihood function, under some transformation of the data, that produces the same shape for all datasets and simply changes the location of its peak. Thus, a non-informative prior in this translation would be ambiguous, i.e. flat. Although it is often impossible to determine such a likelihood function, Jeffreys developed a useful approximation given by

$$\pi(\theta) = [I(\theta)]^{1/2}$$

where $I(\theta)$ is the expected Fisher information in the model:

$$I(\theta) = -E_{X|\theta}\left[\frac{\partial^2}{\partial\theta^2}\log l(X|\theta)\right]$$

The formula is averaging, over all values of x (the data), the second-order partial derivative of the loglikelihood function. The form of the likelihood function is helping determine the prior, but the data themselves are not. This is important since the prior must be "blind" to the data. [Interestingly, empirical Bayes methods (another field of Bayesian inference though not discussed in this book) *do* use the data to determine the prior distribution and then try to make appropriate corrections for the bias this creates.]

Some of the Jeffreys prior results are a little counterintuitive. For example, the Jeffreys prior for a binomial probability is the Beta$(\frac{1}{2}, \frac{1}{2})$ shown in Figure 9.15. It peaks at $p = 0$ and $p = 1$, dipping to its lowest value at $p = 0.5$, which does not equate well with most people's intuitive notion of uninformed. The Jeffreys prior for the Poisson mean λ is $\pi(\lambda) \propto 1/\lambda^{1/2}$. But, using the Jacobian transformation, we see that this gives a prior for $\beta = 1/\lambda$ of $p(\beta) \propto \beta^{-3/2}$, so the prior is not transformation invariant.

Improper priors

We have seen how a uniform prior can be used to represent uninformed knowledge about a parameter. However, if that parameter can take on any value between zero and infinity, for example, then it is not strictly possible to use the uniform prior $\pi(\theta) = c$, where c is some constant, since no value of c will let the area of the distribution sum to 1, and the prior is called *improper*. Other common improper priors include using $1/\sigma$ for the standard deviation of a normal distribution and $1/\sigma^2$ for the variance. It turns out that we can use improper priors provided the denominator in Equation (9.8) equals some constant (i.e. is not infinite), because this means that the posterior distribution can be normalised.

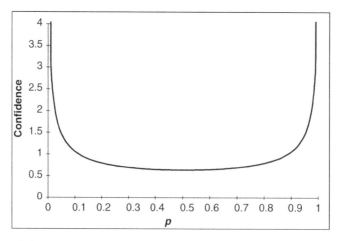

Figure 9.15 The Beta$(\frac{1}{2}, \frac{1}{2})$ distribution.

Savage *et al.* (1962) has pointed out that an uninformed prior can be uniformly distributed over the area of interest, then slope smoothly down to zero outside the area of interest. Such a prior can, of course, be designed to have an area of 1, eliminating the need for improper priors. However, the extra effort required in designing such a prior is not really necessary if one can accept using an improper prior.

Hyperpriors

Occasionally, one may wish to specify a prior that itself has one or more uncertain parameters. For instance, in Example 9.3 we used a Binomial(20, 0.5) prior because we believed that about 50 % of the population were female, and we discussed the effect of changing this value to a distribution representing the uncertainty about the true female prevalence. Such a distribution is described as a *hyperprior* for the *hyperparameter* p in Binomial(20, p). As previously discussed, Bayesian inference can account for hyperpriors, but we are then required to do an integration over all values of the hyperparameter to determine the shape of the prior, and that can be time consuming and at times very difficult. An alternative to the algebraic approach is to find the prior distribution by Monte Carlo simulation. We run a simulation for this model, naming as outputs the array of cells calculating the prior. At the end of the simulation, we collect the mean values for each output cell, which together form our prior. The posterior distribution will naturally have a greater spread if there is uncertainty about any parameters in the prior. If we had used a Beta(a, b) distribution for p, the prior would have been a *Beta–Binomial*(20, a, b) distribution and a beta–binomial distribution always has a greater spread than the best-fitting binomial.

Theoretically, one could continue applying uncertainty distributions to the parameters of hyperpriors, etc., but there is little if any accuracy to be gained by doing so, and the model starts to seem pretty silly. It is also worth remembering that the likelihood function often quickly overpowers the prior distribution as more data become available, so the effort expended in subtle changes to defining a prior will often be wasted.

Conjugate priors

A conjugate prior has the same functional form in θ as the likelihood function which leads to a posterior distribution belonging to the same distribution family as the prior. For example, the Beta(α_1, α_2) distribution has probability density function $f(\theta)$ given by

$$f(\theta) = \frac{\theta^{\alpha_1 - 1}(1 - \theta)^{\alpha_2 - 1}}{\int_0^1 t^{\alpha_1 - 1}(1 - t)^{\alpha_2 - 1}\, dt}$$

The denominator is a constant for particular values of α_1 and α_2, so we can rewrite the equation as

$$f(\theta) \propto \theta^{\alpha_1 - 1}(1 - \theta)^{\alpha_2 - 1}$$

If we had observed s successes in n trials and were attempting to estimate the true probability of success p, the likelihood function $l(s, n; \theta)$ would be given by the binomial distribution probability mass function written (using θ to represent the unknown parameter p) as

$$l(s, n\,;\,\theta) = \binom{n}{s} \theta^s (1 - \theta)^{n - s}$$

Since the binomial coefficient $\binom{n}{s}$ is constant for the given dataset (i.e. known n, s), we can rewrite the equation as

$$l(s, n; \theta) \propto \theta^s (1 - \theta)^{n-s}$$

We can see that the beta distribution and the binomial likelihood function have the same functional form in θ, i.e. $\theta^a (1 - \theta)^b$, where a and b are constants. Since the posterior distribution is a product of the prior and likelihood function, it too will have the same functional form, i.e. using Equation (9.9) we have

$$f(\theta|s, n) \propto \theta^{\alpha_1 - 1 + s} (1 - \theta)^{\alpha_2 - 1 + n - s} \tag{9.10}$$

Since this is a true distribution, it must normalise to 1, so the probability distribution function is actually

$$f(\theta|s, n) = \frac{\theta^{\alpha_1 - 1 + s} (1 - \theta)^{\alpha_2 - 1 + n - s}}{\int_0^1 t^{\alpha_1 - 1 + s} (1 - t)^{\alpha_2 - 1 + n - s} \, dt}$$

which is just the Beta$(\alpha_1 + s, \alpha_2 + n - s)$ distribution. (In fact, with a bit of practice, one starts to recognise distributions because of their functional form, e.g. that Equation (9.10) represents a beta distribution, without having to go through the step of obtaining the normalised equation.) Thus, if one uses a beta distribution as a prior for p with a binomial likelihood function, the posterior distribution is also a beta. The value of using conjugate priors is that we can avoid actually doing any of the mathematics and get directly to the answer. Conjugate priors are often called *convenience priors* for obvious reasons.

The Beta(1, 1) distribution is exactly the same as a Uniform(0, 1) distribution, so, if we want to start with a Uniform(0, 1) prior for p, our posterior distribution is given by Beta$(s + 1, n - s + 1)$. This is a particularly useful result that will be used repeatedly in this book. By comparison, the Jeffreys prior for a binomial probability is a Beta$(\frac{1}{2}, \frac{1}{2})$. Haldane (1948) discusses using a Beta(0, 0) prior, which is mathematically undefined and therefore meaningless by itself, but gives a posterior distribution of Beta$(s, n - s)$ that has a mean of s/n: in other words, it provides an unbiased estimate for the binomial probability.

Table 9.1 lists other conjugate priors and the associated likelihood functions. Morris (1983) has shown that exponential families of distributions, from which one often draws the likelihood function, all have conjugate priors, so the technique can be used frequently in practice. Conjugate priors are also often used to provide approximate but very convenient representations to subjective priors, as described in the next section.

Subjective priors

A subjective prior (sometimes called an elicited prior) describes the informed opinion of the value of a parameter prior to the collection of data. Chapter 14 discusses in some depth the techniques for eliciting opinions. A subjective prior can be represented as a series of points on a graph, as shown in Figure 9.16. It is a simple enough exercise to read off a number of points from such graphs and use the height of each point as a substitute for $\pi(\theta)$. That makes it quite difficult to normalise the posterior distribution,

Table 9.1 Likelihood functions and their associated conjugate priors.

Distribution	Probability density function	Estimated parameter	Prior	Posterior
Binomial	$\binom{n}{x} p^x (1-p)^{n-x}$	Probability p	Beta(α_1, α_2)	$\alpha_1' = \alpha_1 + x$ $\alpha_2' = \alpha_2 + n - x$
Exponential	$\lambda e^{-\lambda x}$	Mean$^{-1} = \lambda$	Gamma(α, β)	$\alpha' = \alpha + n$ $\beta' = \dfrac{\beta}{1 + \beta \sum_i x_i}$
Normal (with known σ)	$\dfrac{1}{\sqrt{2\pi}\sigma} \exp\left[-\dfrac{1}{2}\left(\dfrac{x-\mu}{\sigma}\right)^2 \right]$	Mean μ	Normal(μ_μ, σ_μ)	$\mu_\mu' = \dfrac{\mu_\mu(\sigma^2/n) + \bar{x}\sigma_\mu^2}{\sigma^2/n + \sigma_\mu^2}$ $\sigma_\mu' = \sqrt{\dfrac{\sigma_\mu^2 \sigma^2}{n\sigma_\mu^2 + \sigma^2}}$
Poisson	$e^{-\lambda t}\dfrac{(\lambda t)^x}{x!}$	Mean events per unit time λ	Gamma(α, β)	$\alpha' = \alpha + x$ $\beta' = \dfrac{\beta}{1 + \beta t}$

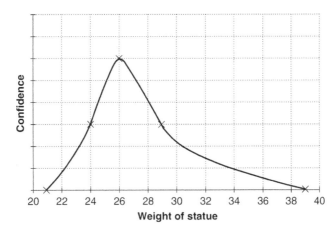

Figure 9.16 Example of a subjective prior.

but we will see in Section 9.2.4 a technique that one can use in Monte Carlo modelling that removes that problem.

Sometimes it is possible reasonably to match a subjective opinion like that of Figure 9.16 to a convenience prior for the likelihood function one is intending to use. Software products like ModelRisk, BestFit® and RiskView Pro® can help in this regard. An exact match is not usually important because (a) the subjective prior is not usually specified that accurately anyway and (b) the prior has progressively less influence on the posterior the larger the set of data used in calculating the likelihood function. At other times, a single conjugate prior may be inadequate for describing a subjective prior, but a composite of two or more conjugate priors will produce a good representation.

Multivariate priors

I have concentrated discussion on the quantification of uncertainty in this chapter to a single parameter θ. In practice one may find that θ is multivariate, i.e. that it is multidimensional, in which case one needs multivariate priors. In general, such techniques are beyond the scope of this book, and the reader is referred to more specialised texts on Bayesian inference: I have listed some texts I have found useful (and readable) in Appendix IV. Multivariate priors are, however, discussed briefly with respect to fitting distributions to data in Section 10.2.2.

9.2.3 Likelihood functions

The likelihood function $l(X|\theta)$ is a function of θ with the data X fixed. It calculates the probability of observing the X observed data as a function of θ. Sometimes the likelihood function is simple: often it is just the probability distribution function of a distribution like the binomial, Poisson or hypergeometric. At other times, it can quickly become very complex.

Examples 9.2, 9.3 and 9.6 to 9.8 illustrate some different likelihood functions. As likelihood functions are calculating probabilities (or probability densities), they can be combined in the same way as we usually do in probability calculus, discussed in Section 6.3.

The *likelihood principle* states that all relevant evidence about θ from an experiment and its observed outcome should be present in the likelihood function. For example, in binomial sampling with n fixed, s is binomially distributed for a given p. If s is fixed, n is negative binomially distributed for a given p. In both cases the likelihood function is proportional to $p^s(1-p)^{n-s}$, i.e. it is independent of how the sampling was carried out and dependent only on the type of sampling and the result.

9.2.4 Normalising the posterior distribution

A problem often faced by those using Bayesian inference is the difficulty of determining the normalising integral that is the denominator of Equation (9.8). For all but the simplest likelihood functions this can be a complex equation. Although sophisticated commercial software products like Mathematica®, Mathcad® and Maple® are available to perform these equations for the analyst, many integrals remain intractable and have to be solved numerically. This means that the calculation has to be redone every time new data are acquired or a slightly different problem is encountered.

For the risk analyst using Monte Carlo techniques, the normalising part of the Bayesian inference analysis can be bypassed altogether. Most Monte Carlo packages offer two functions that enable us to do this: a Discrete($\{x\}, \{p\}$) distribution and a Relative(min, max, $\{x\}, \{p\}$). The first defines a discrete distribution where the allowed values are given by the $\{x\}$ array and the relative likelihood of each of these values is given by the $\{p\}$ array. The second function defines a continuous distribution with a minimum = min, a maximum = max and several x values given by the array $\{x\}$, each of which has a relative likelihood "density" given by the $\{p\}$ array. The reason that these two functions are so useful is that the user is not required to ensure that for the discrete distribution the probabilities in $\{p\}$ sum to 1 and for the relative distribution the area under the curve equals 1. The functions normalise themselves automatically.

9.2.5 Taylor series approximation to a Bayesian posterior distribution

When we have a reasonable amount of data with which to calculate the likelihood function, the posterior distribution tends to come out looking approximately normally distributed. In this section we will examine why that is, and provide a shorthand method to determine the approximating normal distribution directly without needing to go through a complete Bayesian analysis.

Our best estimate θ_0 of the value of a parameter θ is the value for which the posterior distribution $f(\theta)$ is at its maximum. Mathematically, this equates to the condition

$$\frac{\mathrm{d}f(\theta)}{\mathrm{d}\theta}\bigg|_{\theta_0} = 0 \tag{9.11}$$

That is to say, θ_0 occurs where the gradient of $f(\theta)$ is zero. Strictly speaking, we also require that the gradient of $f(\theta)$ go from positive to negative for θ_0 to be a maximum, i.e.

$$\frac{\mathrm{d}^2 f(\theta)}{\mathrm{d}\theta^2}\bigg|_{\theta_0} < 0$$

The second condition is only of any importance if the posterior distribution has two or more peaks, for which a normal approximation to the posterior distribution would be inappropriate anyway. Taking the first and second derivatives of $f(\theta)$ assumes that θ is a continuous variable, but the principle applies equally to discrete variables, in which case we are just looking for that value of θ for which the posterior distribution has the highest value.

The Taylor series expansion of a function (see Section 6.3.6) allows one to produce a polynomial approximation to some function $f(x)$ about some value x_0 that usually has a much simpler form than the original function. The Taylor series expansion says

$$f(x) = \sum_{m=0}^{\infty} \frac{f^{(m)}(x_0)}{m!}(x - x_0)^m$$

where $f^{(m)}(x)$ represents the mth derivative of $f(x)$ with respect to x.

To make the next calculation a little easier to manage, we first define the log of the posterior distribution $L(\theta) = \log_e[f(\theta)]$. Since $L(\theta)$ increases with $f(\theta)$, the maximum of $L(\theta)$ occurs at the same value of θ as the maximum of $f(\theta)$. We now apply the Taylor series expansion of $L(\theta)$ about θ_0 (the MLE) for the first three terms:

$$L(\theta) = L(\theta_0) + \frac{\mathrm{d}L(\theta)}{\mathrm{d}\theta}\bigg|_{\theta_0}(\theta - \theta_0) + \frac{1}{2}\frac{\mathrm{d}^2 L(\theta)}{\mathrm{d}\theta^2}\bigg|_{\theta_0}(\theta - \theta_0)^2 + \cdots$$

The first term in this expansion is just a constant value (k) and tells us nothing about the shape of $L(\theta)$; the second term equals zero from Equation (9.11), so we are left with the simplified form

$$L(\theta) = k + \frac{1}{2}\frac{\mathrm{d}^2 L(\theta)}{\mathrm{d}\theta^2}\bigg|_{\theta_0}(\theta - \theta_0)^2 + \cdots$$

This approximation will be good providing the higher-order terms ($m = 3$, 4, etc.) have much smaller values than the $m = 2$ term here.

We can now take the exponential of $L(\theta)$ to get back to $f(\theta)$:

$$f(\theta) \approx K \exp\left(\frac{1}{2} \left.\frac{\mathrm{d}^2 L(\theta)}{\mathrm{d}\theta^2}\right|_{\theta_0} (\theta - \theta_0)^2\right)$$

where K is a normalising constant. Now, the Normal(μ, σ) distribution has probability density function $f(x)$ given by

$$f(x) = \frac{1}{\sqrt{2\pi\sigma^2}} \exp\left(-\frac{(x-\mu)^2}{2\sigma^2}\right)$$

Comparing the above two equations, we can see that $f(\theta)$ has the same functional form as a normal distribution, where

$$\mu = \theta_0 \quad \text{and} \quad \sigma = \left[-\left.\frac{\mathrm{d}^2 L(\theta)}{\mathrm{d}\theta^2}\right|_{\theta_0}\right]^{-1/2}$$

and we can thus often approximate the Bayesian posterior distribution with the following normal distribution:

$$\theta = \text{Normal}\left(\theta_0, \left[-\left.\frac{\mathrm{d}^2 L(\theta)}{\mathrm{d}\theta^2}\right|_{\theta_0}\right]^{-1/2}\right)$$

We shall illustrate this normal (or quadratic) approximation with a few simple examples.

Example 9.5 Approximation to the beta distribution

We have seen above that the beta distribution $(s + 1, n - s + 1)$ provides an estimate of the binomial probability p when we have observed s successes in n independent trials, and assuming a prior Uniform(0, 1) distribution. The posterior density has the function

$$f(\theta) \propto \theta^s (1 - \theta)^{(n-s)}$$

Taking logs gives

$$L(\theta) = k + s \log_e[\theta] + (n - s) \log_e[1 - \theta]$$

and

$$\frac{\mathrm{d}L(\theta)}{\mathrm{d}\theta} = \frac{s}{\theta} - \frac{n-s}{1-\theta}, \quad \frac{\mathrm{d}^2 L(\theta)}{\mathrm{d}\theta^2} = -\frac{s}{\theta^2} - \frac{n-s}{(1-\theta)^2}$$

We first find our best estimate θ_0 of θ

$$\left.\frac{\mathrm{d}L(\theta)}{\mathrm{d}\theta}\right|_{\theta_0} = \frac{s}{\theta_0} - \frac{n-s}{1-\theta_0} = 0$$

which gives the intuitively encouraging answer

$$\theta_0 = s/n \tag{9.12}$$

i.e. our best guess for the binomial probability is the proportion of trials that were successes.

Next, we find the standard deviation σ for the normal approximation to this beta distribution:

$$\frac{d^2 L(\theta)}{d\theta^2}\bigg|_{\theta_0} = -\frac{s}{\theta_0^2} - \frac{n-s}{(1-\theta_0)^2} = -\frac{n}{\theta_0(1-\theta_0)}$$

which gives

$$\sigma = \left[-\frac{d^2 L(\theta)}{d\theta^2}\bigg|_{\theta_0} \right]^{-1/2} = \left[\frac{\theta_0(1-\theta_0)}{n} \right]^{1/2} \tag{9.13}$$

and so we get the approximation

$$\theta \approx \text{Normal}\left(\theta_0, \left[\frac{\theta_0(1-\theta_0)}{n} \right]^{1/2} \right)$$

$$= \text{Normal}\left(\frac{s}{n}, \left[\frac{s(n-s)}{n^3} \right]^{1/2} \right) \tag{9.14}$$

The equation for σ allows us some useful insight into the behaviour of the beta distribution. We can see in the numerator that the spread of the beta distribution, and therefore our measure of uncertainty about the true value of θ, is a function of our best estimate for θ. The function $[\theta_0(1-\theta_0)]$ is at its maximum when $\theta_0 = \frac{1}{2}$, so, for a given set of trials n, we will be more uncertain about the true value of θ if the proportion of successes is close to $\frac{1}{2}$ than if it were closer to 0 or 1. Looking at the denominator, we see that the degree of uncertainty, represented by σ, is proportional to $n^{-1/2}$. We will see time and again that the level of uncertainty of some parameter is inversely proportional to the square root of the amount of data available. Note also that Equation (9.14) is exactly the same as the classical statistics result of Equation (9.7). But when is this quadratic approximation to $L(\theta)$, i.e. the normal approximation to $f(\theta)$, a reasonably good fit? The mean μ and variance V of a Beta$(s+1, n-s+1)$ distribution are as follows:

$$\mu = \frac{s+1}{n+2}, \quad V = \frac{(s+1)(n-s+1)}{(n+2)^2(n+3)}$$

Comparing these identities with Equation (9.13), we can see that the normal approximation works when s and $(n-s)$ are both sufficiently large for adding 1 to s and adding 3 to n proportionally to have little effect, i.e. when

$$\frac{s+1}{s} \approx 1 \quad \text{and} \quad \frac{n+3}{n} \approx 1$$

Figure 9.17 compares the beta distribution with its normal approximation for several combinations of s successes in n trials. ◆

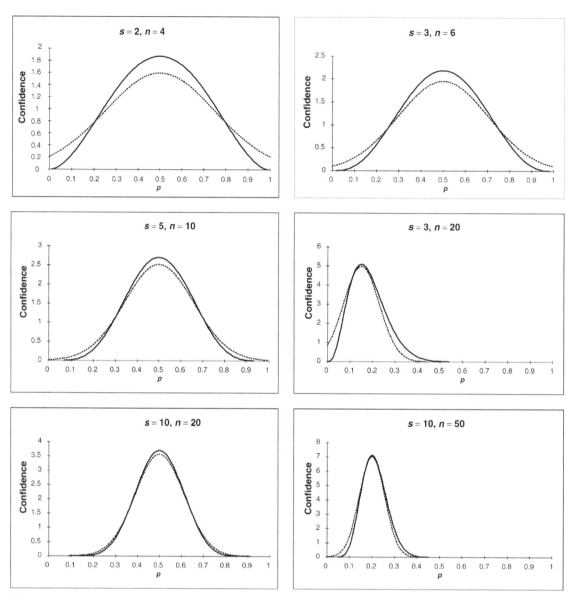

Figure 9.17   Comparisons of the Beta$(s + 1, n - s + 1)$ distribution and its normal approximation for several combinations of s and n (beta distributions in filled lines, normal approximations in dashed lines).

Example 9.6   Uncertainty of λ in a Poisson process

The number of earthquakes that have occurred in a region of the Pacific during the last 20 years are shown in Table 9.2. What is the probability that there will be more than 10 earthquakes next year?

Let us assume that the earthquakes come from a Poisson process (it probably doesn't, I admit, since one big earthquake can release built-up pressure and give a hiatus until the next one), i.e. that there is a constant probability per unit time of an earthquake and that all earthquakes are independent of each

Table 9.2 Pacific earthquakes.

Year	Earthquakes	Year	Earthquakes
1979	8	1989	11
1980	7	1990	4
1981	9	1991	13
1982	5	1992	4
1983	7	1993	9
1984	7	1994	3
1985	6	1995	11
1986	5	1996	3
1987	6	1997	7
1988	4	1998	8

other. If such an assumption is acceptable, then we need to determine the value of the Poisson process parameter λ, the theoretical true mean number of earthquakes there would be per year. Assuming no prior knowledge, we can proceed with a Bayesian analysis, labelling $\lambda = \theta$ as the parameter to be estimated. The prior distribution should be uninformed, which, as discussed in Section 9.2.2, leads us to use a prior $\pi(\theta) = 1/\theta$. The likelihood function $l(\theta|X)$ for the x_i observations in n years is given by

$$l(X|\theta) \propto \prod_{i=1}^{n} e^{-\theta} \theta^{x_i}$$

which gives a posterior function

$$f(\theta) = \pi(\theta)l(X|\theta) \propto e^{-n\theta} \theta^{\sum_{i=1}^{n} x_i - 1}$$

Taking logs gives

$$L(\theta) = k - n\theta + \left(\sum_{i=1}^{n} x_i - 1 \right) \log_e[\theta]$$

Our best estimate θ_0 is determined by

$$\left. \frac{dL(\theta)}{d\theta} \right|_{\theta_0} = -n + \frac{\sum_{i=1}^{n} x_i - 1}{\theta_0} = 0$$

which gives

$$\theta_0 = \frac{\sum_{i=1}^{n} x_i - 1}{n}$$

and the standard deviation for the normal approximation is given by

$$\sigma = \left[-\frac{d^2 L(\theta)}{d\theta^2} \bigg|_{\theta_0} \right]^{-1/2} = \left[\frac{\theta_0^2}{\sum_{i=1}^{n} x_i - 1} \right]^{1/2} = \sqrt{\frac{\theta_0}{n}} \qquad (9.15)$$

since

$$\theta_0 = \frac{\sum_{i=1}^{n} x_i - 1}{n}$$

which gives our estimate for λ:

$$\lambda \approx \text{Normal}\left(\theta_0, \sqrt{\frac{\theta_0}{n}} \right)$$

Again this solution makes sense, and again we see that the uncertainty decreases proportional to the square root of the amount of data n. The central limit theorem (see Section 6.3.3) says that, for large n, the uncertainty about the true mean μ of a population can be described as

$$\mu \approx \text{Normal}(\bar{x}, s/\sqrt{n})$$

where $\bar{x}$ is the mean and s is the standard deviation of the data sampled from the parent distribution. The Poisson distribution has a variance equal to its mean λ, and therefore a standard deviation equal to $\sqrt{\lambda}$. As $\sum_{i=1}^{n} x_i$ gets large, so the "-1" in the above formula for θ_0 gets progressively less important and θ_0 gets closer and closer to the mean of the observations per period $\bar{x}$, and we see that the Bayesian approach and the central limit theorem of classical statistics converge to the same answer. $\sum_{i=1}^{n} x_i$ will be large when either λ is large, so each x_i is large, or when there are a lot of data (i.e. n is large), so that the sum of a lot of small x_i is still large. Figure 9.18 provides three estimates of λ, the true mean number of earthquakes for the system, given the data for earthquakes for the last 20 years, namely: the standard Bayesian approach, the normal approximation to the Bayesian and the central limit theorem approximation. ◆

Example 9.7 Estimate of the mean of a normal distribution with unknown standard deviation

Assume that we have a set of n data samples from a normal distribution with unknown mean μ and unknown standard deviation σ. We would like to determine our best estimate of the mean together with the appropriate level of uncertainty. A normal distribution can have a mean anywhere in $[-\infty, +\infty]$, so we could use a uniform improper prior $\pi(\mu) = k$. From the discussion in Section 9.2.2, the uninformed prior for the standard deviation should be $\pi(\sigma) = 1/\sigma$ to ensure invariance under a linear transformation. The likelihood function is given by the normal distribution density function:

$$l(X|\mu, \sigma) = \frac{1}{(2\pi\sigma^2)^{n/2}} \exp\left(-\frac{1}{2\sigma^2} \sum_{i=1}^{n} (x_i - \mu)^2 \right)$$

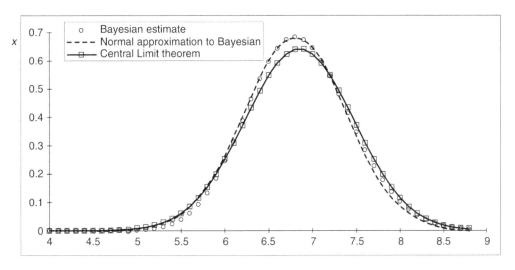

Figure 9.18 Uncertainty distributions for λ by various methods.

Multiplying the priors together with the likelihood function and integrating over all possible values of σ, we arrive at the posterior distribution for μ:

$$f(\mu) \propto [n(\overline{x} - \mu)^2 + ns^2]^{-n/2}$$

where $\overline{x}$ and s are the mean and sample standard deviation of the data values.

Now the Student t-distribution with v degrees of freedom has the probability density

$$f(x) \propto \left[1 + \frac{x^2}{v}\right]^{-(v+1)/2}$$

The equation for $f(\mu)$ is of the same form as the equation for $f(x)$ if we set $v = n - 1$. If we divide the term inside the square brackets for $f(\mu)$ by the constant ns^2, we get

$$f(\mu) \propto \left[\frac{(\overline{x} - \mu)^2}{s^2} + 1\right]^{-n/2}$$

so the equation above for $f(\mu)$ equates to a shifted, rescaled Student t-distribution with $(n - 1)$ degrees of freedom. Specifically, μ can be modelled as

$$\mu = t(n - 1)\frac{s}{\sqrt{n - 1}} + \overline{x}$$

where $t(n - 1)$ represents the Student t-distribution with $(n - 1)$ degrees of freedom. This is the exact result used in classical statistics, as described in Section 9.1.3. ◆

Example 9.8 Estimate of the mean of a normal distribution with known standard deviation

This is a more specific case than the previous example and might occur, for example, if one was making many measurements of the same parameter but believed that the measurements had independent, normally distributed errors and no bias (so the distribution of possible values would be centred about the true value).

We proceed in exactly the same way as before, giving a uniform prior for μ and using a normal likelihood function for the observed n measurements $\{x_i\}$. No prior is needed for σ since it is known, and we arrive at a posterior distribution for μ given by

$$f(\mu) = \frac{1}{(2\pi\sigma^2)^{n/2}} \exp\left(-\frac{1}{2\sigma^2} \sum_{i=1}^{n} (x_i - \mu)^2\right)$$

Taking logs gives

$$L(\mu) = \log_e[f(\mu)] = -\frac{n}{2}\log_e[2\pi] - n\log_e[\sigma] - \frac{1}{2\sigma^2} \sum_{i=1}^{n} (x_i - \mu)^2$$

i.e., since σ is known,

$$L(\mu) = k - \frac{1}{2\sigma^2} \sum_{i=1}^{n} (x_i - \mu)^2$$

where k is some constant. Differentiating twice, we get

$$\frac{dL(\mu)}{d\mu} = \frac{1}{\sigma^2}\left(\sum_{i=1}^{n} x_i - \mu n\right)$$

$$\frac{d^2 L(\mu)}{d\mu^2} = \frac{-n}{\sigma^2}$$

The best estimate μ_0 of μ is that value for which $\frac{dL(\mu)}{d\mu} = 0$:

$$\left.\frac{dL(\mu)}{d\mu}\right|_{\mu_0} = \frac{1}{\sigma^2}\left(\sum_{i=1}^{n} x_i - \mu_0 n\right) = 0$$

i.e. μ_0 is the average of the data values $\bar{x}$ – no surprise there! A Taylor series expansion of this function about μ_0 gives

$$L(\mu) = L(\mu_0) + \left.\frac{d^2 L(\mu)}{d\mu^2}\right|_{\mu_0} \frac{(\mu - \mu_0)^2}{2} = -\frac{n}{\sigma^2}\frac{(\mu - \mu_0)^2}{2} \tag{9.16}$$

The second term is missing because it equals zero and there are no other higher-order terms since $(d^2 L(\mu)/d\mu^2) = (-n/\sigma^2)$ is independent of μ and any further differential therefore equals zero. Consequently, Equation (9.16) is an exact result.

Taking natural exponents to convert back to $f(\mu)$, and rearranging a little, we get

$$f(\mu) = K \exp\left(\frac{(\mu - \overline{x})^2}{2\left(\frac{\sigma}{\sqrt{n}}\right)^2}\right)$$

where K is a normalising constant. By comparison with the probability density function for the normal distribution, it is easy to see that this is just a normal density function with mean $\overline{x}$ and standard deviation $\sigma/\sqrt{n}$. In other words

$$\mu = \text{Normal}(\overline{x}, \sigma/\sqrt{n})$$

which is the classical statistics result of Equation (9.4) and a result predictable from the central limit theorem. ◆

Exercise 9.4: Bayesian uncertainty for the standard deviation of a normal distribution.

  Show that the Bayesian inference results of uncertainty about the standard deviation of a normal distribution take a similar form to the classical statistics results of Section 9.1.2.

9.2.6 Markov chain simulation: the Metropolis algorithm and the Gibbs sampler

Gibbs sampling is a simulation technique to obtain a required Bayesian posterior distribution and is particularly useful for multiparameter models where it is difficult algebraically to define, normalise and draw from a posterior distribution. The method is based on Markov chain simulation: a technique that creates a Markov process (a type of random walk) whose stationary distribution (the distribution of the values it will take after a very large number of steps) is the required posterior distribution. The technique requires that one runs the Markov chain a sufficiently large number of steps to be close to the stationary distribution, and then records the generated values. The trick to a Markov chain model is to determine a transition distribution $T_t(\theta^t | \theta^{t-1})$ (the distribution of possible values for the Markov chain at its ith step θ^i, conditional on the value generated in the $(i - 1)$th step θ^{i-1}) that converges to the posterior distribution.

The metropolis algorithm

The transition distribution T_t is a combination of some symmetric jumping distribution $J_t(\theta^i | \theta^{i-1})$, which lets one move from one value θ^{i-1} to another randomly selected θ^*, and a weighting function that assigns the probability of jumping to θ^* (as opposed to staying still) as the ratio r, where

$$r = \frac{p(\theta^* | X)}{p(\theta^{t-1} | X)}$$

so that

$$\begin{aligned} \theta^i &= \theta^* \quad \text{with probability} \min[1, r] \\ &= \theta^{i-1} \quad \text{otherwise} \end{aligned}$$

The technique relies on being able to sample from J_t for all i and θ^{i-1}, as well as being able to calculate r for all jumps. For multiparameter problems, the Metropolis algorithm is very inefficient: the Gibbs sampler provides a method that achieves the same posterior distribution but with far fewer model iterations.

The Gibbs sampler

The Gibbs sampler, also called *alternating conditional sampling*, is used in multiparameter problems, i.e. where θ is a d-dimensional vector with components $(\theta_1, \ldots, \theta_d)$. The Gibbs sampler cycles through all the components of θ for each iteration, so there are d steps in each iteration. The order in which the components are taken is changed at random from one iteration to the next. In a cycle, the kth component is replaced ($k = 1$ to d, while all of the other components are kept fixed in turn) with a value drawn from a distribution with probability density

$$f(\theta_k | \theta_{-k}^{i-1}, X)$$

where θ_{-k}^{i-1} are all the other components of θ except for θ_k at their current value. This may look rather awkward as one has to determine and sample from d separate distributions for each iteration of the Gibbs sampler. However, the conditional distributions are often conjugate distributions, which makes sampling from them a lot simpler and quicker. Have a look at Gelman *et al.* (1995) for a very readable discussion of various Markov chain models, and for a number of examples of their use. Gilks *et al.* (1996) is written by some of the real gurus of MCMC methods.

MCMC in practice

Some terribly smart people write their own Gibbs sampling programs, but for the rest of us there is a product called WinBUGS developed originally at Cambridge University. It is free to download and the software most used for MCMC modelling. It isn't that easy to get the software to work for you unless you are familiar with S-plus or R type script, and one always waits with baited breathe for the message "Compiled successfully" because there is rather little in the way of hints about what to do when it doesn't compile. On the plus side, the actual probability model is quite intuitive to write and WinBUGS has the flexibility to allow different datasets to be incorporated into the same model. The software is also continuously improving, and several people have written interfaces to it through the OpenBUGS project. To use the WinBUGS output, you will need to export the CODA file for data (after a sufficient burn-in) to a spreadsheet, move the data around to have one column per parameter and then randomly sample across a line (i.e. one MCMC iteration) in just the same way I explain for bootstrapping paired data. The ModelRisk function VoseNBootPaired allows you to do this very simply.

9.3 The Bootstrap

The bootstrap was introduced by Efron (1979) and is explored in great depth in Efron and Tibshirani (1993) and perhaps more practically in Davison and Hinkley (1997). This section presents a rather brief introduction that covers most of the important concepts. The bootstrap appears at first sight to be rather dubious, but it has earned its place as a useful technique because (a) it corresponds well to traditional techniques where they are available, particularly when a large dataset has been obtained, and (b) it offers an opportunity to assess the uncertainty about a parameter where classical statistics has no technique available and without recourse to determining a prior.

The "bootstrap" gets its name from the phrase "to pull yourself up by your bootstraps", which is thought to originate from one of the tales in the Adventures of Baron Munchausen by Rudolph Erich Raspe (1737–1794). Baron Munchausen (1720–1797) actually existed and was known as an enormous boaster, especially of his exploits during his time as a Russian cavalry officer. Raspe wrote ludicrous stories supposedly in his name (he would have been sued these days). In one story, the Baron was at the bottom of a deep lake and in some trouble, until he thought of pulling himself up by his bootstraps. The name "bootstrap" does not perhaps engender much confidence in the technique: you get the impression that there is an attempt somehow to get something from nothing – actually, it *does* seem that way when one first looks at the technique itself. However, the bootstrap has shown itself to be a powerful method of statistical analysis and, if used with care, can provide results very easily and in areas where traditional statistical techniques are not available.

In its simplest form, which is the *non-parametric bootstrap*, the technique is very straightforward indeed. The standard notation as used by Efron is perhaps a little confusing, though, to the beginner, and, since I am not going into any great sophistication in this book, I have modified the notation a little to keep it as simple as possible. The bootstrap is used in similar conditions to Bayesian inference, i.e. we have a set of data x randomly drawn from some population distribution F for which we wish to estimate some statistical parameter.

The jackknife

The bootstrap was originally developed from a much earlier technique called the jackknife. The jackknife was used to review the accuracy of a statistic calculated from a set of data. A *jackknife value* was the statistic of interest calculated with the ith value removed from the dataset and is given the notation $\hat{\theta}_{(i)}$. With a dataset of n values, one thus has n jackknife values, the distribution of which gives a feel for the uncertainty one has about the true value of the statistic. I say "gives a feel" because the reader is certainly *not* recommended to use the jackknife as a method for obtaining any precise estimate of uncertainty. The jackknife turns out to be quite a poor estimation of uncertainty and can be greatly improved upon.

9.3.1 The non-parametric bootstrap

Imagine that we have a set of n random measurements of some characteristic of a population (the height of 100 blades of grass from my lawn, for example) and we wish to estimate some parameter of that population (the true mean height of all blades of grass from my lawn, for example). Bootstrap theory says that the true distribution F of these blades of grass can be reasonably approximated by the distribution $\hat{F}$ of observed values. Obviously, this is a more reasonable assumption the more data one has collected. The theory then constructs this distribution $\hat{F}$ of the n observed values and takes another n random samples (with replacement) from that constructed distribution and calculates the statistic of interest from that sample. The sampling from the constructed distribution and statistic calculation is repeated a large number of times until a reasonably stable distribution of the statistic of interest is obtained. This is the distribution of uncertainty about the parameter.

The method is best illustrated with a simple example. Imagine that I work for a contact lens manufacturer in Auckland and for some reason would really like to know the mean diameter of the pupils of the eyes of New Zealand's population under some specific light condition. I have a limited budget, so I randomly select 10 people off the street and measure their pupils while controlling the ambient light. The results I get are (in mm): 5.92, 5.06, 6.16, 5.60, 4.87, 5.61, 5.72, 5.36, 6.03 and 5.71. This dataset forms my bootstrap estimate of the true distribution for the whole population, so I now randomly sample

	A	B	C	D	E	F	G
1							
2			*Bootstrap*			*Formulae table*	
3		*Data*	*sample*		B4:B13	Data values	
4		5.92	6.03		C4:C13	=VoseDUniform($B$4:$B$13)	
5		5.06	5.60		C14	=AVERAGE(C4:C13)	
6		6.16	5.60				
7		5.60	5.72				
8		4.87	5.92				
9		5.61	5.71				
10		5.72	5.72				
11		5.36	5.92				
12		6.03	5.71				
13		5.71	6.03				
14		Average	5.80				
15							

Figure 9.19   Example of a non-parametric bootstrap model.

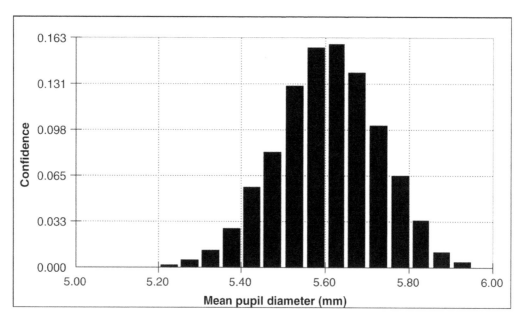

Figure 9.20   Uncertainty distribution resulting from the model of Figure 9.19.

with replacement from the distribution $\hat{F}$ to get 10 bootstrap samples. The spreadsheet in Figure 9.19 illustrates the bootstrap sampling: column B lists the original data and column C gives 10 bootstrap samples from these data using the Duniform($\{x\}$) distribution (Duniform($\{x\}$) is a discrete distribution where all values in the $\{x\}$ array are equally likely). Cell C14 then calculates the statistic of interest (the mean) from this sample. Running a 10 000 iteration simulation on this cell produces the bootstrap uncertainty distribution shown in Figure 9.20. The distribution is roughly normal (skewness $= -0.16$, kurtosis $= 3.02$) with mean $= 5.604$ – the mean of the original dataset.

In summary, the non-parametric bootstrap proceeds as follows:

- Collect the dataset of n samples $\{x_1, \ldots, x_n\}$.
- Create B bootstrap samples $\{x_1^*, \ldots, x_n^*\}$ where each x_i^* is a random sample with replacement from $\{x_1, \ldots x_n\}$.
- For each bootstrap sample $\{x_1^*, \ldots, x_n^*\}$, calculate the required statistic $\hat{\theta}$. The distribution of these B estimates of θ represents the bootstrap estimate of uncertainty about the true value of θ.

Example 9.9 Bootstrap estimate of prevalence

Prevalence is the proportion of a population that has a particular characteristic. An estimate of the prevalence P is usually made by randomly sampling from the population and seeing what proportion of the sample has that particular characteristic. Our confidence around this single-point estimate can be obtained quite easily using the non-parametric bootstrap. Imagine that we have randomly surveyed 50 voters in Washington, DC, and asked them how many will be voting for the Democrats in a presidential election the following day. Let's rather naïvely assume that they all tell the truth and that none of them will have a change of mind before tomorrow. The result of the survey is that 19 people said they will vote Democrat. Our dataset is therefore a set of 50 values, 19 of which are 1 and 31 of which are 0. A non-parametric bootstrap would sample from this dataset. Thus, the bootstrap replicate would be equivalent to a Binomial(50, 19/50). The estimate of prevalence is then just the proportion of the bootstrap samples that are 1, i.e. $P = $ Binomial(50, 19/50)/50. This is exactly the same as the classical statistics estimate given in Equation (9.6), and, interestingly, the parametric bootstrap (see next section) has exactly the same estimate in this example too. The distribution being sampled in a parametric bootstrap is a Binomial(1, P) from which we have 50 samples and our MLE (maximum likelihood estimator) for P is 19/50. Thus, the 50 parametric bootstrap replicates could be summed together as a Binomial(50, 19/50), and our estimate for P is again Binomial(50, 19/50)/50.

We could have used a Bayesian inference approach. With a Uniform(0, 1) prior, and a binomial likelihood function (which assumes the population is much larger than the sample), we would have an estimate of prevalence using the beta distribution (see Section 8.2.3):

$$P = \text{Beta}(20, 32)$$

Figure 9.21 plots the Bayesian estimate alongside the bootstrap for comparison. They are very close, except that the bootstrap estimate is discrete and the Bayesian is continuous, and, as the sample size increases, they would become progressively closer. ♦

9.3.2 The parametric bootstrap

The non-parametric bootstrap in the previous section made no assumptions about the distributional form of the population (parent) distribution. However, there will be many times that we will know to which family of distributions the parent distribution belongs. For example, the number of earthquakes each year and the number of Giardia cysts in litres of water drawn from a lake will logically both be approximately Poisson distributed; the time between phone calls to an exchange will be roughly exponentially distributed and the number of males in randomly sampled groups of a certain size will be

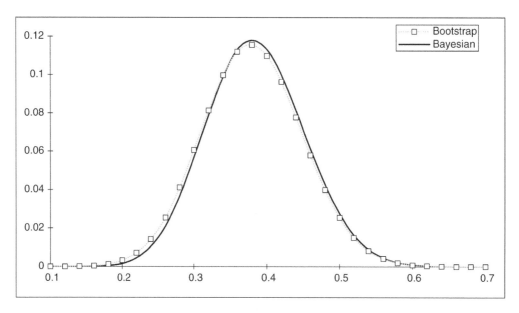

Figure 9.21 Bootstrap and Bayesian estimates of prevalence for Example 9.9.

binomially distributed. The parametric bootstrap gives us a means to use the extra information we have about the population distribution. The procedure is as follows:

- Collect the dataset of n samples $\{x_1, \ldots, x_n\}$.
- Determine the parameter(s) of the distribution that best fit(s) the data from the known distribution family using maximum likelihood estimators (MLEs – see Section 10.3.1).
- Generate B bootstrap samples $\{x_1^*, \ldots, x_n^*\}$ by randomly sampling from this fitted distribution.
- For each bootstrap sample $\{x_1^*, \ldots, x_n^*\}$, calculate the required statistic $\hat{\theta}$. The distribution of these B estimates of θ represents the bootstrap estimate of uncertainty about the true value of θ.

We can illustrate the technique by using the pupil measurement data again. Let us assume that we know for some reason (perhaps experience from other countries) that this measurement should be normally distributed for a population. The normal distribution has two parameters – its mean and standard deviation, both of which we will assume to be unknown – and their MLEs are the mean and standard deviation of the data to be fitted. The mean and standard deviation of the pupil measurements are 5.604 mm and 0.410 mm respectively. Figure 9.22 shows a spreadsheet model where, in column C, 10 Normal(5.604, 0.410) distributions are randomly sampled to give the bootstrap sample. Cell D14 is calculating the mean (the statistic of interest) of the bootstrap sample. Figure 9.23 shows the results of this parametric bootstrap model, together with the result from applying the classical statistics method of Equation 9.2 – they are very similar. The result also looks very similar to the non-parametric distribution of Figure 9.20. In comparison with the classical statistics model, which happens to be exact for this particular problem (i.e. when the parent distribution is normal), both bootstrap methods provide a narrower range. In other words, the bootstrap in its simplest form tends to underestimate the uncertainty associated with the parameter of interest. A number of corrective measures are proposed in Efron and Tibshirani (1993).

	A	B	C	D	E	F	G	H
1								
2				*Bootstrap*			*Formulae table*	
3			*Data*	*sample*		C4:C13	Data values	
4			5.92	5.57		C14	=AVERAGE(C4:C13)	
5			5.06	5.72		C15	=STDEV(C4:C13)	
6			6.16	5.25		D4:D13	=VoseNormal($C$14,$C$15)	
7			5.60	6.01		D14 (output)	=AVERAGE(D4:D13)	
8			4.87	4.91				
9			5.61	6.06				
10			5.72	5.57				
11			5.36	5.54				
12			6.03	4.68				
13			5.71	4.69				
14		*Mean*	5.60	5.40				
15		*Stdev*	0.4095					
16								

Figure 9.22 Example of a parametric bootstrap model.

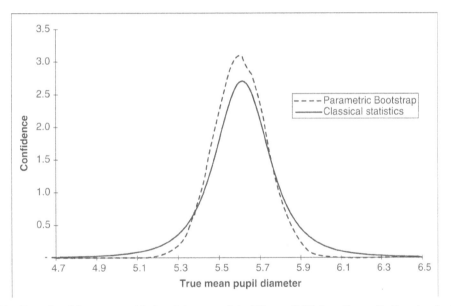

Figure 9.23 Results of the parametric bootstrap model of Figure 9.22, together with the classical statistics result.

Imagine that we wish to estimate the true depth of a well using some sort of sonic probe. The probe has a known standard error $\sigma = 0.2$ m, i.e. σ is the standard deviation of the normally distributed variation of results the probe will produce when repetitively measuring the same depth. In order to estimate this depth, we take n separate measurements. These measurements have a mean of $\bar{x}$ metres. The parametric bootstrap model would take the average of n Normal$(\bar{x}, \sigma)$ distributions to estimate the true mean μ of the distribution of possible measurement results, i.e. the true well depth. From the central limit theorem, we know that this calculation is equivalent to

$$\mu = \text{Normal}\left(\bar{x}, \frac{\sigma}{\sqrt{n}}\right)$$

which is the classical statistics result of Equation (9.3). ◆

Parametric bootstrap estimate of the standard deviation of a normal distribution

It can also be shown that the parametric bootstrap estimates of the standard deviation of a normal distribution when the mean is and is not known are exactly the same as the classical statistics estimates given in Equations (9.5) and (9.6) (the reader may like to prove this, bearing in mind that the ChiSq(v) distribution is the sum of the squares of v independent unit normal distributions).

Example 9.10 Parametric bootstrap estimate of mean time between calls at a telephone exchange

Imagine that we want to predict the number of phone calls there will be at an exchange during a particular hour in the working day (say 2 p.m. to 3 p.m.). Imagine that we have collected data from this period on n separate, randomly selected days. It is reasonable to assume that telephone calls will arrive at a Poisson rate since each call will be, roughly speaking, independent of every other. Thus, we could use a Poisson distribution to model the number of calls in an hour. The maximum likelihood estimate (MLE) of the mean number of calls per hour at this time of day is simply the average number of calls observed in the test periods $\bar{x}$ (see Example 10.3 for proof). Thus, our bootstrap replicate is a set of n independent Poisson($\bar{x}$) distributions. To generate our uncertainty about the true mean number of phone calls per hour at this time of the day, we calculate the mean of the sum of the bootstrap replicate, i.e. the average of n independent Poisson($\bar{x}$) distributions. The sum of n independent Poisson($\bar{x}$) distributions is simply Poisson($n\bar{x}$), so the average of n Poisson($\bar{x}$) distributions is Poisson($n\bar{x}$)/n, where ($n\bar{x}$) is simply the sum of the observations. So, in general, if one has observations from n periods, the Poisson parametric bootstrap for the mean number of observations per period λ is given by

$$\lambda = \text{Poisson}(S)/n$$

where S is the sum of observations in the n periods.

The uncertainty distribution of λ should be continuous, as λ can take any positive real value. However, the bootstrap will only generate discrete values for λ, i.e. $\{0, 1/n, 2/n, \ldots\}$. When n is large this is not a problem since the allowable values are close together, but when S is small the approximation starts to fall down. Figure 9.24 illustrates three Poisson parametric bootstrap estimates for λ for $S = 2$, 10 and 20 combined with $n = 5$. For $S = 2$, the discreteness will in some circumstances be an inadequate uncertainty model for λ, and a different technique like Bayesian inference would be preferable. However, for values of S around 20 or more, the allowable values are relatively close together. For large S, one can also add back the continuous characteristic of the parameter by making a normal approximation to the Poisson, i.e. since Poisson(α) $\approx$ Normal(α, $\sqrt{\alpha}$) we get

$$\lambda \approx \text{Normal}(S/n, \sqrt{S}/n)$$

or, replacing S/n with $\bar{x}$, we get

$$\lambda \approx \text{Normal}\left(\bar{x}, \sqrt{\frac{\bar{x}}{n}}\right)$$

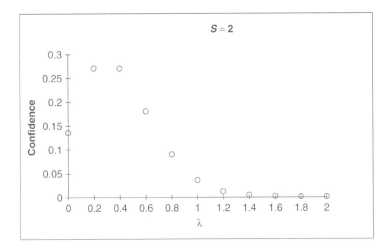

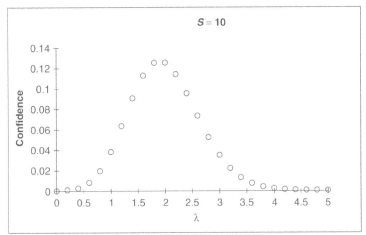

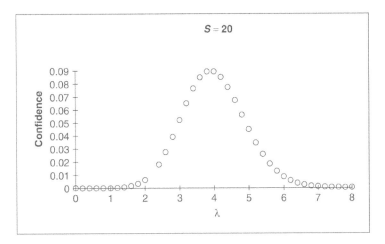

Figure 9.24   Three Poisson parametric bootstrap estimates for λ for S = 2, 10 and 20 from Example 9.10.

which also illustrates the familiar reduction in uncertainty as the square root of the number of data points n. ◆

9.3.3 The Bayesian bootstrap

The Bayesian bootstrap is considered to be a robust Bayesian approach for estimating a parameter of a distribution where one has a random sample x from that distribution. It proceeds in the usual bootstrap way, determining a distribution of $\hat{\theta}$, the distribution density of which is then interpreted as the likelihood function $l(x|\theta)$. This is then used in the standard Bayesian inference formula (Equation (9.8)) along with a prior distribution $\pi(\theta)$ for θ to determine the posterior distribution. In many cases, the bootstrap distribution for $\hat{\theta}$ closely approximates a normal distribution, so, by calculating the mean and standard deviation of the B bootstrap replicates $\hat{\theta}$, one can quickly define a likelihood function.

9.4 Maximum Entropy Principle

The maximum entropy formalism (sometimes known as MaxEnt) is a statistical method for determining a distribution of maximum logical uncertainty about some parameter, consistent with a certain limited amount of information. For a discrete variable, MaxEnt determines the distribution that maximises the function $H(x)$, where

$$H(x) = -\sum_{i=1}^{M} p_i \ln[p_i]$$

and where p_i is the confidence for each of the M possible values x_i of the variable x. The function $H(x)$ takes the equation of a statistical mechanics property known as entropy, which gives the principle its name. For a continuous variable, $H(x)$ takes the form of an integral function:

$$H(x) = -\int_{min}^{max} f(x) \ln[f(x)] \, dx$$

The appropriate uncertainty distribution is determined by the method of Lagrange multipliers, and, in practice, the continuous variable equation for $H(x)$ is replaced by its discrete counterpart. It is beyond the scope of this book to look too deeply into the mathematics, but there are a number of results that are of general interest. MaxEnt is often used to determine appropriate priors in a Bayesian analysis, so the results listed in Table 9.3 give some reassurance to prior distributions we might wish to use conservatively to represent our prior knowledge.

The reader is recommended Sivia (1996) for a very readable explanation of the principle of MaxEnt and derivation of some of its results. Gzyl (1995) provides a far more advanced treatise on the subject, but requires a much higher level of mathematical understanding. The normal distribution result is interesting and provides some justification for the common use of the normal distribution when all we know is the mean and variance (standard deviation), since it represents the most reasonably conservative estimate of the parameter given that set of knowledge. The uniform distribution result is also very encouraging when estimating a binomial probability, for example. The use of a Beta$(s + a, n - s + b)$ to represent the uncertainty about the binomial probability p when we have observed s successes in n trials assumes a Beta(a, b) prior. A Beta$(1, 1)$ is a Uniform$(0, 1)$ distribution, and thus our most honest estimate of p is given by Beta$(s + 1, n - s + 1)$.

Table 9.3 Maximum entropy method.

State of knowledge	MaxEnt distribution
Discrete parameter, n possible values $\{x_i\}$	DUniform($\{x_i\}$), i.e. $p(x_i) = 1/n$
Continuous parameter, minimum and maximum	Uniform(min, max), i.e. $f(x) = 1/(\text{max} - \text{min})$
Continuous parameter, known mean μ and variance σ^2	Normal(μ, σ)
Continuous parameter, known mean μ	Expon(μ)
Discrete parameter, known mean μ	Poisson(μ)

9.5 Which Technique Should You Use?

I have discussed a variety of methods for estimating your uncertainty about some model parameter. The question now is which one is best? There are some situations where classical statistics has exact methods for determining confidence intervals. In such cases, it is sensible to use those methods of course, and the results are unlikely to be challenged. In situations where the assumptions behind traditional statistical methods are being stretched rather too much for comfort, you will have to use your judgement as to which technique to use. Bootstraps, particularly the parametric bootstrap, are powerful classical statistics techniques and have the advantage of remaining purely objective. They are widely accepted by statisticians and can also be used to determine uncertainty distributions for statistics like the median, kurtosis or standard deviation for parent distributions where classical statistics have no method to offer. However, it is a fairly new (in statistics terms) technique, so you may find people resisting making decisions based on its results, and the results can be rather "grainy".

The Bayesian inference technique requires some knowledge of an appropriate likelihood function, which may be difficult and will often require some subjectivity in assessing what is a sufficiently accurate function to use. Bayesian inference also requires a prior, which can be contentious at times, but has the potential to include knowledge that the other techniques cannot allow for. Traditional statisticians will sometimes offer a technique to use on your data that implicitly assumes a random sample from a normal distribution, though the parent distribution is clearly not normal. This usually involves some sort of approximation or a translation of the data (e.g. by taking logs) to make the data better fit a normal distribution. While I appreciate the reasons for doing this, I do find it difficult to know what errors one is introducing by such data manipulation.

Pretty often in our consulting work there is no option but to use Gibbs sampling because it is the only way to handle multivariate estimates that are good for risk analysis. The WinBUGS program may be a little difficult to use but the models can be made very transparent. I suggest that, if the parameter to your model is important, it may well be worth comparing two techniques (for example, non-parametric bootstrap (or parametric, if possible) and Bayesian inference with an uninformed prior). It will certainly give you greater confidence if there is reasonable agreement between any two methods you might choose. What is meant by *reasonable* will depend on your model and the level of accuracy your decision-maker needs from that model. If you find there appears to be some reasonable disagreement between two methods that you test, you could try running your model twice, once with each estimate, and seeing if the model outputs are significantly different. Finally, if the uncertainty distributions between two methods are significantly different and you cannot choose between them, it makes sense to accept that this is another source of uncertainty and simply combine the two distributions, using a discrete distribution, in the same way I describe in Section 14.3.4 on combining differing expert opinions.

9.6 Adding uncertainty in Simple Linear Least-Squares Regression Analysis

In least-squares regression, one is attempting to model the change in one variable y (the response or dependent variable) as a function of one or more other variables $\{x\}$ (the explanatory or independent variables). The regression relationship between $\{x\}$ and y minimises the sum of squared errors between a fitted equation for y and the observations. The theory of least-squares regression assumes the random variations about this line (resulting from effects not explained by the explanatory variables) to be normally distributed with constant variance across all $\{x\}$ values, which means the fitted line describes the mean y value for a given set of $\{x\}$. For simplicity we will consider a single explanatory variable x (i.e. simple regression analysis), and that the relationship between x and y is linear (which is linear regression analysis), i.e. we will use a model of the variability in y as a result of changes in x with the following equation:

$$y = \text{Normal}(mx + c, \sigma)$$

where m and c are the gradient and y intercept of the straight-line relationship between x and y, and σ is the standard deviation of the additional variation observed in y that is not explained by the linear equation in x. Figure 6.11 illustrates these concepts. In least-squares linear regression, we typically have a set of n paired observations $\{x_i, y_i\}$ for which we wish to fit this linear relationship.

9.6.1 Classical statistics

Classical statistics theory (see Section 6.3.9) provides us with the best-fitting values for m, c and σ, assuming the model's assumptions to be correct, which we will name $\hat{m}, \hat{c}$ and $\hat{\sigma}$. It also gives us exact distributions of uncertainty for the estimate $\hat{y}_P = (mx_P + c)$ at some value x_P (see, for example, McClave, Dietrich and Sincich, 1997) and σ as follows:

$$\hat{y}_P = t(n-2)s\sqrt{\frac{1}{n} + \frac{(x_P - \overline{x})^2}{SS_{xx}}}$$

$$\sigma = \sqrt{\frac{(n-1)s^2}{\chi^2(n-1)}}$$

where

$$SS_{xx} = \sum_{i=1}^{x} (x_i - \overline{x})^2$$

$t(n-2)$ is a Student t-distribution with $(n-2)$ degrees of freedom, $\chi^2(n-1)$ is a chi-square distribution with $(n-1)$ degrees of freedom and s is the standard deviation of the differences e_i between the observed value y_i and its predictor $\hat{y}_i = \hat{m}x_i + \hat{c}$, i.e.

$$s = \sum_{i=1}^{n} \frac{(y_i - (\hat{m}x_i + \hat{c}))^2}{n-1}$$

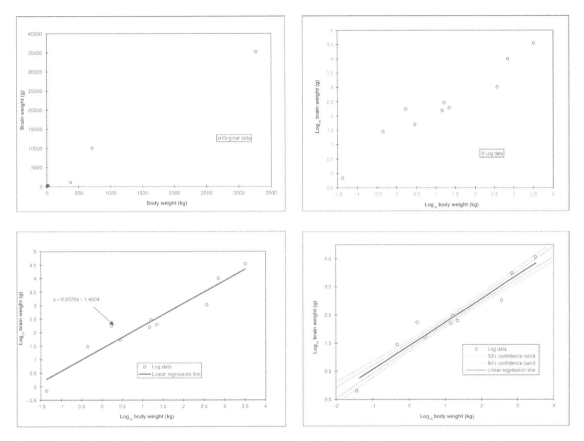

Figure 9.25 Simple least-squares regression uncertainty about $\hat{y}$ for the dataset of Table 9.4.

The uncertainty distribution for σ is independent of the uncertainty distribution for $(mx + c)$, since the model assumes that the random variations about the regression line are constant, i.e. that they are independent of the values of x and y. It turns out that these same results are given by Bayesian inference with uninformed priors, i.e. $\pi(m, c, \sigma) \propto 1/\sigma$.

The uncertainty equation for $\hat{y}_i = mx_i + c$ produces a relationship between x and y with uncertainty that is pinched at the middle, as shown in the simple least-squares regression analysis of Figure 9.25 for the data in Table 9.4. This makes sense as, the further we move towards the extremes of the set of observations, the more uncertain we should be about the relationship. This describes the relationship between the weight of a mammal in kilograms and the mean weight of the brain of a mammal in grams at that body weight. Strictly speaking, the theory of regression analysis says that the relationship can only be considered to hold within the range of observed values for x. However, with caution, one can reasonably extrapolate a little past the range of observed body weights, although, the further one extends beyond the observed range, the more tenuous the validity of the analysis becomes.

Including uncertainty in a regression analysis means that we now have a family of normal distributions representing the possible value of y, given a specific value for x. The normal distribution reflects the observed variability about the regression line. That there is a family of these distributions reflects our

Table 9.4 Experimental measurements of the weight of mammals' bodies and brains.

Brain weight (g)	Body weight (kg)
2.844	50.856
713.72	9 958.02
22.309	193.49
16.265	294.52
14.69	155.74
0.0436	0.685
0.4492	29.05
3 270.15	35 160.5
1.698	175.92
372.97	1 034.4

uncertainty about the coefficients for the regression equation and therefore the parameters for the normal distribution.

The bootstrap

The variables x and y will fit a simple least-squares regression model if the underlying relationship between these two variables is one of two forms: type A where the $\{x_i, y_i\}$ observations are drawn from a bivariate normal distribution in x and y, or type B where, for any value x, the distribution of possible response values in y are Normal($mx + c$, $\sigma(x)$) distributed and, for the time being, $\sigma(x) = \sigma$, i.e. the random variations about the line have the same standard deviation (known as homoscedasticity). In order to use the bootstrap to determine the uncertainty about the regression coefficients, we must first determine which of these two relationships is occurring. Essentially, this is equivalent to the design of the experiment that produced the $\{x_i, y_i\}$ observations. The experiment design is of type A if we are making random observations of x and y together, whereas the experiment design is of type B if we are testing at different specific values of x to determine the response in y. So, for example, the {body weight, brain weight} data from Table 9.4 are of type A if we have attempted to pick a fairly random sample of mammals, whereas they would be of type B if we had picked an animal from each of the 20 subspecies of a species of some particular mammal. If, for example, we were doing an experiment to demonstrate Hooke's law by adding incremental weights to a hanging spring and observing the resultant extension beyond the spring's original length, the {mass, extension} observations would again be of type B, because we are specifically controlling the x values to observe the resultant y values.

For type A data, the regression coefficients can be thought of as parameters of a bivariate normal distribution. Thus, using the non-parametric bootstrap, we simply resample from the paired observations $\{x_i, y_i\}$ and, at each bootstrap replicate, calculate the regression coefficients. Figure 9.26 illustrates this type of analysis set out in a spreadsheet model for the dataset of Table 9.4.

For type B data, the x values are fixed since they were predetermined rather than resulting from a random sample from a distribution. Assuming the random variations about the regression line to be homoscedastic and the straight-line relationship to be correct, the only random variable involved is

	A	B	C	D	E	F	G	H
1								
2							Bootstrap	
3		Brain weight (gm)	Body weight (kg)	Log(Brain weight)	Log(Body weight)	Log(Brain weight)	Log(Body weight)	
4		0.0436	0.685	−1.361	−0.164	1.348	2.287	
5		0.4492	29.05	−0.348	1.463	0.230	2.245	
6		1.698	175.92	0.230	2.245	0.454	1.706	
7		2.844	50.856	0.454	1.706	1.348	2.287	
8		14.69	155.74	1.167	2.192	3.515	4.546	
9		16.265	294.52	1.211	2.469	−0.348	1.463	
10		22.309	193.49	1.348	2.287	1.211	2.469	
11		372.97	1034.4	2.572	3.015	−1.361	−0.164	
12		713.72	9958.02	2.854	3.998	−1.361	−0.164	
13		3270.15	35160.5	3.515	4.546	0.454	1.706	
14						m	0.91011188	
15			Formulae table			c	1.3382687	
16		B4:C13	Data			Steyx	0.35032446	
17		D4:E13	=LOG(B4)					
18		F4:F13	=VoseDuniform($D$4:$D$13)					
19		G4:G13	=VLOOKUP(F4,$D$4:$E$13,2)					
20		G14	=SLOPE(G4:G13,F4:F13)					
21		G15	=INTERCEPT(G4:G13,F4:F13)					
22		G16	=STEYX(G4:G13,F4:F13)					
23								

Figure 9.26 Example model for a data pairs resampling (type A) bootstrap regression analysis.

	A	B	C	D	E	F	G	H	I
1									
2								Bootstrap	
3		Brain weight (gm)	Body weight (kg)	Log(Brain weight)	Log(Body weight)		Residual	Log(Body weight)	
4		0.0436	0.685	−1.3605	−0.164		−0.425	0.260	
5		0.4492	29.05	−0.348	1.463		0.354	1.109	
6		1.698	175.92	0.230	2.245		0.652	1.593	
7		2.844	50.856	0.454	1.706		−0.074	1.781	
8		14.69	155.74	1.167	2.192		−0.186	2.378	
9		16.265	294.52	1.211	2.469		0.054	2.415	
10		22.309	193.49	1.348	2.287		−0.243	2.530	
11		372.97	1034.4	2.572	3.015		−0.540	3.555	
12		713.72	9958.02	2.854	3.998		0.207	3.791	
13		3270.15	35160.5	3.515	4.546		0.201	4.345	
14							stdev		
15			Formulae table				0.366		
16		B4:C13	Data						
17		D4:E13	=LOG(B4)				m	0.838	
18		G4:G13	=E4−TREND($E$4:$E$13,$D$4:$D$13,D4)				c	1.400	
19		G15	=STDEV(G4:G13)				Steyx	0.24436273	
20		H4:H13	=VoseNormal(E4−G4,$G$15)						
21		H17 (output)	=SLOPE(H4:H13,D4:D13)						
22		H18 (output)	=INTERCEPT(H4:H13,D4:D13)						
23		H19 (output)	=STEYX(H4:H13,D4:D13)						
24									

Figure 9.27 Example model for a residuals resampling (type B) parametric bootstrap regression analysis.

that producing the variations about the line, and so we seek to bootstrap the residuals. If we know the residuals are normally distributed, we can use a parametric bootstrap model, as follows:

1. Determine S_{yx} – the standard deviation of the residuals about the least-squares regression line for the original dataset.
2. For each of the x values in the dataset, randomly sample from a Normal($\hat{y}$, S_{yx}) where $\hat{y} = \hat{m}x + \hat{c}$ and $\hat{m}$ and $\hat{c}$ are the least-squares regression coefficients for the original dataset.
3. Determine the least-squares regression coefficients for this bootstrap sample.
4. Repeat for B iterations.

Figure 9.27 illustrates this procedure in a spreadsheet model for the {body weight, brain weight} data.
Although this procedure works quite well, it would be better to use the classical statistics approach described above, which offers exact answers under these conditions. However, a slight modification to the above approach allows one to use a non-parametric bootstrap, i.e. where we can remove the assumption of normally distributed residuals which may often not be very accurate. For the non-parametric model,

	A	B	C	D	E	F	G	H	I
1									
2		Mass (kg)	Extension (mm)	Residual ε_i	Leverage h_i	Modified residual r_i	Bootstrap Extension		
3		0.0	137.393	0.720	0.228	0.820	127.4		
4		0.1	138.954	2.281	0.187	2.530	132.7		
5		0.2	139.977	3.304	0.151	3.587	136.4		
6		0.3	140.107	3.434	0.122	3.665	132.8		
7		0.4	142.765	6.093	0.099	6.417	151.4		
8		0.5	145.606	8.933	0.081	9.318	134.7		
9		0.6	147.881	11.208	0.069	11.616	149.8		
10		0.7	147.011	10.338	0.063	10.681	142.9		
11		0.8	144.194	7.521	0.063	7.771	145.2		
12		0.9	144.949	8.277	0.069	8.578	154.2		
13		1.0	152.161	15.488	0.081	16.155	160.2		
14		1.1	149.694	13.021	0.099	13.714	150.3		
15		1.2	154.700	18.027	0.122	19.239	153.2		
16		1.3	162.037	25.364	0.151	27.535	147.6		
17		1.4	155.275	18.602	0.187	20.628	156.1		
18		1.5	160.221	23.548	0.228	26.800	167.5		
19		*mean*			*mean*	11.8			
20		0.8							
21		SS_x				*m*	19.81		
22		3.4				*c*	131.54		
23									
24				Formulae table					
25		B3:C18	Data						
26		B20	=AVERAGE(B3:B18)						
27		B22	{=SUM((B3:B18-$B$20)^2)}						
28		D3:D18	=C3-TREND($C$3:$C$18,$B$3:$B$18,0)						
29		E3:E18	=1/16+(B3-$B$20)^2/$B$22						
30		F3:F18	=D3/SQRT(1-E3)						
31		G3:G18	=TREND($C$3:$C$18,$B$3:$B$18,B3)+Duniform($F$3:$F$18)-$F$19						
32		G21 (output)	=SLOPE(G3:G18,B3:B18)						
33		G22 (output)	=INTERCEPT(G3:G18,B3:B18)						
34									

Figure 9.28 Example model for a residuals resampling (type B) non-parametric bootstrap regression analysis.

we must first develop a non-parametric distribution of residuals by changing them to have constant variance. We define the *modified residual* r_i as follows:

$$r_i = \frac{e_i}{(1 - h_i)^{1/2}}$$

where the *leverage* h_i is given by

$$h_i = \frac{1}{n} + \frac{(x_i - \overline{x})^2}{SS_{xx}}$$

The mean of the modified residuals $\overline{r}$ is calculated. Then a bootstrap sample r_i^* is drawn from the set of r_i values and used to determine the quantity $(\hat{y}_j + r_j^* - \overline{r})$ for each x_j value which is used in step 2 of the algorithm above. Figure 9.28 provides a spreadsheet illustration of this type of model using data from Table 9.5.

In certain problems, it is logical that the y-intercept value c be set to zero. In this situation, the leverage values are different:

$$h_i = \frac{x_i^2}{\sum\limits_{j=1}^{n} x_j^2}$$

The modified residuals are thus also different and won't sum to zero, so it is essential to mean-correct the residuals before they are used to simulate random errors.

Table 9.5 Experimental measurements of the variation in length of a vertical spring as weight is attached to its end.

Mass (kg)	Extension (mm)
0.0	137.393
0.1	138.954
0.2	139.977
0.3	140.107
0.4	142.765
0.5	145.606
0.6	147.881
0.7	147.011
0.8	144.194
0.9	144.949
1.0	152.161
1.1	149.694
1.2	154.700
1.3	162.037
1.4	155.275
1.5	160.221

Bootstrapping the data pairs is more robust than bootstrapping the residuals, as it is less sensitive to any deviation from the regression assumptions, but won't be as accurate where the assumptions are correct. However, as the dataset increases in size, the results from bootstrapping the pairs approach those from bootstrapping the residual, and it is also easier to execute, of course. These techniques can be extended to non-linear, non-constant variance and to multiple linear regressions, described in detail in Efron and Tibshirani (1993) and Davison and Hinkley (1997).

Chapter 10

Fitting distributions to data

In this chapter I use the statistical methods I've described in Chapter 9 to fit probability distributions to data. I also briefly describe how regression models are fitted to data. There are other types of probability models we use in risk analysis: fitting time series and copulas are described elsewhere in this book.

This chapter is concerned with a problem frequently confronted by the risk analyst: that of determining a distribution to represent some variable in a risk analysis model. There are essentially two sources of information used to quantify the variables within a risk analysis model. The first is available data and the second is expert opinion. Chapter 14 deals with the quantification of the parameters that describe the variability purely from expert opinion. Here I am going to look at techniques to interpret observed data for a variable in order to derive a distribution that realistically models its true variability and our uncertainty about that true variability. Any interpretation of data by definition requires some subjective input, usually in the form of assumptions about the variable. The key assumption here is that the observed data can be thought of as a random sample from some probability distribution that we are attempting to identify.

The observed data may come from a variety of sources: scientific experiments, surveys, computer databases, literature searches, even computer simulations. It is assumed here that the analyst has satisfied himself that the observed data are both reliable and as representative as possible. Anomalies in the data should be checked out first where possible and any unreliable data points discarded. Thought should also be given to any possible biases that could be produced by the method of data collection, for example: a high-street survey may have visited an unrepresentative number of large or affluent towns; the data may have come from an organisation that would benefit from doctoring the data, etc.

I start by encouraging analysts to review the data they have available and the characteristics of the variable that is to be modelled. Several techniques are then discussed that enable analysts to fit the available data to an empirical (non-parametric) distribution. The key advantages of this intuitive approach are the simplicity of use, the avoidance of assuming some distribution form and the omission of inappropriate or confusing theoretical (parametric or model-based) distributions. Techniques are then described for fitting theoretical distributions to observed data, including the use of maximum likelihood estimators, optimising goodness-of-fit statistics and plots.

For both non-parametric and parametric distribution fitting, I have offered two approaches. The first approach provides a first-order distribution, i.e. a best-fitting (best-guess) distribution that describes the variability only. The second approach provides second-order distributions that describe both the variability of the variable and the uncertainty we have about what that true distribution of variability really is. Second-order distributions are more complete than their first-order counterparts and require more effort: if there is a sufficiently large set of data such that the inclusion of uncertainty provides only marginally more information, it is quite reasonable to approximate the distribution to one of variability only. That said, it is often difficult to gauge the degree of uncertainty one has about a distribution without having first formally determined its uncertainty. The reader is therefore encouraged at least to go through the exercise of describing the uncertainty of a variability distribution to determine whether the uncertainty needs to be included.

10.1 Analysing the Properties of the Observed Data

Before attempting to fit a probability distribution to a set of observed data, it is worth first considering the properties of the variable in question. The properties of the distribution or distributions chosen to be fitted to the data should match those of the variable being modelled. Software like BestFit, EasyFit, Stat::Fit and ExpertFit have made fitting distributions to data very easy and removed the need for any in-depth statistical knowledge. These products can be very useful but, through their automation and ease of use, inadvertently encourage the user to attempt fits to wholly inappropriate distributions. It is therefore worth considering the following points before attempting a fit:

- *Is the variable to be modelled discrete or continuous?* A *discrete* variable may only take certain specific values, for example the number of bridges along a motorway, but a measurement such as the volume of tarmac, for example, is continuous. A variable that is discrete in nature is usually, but not always, best fitted to a discrete distribution. A very common exception is where the increment between contiguous allowable values is insignificant compared with the range that the variable may take. For example, consider a distribution of the number of people using the London Underground on any particular day. Although there can only be a whole number of people using the Tube, it is easier to model this number as a continuous variable since the number of users will number in the millions and there is little importance and considerable practical difficulty in recognising the discreteness of the number.

   In certain circumstances, discrete distributions can be very closely approximated by continuous distributions for large values of x. If a discrete variable has been modelled by a continuous distribution for convenience, its discrete nature can easily be put back into the risk analysis model by using the ROUND(...) function in Excel.

   The reverse of the above, however, never occurs, i.e. data from a continuous variable are always fitted to a continuous distribution and never a discrete distribution.

- *Do I really need to fit a mathematical (parametric) distribution to my data?* It is often practical to use the data points directly to define an empirical distribution, without having to attempt a fit to any theoretical probability distribution type. Section 10.2 describes these methods.

- *Does the theoretical range of the variable match that of the fitted distribution?* The fitted distribution should, within reason, cover the range over which the variable being modelled may theoretically extend. If the fitted distribution extends beyond the variable's possible range, a risk analysis model will produce impossible scenarios. If the distribution fails to extend over the entire possible range of the variable, the risk analysis will not reflect the true uncertainty of the problem. For example, data on the oil saturation of a hydrocarbon reserve should be fitted to a distribution that is bounded at zero and 1, as values outside that range are nonsensical. It may turn out that a normal distribution, for example, fits the data far better than any other shape, but, of course, it extends from $-\infty$ to $+\infty$. In order to ensure that the risk analysis only produces meaningful scenarios, the normal distribution would be truncated in the risk analysis model at zero and 1.

   Note that a correctly fitted distribution will usually cover a range that is greater than that displayed by the observed data. This is quite acceptable because data are rarely observed at the theoretical extremes for the variable in question.

- *Do you already know the value of the distribution parameters?* This applies most often to discrete variables. For example, a Hypergeometric(n, D, M) distribution describes the number of successes we might have from n independent individuals without replacement from a population of size M

where a success means the individual comes from a subpopulation of size D. It seems unlikely that we would not know how many samples were taken to have observed our dataset of successes. More likely is that we already know n and D and are trying to estimate M, or we know n and M and are trying to estimate D. Discrete distributions like the binomial, beta–binomial, negative binomial, beta negative binomial, hypergeometric and inverse hypergeometric have either the number of samples n or the number of required successes s as parameters and will generally be known.

- *Is this variable independent of other variables in the model?* The variable may be correlated with, or a function of, another variable within the model. It may also be related to another variable outside the model but which, in turn, affects a third variable within the risk analysis model. Figure 10.1 illustrates a couple of examples. In example (a), a high-street bank's revenue is modelled as a function of the interest and mortgage rates, among other things. The mortgage rate is correlated to the interest rate since the interest rate largely defines what the mortgage rate is to be. This relationship must be included in the model to ensure that the simulation will only produce meaningful scenarios. There are two approaches to modelling such dependency relationships:

1. Determine distributions for the mortgage and interest rates on the basis of historical data and then correlate the sampling from these distributions during simulation.

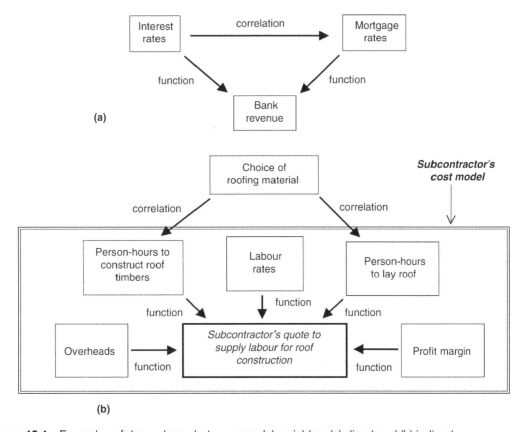

Figure 10.1 Examples of dependency between model variables: (a) direct and (b) indirect.

2. Determine the distribution of interest rate from historical data and a (stochastic) functional relationship with the mortgage rate.

Method 1 is tempting because of its simple execution, but method 2 offers greater opportunity to reproduce any observed relationship between the two variables.

In example (b) of Figure 10.1, a construction subcontractor is calculating her bid price to supply labour for a roofing job. The choice of roofing material has not yet been decided and this uncertainty has implications for the person-hours that will be needed to construct the roofing timbers and to lay the roof. There is therefore an *indirect* dependency between these two variables that could easily have been missed, had she not looked outside the immediate components of her cost calculation. Missing this correlation would have resulted in an underestimation of the spread of the subcontractor's cost and potentially could have led her to quote a price that exposed her to significant loss. Correlation and dependency relationships form a vital part of many risk analyses. Chapter 13 describes several techniques to model correlation and dependencies between variables.

*   *Does a theoretical distribution exist that fits the mathematics of this variable?* Many theoretical distributions have developed as a result of modelling specific types of problem. These distributions then find a wider use in other problems that have the same mathematical structure. Examples include: the times between telephone calls at a telephone exchange or fires in a railway system may be accurately represented by an exponential distribution; the time until failure of an electronics component may be represented by a Weibull distribution; how many treble 20s a darts player will score with a specific number of darts may be represented by a binomial distribution; the number of cars going through a road junction in any one hour may be represented by a Poisson distribution; and the heights of the tallest and shortest children in UK school classes may be represented by Gumbel distributions. If a distribution can be found with the same mathematical basis as the variable being modelled, it only remains to find the appropriate parameters to define the distribution, as explained in Section 10.3.

*   *Does a theoretical distribution exist that is well known to fit this type of variable?* Many types of variable have been observed closely to follow specific distribution types without any mathematical rationale being available to explain such close matching. Examples abound with the normal distribution: the weight of babies and other measures that come from nature, which is how the normal distribution got its name; measurement errors in engineering, variables that are the sum of other variables (e.g. means of samples from a population), etc. However, there are many other examples for distributions like the lognormal, Pareto and Rayleigh, some of which are noted in Appendix III.

If a distribution is known to be a close fit to the type of variable being modelled, usually as a result of published academic work, all that remains is to find the best-fitting distribution parameters, as explained in Section 10.3.

Errors – systematic and non-systematic

The collected data will at times have measurement errors that add another level of uncertainty. In most scientific data collection, the random error is well understood and can be quantified, usually by simply repeating the same measurement and reviewing the distribution of results. Such random errors are described as non-systematic. Systematic errors, on the other hand, mean that the values of a measurement deviate from the true value in a systematic fashion, consistently either over- or underestimating the true value. This type of error is often very difficult to identify and quantify. One will often attempt to estimate the degree of suspected systematic measurement error by comparing with measurements using another technique that is known (or believed) to have little or no systematic error.

Systematic and non-systematic error can both be accounted for in determining a distribution of fit. In determining a first-order distribution, one need only adjust the data by the systematic error (the non-systematic error has, by definition, a mean shift of zero). In second-order distribution fitting, one can model the data as being uncertain, with appropriate distributions representing both the non-systematic error and the systematic error (including uncertainty about what these error parameters are).

Sample size

Is the number of data points available sufficient to give a good idea of the true variability? Consider the 20 plots of Figure 10.2 which each show random samples of twenty values drawn from a Normal(100, 10) distribution. These samples are all plotted as histograms with six evenly spaced bars, three either side of 100. The variation in shapes is something of an eye-opener to a lot of people, who expect to see plots that look at least *reasonably* like bell-shaped curves and symmetric about 100. After all, one might think that 20 data points is a reasonable number from which to draw some inference. The bottom-right panel in Figure 10.2 shows all 400 data values (i.e. 20 plots * 20 data values each), which looks something like a normal distribution but nonetheless still has a significant degree of asymmetry. It is an interesting and useful exercise when attempting to fit data to a distribution to see what sort of patterns one would observe if the data did truly come from the distribution that is being fitted. So, for example, if I had 30 data values that I was fitting to a Lognormal(10, 2) distribution, I could plot a variety of 30 Monte Carlo samples (not Latin hypercube samples, which forces a better-fitting sample to the true distribution than a random sample would produce) from a Lognormal(10, 2) distribution in histogram form and see the different patterns they produce. I am at least then aware of the range of data patterns that I should accept as feasibly coming from that distribution for that size of sample.

Overdispersion of data

Sometimes we wish to fit a parametric distribution to observations, but note that the data appear to show a much larger spread than the fitted distribution would suggest. For example, in fitting a binomial distribution to the results of a multiple question exam taken by a large class, one might imagine that the distribution of a number of correct answers could be modelled by a Binomial(n, p) distribution, where n = the number of questions and p is the average probability for the class of correctly answering a question. The spread of the fitted binomial distribution is essentially determined by the mean = np, since n is fixed, so there is no opportunity to attempt to match the fitted distribution to the data in terms of the observed spread in results as well as the average result. One plausible reason for the fit being poor is that there will be a range of abilities in the class. If one models the range of probabilities of successfully answering a question across all the individuals as a beta distribution, the resultant distribution of results will be drawn from a beta–binomial distribution, which is then the appropriate distribution to fit to the data. The extra variability added to the binomial distribution by making p beta distributed means that the beta–binomial distribution will always have more spread than the binomial. The beta–binomial distribution has three parameters: α, β and n, where α and β (sometimes written as α_1 and α_2) are the parameters of the beta distribution and n remains the number of trials. These three parameters allow a better and logical match to the mean and variance of the observations. As α and β become larger, the beta distribution becomes narrower, i.e. the participants have a narrow range of probabilities of successfully answering a question (the population is more homogeneous), and the Beta–Binomial(n, α, β) is then approximated well by a Binomial(n, $\alpha/(\alpha + \beta)$).

The same type of problem applies in fitting the Poisson(λ) distribution to data. Since the mean and variance are both equal to λ, the spread of the distribution is determined by the mean. Observed data are often more widely dispersed than a Poisson distribution might suggest, and this is often because the

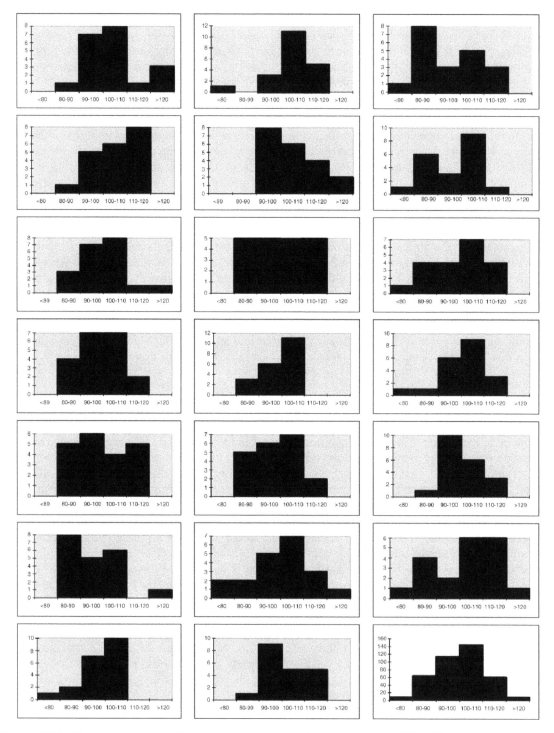

Figure 10.2 Examples of distributions of 20 random samples from a Normal(100, 10) distribution.

n observations come from Poisson processes with different means $\lambda_1, \ldots, \lambda_n$. For example, one might be looking at the failure rates of computers. Each computer will be slightly different from the next and so will have its own λ. If one models the distribution of variability of the λs using a Gamma(α, β) distribution, the resultant distribution of failures in a single time period is a Pólya(α, β). The Pólya distribution always has a variance greater than the mean, and its two parameters allow a greater flexibility in matching the distribution to the mean and variance of the observations.

Finally, data fitted to a normal distribution can often demonstrate longer tails than a normal distribution. In such cases, the three-parameter Student t-distribution can be used, i.e. Student(ν) $* \sigma + \mu$, where μ is the fitted distribution's mean, σ is the fitted distribution's standard deviation and ν is the "degrees of freedom" parameter that determines the shape of the distribution. For $\nu = 1$, this is the Cauchy distribution which has infinite (i.e. undeterminable) mean and standard deviation. As ν gets larger, the tails shrink until at very large ν (some 50 or more) this looks like a Normal(μ, σ) distribution. The three-parameter Student t-distribution can be derived as the mixture of normal distributions with the same mean and different variances distributed as a scaled inverse χ^2. So, in attempting to fit data to the three-parameter Student t-distribution instead of a normal distribution, you would need to be able reasonably to convince yourself that the observations were drawn from normal distributions with the same mean and different variances.

10.2 Fitting a Non-Parametric Distribution to the Observed Data

This section discusses techniques for fitting an empirical distribution to data. We look at continuous and then discrete variables, and both first-order (variability only) and second-order (variability and uncertainty) fitting.

10.2.1 Modelling a continuous variable (first order)

If the observed variable is continuous and reasonably extensive, it is often sufficient to use a cumulative frequency plot of the data points themselves to define its probability distribution. Figure 10.3 illustrates an example with 18 data points. The observed $F(x)$ values are calculated as the expected $F(x)$ that would correspond to a random sampling from the distribution, i.e. $F(x) = i/(n+1)$, where i is the rank of the observed data point and n is the number of data points. An explanation for this formula is provided in the next section. Determination of the empirical cumulative distribution proceeds as follows:

- The minimum and maximum for the empirical distribution are subjectively determined on the basis of the analyst's knowledge of the variable. For a continuous variable, these values will generally be outside the observed range of the data. The minimum and maximum values selected here are 0 and 45.

- The data points are ranked in ascending order between the minimum and maximum values.

- The cumulative probability $F(x_i)$ for each x_i value is calculated as follows:

$$F(x_i) = \frac{i}{n+1} \tag{10.1}$$

This formula maximises the chance of replicating the true distribution.

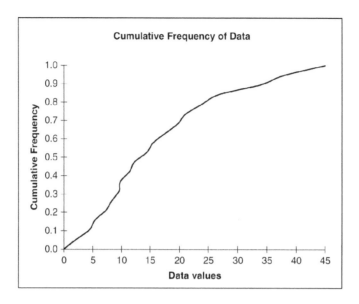

Number of data points $n = 18$

i	x	$F(x) = i/19$
	0.000	0.000
1	2.058	0.053
2	4.382	0.105
3	5.348	0.158
4	7.296	0.211
5	8.334	0.263
6	9.596	0.316
7	9.805	0.368
8	11.385	0.421
9	12.241	0.474

i	x	$F(x) = i/19$
10	14.392	0.526
11	15.566	0.579
12	17.615	0.632
13	19.745	0.684
14	21.077	0.737
15	23.894	0.789
16	26.804	0.842
17	33.879	0.895
18	38.018	0.947
	45.000	1.000

Figure 10.3   Fitting a continuous empirical distribution to data using a cumulative distribution.

- The two arrays, $\{x_i\}$ and $\{F(x_i)\}$, along with the minimum and maximum values, can then be used as direct inputs into a cumulative distribution CumulA(min, max, $\{x_i\}$, $\{F(x_i)\}$).

The VoseOgive function in ModelRisk will simulate values from a distribution constructed using the method above.

If there is a very large amount of data, it becomes impracticable to use all of the data points to define the cumulative distribution. In such cases it is useful to batch the data first. The number of batches should be set to the practical maximum that balances fineness of detail (large number of bars) with the practicalities of having large arrays defining the distribution (lower number of bars).

Example 10.1   Fitting a continuous non-parametric distribution to data

Figure 10.4 illustrates an example where 221 data points are plotted in histogram form over the range of the observed data. The analyst considers that the variable could conceivably range from 0 to 300. Since there are no observed data with values below 20 and above 280, the histogram bar ranges need

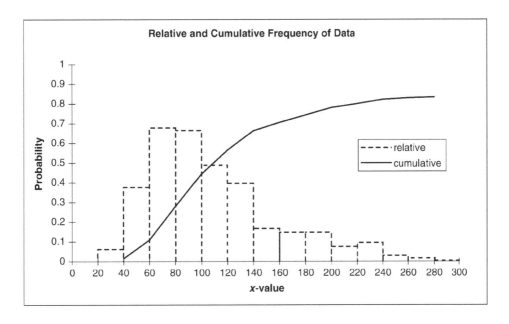

Number of data points $n = 221$

Observed frequencies			Modelled distribution		
Histogram bar		Histogram	Cumulative	Histogram bar		Cumulative
From A	To B	probability $f(A<x \le B)$	probability $F(x \le B)$	From A	To B	probability $F(x \le B)$
20	40	0.018	0.018	0	40	0.018
40	60	0.113	0.131	40	60	0.131
60	80	0.204	0.335	60	80	0.335
80	100	0.199	0.534	80	100	0.534
100	120	0.145	0.679	100	120	0.679
120	140	0.118	0.796	120	140	0.796
140	160	0.050	0.846	140	160	0.846
160	180	0.045	0.891	160	180	0.891
180	200	0.045	0.937	180	200	0.937
200	220	0.023	0.959	200	220	0.959
220	240	0.027	0.986	220	240	0.986
240	260	0.009	0.995	240	260	0.995
260	280	0.005	1.000	260	300	1.000

Figure 10.4   Fitting an empirical distribution to histogrammed data using a cumulative distribution.

to be altered to accommodate the subjective minimum and maximum. The easiest way to achieve this is to extend the range of the first and last bars with non-zero probability to cover the required range, but without altering its probability. In this example, the histogram bar with range 20–40 is expanded to a range 0–40, and the bar with range 260–280 is expanded to range 260–300. We will probably have *slightly* exaggerated the tails of the distribution. However, if the number of bars initially selected is quite large, there will be little real effect on the model. The $\{x_i\}$ array input into the cumulative distribution is then $\{40, 60, \ldots, 240, 260\}$, the $\{P_i\}$ array is $\{0.018, 0.131, \ldots, 0.986, 0.995\}$ and the minimum and maximum are, of course, 0 and 300 respectively. ♦

Converting a histogram distribution into a cumulative distribution may seem a little pointless when the histogram can be used in a risk analysis model. However, this technique allows analysts to select varying bar widths to suit their needs, as in the above example, and therefore to maximise detail in the distribution where it is needed.

10.2.2 Modelling a continuous variable (second order)[1]

When we do not have a great deal of data, a considerable amount of uncertainty will remain about an empirical distribution determined directly from the data. It would be very useful to have the flexibility of using an empirical distribution, i.e. not having to assume a parametric distribution, and also to be able to quantify the uncertainty about that distribution. The following technique provides these requirements.

Consider a set of n data values $\{x_j\}$ drawn from a distribution and ranked in ascending order $\{x_i\}$ so $x_i < x_{i+1}$. Data thus ranked are known as the order statistics of $\{x_j\}$. Individually, each of the values of $\{x_j\}$ may map as a U(0, 1) onto the cumulative probability of the parent distribution $F(x)$. We take a U(0, 1) distribution as the prior distribution for the cumulative probability for any value of x. We can thus use a U(0, 1) prior for $P_i = F(x_i)$ for the value of the ith observation. However, we have the additional information that, of n values drawn randomly from this distribution, x_i ranked ith, i.e. $(i-1)$ of the data values are less than x_i, and $(n-i)$ values are greater than x_i. Using Bayes' theorem and the binomial theorem, the posterior marginal distribution for P_i can readily be determined, remembering that P_i has a U(0, 1) prior and therefore a prior probability density $= 1$:

$$f(P_i|x_i; i = 1, n) \propto (P_i)^{i-1}(1 - P_i)^{n-i}$$

which is simply the standard beta distribution Beta$(i, n - i + 1)$:

$$P_i = \text{Beta}(i, n - i + 1) \tag{10.2}$$

Equation (10.2) could actually be determined directly from the fact that the beta distribution is the conjugate to the binomial likelihood function and that a U(0, 1) = Beta(1, 1). The mean of the Beta$(i, n - i + 1)$ distribution equals $i/(n + 1)$: a formula that has been used in Equation (10.1) to estimate the best-fitting first-order non-parametric cumulative distribution.

Since $P_{i+1} > P_i$, these beta distributions are not independent, so we need to determine the conditional distribution $f(P_{i+1}|P_i)$, as follows. The joint distribution $f(P_i, P_j)$ for any two P_i, P_j is calculated using the binomial theorem in a similar manner to the numerator of the equation for $f(P_i|x_i; i = 1, n)$, that is

$$f(P_i, P_j) \propto P_i^{i-1}(P_j - P_i)^{j-i-1}(1 - P_j)^{n-j}$$

where $P_j > P_i$, and remembering that the prior probability densities for P_i and P_j equal 1 since they have U(0, 1) priors.

Thus, for $j = i + 1$,

$$f(P_i, P_{i+1}) \propto P_i^{i-1}(1 - P_{i+1})^{n-i-1}$$

---

[1] I submitted a paper on this technique (I developed the idea) for publication in a journal a long time ago. One reviewer was horribly dismissive, saying that the derivation was one of the most drunken s/he had ever seen, and anyway it was a Bayesian method (it isn't) so it was of no value. Actually, this has proven to be one of the most useful things I ever figured out.

The conditional probability $f(P_{i+1}|P_i)$ is thus given by

$$f(P_{i+1}|P_i) = \frac{f(P_i, P_{i+1})}{f(P_i)} = k \frac{P_i^{i-1}(1 - P_{i+1})^{n-i-1}}{P_i^{i-1}(1 - P_i)^{n-i}} = k \frac{(1 - P_{i+1})^{n-i-1}}{(1 - P_i)^{n-i}}$$

where k is some constant. The corresponding cumulative distribution function $F(P_{i+1}|P_i)$ is then given by

$$F(P_{i+1}|P_i) = \int_{P_i}^{P_{i+1}} k \frac{(1 - y)^{n-i-1}}{(1 - P_i)^{n-i}} \, dy = \frac{k}{(n - i)} \left[1 - \left(\frac{1 - P_{i+1}}{1 - P_i} \right)^{n-i} \right]$$

$$F(P_{i+1}|P_i) = 1 \text{ at } P_{i+1} = 1$$

and thus $k = n - i$ and the formula reduces to

$$F(P_{i+1}|P_i) = 1 - \left(\frac{1 - P_{i+1}}{1 - P_i} \right)^{n-i} \tag{10.3}$$

Together, Equations (10.2) and (10.3) provide us with the tools to construct a non-parametric second-order distribution for a continuous variable given a dataset sampled from that distribution. The distribution for the cumulative probability P_1 that maps onto the first-order statistic X_1 can be obtained from Equation (10.2) by setting $i = 1$:

$$P_1 = \text{Beta}(1, n) \tag{10.4}$$

The distribution for the cumulative probability P_2 that maps onto the first-order statistic X_2 can be obtained from Equation (10.3). Being a cumulative distribution function, $F(P_{i+1}|P_i)$ is Uniform(0, 1) distributed. Thus, writing U_{i+1} to represent a Uniform(0, 1) distribution in place of $F(P_{i+1}|P_i)$, using the identity $1 - U(0, 1) = U(0, 1)$, and rewriting for P_{i+1}, we obtain

$$P_{i+1} = 1 - \sqrt[n-i]{U_{i+1}(1 - P_i)} \tag{10.5}$$

which gives

$$P_2 = 1 - \sqrt[n-1]{U_2(1 - P_1)}$$

$$P_3 = 1 - \sqrt[n-2]{U_3(1 - P_2)}$$

etc.

Note that each of the $U_2, U_3, \ldots, U_n$ uniform distributions are independent of each other.

The formulae from Equations (10.4) and (10.5) can be used as inputs into a cumulative distribution function available from standard Monte Carlo software tools like @RISK and Crystal Ball, together with subjective estimates of the minimum and maximum values that the variable may take. The variability ("inner loop") is described by the range for the variable in question, and estimates of the cumulative distribution shape via the $\{X_i\}$ and $\{P_i\}$ values. The uncertainty ("outer loop") is catered for by the uncertainty distributions for the minimum, maximum and P_i values.

The RiskCumul distribution function in @RISK, the VoseCumulA function in ModelRisk and the cumulative version of the custom distribution in Crystal Ball have the same cumulative distribution function, namely

$$F(x) = \left(\frac{x - X_i}{X_{i+1} - X_i} \right)(P_{i+1} - P_i) + P_i$$

where X_0 = minimum, X_{n+1} = maximum, $P_0 = 0$, $P_{n+1} = 1$ and $X_i \le x < X_{i+1}$.

Figure 10.5 illustrates a model where a dataset is being used to create a second-order distribution using this technique. If the model is created in the current version of @RISK, the uncertainty distributions for $F(x)$ in column D are nominated as outputs, a smallish number of iterations are run and the resultant data are exported back to a spreadsheet. Those data are then used to perform multiple simulations (the "outer loop") of uncertainty using @RISK's RiskSimtable function: the "inner loop" of variability comes

	A	B	C	D	E	F	G	H
1								
2		**Rank (i)**	**Order statistics (x)**	**F(x)**			**Formulae table**	
3		minimum	0	0		B4:B103	1:100	
4		1	0.473	0.0099		C3, C104	Input: estimates of min, max	
5		2	3.170	0.0168		C4:C103	Input: data values	
6		3	4.254	0.0237		D4	=VoseBeta(1,100)	
7		4	4.540	0.0307		D5:D103	=1-(VoseUniform(0,1)^(1/(100-B4)))*(1-D4)	
102		99	95.937	0.9453				
103		100	96.936	0.9726				
104		maximum	100	1				
105								

Figure 10.5 Model to produce a second-order non-parametric continuous distribution.

	A	B	C	D	CW	CX	CY
1							
2		**Iteration# / Cell**	**D4**	**D5**	**D102**	**D103**	
3		1	5.04%	6.83%	99.08%	99.60%	
4		2	0.29%	1.63%	99.20%	99.90%	
101		99	0.05%	0.69%	98.99%	99.67%	
102		100	0.93%	4.28%	99.45%	99.88%	
103		**Simtable functions**	5.04%	6.83%	99.08%	99.60%	
104		**Order statistics**	0.473	3.170	95.937	96.936	
105							
106		**Distribution for model**	46.000489				
107							
108				Formulae table			
109		Rows 3 to 102:	List samples from the distribution for $F(X^i)$				
110		C103:CX103	=RiskSimtable(C3:C102)				
111		Row 104:	Lists the observed data values				
112		C106 (output)	=VoseCumulA(0,100,C104:CX104,C103:CX103)				
113							

Figure 10.6 @RISK model to run a second-order risk analysis using the data generated from the model of Figure 10.5.

	A	B	C	D	E	F	G	H
1								
2		Rank (*i*)	Order statistics (*x*)	F(*x*)			Crystal Ball Pro formulae table	
3		minimum	0	0		B4:B103	1:100	
4		1	0.473	0.0324		C3, C104	Input: estimates of min, max	
5		2	3.170	0.0383		C4:C103	Input: data values	
6		3	4.254	0.0438		D4	=CB.Beta(1,100,1)	
7		4	4.540	0.0511		D5:D103	=1-(CB.Uniform(0,1)^(1/(100-B3)))*(1-D3)	
101		98	93.301	0.9414		D106 (output)	=CB.Custom(C3:C104)	
102		99	95.937	0.9766			*D4:D103 are nominated as uncertainty distributions*	
103		100	96.936	0.9901			*D106 is nominated as a variability distribution*	
104		maximum	100	1				
105								
106		**Second order distribution:**		41.640				
107								

Figure 10.7 Crystal Ball Pro model to run a second-order risk analysis using the data generated from the model of Figure 10.5.

from the cumulative distribution itself, as shown in Figure 10.6. If one creates the model in Crystal Ball Pro, the $F(x)$ distributions can be nominated as uncertainty distributions and the cumulative nominated as the variability distribution, and the inner/outer loop procedure will run automatically (Figure 10.7).

There are a few limitations to this technique. In using a cumulative distribution function, one is assuming a histogram style probability density function. When there are a large number of data points, this approximation becomes irrelevant. However, for small datasets the approximation tends to accentuate the tails of the distribution: a result of the histogram "squaring-off" effect of using the cumulative distribution. In other words, the variability will be slightly exaggerated. However, the squaring effect can be reduced, if required, by using some sort of smoothing algorithm and defining points between each observed value. In addition, for small datasets, the tails' contribution to the variability will often be more influenced by the subjective estimates of the minimum and maximum values: a fact one can view positively (one is recognising the real uncertainty about a distribution's tail), and negatively (the smaller the dataset, the more the technique relies on subjective assessment).

The fewer the data points, the wider the confidence intervals will become, quite naturally, and, in general, the more emphasis will be placed on the subjectively defined minimum and maximum values. Conversely, the more data points available, the less influence the minimum and maximum estimates will have on the estimated distribution. In any case, the values of the minimum and maximum only have influence on the width (and therefore height) of the end two histogram bars in the fitted distribution. The fact that the technique is non-parametric, i.e. that no statistical distribution with a particular cumulative distribution function is assumed to be underlying the data, allows the analyst a far greater degree of flexibility and objectivity than that afforded by fitting parametric distributions.

A further sophistication to this technique would be to correlate the uncertainty distributions for the minimum and maximum parameter values to the uncertainty distributions for P_1 and P_n respectively. If P_1 were to be sampled with a high value, it would make sense that the variability distribution had a long left tail and the value sampled for the minimum should be towards its lowest value. Similarly, a high value for P_n would suggest a low value for the maximum. One could model these relationships using either very high levels of negative rank order correlation for simplicity or some more involved but more explicit equation.

Example 10.2 Fitting a second-order non-parametric distribution to continuous data

Three datasets of five, then a further 15 and then another 80 random samples were drawn from a Normal(100, 10) distribution to give sets of five, 20 and 100 samples. The graphs of Figure 10.8 show, naturally enough, that the population distribution is approached with increasing confidence the more data values one has available.

There are classical statistical techniques for determining confidence distributions for the mean and standard deviation of a normal distribution that is fitted to a dataset with a population normal distribution, as discussed in Section 9.1, namely:

$$\text{Mean } \mu = \overline{x} + t(n-1)\frac{s}{\sqrt{n-1}}$$

$$\text{Standard deviation } \sigma = \sqrt{\frac{ns^2}{\chi^2(n-1)}}$$

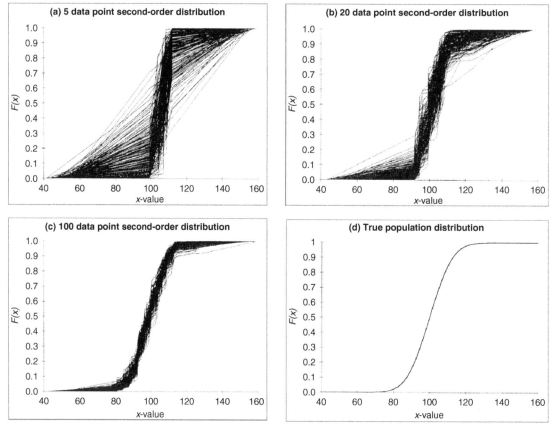

Figure 10.8 Results of fitting a non-parametric distribution to data from a normal parent distribution: (a) five data points; (b) 20 data points; (c) 100 data points; (d) the true population distribution.

where:

- μ and σ are the mean and standard deviation of the population distribution;
- x and s are the mean and sample standard deviation of the n data points being fitted;
- $t(n-1)$ is a t-distribution with $n-1$ degrees of freedom, and $\chi^2(n-1)$ is a chi-square distribution with $n-1$ degrees of freedom.

The second-order distribution that would be fitted to the 100 data point set using the non-parametric technique is shown in the right-hand panel of Figure 10.9. The second-order distribution produced using the above statistical theory with the assumption of a normal distribution is shown in the left-hand panel of Figure 10.9. There is a strong agreement between these two techniques. The statistical technique produces less uncertainty in the tails because the assumption of normality adds extra information that the non-parametric technique does not provide. This is, of course, fine providing we *know* that the population distribution is truly normal, but leads to overconfidence in the tails if the assumption is incorrect. ♦

The advantage of the technique offered here is that it works for all continuous smooth distributions, not just the normal distribution. It can also be used to determine distributions of uncertainty for specific percentiles and quantiles of the population distribution, essentially by reading off values from the fitted cumulative distribution and interpolating as necessary between the defined points. Figure 10.10 shows a spreadsheet model for determining the percentile, defined in cell E3, of the population distribution, given the 100 data points from the normal distribution used previously. The uncertainty distribution for the percentile is produced by running a simulation with cell G3 as the output. Similarly, Figure 10.11 illustrates a spreadsheet to determine the cumulative probability that the value in cell F2 represents in the population distribution. The distribution of uncertainty of this cumulative probability is produced by running a simulation with cell H2 as the output. In other words, the model in Figure 10.10 is slicing horizontally through the second-order fitted distribution at $F(x) = 50\%$, while the model of Figure 10.11 is slicing vertically at $x = 99$. The spreadsheets can, of course, be expanded or contracted to suit the number of data points available. ModelRisk includes the VoseOgive2 function that generates the array of $F(x)$ variables required for second-order distribution modelling.

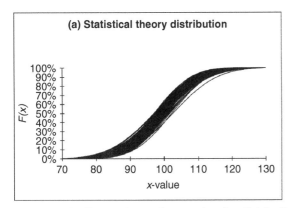
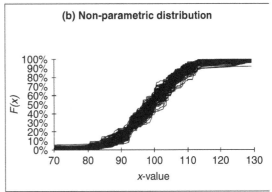

Figure 10.9 Comparison of second-order distributions using the non-parametric technique and classical statistics.

	A	B	C	D	E	F	G	H	I
1									
2		rank (i)	data (x)						
3		0	60			50% ile:	100.122		
4		1	75.799						
103		100	129.176			Lower i	56		
104		101	140			Upper i	57		
105						Lower F(x)	49.58%		
106		rank(i)	F(x)	rank(i)		Upper F(x)	50.67%		
107		0	0%	0		Lower x	100.027		
108		1	6%	1		Upper x	100.276		
207		100	94%	100					
208		101	100%	101					
209									
210					Formulae table				
211		B3:B104	0:101						
212		C4:C103	Input: data values						
213		C3, C104	Input: estimates of min, max						
214		B107:B208	=B3						
215		C107, C208	0, 1						
216		C108	=VoseBeta(1,100)						
217		C109:C207	=1-(VoseUniform(0,1)^(1/(100-B108)))*(1-C108)						
218		D107:D208	=B3						
219		G103	=VLOOKUP(E3,C107:D208,2)						
220		G104	=G103+1						
221		G105	=VLOOKUP(G103,B107:C208,2)						
222		G106	=VLOOKUP(G104,B107:C208,2)						
223		G107	=VLOOKUP(G103,B3:C104,2)						
224		G108	=VLOOKUP(G104,B3:C104,2)						
225		E3	Input target percentile						
226		G3 (output)	=(E3-G105)/(G106-G105)*(G108-G107)+G107						
227									

Figure 10.10 Model to determine the uncertainty distribution for a percentile.

10.2.3 Modelling a discrete variable (first order)

Data from a discrete variable can be used to define an empirical distribution in two ways: if the number of allowable x values is not very large, the frequency of data at each x value can be used directly to define a discrete distribution; and if the number of allowable x values is very large, it is usually easier to arrange the data into histogram form and then define a cumulative distribution, as above. The discrete nature of the variable can be reintroduced by imbedding the cumulative distribution inside the standard spreadsheet ROUND(...) function.

10.2.4 Modelling a discrete variable (second order)

Uncertainty can be added to the discrete probabilities in the previous technique to provide a second-order Discrete distribution. Assuming that the variable in question is stable (i.e. is not varying with time), there is a constant (i.e. binomial) probability p_i that any observation will have a particular value x_i. If k of the n observations have taken the value x_i, then our estimate of the probability p_i is given by Beta$(k + 1, n - k + 1)$ from Section 8.2.3. However, all these p_i probabilities have to sum to equal

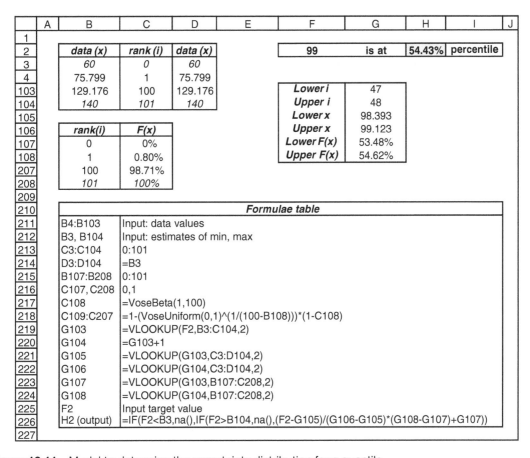

Figure 10.11 Model to determine the uncertainty distribution for a quantile.

1.0, so we normalise the p_i values. Figure 10.12 illustrates a spreadsheet that calculates the discrete second-order non-parametric distribution for the set of data in Table 10.1 where the distribution has been assumed to finish with the maximum observed value.

There remains a difficulty in selecting the range of this distribution, and it will be a matter of judgement how far one extends the range beyond the observed values. In the simple form described here there is also a problem in determining the p_i values for these unobserved tails, and any middle range that has no observed values, since all p_i values will have the same (normalised) Beta$(1, n + 1)$ distribution, no matter how extreme their position in the distribution's tail. This obviously makes no sense, and, if it is important to recognise the possibility of a long tail beyond observed data, a modification is necessary. The tail can be forced to zero by multiplying the beta distributions by some function that attenuates the tail, although the choice of function and severity of the attenuation will ultimately be a subjective matter.

These last two techniques have the advantages that the distribution derived from the observed data would be unaffected by any subjectivity in selecting a distribution type and that the maximum use of the data has been made in defining the distribution. There is an obvious disadvantage in that theprocess is

	A	B	C	D	E	F	G	H	I
1									
2		Value	Frequency	Estimate of probability	Normalised probability				
3		0	0	0.20%	0.19%			Formulae table	
4		1	1	0.40%	0.38%		B3:C22	Data	
5		2	1	0.40%	0.38%		B23:E23	=SUM(C3:C22)	
6		3	12	2.59%	2.50%		D3:D22	=VoseBeta(C3+1,$C$23-C3+1)	
7		4	35	7.17%	6.92%		E3:E22 (output)	=D3/$D$23	
8		5	52	10.56%	10.19%				
9		6	61	12.35%	11.92%				
10		7	65	13.15%	12.69%				
11		8	69	13.94%	13.46%				
12		9	68	13.75%	13.27%				
13		10	46	9.36%	9.04%				
14		11	33	6.77%	6.54%				
15		12	26	5.38%	5.19%				
16		13	12	2.59%	2.50%				
17		14	10	2.19%	2.12%				
18		15	2	0.60%	0.58%				
19		16	5	1.20%	1.15%				
20		17	1	0.40%	0.38%				
21		18	0	0.20%	0.19%				
22		19	1	0.40%	0.38%				
23		Total	500	1.03585657	1				
24									

Figure 10.12 Model to determine a discrete non-parametric second-order distribution.

Table 10.1 Dataset to fit a discrete second-order non-parametric distribution.

Value	Frequency	Value	Frequency
0	0	10	46
1	1	11	33
2	1	12	26
3	12	13	12
4	35	14	10
5	52	15	2
6	61	16	5
7	65	17	1
8	69	18	0
9	68	19	1

fairly laborious for large datasets. However, the FREQUENCY() function and Histogram facility in Excel and the BestFit statistics report and other statistics packages can make sorting the data and calculating the cumulative frequencies very easy. More importantly, there remains a difficulty in estimating probabilities for values of the variable that have not been observed. If this is important, it may well be better to fit the data to a parametric distribution.

10.3 Fitting a First-Order Parametric Distribution to Observed Data

This section describes methods of finding a theoretical (parametric) distribution that best fits the observed data. The following section deals with fitting a second-order parametric distribution, i.e. a distribution where the uncertainty about the parameters needs to be recognised. A parametric distribution type may be selected as the most appropriate to fit the data for three reasons:

- The distribution's mathematics corresponds to a model that accurately represents the behaviour of the variable being considered (see Section 10.1).

- The distribution to be fitted to the data is well known to fit this type of variable closely (see Section 10.1 again).

- The analyst simply wants to find the theoretical distribution that best fits the data, whatever it may be.

The third option is very tempting, especially when distribution-fitting software is available that can automatically attempt fits to a large number of distribution types at the click of an icon. However, this option should be used with caution. Analysts must ensure that the fitted distribution covers the same range over which, in theory, the variable being modelled may extend; for example, a four-parameter beta distribution fitted to data will not extend past the range of the observed data if its minimum and maximum are determined by the minimum and maximum of the observed data. Analysts should ensure that the discrete or continuous nature of the distribution matches that of the variable. They should also be flexible about using a different distribution type in a later model, should more data become available, although this may cause confusion when comparing old and new versions of the same model. Finally, they may find it difficult to persuade the decision-maker of the validity of the model: seeing an unusual distribution in a model with no intuitive logic associated with its parameters can easily invoke distrust of the model itself. Analysts should consider including in their report a plot of the distribution being used against the observed data to reassure the decision-maker of its appropriateness.

The distribution parameters that make a distribution type best fit the available data can be determined in several ways. The most common and most flexible technique is to determine parameter values known as maximum likelihood estimators (MLEs), described in Section 10.3.1. The MLEs of the distribution are the parameters that maximise the joint probability density or probability mass for the observed data. MLEs are very useful because, for several common distributions, they provide a quick way to arrive at the best-fitting parameters. For example, the normal distribution is defined by its mean and standard deviation, and its MLEs are the mean and standard deviation of the observed data. More often than not, however, when we fit a distribution to data using maximum likelihood, we need to use an optimiser (like Microsoft Solver which comes with Microsoft Excel) to find the combination of parameter values that maximises the likelihood function. Other methods of fit tend to find parameter values that minimise some measure of goodness of fit, some of which are described in Section 10.3.4. Both using MLEs and minimising goodness-of-fit statistics enable us to determine first-order distributions. However, for fitting second-order distributions we need additional techniques for quantifying the uncertainty about parameter values, like the bootstrap, Bayesian inference and some classical statistics.

10.3.1 Maximum likelihood estimators

The maximum likelihood estimators (MLEs) of a distribution type are the values of its parameters that produce the maximum joint probability density for the observed dataset x. In the case of a discrete distribution, MLEs maximise the actual probability of that distribution type being able to generate the observed data.

Consider a probability distribution type defined by a single parameter α. The likelihood function $L(\alpha)$ that a set of n data points (x_i) could be generated from the distribution with probability density $f(x)$ – or, in the case of a discrete distribution, probability mass – is given by

$$L(X|\alpha) = \prod_i f(x_i, \alpha), \text{ i.e. } L(\alpha) = f(x_1, \alpha) f(x_2, \alpha) \cdots f(x_{n-1}, \alpha) \, f(x_n, \alpha)$$

The MLE $\hat{\alpha}$ is then that value of α that maximises $L(\alpha)$. It is determined by taking the partial derivative of $L(\alpha)$ with respect to α and setting it to zero:

$$\left. \frac{\partial L(\alpha)}{\partial \alpha} \right|_{\hat{a}} = 0$$

For some distribution types this is a relatively simple algebraic problem, for others the differential equation is extremely complicated and is solved numerically instead. This is the equivalent of using Bayesian inference with a uniform prior and then finding the peak of the posterior uncertainty distribution for α. Distribution fitting software have made this process very easy to perform automatically.

Example 10.3 Determining the MLE for the Poisson distribution

The Poisson distribution has one parameter, the product λt, or just λ if we let t be a constant. Its probability mass function $f(x)$ is given by

$$f(x) = \frac{e^{-\lambda t} (\lambda t)^x}{x!}$$

Because of the memoryless character of the Poisson process, if we have observed x events in a total time t, the likelihood function is given by

$$L(\lambda) = \frac{e^{-\lambda t} (\lambda t)^x}{x!}$$

Let $I(\lambda) = \ln L(\lambda)$, and using the fact that t is a constant:

$$I(\lambda) = -\lambda t + x \ln(\lambda) + x \ln(t) - \ln(x!)$$

The maximum value of $I(\lambda)$, and therefore of $L(\lambda)$, occurs when the partial derivative with respect to λ equals zero, i.e.

$$\left. \frac{\partial I(\lambda)}{\partial \lambda} \right|_{\hat{\lambda}} = -t + \frac{x}{\hat{\lambda}} = 0$$

Rearranging yields

$$\hat{\lambda} = \frac{x}{t}$$

i.e. it is the average number of observations per unit time. ◆

10.3.2 Finding the best-fitting parameters using optimisation

Figure 10.13 illustrates a Microsoft Excel spreadsheet set up to find the parameters of a gamma distribution that will best match the observed data. Excel provides the GAMMADIST function that will return the probability density of a gamma distribution.

The Microsoft Solver in Excel is set to find the maximum value for cell F5 (or equivalently F7) by changing the values of α and β in cells F2 and F3.

10.3.3 Fitting distributions to truncated, censored or binned data

Maximum likelihood methods offer the greatest flexibility for distribution fitting because we need only be able to write a probability model that corresponds with how our data are observed and then maximise that probability by varying the parameters.

Censored data are those observations that we do not know precisely, only that they fall above or below a certain value. For example, a weight scale will have a maximum value X it can record: we might have some measurement off the scale and all we can say is that they are greater than X.

Truncated data are those observations that we do not see above or below some level. For example, at a bank it may not be required to record an error below \$100, and a sieve system may not select out diamonds from a river below a certain diameter.

Binned data are those observations that we only know the value of in terms of bins or categories. For example, one might record in a survey that customers were (0, 10], (10, 20], (20−40] and (40+) years of age.

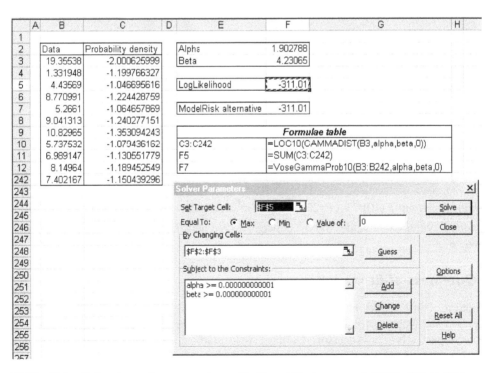

Figure 10.13 Using Solver to perform a maximum likelihood fit of a gamma distribution to data.

It is a simple matter to produce a probability model for each category or combination, as shown in the following examples where we are fitting to a continuous variable with density $f(x)$ and cumulative probability $F(x)$:

Example 10.4 Censored data

- *Observations*. Measurement censored at *Min* and *Max*. Observations between *Min* and *Max* are a, b, c, d and e; p observations below *Min* and q observations above *Max*.
- *Likelihood function*: $f(a) * f(b) * f(c) * f(d) * f(e) * F(Min)^p * (1 - F(Max))^q$.
- *Explanation*. For p values we only know that they are below some value *Min*, and the probability of being below *Min* is $F(Min)$. We know q values are above *Max*, each with probability $(1 - F(Max))$. The other values we have the exact measurements for. ♦

Example 10.5 Truncated data

- *Observations*. Measurement truncated at *Min* and *Max*. Observations between *Min* and *Max* are a, b, c, d and e.
- *Likelihood function*: $f(a) * f(b) * f(c) * f(d) * f(e)/(F(Max) - F(Min))^5$.
- *Explanation*. We only observe a value if it lies between *Min* and *Max* which has the probability $(F(Max) - F(Min))$. ♦

Example 10.6 Binned data

- *Observations*. Measurement binned into continuous categories as follows:

Bin	Frequency
0–10	10
10–20	23
20–50	42
50+	8

- *Likelihood function*: $F(10)^{10} * (F(20) - F(10))^{23} * (F(50) - F(20))^{42} * (1 - F(50))^8$.
- *Explanation*. We observe values in bins between a *Low* and *High* value with probability $F(High) - F(Low)$. ♦

10.3.4 Goodness-of-fit statistics

Many goodness-of-fit statistics have been developed, but two are in most common use. These are the chi-square (χ^2) and Kolmogorov–Smirnoff (K–S) statistics, generally used for discrete and continuous distributions respectively. The Anderson–Darling (A–D) statistic is a sophistication of the K–S statistic. The lower the value of these statistics, the closer the theoretical distribution appears to fit the data.

Goodness-of-fit statistics are not intuitively easy to understand or interpret. They do not provide a true measure of the probability that the data actually come from the fitted distribution. Instead, they provide a probability that random data generated from the fitted distribution would have produced a goodness-of-fit statistic value as low as that calculated for the observed data. By far the most intuitive measure of goodness of fit is a visual comparison of probability distributions, as described in Section 10.3.5. The reader is encouraged to produce these plots to assure himself or herself of the validity of the fit before labouring over goodness-of-fit statistics.

Critical values and confidence intervals for goodness-of-fit statistics

Analysis of the χ^2, K–S and A–D statistics can provide confidence intervals proportional to the probability that the fitted distribution could have produced the observed data. It is important to note that this is *not* equivalent to the probability that the data did, in fact, come from the fitted distribution, since there may be many distributions that have similar shapes and that could have been quite capable of generating the observed data. This is particularly so for data that are approximately normally distributed, since many distributions tend to a normal shape under certain conditions.

Critical values are determined by the required confidence level α. They are the values of the goodness-of-fit statistic that have a probability of being exceeded that is equal to the specified confidence level. Critical values for the χ^2 test are found directly from the χ^2 distribution. The shape and range of the χ^2 distribution are defined by the degrees of freedom ν, where $\nu = N - a - 1$, $N =$ number of histogram bars or classes and $a =$ number of parameters that are estimated to determine the best-fitting distribution.

Figure 10.14 shows a descending cumulative plot for the $\chi^2(11)$ distribution, i.e. a χ^2 distribution with 11 degrees of freedom. This plots an 80 % chance α (the confidence interval) that a value would have occurred that was higher than 6.988 (the critical value at an 80 % confidence level) for data that *were* actually drawn from the fitted distribution, i.e. there is only a 20 % chance that the χ^2 value could be this small. If analysts are conservative and accept this 80 % chance of falsely rejecting the fit, their confidence interval α equals 80 % and the corresponding critical value is 6.988, and they will not accept any distribution as a good fit if its χ^2 is greater than 6.988.

Critical values for K–S and A–D statistics have been found by Monte Carlo simulation (Stephens, 1974, 1977; Chandra, Singpurwalla and Stephens, 1981). Tables of critical values for the K–S statistic

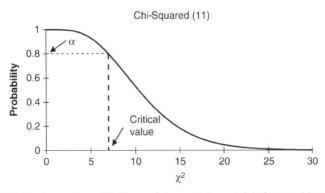

Figure 10.14 The critical value at an 80 % confidence interval (α) for a chi-square distribution with 11 degrees of freedom.

are very commonly found in statistical textbooks. Unfortunately, the standard K–S and A–D values are of limited use for comparing critical values if there are fewer than about 30 data points. The problem arises because these statistics are designed to test whether a distribution with *known* parameters could have produced the observed data. If the parameters of the fitted distribution have been estimated from the data, the K–S and A–D statistics will produce conservative test results, i.e. there is a smaller chance of a well-fitting distribution being accepted. The size of this effect varies between the types of distribution being fitted. One technique for getting round this problem is to use the first two-fifths or so of the data to estimate the parameters of a distribution, using MLEs for example, and then to use the remaining data to check the goodness of fit.

Modifications to the K–S and A–D statistics have been determined to correct for this problem, as shown in Tables 10.2 and 10.3 (see the BestFit manual published in 1993), where n is the number of data points and D_n and A_n^2 are the unmodified K–S and A–D statistics respectively.

Another goodness-of-fit statistic with intuitive appeal, similar to the A–D and K–S statistics, is the Cramer–von Mises statistic Y:

$$Y = \frac{1}{12n} + \sum_{i=1}^{n}\left[F_0(X_i) - \frac{2i-1}{2n}\right]^2$$

The statistic essentially sums the square of differences between the cumulative percentile $F_0(X_i)$ for the fitted distribution for each X_i observation and the average of i/n and $(i-1)/n$: the low and high plots of the empirical cumulative distribution of X_i values. Tables for this statistic can be found in Anderson and Darling (1952).

Table 10.2 Kolmogorov–Smirnoff statistic.

Distribution	Modified test statistic
Normal	$\left(\sqrt{n} - 0.01 + \dfrac{0.85}{\sqrt{n}}\right)D_n$
Exponential	$\left(D_n = \dfrac{0.2}{n}\right)\left(\sqrt{n} + 0.26 + \dfrac{0.5}{\sqrt{n}}\right)$
Weibull and extreme value	$\sqrt{n}D_n$
All others	$\left(\sqrt{n} + 0.12 + \dfrac{0.11}{\sqrt{n}}\right)D_n$

Table 10.3 Anderson–Darling statistics.

Distribution	Modified test statistic
Normal	$\left(1 + \dfrac{4}{n} - \dfrac{25}{n^2}\right)A_n^2$
Exponential	$\left(1 + \dfrac{0.6}{n}\right)A_n^2$
Weibull and extreme value	$\left(1 + \dfrac{0.2}{\sqrt{n}}\right)A_n^2$
All others	A_n^2

The chi-square goodness-of-fit statistic

The chi-square (χ^2) statistic measures how well the expected frequency of the fitted distribution compares with the observed frequency of a histogram of the observed data. The chi-square test makes the following assumptions:

1. The observed data consist of a random sample of n independent data points.
2. The measurement scale can be nominal (i.e. non-numeric) or numerical.
3. The n data points can be arranged into histogram form with N non-overlapping classes or bars that cover the entire possible range of the variable.

The chi-square statistic is calculated as follows:

$$\chi^2 = \sum_{i=1}^{N} \frac{\{O(i) - E(i)\}^2}{E(i)} \tag{10.6}$$

where $O(i)$ is the observed frequency of the ith histogram class or bar and $E(i)$ is the expected frequency from the fitted distribution of x values falling within the x range of the ith histogram bar. $E(i)$ is calculated as

$$E(i) = \{F(i_{max}) - F(i_{min})\} * n \tag{10.7}$$

where $F(x)$ is the distribution function of the fitted distribution, (i_{max}) is the x value upper bound of the ith histogram bar and (i_{min}) is the x value lower bound of the ith histogram bar.

Since the χ^2 statistic sums the *squares* of all of the errors $\{O(i) - E(i)\}$, it can be disproportionately sensitive to any large errors, e.g. if the error of one bar is 3 times that of another bar, it will contribute 9 times more to the statistic (assuming the same $E(i)$ for both).

χ^2 is the most commonly used of the goodness-of-fit statistics described here. However, it is very dependent on the number of bars, N, that are used. By changing the value of N, one can quite easily switch ranking between two distribution types. Unfortunately, there are no hard and fast rules for selecting the value of N. A good guide, however, is Scott's normal approximation which generally appears to work very well:

$$N = (4n)^{2/5}$$

where n is the number of data points. Another useful guide is to ensure that no bar has an expected frequency smaller than about 1, i.e. $E(i) \geq 1$ for all i. Note that the χ^2 statistic does not require that all or any histogram bars are of the same width.

The χ^2 statistic is most useful for fitting distributions to discrete data and is the only statistic described here that can be used for nominal (i.e. non-numeric) data.

Example 10.7 Use of χ^2 with continuous data

A dataset of 165 points is thought to come from a normal(70, 20) distribution. The data are first put into histogram form with 14 bars, as suggested by Scott's normal approximation (Table 10.4(a)). The four extreme bars have expected frequencies below 1 for a Normal(70, 20) distribution with 165 observations. These outside bars are therefore combined to produce a revised set of bar ranges. Table 10.4(b) shows the χ^2 calculation with the revised bar ranges.

Table 10.4 Calculation of the χ^2 statistic for a continuous dataset: (a) determining the bar ranges to be used; (b) calculation of χ^2 with revised bar ranges.

(a)

Histogram bars		Expected frequency
From A	To B	of Normal(70, 20)
$-\infty$	10	0.22
10	20	0.80
20	30	2.73
30	40	7.27
40	50	15.15
50	60	24.73
60	70	31.59
70	80	31.59
80	90	24.73
90	100	15.15
100	110	7.27
110	120	2.73
120	130	0.80
130	$+\infty$	0.22

(b)

Revised bars		$E(i)$ of	$O(i)$	Chi-square calc.
From A	To B	Normal(70, 20)		$\{O(i) - E(i)\}^2 / E(i)$
$-\infty$	20	1.02	3	3.80854
20	30	2.73	5	1.88948
30	40	7.27	6	0.22168
40	50	15.15	10	1.75344
50	60	24.73	21	0.56275
60	70	31.59	25	1.37523
70	80	31.59	37	0.92601
80	90	24.73	21	0.56275
90	100	15.15	17	0.22463
100	110	7.27	11	1.91447
110	120	2.73	6	3.92002
120	$+\infty$	1.02	3	3.80854
			Chi-square:	20.96754

Table 10.5 Calculation of the χ^2 statistic for a discrete dataset: (a) tabulation of the data; (b) calculation of χ^2.

(a)

x value	Observed frequency $O(i)$	Frequency $E(i)$ of Poisson (4.456)
0	0	1.579
1	8	7.036
2	18	15.675
3	20	23.282
4	29	25.936
5	21	23.113
6	18	17.165
7	10	10.926
8	8	6.086
9	2	3.013
10	1	1.343
11+	1	0.846
Total:	136	

(b)

x-value	Observed frequency $O(i)$	Frequency $E(i)$ of Poisson (4.456)	Chi Squared calc. $\{O(i) - E(i)\}^2/E(i)$
0	0	1.579	1.5790
1	8	7.036	0.1322
2	18	15.675	0.3448
3	20	23.282	0.4627
4	29	25.936	0.3621
5	21	23.113	0.1932
6	18	17.165	0.0406
7	10	10.926	0.0786
8	8	6.086	0.6020
9	2	3.013	0.3406
10+	2	2.189	0.0163
		Chi Squared:	4.1521

Hypotheses

- H_0: the data come from a Normal(70, 20) distribution.
- H_1: the data do not come from the Normal(70, 20) distribution.

Decision

The χ^2 test statistic has a value of 21.0 from Table 10.4(b). There are $\nu = N - 1 = 12 - 1 = 11$ degrees of freedom ($a = 0$ since no distribution parameters were determined from the data). Looking this up in a $\chi^2(11)$ distribution, the probability that we will have such a high value of χ^2 when H_0 is true is around 3%. We therefore conclude that the data did not come from a Normal(70, 20) distribution. ♦

Example 10.8 Use of χ^2 with discrete data

A set of 136 data points is believed to come from a Poisson distribution. The MLE for the parameter λ for the Poisson is estimated by taking the mean of the data points: $\lambda = 4.4559$. The data are tabulated in frequency form in Table 10.5(a) and, next to it, the expected frequency from a Poisson(4.4559) distribution, i.e. $E(i) = f(x) * 136$, where

$$f(x) = \frac{e^{-4.4559}4.4559^x}{x!}$$

The expected frequency for a value of 11+, calculated as $136 -$ (the sum of all the other expected frequencies), is less than 1. The number of bars is therefore decreased, as shown in Table 10.5(b), to ensure that all expected frequencies are greater than 1.

Hypotheses

- H_0: the data come from a Poisson distribution.
- H_1: the data do not come from a Poisson distribution.

Decision

The χ^2 test statistic has a value of 4.152 from Table 10.5(b). There are $\nu = N - a - 1 = 11 - 1 - 1 = 9$ degrees of freedom ($a = 1$ since one distribution parameter, the mean, was determined from the data). Looking this up in a $\chi^2(9)$ distribution, the probability that we will have such a high value of χ^2 when H_0 is true is just over 90%. Since this is such a large probability, we cannot reasonably reject H_0 and therefore conclude that the data fit a Poisson (4.4559) distribution. ♦

I've covered the chi-square statistic quite a bit here, because it is used often, but let's just trace back a moment to the assumptions behind it. The $\chi^2(\nu)$ distribution is the sum of ν unit normal distributions squared. Equation (10.6) says

$$\chi^2 = \sum_{i=1}^{N} \frac{\{O(i) - E(i)\}^2}{E(i)}$$

so the test is assuming that each $\frac{\{O(i)-E(i)\}^2}{E(i)}$ is approximately a Normal(0, 1)^2, i.e. that $O(i)$ is approximately Normal($E(i), \sqrt{E(i)}$) distributed. $O(i)$ is a Binomial(n, p) variable, where $p = F(i_{max}) - F(i_{min})$ and will only look somewhat normal when n is large and p is not near 0 or 1, in which case it will be approximately Normal$(np, \sqrt{np(1 - p)})$. The point is that the chi-square test is based on an implicit assumption that there are a *lot* of observations for each bin – so don't rely on it. Maximum likelihood methods will give better fits than optimising the chi-square statistic and have more flexibility, and the ability of the chi-square statistic as a measure of comparisons between goodness of fits is highly questionable since one should change the bin widths for each fitted distribution to give the same probability of a random sample lying within, but those bin ranges will be different for each fitted distribution.

Kolmogorov–Smirnoff (K–S) statistic

The K–S statistic D_n is defined as

$$D_n = \max[|F_n(x) - F(x)|]$$

where D_n is known as the K–S distance, n is the total number of data points, $F(x)$ is the distribution function of the fitted distribution, $F_n(x) = i/n$ and i is the cumulative rank of the data point.

The K–S statistic is thus only concerned with the maximum vertical distance between the cumulative distribution function of the fitted distribution and the cumulative distribution of the data. Figure 10.15 illustrates the concept for data fitted to a Uniform(0, 1) distribution.

- The data are ranked in ascending order.
- The upper $F_U(i)$ and lower $F_L(i)$ cumulative percentiles are calculated as follows:

$$F_L(i) = \frac{i - 1}{n}$$

$$F_U(i) = \frac{i}{n}$$

where i is the rank of the data point and n is the total number of data points.

- $F(x)$ is calculated for the Uniform distribution (in this case $F(x) = x$).

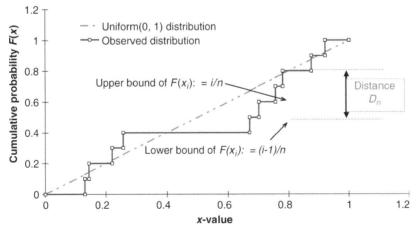

Figure 10.15 Calculation of the Kolmogorov–Smirnoff distance D_n for data fitted to a Uniform(0, 1) distribution.

- The maximum distance D_i between $F(i)$ and $F(x)$ is calculated for each i:

$$D_i = \text{MAX}(\text{ABS}(F(x) - F_L(i)), \text{ABS}(F(x) - F_U(i)))$$

where ABS $(\ldots)$ finds the absolute value.

- The maximum value of the D_i distances is then the K–S distance D_n:

$$D_n = \text{MAX}(\{D_i\})$$

The K–S statistic is generally more useful than the χ^2 statistic in that the data are assessed at all data points which avoids the problem of determining the number of bands into which to split the data. However, its value is only determined by the one largest discrepancy and takes no account of the lack of fit across the rest of the distribution. Thus, in Figure 10.16 it would give a worse fit to the distribution in (a) which has one large discrepancy than to the distribution in (b) which has a poor general fit over the whole x range.

The vertical distance between the observed distribution $F_n(x)$ and the theoretical fitted distribution $F(x)$ at any point, say x_0, itself has a distribution with a mean of zero and a standard deviation σ_{K-S} given by binomial theory:

$$\sigma_{K-S} = \sqrt{\frac{F(x_0)[1 - F(x_0)]}{n}}$$

The size of the standard deviation σ_{K-S} over the x range is shown in Figure 10.17 for a number of distribution types with $n = 100$. The position of D_n along the x axis is more likely to occur where σ_{K-S} is greatest, which, Figure 10.17 shows, will generally be away from the low-probability tails. This insensitivity of the K–S statistic to lack of fit at the extremes of the distributions is corrected for in the Anderson–Darling statistic.

The enlightened statistical literature is quite scathing about distribution-fitting software that use the KS statistic as a goodness of fit – particularly if one has estimated the parameters of a fitted distribution from data (as opposed to comparing data against a predefined distribution). This was not the intention of the K–S statistic, which assumes that the fitted distribution is fully specified. In order to use it as a goodness-of-fit measure that ranks levels of distribution fit, one must perform simulation experiments to determine the critical region of the K–S statistic in each case.

Anderson–Darling (A–D) statistic

The A–D statistic A_n^2 is defined as

$$A_n^2 = \int_{-\infty}^{\infty} |F_n(x) - F(x)|^2 \Psi(x) f(x) \, dx$$

where

$$\Psi(x) = \frac{n}{F(x)\{1 - F(x)\}}$$

n is the total number of data points, $F(x)$ is the distribution function of the fitted distribution, $f(x)$ is the density function of the fitted distribution, $F_n(x) = i/n$ and i is the cumulative rank of the data point.

The Anderson–Darling statistic is a more sophisticated version of the Kolmogorov–Smirnoff statistic. It is more powerful for the following reasons:

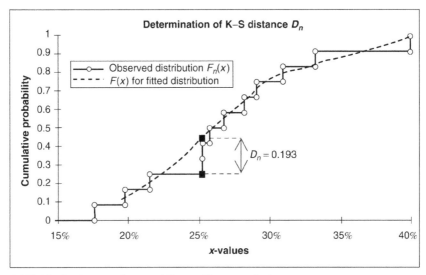

(a) Distribution is generally a good fit except in one particular area

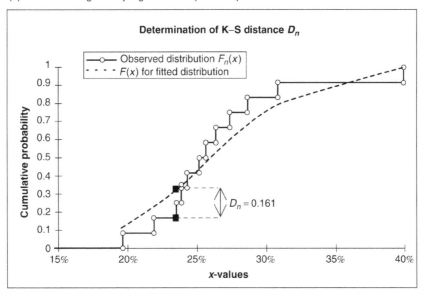

(b) Distribution is generally a poor fit but with no single large discrepancies

Figure 10.16 How the K–S distance D_n can give a false measure of fit because of its reliance on the single largest distance between the two cumulative distributions rather than looking at the distances over the whole possible range.

- $\Psi(x)$ compensates for the increased variance of the vertical distances between distributions (σ^2_{K-S}), which is described in Figure 10.17.

- $f(x)$ weights the observed distances by the probability that a value will be generated at that x value.

- The vertical distances are integrated over *all* values of x to make maximum use of the observed data (the K–S statistic only looks at the maximum vertical distance).

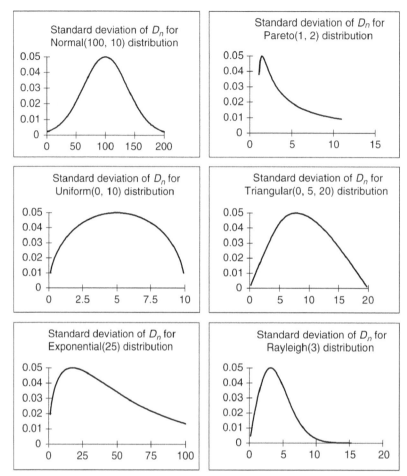

Figure 10.17 Variation in the standard deviation of the K–S statistic D_n over the range of a variety of distributions. The greater the standard deviation, the more chance that D_n will fall in that part of the range, which shows that the K–S statistic will tend to focus on the degree of fit at x values away from a distribution's tails.

The A–D statistic is therefore a generally more useful measure of fit than the K–S statistic, especially where it is important to place equal emphasis on fitting a distribution at the tails as well as the main body. Nonetheless, it still suffers from the same problem as the K–S statistic in that the fitted distribution should in theory be fully specified, not estimated from the data. It suffers from a larger problem in that the confidence region has been determined for only a very few distributions.

A better goodness-of-fit measure

For reasons I have explained above, the chi-square, Kolmogorov–Smirnoff and Anderson–Darling goodness-of-fit statistics are technically all inappropriate as a method of comparing fits of distributions to data. They are also limited to having precise observations and cannot incorporate censored, truncated or binned data. Realistically, most of the time we are fitting a continuous distribution to a set of precise observations, and then the Anderson–Darling does a reasonable job. However, for important work you should instead consider using statistical measures of fit called *information criteria*.

Let n be the number of observations (e.g. data values, frequencies), k be the number of parameters to be estimated (e.g. the normal distribution has two parameters: mu and sigma) and $\log L_{max}$ be the maximized value of the log-likelihood for the estimated.

1. **SIC (Schwarz information criterion, aka Bayesian information criterion, BIC)**

$$SIC = \ln[n]k - 2\ln[L_{max}]$$

2. **AIC$_C$ (Akaike information criterion)**

$$AIC_c = \left(\frac{2n}{n-k-1}\right)k - 2\ln[L_{max}]$$

3. **HQIC (Hannan–Quinn information criterion)**

$$HQIC = 2\ln[\ln[n]]k - 2\ln[L_{max}]$$

The aim is to find the model with the *lowest* value of the selected information criterion. The $-2\ln[L_{max}]$ term appearing in each formula is an estimate of the deviance of the model fit. The coefficients for k in the first part of each formula shows the degree to which the number of model parameters is being penalised. For $n \gtrsim 20$ or so the SIC (Schwarz, 1997) is the strictest in penalising loss of degree of freedom by having more parameters in the fitted model. For $n \gtrsim 40$ the AIC$_C$ (Akaike, 1974, 1976) is the least strict of the three and the HQIC (Hannan and Quinn, 1979) holds the middle ground, or is the least penalising for $n \lesssim 20$.

ModelRisk applies modified versions of these three criteria as a means of ranking each fitted model, whether it be fitting a distribution, a time series model or a copula. If you fit a number of models to your data, try not to pick automatically the fitted distribution with the best statistical result, particularly if the top two or three are close. Also, look at the range and shape of the fitted distribution and see whether they correspond to what you think is appropriate.

10.3.5 Goodness-of-fit plots

Goodness-of-fit plots offer the analyst a visual comparison between the data and fitted distributions. They provide an overall picture of the errors in a way that a goodness-of-fit statistic cannot and allow the analyst to select the best-fitting distribution in a more qualitative and intuitive way. Several types of plot are in common use. Their individual merits are discussed below.

Comparison of probability density

Overlaying a histogram plot of the data with a density function of the fitted distribution is usually the most informative comparison (see Figure 10.18(a)). It is easy to see where the main discrepancies are and whether the general shape of the data and fitted distribution compare well. The same scale and number of histogram bars should be used for all plots if a direct comparison of several distribution fits is to be made for the same data.

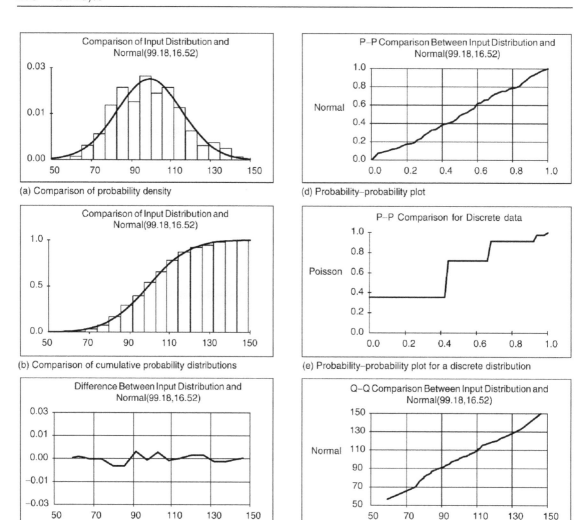

Figure 10.18 Examples of goodness-of-fit plots.

Comparison of probability distributions

An overlay of the cumulative frequency plots of the data and the fitted distribution is sometimes used (see Figure 10.18(b)). However, this plot has a very insensitive scale and the cumulative frequency of most distribution types follow very similar S-curves. This type of plot will therefore only show up very large differences between the data and fitted distributions and is not generally recommended as a visual measure of the goodness of fit.

Difference between probability densities

This plot is derived from the above comparison of probability density, plotting the *difference* between the probability densities (see Figure 10.18(c)). It has a far more sensitive scale than the other plots described here. The size of the deviations is also a function of the number of classes (bars) used to plot the histogram. In order to make a direct comparison between other distribution function fits using this type of plot, analysts must ensure that the same number of histogram classes is used for all plots. They must also ensure that the same vertical scale is used, as this can vary widely between fits.

Probability–probability (P–P) plots

This is a plot of the cumulative distribution of the fitted curve $F(x)$ against the cumulative frequency $F_n(x) = i/(n + 1)$ for all values of x_i (see Figure 10.18(d)). The better the fit, the closer this plot resembles a straight line. It can be useful if one is interested in closely matching cumulative percentiles, and it will show significant differences between the middles of the two distributions. However, the plot is far less sensitive to any discrepancies in fit than the comparison of probability density plot and is therefore not often used. It can also be rather confusing when used to review discrete data (see Figure 10.18(e)) where a fairly good fit can easily be masked, especially if there are only a few allowable x values.

Quantile–Quantile (Q–Q) plots

This is a plot of the observed data x_i against the x values where $F(x) = F_n(x)$, i.e. $= i/(n + 1)$ (see Figure 10.18(f)). As with P–P plots, the better the fit, the closer this plot resembles a straight line. It can be useful if one is interested in closely matching cumulative percentiles, and it will show significant differences between the tails of the two distributions. However, the plot suffers from the same insensitivity problem as the P–P plots.

10.4 Fitting a Second-Order Parametric Distribution to Observed Data

The techniques for quantifying uncertainty, described in the first part of this chapter, can be used to determine the distribution of uncertainty for parameters of a parametric distribution fitted to data. The three main techniques are classical statistics methods, the bootstrap and Bayesian inference by Gibbs sampling. The main issue in estimating the parameters of a distribution from data is that the uncertainty distributions of the estimated parameters are usually linked together in some way.

Classical statistics tends to overcome this problem by assuming that the parameter uncertainty distributions are normally distributed, in which case it determines a covariance between these distributions. However, in most situations one comes across, the parameter uncertainty distributions are not normal (they will tend to be as the amount of data gets very large), so the approach is very limited.

The parametric bootstrap is much better, since one simply resamples from the MLE fitted distribution in the same fashion in which the data appear, and in the same amount, of course. Then, refitting using MLE again gives us random samples from the joint uncertainty distribution for the parameters. The main limitation to the bootstrap is in fitting a discrete distribution, particularly one where there are few allowable values, as this will make the joint uncertainty distribution very "grainy".

Markov chain Monte Carlo will also generate random samples from the joint uncertainty density. It is very flexible but has the small problem of setting the prior distributions.

Example 10.9 Fitting a second-order normal distribution to data with classical statistics

The normal distribution is easy to fit to data since we have the z-test and chi-square test giving us precise formulae. There are not many other distributions that can be handled so conveniently. Classical statistics tells us that the uncertainty distributions for the mean and standard deviation of the normal distribution are given by Equation (9.3)

$$\sigma = \sqrt{\frac{(n-1)V_s}{\chi^2(n-1)}}$$

when we don't know the mean, and by Equation (9.1)

$$\mu = N\left(\overline{x}, \frac{\sigma}{\sqrt{n}}\right)$$

when we know the standard deviation.

So, if we simulate possible values for the standard deviation first with Equation (9.3), we can feed these values into Equation (9.1) to determine the mean. ◆

Example 10.10 Fitting a second-order normal distribution to data using the parametric bootstrap

The sample mean (Excel: AVERAGE) and sample standard deviation (Excel: STDEV) are the MLE estimates for the normal distribution. Thus, if we have n data values with mean $\overline{x}$ and standard deviation s, we generate n independent Normal($\overline{x}, s$) distributions and recalculate their mean and standard deviation using AVERAGE and STDEV to generate uncertainty values for the population parameters. ◆

Example 10.11 Fitting a second-order gamma distribution to data using the parametric bootstrap

There are no equations for direct determination of the MLE parameter values for a gamma distribution, so one needs to construct the likelihood function and optimise it by varying the parameters, which is rather tiresome but by far the more common situation encountered. ModelRisk offers distribution-fitting algorithms that do this automatically. For example, the two-cell array {VoseGammaFitP(*data*, TRUE)} will generate values from the joint uncertainty distribution for a gamma distribution fit to the set of values *data*. The array {VoseGammaFitP(*data*, FALSE)} will return just the MLE values. The function VoseGammaFit(*data*, TRUE) returns random samples from a gamma distribution. with the parameter uncertainty imbedded, and VoseGammaFit(*data*, 0.99, TRUE) will return random samples from the uncertainty distribution for the 99th percentile of a gamma distribution fit to *data*. ◆

Example 10.12 Fitting a second-order gamma distribution to data using WinBUGS

The following WinBUGS model takes 47 data values (that were in fact drawn from a Gamma(4,7) distribution) and fits a gamma distribution. There are two important things to note here: in WinBUGS the scale parameter *lambda* is defined as the reciprocal of the beta scale parameter more commonly used (and this book's convention); and I have used a prior for each parameter of Gamma(1, 1000) [in more standard convention] which is an exponential with mean 1000. The exponential distribution is used because it extends from zero to infinity which matches the parameters' domains, and an exponential with such a large mean will appear quite flat over the range of interest (so it is reasonably uninformed). The model is:

```
model
    {
          for(i in 1 : M) {
            x[i] ~ dgamma(alpha, lambda)
          }
```

```
        alpha ~ dgamma(1.0, 1.0E-3)
        beta ~ dgamma(1.0, 1.0E-3)
        lambda<-1/beta
    }

list(M = 47, x = c(15.31, 17.63, 17.53, 34.59, 27.59, 27.34, 17.96, 16.95, 11.63, 31.15,
    36.41, 29.53, 56.35, 20.53, 16.23, 23.14, 35.5, 35.5, 31.63, 14.26, 10.29, 29.86,
    24.49, 13.23, 12.91, 20.18, 66.18, 23.25, 30.58, 14.1, 11.25, 37.75, 52.35, 44.46,
    13.52, 10.56, 27.62, 30.06, 11.46, 29.12, 21.57, 54.03, 28.06, 42.97, 5.42, 11.23,
    19.05))
```

After a burn-in of 100 000 iterations, the estimates are as shown in Figure 10.19.

The estimates are centred roughly around 4 (mean = 4.111) and 7 (mean = 6.288), as we might have hoped having generated the samples from a Gamma(4, 7). We can check to see whether the choice of prior has much effect. For alpha the uncertainty distribution ranges from about 2 to 6: the Exponential(1000)

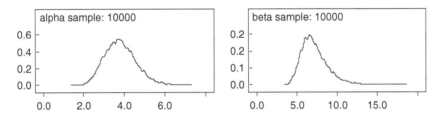

Figure 10.19 WinBUGS estimates of gamma distribution parameters for Example 10.12.

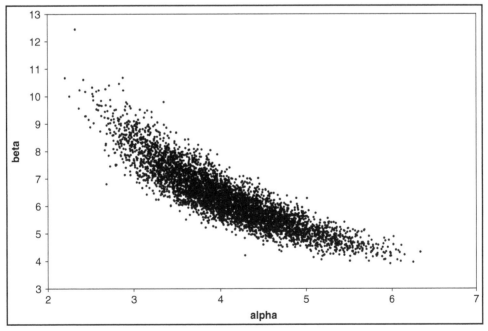

Figure 10.20 5000 posterior distribution samples from the WinBUGS model to estimate gamma distribution parameters for Example 10.12.

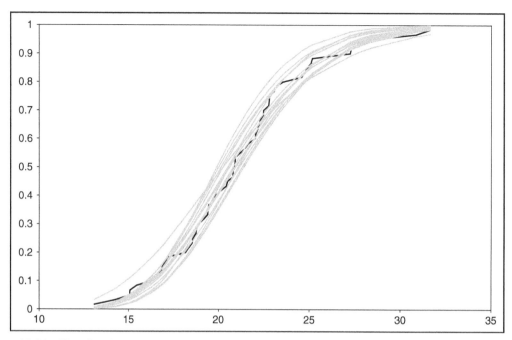

Figure 10.21 Plot showing the empirical cumulative distribution of the data in bold and the second-order fitted lognormal distribution in grey.

density at 2 and 6 respectively are 9.98E-4 and 9.94E-4, a ratio of 1.004, so essentially flat over the posterior region. Between 4 and 13, the range for the beta parameter, the ratio is 1.009 – again essentially flat.

Figure 10.20 shows why it is necessary to estimate the joint uncertainty distribution. The banana shape of this scatter plot shows that there is a strong correlation between the parameter estimates. You can understand why this relationship occurs intuitively as follows: the mean of a population distribution can be estimated quite quickly from the data and will have roughly normally distributed uncertainty: in this case the 47 observations have sample mean = 25.794 and sample variance = 184.06, so the population mean uncertainty is Normal(25.794, SQRT(184.06/47)) = Normal(25.794, 1.979). The mean of a Gamma(α, β) distribution is $\alpha\beta$. Equating the two says that if $\alpha = 6$ then β must be about 4.3 ± 0.3, and if $\alpha = 3$ then β is about 8.6 ± 0.6, which can be seen in Figure 10.20. ♦

10.4.1 Second-order goodness-of-fit plots

Second-order goodness-of-fit plots are the same as the first-order plots in Figure 10.18, except that uncertainty about the distribution is expressed as a series of lines describing possible true distributions (sometimes called a candyfloss or spaghetti plot). Figure 10.21 gives an example.

In Figure 10.21 the grey lines represent the fitted lognormal cumulative distribution function for 15 samples from the joint uncertainty distribution for the lognormal's mean and standard deviation. This gives an intuitive visual description of how certain we are about the fitted distribution. ModelRisk's distribution-fitting facility will show these plots automatically with a user-defined number of "spaghetti" lines.

Chapter 11

Sums of random variables

One of the most common mistakes people make in producing even the most simple Monte Carlo simulation model is in calculating sums of random variables.

In this chapter we look at a number of techniques that have extremely broad use in risk analysis in estimating the sum of random variables. We start with the basic problem and how this can be simulated. Then we examine how simulation can be improved, and then how it can often be replaced with a direct construction of the distribution of the sum of the random variables. Finally, I introduce the ability to model correlation between variables that are being summed.

11.1 The Basic Problem

We are very often in the situation of wanting to estimate the aggregate (sum) of a number n of variables, each of which follow the same distribution or have the same value X (see Table 11.1, for example).

We have six situations to deal with (Table 11.2).

Situations A, B, D and E

For situations A B, D and E the mathematics is very easy to simulate:

$$\text{SUM} = n * X$$

Situation C

For situation C, where X are independent random variables (i.e. each X being summed can take a different value) and n is fixed, we often have a simple way to determine the aggregate distribution based on known identities. The most common identities are listed in Table 11.3.

We also know from the central limit theorem that, if n is large enough, the sum will often look like a normal distribution. If X has a mean μ and standard deviation σ, then, as n becomes large, we get

$$Sum \approx \text{Normal}(n * \mu, \sqrt{n} * \sigma)$$

which is rather nice because it means we can have a distribution like the relative distribution and determine the moments (ModelRisk function VoseMoments will do this automatically for you), or just the mean and standard deviation of relevant observations of X and use them. It also explains why the distributions in the right-hand column of Table 11.3 often look approximately normal.

When none of these identities applies, we have to simulate a column of X variables of length n and add them up, which is usually not too onerous in computing time or spreadsheet size because if n is large we can usually use the central limit theorem approximation.

Table 11.1 Variables and their aggregate distribution.

N	X	Aggregate distribution
Customers in a year	Purchase of each customer	Total receipts in a year
Contaminated egg	Bacteria in a contaminated egg	Bacteria in my three-raw-egg milkshake
Credit defaults	Amount owed by a creditor	Total credit default exposure
Life insurance holders who die next year	Amount due on death for a policyholder	Total financial exposure of insurance company

Table 11.2 Different situations where aggregate distributions are needed.

Situation	N	X
A	Fixed value	Fixed value
B	Fixed value	Random variable, all n take same value
C	Fixed value	Random variable, all n take different values (iids)
D	Random variable	Fixed value
E	Random variable	Random variable, all n take same value
F	Random variable	Random variable, all n take different values (iids)

Table 11.3 Known identities for aggregate distributions.

X	Aggregate distribution
Bernoulli(p)	Binomial(n, p)
BetaBinomial(m, α, β)	BetaBinomial($n * m, \alpha, \beta$)
Binomial(m, p)	Binomial($n * m, p$)
Cauchy(a, b)	$n *$ Cauchy(a, b)
ChiSq(v)	ChiSq($n * v$)
Erlang(m, β)	Erlang($n * m, \beta$)
Exponential(β)	Gamma(n, β)
Gamma(α, β)	Gamma($n * \alpha, \beta$)
Geometric(p)	NegBin(n, p)
Levy(c, a)	$n^2 *$ Levy(c, a)
NegBin(s, p)	NegBin($n * s, p$)
Normal(μ, σ)	Normal($n * \mu$, SQRT(n) $* \sigma$)
Poisson(λ)	Poisson($n * \lambda$)
Student(v)	Student($n * v$)

An alternative for situation C available in ModelRisk is to use the VoseAggregateMC(n, distribution) function; for example, if we write

$$= \text{VoseAggregateMC}(1000, \text{VoseLognormalObject}(2, 6))$$

the function will generate and add together 1000 independent random samples from a lognormal(2, 6) distribution. However, were we to write

$$= \text{VoseAggregateMC}(1000, \text{VoseGammaObject}(2, 6))$$

the function would generate a single value from a Gamma(2 * 1000, 6) distribution because all of the identities in Table 11.3 are programmed into the function.

Situation F

This leaves us with situation F – the sum of a random number of random variables. The most basic simulation method is to produce a model where a value for n is generated in one spreadsheet cell and then a column of X variables is created that varies in size according to the value on n (see, for example, Figure 11.1).

In this model, n is a Poisson(12) random being generated at cell C2. The Lognormal(100, 10) X values are generated in column C only if the count value in column B is smaller than or equal to n. For example, in the iteration shown, a value of 14 is generated for n, so 14 X values are generated in column C.

The method is quite generally applicable, but among other problems is inefficient. Imagine if n had been Poisson(10 000), for example – we would need huge B and C columns to make the model work. It is also difficult from a modelling perspective because the model has to be written for a specific range of n. One cannot simply change the parameter in the Poisson distribution.

We have a couple of options based on the techniques described above for situation C. If we are adding together X variables shown in Table 11.3, then we can apply those identities by simulating n

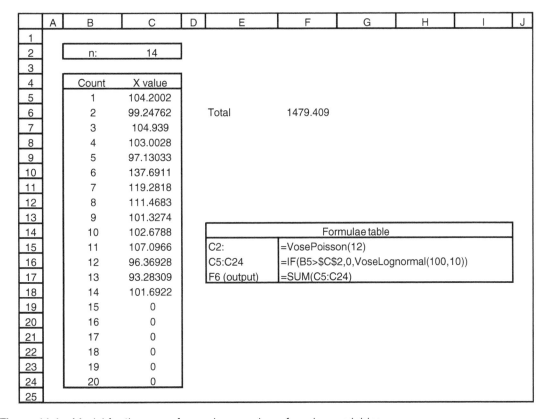

Figure 11.1 Model for the sum of a random number of random variables.

in one cell and linking that to a cell that simulates from the aggregate variable conditioned on n. For example, imagine we are summing Poisson(100) X variables where each X variable takes a Gamma(2, 6) distribution. Then we can write

$$\text{Cell A1} := \text{VosePoisson}(100)$$

$$\text{Cell A2(output)} := \text{VoseGamma(A1 * 2, 6)}$$

We can also use the central limit theorem method. Imagine we have $n = \text{Poisson}(1000)$ and $X = \text{Beta4}(3, 7, 0, 8)$, which is illustrated in Figure 11.2.

The distribution is not terribly asymmetric, so adding roughly 1000 of them will look very close to a normal distribution, which means that we can be confident in applying the central limit theorem approximation, shown in the model of Figure 11.3.

Here we have made use of the VoseMoments array function which returns the moments of a distribution object. Most software, however, will allow you at least to view the moments of a distribution, and, if not, you can simulate the distribution on its own and empirically determine its moments from the values or, if you need greater accuracy or speed, apply the equations given in the distribution compendium in Appendix III. The VoseCLTSum performs the same calculation as that shown in F5 but is a little more intuitive. Alternatively, the VoseAggregateMC will, in this iteration, add together 957 values drawn from the Beta4 distribution because there is no known identity for sums of Beta4 distributions.

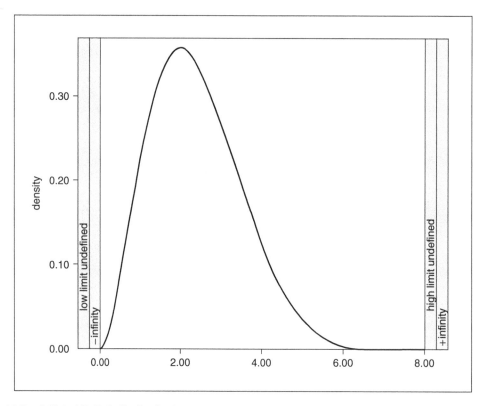

Figure 11.2 A Beta4(3, 7, 0, 8) distribution.

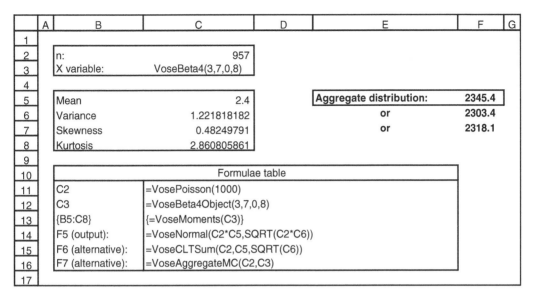

Figure 11.3 Model for the central limit theorem approximation.

11.2 Aggregate Distributions

11.2.1 Moments of an aggregate distribution

There are general formulae for determining the moments of an aggregate distribution given that one has the moments for the frequency distribution for n and the severity distribution for X. If the frequency distribution has mean, variance and skewness of μ_F, V_F and S_F respectively, and the severity distribution has mean, variance and skewness of μ_C, V_C and S_C respectively, then the aggregate distribution has the following moments:

$$\text{Mean} = \mu_F \mu_C \qquad (11.1)$$

$$\text{Variance} = \mu_F V_C + V_F \mu_C^2 \qquad (11.2)$$

$$\text{Skewness} = \frac{\mu_F S_C V_C^{3/2} + 3 V_F \mu_C V_C + S_F V_F^{3/2} \mu_C^3}{(\text{Variance})^{3/2}} \qquad (11.3)$$

There is also a formula for kurtosis, but it is rather ugly. The ModelRisk function VoseAggregate-Moments determines the first four moments of an aggregate distribution for any frequency and severity distribution, even if they are bounded and/or shifted.

Equations (11.1) to (11.3) deserve a little more exploration. Firstly, let's consider the situation where n is a fixed value, so $\mu_F = n$, $V_F = 0$ and $S_F =$ undefined. Then we have moments for the aggregate distribution of

$$\text{Mean} = n\mu_C$$

$$\text{Variance} = n V_C$$

$$\text{Skewness} = \frac{S_C}{\sqrt{n}}$$

You can see that this gives support to the central limit theorem which states that, if n is large enough, the aggregate distribution approaches a normal distribution with mean $= n\mu_C$ and variance $= n V_C$. The skewness equation shows that the aggregate skewness is proportional to the skewness of X but decreases rapidly at first with increasing n, then more slowly, and asymptotically towards zero.

Another interesting example is to consider the aggregate moment equations when n follows a Poisson(λ) distribution, which is very commonly the most appropriate distribution for n, and also has the convenience of being described by just one parameter. Now we have $\mu_F = \lambda$, $V_F = \lambda$ and $S_F = \frac{1}{\sqrt{\lambda}}$, and the aggregate moments are

$$\text{Mean} = \lambda \mu_C$$

$$\text{Variance} = \lambda \left(V_C + \mu_C^2 \right)$$

$$\text{Skewness} = \frac{\left(S_C V_C^{3/2} + 3\mu_C V_C + \mu_C^3 \right)}{\left(V_C + \mu_C^2 \right)^{\frac{3}{2}} \sqrt{\lambda}}$$

The mean and variance equations are simple formulae. We can see that the skewness decreases with $\frac{1}{\sqrt{\lambda}}$ in the same way as it does for a fixed value for n. If X is symmetrically distributed, then, for a given λ, the skewness is at its maximum when the mean and standard deviation of X are the same, and at its lowest when the standard deviation is very high. Thus, the aggregate distribution will be more closely normal when V_C is large.

Being able to determine the aggregate moments is pretty useful. One can directly compare sums of random variables, which I will discuss more in Chapter 21. One can also match these moments to some parametric distribution and use that as an approximation to the aggregate distribution. An aggregate distribution is almost always right skewed, so we can select from a number of right-skewed distributions like the lognormal and gamma and match moments. For example, a Gamma(α, β) distribution shifted by a value T has

$$\text{Mean} = \alpha\beta + T \tag{11.4}$$

$$\text{Variance} = \alpha\beta^2 \tag{11.5}$$

$$\text{Skewness} = \frac{2}{\sqrt{\alpha}} \tag{11.6}$$

Thus, matching skewness gives us a value for α. Then, matching variance gives us β, and, finally, matching mean gives us T. Adding a shift gives us three parameters to estimate, so we can match three moments. The model in Figure 11.4 offers an example.

Cells C3:C5 are the parameters for the model. Cells D3 and D4 use ModelRisk functions to create distribution objects. B8:C11 and D8:E11 use the VoseMoments function to calculate the moments of the two distributions. Alternatively, you can use the equations in the distribution compendium in Appendix III. F8:F10 manually calculates the first three aggregate moments from Equations (11.1) to (11.3), and G8:H11 calculates all four using the VoseAggregateMoments function as a check. In C15:C17, Equations (11.4) to (11.6) are inverted to determine the gamma distribution parameters. Finally, G14:H17 uses the VoseMoments function again to determine the moments of the gamma distribution. You can see that they match the mean, variance and skewness of the aggregate distribution – as they should – but also that the kurtosis is very close, so the gamma distribution would likely be a good substitute for the aggregate distribution. To be sure, we would need to plot the two together, which we'll look

	A	B	C	D	E	F	G	H	I
1									
2			**Parameters**		**Distribution**				
3		Lambda		25	VosePoisson($C$3)				
4		Mu		5	VoseLognormal($C$4,$C$5)				
5		Sigma		7					
6									
7			**Frequency**		**Severity**		**Aggregate**	**VoseAMoments**	
8		Mean		25	Mean	5	125	Mean	125
9		Variance		25	Variance	49	1850	Variance	1850
10		Skewness		0.2	Skewness	6.944	1.018515312	Skewness	1.018515
11		Kurtosis		3.04	Kurtosis	75.1056		Kurtosis	4.723443
12									
13								**Gamma Moments**	
14			**Fitted Gamma parameters**					Mean	125
15		Shape alpha	3.85589205					Variance	1850
16		Scale beta	21.904					Skewness	1.018515
17		Shift T	40.54054054					Kurtosis	4.55606
18									
19				**Formulae table**					
20		D3:		=VosePoissonObject(C3)					
21		D4:		=VoseNormalObject(C4,C5)					
22		{B8:C11}:		{=VoseMoments(D3)}					
23		{D8:E11}:		{=VoseMoments(D4)}					
24		F8		=C8*E8					
25		F9		=C8*E9+C9*E8^2					
26		F10		=(C8*E10*E9^1.5+3*C9*E8*E9+C10*C9^1.5*E8^3)/(F9^1.5)					
27		{G8:H11}:		{=VoseAggregateMoments(D3,D4)}					
28		C15		=(2/H10)^2					
29		C16		=SQRT(H9/C15)					
30		C17		=H8-C15*C16					
31		{G14:H17}		{=VoseMoments(VoseGammaObject(C15,C16,VoseShift(C17)))}					
32									

Figure 11.4 Model for determining aggregate moments.

at later: a feature in ModelRisk uses the matching moments principle to match shifted versions of the gamma, inverse gamma, lognormal, Pearson5, Pearson6 and fatigue distributions to constructed aggregate distributions and overlay the distributions for an extra visual comparison.

11.2.2 Methods for constructing an aggregate distribution

In this section I want to turn to a range of very neat techniques for constructing the aggregate distribution when n is a random variable and X are independent identically distributed random variables. There are a lot of advantages to being able to construct such an aggregate distribution, among which are:

- We can determine tail probabilities to a high precision.
- It is much faster than Monte Carlo simulation.
- We can manipulate the aggregate distribution as with any other in Monte Carlo simulation, e.g. correlate it with other variables.

The main disadvantage to these methods is that they are computationally intensive and need to run calculations through often very long arrays. This makes them impractical to show in a spreadsheet environment, so I will only describe the theory here. All methods are implemented in ModelRisk, however, which runs the calculations internally in C++.

We start by looking at the Panjer recursive method, and then the fast Fourier transform (FFT) method. These two have a similar feel to them, and similar applications, although their mathematics is quite different. Then we'll look at a multivariate FFT method that allows us to extend the aggregate calculation to a set of $\{n, X\}$ variables. The de Pril recursive method is similar to Panjer's and has specific use.

Finally, I give a summary of these methods and when and why they are useful.

Panjer's recursive method

Panjer's recursive method (Panjer, 1981; Panjer and Willmot, 1992) applies where the number of variables n being added together follows one of these distributions:

- binomial;
- geometric;
- negative binomial;
- Poisson;
- Pólya.

The technique begins by taking the claim size distribution and discretising it into a number of values with increment C. Then the probability is redistributed so that the discretised claim distribution has the same mean as the continuous variable. There are a few ways of doing this, but if the discretisation steps are small they give essentially the same answer. A simple method is to assign the value $(i * C)$ the probability s_i as follows:

$$s_i = F((i + 0.5)C) - F((i - 0.5)C)$$

In the discretisation process we have to decide on a maximum value of i (called r) so we don't have an infinite number of calculations to perform. Now comes the clever part. The above discrete distributions lead to a simple one-time summation through a recursive formula to calculate the probability $p(j)$ that the aggregate distribution will equal $j * C$:

$$p_j = \frac{1}{1 - a \cdot s_0} \sum_{i=1}^{\min(j,r)} \left(a + \frac{i \cdot b}{j}\right) \cdot s_i \cdot p_{j-i}, \, j = 1, 2, \ldots \tag{11.7}$$

The formula works for all frequency distributions for n that are of the $(a, b, 0)$ class, which means that, from $P(n = 0)$ up, we have a recursive relationship between $P(n = i)$ and $P(n = i - 1)$ of the form

$$P(n = i) = \left(a + \frac{b}{i}\right) * P(n = i - 1) \tag{11.8}$$

a and b are fixed values that depend on which of the discrete distributions is used and their parameter value. The specific formula for each case is given below for the $(a, b, 0)$ class of discrete distributions:

- For the Binomial(n,p)

$$p_0 = \left(\frac{a - 1}{a \cdot s_0 - 1}\right)^{\frac{a+b}{a}}, a = -\frac{p}{1 - p}, b = \frac{(n + 1)p}{1 - p}$$

- For the Geometric(p)

$$p_0 = \frac{p}{1 - s_0 + ps_0}, a = 1 - p, b = 0$$

- For the NegBin(s,p)

$$p_0 = \left(\frac{p}{1 - s_0 + ps_0} \right)^s, a = 1 - p, b = (s - 1)(1 - p)$$

- For the Poisson(λ)

$$p_0 = \exp[\lambda \cdot s_0 - \lambda], a = 0, b = \lambda$$

- For the Pólya(α,β)

$$p_0 = \left(1 + \frac{a \cdot \alpha\beta \cdot (1 - s_0)}{a + b} \right)^{-\frac{a+b}{a}}, a = \frac{\beta}{\beta + 1}, b = \frac{(\alpha - 1) \cdot \beta}{\beta + 1}$$

The output of the algorithm is two arrays $\{i\}, \{p(i)\}$ that can be constructed into a distribution, for example as VoseDiscrete($\{i\}$, $p\{i\}$) * C. Panjer's method can occasionally numerically "blow up" with the binomial distribution, but when it does so it generates negative probabilities, so is immediately obvious.

A small change to Panjer's algorithm allows the formula to be applied to $(a, b, 1)$ distributions, which means that the recursive formula (11.8) works from $P(n = 1)$ onwards. This allows us to include the logarithmic distribution using the formulae

$$p_j = \theta \left[\frac{s(j)}{|\log(1 - \theta)|} + \sum_{i=1}^{\min(j-1,r)} \left(1 - \frac{i}{j} \right) s(i)p(j - i) \right], \quad j = 1, 2, \dots p_0 = 0$$

Panjer's method cannot, however, be applied to the Delaporte distribution. Panjer's method requires a bit of hands-on management because one has to experiment with the maximum value r to ensure sufficient coverage and accuracy of the distribution. ModelRisk uses two controls for this: MaxP specifies the upper percentile value of the distribution of X at which the algorithm will stop, and Intervals specifies how many steps will be used in the discretisation of the X distribution. In general, the larger one makes Intervals, the more accurate the model will be, but at the expense of computation time. The MaxP value should be set high enough realistically to cover the distribution of X, but, if one sets it too high for a long tailed distribution, there will be an insufficient number of increments in the main body of the distribution. In ModelRisk one can compare the exact moments of the aggregate distribution with those of the Panjer constructed distribution to ensure that the two correspond with sufficient accuracy for the analyst's needs.

Fast fourier transform (FFT) method

The density function $f(x)$ of a continuous random variable can always be converted into its Fourier transform $\phi_x(t)$ (also called its characteristic function) as follows:

$$\phi_x(t) = \int\limits_{\min}^{\max} e^{itx} f(x) \, dx = E[e^{itx}]$$

and we can transform back using

$$f(x) = \frac{1}{2\pi} \int\limits_{\min}^{\max} e^{-itx} \phi_x(t) dt$$

Characteristic functions are really useful for determining the sums of random variables because $\phi_{X+Y}(t) = \phi_X(t) * \phi_Y(t)$, i.e. we just multiply the characteristic functions of variables X and Y to get the characteristic function of $(X + Y)$. For example, the characteristic function for a normal distribution is $\phi(t) = \exp\left[i\mu t - \frac{\sigma^2 t^2}{2}\right]$. Thus, for variables $X = \text{Normal}(\mu_X, \sigma_X)$ and $Y = \text{Normal}(\mu_Y, \sigma_Y)$ we have

$$\phi_{X+Y}(t) = \phi_X(t)\phi_Y(t) = \exp\left[i\mu_X t - \frac{\sigma_X^2 t^2}{2}\right] \exp\left[i\mu_Y t - \frac{\sigma_Y^2 t^2}{2}\right]$$

$$= \exp\left[i(\mu_X + \mu_Y)t - \frac{(\sigma_X^2 + \sigma_Y^2)t^2}{2}\right]$$

In this particular example, the function form of $\phi_{X+Y}(t)$ equates to another normal distribution with mean $(\mu_X + \mu_Y)$ and variance $(\sigma_X^2 + \sigma_Y^2)$, so we don't have to apply a transformation back – we can already recognise the result.

The fast Fourier transform method of constructing an aggregate distribution where there are a random number n of identically distributed random variables X to be summed is described fully in Robertson (1992). The technique involves discretising the severity distribution X like Panjer's method so that one has two sets of discrete vectors, one each for the frequency and severity distributions. The mathematics involves complex numbers and is based on the convolution theory of discrete Fourier transforms, which states that to obtain the aggregate distribution one multiplies the two discrete Fourier transforms of these vectors pointwise and then computes the inverse discrete Fourier transform. The fast Fourier transform is used as a very quick method for computing the discrete Fourier transform for long vectors.

The main advantage of the FFT method is that it is not recursive, so, when one has a large array of possible values, the FFT won't suffer the same error propagation that Panjer's recursion will. The FFT can also take any discrete distribution for its frequency distribution (and, in principle, any other non-negative continuous distribution if one discretises it). The FFT can also be started away from zero, whereas the Panjer method must calculate the probability of every value starting at zero. Thus, as a rough guide, consider using Panjer's method where the frequency distribution does not take very large values and where it is one of those for which Panjer's method applies, otherwise use the FFT method. ModelRisk offers a version of the FFT method with some adjustments to improve efficiency and allow for a continuous aggregate distribution.

FFT methods can also be extended to a group of $\{n, X\}$ paired distributions, which ModelRisk makes available via its VoseAggregateMultiFFT function.

De Pril method

For a portfolio of n independent life insurance policies, each policy y has a particular probability of a claim p_y in some period (usually a year) and benefit B_y. There are various methods for calculating the aggregate payout. Dickson (2005) is an excellent (and very readable) review of these methods and other areas of insurance risk and ruin.

The De Pril method is an exact method for determining the aggregate payout distribution. The compound Poisson approximation discussed next is a faster method that will usually work too.

De Pril (1986) offers an exact calculation of the aggregate distribution under the assumptions that:

- The benefits are fixed values rather than random variables and take integer multiples of some convenient base (e.g. \$1000) with a maximum value M * base, i.e. $B_i = \{1 \dots M\}$ * base.
- The probability of claims can similarly be grouped into a set of J values (i.e. into tranches of mortality rates) $p_j = \{p_1 \dots p_J\}$.

Let n_{ij} be the number of policies with benefit i and probability of claim p_j. Then De Pril's paper demonstrates that $p(y)$, the probability that the aggregate payout will be equal to y * base, is given by the recursive formula

$$p(y) = \frac{1}{y} \sum_{i=1}^{\min[y,M]} \sum_{k=1}^{\lfloor y/i \rfloor} p(y - ik)h(i, k) \text{ for } y = 1, 2, 3 \dots$$

and

$$p(0) = \prod_{i=1}^{M} \prod_{j=1}^{J} (1 - p_j)^{n_{ij}}$$

where

$$h(i, k) = i(-1)^{k-1} \sum_{j=1}^{J} n_{ij} \left(\frac{p_j}{1 - p_j} \right)^k$$

The formula has the benefit of being exact, but it is very computationally intensive. However, the number of computations can usually be significantly reduced if one accepts ignoring small aggregate costs to the insurer. Let K be a positive integer. Then the recursive formulae above are modified as follows:

$$p_K(0) = p(0)$$

$$p_K(y) = \frac{1}{y} \sum_{i=1}^{\min[x,M]} \sum_{k=1}^{\min[K,y/i]} p_K(y - ik)h(i, k)$$

Dickson (2005) recommends using a value of 4 for K. The De Pril method can be seen as the counterpart to Panjer's recursive method for the collective model. ModelRisk offers a set of functions for implementing De Pril's method.

Compound Poisson approximation

The compound Poisson approximation assumes that the probability of payout for an individual policy is fairly small – which is usually true, but has the advantage over the De Pril method in allowing that the payout distribution is a random variable rather than a fixed amount.

Let n_j be the number of policies with probability of claim p_j. The number of payouts in this stratum is therefore Binomial(n_j, p_j). If n_j is large and p_j is small, the binomial is well approximated by a Poisson$(n_j * p_j) = $ Poisson(λ_i) distribution. The additive property of the Poisson distribution tells us that the frequency distribution for payouts over all groups of lines of insurance is given by

$$\lambda_{\text{all}} = \sum_{i=1}^{k} \lambda_i = \sum_{i=1}^{k} n_i p_i$$

and the total number of claims = Poisson(λ_{all}).

The probability that one of these claims, randomly selected, comes from stratum j is given by

$$P(j) = \frac{\lambda_j}{\displaystyle\sum_{i=1}^{k} \lambda_i}$$

Let $F_j(x)$ be the cumulative distribution function for the claim size of stratum j. The probability that a random claim is less than or equal to some value is therefore

$$F(x) = \frac{\displaystyle\sum_{j=1}^{k} F_j(x)\lambda_j}{\displaystyle\sum_{i=1}^{k} \lambda_i}$$

Thus, we can consider the aggregate distribution for the total claims to have a frequency distribution equal to Poisson(λ_{all}) and a severity distribution given by $F(x)$.

Adding correlation in aggregate calculations

Simulation

The most common method for determining the aggregate distribution of a number of correlated random variables is to simulate each random variable in its own spreadsheet cell, using one of the correlation methods described elsewhere in this book, and then sum them up in another cell. For example, the model in Figure 11.5 adds together Poisson(100) random variables each following a Lognormal(2, 5) distribution but where these variables are correlated through a Clayton(10) copula.

Cell C7 determines the 99.99th percentile of the Poisson(100) distribution – a value of 139 – which is used as a guide to set the maximum number of rows in the table. The Clayton copula values are used as "U-parameter" inputs into the lognormal distributions, meaning that they make the lognormal distributions return the percentile equating to the copula value; for example, cell D12 returns a value of 2.5539..., which is the 80.98...th percentile of the Lognormal(2, 5) distribution.

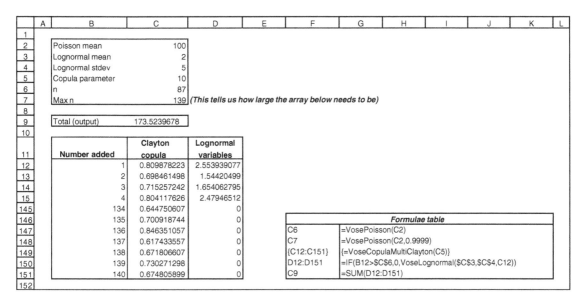

	A	B	C	D	E	F	G	H	I	J	K	L
1												
2		Poisson mean	100									
3		Lognormal mean	2									
4		Lognormal stdev	5									
5		Copula parameter	10									
6		n	87									
7		Max n	139	*(This tells us how large the array below needs to be)*								
8												
9		Total (output)	173.5239678									
10												
11		**Number added**	**Clayton copula**	**Lognormal variables**								
12		1	0.809878223	2.553939077								
13		2	0.698461498	1.54420499								
14		3	0.715257242	1.654062795								
15		4	0.804117626	2.47946512								
145		134	0.644750607	0								
146		135	0.700918744	0								
147		136	0.846351057	0								
148		137	0.617433557	0								
149		138	0.671806607	0								
150		139	0.730271298	0								
151		140	0.674805899	0								
152												

Formulae table	
C6	=VosePoisson(C2)
C7	=VosePoisson(C2,0.9999)
{C12:C151}	{=VoseCopulaMultiClayton(C5)}
D12:D151	=IF(B12>$C$6,0,VoseLognormal($C$3,$C$4,C12))
C9	=SUM(D12:D151)

Figure 11.5 Model for simulating the aggregate distribution of correlated random variables .

A Clayton copula provides a particularly high level of correlation of the variables at their low end. For example, the plot in Figure 11.6 shows the level of correlation of two variables with a Clayton(10).

Thus, the model will produce a wider range for the sum than an uncorrelated set of variables but in particular will produce more extreme low-end values from a probabilistic view (the correlated sum has about a 70 % probability of taking a lower value than the uncorrelated sum). The use of one of the Archimedean copulas is an appropriate tool here because we are adding up a random number of these variables but the number being summed does not affect the copula's behaviour – all variables will be related to the same degree no matter how many are being summed. The effect of the correlation is readily observed by repeating the model without any correlation. The plot in Figure 11.7 compares the two cumulative distributions.

Complete correlation

In the situation where the source of the randomness or uncertainty of the distribution associated with a random variable is the same for the whole group you are adding up, there is really just one random variable. For example, imagine that a railway network company must purchase 127 000 sleepers (the beams under the rails) next year. The sleepers will be made of wood, but the price is uncertain because the cost of timber may fluctuate. It is estimated that the cost will be $PERT(22.1, 22.7, 33.4) each. If all the timber is being purchased at the same time, it might be reasonable to believe that all the sleepers will have the same price. In that case, the total cost can be modelled simply:

$$= 127\ 000 * \text{VosePert}(22.1, 22.7, 33.4).$$

Using covariance

If there are a large number n of random variables $X_i (i = 1, \ldots, n)$ being summed and the uncertainty of the sum is not dominated by a few of these distributions, the sum is approximately normally distributed

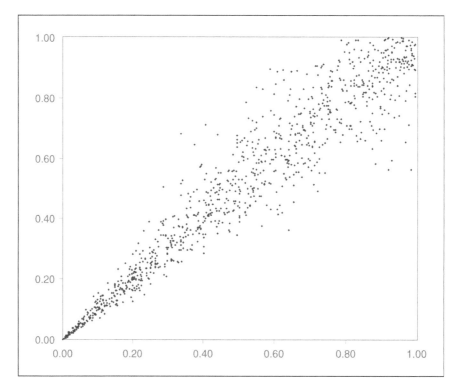

Figure 11.6 Correlation of two variables with a Clayton(10).

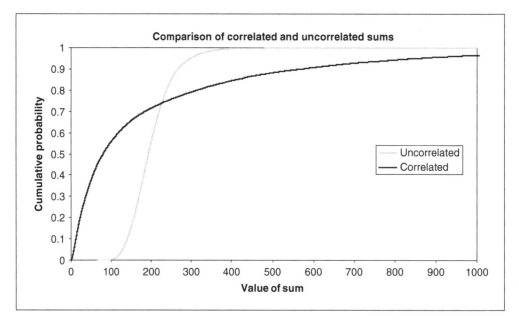

Figure 11.7 Comparison of correlated and uncorrelated sums.

according to the central limit theory as follows:

$$\sum_{i=1}^{n} X_i = \text{Normal}\left(\sum_{i=1}^{n} \mu_i, \sqrt{\sum_{i=1}^{n}\sum_{j=1}^{n} \sigma_{ij}}\right)$$

The equation states that the aggregate sum takes a normal distribution with a mean equal to the sum of the means for the individual distributions being added together. It also states that the variance (the square of the standard deviation in the formula) of the normal distribution is equal to the square of the covariance terms between each variable. The covariance terms σ_{ij} are calculated as follows:

$$\sigma_{ij} = \rho_{ij}\sigma_i\sigma_j \quad \text{or} \quad \sigma_{ij} = E[(x_i - \mu_i)(x_j - \mu_j)]$$

where σ_i and σ_j are the standard deviations of variables i and j, ρ_{ij} is the correlation coefficient and $E[\cdot]$ means "the expected value of" the thing in the brackets.

If we have datasets for the variables being modelled, Excel can calculate the covariance and correlation coefficients using the functions COVAR() and CORREL() respectively. If we were thinking of using a rank order correlation matrix, each element corresponds reasonably accurately to ρ_{ij} for roughly normal distributions (at least, not very heavily skewed distributions), so the standard deviation of the normally distributed sum could be calculated directly from the correlation matrix.

Correlating partial sums

We will sometimes be in the situation of having two or more sums of random variables that have some correlation relationship between them. For example, imagine that you are a hospital trying to forecast the number of patient-days you will need to provide next year, and you split the patients into three groups: surgery, maternity and chronic illness (e.g. cancer). Let's say that the distribution of days that a person will spend in hospital under each category is independent of the other categories, but the number of individuals being treated is correlated with the number of people in the catchment area, which is uncertain because hospital catchments are being redefined in your area. There are plenty of ways to model this problem, but perhaps the most convenient is to start with the uncertainty of size of the number of people in the catchment area and derive what the demand will be for each type of care as a consequence, then make a projection of what the total patient-days might be as a result, as shown in the model in Figure 11.8.

In this model the uncertainty about the catchment area population is modelled with a PERT distribution, the bed-days for each category of healthcare are modelled by lognormal distributions with different parameters and the number of patients in each category is modelled with a Poisson distribution with a mean equal to (population size-000s) * (expected cases/year/1000 people). I have shown three different methods for simulating the aggregate distribution in each class: pure Monte Carlo for surgery; FFT for maternity and Panjer's recursive method for chronic. Any of the three could be used to model each category. You'll notice that the Monte Carlo method is slightly different from the others in that I've used VosePoisson(...) instead of VosePoissonObject(...) because the VoseAggregateMC function requires a numerical input for how many variables to sum (allowing the flexibility that this could be a calculated value), whereas the FFT and Panjer methods perform calculations on the Poisson distribution and therefore need it to be defined as an object. Note that the same model could be achieved with other Monte Carlo simulation software by making randomly varying arrays for each category, the technique illustrated in Figure 11.1, but the numbers in this problem would require very long arrays.

Using the same basic problem, let us now consider the situation where the frequency distribution for each category is correlated in some fashion, as we had before, but not because of their direct relationship

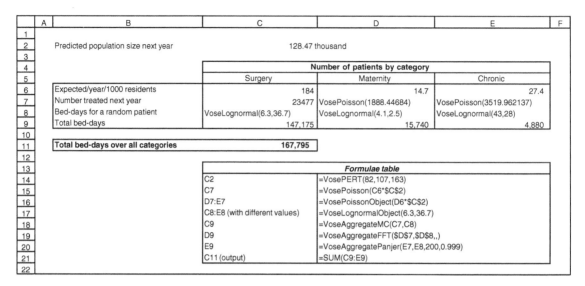

	A	B	C	D	E	F
1						
2		Predicted population size next year	128.47 thousand			
3						
4			**Number of patients by category**			
5			Surgery	Maternity	Chronic	
6		Expected/year/1000 residents	184	14.7	27.4	
7		Number treated next year	23477	VosePoisson(1888.44684)	VosePoisson(3519.962137)	
8		Bed-days for a random patient	VoseLognormal(6.3,36.7)	VoseLognormal(4.1,2.5)	VoseLognormal(43,28)	
9		Total bed-days	147,175	15,740	4,880	
10						
11		Total bed-days over all categories	167,795			
12						
13			**Formulae table**			
14			C2	=VosePERT(82,107,163)		
15			C7	=VosePoisson(C6*$C$2)		
16			D7:E7	=VosePoissonObject(D6*$C$2)		
17			C8:E8 (with different values)	=VoseLognormalObject(6.3,36.7)		
18			C9	=VoseAggregateMC(C7,C8)		
19			D9	=VoseAggregateFFT($D$7,$D$8,,)		
20			E9	=VoseAggregatePanjer(E7,E8,200,0.999)		
21			C11 (output)	=SUM(C9:E9)		
22						

Figure 11.8 Model for forecasting the number of patient-days in a hospital.

	A	B	C	D	E	F
1						
2		Predicted population size next year	107.00 thousand			
3						
4			Correlation matrix			
5						
6			Surgery	Maternity	Chronic	
7		Surgery	1	-0.3	0.2	
8		Maternity	-0.3	1	-0.25	
9		Chronic	0.2	-0.25	1	
10						
11		Normal copula	0.441	0.918	0.745	
12						
13			**Number of patients by category**			
14			Surgery	Maternity	Chronic	
15		Expected/year/1000 residents	184	14.7	27.4	
16		Number treated next year	19,667	1,628	2,967	
17		Bed-days for a random patient	VoseLognormal(6.3,36.7)	VoseLognormal(4.1,2.5)	VoseLognormal(43,28)	
18		Total bed-days	120,831	6,715	127,904	
19						
20		Total bed-days over all categories	255,450			
21						
22			**Formulae table**			
23			{C11:E11}	{=VoseCopulaMultiNormal(C7:E9)}		
24			C16:E16	=VosePoisson(C15*$D$2,C11)		
25			C17:E17 (with different values)	=VoseLognormalObject(6.3,36.7)		
26			C18:E18	=VoseAggregateMC(C16,C17)		
27			C20 (output)	=SUM(C18:E18)		
28						

Figure 11.9 Using a normal copula to correlate the Poisson frequency distributions.

to any observable variable. Imagine that the population size is known, but we want to model the effects of increased pollution in the area, so we want the surgery and chronic Poisson variables to be positively correlated with each other but negatively correlated with maternity. The following model uses a normal copula to correlate the Poisson frequency distributions (Figure 11.9).

There is in fact an FFT method to achieve this correlation between frequency distributions, but the algorithm is not particularly stable.

Turning now to the severity (length of hospital stay) distributions, we may wish to correlate the length of stay for all individuals in a certain category. In the above model, this can be achieved by creating a separate scaling variable for each lognormal distribution with a mean of 1, for example a $\text{Gamma}\left(\frac{1}{h^2}, h^2\right)$ distribution with the required mean and a standard deviation of h (Figure 11.10). Note that this means that the lognormal distributions will no longer have the standard deviations they were given before.

Finally, let's consider how to correlate the aggregate distributions themselves. We can construct the distribution of the number of bed-days required for each type of healthcare using either the FFT or Panjer method. Since the distribution is constructed rather than simulated, we can easily correlate the aggregate distributions by controlling how they are sampled. In the example in Figure 11.11, the model uses the FFT method to construct the aggregate variables and correlates them together using a Frank copula.

	A	B	C	D	E	F
1						
2		Predicted population size next year	107.00 thousand			
3						
4			Number of patients by category			
5			Surgery	Maternity	Chronic	
6		Expected/year/1000 residents	184	14.7	27.4	
7		Number treated next year	19,858	1,610	2,874	
8		Scaling variable stdev (h)	0.2	0.15	0.3	
9		Hospital days scaling variable	1.0267	0.8740	0.4937	
10		Bed-days for a random patient	VoseLognormal(6.47,37.68)	VoseLognormal(5.51,32.08)	VoseLognormal(3.11,18.12)	
11		Total bed-days	129,922	9,602	8,996	
12						
13		Total bed-days over all categories	148,520			
14						
15			Formulae table			
16			C7:E7	=VosePoisson(C6*$C$2)		
17			C9:E9	=VoseGamma(C8^-2,C8^2)		
18			C10:E10 (with different values)	=VoseLognormalObject(6.3*C9,36.7*C9)		
19			C11:E11	=VoseAggregateMC(C7,C10)		
20			C13 (output)	=SUM(C11:E11)		
21						

Figure 11.10   Creating separate scaling variables for each lognormal distribution.

	A	B	C	D	E	F
1						
2		Predicted population size next year	107.00 thousand			
3						
4			Number of patients by category			
5			Surgery	Maternity	Chronic	
6		Expected/year/1000 residents	184	14.7	27.4	
7		Number treated next year	VosePoisson(19688)	VosePoisson(1572.9)	VosePoisson(2931.8)	
8		Bed-days for a random patient	VoseLognormal(6.3,36.7)	VoseLognormal(4.1,2.5)	VoseLognormal(43,28)	
9		Frank copula	0.6284	0.6507	0.5676	
10		Total bed-days	7,746	7,758	7,712	
11						
12		Total bed-days over all categories	23,216			
13						
14			Formulae table			
15			C7:E7	=VosePoissonObject(C6*$C$2)		
16			C8:E8 (with different values)	=VoseLognormalObject(6.3,36.7)		
17			{C9:E9}	{=VoseCopulaMultiFrank(15)}		
18			C10:E10	=VoseAggregateFFT($D$7,$D$8,,C9)		
19			C12 (output)	=SUM(C10:E10)		
20						

Figure 11.11   Using the FFT method to combine correlated aggregate variables.

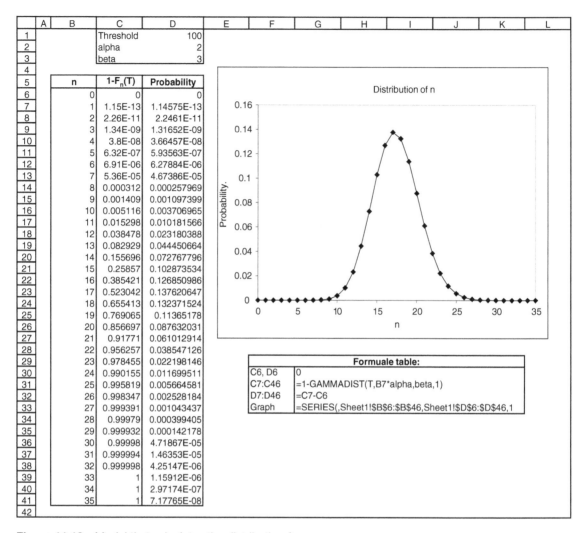

Figure 11.12 Model that calculates the distribution for *n*.

11.2.3 Number of variables to reach a total

So far in this chapter we have focused on determining the distribution of the sum of a (usually random) number of random variables. We are also often interested in the reverse question: how many random variables will it take to exceed some total? For example, we might want to answer the following questions:

- How many random people entering a lift will it take to exceed the maximum load allowed?
- How many sales will a company need to make to reach its year-end target?
- How many random exposures to a chemical will it take to reach the exposure limit?

Some questions like this are directly answered by known distributions, for example the negative binomial, beta–negative binomial and inverse hypergeometric describe how many trials will be needed to achieve s successes for the binomial, beta–binomial and hypergeometric processes respectively. However, if the random variables are not 0 or 1 but are continuous distributions, there are no distributions available that are directly useful.

The most general method is to use Monte Carlo simulation with a loop that consecutively adds a random sample from the distribution in question until the required sum is produced. ModelRisk offers such a function called VoseStopSum(Distribution, Threshold). This can, however, be quite computationally intensive when the required number is large, so it would be useful to have some quicker methods available.

Table 11.3 gives us some identities that we can use. For example, the sum of n independent variables following a Gamma(α, β) distribution is equal to a Gamma($n * \alpha$, β). If we require a total of at least T, then the probability that $(n - 1)$ Gamma(α, β) variables will exceed T is $1 - F_{(n-1)}(T)$, where $F_{(n-1)}(T)$ is the cumulative probability for a Gamma($(n - 1) * \alpha$, β). Excel has the GAMMADIST function which calculates $F(x)$ for a gamma distribution (ModelRisk has the function VoseGammaProb which performs the same task but without the errors GAMMADIST sometimes produces). The probability that n variables will exceed T is given by $1 - F_n(T)$. Thus, the probability that it was the nth random variable that took the sum over the threshold is $(1 - F_n(T)) - (1 - F_{(n-1)}(T)) = F_{(n-1)}(T) - F_n(T)$. You can therefore construct a model that calculates the distribution for n directly, as shown in the spreadsheet in Figure 11.12.

The same idea can be applied with the Cauchy, chi-square, Erlang, exponential, Levy, normal and Student distributions. The VoseStopSum function in ModelRisk implements this shortcut automatically.

Chapter 12

Forecasting with uncertainty

This chapter looks at several forecasting methods in common use and how variability and uncertainty can be incorporated into their forecasts. Time series modelling is usually based on extrapolating a set of observations from the past, or, where data are not available or inadequate, the modelling focuses on expert opinion of how the variable may behave in the future. In this chapter we will look first of all at the more formal techniques of time series modelling based on past observations, then look at some ways that the reader may find useful to model expert opinion of what the future holds.

The prerequisites of formal quantitative forecasting techniques are that a reliable time series of past observations is available and that it is believed that the factors determining the patterns exhibited in that time series are likely to continue to exist, or, if not, that we can determine the effect of changes in these factors. We begin by discussing ways of measuring the performance of a forecasting technique. Then we look at the naïve forecast, which is simply repeating the last, deseasonalised, value in the available time series. This simplistic forecasting technique is useful for providing a benchmark against which the performance of the other techniques can be compared. This is followed by a look at various forecasting techniques, divided into three sections according to the length of the period that is to be forecast. Finally, we will look at a couple of examples of a different approach that aim at modelling the variability based on a reasonable theoretical model of the actual system.

There are a few useful basic tips I recommend when you are producing a stochastic time series as part of your risk analysis:

- Check the model's behaviour with imbedded Excel $x-y$ scatter plots.
- Split the model up into components rather than create long, complicated formulae. That way you'll see that each component is working correctly, and therefore have confidence in the time series projection as a whole.

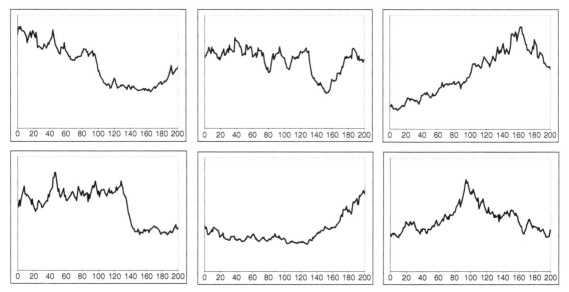

Figure 12.1 Six plots from the same geometric Brownian motion model. Each pattern could easily be what follows on from any other pattern.

- Be realistic about the match between historic patterns and projections. For example, write a simple geometric Brownian motion model, plot the series and hit the F9 key (recalculate) a few times and see the variation in patterns you get. Remember that these all come from the same stochastic model – but they will often look convincingly different (see Figure 12.1): if any of these had been our historical data, a statistical analysis of the data would have tended to agree with you and reinforced any preconception about the appropriate model, because statistical analysis requires you to specify the model to test. So, don't always go for a forecast model because it fits the data the best – also look at whether there is a logical reason for choosing one model over another.

- Be creative. Short-term forecasts (say 20–30 % of the historic period for which you have good data) are often adequately produced from a statistical analysis of your data. Even then, be selective about the model. However, beyond that timeframe we move into crystal ball gazing. Including your perceptions of where the future may go, possible influencing events, etc., will be just as valid as an extrapolation of historic data.

12.1 The Properties of a Time Series Forecast

When producing a risk analysis model that forecasts some variable over time, I recommend you go through a list of several properties that variable might exhibit over time, as this will help you both statistically analyse any past data you have and select the most appropriate model to use. The properties are: trend, randomness, seasonality, cyclicity or shocks and constraints.

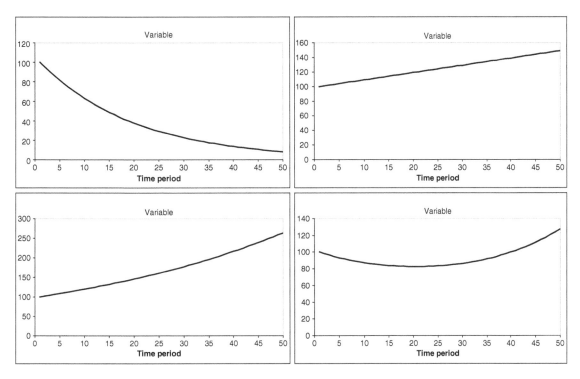

Figure 12.2 Examples of expected value trend over time.

12.1.1 Trend

Most variables we model have a general direction in which they have been moving, or in which we believe they will move in the future. The four plots in Figure 12.2 give some examples of the expected value of a variable over time: top left – a steady relative decrease, such as one might expect for sales of an old technology, or the number of individuals remaining alive from a group; top right – a steady (straight-line) increase, such as is often assumed for financial returns over a reasonably short period (sometimes called "drift"); bottom left – a steady relative increase, such as bacterial growth or take-up of new technology; and bottom right – a drop turning into an increase, such as the rate of component failures over time (like the bathtub curve in reliability modelling) or advertising expenditure (more at a launch, then lower, then ramping up to offset reduced sales).

12.1.2 Randomness

The second most important property is randomness. The four plots in Figure 12.3 give some examples of the different types of randomness: top left – a relatively small and constant level of randomness that doesn't hide the underlying trend; top right – a relatively large and constant level of randomness that can disguise the underlying trend; bottom left – a steadily increasing randomness, which one typically sees in forecasting (care needs to be taken to ensure that the extreme values don't become unrealistic); and bottom right – levels of randomness that vary seasonally.

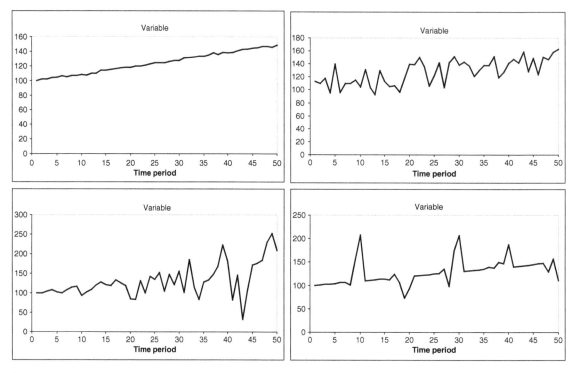

Figure 12.3 Examples of the behaviour of randomness over time.

12.1.3 Seasonality

Seasonality means a consistent pattern of variation in the expected value (but also sometimes its randomness) of the variable. There can be several overlaying seasonal periods, but we should usually have a pretty good guess at what the periods of seasonality might be: hour of the day; day of the week; time of the year (summer/winter, for example, or holidays, or end of financial year). The plot in Figure 12.4 shows the effect of two overlaying seasonal periods. The first is weekly with a period of 7, the second is monthly with a period of 30, which complicates the pattern. Monthly seasonality often occurs with financial transactions that take place on a certain day of the month: for example, volumes of documents that a bank's printing facility must produce each day – at the end of the month they have to churn out bank and credit card statements and get them in the post within some legally defined time.

One difficulty in analysing monthly seasonality from data is that months have different lengths, so one cannot simply investigate a difference each 30 days, say. Another hurdle in analysing data on variables with monthly and holiday peaks is that there can be some spread of the effect over 2 or 3 days. For example, we performed an analysis recently looking at the calls received into a US insurance company's national call centre to help them optimise how to staff the centre. We were asked to produce a model that predicted every 15 minutes for the next 2 weeks, and another model to predict out 6 weeks. We looked at the patterns by individual state and language (Spanish and English). There was a very obvious and stable pattern through the day that was constant during the working week, but a different pattern on Saturday and on Sunday. The pattern was largely the same between states but different between languages. Holidays like Thanksgiving (the last Thursday of November, so not even a fixed date) were

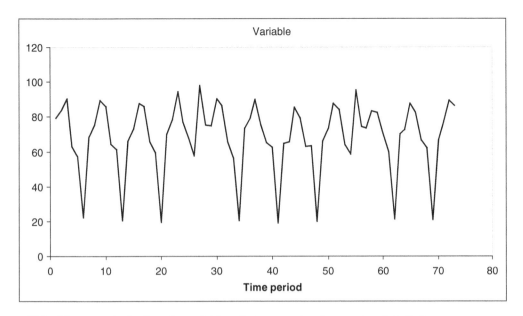

Figure 12.4 The expected value of a variable with two overlapping seasonal periods.

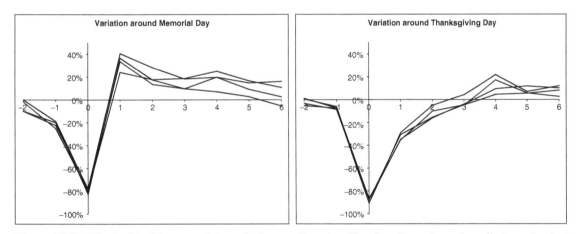

Figure 12.5 Effect of holidays on daily calls to a call centre. The four lines show the effect on the last 4 years. Zero on the *x* axis is the day of the holiday.

very interesting: call rates dropped hugely on the holiday to 10 % of the level one would have usually expected, but were slightly lower than normal the day before (Wednesday), significantly lower the day after (Friday), a little lower during the following weekend and then significantly higher the following Monday and Tuesday (presumably because people were catching up on calls they needed to make). Memorial Day, the last Monday of May, exhibited a similar pattern, as shown in Figure 12.5.

The final models had logic built into them to look for forthcoming holidays and apply these patterns to forecast expected levels which had a trend by state and a daily seasonality. For the 15-minute models we also had to take into account the time zone of the state, since all calls from around the US were received

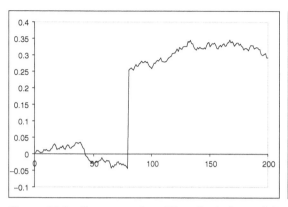 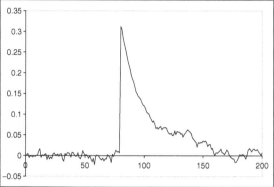

Figure 12.6 Two examples of the effect of a cyclicity shock. On the left, the shock produces a sudden and sustained increase in the variable; on the right, the shock produces a sudden increase that gradually reduces over time – an exponential distribution is often used to model this reduction.

into one location, which also involved thinking about when states changed their clocks from summer to winter and little peculiarities like some states having two time zones (Arizona doesn't observe daylight saving to conserve energy used by air conditioners, etc.).

12.1.4 Cyclicity or shocks

Cyclicity is a confusing term (being rather similar to seasonality) that refers to the effect of obvious single events on the variable being modelled (Figure 12.6 illustrates two basic forms). For example, the Hatfield rail crash in the UK on 12 October 2000 was a single event with a long-term effect on the UK railway network. The accident was caused by the lapsed maintenance of the track which led to "gauge corner cracking", resulting in the rail separating. Investigators found many more such cracks in the area and a temporary speed restriction was imposed over very large lengths of track because of fears that other track might be suffering from the same degradation. The UK network was already at capacity levels, so slowing down trains resulted in huge delays. The cost of repairs to the undermaintained track also sent RailTrack, the company managing the network, into administration. In analysing the cause of train delays for our client, NetworkRail, a not-for-dividend company that took over from RailTrack, we had to estimate and remove the persistent effect of Hatfield.

Another obvious example is 9/11. Anyone who regularly flies on commercial airlines will have experienced the extra delays and security checks. The airline industry was also greatly affected, with several US carriers filing for protection under Chapter 11 of the US Bankruptcy Code, although other factors also played a part, such as oil price increases and other terrorist attacks (also cyclicity events) which dissuaded people from going abroad. We performed a study to determine what price should be charged for parking at a US national airport, part of which included estimating future demand. From analysing historic data it was evident that the effect of 9/11 on passenger levels was quite immediate, and, as of 2006, they were only just returning to 2000 levels, where previously there had been consistent growth in passenger numbers, so levels still remain far below what would have been predicted before the terrorist attack.

Events like Hatfield and 9/11 are, of course, almost impossible to predict with any confidence. However, other types of cyclicity event are more predictable. As I write this (20 June 2007), there are 7 days left before Tony Blair steps down as Prime Minister of the UK, which he announced on 10 May, and Gordon Brown takes over. Newspaper columnists are debating what changes will come about, and, for people in the know, there are probably some predictable elements.

12.1.5 Constraints

Randomly varying time series projections can quite easily produce extreme values far beyond the range that the variable might realistically take. There are a number of ways to constrain a model. Mean reversion, discussed later, will pull a variable back to its mean so that it is far less likely to produce extreme values. Simple logical bounds like IF($S_t > 100$, 100, S_t) will constrain a variable to remain at or below 100, and one can make the constraining parameter (100) a function of time too. The section describing market modelling below offers some other techniques that are based on more modelling-based constraints.

12.2 Common Financial Time Series Models

In this section I describe the most commonly used time series for financial models of variables such as stock prices, exchange rates, interest rates and economic indicators such as producers' price index (PPI) and gross domestic product (GDP). Although they have been developed for financial markets, I encourage you to review the ideas and models presented here because they have much wider applications.

Financial time series are considered to vary continuously, even if perhaps we only observe them at certain moments in time. They are based on stochastic differential equations (SDEs), which are the most general descriptions of continuously evolving random variables. The problem with SDEs from a simulation perspective is that they are not always amenable to being exactly converted to algorithms that will generate random possible observations at specific moments in time, and there are often no exact methods for estimating their parameters from data. On the other hand, the advantage is that we have a consistent framework for comparing the time series and there are sometimes analytical solutions available to us for determining, say, the probability that the variable exceeds some value at a certain point in time – answers that are useful for pricing derivatives and other financial instruments, for example. We can get around the problems with a bit of intense computing, as I will explain for each type of time series.

Financial time series model a variable in one of two forms: the actual price S_t of the stock (or the value of a variable such as exchange rate, interest rate, etc., if it is not a stock) at some time t, or its return (aka its relative change if it is not an investment) r_t over a period Δt, $\Delta S / S_t$. It might seem that modelling S_t would be more natural, but in fact modelling the return of the variable is often more helpful: apart from making the mathematics simpler, it is usually the more fundamental variable. In this section, I will refer to S_t when talking specifically about a price, to r_t when talking specifically about a return and to x_t when it could be either.

I introduce geometric Brownian motion (GBM) first, as it is the simplest and most common financial times series, the basis of the Black–Scholes model, etc., and the launching pad for a number of more advanced models. I have developed the theory a little for GBM, so you get the feel of the thinking, but keep the theory to a minimum after that, so don't be too put off.

ModelRisk provides facilities (Figure 12.7) to fit and/or model all of the time series described in the chapter. For financial models, data and forecasts can be either returns or prices, and the fitting algorithms can automatically include uncertainty about parameter estimates if required.

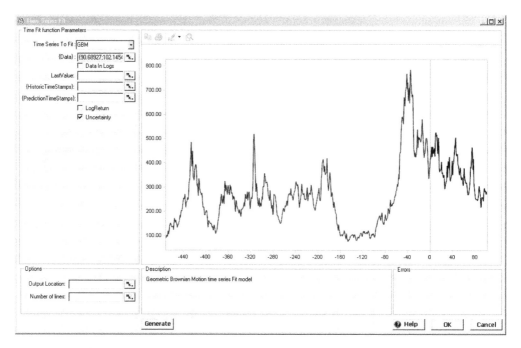

Figure 12.7 ModelRisk time series fit window.

12.2.1 Geometric Brownian motion

Consider the formula

$$x_{t+1} = x_t + \text{Normal}(\mu, \sigma) \tag{12.1}$$

It states that the variable's value changes in one unit of time by an amount that is normally distributed with mean μ and variance σ^2. The normal distribution is a good first choice for a lot of variables because we can think of the model as stating (from the central limit theorem) that the variable x is being affected additively by many independent random variables. We can iterate the equation to give us the relationship between x_t and x_{t+2}:

$$x_{t+2} = x_{t+1} + \text{Normal}(\mu, \sigma) = [x_t + \text{Normal}(\mu, \sigma)] + \text{Normal}(\mu, \sigma) = x_t + \text{Normal}(2\mu, \sqrt{2}\sigma)$$

and generalise to any time interval T:

$$x_{t+T} = x_t + \text{Normal}(\mu T, \sigma \sqrt{T})$$

This is a rather convenient equation because (a) we keep using normal distributions and (b) we can make a prediction between any time intervals we choose. The above equation deals with discrete units of time but can be written in a continuous time form, where we consider any small time interval Δt:

$$\Delta x = \text{Normal}(\mu(\Delta t), \sigma \sqrt{\Delta t})$$

The SDE equivalent is

$$dx = \mu \, dt + \sigma \, dz$$

$$dz = \varepsilon \sqrt{dt} \tag{12.2}$$

where dz is the generalised Wiener process, called variously the "perturbation", "innovation" or "error", and ε is a Normal(0, 1) distribution. The notation might seem to be a rather unnecessary complication, but when you get used to the SDEs they give us the most succinct description of a stochastic time series. A more general version of Equations (12.2) is

$$dx = g(t) \, dt + f(t) \, dz$$

$$dz = \varepsilon \, dt$$

where g and f are two functions. It is really just shorthand for writing

$$x(t) = \int_0^t g(\tau) \, d\tau + \int_0^t f(\tau) \, dz(\tau)$$

Equation (12.1) can allow the variable x to take any real value, including negative values, so it would not be much good at modelling a stock price, interest rate or exchange rate, for example. However, it has the desirable property of being memoryless, i.e. to make a prediction of the value of x some time T from now, we only need to know the value of x now, not anything about the path it took to get to the present value. We can use Equations (12.2) to model the return of a stock:

$$\frac{dS}{S} = r = \mu \, dt + \sigma \, dz \tag{12.3}$$

or

$$dS = \mu S \, dt + \sigma S \, dz \tag{12.4}$$

There is an identity known as Itô's lemma which states that for a function F of a stochastic variable X following an Itô process of the form $dx(t) = a(x, t) \, dt + b(x, t) \, dz$ we have

$$dF = \left(\frac{\partial F}{\partial t} + a(x, t) \frac{\partial F}{\partial x} + \frac{1}{2} b(x, t)^2 \frac{\partial^2 F}{\partial x^2} \right) dt + b(x, t) \frac{\partial F}{\partial x} \, dz_t \tag{12.5}$$

Choosing $F(S) = \log[S]$ together with Equation (12.3) where $x = S$, $a(x, t) = \mu$ and $b(x, t) = \sigma$:

$$d(\ln[S]) = \left(\frac{\partial \ln[S]}{\partial t} + \mu \frac{\partial \ln[S]}{\partial S} + \frac{1}{2} \sigma^2 \frac{\partial^2 \ln[S]}{\partial S^2} \right) dt + \sigma \frac{\partial \ln[S]}{\partial S} \, dz_t$$

$$= \left(\mu - \frac{\sigma^2}{2} \right) dt + \sigma \, dz$$

Integrating over time T, we get the relationship between some initial value S_t and some later value S_{t+T}:

$$S_{t+T} = S_t \exp \left[\text{Normal} \left(\left(\mu - \frac{\sigma^2}{2} \right) T, \sigma \sqrt{T} \right) \right] = S_t \exp[r_T] \tag{12.6}$$

where r_T is called the *log return*[1] of the stock over the period T. The exp $[\cdot]$ term in Equation (12.6) means that S is always > 0, so we still retain the memoryless property which corresponds to some financial thinking that a stock's value encompasses all information available about a stock at the time, so there should be no memory in the system (I'd argue against that, personally).

The log return r of a stock S is (roughly) the fractional change in the stock's value. For stocks this is a more interesting value than the stock's actual price because it would be more profitable to own 10 shares in a \$1 stock that increased by 6% over a year than one share in a \$10 stock that increased by 4%, for example.

Equation (12.6) is the GBM model: the "geometric" part comes because we are effectively multiplying lots of distributions together (adding them in log space). From the definition of a lognormal random variable, if $ln[S]$ is normally distributed, then S is lognormally distributed, so Equation (12.6) is modelling S_{t+T} as a lognormal random variable. From the equation of the mean of the lognormal distribution in Appendix III you can see that S_{t+T} has a mean given by

$$E(S_{t+T}) = S_t \exp[\mu T]$$

hence μ is also called the exponential growth rate, and a variance given by

$$V(S_{t+T}) = \exp[2\mu T](\exp[\sigma^2 T] - 1)$$

GBM is very easy to reproduce in Excel, as shown by the model in Figure 12.8, even with different time increments.

It is also very easy to estimate its parameters from a dataset when the observations have a constant time increment between them, as shown by the model in Figure 12.9.

			Mu	0.01								
			Sigma	0.033								
	Period	Return	Price S									
	0		100									
	1	0.027807	102.8197				**Formulae table**					
	2	-0.031105	99.67078		C7:C42	=VoseNormal((Mu-(Sigma^2)/2)*(B7-B6),Sigma*SQRT(B7-B6))						
	3	0.015708	101.2487		D7:D42	=D6*EXP(C7)						
	4	-0.010917	100.1494									
	5	-0.029635	97.22498									
	8	0.037244	100.9143									
	9	-0.009822	99.92796									
	10	-0.008984	99.03423									
	11	0.071986	106.4262									
	40	0.02078	144.1044									
	43	0.005866	144.9522									
	44	0.03901	150.7184									
	45	-0.01083	149.0949									
	46	-0.010239	147.5762									
	47	0.024494	151.2356									
	50	0.027545	155.4593									

Figure 12.8 GBM model with unequal time increments.

---

[1] Not to be confused with the *simple return* R_t, which is the fractional increase of the variable over time t, and where $r_t = ln[1 + R_t]$.

	A	B	C	D	E	F	G	H	I
1									
2		Period	Price S	$LN(S_t)-LN(S_{t-1})$		Time increment	1		
3		1	131.2897						
4		2	139.8505	0.063167908		Innovations			
5		3	151.8574	0.082367645		Mean	0.01391		
6		4	152.7159	0.005637288		Stdev	0.032387		
7		5	161.5825	0.056436531					
8		6	165.1629	0.021916209		Parameter estimates			
9		7	157.3468	-0.048479708		Sigma	0.032387		
10		8	160.6972	0.021069702		Mu	0.014434		
11		9	157.7477	-0.018525353					
12		10	152.9904	-0.030621756		*Formulae table*			
13		11	159.0034	0.038550398		D4:D105	=LN(C4)-LN(C3)		
14		12	168.8502	0.060086715		G5	=AVERAGE(D4:D105)		
15		13	161.8312	-0.042458444		G6	=STDEV(D4:D105)		
16		14	160.6408	-0.007382664		G9	=G6/SQRT(G2)		
17		15	173.5187	0.077114246		G10	=G5/G2+G9^2/2		
104		102	521.6434	0.034478322					
105		103	542.4933	0.039191541					
106									

Figure 12.9 Estimating GBM model parameters with equal time increments.

	A	B	C	D	E	F	G	H	I
1									
2		Period	Price S	z		Mu	0.05		
3		1	100.789			Sigma	0.08		
4		2	103.0675	-0.305560011					
5		3	102.8591	-0.610305645		ABS(Mean{z})	0.525061		
6		4	103.6719	-0.48660819		ABS(Stdev{z}-1)	0.569811		
7		5	99.8012	-1.060637884					
8		8	107.2738	-0.492158354		Error sum	1.094871		
9		9	111.2296	-0.132347657					
10		10	110.0289	-0.7206778		*Formulae table*			
11		11	114.0051	-0.141243519		D4:D187	=(LN(C4)-LN(C3)-(Mu-Sigma^2/2)*(B4-B3))/(Sigma*SQRT(B4-B3))		
12		12	111.989	-0.808033736		G5	=ABS(AVERAGE(D4:D187))		
13		15	112.9895	-0.949059593		G6	=ABS(STDEV(D4:D187)-1)		
185		255	1685.406	-0.866893734		G8	=G5+G6		
186		256	1637.663	-0.944206129					
187		257	1667.555	-0.358896539					
188									

Figure 12.10 Estimating GBM model parameters with unequal or missing time increments.

If there are missing observations or observations with different time increments, it is still possible to estimate the GBM parameters. In the model in Figure 12.10, the observations are transformed to Normal(0, 1) variables $\{z\}$, and then Excel's Solver is used to vary mu and sigma to make the $\{z\}$ values have a mean of zero and a standard deviation of 1 by minimising the value of cell G8.

An alternative method would be to regress $\dfrac{\ln[S_{t+T}] - \ln[S_t]}{\sqrt{T}}$ against $\sqrt{T}$ with zero intercept: the slope estimates μ and the standard error estimates σ.

The spread of possible values in a GBM increases rapidly with time. For example, the plot in Figure 12.11 shows 50 possible forecasts with $S_0 = 1$, $\mu = 0.001$ and $\sigma = 0.02$.

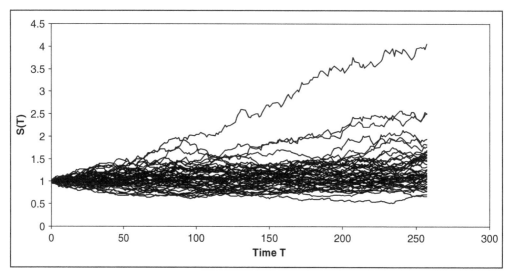

Figure 12.11 Plot of 50 possible scenarios with a GBM($\mu = 0.001$, $\sigma = 0.02$) model with a starting value of 1.

Mean reversion, discussed next, is a modification to GBM that progressively encourages the series to move back towards a mean the further it strays away. Jump diffusion, discussed after that, acknowledges that there may be shocks to the variable that result in large discrete jumps. ModelRisk has functions for fitting and projecting GBM and GBM + mean reversion and/or jump diffusion. The functions work with both returns r and stock prices S.

12.2.2 GBM with mean reversion

The long-run time series properties of equity prices (among other variables) are, of course, of particular interest to financial analysts. There is a strong interest in determining whether stock prices can be characterised as random-walk or mean reverting processes because this has an important effect on an asset's value. A stock price follows a mean reverting process if it has a tendency to return to some average value over time, which means that investors may be able to forecast future returns better by using information on past returns to determine the level of reversion to the long-term trend path. A random walk has no memory, which means that any large move in a stock price following a random-walk process is permanent and there is no tendency for the price level to return to a trend path over time. The random-walk property also implies that the volatility of stock price can grow without bound in the long run: increased volatility lowers a stock's value, so a reduction in volatility (Figure 12.12) owing to mean reversion would increase a stock's value.

For a variable x following a Brownian motion random walk, we have the SDE of Equation (12.2):

$$\mathrm{d}x = \mu\,\mathrm{d}t + \sigma\,\mathrm{d}z$$

For mean reversion, this equation can be modified as follows:

$$\mathrm{d}x = \alpha(\mu - x)\,\mathrm{d}t + \sigma\,\mathrm{d}z \tag{12.7}$$

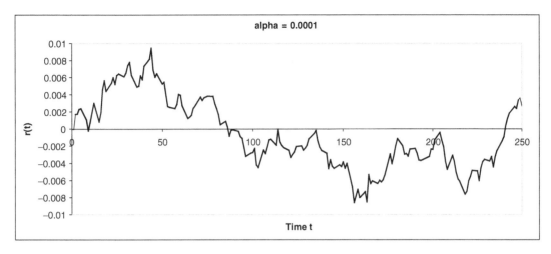

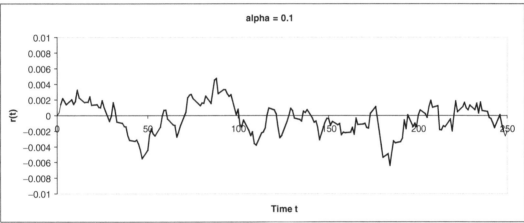

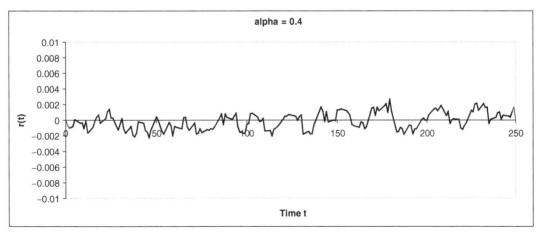

Figure 12.12 Plots of sample GBM series with mean reversion for different values of alpha ($\mu = 0, \sigma = 0.001$).

where $\alpha > 0$ is the speed of reversion. The effect of the dt coefficient is to produce an expectation of moving downwards if x is currently above μ, and vice versa. Mean reversion models are produced in terms of S or r:

$$dS = \alpha(\mu - S)\,dt + \sigma\,dz$$

known as the Ornstein–Uhlenbeck process, and was one of the first models used to describe short-term interest rates, where it is called the Vasicek model. The problem with the equation is that we can get negative stock prices; modelling in terms of r, however,

$$dr = \alpha(\mu - r)\,dt + \sigma\,dz$$

keeps the stock price positive. Integrating this last equation over time gives

$$r_{t+T} = \text{Normal}\left(\mu + \exp[-\alpha T](r_t - \mu), \sigma\sqrt{\frac{1 - \exp[-2\alpha T]}{2\alpha}}\right) \tag{12.8}$$

which is very easy to simulate. The following plots show some typical behaviour for r_t. Typical values of α would be in the range 0.1–0.3.

A slight modification to Equation (12.7) is called the Cox–Ingersoll–Ross or CIR model (Cox, Ingersoll and Ross, 1985), again used for short-term interest rates, and has the useful property of not allowing negative values (so we can use it to model the variable S) because the volatility goes to zero as S approaches zero:

$$dS = \alpha(\mu - S)\,dt + \sigma\sqrt{S}\,dz$$

Integrating over time, we get

$$S_{t+T} = S_t + cY$$

where

$$c = \frac{(1 - \exp[-\alpha T])\sigma^2}{2\alpha}$$

and Y is a non-central chi-square distribution with $\dfrac{4\alpha\mu}{\sigma^2}$ degrees of freedom and non-centrality parameter $2cr_t \exp[-\alpha T]$. This is a little harder to simulate since you need the uncommon non-central chi-square distribution in your simulation software, but it has the attraction of being tractable (we can precisely determine the form of the distribution for the variable S_{t+T}), which makes it easier to determine its parameters using maximum likelihood methods.

12.2.3 GBM with jump diffusion

Jump diffusion refers to sudden shocks to the variable that occur randomly in time. The idea is to recognise that, beyond the usual background randomness of a time series variable, there will be events that have a much larger impact on the variable, e.g. a CEO resigns, a terrorist attack takes place, a drug gets FDA approval. The frequency of the jumps is usually modelled as a Poisson distribution with intensity λ, so that in some time increment T there will be Poisson(λT) jumps. The jump size for r is usually modelled as Normal(μ_J, σ_J) for mathematical convenience and ease of estimating the parameters. Adding jump diffusion to the discrete time Equation (12.6) for one period, we get the following:

$$r_1 = \text{Normal}\left(\mu - \frac{\sigma^2}{2}, \sigma\right) + \sum_{i=1}^{\text{Poisson}(\lambda)} \text{Normal}(\mu_J, \sigma_J)$$

If we define $k = \text{Poisson}(\lambda)$, this reduces to

$$r_1 = \text{Normal}\left(\mu - \frac{\sigma^2}{2} + k\mu_J, \sqrt{\sigma^2 + k\sigma_J^2}\right) \tag{12.9}$$

or for T periods we have

$$r_T = \text{Normal}\left(\left(\mu - \frac{\sigma^2}{2}\right)T + k\mu_J, \sqrt{\sigma^2 T + k\sigma_J^2}\right)$$

$$k = \text{Poisson}(\lambda T)$$

which is easy to model with Monte Carlo simulation and easy to estimate parameters for by matching moments, although one must be careful to ensure that the λ estimate isn't too high (e.g. > 0.2) because the Poisson jumps are meant to be rare events, not form part of each period's volatility. The plot in Figure 12.13 shows a typical jump diffusion model giving both r and S values and with jumps marked as circles.

12.2.4 GBM with jump diffusion and mean reversion

You can imagine that, if the return r has just received a large shock, there might well be a "correction" over time that brings it back to the expected return μ of the series. Combining mean reversion with jump diffusion will allow us to model these characteristics quite well and with few parameters. However, the additive model of Equation (12.9) for mean and variance no longer applies, particularly when the reversion speed is large because one needs to model when within the period the jump took place: if it was at the beginning of the period, it may well have already strongly reverted before one observes the value at the period's end. The most practical solution, called Euler's method, is to split up a time period into many small increments. The number of increments will be sufficient when the model produces the same output for decision purposes as any greater number of increments.

12.3 Autoregressive Models

An ever-increasing number of autoregressive models are being developed in the financial area. The ones of more general interest discussed here are AR, MA, ARMA, ARCH and GARCH, and it is more standard to apply the models to the return r rather than to the stock price S. I also give the equations for EGARCH and APARCH. Let me just repeat my earlier warning that, before being convinced that some subtle variation of the model gives a genuine advantage, try generating a few samples for simpler models that you have fit to the data and see whether they can create scenarios of a similar pattern. ModelRisk offers functions that fit each of these series to data and produce forecasts. The data can be live linked to historical values, which is very convenient for keeping your model automatically up to date.

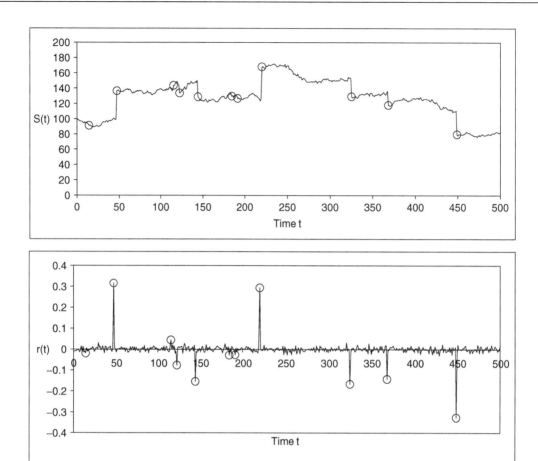

Figure 12.13 Sample of a GBM with jump diffusion with parameters $\mu = 0$, $\sigma = 0.01$, $\mu_J = 0.04$, $\sigma_J = 0.2$ and $\lambda = 0.02$.

12.3.1 AR

The equation for an autoregressive process of order p, or AR(p), is

$$r_t = K + \sum_{i=1}^{p} a_i r_{t-i} + \varepsilon_t$$

where ε_t are independent Normal(0, σ) random variables. Some constraints on the parameters $\{a_i\}$ are needed if one wants to keep the model stationary (meaning the marginal distribution of r is the same for all t), e.g. for an AR(1), $|a_1| < 1$. In most situations, an AR(1) or AR(2) is sufficiently elaborate, i.e:

$$AR(1) : r_t = K + a r_{t-1} + \varepsilon_t$$
$$AR(2) : r_t = K + a_1 r_{t-1} + a_2 r_{t-2} + \varepsilon_t$$

You can see that this is just a regression model where r_t is the dependent variable and r_{t-i} are the explanatory variables. It is usual, though not essential, that $a_i > a_{i+1}$, i.e. that r_t is explained more by more recent values $(t-1, t-2, \ldots)$ rather than by older values $(t-10, t-11, \ldots)$.

12.3.2 MA

The equation for a moving-average process of order q, or MA(q), is

$$r_t = \mu + \varepsilon_t + \sum_{j=1}^{q} b_j \varepsilon_{t-j}$$

This says that the variable r_t is normally distributed about a mean equal to

$$\mu + \sum_{j=1}^{q} b_j \varepsilon_{t-j}$$

where ε_t are independent Normal$(0, \sigma)$ random variables again. In other words, the mean of r_t is the mean of the process as a whole μ plus some weighting of the variation of q previous terms from the mean. Similarly to AR models, it is usual that $b_i > b_{i+1}$, i.e. that r_t is explained more by more recent terms $(t-1, t-2, \ldots)$ rather than by older terms $(t-10, t-11, \ldots)$.

12.3.3 ARMA

We can put the AR(p) and MA(q) processes together to create an autoregressive, moving-average model ARMA(p, q) process with mean μ that is described by the following equation:

$$r_t - \mu = \sum_{i=1}^{p} a_i (r_{t-i} - \mu) + \varepsilon_t + \sum_{j=1}^{q} b_j \varepsilon_{t-j}$$

or

$$r_t = K + \sum_{i=1}^{p} a_i r_{t-i} + \varepsilon_t + \sum_{j=1}^{q} b_j \varepsilon_{t-j}, \, K = \mu \left(1 - \sum_{i=1}^{p} a_i \right)$$

In practice, the ARMA(1, 1) is usually sufficiently complex, so the equation simplifies to

$$r_t = K + a r_{t-1} + \varepsilon_t + b \varepsilon_{t-1}, \, K = \mu (1 - a)$$

12.3.4 ARCH/GARCH

ARCH models were originally developed to account for fat tails by allowing clustering of periods of volatility (heteroscedastic, or heteroskedastic, means "having different variances"). One of the assumptions in regression models that were previously used for analysis of high-frequency financial data was that the error terms have a constant variance. Engle (1982), who won the 2003 Nobel Memorial Prize for Economics, introduced the ARCH model, applying it to quarterly UK inflation data. ARCH was later generalised to GARCH by Bollerslev (1986), which has proven more successful in fitting to financial data. Let r_t denote the returns or return residuals and assume that $r_t = \mu + \sigma_t z_t$, where z_t are independent, Normal(0,1) distributed, and the σ_t^2 is modelled by

$$\sigma_t^2 = \omega + \sum_{i=1}^{q} a_i (r_{t-i} - \mu)^2$$

where $\omega > 0$, $a_i \geq 0$, $i = 1, \ldots, q$ and at least one $a_i > 0$. Then r_t is said to follow an *autoregressive conditional heteroskedastic*, ARCH(q), process with mean μ. It models the variance of the current error term as a function of the variance of previous error terms $(r_{t-1} - \mu)$. Since each $a_i > 0$, it has the effect of grouping low (or high) volatilities together.

If an autoregressive moving-average process (ARMA process) is assumed for the variance, then r_t is said to be a *generalised autoregressive conditional heteroskedastic* GARCH(p, q) process with mean μ:

$$\sigma_t^2 = \omega + \sum_{i=1}^{q} a_i (r_{t-i} - \mu)^2 + \sum_{j=1}^{p} b_j \sigma_{t-j}^2$$

where p is the order of GARCH terms and q is the order of ARCH terms, $\omega > 0$, $a_i \geq 0$, $i = 1, \ldots, q$; $b_j \geq 0$, $j = 1, \ldots, p$ and at lease one a_i or $b_j > 0$.

In practice, the model most generally used is a GARCH(1, 1):

$$r_t = \mu + \sigma_t z_t$$
$$\sigma_t^2 = \omega + a(r_{t-1} - \mu)^2 + b\sigma_{t-1}^2$$

12.3.5 APARCH

The *asymmetric power autoregressive conditional heteroskedasticity*, APARCH(p, q), model was introduced by Ding, Granger and Engle (1993) and is defined as follows:

$$r_t = \mu + \sigma_t z_t$$
$$\sigma_t^\delta = \omega + \sum_{i=1}^{q} a_i (|r_{t-i} - \mu| - \gamma_i (r_{t-i} - \mu))^\delta + \sum_{j=1}^{p} b_j \sigma_{t-j}^\delta$$

where $-1 < \gamma_i < 1$ and at least one a_i or $b_j > 0$. δ plays the role of a Box–Cox transformation of the conditional standard deviation σ_t, while γ_i reflect the so-called leverage effect. APARCH has proved very promising and is now quite widespread because it nests several other models as special cases, e.g. the ARCH($\delta = 1$, $\gamma_i = 0$, $b_i = 0$), GARCH($\delta = 2$, $\gamma_i = 0$), (TS-GARCH($\delta = 1$, $\gamma_i = 0$), GJR-GARCH($\delta = 2$), TARCH($\delta = 1$) and NARCH($b_i = 1$, $\gamma_i = 0$).

In practice, the model most generally used is an APARCH(1, 1):

$$\sigma_t^\delta = \omega + a(|r_{t-1} - \mu| - \gamma (r_{t-1} - \mu))^\delta + b\sigma_{t-1}^\delta$$

12.3.6 EGARCH

The *exponential general autoregressive conditional heteroskedastic*, EGARCH(p, q), model was another form of GARCH model with the purpose of allowing negative values in the linear error variance equation. The GARCH model imposes non-negative constraints on the parameters, a_i and b_j, while there are no such restrictions on these parameters in the EGARCH model. In the EGARCH(p, q) model, the conditional variance, σ_t^2, is formulated by an asymmetric function of lagged disturbances r_t:

$$\ln(\sigma_t^2) = \omega + \sum_{i=1}^{q} a_i g(z_{t-i}) + \sum_{j=1}^{p} b_j \ln(\sigma_{t-j}^2)$$

where

$$g(z_t) = \theta z_t + |z_t| - E[z_t]$$

and

$$E[z_t] = \sqrt{\frac{2}{\pi}}$$

when z_t is a standard normal variable.

Again, in practice the model most generally used has $p = q = 1$, i.e. is an EGARCH(1, 1):

$$\ln(\sigma_t^2) = \omega + a g(z_{t-1}) + b \ln(\sigma_{t-1}^2)$$

12.4 Markov Chain Models

Markov[2] chains comprise a number of individuals who begin in certain allowed states of the system and who may or may not randomly change (transition) into other allowed states over time. A Markov chain has no memory, meaning that the joint distribution of how many individuals will be in each allowed state depends only on how many were in each state the moment before, not on the pathways that led there. This lack of memory is known as the *Markov property*. Markov chains come in two flavours: continuous time and discrete time. We will look at a discrete-time process first because it is the easiest to model.

12.4.1 Discrete-time Markov chain

In a discrete-time Markov process the individuals can move between states only at set (usually equally spaced) intervals of time. Consider a set of 100 individuals in the following four marital states:

- 43 are single;
- 29 are married;
- 11 are separated;
- 17 are divorced.

---

[2] Named after Andrey Markov (1856–1922), a Russian mathematician.

We write this as a vector:

$$\begin{pmatrix} 43 \\ 29 \\ 11 \\ 17 \end{pmatrix}$$

Given sufficient time (let's say a year) there is a reasonable probability that the individuals can change state. We can construct a matrix of the transition probabilities as follows:

Transition matrix		Is now:			
		Single	**Married**	**Separated**	**Divorced**
Was:	**Single**	0.85	0.12	0.02	0.01
	Married	0	0.88	0.08	0.04
	Separated	0	0.13	0.45	0.42
	Divorced	0	0.09	0.02	0.89

We read this matrix row by row. For example, it says (first row) that a single person has an 85 % chance of still being single 1 year later, a 12 % chance of being married, a 2 % chance of being separated and a 1 % chance of being divorced. Since these are the only allowed states (e.g. we haven't included "engaged" so that must be rolled up into "single"), the probabilities must sum to 100 %. Of course, we'd have to decide what a death would mean: the transition matrix could either be defined such that if a person dies they retain their marital status for this model, or we could make this a transition matrix conditional on them surviving a year.

Notice that the "single" column is all 0s, except the single/single cell, because, once one is married, the only states allowed after that are married, separated and divorced. Also note that one can go directly from single to separated or divorced, which implies that during that year the individual had passed through the married state. Markov chain transition matrices describe the probability that one is in a state at some precise time, given some state at a previous time, and is not concerned with how one got there, i.e. all the other states one might have passed through.

We now have the two elements of the model, the initial state vector and the transition matrix, to estimate how many individuals will be in each state after a year. Let's go through an example calculation to estimate how many people will be married in one year:

- for the single people, Binomial(43, 0.12) will be married;
- for the married people, Binomial(29, 0.88) will be married;
- for the separated people, Binomial(11, 0.13) will be married;
- for the divorced people, Binomial(17, 0.09) will be married.

Add together these four binomial distributions and we get an estimate of the number of people from our group who will be married next year. However, the above calculation does not work when we want to look at the joint distribution of how many people will be in each state: clearly we cannot add four sets of four binomial distributions because the total must sum to 100 people. Instead, we need to use the multinomial distribution. The number of people who were single but are now {Single, Married, Separated, Divorced} equals Multinomial(43, {0.85, 0.12, 0.02, 0.01}). Applying the multinomial distribution for the other three initial states, we can take a random sample from each multinomial and add up how many are in each state, as shown in the model in Figure 12.14.

	Number in initial state	Transition matrix		Is now:					Number in final state			
				Single	Married	Separated	Divorced		Single	Married	Separated	Divorced
	43		Single	0.85	0.12	0.02	0.01		40	3	0	0
	29	Was:	Married	0	0.88	0.08	0.04		0	25	1	3
	11		Separated	0	0.13	0.45	0.42		0	1	7	3
	17		Divorced	0	0.09	0.02	0.89		0	2	0	15
								Totals	40	31	8	21

Formulae table	
Input data	B4:B7, F4:I7
{L4:O4}	{=VoseMultinomial(B4,F4:I4)}
to	
{L7:O7}	{=VoseMultinomial(B7,F7:I7)}
L8:O8 (outputs)	=SUM(L4:L7)

Figure 12.14 Multinomial method of performing a Markov chain model.

Let's now look at extending the model to predict further ahead in time, say 5 years. If we can assume that the probability transition matrix remains valid for that period, and that nobody in our group dies, we could repeat the above exercise 5 times – calculating in each year how many individuals are in each state and using that as the input into the next year, etc. However, there is a more efficient method.

The probability a person starting in state i is in state j after 2 years is determined by looking at the probability of the person going from state i to each state after 1 year, and then going from that state to state j in the second year. So, for example, the probability of changing from single to divorced after 2 years is

$$P(\text{Single to Single}) * P(\text{Single to Divorced})$$

$$+ P(\text{Single to Married}) * P(\text{Married to Divorced})$$

$$+ P(\text{Single to Separated}) * P(\text{Separated to Divorced})$$

$$+ P(\text{Single to Divorced}) * P(\text{Divorced to Divorced})$$

$$= 0.85 * 0.01 + 0.12 * 0.04 + 0.02 * 0.42 + 0.01 * 0.89 = 0.0306$$

Notice how we have multiplied the elements in the first row (single) by the elements in the last column (divorced) and added them. This is the operation performed in matrix multiplication. We can therefore determine the probability transition matrix over the 2 year period by simply multiplying the 1 year transition matrix by itself (using Excel's MMULT function) in the model in Figure 12.15.

When one wants to forecast T periods in advance, where T is large, performing the matrix multiplication $(T - 1)$ times can become rather tedious, but there is some mathematics based on transforming the matrix that allows one directly to determine the transition matrix over any number of periods. ModelRisk provides some efficient means to do this: the VoseMarkovMatrix function calculates the transition matrix for any time length, and the VoseMarkovSample goes the next step, simulating how many individuals are in each final state after some period. In this next example (Figure 12.16) we calculate the transition matrix and simulate how many individuals will be in each state after 25 years.

Notice how after 25 years the probability of being married is about 45 %, irrespective of what state one started in: a similar situation occurs for separated and divorced. This stabilising property is very common and, as a matter of interest, is the basis of a statistical technique discussed briefly elsewhere in this book called Markov chain Monte Carlo. Of course, the above calculation does assume that the transition matrix for 1 year is valid to apply over such a long period (a *big* assumption in this case).

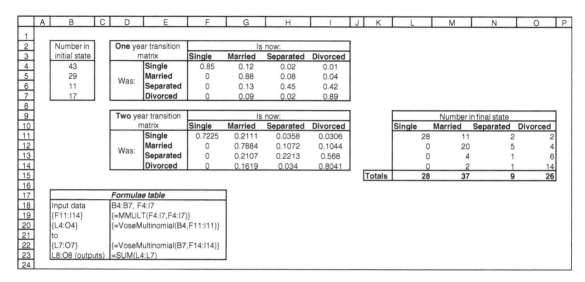

Figure 12.15 Multinomial method of performing a Markov chain model with time an integer > 1 unit.

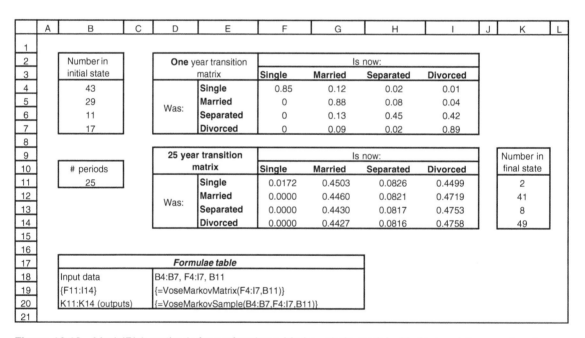

Figure 12.16 ModelRisk methods for performing a Markov chain model with time an integer > 1 unit.

12.4.2 Continuous-time Markov chain

For a continuous-time Markov process we need to be able to produce the transition matrix for any positive time increment, not just an integer multiple of the time that applies to the base transition matrix. So, for example, we might have the above marital status transition matrix for a single year but wish to know what the matrix is for half a year, or 2.5 years.

There is a mathematical technique for finding the required matrix, based on converting the multinomial probabilities in the matrix into Poisson intensities that match the required probability. The mathematical manipulation is somewhat complex, particularly when one has to wrestle with numerical stability. The ModelRisk functions VoseMarkovMatrix and VoseMarkovSample detect when you are using non-integer time and automatically convert to the alternative mathematics. So, for example, we can have the model described above for a half-year.

12.5 Birth and Death Models

There are two strongly related probabilistic time series models called the Yule (or pure birth) and pure death models. We have certainly found them very useful in modelling numbers in a bacterial population, but they could be helpful in modelling other variables, modelling numbers of individuals that increase or decrease according to their population size.

12.5.1 Yule growth model

This is a pure birth growth model and is a stochastic analogue to the deterministic exponential growth models one often sees in, for example, microbial risk analysis. In exponential growth models, the rate of growth of a population of n individuals is proportional to the size of the population:

$$\frac{\partial n}{\partial t} = \beta n$$

where β is the mean rate of growth per unit time t. This gives the number of individuals n_t in the population after time t as

$$n_t = n_0 \exp(\beta t)$$

where n_0 is the initial population size. The model is limited because it takes no account of any randomness in the growth. It also takes no account of the discrete nature of the population, which is important at low values of n. Moreover, there are no defensible statistical tests to apply to fit an exponential growth curve to observations (regression is often used as a surrogate) because an exponential growth model is not probabilistic, so no probabilistic (i.e. statistical) interpretation of data is possible.

The Yule model starts with the premise that individuals have offspring on their own (e.g. by division), that they procreate independently, that procreating is a Poisson process in time and that all individuals in the population are the same. The expected number of offspring from an individual per unit time (over some infinitesimal time increment) is defined as β. This leads to the results that an individual will have, after time t, Geometric$(\exp(-\beta t))$ offspring, giving a new total population of Geometric$(\exp(-\beta t)) + 1$. Thus, if we start with n_0 individuals, then by some later time t we will have

$$n_t = \text{NegBin}(n_0, e^{-\beta t}) + n_0$$

from the relationship

$$\text{NegBin}(s, p) = \sum_{i=1}^{s} \text{Geometric}(p)$$

with mean $\bar{n}_t = n_0 e^{\beta t}$, corresponding to the exponential growth model.

A possible problem in implementing this type of model is that n_0 and n_t can be very large, and simulation programs tend to produce errors for discrete distributions like the negative binomial for large input parameters and output values. ModelRisk has two time series functions to model the Yule process that work for all input values:

$$\text{VoseTimeSeriesYule}(n_0, \beta, t)$$

which generates values for n_t, and

$$\text{VoseTimeSeriesYule10}(\text{Log}_{10}n_0, LogIncrease, t)$$

which generates values for $\text{Log}_{10}(n_t)$, as one often finds it more convenient to deal with logs for exponentially growing populations because of the large numbers that can be generated. *LogIncrease* is the number of logs (in base 10) by which one expects the population to increase per time unit. The parameters β and *LogIncrease* are related by

$$LogIncrease = \text{Log}_{10}[\exp(\beta)]$$

12.5.2 Death model

The pure death model is a stochastic analogue to the deterministic exponential death models one often sees in, for example, microbial risk analysis. Individuals are assumed to die independently and randomly in time, following a Poisson process. Thus, the time until death can be described by an exponential distribution, which has a cdf:

$$P(X \leq x) = 1 - \exp(-\lambda x)$$

where λ is the expected instantaneous death of an individual. The probability that an individual is still alive at time t is therefore

$$P(\text{alive}) = \exp(-\lambda t)$$

Thus, if n_0 is the initial population, the number n_t surviving until time t follows a binomial distribution:

$$n_t = \text{Binomial}(n_0, \exp(-\lambda t))$$

which has a mean of

$$n_t = n_0 \exp(-\lambda t)$$

i.e. the same as the exponential death model. The cdf for the time until extinction t_E of the population is given by

$$P(t_E < t) = (1 - \exp(-\lambda t))^{n_0}$$

The binomial death model offered here is an improvement over the exponential death model for several reasons:

- The exponential death model takes no account of any randomness in the growth, so cannot interpret variations from an exponential line fit.

- The exponential death model takes no account of the discrete nature of the population, which is important at low values of n.

- There are no defensible statistical tests to apply to fit an exponential growth curve to observations (regression is often used as a surrogate) because an exponential model is not probabilistic, so there can be no probabilistic interpretation of data. A likelihood function is possible, however, for the death model described here.

A possible difficulty in implementing this death model is that n_0 and n_t can be very large, and simulation programs tend to produce errors for discrete distributions like the binomial for large input parameters and output values. ModelRisk has two time series functions to model the death model that eliminate this problem:

$$\text{VoseTimeSeriesDeath}(n_0, \lambda, t)$$

which generates values for n_t, and

$$\text{VoseTimeSeriesDeath10}(\text{Log}_{10} n_0, LogDecrease, t)$$

which generates values for $\text{Log}_{10}(n_t)$, as one often finds it more convenient to deal with logs for bacterial populations (for example) because of the large numbers that can be involved. The *LogDecrease* parameter is the number of logs (in base 10) that one expects the population to decrease by per time unit. The parameters λ and *LogDecrease* are related by

$$LogDecrease = \lambda \text{Log}_{10}(e)$$

12.6 Time Series Projection of Events Occurring Randomly in Time

Many things we are concerned about occur randomly in time: people arriving at a queue (customers, emergency patients, telephone calls into a centre, etc.), accidents, natural disasters, shocks to a market, terrorist attacks, particles passing through a bubble chamber (a physics experiment), etc. Naturally, we may want to model these over time, perhaps to figure out whether we will have enough stock vaccine, storage space, etc. The natural contender for modelling random events is the Poisson distribution – see Section 8.3 which returns the number of random events occurring in time t when λ events are expected per unit time within t. Often we might think that the expected number of events may increase or decrease over time, so we make λ a function of t as shown by the model in Figure 12.17.

A variation of this model is to take account of seasonality by multiplying the expected number of events by seasonal indices (which should average to 1).

In Section 8.3.7 I have discussed the Pólya and Delaporte distributions which are counting distributions similar to the Poisson but which allow λ to be a random variable too. The Pólya is particularly helpful because, with one extra parameter, h, we can add some volatility to the expected number of events, as shown by the model in Figure 12.18.

Notice the much greater peaks in the plot for this model compared with that of the previous model in Figure 12.17. Mixing a Poisson with a gamma distribution to create the Pólya is a helpful tool because we can get the likelihood function directly from the probability mass function (pmf) of the Pólya and therefore fit to historical data. If the MLE value for h is very small, then the Poisson model will be as good a fit and has one less parameter to estimate, so the Pólya model is a useful first test.

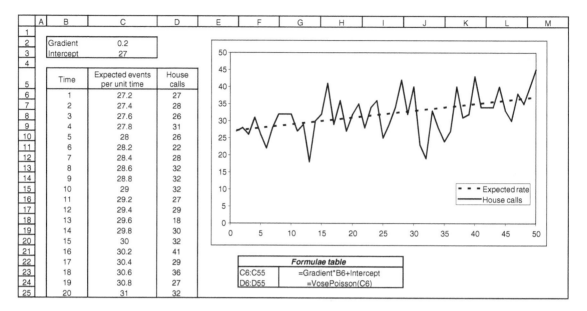

Figure 12.17 A Poisson time series with intensity as a linear function of time.

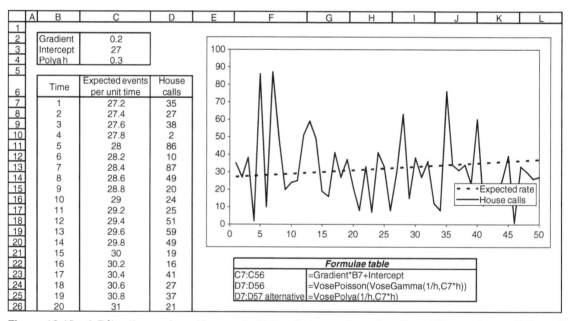

Figure 12.18 A Pólya time series with expected intensity λ as a linear function of time and a coefficient of variation of $h = 0.3$.

The linear equation used in the above two models for giving an approximate description of the relationship of the expected number with time is often quite convenient, but one needs to be careful because a negative slope will ultimately produce a negative expected value, which is clearly nonsensical (which is why it is good practice to plot the expected value together with the modelled counts as shown in the two figures above). The more correct Poisson regression model considers the log of the expected value of the number of counts to be a linear function of time, i.e.

$$\ln E[X] = \ln(e) + \beta_1 * t + \beta_0 \tag{12.10}$$

where β_0 and β_1 are regression parameters. The $\ln(e)$ term in Equation (12.10) is included for data where the amount of exposure e varies between observations; for example, if we were analysing data to determine the annual increase in burglaries across a country where our data are given for different parts of the country with different population levels, or where the population size is changing significantly (so the exposure measure e would be person-years). Where e is constant, we can simplify Equation (12.10) to

$$\ln \lambda e = \beta_1 * t + \beta_0 \tag{12.11}$$

The model in Figure 12.19 fits a Pólya regression to data (year $<= 0$) and projects out the next 3 years on annual sports accidents where the population is considered constant so we can use Equation (12.11).

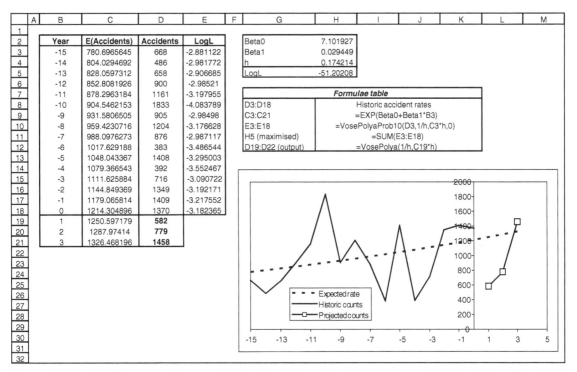

Figure 12.19 A Pólya regression model fitted to data and projected 3 years into the future. The Log*L* variable is optimised using Excel's Solver with the constraint that $h > 0$. ModelRisk offers Poisson and Pólya regression fits for multiple explanatory variables and variable exposure levels.

12.7 Time Series Models with Leading Indicators

Leading indicators are variables whose movement has some relationship to the movement of the variable you are actually interested in. The leading indicator may move in the same or opposite direction as the variable of interest, as shown in Figure 12.20.

In order to evaluate the leading indicator relationship, you will have to determine:

- the causal relationship;
- the quantitative nature of the relationship.

The causal relationship is critical. It gives a plausible argument for why the movement in the leading indicator should in some way presage the movement of the variable of interest. It will be very easy to find *apparent* leading indicator patterns if you try out enough variables, but, if you can't logically argue why there should be any relationship (preferably make the argument *before* you do the analysis on the potential indicator variable, it's much easier to convince yourself of a causal argument when you've seen a temptingly strong statistical correlation), it's likely that the observed relationship is spurious.

The quantitative nature of the relationship should come from a mixture of analysis of historic data and practical thinking. Some leading indicators will have a cumulative effect over time (e.g. rainfall as an indicator of the water available for use at a hydroelectric plant) and so need to be summed or averaged. Other leading indicators may have a shorter response time to the same, perhaps unmeasurable, causal variable as the variable in which you are interested (if the causal variable was measurable, you would use that as the leading indicator instead), and so your variable may exhibit the same pattern with a time lag.

The analysis of historic data to determine the leading indicator relationship will depend largely on the type of causal relationship. Linear regression is one possible method, where one regresses historic values of the variable of interest against the lead indicator values, with either a specific lag time if that can be causally deduced or with a varying lag time to produce the greatest r-squared fit if one is estimating the lag time. Note that any forecast can only be made a distance into the future equal to the lag time: otherwise one needs to make a forecast of the lead indicator too.

The model in Figure 12.21 provides a fairly simple example in which the historic data (used to create the left pane of Figure 12.20 below) of the variable of interest Y are compared visually with lead indicator X data for different lag periods. The closest pattern match occurs for a lag δ of 11 periods (Figure 12.22).

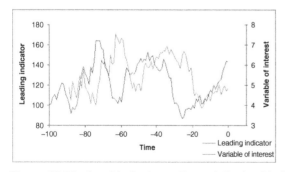
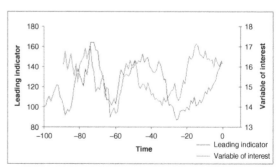

Figure 12.20 Lead indicator patterns: left – lead indicator variable is positively correlated with variable of interest; right – negatively correlated.

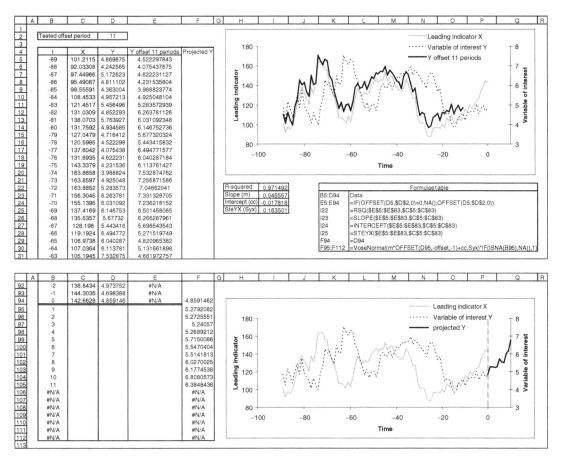

Figure 12.21 Leading indicator fit and projection model.

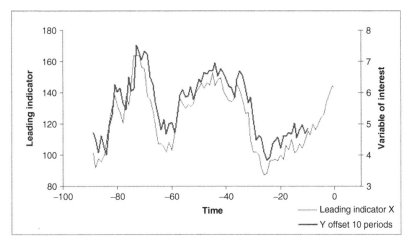

Figure 12.22 Overlay of variable of interest and lead indicator variable lagged by 10, 11 and 12 periods, showing the closest pattern correlation at 11 periods.

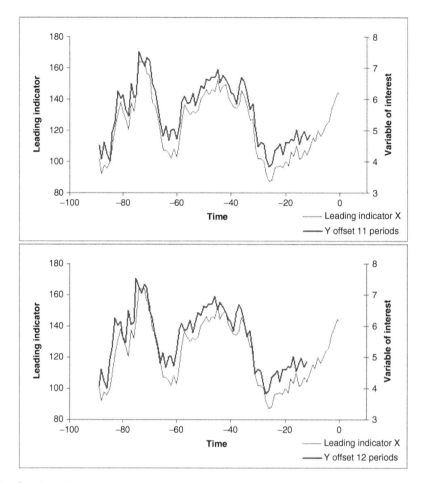

Figure 12.22 Continued.

A scatter plot of $Y(t)$ against $X(t-11)$ shows a strong linear relationship, so a least-squares regression seems appropriate (Figure 12.23).

The regression parameters are:

- slope $= 0.04555$
- intercept $= -0.01782$
- Ste$YX = 0.1635$

(We could use the linear regression parametric bootstrap to give us uncertainty about these parameters if we wished.)

The resultant model is then

$$Y(i) = \text{Normal}(0.04555 * X(i-11) - 0.01782, 0.1635)$$

which we can use to predict $\{Y(1)\ldots Y(11)\}$:

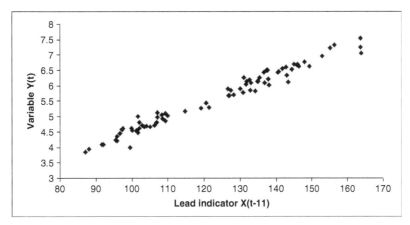

Figure 12.23   Scatter plot of variable of interest observations against lead indicator observations lagged by 11 periods.

12.8 Comparing Forecasting Fits for Different Models

There are three components to evaluating the relative merits of the various forecasting models fitted to data. The first is to take an honest look at the data you are going to fit: do they come from a world that you think is similar to the one you are forecasting into? If not (e.g. there are fewer companies in the market now, there are stricter controls, the product for which you are forecasting sales is getting rather old and uninteresting, etc.), then consider some of the forecasting techniques I describe in Chapter 17 which are based more on intuition than mathematics and statistics. The second step is also common sense: ask yourself whether the assumptions behind the model could actually be true and why that might be. Perhaps you can investigate whether this type of model has been used successfully for similar variables (e.g. a different exchange rate, interest rate, share price, water levels, hurricane frequencies than the one you are modelling). In fact, I recommend that you use this as a first step in selecting which models might be appropriate for the variable you are modelling.

Then you will need statistically to evaluate the degree to which each model fits the data and to compensate for the fact that a model with more parameters will have greater flexibility to fit the data but may not mean anything. Statistical techniques for model selection and comparison have improved, and the best methods now use "information criteria" of which there are three in common usage, described at the end of Section 10.3.4. The main advantage over the older log-likelihood ratio method is that the models don't have to be nested – meaning that each tested model does not need to be a simplified (some parameters removed) version of a more complex model. For ARCH, GARCH, APARCH and EGARCH you should subtract $n(1 + \ln[2\sigma])$, where n is the number of data points, from each of the criteria. If you fit a number of models to your data, try not to pick automatically the model with the best statistical result, particularly if the top two or three are close. Also, simulate projections out into the future and see whether the range and behaviour correspond to what you think is realistic (you can do this automatically in the time series fitting window in ModelRisk, overlaying any number of paths).

12.9 Long-Term Forecasting

By long-term forecasts I mean making projections out into the future that span more than, say, 20–30 % of your historical experience. I am not a big believer in using very technical models in these situations. For a start, there should be a lot of uncertainty to the projections, but more importantly the world is ever-changing and the key assumption you implicitly make by producing a forecast with a model fitted to historic data is that the world will carry on behaving in the same way. I know that historically I have been hopeless at predicting what my life will be like in 5 years time: in 1985 I fully expected to be a physical oceanographer in the UK; in 1987 I'd become a qualified photographer living in New Zealand, etc. I'd fixed on being a risk analyst by 1988, but then moved to the UK, Ireland, France and now Belgium.[3] Five years ago I had no idea that our company would have grown in the way it has, or that we would have developed such a strong software capability. Try applying the same test to the world you are attempting to model.

The alternative is to combine lessons learned from the past (e.g. how sensitive your sales are to the US economy) with a good look around to see how the world is changing (mergers coming up, wars starting or ending, new technology, etc.) and draw up scenarios of what the world might look like and how it would affect the variables you want to forecast. I give a number of techniques for this in Chapter 14.

---

[3] Now I have three kids, a partner, a nice home, a dog and an estate car, so maybe things are settling down.

Chapter 13

Modelling correlation and dependencies

13.1 Introduction

In previous chapters we have looked at building a risk analysis model and assigning distributions to various components of the model. We have also seen how risk analysis models are more complex than the deterministic models they are expanding upon. The chief reason for this increase in complexity is that a risk analysis model is dynamic. In most cases there are a potentially infinite number of possible combinations of scenarios that can be generated for a risk analysis model. We have seen in Chapter 4 that a golden rule of risk analysis is that each one of these scenarios *must be potentially observable in real life*. The model, therefore, must be restricted to prevent it from producing, in any iteration, a scenario that could not physically occur.

One of the restrictions we must place on our model is to recognise any interdependencies between its uncertain components. For example, we may have both next year's interest rate and next year's mortgage rate represented as distributions. Figure 13.1 gives an example of two distributions modelling these interest rate and mortgage rate predictions. Clearly, these two components are strongly positively correlated, i.e. if the interest rate turns out to be at the high end of the distribution, the mortgage rate should show a correspondingly high value. If we neglect to model the interdependency between these two components, the joint probabilities of the various combinations of these two parameters will be incorrect. Impossible combinations will also be generated. For example, a value for the interest rate of 6.5 % could occur with a value for the mortgage rate of 5.5 %.

There are three reasons why we might observe a correlation between observed data. The first is that there is a logical relationship between the two (or more) variables. For example, the interest rate statistically determines the mortgage rate, as discussed above. The second is that there is another external factor that is affecting both variables. For example, the weather during construction of a building will affect how long it takes both to excavate the site and to construct the foundations. The third reason is that the observed correlation has occurred purely by chance and no correlation actually exists. Chapter 6 outlines some statistical confidence tests to help determine whether the observed correlations are real. However, there are many examples of strong correlation between variables that would pass any tests of significance but where there is no relationship between the variables. For example, the number of personal computer users in the UK over the last 8 years and the population of Asia will probably be strongly correlated – not because there is any relationship but because both have steadily increased over that period.

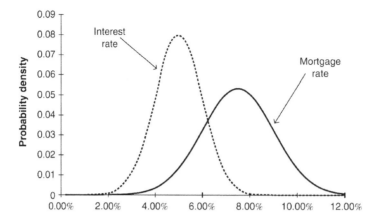

Figure 13.1 Distributions of interest and mortgage rate predictions.

13.1.1 Explanation of dependency, correlation and regression

The terms *dependency, correlation*, and *regression* are often used interchangeably, causing some confusion, but they have quite specific meanings. A *dependency* relationship in risk analysis modelling is where the sampled value from one variable (called the *independent*) has a statistical relationship that approximately determines the value that will be generated for the other variable (called the *dependent*). A statistical relationship has an underlying or average relationship between the variables around which the individual observations will be scattered. Its chief difference to correlation is that it presumes a causal relationship. As an example, the interest rate and mortgage rate will be highly correlated. Moreover, the mortgage rate will be in essence *dependent* on the interest rate, but not the other way round.

Correlation is a statistic used to describe the degree to which one variable is related to another. Pearson's correlation coefficient (also known as Pearson's product moment correlation coefficient) is given by

$$r = \frac{\mathrm{Cov}(X, Y)}{\sigma(X)\sigma(Y)}$$

where $\mathrm{Cov}(X, Y)$ is the covariance between datasets X and Y, and $\sigma(X)$ and $\sigma(Y)$ are the sample standard deviations as defined in Chapter 6. Correlation can be considered to be a normalised covariance between the two datasets: dividing by the standard deviation of each dataset produces a unitless index between -1 and $+1$. The correlation coefficient is frequently used alongside a regression analysis to measure how well the regression line explains the observed variations of the dependent variable. The above correlation statistic is not to be confused with Spearman's rank order correlation coefficient which provides an alternative, non-parametric approach to measuring the correlation between two variables. A little care is needed in interpreting covariance. Independent variables are always uncorrelated, but uncorrelated variables are not always independent. A classic, if somewhat theoretical, example is to consider the variables $X = \mathrm{Uniform}(-1, 1)$ and $Y = X^2$. There is a direct link between X and Y, but they have zero covariance since $\mathrm{Cov}(X, Y) = E[XY] - E[X]E[Y]$[1] (the definition) $= E[X^3] - E[X]E[X^2]$, and both $E[X]$ and $E[X^3] = 0$. This is one reason we look at scatter plots of data as well as calculating correlation statistics.

---

[1] E[ ] denotes the expectation, i.e. the mean of all values weighted by their probability

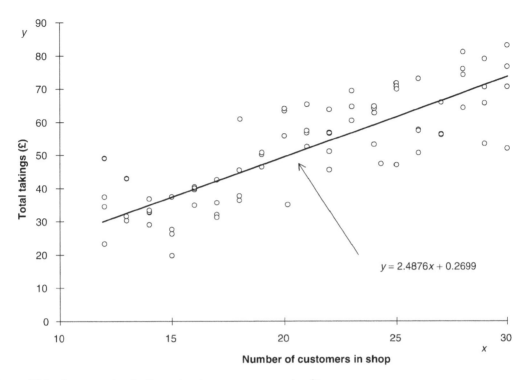

Figure 13.2   An example of a linear least-squares regression fit.

Regression is a mathematical technique used to determine the equation that relates the independent and dependent variables with the least margin of error. If we were to plot a scatter plot of the available data, this equation would be represented by a line that passed as close as possible through the data points (see Figure 13.2). The most common technique is that of simple least-squares linear regression. This objectively determines the straight line ($Y = aX + b$) such that the sum of the squares of the vertical deviations of the data points from the line is a minimum. The assumptions, mathematics and statistics relating to least-squares linear regression are provided in Section 6.3.9.

13.1.2 General comments on dependency modelling

The remainder of this chapter offers several techniques for modelling correlation and dependencies between uncertain components, with examples of where and how they are used. The sections on rank order correlation and copulas provide techniques for modelling correlation. The other sections offer techniques for dependency modelling. The analyst will need to determine whether it is important to focus on any particular correlation or dependency structure in the model. A simple way to determine this is to run two simulations, one with a zero rank order correlation and one with a +1 or −1 correlation, using two approximate distributions to define the correlated pair. If the model's results from these two simulations are significantly different, the correlation is obviously an important component of the general model.

Scatter plots are an extremely useful way of visualising the form of a correlation or dependency. The common practice is to plot observed data for the independent (when known) variable on the x axis

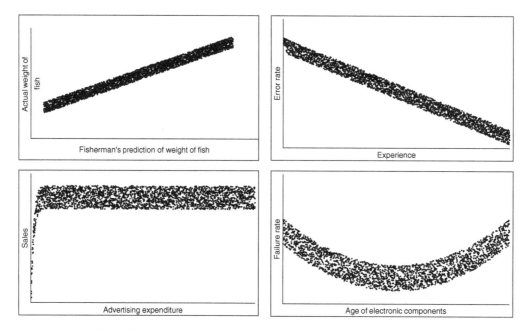

Figure 13.3   Examples of dependency patterns.

and corresponding data for the dependent (again, when known) variable on the y axis. Figure 13.3 illustrates four dependency patterns that you may meet: top left – positive linear; top right – negative linear; bottom left – positive curvilinear; and bottom right – mixed curvilinear.

Scatter plots also provide an excellent way of previewing a correlation pattern that you have defined in your own models. Most risk analysis packages allow the user to export the Monte Carlo generated values for any component in your model to the Windows clipboard or directly into a spreadsheet. The data can then be plotted in a scatter plot using the standard spreadsheet-charting facilities. The number of iterations (and therefore the number of generated data points) should be set to a value that will produce a scatter plot that fills out the low-probability areas reasonably well while avoiding overpopulation of the high-probability areas. High-resolution screens now make it reasonable to plot around 3000 data points as little dots that will show the pattern and give an impression of density quite nicely.

13.2 Rank Order Correlation

Most risk analysis software products now offer a facility to correlate probability distribution within a risk analysis model using rank order correlation. The technique is very simple to use, requiring only that the analyst nominates the two distributions that are to be correlated and a correlation value between -1 and $+1$. This coefficient is known as the *Spearman's Rank Order Correlation Coefficient*:

- *A correlation value of -1* forces the two probability distributions to be exactly negatively correlated, i.e. the X percentile value in one distribution will appear in the same iteration as the $100 - X$ percentile value of the other distribution.

- *A correlation value of* $+1$ forces the two probability distributions to be exactly positively correlated, i.e. the X percentile value in one distribution will appear in the same iteration as the X percentile value of the other distribution. In practice, one rarely uses correlation values of -1 and $+1$.
- *Negative correlation values between 0 and* -1 produce varying degrees of inverse correlation, i.e. a low value from one distribution will correspond to a high value in the other distribution, and vice versa. The closer the correlation to zero, the looser will be the relationship between the two distributions.
- *Positive correlation values between 0 and* $+1$ produce varying degrees of positive correlation, i.e. a low value from one distribution will correspond to a low value in the other distribution and a high value from one distribution will correspond to a high value from the other.
- *A correlation value of 0* means that there is no relationship between the two distributions.

13.2.1 How rank order correlation works

The rank order correlation coefficient uses the ranking of the data, i.e. what position (rank) the data point takes in an ordered list from the minimum to maximum values, rather than the actual data values themselves. It is therefore independent of the distribution shapes of the datasets and allows the integrity of the input distributions to be maintained. Spearman's ρ is calculated as

$$\rho = 1 - \left(\frac{6 \sum (\Delta R)^2}{n(n^2 - 1)} \right)$$

where n is the number of data pairs and ΔR is the difference in the ranks between data values in the same pair. This is in fact a short-cut formula where there are few or no ties: the exact formula is discussed in Section 6.3.10.

Example 13.1

The spreadsheet in Figure 13.4 calculates the Spearman's ρ for a small dataset. This correlation coefficient is symmetric about the distributions being correlated, i.e. only the difference between ranks

	B	C	D	E	F
2	Variable	Variable	Rank	Rank	Difference
3	A value	B value	of A	of B	in ranks^2
4	90.86	77.57	4	9	25
5	110.89	95.04	18	17	1
6	86.84	66.35	2	4	4
7	92.24	71.11	5	6	1
8	95.88	75.90	7	8	1
9	115.14	89.06	19	15	16
10	83.53	51.16	1	1	0
22	96.96	87.34	8	14	36
23	87.88	59.84	3	2	1

Number of data pairs:	20
Rank order correlation :	**0.72**

Formulae table	
D4:D23	=RANK(B4,BS4:B$23,1)
E4:E23	=RANK(C4,C$4:C$23,1)
F4:F23	=(D4-E4)^2
J3	=COUNT(B4:B23)
J4 (output)	=1-(6*SUM(F4:F23)/(J3*(J3^2-1)))

Figure 13.4 An example of the calculation of Spearman's rank order correlation coefficient.

is important and not whether distribution *A* is being correlated with distribution *B* or the other way round. ♦

In order to apply rank order correlation to a pair of probability distributions, risk analysis software has to go through several steps. Firstly, a number of rank scores equivalent to the number of iterations is generated for each distribution that is to be correlated. Secondly, these rank score lists are jumbled up so that the specified correlation is achieved between correlated pairs. Thirdly, the same number of samples are drawn from each distribution and sorted from minimum to maximum. Finally, these values are used during the simulation: the first to be used has the same ranking in the list as the first value in its rank score list, and so on, until all rank scores and all generated values have been used.

13.2.2 Use, advantages and disadvantages of rank order correlation

Rank order correlation provides a very quick and easy to use method of modelling correlation between probability distributions. The technique is "distribution independent", i.e. it has no effect on the shape of the correlated distributions. One is therefore guaranteed that the distributions used to model the correlated variables will still be replicated.

The primary disadvantage of rank order correlation is the difficulty in selecting the appropriate correlation coefficient. If one is simply seeking to reproduce a correlation that has been observed in previous data, the correlation coefficient can be calculated directly from the data using the formula in the previous section. The difficulty appears when attempting to model an expert's opinion of the degree of correlation between distributions. A rank order correlation lacks intuitive appeal, and it is therefore very difficult for experts to decide which level of correlation best represents their opinion.

This difficulty is compounded by the fact that the same degree of correlation will look quite different on a scatter plot for different distribution types, e.g. two lognormals with a 0.7 correlation will produce a different scatter pattern to two uniform distributions with the same correlation. Determining the appropriate correlation coefficient is more difficult still if the two distributions do not share the same geometry, e.g. one is normal and the other uniform, or one is a negatively skewed triangle and the other a positively skewed triangle. In such cases, the scatter plot will often show quite surprising results (Figure 13.5 illustrates some examples).

Figure 13.6 shows that correlation only becomes visually evident at levels of about 0.5 or above (or about −0.5 or below for negative correlation). Producing scatter plots like this at various levels of correlation for two variables can help subject matter experts provide estimates of levels of correlation to be applied.

Another disadvantage of rank order correlation is that it ignores any causal relationship between the two distributions. It is usually more logical to think of a dependency relationship along the lines of that described in Sections 13.4 and 13.5.

A further disadvantage of which most people are unaware is that an assumption of the correlation *shape* has already been built into the simulation software. The programming technique was originally developed in a seminal paper by Iman and Connover (1982) who used an intermediate step of translating the random numbers through van der Waerden scores. Iman and Conover found that these scores produced "natural-looking" correlations: variables correlated using van der Waerden scores produced elliptical-shaped scatter plots, while using the ranking of the variables directly produced scatter patterns that were pinched in the middle and fanned out at each end. For example, correlating two Uniform(0, 1) distributions together (the same as plotting the cdfs of any two continuous rank order correlated distributions) produces the patterns in Figure 13.7.

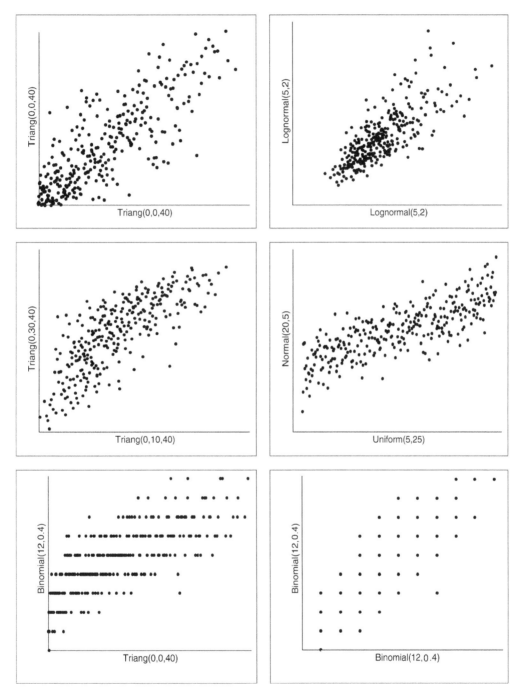

Figure 13.5 Examples of patterns produced by correlating different distribution types with a rank order correlation of 0.8.

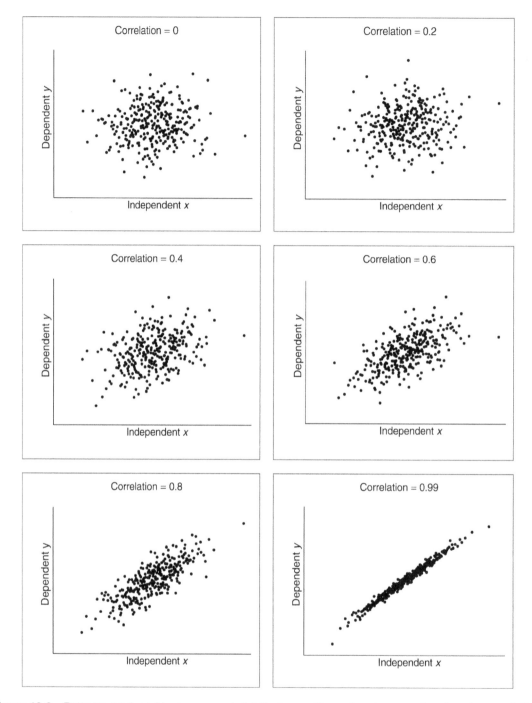

Figure 13.6 Patterns produced by two normal distributions with varying degrees of rank order correlation.

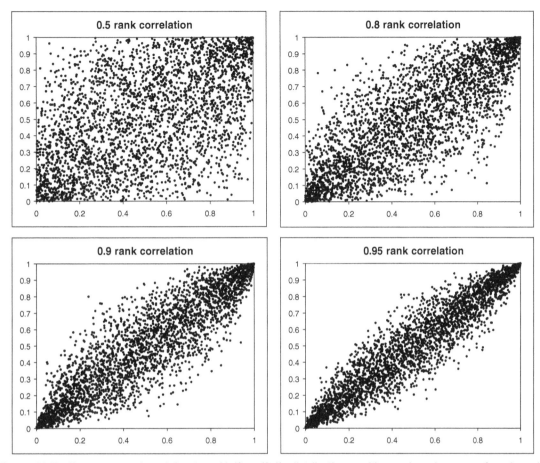

Figure 13.7 Patterns produced by two Uniform(0,1) distributions with varying degrees of rank order correlation.

Notice that the patterns are symmetric about the diagonals of Figure 13.7. In particular, rank order correlation will "pinch" the variables to the same extent at each extreme. In fact there are a wide variety of different patterns that could give us the same level of rank correlation. To illustrate the point, the following plots in Figure 13.8 give the same 0.9 correlation as the bottom-left pane of Figure 13.7, but are based on copulas which I discuss in the next section.

There are times in which two variables are perhaps much more correlated at one end of their distribution than the other. In financial markets, for example, we might believe that returns from two correlated stocks of companies in the same area (let's say mobile phone manufacture) are largely uncorrelated except when the mobile phone market takes a huge dive, in which case the returns are highly correlated. Then the Clayton copula in Figure 13.7 would be a much better candidate than rank order correlation.

The final problem with rank order correlation is that it is a simulation technique rather than a probability model. This means that, although we can calculate the rank order correlation between variables (ModelRisk has the VoseSpearman function to do this; it is possible in Excel but one has to create a large array to do it), and although we can use a bootstrap technique to gauge the uncertainty about that

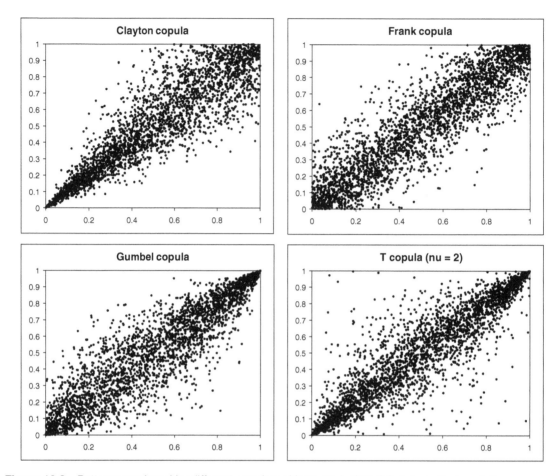

Figure 13.8 Patterns produced by different copulas with an equivalent 0.9 rank order correlation.

correlation coefficient (VoseSpearmanU), it is not possible to compare correlation structures statistically; for example, it is not possible to use maximum likelihood methods and produce goodness-of-fit statistics. Copulas, on the other hand, are probability models and can be compared, ranked and tested for significance.

In spite of the inherent disadvantages of rank order correlation, its ease of use and its speed of implementation make it a very practical technique. In summary, the following guidelines in using rank order correlation will help ensure that the analyst avoids any problems:

- Use rank order correlation to model dependencies that only have a small impact on your model's results. If you are unsure of its impact, run two simulations: one with the selected correlation coefficient and one with zero correlation. If there is a substantial difference between the model's final results, you should choose one of the other more precise techniques explained later in this chapter.
- Wherever possible, restrict its use to pairs of similarly shaped distributions.

- If differently shaped distributions are being correlated, preview the correlation using a scatter plot before accepting it into the model.
- If using subject matter experts (SMEs) to estimate correlations, use charts at various levels of correlation to help the expert determine the appropriate level of correlation.
- Consider using copulas if the correlation is important or shows an unusual pattern.
- Avoid modelling a correlation where there is neither a logical reason nor evidence for its existence.

This last point is a contentious issue, since many would argue that it is safer to assume a 100% positive or negative correlation (whichever increases the spread of the model output) rather than zero. In my view, if there is neither a logical reason that would lead one to believe that the variables are related in some way nor any statistical evidence to suggest that they are, it seems that one would be unjustified in assuming high levels of correlation. On the other hand, using levels of correlation throughout a model that maximise the spread of the output, and other correlation levels that minimise the spread of the output, does provide us with bounds within which we know the true output distribution(s) must lie. This technique is sometimes used in project risk analysis, for example, where for the sake of reassurance one would like to see the most widely spread output feasible given the available data and expert estimates. I suspect that using such pessimistic correlation coefficients proves helpful because it in some general way compensates for the tendency we all have to be overconfident about our estimates (of time to complete the project's tasks, for example, thereby reducing the distribution of possible outcomes for the model outputs like the date of completion) as well as quietly recognising that there are elements running through a whole project like management competence, team efficiency and quality of the initial planning – factors that it would be uncomfortable to model explicitly.

13.2.3 Uncertainty about the value of the correlation coefficient

We will often be uncertain about the level of rank order correlation to apply. We will be guided by either available data or expert opinion. In the latter case, determining an uncertainty distribution for the correlation coefficient is simply a matter of asking for a subject matter expert to estimate a feasible correlation coefficient: perhaps just minimum, most likely and maximum values which can then be fed into a PERT distribution, for example. The expert can be helped in providing these three values by being shown scatter plots of various degrees of correlation for the two variables of interest.

In the case where data are available on which the estimate of the level of correlation is to be based, we need some objective technique for determining a distribution of uncertainty for the correlation coefficient. Classic statistics and the bootstrap both provide techniques that accomplish this. In classical statistics, the uncertainty about the correlation coefficient, given the data set $(\{x_i\}, \{y_i\}), i = 1, \ldots, n,$ was shown by R. A. Fisher to be as follows (Paradine and Rivett, 1964, pp. 208–210):

$$\rho = \tanh[\text{Normal}(\tanh^{-1}[\hat{\rho}], 1/\sqrt{n-3})]$$

where tanh is the hyperbolic tangent, $\tanh^{-1}$ is the inverse hyperbolic tangent, $\hat{\rho}$ is the rank correlation of the set of observations and ρ is the true rank correlation between the two variables.

The bootstrap technique that applies here is the same technique usually used to estimate some statistic, except that we have to sample the data in pairs rather than individually. Figure 13.9 illustrates a spreadsheet where this has been done. Note that the formula that calculates the rank is modified from the Excel function RANK( ), since this function assigns the same lowest-value rank to all data values that are equal: in calculating ρ we require the ranks of tied data values to equal the average of the ranks

	A	B	C	D	E	F	G	H	I
1									
2		Sorted data		Correlation Calculation		Bootstrap sample		Correlation Calculation	
3		x	y	Rank x	Rank y	x	y	Rank x	Rank y
4		84.61	1.41	25	25	111.99	8.30	5	6
5		87.78	1.68	24	24	90.18	5.13	19.5	16.5
27		116.90	9.13	2	3	110.98	8.88	7	4
28		119.64	9.90	1	2	88.67	4.59	24	19
29				Data	0.719231			Bootstrap	0.570769
30								Fischer	0.753599
31									
32				*Formulae table*					
33		B4:C28	25 data pairs sorted in order of x						
34		D4:D28	=RANK(B4,B$4:B$28)+(COUNTIF(B$4:B$28,B4)-1)/2						
35		E29	{=1-6*SUM((E4:E28-D4:D28)^2)/(25*(25^2-1))}						
36		F4:F28	=VoseDuniform(B$4:B$28)						
37		G4:G28	=VLOOKUP(F4,B$4:C$28,2)						
38		H4:I28	=RANK(F4,F$4:F$28)+(COUNTIF(F$4:F$28,F4)-1)/2						
39		I29	{=1-6*SUM((I4:I28-H4:H28)^2)/(25*(25^2-1))}						
40		I30	=TANH(VoseNormal(ATANH(E29),1/SQRT(22)))						

Figure 13.9   Model to determine uncertainty of a correlation coefficient using the bootstrap.

that the tied values would have had if they had been infinitesimally separated. So, for example, the dataset $\{1, 2, 2, 3, 3, 3, 4\}$ would be assigned the ranks $\{1, 2.5, 2.5, 5, 5, 5, 7\}$. The 2s have to share the ranks 2 and 3, so get allocated the average 2.5. The 3s have to share the ranks 4, 5, 6, so get allocated the average 5. The Duniform distribution has been used randomly to sample from the $\{x_i\}$ values, and the VLOOKUP() function has been used to sample the $\{y_i\}$ values to ensure that the data are sampled in appropriate pairs. For this reason, the data pairs have to be ranked in ascending order by $\{x_i\}$ so that the VLOOKUP function will work correctly. Note in cell I30 that the uncertainty distribution for the correlation coefficient is calculated for comparison using the traditional statistics technique above. While the results from the two techniques will not normally be in exact agreement, the difference is not excessive and they will return almost exactly the same mean values. The ModelRisk function VoseSpearmanU simulates the bootstrap estimate directly.

Uncertainty about correlation coefficients can only be included by running multiple simulations, if one uses rank order correlation. As discussed previously (Chapter 7), simulating uncertainty and randomness together produces a single combined distribution that quite well expresses the total indeterminability of our output, but without showing the degree due to uncertainty and that due to randomness. However, it is not possible to do this with uncertainty about rank order correlation coefficients, as the scores used to simulate the correlation between variables are generated *before* the simulation starts. If one is intending to simulate uncertainty and randomness together, a representative value for the correlation needs to be determined, which is not easy because of the difficulty of assessing the effect of a correlation coefficient on a model's output(s). The reader may choose to use the mean of the uncertainty distribution for the correlation coefficient or may choose to play safe and pick a value somewhere at an extreme, say the 5 percentile or 95 percentile, whichever is the most conservative for the purposes of the model.

13.2.4 Rank order correlation matrices

An important benefit of rank order correlation is that one can apply it to a set of several variables together. In this case, we must construct a matrix of correlation coefficients. Each distribution must clearly have a correlation of 1.0 with itself, so the top-left to bottom-right diagonal elements are all 1.0. Furthermore, because the formula for the rank order correlation coefficient is symmetric, as explained above, the matrix elements are also symmetric about this diagonal line.

Example 13.2

Figure 13.10 shows a simple example for a three-phase engineering project. The cost of each phase is considered to be strongly correlated with the amount of time it takes to complete (0.8). The construction time is moderately correlated (0.5) with the design time: it is considered that the more complex the design, the longer it will take to finish the design and construct the machine, etc. ♦

There are some restrictions on the correlation coefficients that may be used within the matrix. For example, if A and B are highly positively correlated and B and C are also highly positively correlated, A and C cannot be highly negatively correlated. For the mathematically minded, the restriction is that there can be no negative eigenvalues for the matrix. In practice, the risk analysis software should determine whether the values entered are valid and alter your entries to the closest allowable values or, at least, reject the entered values and post a warning.

While correlation matrices suffer from the same drawbacks as those outlined for simple rank order correlation, they are nonetheless an excellent way of producing a complex multiple correlation that is laborious and quite difficult to achieve otherwise.

	Design cost	Design time	Construction cost	Construction time	Testing cost	Testing time
Design cost	1	0.8	0	0	0	0
Design time	0.8	1	0	0.5	0	0.4
Construction cost	0	0	1	0.8	0	0
Construction time	0	0.5	0.8	1	0	0.4
Testing cost	0	0	0	0	1	0.8
Testing time	0	0.4	0	0.4	0.8	1

Figure 13.10 An example of a rank order correlation matrix.

Adding uncertainty to a correlation matrix

Uncertainty about the correlation coefficients in a correlation matrix can be easily added when there are data available. The technique requires a repeated application of the bootstrap procedure described in the previous section for determining the uncertainty about a single parameter.

Example 13.3

Figure 13.11 provides a spreadsheet model where a dataset for three variables is used to determine the correlation coefficient between each variable. By using the bootstrap method, we retain the correlation between the uncertainty distributions of each correlation coefficient automatically. Cells C32:E32 are the outputs to this model, providing the uncertainty distributions for the correlation coefficients for $A : B$, $B : C$ and $A : C$. The exact formula has been used to calculate the correlation coefficients because

A	B	C	D	E	F	G	H	I	J	K
1										
2		Data ranked by A			Bootstrapped sample				Ranks		
3		A	B	C	A	B	C	A	B	C
4		78.07	2.05	0.34	94.91734	4.9082	0.0521	9.5	9.5	9.5
5		90.45	3.34	0.27	109.5817	6.4938	0.5103	3	6	2
12		109.58	6.49	0.51	103.5621	9.4092	0.1097	5.5	1.5	7.5
13		115.03	5.34	0.41	109.5817	6.4938	0.5103	3	6	2
14							average	5.5	5.5	5.5
15										
16					Calculations					
17			SS(AA)	SS(BB)	SS(CC)	SS(AB)	SS(BC)	SS(AC)		
18			16	16	16	16	16	16		
19			6.25	0.25	12.25	-1.25	-1.75	8.75		
26			0	16	4	0	-8	0		
27			6.25	0.25	12.25	-1.25	-1.75	8.75		
28		sums	79	79	79	9	7	65		
29										
30			Correlation calculations							
31			A-B	B-C	A-C					
32		ρ	0.114	0.089	0.823					
33										
34			Formulae table							
35		B4:D13	Data ranked in triplets by variable A							
36		E4:E13	=VoseDuniform(B$4:B$13)							
37		F4:F13	=VLOOKUP(E4,B$4:D$13,2)							
38		G4:G13	=VLOOKUP(E4,B$4:D$13,3)							
39		H4:J13	=RANK(E4,E$4:E$13)+(COUNTIF(E$4:E$13,E4)−1)/2							
40		H14:J14	=AVERAGE(H4:H13)							
41		C18:E27	=(H4-H$14)^2							
42		F18:F27	=(H4-H$14)*(I4-I$14)							
43		G18:G27	=(I4-I$14)*(J4-J$14)							
44		H18:H27	=(J4-J$14)*(H4-H$14)							
45		C32 (output)	=F28/SQRT(C28*D28)							
46		D32 (output)	=G28/SQRT(D28*E28)							
47		E32 (output)	=H28/SQRT(C28*E28)							
48										

Figure 13.11 Model to add uncertainty to a correlation matrix.

	A	B	C	D	E	F	G	H	I	J	K	L	M	N	O	P
1		Observations for the variable A:F														
2		A	B	C	D	E	F			A	B	C	D	E	F	
3		0.583	5.555	0.176	1.256	4.436	0.755		A	1	0.8765702	0.8711951	0.8673862	0.8790944	0.8664273	
4		1.417	7.119	22.78	3.745	6.319	2.169		B	0.8765702	1	0.8936254	0.8975755	0.9047335	0.8843717	
5		3.368	6.109	0.741	2.078	5.208	1.493		C	0.8711951	0.8936254	1	0.8902975	0.8910415	0.8811859	
6		0.408	4.628	0.05	0.807	1.891	0.717		D	0.8673862	0.8975755	0.8902975	1	0.8916671	0.8738415	
7		1.079	6.105	0.415	2.807	5.492	1.871		E	0.8790944	0.9047335	0.8910415	0.8916671	1	0.8919163	
8		2.471	6.666	2.039	8.148	8.262	4.127		F	0.8664273	0.8843717	0.8811859	0.8738415	0.8919163	1	
9		3.381	6.509	0.565	2.473	7.182	2.292									
10		0.236	5.053	0.095	0.692	2.171	0.262			A	B	C	D	E	F	
11		0.524	5.039	0.278	1.005	2.983	0.597		A	1	0.8765702	0.8711951	0.8673862	0.8790944	0.8664273	
12		3.075	6.732	2.971	3.582	6.44	3.716		B	0.8765702	1	0.8936254	0.8975755	0.9047335	0.8843717	
13		0.617	5.819	0.316	1.417	2.867	0.602		C	0.8711951	0.8936254	1	0.8902975	0.8910415	0.8811859	
14		1.427	4.787	0.068	0.788	3.605	0.366		D	0.8673862	0.8975755	0.8902975	1	0.8916671	0.8738415	
15		5.38	7.694	1.338	4.933	7.829	3.252		E	0.8790944	0.9047335	0.8910415	0.8916671	1	0.8919163	
16		0.964	5.106	0.088	1.043	3.108	0.22		F	0.8664273	0.8843717	0.8811859	0.8738415	0.8919163	1	
17		0.952	5.82	0.67	1.977	6.806	1.741									
430		2.454	6.38	0.965	3.299	8.534	3.385				*Formulae table*					
431		0.943	5.691	0.37	2.02	3.979	0.796		{J3:O8}	{=VoseCorrMatrix(B3:G431)}		Generates the correlation matrix				
432									{J11:O16}	{=VoseCorrMatrix(UB3:G431)}		Adds uncertainty to the matrix				
433																

Figure 13.12   Using VoseCorrMat and VoseCorrMatU to calculate a rank order correlation matrix from data.

the number of ties can be large compared with the number of data pairs because there are few data pairs. ◆

ModelRisk offers two functions VoseCorrMatrix and VoseCorrMatrixU that will construct the correlation matrix of the data and generate uncertainty about those matrix values respectively, as shown in the model in Figure 13.12. The functions are particularly useful when you have a large data array because they use less memory and spreadsheet space and calculate far faster than trying to do the entire analysis in Excel.

Note that, since the uncertainty distributions for the correlation coefficients in a correlation matrix are correlated together, the traditional statistics technique by Fisher cannot be used here. Fisher's technique described the uncertainty about an individual correlation coefficient, but not its relationship to other correlation coefficients in a matrix, whereas the bootstrap does so automatically.

13.3 Copulas

Quantifying dependence has long been a major topic in finance and insurance risk analysis and has led to an intense interest in, and development of, copulas, but they are now enjoying increasing popularity in other areas of risk analysis where one has considerable amounts of data. The rank order correlation employed by most Monte Carlo simulation tools is certainly a meaningful measure of dependence but is very limited in the patterns it can produce, as discussed above. Copulas offer a far more flexible method for combining marginal distributions into multivariate distributions and offer an enormous improvement in capturing the real correlation pattern. Understanding the mathematics is a little more onerous but is not all that important if you just want to use it as a correlation tool, so feel free to skim over the equations a bit. In the following presentation of copulas, I have used the formulae for a bivariate copula to keep them reasonably readable and show graphs of bivariate copulas, but keep in mind that the ideas extend to multivariate copulas too. I start off with an introduction to some copulas from a theoretical viewpoint, and then look at how we can use them in models. Cherubini *et al.* (2004) is a very thorough and readable exploration of copulas and gives algorithms for their generation and estimation, some of which we use in ModelRisk.

A d-dimensional copula C is a multivariate distribution with uniformly distributed marginals U(0, 1) on [0, 1]. Every multivariate distribution F with marginals $F_1, F_2, \ldots, F_d$ can be written as

$$F(x_1, \ldots, x_d) = C(F_1(x_1), F_2(x_2), \ldots, F_d(x_d))$$

for some copula C (this is known as Sklar's theorem). Because the copula of a multivariate distribution describes its dependence structure, we can use measures of dependence that are copula based. The concordance measures Kendall's tau and Spearman's rho, as well as the coefficient of tail dependence, can, unlike the rank order correlation coefficient, be expressed in terms of the underlying copula alone. I will focus particularly on Kendall's tau, as the relationships between the value of Kendall's tau (τ) and the parameters of the copulas discussed in this section are quite straightforward.

The general relationship between Kendall's tau of two variables X and Y and the copula $C(u, v)$ of the bivariate distribution function of X and Y is

$$\tau(X, Y) = 4 \int_0^1 \int_0^1 C(u, v) \, \mathrm{d}C(u, v) - 1$$

This relationship gives us a tool for fitting a copula to a dataset: we simply determine Kendall's tau for the data and then apply a transformation to get the appropriate parameter value(s) for the copula being fitted.

13.3.1 Archimedean copulas

An important class of copulas – because of the ease with which they can be constructed and the nice properties they possess – are the Archimedean copulas, which are defined by

$$C(u, v) = \varphi^{-1}(\varphi(u) + \varphi(v))$$

where φ is the generator of the copula, which I will explain later. The general relationship between Kendall's tau and the generator of an Archimedean copula $\varphi_\alpha(t)$ for a bivariate dataset can be written as

$$\tau = 1 + 4 \int_0^1 \frac{\varphi_\alpha(t)}{\varphi_\alpha(t)} \mathrm{d}t$$

For example, the relationship between Kendall's tau and the Clayton copula parameter α for a bivariate dataset is given by

$$\hat{\alpha} = \frac{2\tau}{1 - \tau}$$

The definition doesn't extend to a multivariate dataset of n variables because there will be multiple values of tau, one for each pairing. However, one can calculate tau for each pair and use the average, i.e.

$$\hat{\alpha} = \frac{2\overline{\tau}}{1 - \overline{\tau}}, \overline{\tau} = \frac{\displaystyle\sum_{i=1}^{n} \sum_{j=1}^{n, i \neq j} \tau_{ij}}{n(n-1)}$$

There are three Archimedean copulas in common use: the Clayton, Frank and Gumbel. These are discussed below.

The Clayton copula

The Clayton copula is an asymmetric Archimedean copula exhibiting greater dependence in the negative tail than in the positive, as shown in Figure 13.13.

This copula is given by:

$$C_\alpha(u, v) = \max[u^{-\alpha} + v^{-\alpha} - 1, 0]$$

and its generator is

$$\varphi_\alpha(t) = \frac{1}{\alpha}(t^{-\alpha} - 1)$$

where $\alpha \in [-1, \infty)$ {0}, meaning α is greater than or equal to -1 but can't take a value of zero.

The relationship between Kendall's tau and the Clayton copula parameter α for a bivariate dataset is given by

$$\hat{\alpha} = \frac{2\tau}{1 - \tau}$$

The model in Figure 13.14 generates a Clayton copula for four variables.

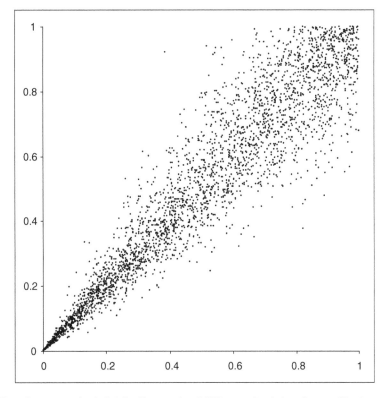

Figure 13.13 Plot of two marginal distributions using 3000 samples taken from a Clayton copula with $\alpha = 8$.

	A	B	C	D	E	F	G
1							
2		Alpha	15				
3							
4		No. variables n min = 2	Random number	Random^–alpha	Running sum	**Clayton Copula**	
5		1	0.934	2.79E+00	2.79E+00	**0.9338**	
6		2	0.605	2.68E+00	5.47E+00	**0.9363**	
7		3	0.473	2.95E+00	8.43E+00	**0.9304**	
8		4	0.664	1.92E+00	1.03E+01	**0.9575**	
9							
10				*Formulae table*			
11		C5:C8	=RAND()				
12		D5:D8	=F5^–Alpha				
13		E5:E8	=SUM($D$5:D5)				
14		F5 (output)	=C5				
15		F6:F8 (outputs)	= ((E5–B6+2) *((C6^(Alpha /((Alpha*(1–B6)) –1)))–1)+1)^(–1/ Alpha)				
16							

Figure 13.14 Model to generate values from a Clayton(alpha) copula.

The Gumbel copula

The Gumbel copula (aka Gumbel–Hougard copula) is an asymmetric Archimedean copula, exhibiting greater dependence in the positive tail than in the negative as shown in Figure 13.15.

This copula is given by

$$C_\alpha(u, v) = \exp\left\{ -\left[(-\ln u)^\alpha + (-\ln v)^\alpha\right]^{1/\alpha} \right\}$$

and its generator is

$$\varphi_\alpha(t) = (-\ln t)^\alpha$$

where $\alpha \in [-1, \infty)$. The relationship between Kendall's tau and the Gumbel copula parameter α for a bivariate dataset is given by

$$\hat{\alpha} = \frac{1}{1 - \tau}$$

The model in Figure 13.16 shows how to generate the Gumbel copula.

The Frank copula

The Frank copula is a symmetric Archimedean copula, exhibiting an even, sausage-type correlation structure as shown in Figure 13.17.

This copula is given by

$$C_\alpha(u, v) = -\frac{1}{\alpha} \ln\left(1 + \frac{(e^{-\alpha u} - 1)(e^{-\alpha v} - 1)}{e^{-\alpha} - 1}\right)$$

and its generator is

$$\varphi_\alpha(t) = -\ln\left[\frac{\exp(-\alpha t) - 1}{\exp(-\alpha) - 1}\right]$$

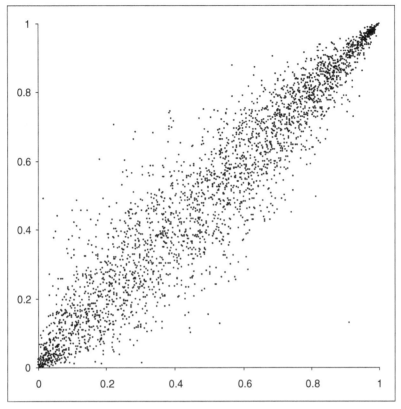

Figure 13.15 Plot of two marginal distributions using 3000 samples taken from a Gumbel copula with $\alpha = 5$.

where $\alpha \in (-\infty, \infty)\{0\}$. The relationship between Kendall's tau and the Frank copula parameter α for a bivariate dataset is given by

$$\frac{D_1(\alpha) - 1}{\alpha} = \frac{1 - \tau}{4}$$

where

$$D_1(\alpha) = \frac{1}{\alpha} \int_0^{\alpha} \frac{t}{e^t - 1} \, \mathrm{d}t$$

is a Debye function of the first kind. There is a simple way to generate values for the Frank copula using the logarithmic distribution, as shown by the following model in Figure 13.18.

13.3.2 Elliptical copulas

Elliptical copulas are simply the copulas of elliptically contoured (or elliptical) distributions. The most commonly used elliptical distributions are the multivariate normal and Student t-distributions. The key advantage of elliptical copulas is that one can specify different levels of correlation between the

	A	B	C	D	E	F
1						
2		Theta		2		
3						
4		alpha	gamma	t	Theta0	
5			0.5	0.5	1.070346954	1.570796327
6						
7		part1	part2	Z	X	
8		10.99984836	19.51736078	214.688009	107.3440045	
9						
10		No. variables	Random number	s	**Gumbel copula**	
11		1	0.960	0.009	**0.9098**	
12		2	0.611	0.006	**0.9273**	
13		3	0.642	0.006	**0.9256**	
14		4	0.223	0.002	**0.9555**	
15						
16			*Formulae table*			
17		B5 (alpha)	=1/theta			
18		C5 (gamma)	=COS(PI()/(2*theta))^theta			
19		D5 (t)	=VoseUniform(−PI()/2,PI()/2)			
20		E5 (Theta0)	=ATAN(TAN(PI()*Alpha/2))/Alpha			
21		B8 (part1)	=(SIN(Alpha)*(Theta0+t))/((COS(Alpha*Theta0)*COS(t))^(1/Alpha))			
22		C8 (part2)	=(COS(Alpha*Theta0+(Alpha−1)*t)/VoseExpon(1))^((1−Alpha)/Alpha)			
23		D8 (z)	=B8*C8			
24		E8 (x)	=gamma*Z			
25		C11:C14	=VoseUniform(0,1)			
26		D11:D14	=C11/$E$8			
27		E11:E14 (Output)	=EXP(−(D11^(1/theta)))			
28						

Figure 13.16 Model to generate values from a Gumbel(theta) copula.

marginals, and the key disadvantages are that elliptical copulas do not have closed-form expressions and are restricted to having radial symmetry. For elliptical copulas the relationship between the linear correlation coefficient ρ and Kendall's tau is given by

$$\rho(X, Y) = \sin\left(\frac{\pi}{2}\tau\right)$$

The normal and Student t-copulas are described below.

The normal copula

The normal copula (Figure 13.19) is an elliptical copula given by

$$C_\rho(u, v) = \int_{-\infty}^{\Phi^{-1}(u)} \int_{-\infty}^{\Phi^{-1}(v)} \frac{1}{2\pi(1-\rho^2)^{1/2}} \exp\left\{-\frac{x^2 - 2\rho x y + y^2}{2(1-\rho)^2}\right\} dx\, dy$$

where Φ^{-1} is the inverse of the univariate standard normal distribution function, and ρ, the linear correlation coefficient, is the copula parameter.

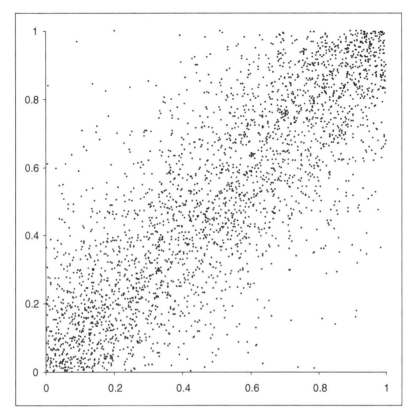

Figure 13.17 Plot of two marginal distributions using 3000 samples taken from a Frank copula with $\alpha = 8$.

The relationship between Kendall's tau and the normal copula parameter ρ is given by

$$\rho(X, Y) = \sin\left(\frac{\pi}{2}\tau\right)$$

The normal copula is generated by first generating a multinormal distribution with mean vector $\{0\}$ and then transforming these values into percentiles of a Normal(0, 1) distribution, as shown by the model in Fig. 13.20.

The Student t-copula (or Just "the t-copula")

The Student t-copula is an elliptical copula defined as

$$C_{\rho,v} = (u, v) = \int\limits_{-\infty}^{t_v^{-1}(u)} \int\limits_{-\infty}^{t_v^{-1}(v)} \frac{1}{2\pi (1-\rho^2)^{1/2}} \left\{1 + \frac{x^2 - 2\rho x y + y^2}{v(1-\rho^2)}\right\}^{-(v+2)/2} dx\, dy$$

where v (the number of degrees of freedom) and ρ (the linear correlation coefficient) are the parameters of the copula. When the number of degrees of freedom v is large (around 30 or so), the copula converges

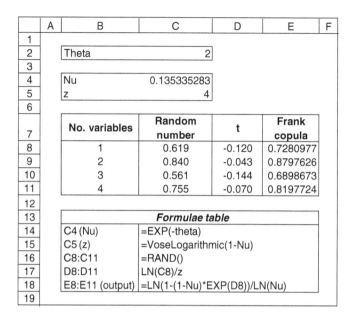

Figure 13.18 Model to generate values from a Frank(theta) copula.

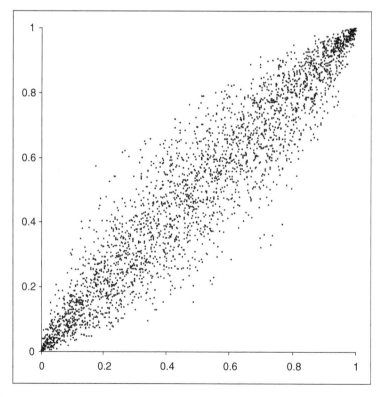

Figure 13.19 Graph of 3000 samples taken from a bivariate normal copula with parameter $\rho = 0.95$.

	A	B	C	D	E	F	G	H	I	J	K
1											
2		Means		\multicolumn{4}{c}{Covariance matrix}				MultiNormal	Normal copula	
3		0		1.00	0.95	0.95	0.95		0.19530725	**0.5774**	
4		0		0.95	1.00	0.95	0.95		0.16428688	**0.5652**	
5		0		0.95	0.95	1.00	0.95		0.37788608	**0.6472**	
6		0		0.95	0.95	0.95	1.00		0.39489876	**0.6535**	
7											
8						*Formulae table*					
9				{I3:I6}		{=VoseMultiNormal(Means,CovMatrix)}					
10				J3:J6 (output)		=VoseNormalProb(I3,0,1,1)					
11											

Figure 13.20   Model to generate values from a normal copula.

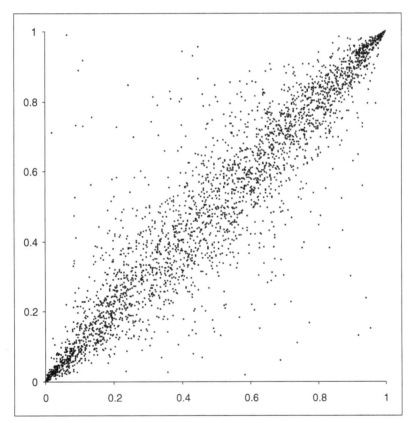

Figure 13.21   Graph of 3000 samples taken from a bivariate Student t-copula with $v = 2$ degrees of freedom and parameter $\rho = 0.95$.

to the normal copula just as the Student distribution converges to the normal. But for a limited number of degrees of freedom the behaviour of the copulas is different: the t-copula has more points in the tails than the gaussian one and a star-like shape (Figure 13.21).

As in the normal case (and also for all other elliptical copulas), the relationship between Kendall's tau and the Student t-copula parameter ρ is given by

$$\rho(X, Y) = \sin\left(\frac{\pi}{2}\,\tau\right)$$

Fitting a Student t-copula is slightly more complicated than fitting the normal. We first estimate τ and then, starting with $\nu = 2$, we determine the likelihood of observing the dataset. Then we repeat the exercise for $\nu = 3, 4, \ldots, 50$ and find the combination that produces the maximum likelihood. For ν values of 50 or more there will be no discernible difference to using a fitted normal copula which is simpler to generate values from.

Generating values from a Student copula requires determining the Cholesky decomposition of the covariance matrix, as shown by the model in Figure 13.22.

	A	B	C	D	E	F	G
1							
2		nu	3		Chisq distribution	2.7443	
3							
4			Covariance matrix (lower diagonal)				
5		1	0	0	0	0	
6		0.99	1	0	0	0	
7		0.98	0.98	1	0	0	
8		0.97	0.97	0.98	1	0	
9		0.97	0.97	0.98	0.99	1	
10							
11			Cholesky Decomposition				
12		1	0	0	0	0	
13		0.99	0.14106736	0	0	0	
14		0.98	0.069470358	0.18647753	0	0	
15		0.97	0.068761477	0.132043338	0.192188491	0	
16		0.97	0.068761477	0.132043338	0.140156239	0.131501501	
17							
18		Unit Normal	Mult	Student(nu)	**Student copula**		
19		−0.894966446	−0.894966446	−0.935740492	**0.209217857**		
20		1.742287149	−0.640236933	−0.669405681	**0.275574275**		
21		0.105547379	−0.73634759	−0.769895072	**0.24871516**		
22		−0.014095942	−0.737087464	−0.770668655	**0.248516973**		
23		1.926302143	−0.483042398	−0.505049472	**0.324145046**		
24							
25			*Formulae table*				
26		F2	=VoseChisq(nu)				
27		{B12:F16}	{=VoseCholesky(B4:F8)}				
28		B19:B23	=VoseNormal(0,1)				
29		C19:C23	{=MMULT(B12:F16,B19:B23)}				
30		D19:D23	=C19*SQRT(nu/ChiSqDist)				
31		E19:E23 (outputs)	=IF(D19<0,TDIST(−D19,nu,1),1−TDIST(D19,nu,1))				
32							

Figure 13.22   Model to generate values from a Student copula.

13.3.3 Modelling with copulas

In order to make use of copulas in your risk analysis, you need three things:

1. A method to estimate its parameter(s), which has been described above.
2. A model that generates the copula described above.
3. Functions that use the inversion method to generate values from the marginal distributions to which you wish to apply the copula. Excel offers a very limited number of such functions,[2] but they are notoriously inaccurate and unstable. You can derive many other inversion functions from the F(x) equations in Appendix III.

Let's say that we have a dataset of 1000 joint observations for each of five variables, we fit the data to gamma distributions for each variable and we correlate them together with a normal copula. In principle one could do all these things in Excel, but it would be a pretty large spreadsheet, so I am going to compromise a little. (By the way, I am using gamma distributions here so I can make a model that works with Excel, though be warned that Excel's GAMMAINV is one of the most unstable). In the model in Figure 13.23 I am also fitting a marginal gamma distribution to each variable using the method

	A	B	C	D	E	F	G	H	I	J	K	L	M	N	O
1		Joint observations for variables:							Normal copula parameter estimates						
2		1	2	3	4	5			1	2	3	4	5		
3		4.2953	12.769	5.6258	21.734	21.849		1	1.000	0.578	0.490	0.393	0.242		
4		17.544	32.924	14.971	35.321	27.799		2	0.578	1.000	0.373	0.281	0.139		
5		4.8865	2.7555	14.085	19.687	17.224		3	0.490	0.373	1.000	0.252	0.169		
6		2.2816	4.2633	8.3166	25.215	12.18		4	0.393	0.281	0.252	1.000	0.035		
7		5.4732	10.366	7.2923	5.4288	17.656		5	0.242	0.139	0.169	0.035	1.000		
8		15.073	24.038	41.372	19.957	19.139									
9		0.9581	4.2373	3.8137	12.819	1.9824					Data statistics				
10		1.4401	10.711	1.0511	11.975	7.9597		Mean	5.974	12.118	9.909	18.054	12.140		
11		4.0238	7.4557	12.291	11.627	14.717		Variance	17.884	46.878	49.397	117.292	26.045		
12		4.7946	4.967	9.2351	5.1999	9.2756									
13		10.943	24.14	10.191	22.018	17.204				Distribution Gamma parameter estimates					
14		2.2683	9.9109	12.455	14.784	18.206		Alpha	1.996	3.132	1.988	2.779	5.658		
15		0.7928	12.434	4.5066	32.179	12.783		Beta	2.994	3.869	4.985	6.497	2.145		
16		7.8518	27.508	14.434	27.597	18.576									
17		5.9436	8.5434	24.088	11.487	16.876					Fitted Normal copula				
18		6.9022	16.847	8.3371	17.772	12.025			0.470	0.710	0.357	0.524	0.072		
19		4.2686	12.562	4.5681	32.628	10.44									
20		3.6353	5.2728	5.6276	8.1151	7.6885					Correlated Gamma variables				
21		4.3357	12.094	5.2264	22.58	10.647			4.732	14.811	6.205	16.561	5.660		
22		10.947	9.6294	14.573	17.219	11.977									
23		3.9473	2.9792	8.0411	18.909	8.403					Formulae table				
24		4.2977	17.748	8.0677	7.0939	15.242		I3:M7	{=CORREL(OFFSET($B$3:$B$1002,0,I$2−1),OFFSET($B$3:$B$1002,0,$H3−1))}						
1001		7.1342	30.602	19.104	29.436	10.365		I10:M10	=AVERAGE(B3:B1002)						
1002		7.1934	16.667	5.4139	22.768	16.905		I11:M11	=VAR(B3:B1002)						
1003								I14:M14	=I10^2/I11						
1004								I15:M15	=I11/I10						
1005								{I18:M18}	{=VoseCopulaMultiNormal(I3:M7)}						
1006								I21:M21	=GAMMAINV(I18,I14,I15)						
1007															

Figure 13.23 A model using copulas.

---

[2] BETAINV, CHIINV, FINV, GAMMAINV, LOGINV, NORMINV, NORMSINV and TINV.

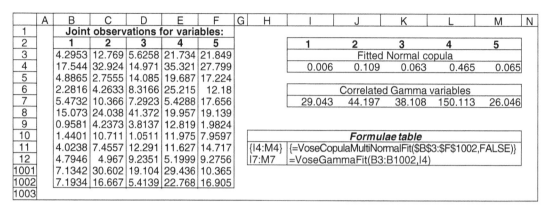

Figure 13.24 The same model as in Figure 13.23, but now in ModelRisk.

of moments: usually you would want to use maximum likelihood, but this involves optimisation, so the method of moments is easier to follow, and with 1000 data points there won't be much difference. I am also foregoing the rather elaborate calculations needed to estimate the normal copula's covariance matrix by using Excel's CORREL as an approximation. I have used ModelRisk's normal copula function because it takes up less space, and I have already shown you how to generate this copula above.

The model in Figure 13.24 is the equivalent with ModelRisk.

13.3.4 Making a special case of bivariate copulas

In the standard formulation for copulas there is no distinction between a bivariate (only two marginals) and a multivariate (more than two marginals) copula. However, we can manipulate a bivariate copula greatly to extend its applicability.

Sometimes, when creating a certain model, one is interested in a particular copula (say the Clayton copula), but with a greater dependence in the positive tails than in the negative (a Clayton copula has greater dependence in the negative tail than in the positive, see Figure 13.13 above).

For a bivariate copula it is possible to change the direction of the copulas by calculating $1 - X$, where X is one of the copula outputs. For example:

$$\{A1:A2\} \quad \text{Clayton copula with } \alpha = 8$$
$$B1 \qquad = 1 - A1$$
$$B2 \qquad = 1 - A2$$

A scatter plot of B1:B2 is now as in Figure 13.25.

ModelRisk offers an extra parameter to allow control over the possible directional combinations. For Clayton and Gumbel copulas there are four possible directions, but for the Frank there are just two possibilities since it is symmetric about its centre. The plots in Figures 13.26 and 13.27 illustrate the four possible bivariate Clayton copulas (1000 samples) with parameter $\alpha = 15$ and the two possible bivariate Frank copulas (1000 samples) with parameter 21.

Estimation of which direction gives the closest fit to data simply requires that one repeat the fitting methods described above, calculate the likelihood of the data for each direction and select the direction with the maximum likelihood. ModelRisk has bivariate copula functions that do this directly, returning either the parameters of the fitted copula or generating values from a fitted copula.

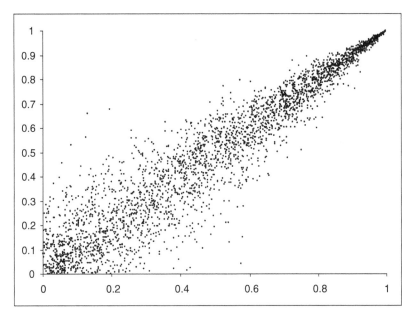

Figure 13.25 Graph of 3000 samples taken from a bivariate Clayton(8) with both directions reversed.

13.3.5 An empirical copula

In spite of the extra flexibility afforded by copulas I have introduced in the chapter over rank order correlation, you can see that they still rely on a symmetrical relationship between the variables: draw a line between (0, 0) and (1, 1) and you get a symmetric pattern about that line (assuming you didn't alter the copula direction). Unfortunately, real-world variables tend to have other ideas. As risk analysts, we put ourselves in a difficult situation if we try to squeeze data into a model that just doesn't fit. An empirical copula gives us a possible solution. Provided we have a good amount of observations, we can bootstrap the ranks of the data to construct an approximation to an empirical copula, as the model in Figure 13.28 demonstrates.

The model above uses the empirical estimate rank/$(n + 1)$ described in Section 10.2 for the quantile which should be associated with a value in a set of n data points. The VoseStepUniform distribution simply randomly picks an integer value between 1 and the number of observations (1000).

This method is very general and will replicate any correlation structure that the data show. It will be rather slow in Excel when you have large datasets because each RANK function goes through the whole array of data for a variable to determine its rank – it would be more efficient to use the VoseRank array function which will take far fewer passes through the data. However, the main drawback to this method occurs when we have relatively few observations. For example, if we have just nine observations, the empirical copula will only generate values of {0.1, 0.2, ... , 0.9} so our model will only generate between the 10th and 90th percentiles of the marginal distributions.

This problem can be corrected by applying some order statistics thinking along the lines of Equations 10.4 and 10.5. The ModelRisk function VoseCopulaData encapsulates that thinking. In the model in Figure 13.29 there are just 21 observations, so any correlation structure is only vaguely known.

The plots in Figure 13.30 show how the VoseCopulaData performs. The large grey dots are the data and the small dots are 3000 samples from the empirical copula: notice that the copula extends over

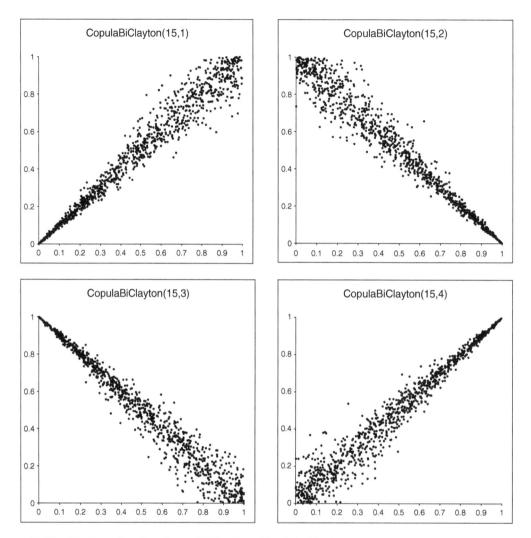

Figure 13.26 The four directional possibilities for a bivariate Clayton copula.

(0, 1) for all variables and fills in the areas between the observations with greatest density concentrated around the observations.

13.4 The Envelope Method

The *envelope method* offers a more flexible technique for modelling dependencies that is both intuitive and easy to control. It models the logic whereby the value of the independent variable statistically determines the value of the dependent variable. Its drawback is that it requires considerably more effort than rank order correlation and is therefore only really used where the dependency relationship is going to produce a significant effect on the final outcome of the model.

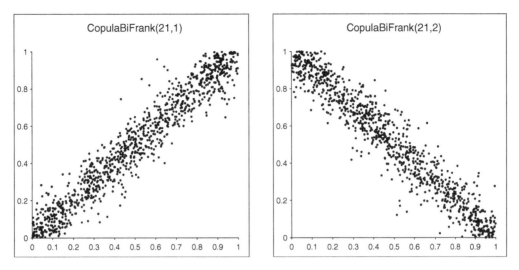

Figure 13.27   The two directional possibilities for a bivariate Frank copula.

	A	B	C	D	E	F	G	H	I	J	K	L	M
1		Joint observations for variables:						Ranks of observations					
2		1	2	3	4	5		1	2	3	4	5	
3		4.2953	12.769	5.6258	21.734	21.849		409	607	330	705	957	
4		17.544	32.924	14.971	35.321	27.799		985	990	808	925	994	
5		4.8865	2.7555	14.085	19.687	17.224		480	28	778	641	834	
6		2.2816	4.2633	8.3166	25.215	12.18		179	93	493	786	572	
7		5.4732	10.366	7.2923	5.4288	17.656		533	483	430	68	854	
1001		7.1342	30.602	19.104	29.436	10.365		684	982	891	857	422	
1002		7.1934	16.667	5.4139	22.768	16.905		694	772	317	736	819	

Number of observations	1000		
Row to select	42		

Empirical copula				
0.6434	0.8072	0.9151	0.3676	0.6533

Formulae table	
H3:L1002	=RANK(B3,B$3:B$1002,1)
E1004	=COUNT(E3:E1002)
H1007	=VoseStepUniform(1,E1004)
B1006:F1006 (ouput)	=OFFSET(I2,$E$1005,0)/($E$1004+1)

Figure 13.28   Constructing an approximate empirical copula from data.

13.4.1 Using the envelope method for approximate modelling of straight-line correlation in observed data

A large number of observed correlations can be quite adequately modelled using a straight-line relationship, as already discussed. If this is the case, the following techniques can prove very valuable. However, you may sometimes come across a dependency relationship that is curvilinear and/or has a vertical spread that changes across the range of the independent variable. The bottom graphs in Figure 13.3 illustrate curvilinear relationships. The following section offers some advice on how the envelope method can still be used to model such relationships.

	A	B	C	D	E
1		Joint observations for variables:			
2		1	2	3	
3		0.15227	0.46077	−2.09686	
4		1.50858	3.21206	3.41432	
5		−0.38116	0.64020	−2.08234	
6		−0.65663	1.95979	0.29414	
7		0.70030	1.34840	1.49071	
8		0.20642	0.14370	−1.49062	
9		0.03227	0.06054	−3.40363	
10		−0.23759	0.39242	−2.09327	
11		−1.61737	3.07033	0.48285	
12		−0.55439	0.74408	−2.92683	
13		−0.24406	0.40630	−0.63836	
14		−0.98675	4.17842	−1.02711	
15		−2.38768	17.72537	10.05931	
16		−1.02131	3.54146	−0.18354	
17		−0.59810	0.49291	−1.94212	
18		−0.24517	0.77250	−2.75109	
19		0.22220	0.65293	−0.47101	
20		−0.40109	0.98979	−1.24541	
21		0.62228	1.21112	0.43523	
22		−1.01850	1.31129	−1.16206	
23		−0.38151	0.83325	−0.65962	
24					
25		Empirical copula			
26		**0.34079**	**0.95104**	**0.55442**	
27					
28		*Formulae table*			
29		{B26:D26}	{=VoseCopulaData($B$3:$D$23)}		
30					

Figure 13.29 Constructing an empirical copula with few data using ModelRisk.

Using a uniform distribution

The envelope method first requires that all available data are plotted in a scatter plot. The independent variable is plotted on the x axis and the dependent variable on the y axis. Bounding lines are then determined that contain the minimum and maximum observed values of the dependent variable for all values of the independent variable.

Example 13.4

Data on the time that 40 participants took to practise making a wicker basket were negatively correlated to the time they took to make the basket in a subsequent test, shown in Figure 13.31. Two straight lines, drawn by eye, neatly contain all of the data points: a minimum line of $y = -0.28x + 57$ and a maximum line of $y = -0.42x + 88$. The data look to be roughly vertically uniformly distributed between these two lines for all values of the x axis. We could therefore predict the test time that would be taken for any value of the practice time as follows:

$$\text{Test time} = \text{Uniform}(-0.28 * \text{Practice time} + 57, -0.42 * \text{Practice time} + 88)$$

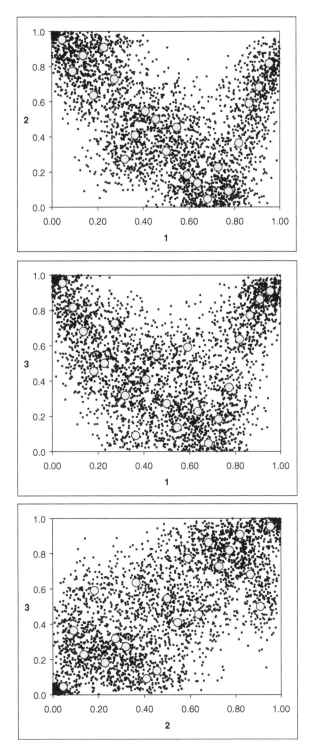

Figure 13.30 Scatter plots of random samples from the empirical copula fitted to the data in Figure 13.29.

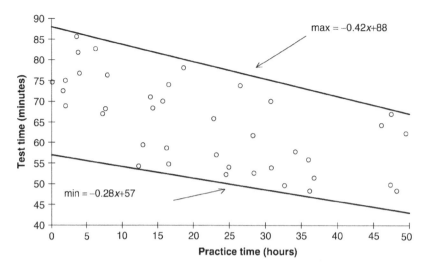

Figure 13.31 Setting boundary lines for the envelope method of modelling dependencies.

	A	B	C	D	E
1					
2			Practice time	26.67	
3			Minimum test time	49.53	
4			Maximum test time	76.80	
5			Modelled test time	63.17	
6					
7			*Formulae Table*		
8		D2	=VoseTriangle(0,20,60)		
9		D3	=−0.28*D2+57		
10		D4	=−0.42*D2+88		
11		D5	=VoseUniform(D3,D4)		
12					

Figure 13.32 Dependency model using the envelope method with a uniform distribution.

We have thus defined a uniform distribution for the test time that varies according to the practice time taken. If we believe that the practice time that will be taken by future workers is Triangle(0, 20, 60), we can use this dependency model to generate the distribution of test times as illustrated in the spreadsheet of Figure 13.32.

Consider the Triangle(0, 20, 60) generating a value of 30 in one iteration (see Figure 13.33). The equation for the minimum test time produces a value of $-0.28 * 30 + 57 = 48.6$. The equation for the maximum test time produces a value of $-0.42 * 30 + 88 = 75.4$. Thus, for this iteration, the value for the test time will be generated from a Uniform(48.6, 75.4) distribution. ◆

The above example is a little simplistic. Using a uniform distribution to model the dispersion between the minimum and maximum lines obviously gives equal weighting to all values within the range. It is quite simple to extend this technique to using a triangular or normal distribution in place of the uniform approximation, both of which provide a central tendency that is more realistic.

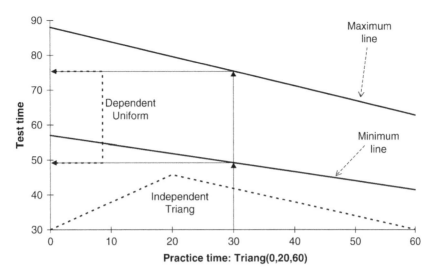

Figure 13.33   Illustration of how the dependency model of Figure 13.32 works.

Using a triangular distribution

Employing a triangular distribution requires that, in addition to the minimum and maximum lines, we also provide the equation of a line that defines the most likely value for the dependent variable for each value of the independent variable. The triangular distribution is still a fairly approximate modelling tool. It is therefore quite reasonable to *draw* a line through the points of greatest vertical density. Alternatively, you may prefer to find the least-squares fit line through the available data. All professional spreadsheet programs now offer the facility to find this line automatically, making the task very simple. A third option is to say that the most likely value lies midway between the minimum and maximum.

Example 13.5

Figures 13.34 and 13.35 provide an illustration of the envelope method with triangular distributions. ◆

	A	B	C	D	E
1					
2			Practice time	26.67	
3			Minimum test time	49.53	
4			Most likely test time	63.17	
5			Maximum test time	76.80	
6			Modelled test time	63.17	
7					
8			*Formulae table*		
9		D2	=VoseTriangle(0,20,60)		
10		D3	=−0.28*D2+57		
11		D4	=−0.35*D2+72.5		
12		D5	=−0.42*D2+88		
13		D6	=VoseTriangle(D3,D4,D5)		
14					

Figure 13.34   Dependency model using the envelope method with a triangular distribution.

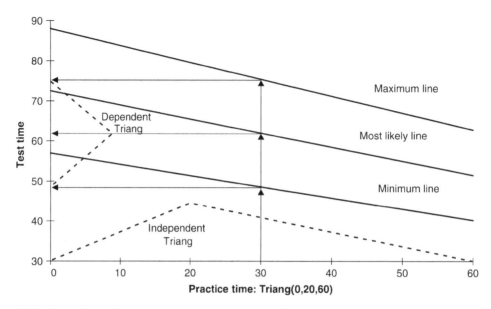

Figure 13.35 Illustration of how the dependency model of Figure 13.34 works.

Using a normal distribution

This option involves running a least-squares regression analysis and finding the equation of the least-squares line and the standard error of the y-estimate Syx. The Syx statistic is the standard deviation of the vertical distances of each point from the least-squares line. Least-squares regression assumes that the error of the data about the least-squares line is normally distributed. Thus, if $y = ax + b$ is the equation of the least-squares line, we can model the dependent distribution as $y = \text{Normal}(ax + b, Syx)$.

Example 13.6

Figure 13.36 provides an illustration of the envelope method with normal distributions. ♦

Comparison of the uniform, triangular and normal methods

Figure 13.37 compares how the three envelope methods behave. The graphs on the left cross-plot a Triangle(0, 20, 60) for the practice time (x axis) against the resulting test time (y axis). The graphs on the right show histograms of the resulting test time distributions.

The uniform method produces a scatter plot that is vertically evenly distributed and strongly bounded. The test time histogram has the flattest shape with the widest "shoulders" of the three methods. The triangular method produces a scatter plot that has a vertical central tendency and is also strongly bounded. The histogram is the most peaked of the three methods, producing the smallest standard deviation. The normal method produces a scatter plot that has a vertical central tendency but that is unbounded. This will generally be a closer approximation to a plot of available data. The histogram has the widest range of the three methods. Using the normal distribution has two advantages over the other two methods: the equation of the line and standard deviation are both calculated directly from the available data and don't involve any subjective estimation; and the unbounded nature of the normal distribution gives the opportunity for generated values to fall outside the range of the observed values. This second point may help ensure that the range of the dependent distribution is not underestimated.

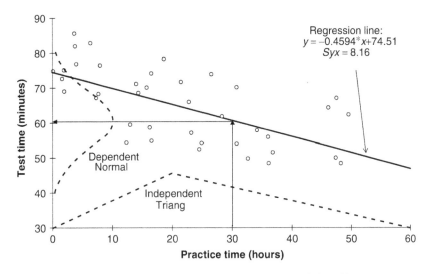

Figure 13.36 Using the normal distribution to model a dependency relationship.

Finally, it is important to be sure that the formula you develop will be valid over the entire range of values that are to be generated for the two variables. For example, the normal formula can potentially generate negative values for test time. It could, however, be mathematically restricted to prevent a negative tail, for example by using an IF (test_time < 0, 0, test_time) statement.

13.4.2 Using the envelope method for non-linear correlation observed from available data

One may come across a correlation relationship that cannot be adequately modelled using a straight-line fit, as in the examples of Section 13.4.1. However, with a little extra work, the techniques described above can be adapted to model most relationships.

The first stage is to find the best curvilinear line that fits the data. Microsoft Excel, for example, offers a choice of automatic line fitting: linear, logarithmic, polynomial (up to sixth order), power and exponential. Several of these fitted lines can be overlaid on the data to help determine the most appropriate equation. The second stage is to use the equation of the selected line to determine the predicted values for the dependent variable for each value of the independent variable. The difference between the observed and predicted values of the dependent variable (i.e. the error terms) are then calculated and cross-plotted against the independent variable. The third stage is to determine how these error terms should be modelled. Any of the three techniques described in Sections 13.4.1 could be used. The final stage is to combine the equation of the best-fit line with the distribution for the error term.

Example 13.7

Data on the amount of money a cosmetic company spends on advertising the launch of a new product are compared with the volume of initial orders it receives (Figure 13.38) and cross-plotted in Figure 13.39. Clearly, the relationship is not linear: an example of the law of diminishing returns. The best-fit line is determined to be logarithmic: $y = 1374.8 * LN(x) - 10\,713$. The error terms appear to have approximately the same distribution across the whole range of advertising budget values. Since the distribution

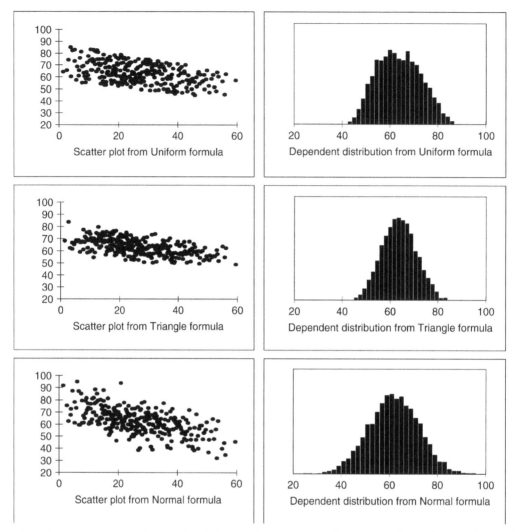

Figure 13.37 Comparison of the results of the envelope method of modelling dependency using uniform, triangular and normal distributions.

of error terms appears to have a greater concentration around zero, we might assume that they are normally distributed and calculate their standard deviation (= 126 from Figure 13.38). The final equation for the total initial order can then be written as

$$\text{Total initial order} = 1374.8 * \text{LN}(\text{advertising\_budget}) - 10\,713 + \text{Normal}(0, 126)$$

or

$$\text{Total initial order} = \text{Normal}(1374.8 * \text{LN}(\text{advertising\_budget}) - 10\,713, 126) \; \blacklozenge$$

	A	B	C	D	E
1					
2		Advertising	Initial	Observed difference	
3		budget (A)	order (O)	to prediction (D)	
4		9743	1973	59	
5		12 011	2132	-70	
6		2818	220	12	
7		24 303	3091	-80	
8		15 082	2536	22	
9		8142	1573	-93	
10		18 183	2652	-120	
11		17 728	2992	255	
12		18 531	2822	24	
13		18 795	2786	-30	
14		16 820	2665	1	
15		18 114	2737	-29	
16		19 603	3003	129	
17		23 290	3032	-80	
18		Standard deviation		126	
19					
20			Formulae table		
21		D4:D17	=C4-(1374.8*LN(B4)-10713)		
22		D18	=STDEV(D4:D17)		
23					

Figure 13.38 Analysis of data and error terms for a curvilinear regression for Example 13.7.

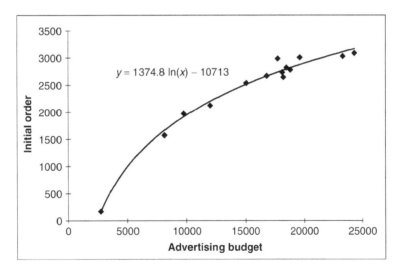

Figure 13.39 The best-fitting non-linear correlation for the data of Example 13.7.

13.4.3 Using the envelope method to model expert opinion of correlation

It is very difficult to get an intuitive feel for rank order correlation coefficients, even when one is familiar with probabilistic modelling. It is therefore recommended that the more intuitive envelope method be employed for the modelling of an expert's opinion of a dependency where that dependency is likely to have a large impact.

The technique involves the following steps:

- Discuss with the expert the logic of how he or she perceives the relationship between the two variables to be correlated. Review any available data.
- Determine the independent and dependent variables. If the causal relationship is unclear, select either to be the independent variable according to which will be easiest.
- Define the range of the independent variable and determine its distribution (using a technique from Chapter 9 or 10).
- Select several values for the independent variable. These values should include the minimum and maximum and a couple of strategic points in between.
- Ask the expert his/her opinion of the minimum, most likely and maximum values for the dependent variable should each of these selected values of the independent variable occur. I often prefer to ask for the *practical* minimum and maximum.
- Plot these values on a scatter diagram and find the best-fit lines through the three sets of points (minima, most likely values and maxima).
- Check that the expert agrees the plot is consistent with his/her opinion.
- Use these equations of the best-fit lines in a triangular or PERT distribution to define the dependent variable.

Example 13.8

Figure 13.40 illustrates an example where the expert is defining the relationship between a bank's average mortgage rate and the number of new mortgages it will sell. The expert has given her opinion of the practical minimum, most likely and practical maximum values of the number of new mortgages for four values of the mortgage rate, as shown in Table 13.1. She has defined *practical* minimum and

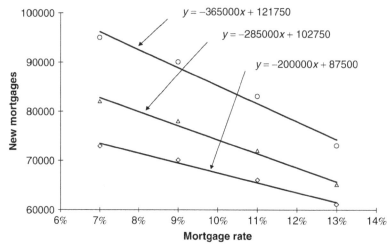

Figure 13.40 An example of the use of the envelope method to model an expert's opinion of a dependency relationship or correlation.

Table 13.1 Data from expert elicitation.

Mortgage rate (%)	New mortgages		
	Min	Most likely	Max
7	73 000	82 000	95 000
9	70 000	78 000	90 000
11	66 000	72 000	83 000
13	61 000	65 000	73 000

maximum to mean, for her, that there is only a 5 % chance that the mortgage will be below and above those values respectively. ♦

This technique has the advantage of being very intuitive. The expert is asked questions that are both meaningful and easy to think about. It also has the advantage of avoiding the need to define the distribution shape for a dependent variable: the shape will be dictated by its relationship to the independent variable.

13.4.4 Adding uncertainty in the envelope method

It is a relatively simple matter to add uncertainty into the envelope method. If data exist to develop the dependency relationship, one can use the bootstrap method or traditional statistics to give uncertainty distributions for the least-squares fit parameters. Uncertainty about the boundaries can be included by simply looking at the best-guess line, as well as extreme possibilities for the minimum and maximum boundaries on y.

13.5 Multiple Correlation Using a Look-Up Table

There may be times when it is necessary to model the simultaneous effect of an external factor on several parameters within a model. An example is the effect of poor weather on a construction site. The times taken to do an archaeological survey of the land, dig out the foundations, put in the form work, build the foundations, construct the walls and floors and assemble the roof could all be affected by the weather to varying degrees.

A simple method of modelling such a scenario is to use a spreadsheet look-up table.

Example 13.9

Figure 13.41 illustrates the example above, showing the values for one particular iteration. The model works as follows:

- Cells D5:D10 list the estimates of duration of each activity if the weather is normal.
- The *look-up table* F4:J10 lists the percentages that the activities will increase or decrease owing to the weather conditions.
- Cell D13 generates a value for the weather from 1 to 5 using a discrete distribution that reflects the relative likelihood of the various weather conditions.

	A	B	C	D	E	F	G	H	I	J
1										
2							% increase:weather condition/index			
3				Base	Revised	VP	Poor	Normal	Good	VG
4				Estimate	Estimate	1	2	3	4	5
5		2	Archeology	4.3	5.52	40%	28%	0%	0%	−2%
6		3	Dig found'n	10.9	13.1	30%	20%	0%	−6%	−10%
7		4	Form work	2.2	2.2	10%	4%	0%	0%	−3%
8		5	Lay found'n	6.7	8.4	40%	25%	0%	−12%	−18%
9		6	Walls & floors	16.7	17.4	10%	4%	0%	0%	−2%
10		7	Lay roofing	7.6	8.3	20%	8%	0%	−4%	−6%
11				Total time	54.93					
12							*Formulae table*			
13			Weather index:	2		D5:D10	=VoseTriangle(3,4,6), VoseTriangle(9,11,13), etc..			
14						E5:E10	=D5*(1+HLOOKUP(D$13,F$4:J$10,B5))			
15						D13	=VoseDiscrete({1,2,3,4,5},{2,5,4,3,2})			
16						E11	=SUM(E5:E10)			

Figure 13.41   Using a look-up table to model multiple dependencies.

- Cells E5:E10 add the appropriate percentage change for that iteration to the base estimate time by looking it up in the look-up table.
- Cell E11 adds up all the revised durations to obtain the total construction time.

It is a simple matter to include uncertainty in this technique. One needs simply to add uncertainty distributions for the magnitude of effect (in this case, the values in cells F5:J10). A little care is needed if the uncertainty distributions overlap for an activity. So, for example, if we used a PERT(30 %, 40 %, 50 %) uncertainty distribution for the parameter in cell F5 and a PERT(20 %, 28 %, 35 %) uncertainty distribution for the parameter in cell G5, we could be modelling a simulation where very poor weather increases the archaeological digging time by 31 % but poor weather increases the time by 33 %. Using high levels of correlation for the uncertainty distributions of effect size across a task will remove this problem quite efficiently and reflect that errors in estimating the effect (in this case weather) will probably be similar for each effect size. ◆

Chapter 14

Eliciting from expert opinion

14.1 Introduction

Risk analysis models almost invariably involve some element of subjective estimation. It is usually impossible to obtain data from which to determine the uncertainty of all of the variables within the model accurately, for a number of reasons:

- The data have simply never been collected in the past.
- The data are too expensive to obtain.
- Past data are no longer relevant (new technology, changes in political or commercial environment, etc.).
- The data are sparse, requiring expert opinion "to fill in the holes".
- The area being modelled is new.

The uncertainty in subjective estimates has two components: the inherent randomness of the variable itself and the uncertainty arising from the expert's lack of knowledge of the parameters that describe that variability. In a risk analysis model, these uncertainties may or may not be distinguished, but both types of uncertainty should at least be accounted for in a model. The variability is best included by assuming some sort of stochastic model, and the uncertainty is then included in the uncertainty distributions for the model parameters.

When insufficient data are available to specify the uncertainty of a variable completely, one or more experts will usually be consulted to provide their opinion of the variable's uncertainty. This chapter offers guidelines for the analyst to model the experts' opinions as accurately as possible.

I will start by discussing sources of bias and error that the analyst will encounter when collecting subjective estimates. We then look at a number of techniques used in the modelling of probabilistic estimates, and particularly the use of various types of distribution. The analyst is then shown how to employ brainstorming sessions to ensure that all of the available information relevant to the problem is disseminated among the experts and the uncertainty of the problem openly discussed. Finally, we look at methods for eliciting expert opinion in one-to-one interviews with the analyst.

Before delving into the techniques of subjective estimation, I would like the reader to consider the following two points that have been the downfall of many a model I have been asked to evaluate:

- Firstly, the most significant subjective estimate in a model is often in designing the structure of the model itself. It is surprising how often the structure of a model evades criticism while the figures within it are given all the scrutiny. Before committing to a specific model structure, it is recommended that the analyst seeks comment from other interested parties as to its validity. In turn, this action will greatly enhance the analyst's chances of having the model's results accepted and of receiving cooperation in determining the input uncertainties. Good analysts should take this stage very seriously and promote an environment where it is possible to provide open criticism of their work.

• The second point is that the analysts should not take it upon *themselves* to provide all of the subjective assessments in a model. This sounds painfully obvious, but it still astounds me how many analysts believe that they can estimate all or most of the variables within their model by themselves without consulting others who are closer to the particular problem.

14.2 Sources of Error in Subjective Estimation

Before looking at the techniques for eliciting distributions from an expert, it is very useful to have an understanding of the biases that commonly occur in subjective estimation. To introduce this subject, Section 14.2.1 describes two exercises I run in my risk analysis training seminars and that the reader might find educational to conduct in his or her own organisation. In each exercise the class members have their own PCs and risk analysis software to help them with their estimates. Section 14.2.2 summarises the sources of heuristic errors and biases: that is, errors produced by the way people mentally approach the task of parameter estimating. Finally, Section 14.2.3 looks at other factors that may cause inaccuracy in the expert's estimates.

14.2.1 Class experiments on estimating

This section looks at two estimating exercises I regularly use in my training seminars on risk analysis modelling. Their purpose is to highlight some of the thought processes (heuristics) people use to produce quantitative estimates. The reader should consider the observations from these exercises in conjunction with the points raised in Section 14.2.2.

Class estimating exercise 1

Each member of the class is asked to provide practical minimum, most likely and practical maximum estimates for a number of quantities (usually 8). The class is instructed that the minimum and maximum should be as close as possible to each other such that they are 90 % confident that the true value falls between them. The class is encouraged to ask questions if anything is unclear.

The quantities being estimated are obscure enough that the class members will not have an exact knowledge of their values, but hopefully familiar enough that they can have a go at estimating the value. The questions are changed to be relevant to the country in which the seminar is run. Examples of these quantities are:

• the distance from Oxford to Edinburgh along main highway routes in kilometres;
• the area of the United Kingdom in square kilometres;
• the mass of the Earth in metric tonnes;
• the length of the Nile in kilometres;
• the number of pages in the December *Vogue* UK magazine;
• the population of Scranton, USA;
• the height of K2, Kashmir, in metres;
• the deepest ocean depth in metres.

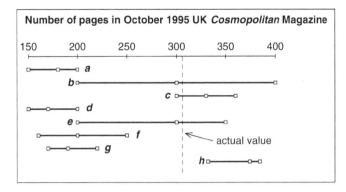

Figure 14.1   How to draw up class estimates from exercises 1 and 2 on a blackboard.

Each member of the class fills out a form giving the three values for each quantity. When everyone has completed their forms, I get the class to pick one of these quantities, e.g. the length of the Nile. I then question each member of the class to find out the minimum and the maximum, i.e. the total range of all of the estimates they have made. On the blackboard, I draw up a plot of each class member's three-point estimate, as illustrated in Figure 14.1, and then superimpose the true value. There is almost invariably an expression of surprise at the true value. Sometimes, after I have drawn all of the estimates up on the blackboard, I will ask if any of the class wishes to change their estimate before I reveal the true value. Some will choose to do so, but this rarely increases their chance of encompassing the true value. I will often repeat this process for four or five of the measurements to collect as many of the lessons to be learned from the exercise as possible.

Now, if the class members were perfectly calibrated, there would be a 90 % chance (i.e. the defined level above) that each true value would lie within their minimum to maximum range. By "calibrated" I mean that their perceptions of the precision of their knowledge were accurate. If there are eight quantities to be estimated, the number that fall within their minimum to maximum range (their score for this exercise) can be estimated by a Binomial(8, 90 %) distribution, as shown in Figure 14.2.

A host of interesting observations invariably comes out of this exercise. The underlying reasons for these observations and those of the following exercise are summarised in Section 14.2.2:

- In the hundred or so seminars in which I have performed this exercise, I have very rarely seen a score higher than 6. From Figure 14.2 we can see that there is only a 4 % chance that anyone would score 5 or less if they were perfectly calibrated. If we take the average score for all members of the class and assume the distribution of scores to be approximately binomial, we can estimate the real probability encompassed by their minimum to maximum range. The mean of a binomial distribution is np, where n is the number of trials (in this case, 8) and p is the probability of success (here, the probability of falling between the minima and maxima). The average individual score for the whole class is usually around 3, giving a probability p of $\frac{3}{8} = 37.5\,\%$. In other words, where they were providing a minimum and maximum for which they believed there was a 90 % chance of the quantity falling between those values, there was in fact only about a 37 % chance. One reason for this "overconfidence" (i.e. the estimated uncertainty is much smaller than the real uncertainty) is anchoring, discussed in Section 14.2.2. Figure 14.3 shows the distribution for the largest class for which I have run this exercise (and the only class for which I kept the results).

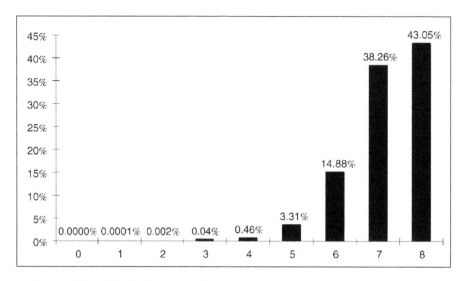

Figure 14.2 Binomial(8, 90 %) distribution for forecasting test scores.

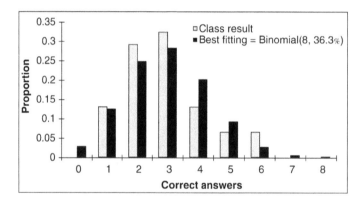

Figure 14.3 Example of scores produced by a large class in the estimating exercise.

- The estimators often confuse the units (e.g. miles instead of kilometres, kilograms instead of tonnes), resulting in a gross error.
- In estimating the population of Scranton, some estimators provide a huge maximum estimate. Since most people have never heard of Scranton, it makes sense that it has a smaller population than London, New York, etc., but some people ignore this obvious deduction and offer a maximum that has no logical basis (their estimation is strongly affected by the fact that they have never heard of Scranton rather than any logic they could apply to the problem).
- When the class discusses the quantities, they can usually agree on a logic for their estimation.
- If estimators are very sure of their quantity, they may nonetheless provide an unrealistically large range given their knowledge ("better to be safe") or, more commonly, provide just slightly too narrow a range (resulting in a protest when I don't award them a correct answer!). I once asked a

class in New Zealand to estimate the area of their country. A gentleman from their Met Office asked if that was at low or high tide, to the amusement of us all. He knew the answer precisely, but the true value fell outside his range because he had not known the precise conversion factor between acres and square kilometres and had made insufficient allowance for that uncertainty.

- If offered the choice of a revision to their estimates after I have drawn them all on the board, those that change will usually gravitate to any grouping of the others' estimates or to the estimate of an individual in the group whose opinion is highly valued. These actions often do not get them closer to the correct answer. This observation has encouraged me to avoid asking for distribution estimates *during* brainstorming sessions (see Section 14.4).

- In many cases, people who have given a vast range to their estimates (to howls of laughter from the others) are the only ones to get it inside their range.

- People attending my seminars are almost always computer literate, but it is surprising how many have little feel for numbers and offer estimates that could not possibly be correct.

- Faced with a quantity that seems impossible to quantify at first, the estimator can often arrive at a reasonable estimate by being encouraged to either break the quantity down into smaller components or to make a comparison with other quantities. For example, the mass of the Earth could be estimated by first estimating the average density of rock and then multiplying it by an estimate of the volume of the Earth (requiring an estimate of its radius or circumference). Occasionally, this method has come up with some huge errors where the estimator has confused formulae for the volume of a sphere with area, etc.

- Very occasionally, individuals lacking confidence will refuse to read out their opinions to the class.

- Sometimes, estimators will provide a set of answers without really understanding the quantity they are estimating (e.g. not knowing that K2 is a mountain, the second highest in the world). Note that the person in question did not seek clarification, even after being encouraged to do so. This "shyness" seems to be much more common in some nationalities than others.

This exercise can legitimately be criticised on several points:

1. The class members are asked to estimate quantities that they have no real knowledge of and their score is therefore not reflective of their ability to estimate quantities that would be required of them in their work.

2. In most real-life problems, the quantity being estimated does not have a fixed known value but is itself uncertain.

3. In real-life problems, if the estimator has provided a range that was small but just missed the true value, that estimate would still be more useful than another estimate with a much wider range but that included the true value.

4. In real-life problems, estimators would presumably check formulae and conversion factors that they were unsure of.

The scores should not be taken very seriously (I don't keep a record of the results). The exercise is simply a good way to highlight some of the issues concerned in estimating. A more realistic exercise would be to compare probabilistic estimates from an expert for real problems with the values that were eventually observed. Of course, such an exercise could take many months or years to complete.

Class estimating exercise 2

The class is grouped in pairs and asked to give the same three-point estimate, as used for the above exercise, of the total weight (mass) of the members of the class in kilograms, including myself, and our total height in metres. While they are estimating, I go round the class and ask each member quietly for their own measurements. At the end of the exercise, I draw up the estimates as in Figure 14.1 and superimpose the true value. Then we discuss how each group produced its estimates. The following points generally come out:

- Three estimating techniques are usually used by the class:
  1. Produce a three-point estimate of the distributions of height and mass for individuals in the class and multiply by the number of people in the class. This logic is incorrect since it ignores the central limit theorem, which states that the spread of the sum of a set of n variables is proportional to $\sqrt{n}$, not n. It generally manages to encompass the true result but with a very wide (and therefore inaccurate) range.
  2. Produce a three-point estimate of each individual in the class and add up the minima to get the final-estimate minimum, add up the most likely values to get the final-estimate most likely and add up the maxima to get the final-estimate maximum. Again, this is incorrect since it ignores the central limit theorem and therefore produces too wide a range.
  3. Produce a three-point estimate of each individual in the class and then run a simulation to add them up. Take the 5%, mode and 95% values of the simulation result as the final three-point estimate. This generally has the narrowest range but is still *quite* likely to encompass the true value.
- There is often a dominant person in a pair who takes over the whole estimating, either because that person is very enthusiastic or more familiar with the software or because the other person is a bit laid back or quiet. This, of course, loses the value of being in pairs.
- The estimators often forget to exclude themselves from their uncertainty estimates. They have given me their measurements, so they should only assign uncertainty to the others' measurements and then add their measurements to the total.

If the central limit theorem corrections are applied to the violating estimates, the class scores average out at about 1.4 compared with the 1.8 it should have been (i.e. 2 * 90%). In other words, their minimum to maximum range, which was supposed to have a 90% probability of including the true value, actually had about a 70% probability.

14.2.2 Common heuristic biases and errors

The analyst should bear in mind the following heuristics that the expert may employ when attempting to provide subjective estimates and that are potential sources of systematic bias and errors. These biases are explained in considerably more detail in Hertz and Thomas (1983) and in Morgan and Henrion (1990) (the latter includes a very comprehensive list of references).

Availability

This is where experts use their recollection of past occurrences of an event to provide an estimate. The accuracy of their estimates is dictated by their ability to remember past occurrences of the event or how easily they can imagine the event occurring. This may work very well if the event is a regular part of their life, e.g. how much they spend on petrol. It also works well if the event is something that sticks in their mind, e.g. the probability of having a flat tyre. On the other hand, it can produce poor estimates if it is difficult for the experts to remember past occurrences of the event: for example, they may not be able confidently to estimate the number of people they passed in the street that day since they would have no interest in noting each passer-by. Availability can produce overestimates of frequency if the experts can remember past occurrences very clearly because of the impact they had on them. For example, if a computer manager was asked how often her mainframe had crashed in the last two years, she might well overestimate the frequency because she could remember every crash and the crises they caused, but, because of the clarity of her recollection ("it seems like only yesterday"), include some crashes that happened well over 2 years ago and therefore overestimate the frequency as a result.

The availability heuristic is also affected by the degree to which we are exposed to information. For example: one might consider that the chance of dying in a motoring accident was much higher than dying from stomach cancer, because car crashes are always being reported in the media and stomach cancer fatalities are not. On the other hand, an older person may have had several acquaintances who have died from stomach cancer and would therefore offer the reverse opinion.

Representativeness

One type of bias is the erroneous belief that the large-scale nature of uncertainty is reflected in small-scale sampling. For example, in the National Lottery, many would say I had no chance of winning if I selected the consecutive numbers 16, 17, 18, 19, 20 and 21. The lottery numbers are randomly picked each week so it is believed that the winning numbers should also exhibit a random pattern, e.g. 3, 11, 15, 21, 29 and 41. Of course, both sets of numbers are actually equally likely.

I once reviewed a paper that noted that, out of 200 houses fitted with a new type of gas supply piping and tested over a period of a year and a half, one of those houses suffered a gas leak due to a rat gnawing through the pipe. It concluded that there was a 1:300 chance of a "rodent attack" per house per year. What should the answer have been?

A second type of representativeness bias is where people concentrate on an enticing detail of the problem and forget the overall picture. In a frequently cited paper by Kahneman and Tversky, described in Morgan and Henrion (1990), subjects in an experiment were asked to determine the probability of a person being an engineer on the basis of a written description of that person. If they were given a bland description that gave no clue to the person's profession, the answer given was usually 50:50, despite being told beforehand that, of the 100 described people, 70 were lawyers and 30 were engineers. However, when the subjects were asked what probability they would give if they had no description of the person, they said 30%, illustrating that they understood how to use the information but had just ignored it.

Adjustment and anchoring

This is probably the most important heuristic of the three. Individuals will usually begin their estimate of the distribution of uncertainty of a variable with a single value (usually the most likely value) and then make adjustments for its minimum and maximum from that first value. The problem is that these adjustments are rarely sufficient to encompass the range of values that could actually occur: the estimators appear to be "anchored" to their first estimated value. This is certainly one source of *overconfidence* and can have a dramatic impact on the validity of a risk analysis model.

14.2.3 Other sources of estimating inaccuracy

There are other elements that may affect the correct assessment of uncertainty, and the analyst should be aware of them in order to avoid unnecessary errors.

Inexpert expert

The person nominated (wrongly) as being able to provide the most knowledgeable opinion occasionally actually has very little idea. Rather than referring the analyst on to another more expert in the problem, that person may try to provide an opinion "to be helpful", even though that opinion is of little real value. The analyst, seeing the inexpertness of the interviewee, should seek an alternative opinion, although this may not be apparent until later.

Culture of the organisation

The environment within which people work may sometimes impact on their estimating. Sales people will often provide unduly optimistic estimates of future sales because of the optimistic culture within which they work. Managers may offer high estimates of running costs because, if they achieve a lower operating cost, their organisation will view them favourably. The analyst should try to be aware of any potential conflict and seek to eliminate it through cross-checking with data and other people in the organisation.

Conflicting agendas

Sometimes the expert will have a vested interest in the values that are submitted to a model. In one model I developed, managers were deliberately providing hugely optimistic growth rate predictions to me because, in the organisation they worked for, it could aid their individual empire building. In another, I was offered very optimistic estimates of completion time and costs for a project because, if that project were given approval, the person in question would become the project's manager with a big wage increase to match. Lawyers may offer a low estimate of the cost of litigation because, if they get the brief, they can usually increase the fees later. The analyst must be aware of such conflicting agendas and seek a second disinterested opinion.

Unwillingness to consider extremes

The expert will frequently find it difficult or be unwilling to envisage circumstances that would cause a variable to be extremely low or high. The analyst will often have to encourage the development of such extreme scenarios in order to elicit an opinion that realistically covers the entire possible range. This can be done by the analyst dreaming up some examples of extreme circumstances and discussing them with the expert.

Eagerness to say the right thing

Occasionally, interviewees will be trying to provide the answer they think the analyst wants to hear. For this reason, it is important not to ask questions that are leading and never to offer a value for the expert to comment on. For example, if I said "How long do you think this task will take? Twelve weeks? More? Less?" I could well get an answer nearer to 12 weeks than if I had simply said "How long do you think this task will take?".

Units used in the estimation

People are frequently confused between the magnitudes of units of measurement. An older (or English) person may be used to thinking of distances in miles and liquid volumes in (UK) gallons and pints. If the model uses SI units, the analyst should let the experts describe their estimates in the units in which they are comfortable and convert the figures afterwards.

Expert too busy

People always seem to be busy and under pressure. A risk analyst coming to ask a lot of difficult questions may not be very welcome. The expert may act brusquely or give the whole process lip service. Obvious symptoms are when the expert offers oversimplistic estimates like $X \pm Y\%$ or minimum, most likely and maximum values that are equally spaced for all estimated variables. The solution to such problems is to get the top management visibly to support the development of the risk model, ensuring that the employees are given the message that this work is a priority.

Belief that the expert should be quite certain

It may be perceived by experts that assigning a large uncertainty to a parameter would indicate a lack of knowledge and thereby undermine their reputation. The expert may need to be reassured that this is not the case. An expert should have a more precise understanding of a parameter's true uncertainty and may, in fact, appreciate that the uncertainty could be greater than the layperson would have expected.

14.3 Modelling Techniques

This section describes a range of techniques including the role of various types of probability distribution that are useful in the eliciting of expert opinion. I have only included those techniques that have worked for me, so the reader will find some omissions when comparing with other risk analysis texts.

14.3.1 Disaggregation

A key technique to eliciting distributions of opinion is to disaggregate the problem sufficiently well so that experts can concentrate on estimating something that is tangible and easy to envisage. For example, it will generally be more useful to ask experts to break down their company's revenue into logical components (like region, product, subsidiary company, etc.) rather than to estimate the total revenue in one go. Disaggregation allows the expert and analyst to recognise dependencies between components of the total revenue. It also means that the risk analysis result will be less critically dependent on the estimate of each model component. Aggregating the estimates of the various revenue components will show a more complex and accurate distribution than ever could have been achieved by directly estimating the sum. The aggregation will also take care of the effects of the central limit theorem automatically – something that is extremely hard for experts to do in their head. Another benefit of disaggregation is that the logic of the problem usually becomes more apparent and the model therefore becomes more realistic.

During the disaggregation process, analysts should be aware of where the key uncertainties lie within their model and therefore where they should place their emphasis. The analyst can check whether an appropriate level of disaggregation has been achieved by running a sensitivity analysis on the model (see Section 5.3.7) and looking to see whether the Tornado chart is dominated by one or two model inputs.

14.3.2 Distributions used in modelling expert opinion

This section describes the role of various types of probability distribution in modelling expert opinion.

Non-parametric and parametric distributions

Probability distribution functions fall into two categories: non-parametric and parametric distributions, the meanings of which are discussed in detail in Appendix III.3. A parametric distribution is based on a mathematical function whose shape and range is determined by one or more distribution parameters. These parameters often have little obvious or intuitive relationship to the distribution shapes they define. Examples of parametric distributions are: lognormal, normal, beta, Weibull, Pareto, loglogistic, hypergeometric – most distribution types, in fact.

Non-parametric distributions, on the other hand, have their shape and range determined by their parameters directly in an obvious and intuitive way. Their distribution function is simply a mathematical description of their shape. Non-parametric distributions are: uniform, relative, triangular, cumulative and discrete.

As a rule, non-parametric distributions are far more reliable and flexible for modelling expert opinion about a model parameter. The questions that the analyst poses to the expert to determine the distribution's parameters are intuitive and easy to respond to. Changes to these parameters also produce an easily predicted change in the distribution's shape and range. The application of each non-parametric distribution type to modelling expert opinion is discussed below.

There are three common exceptions to the above preference for using non-parametric distributions to model expert opinion:

2. The PERT distribution is frequently used to model an expert's opinion. Although it is, strictly speaking, a parametric distribution, it has been adapted so that the expert need only provide estimates of the minimum, most likely and maximum values for the variable, and the PERT function finds a shape that fits these restrictions. The PERT distribution is explained more fully below.

3. The expert may occasionally be very familiar with using the parameters that define the particular distribution. For example, a toxicologist may regularly determine the mean standard error of a chemical concentration in a set of samples. It might be quite helpful to ask the expert for the mean and standard deviation of his/her uncertainty about some concentration in this case.

4. The parameters of a parametric distribution *are* sometimes intuitive and the analyst can therefore ask for their estimation directly. For example, a binomial distribution is defined by n, the number of trials that will be conducted, and p, the probability of success of each trial. In cases where I consider the binomial distribution to be the most appropriate, I generally ask the expert for estimates of n and p, recognising that I will have to insert them into a binomial distribution, but I would try to avoid any discussion of the binomial distribution that might cause confusion. Note that the estimates of n and p can also be distributions themselves.

There are other problems associated with using parametric distributions for modelling expert opinion:

● A model that includes parametric distributions to represent opinion is more difficult to review later because the parameters of the distribution may have no intuitive appeal.

● It is very difficult to get the precise shape right when using parametric distributions to model expert opinion as the effects of changes in the parameters are not usually obvious.

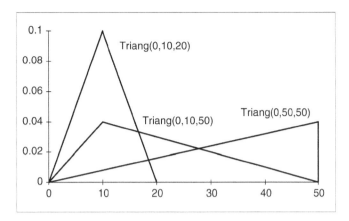

Figure 14.4 Examples of triangular distributions.

The triangular distribution

The triangular distribution is the most commonly used distribution for modelling expert opinion. It is defined by its minimum (a), most likely (b) and maximum (c) values. Figure 14.4 shows three triangular distributions: Triangle(0, 10, 20), Triangle(0, 10, 50) and Triangle(0, 50, 50), which are symmetric, right skewed and left skewed respectively. The triangular distribution has a very obvious appeal because it is so easy to think about the three defining parameters and to envisage the effect of any changes.

The mean and standard deviation of the triangular distribution are determined from its three parameters:

$$\text{Mean} = \frac{(a + b + c)}{3}$$

$$\text{Standard deviation} = \sqrt{\frac{(a^2 + b^2 + c^2 - ab - ac - bc)}{18}}$$

From these formulae it can be seen that the mean and standard deviation are equally sensitive to all three parameters. Many models involve parameters for which it is fairly easy to estimate the minimum and most likely values, but for which the maximum is almost unbounded and could be enormous.

The central limit theorem tells us that, when adding up a large number of distributions (for example, adding costs or task durations), it is the distributions' means and standard deviations that are most important because they determine the mean and standard deviation of the risk analysis result. In situations where the maximum is so difficult to determine, the triangular distribution is not usually appropriate since it will depend a great deal on how the estimation of the maximum is approached. For example, if the maximum is assumed to be the absolutely largest possible value, the risk analysis output will have a far larger mean and standard deviation than if the maximum is assumed to be a "practical" maximum by the estimating experts.

The triangular distribution is often considered to be appropriate where little is known about the parameter outside an approximate estimate of its minimum, most likely and maximum values. On the other hand, its sharp, very localised peak and straight lines produce a very definite and unusual (and very unnatural) shape, which conflicts with the assumption of little knowledge of the parameter.

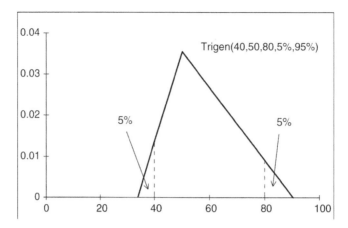

Figure 14.5 Example of a Trigen distribution.

There is another useful variation of the triangular distribution, called Trigen in @RISK and TriangGen in Risk Solver, for example. The Trigen distribution requires five parameters: Trigen(a, b, c, p, q), which have the following meanings:

> a : the practical minimum
>
> b : the most likely value
>
> c : the practical maximum value
>
> p : the probability that the parameter value could be below a
>
> q : the probability that the parameter value could be below c

Figure 14.5 shows a Trigen(40, 50, 80, 5%, 95%) distribution, with the 5% areas extending beyond the minimum and maximum (40 and 80 here). The Trigen distribution is a useful way of avoiding asking experts for their estimate of the absolute minimum and maximum of a parameter: questions that experts often have difficulty in answering meaningfully since there may theoretically be no minimum or maximum. Instead, the analyst can discuss what values of p and q the experts would use to define "practical" minima and maxima respectively. Once this has been decided, the experts only have to give their estimates for practical minimum, most likely and practical maximum for each estimated parameter, and the same p and q estimates are used for all their estimates. One drawback is that the expert may not appreciate the final range to which the distribution may extend, so it is wise to plot the distribution and have it agreed by the expert before using it in the model.

The Tri1090 distribution, featured in @RISK, presumes that p and q are 10 and 90% respectively, which is generally about right, but I prefer to use the Trigen because it adapts to each expert's concept of "practical".

The uniform distribution

The uniform distribution is generally a very poor modeller of expert opinion since all values within its range have equal probability density, but that density falls sharply to zero at the minimum and maximum in an unnatural way. The uniform distribution obeys the maximum entropy formalism (see Section 9.4) where only the minimum and maximum are known, but in my experience it is rare indeed that the expert will be able to define the minimum and maximum but have no opinion to offer on a most likely value.

The uniform distribution does, however, have several uses:

- to highlight or exaggerate the fact that little is known about the parameter;
- to model circular variables (like the direction of wind from 0 to 2π) and other specific problems;
- to produce spider sensitivity plots (see Section 5.3.8).

The PERT distribution

The PERT distribution gets its name because it uses the same assumption about the mean (see below) as PERT networks (used in the past for project planning). It is a version of the beta distribution and requires the same three parameters as the triangular distribution, namely minimum (a), most likely (b) and maximum (c). Figure 14.6 shows three PERT distributions whose shape can be compared with the triangular distributions of Figure 14.4. The equation of a PERT distribution is related to the beta distribution as follows:

$$\text{PERT}(a, b, c) = \text{Beta}(\alpha_1, \alpha_2) \; ^* \; (c - a) + a$$

where

$$\alpha_1 = \frac{(\mu - a) \; ^* \; (2b - a - c)}{(b - \mu) \; ^* \; (c - a)}$$

$$\alpha_2 = \frac{\alpha_1 \; ^* \; (c - \mu)}{(\mu - a)}$$

$$\text{The mean } (\mu) = \frac{a + 4 \; ^* \; b + c}{6}$$

The last equation for the mean is a restriction that is assumed in order to be able to determine values for α_1 and α_2. It also shows how the mean for the PERT distribution is 4 times more sensitive to

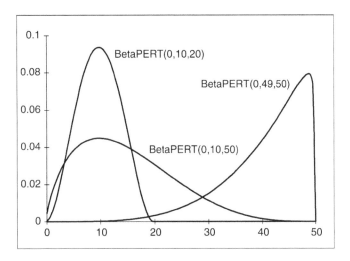

Figure 14.6 Examples of PERT distributions.

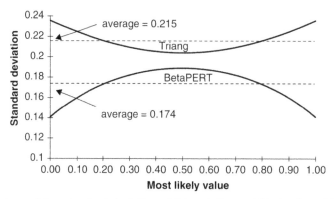

Figure 14.7 Comparison of the standard deviation of Triangle(0, most likely, 1) and PERT(0, most likely, 1) distributions.

the most likely value than to the minimum and maximum values. This should be compared with the triangular distribution where the mean is equally sensitive to each parameter. The PERT distribution therefore does not suffer to the same extent the potential systematic bias problems of the triangular distribution, that is, in producing too great a value for the mean of the risk analysis results where the maximum for the distribution is very large.

The standard deviation of a PERT distribution is also less sensitive to the estimate of the extremes. Although the equation for the PERT standard deviation is rather complex, the point can be illustrated very well graphically. Figure 14.7 compares the standard deviations of triangular and PERT distributions that have the same a, b and c values. To illustrate the point, the figure uses values of 0 and 1 for a and c respectively and allows b to vary between 0 and 1, although the observed pattern extends to any $\{a, b, c\}$ set of values. You can see that the PERT distribution produces a systematically lower standard deviation than the triangular distribution, particularly where the distribution is highly skewed (i.e. b is close to 0 or 1 in this case). As a general rough rule of thumb, cost and duration distributions for project tasks often have a ratio of about 2:1 between the (maximum–most likely) and (most likely–minimum), equivalent to $b = 0.3333$ in Figure 14.7. The standard deviation of the PERT distribution at this point is about 88 % of that for the triangular distribution. This implies that using PERT distributions throughout a cost or schedule model, or any other additive model, will display about 10 % less uncertainty than the equivalent model using triangular distributions.

Some readers would perhaps argue that the increased uncertainty that occurs with triangular distributions will compensate to some degree for the "overconfidence" that is often apparent in subjective estimating. The argument is quite appealing at first sight but is not conducive to the long-term improvement of the organisation's ability to estimate. I would rather see an expert's opinion modelled as precisely as is practical. Then, if the expert is consistently overconfident, this will become apparent with time and his/her estimating can be corrected.

The modified PERT distribution

The PERT distribution can also be manipulated to produce shapes with varying degrees of uncertainty for the same minimum, most likely and maximum by changing the assumption about the mean:

$$\text{The mean } (\mu) = \frac{a + \gamma * b + c}{\gamma + 2}$$

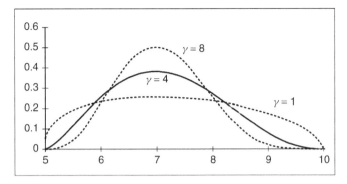

Figure 14.8 Examples of modified PERT distributions with varying most likely weighting γ.

In the standard PERT, $\gamma = 4$, which is the PERT network assumption that $\mu = (a + 4b + c)/6$. However, if we increase the value of γ, the distribution becomes progressively more peaked and concentrated around b (and therefore less uncertain). Conversely, if we decrease γ, the distribution becomes flatter and more uncertain. Figure 14.8 illustrates the effect of three different values of γ for a modified PERT(5, 7, 10) distribution. This modified PERT distribution can be very useful in modelling expert opinion. The expert is asked to estimate the same three values as before (i.e. minimum, most likely and maximum). Then a set of modified PERT distributions is plotted and the expert is asked to select the shape that fits his/her opinion most accurately. It is a fairly simple matter to set up a spreadsheet program that will do all this automatically.

The relative distribution

The relative distribution (also called the general in @RISK, and a version of the Custom in Crystal Ball) is the most flexible of all of the continuous distribution functions. It enables the analyst and expert to tailor the shape of the distribution to reflect, as closely as possible, the opinion of the expert. The relative distribution has the form Relative(minimum, maximum$\{x_i\}$, $\{p_i\}$), where $\{x_i\}$ is an array of x values with probability densities $\{p_i\}$ and where the distribution falls between the minimum and maximum. The $\{p_i\}$ values are not constrained to give an area under the curve of 1, since the software recalibrates the probability scale. Figure 14.9 shows a Relative(4, 15, $\{7, 9, 11\}$, $\{2, 3, 0.5\}$).

The cumulative distribution

The cumulative distribution has the form CumulativeA(minimum, maximum$\{x_i\}$, $\{P_i\}$), where $\{x_i\}$ is an array of x values with cumulative probabilities $\{P_i\}$ and where the distribution falls between the minimum and maximum. Figure 14.10 shows the distribution CumulativeA(0, 10, $\{1, 4, 6\}$, $\{0.1, 0.6, 0.8\}$) as it is defined in its cumulative form and how it looks as a relative frequency plot. The cumulative distribution is used in some texts to model expert opinion. However, I have found it largely unsatisfactory because of the insensitivity of its probability scale. A small change in the shape of the cumulative distribution that would pass unnoticed produces a radical change in the corresponding relative frequency plot that would not be acceptable. Figure 14.11 provides an illustration: a smooth and natural relative frequency plot (A) is converted to a cumulative frequency plot (B) and then altered slightly (C). Converting back to a relative frequency plot (D) shows that the modified distribution is dramatically different to the original, although this would almost certainly not have been appreciated by comparing the cumulative

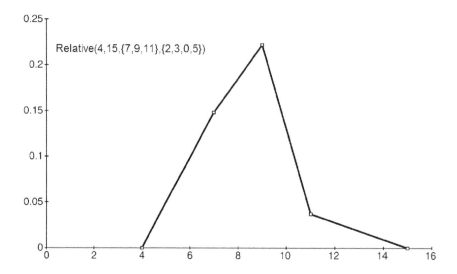

Figure 14.9   Example of a relative distribution.

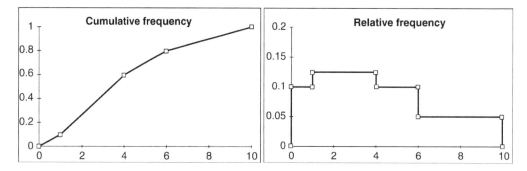

Figure 14.10   Example of a cumulative distribution and its relative frequency plot.

frequency plots. For this reason, I usually prefer to model expert opinion looking at the relative frequency distribution instead.

One circumstance where the cumulative distribution *is* very useful is in attempting to estimate a variable whose range covers several orders of magnitude. For example, the number of bacteria in 1 kg of meat will increase exponentially with time. The meat may contain 100 units of bacteria or 1 million. In such circumstances, it is fruitless to attempt to use a relative distribution directly. This point is discussed more fully in Section 14.3.3.

The discrete distribution

The discrete distribution has the form Discrete($\{x_i\}$, $\{p_i\}$), where $\{x_i\}$ is an array of the possible values of the variable with probability weightings $\{p_i\}$. The $\{p_i\}$ values do not have to add up to unity as the software will normalise them automatically. It is actually often useful just to consider the ratio of likelihood of the different values and not to worry about the actual probability values. The discrete

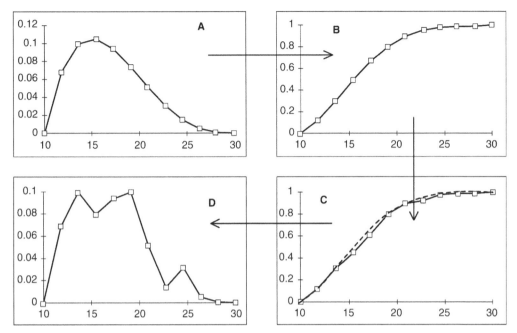

Figure 14.11 Example of how small changes in a distribution's cumulative plot can dramatically affect its shape.

distribution can be used to model a discrete parameter (that is, a parameter that may take one of two or more distinct values), e.g. the number of turbines that will be used in a power station, and to combine two or more conflicting expert opinions (see Section 14.3.4).

14.3.3 Modelling opinion of a variable that covers several orders of magnitude

A continuous parameter whose uncertainty extends over several orders of magnitude generally cannot be modelled in the usual manner. For example, an expert may consider that 1 g of meat could contain any number of units of bacteria from 1 to 10 000 but that this figure is just as likely to be around 100 or 1000. If we were to model this estimate using a Uniform(1, 10 000) distribution, for example, we would almost certainly not match the expert's opinion of the values of the cumulative percentiles. The expert would probably place the 25, 50 and 75 percentiles at about 10, 100 and 1000, where our model places them at 2500, 5000 and 7500 respectively. The reason for such a large discrepancy is that the expert is subconsciously making his/her estimate in log-space, i.e. s/he is thinking of the $\log_{10}$ values: $\log_{10} 1 = 0$, $\log_{10} 10 = 1$, $\log_{10} 100 = 2$, etc. To match the expert's approach to estimating, the analyst can also work in log-space, so the distribution becomes

$$\text{Number of units of bacteria} = 10^{\text{Uniform}(0,4)}$$

Figure 14.12 compares these two interpretations of the expert opinion by looking at the cumulative distributions and statistics they would produce. The Uniform(1, 10 000) has much larger mean and standard deviation than the $10^{\text{Uniform}(0,4)}$ distribution and an entirely different shape.

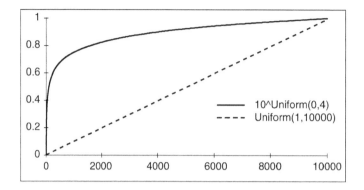

	Uniform(1,10000)	10^Uniform(0,4)
Mean =	5000.5	1085
Std Deviation =	2886	2062
Skewness =	0	2.4
Kurtosis =	1.8	5.2

Figure 14.12   Comparison of two ways to model expert opinion of a variable that covers several orders of magnitude.

If the expert had said instead that there could be between 1 and 10 000 units of bacteria in 1 g of meat, but the most likely number is around 500, we would probably have the greatest success in modelling this variable as

$$\text{Number of units of bacteria} = 10^{\text{PERT}(0, 2.7, 4)}$$

where $\log_{10} 500 = 2.7$.

If the variable is to be modelled as a 10^x type formula described above, it is judicious to compare the cumulative percentiles at a few sensible points with those the expert would expect. Any radical differences would suggest that the expert is not actually thinking in log-space and the cumulative distribution could be used instead.

14.3.4 Incorporating differences in expert opinions

Experts will sometimes produce profoundly different probability distribution estimates of a parameter. This is usually because the experts have estimated different things, made differing assumptions or have different sets of information on which to base their opinion. However, occasionally two or more experts simply genuinely disagree. How should the analyst approach the problem? The first step is usually to confer with someone more senior and find out whether one expert is preferred over the other. If those more senior have some confidence in both opinions, a method is needed to combine these opinions in some way.

Recommended approach

I have used the following method for a number of years with good results. Use a Discrete($\{x_i\}$, $\{p_i\}$) distribution where the $\{x_i\}$ are the expert opinions and the $\{p_i\}$ are the weights given to each opinion according to the emphasis one wishes to place on them. Figure 14.13 illustrates an example combining

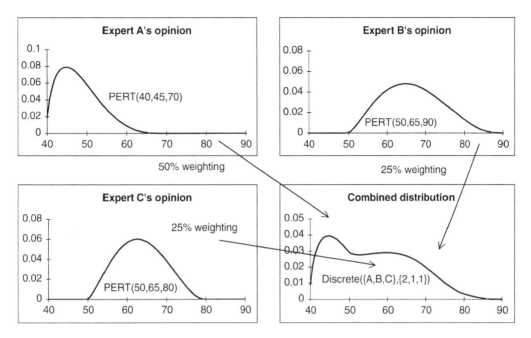

Figure 14.13 Combining three dissimilar expert opinions.

three differing opinions, but where expert A is given twice the emphasis of the others owing to the greater experience of that expert.

Two incorrect approaches are frequently used:

- *Pick the most pessimistic estimate.* This is generally unsatisfactory, as a risk analysis model should be attempting to produce an unbiased estimate of the uncertainty. The caution should only be applied at the decision-making stage after reviewing the risk analysis results.

- *Take the average of the two distributions.* This is incorrect as the resultant distribution will be too narrow. By way of illustration, consider the test situation where both experts believed a parameter should be modelled by a Normal(100, 10) distribution. Whatever technique was used to combine their opinions, the result should be the same Normal(100, 10) distribution. The average of these two distributions, i.e. AVERAGE(Normal(100, 10), Normal(100, 10)), would be a Normal(100, $10/\sqrt{2}$) = Normal(100, 7.07) from the central limit theorem. In other words, we would have produced far too small a spread.

I have been offered suggestions for other approaches to this problem:

- *Take the weighted average of the relative or cumulative percentiles.* This will correctly construct the combined distribution (it is how the ModelRisk function VoseCombined works) but it is very laborious to execute for all but the most simple distributions of opinion unless you have a library of density and cdf functions, so it is somewhat impractical to start from scratch.

- *Multiply together the probability densities at each x value.* This is incorrect because (a) it produces combined distributions with exaggerated peakedness, (b) the area under the curve is no longer 1 and (c) the combined distribution is contained between the highest minimum and the lowest maximum.

	A	B	C	D	E	F	G	H
1								
2		**SME**	**Min**	**Mode**	**Max**	**Distribution**	**Weight**	
3		Peter	11	13	17	VosePERT($C$3,$D$3,$E$3)	0.3	
4		Jane	12	13	16	VosePERT($C$4,$D$4,$E$4)	0.2	
5		Paul	8	10	13	VosePERT($C$5,$D$5,$E$5)	0.4	
6		Susan	9	10	15	VosePERT($C$6,$D$6,$E$6)	0.1	
7								
8			Combined estimate		8.680244			
9			P(>14)		0.878805			
10								
11					*Formulae table*			
12		F3:F6	=VosePERTObject(C3,D3,E3)					
13		E8 (output)	=VoseCombined(F3:F6,G3:G6,B3:B6)					
14		E9 (output)	=VoseCombinedProb(14,F3:F6,G3:G6,B3:B6,1)					
15								

Figure 14.14 Combining weighted SME estimates using VoseCombined functions.

ModelRisk has the function VoseCombined({Distributions}, {Weights}) and related probability calculation functions that perform the combination described above. In the model in Figure 14.14, four expert estimates are combined to construct the one estimate. The advantage of this function is it then allows one to perform a sensitivity analysis on the estimate as a whole: if you were to use the Discrete({Distributions}, {Weights}) method, your Monte Carlo software would, in this case, be performing a sensitivity analysis of five distributions: the four estimates and the discrete distribution, which will dilute the perceived influence of the combined uncertainty.

In the model in Figure 14.4, the VoseCombined function generates random values from a distribution constructed by weighting the four SME estimates. The weights do not need to sum to 1: they will be normalised. The VoseCombinedProb(..., 1) function calculates the probability that this distribution will take a value less than 14. Note that the names of the experts is an optional parameter: this simply records who said what and has no effect on the calculation, but select cell E8 and then click the *Vf* (View Function) icon from the ModelRisk toolbar and you will get the graph shown in Figure 14.15, which allows us to compare each SME's estimate and see how they are weighted.

14.4 Calibrating Subject Matter Experts

When subject matter experts (SMEs) are first asked to provide probabilistic estimates, they usually won't be particularly good at it because it is a new way of thinking. We need some techniques that allow us to help the SMEs gauge how well they are estimating and, over time, correct any biases they have. We may also need a method for selecting between or weighting SMEs estimates.

Imagine that an SME has estimated that a bespoke generator being placed on a ship will cost $PERT(1.2, 1.35, 1.9) million, and we compare the actual outturn costs against that estimate. Let's say it ended up costing $1.83 million. Did the SME provide a good estimate? Well, it fell within the range provided, which is a good start, but it was at the high end, as Figure 14.16 shows.

The 1.83 value fell at the 99.97th percentile of the PERT distribution. That seems rather high considering the SME's estimate lay from 1.2 to 1.9 and 1.83 is only 90 % along that range, but it is the result of how the PERT distribution interprets the minimum, mode and maximum values. The distribution is

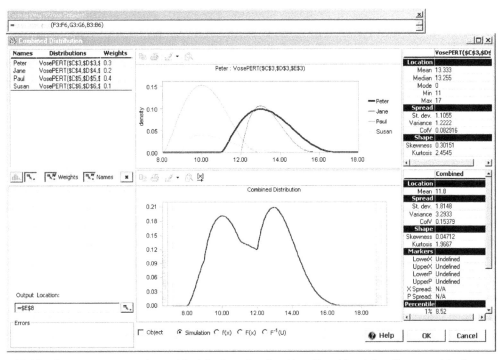

Figure 14.15 Screen capture of graphic interface for the VoseCombined function used in the model of Figure 14.14.

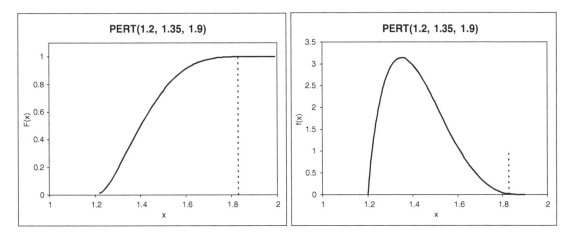

Figure 14.16 An SME estimate.

quite right skewed, in which case the PERT has a thin right tail – in fact it assigns only a 1 % probability to values larger than 1.73.

For this exercise, however, we'll assume that the SME had seen the plots above and was comfortable with the estimate. We can't be certain with just one data point that the SME tends to underestimate. In areas like engineering, capital investment and project planning, one SME will often provide many estimates over time, so let's imagine we repeat the exercise some 10 times and determine the percentile at which each outturn cost lies on each corresponding distribution estimate. In theory, if our SME was perfectly calibrated, these would be random samples from a Uniform(0, 1) distribution, so the mean should rapidly approach 0.5. A Uniform(0, 1) distribution has a variance of 1/12, so the mean of 10 samples from a perfectly calibrated SME should, from central limit theorem, fall on a Normal(0.5, 1/SQRT(12 * 10)) = Normal(0.5, 0.091287). If the 10 values average to 0.7, we can be pretty sure that the SME is overestimating, since there is only a $(1 - \text{NORMDIST}(0.7, 0.5, 0.091287, 1)) = 1.4\%$ chance a perfectly calibrated SME would have produced a value of 0.7 or larger. Similarly, we can analyse the variance of the 10 values. It should be close to 1/12: if the variance is smaller then the SME's distributions are too wide, or, as is more likely, if the variance is larger then the SME's distributions are too narrow. The above analysis assumes, of course, that all the estimates actually fell within the SME's distribution range, which may well not be the case. The plots in Figure 14.17 can help provide a more comprehensive picture.

Experts are also sometimes asked to estimate the probability that an event will occur, which is no easy task. In theory one can roughly estimate how good a SME is at providing these estimates by grouping estimated probabilities into bands (e.g. the same bands as in Figure 14.17) and determining what fraction of those risk events actually occurred. Obviously, around 15% of risks that were thought to have between 10% and 20% chance of occurring should actually occur. However, this breaks down at the lowest and highest categories because many identified potential risks are perceived to have a very small probability of occurrence, so we will almost never actually have any observations.

14.5 Conducting a Brainstorming Session

When the initial structure of the problem has been decided and subjective estimates of the key uncertainties are now required, it is often very useful to conduct one or more *brainstorming sessions* with several experts in the area of the problem being analysed. If the model covers several different disciplines, for example engineering, production, marketing and finance, it may be better to hold a brainstorming session for each discipline group as well as one for everybody.

The objectives of the brainstorming session are to ensure that everyone has the same information pertinent to the problem and then to debate the uncertainties of the problem. In some risk analysis texts, the analyst is encouraged to determine a distribution of each uncertain parameter during these meetings. I have tried this approach and find it very difficult to do well because it relies very heavily on controlling the group's dynamics: ensuring that the loudest voice does not get all the air time; encouraging the individuals to express their own opinion rather than following the leader, etc. These meetings can also end up dragging on, and some of the experts may have to leave before the end of the session, reducing its effectiveness.

My aim in brainstorming sessions is to ensure that all those attending leave with a common perception of the risks and uncertainties of the problem. This is achieved by doing the following:

- Gathering all relevant information and circulating it to the attending experts prior to the meeting. Presenting data in easily digested forms, e.g. using scatter plots, trend charts, statistics and histograms wherever possible rather than columns of figures.
- At the meeting, encouraging discussion of the variability and uncertainty in the problem, including the logical structure and any correlations. Discussing scenarios that would produce extreme values

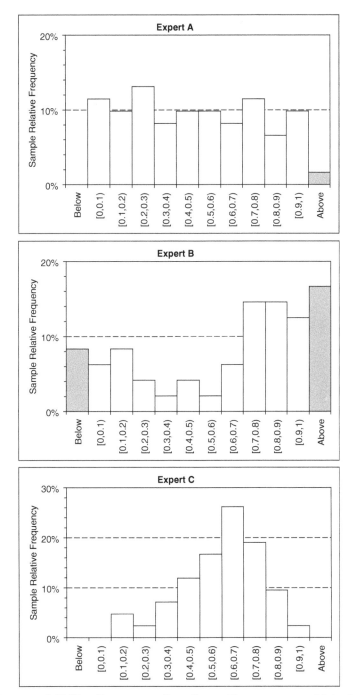

Figure 14.17 Histogram of SME outturn percentiles. Percentiles are grouped into 10 bands so roughly 10 % of the percentile scores should lie in each band (when there are a lot of scores). Expert A is well calibrated. Expert B provides estimates that are too narrow and tends to underestimate. Expert C provides estimates that are far too wide and tends to overestimate.

for the uncertain variables to get a feel for the true extent of the total uncertainty. Some of the experts may also have extra information to add to the pot of knowledge.

- The analyst, acting as chairperson, ensuring that the discussion is structured.
- Taking minutes of the meeting and circulating them afterwards to the attendees.

After a suitable, but short, period for contemplation following the brainstorming session, the analyst conducts individual interviews with each expert and attempts to determine their opinions of the uncertainty of each variable that was discussed. The techniques for eliciting these opinions are discussed in Section 14.6.1. Since all the experts will have the same level of knowledge, they should produce similar estimates of uncertainty. Where there are large differences between opinions, the experts can be reconvened to discuss the issue. If no agreement can be reached, the conflicting opinions can be treated as described in Section 14.3.4.

I believe that this procedure has several distinct benefits over attempting to determine distributions during brainstorming sessions:

- Each expert has been given the time to think about the problem.
- They are encouraged to develop their own opinion after the benefit of discussion with the other experts.
- A quiet individual is given as much prominence as a dominating one.
- Differences in opinion between experts are easier to identify.
- The whole process can be conducted in a much more orderly fashion.

14.6 Conducting the Interview

Initial resistance

Expert opinion of the uncertainty of a parameter is generally determined in a one-to-one interview between the relevant expert and the analyst developing the model. In preparing for such interviews, analysts should make themselves familiar with the various techniques for modelling expert opinion described earlier in this chapter. They should also be familiar with the various sources of biases and errors involved in subjective estimation. The experts, in their turn, having been informed of the interviews well in advance, should have evaluated any relevant information either on their own or in a brainstorming session described above.

There is occasionally some initial resistance by the experts in providing estimates in the form of distributions, particularly if they have not been through the process before. This may be because they are unfamiliar with probability theory. Alternatively, they may feel they know so little about the variable (perhaps because it is so uncertain) that they would find it hard enough to give a single point estimate let alone a whole probability distribution.

I like to start by explaining how, by using uncertainty distributions, we are allowing the experts to express their lack of certainty. I explain that providing a distribution of the uncertainty of a parameter does not require any great knowledge of probability theory. Neither does it demand a greater knowledge of the parameter itself than a single-point estimate – quite the reverse. It gives the experts a means to express their lack of exact knowledge of the parameter. Where in the past their single-point estimates were always doomed never to occur precisely, their estimates now using distributions will be correct if the actual value falls anywhere within the distribution's range.

The next step is to discuss the nature of the parameter's uncertainty. I prefer to let the experts explain how they see the logic of the uncertainty rather than impose on them a structure I may have had in mind and then to model what I hear.

Opportunity to revise estimates

Experts are usually more comfortable about providing estimates if they are told before the interviews that they have the opportunity to revise their estimates at a later date. It is also good practice to leave the experts with a printed copy of each estimate and to get them to sign a copy for the analyst's records. Note that the copy should have a date on it. This is important since the experts' opinion could change dramatically after the occurrence of some event or the acquisition of more data.

14.6.1 Eliciting distributions of the expert opinion

Once the model has been sufficiently disaggregated, it is usually not necessary to provide very precise estimates of each individual component of the model. In fact, three-point estimates are usually quite sufficient, the three points being the minimum, most likely and maximum values the expert believes the value could take. These three values can be used to define either a triangular distribution or some form of PERT distribution. My preference is to use a modified PERT, as described in Section 14.3.2, because it has a natural shape that will invariably match the expert's view better than a triangular distribution would. The analyst should attempt to determine the expert's opinion of the maximum value first and then the minimum, by considering scenarios that could produce such extremes. Then, the expert should be asked for his/her opinion of the most likely value within that range. Determining the parameters in the order (1) *maximum*, (2) *minimum* and (3) *most likely* will go some way to removing the "anchoring" error described in Section 14.2.2.

Occasionally, a model will not disaggregate evenly into sufficiently small components, leaving the model's outputs strongly affected by one or more individual subjective estimates. When this is the case, it is useful to employ a more rigorous approach to eliciting an expert's opinion than a simple three-point estimate. In such cases, the modified PERT distribution is a good start but, on review of the plotted distribution, the expert might still want to modify the shape a little. This can be done with pen and graph paper as shown in Figure 14.18. In this example, the marketing manager believes that the amount of wool her company will sell next month will be at least 5 metric tons (mt), no more than 10 mt and most probably about 7 mt. These figures are then used to define a PERT distribution that is printed

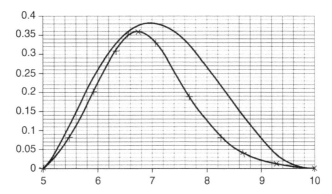

Figure 14.18 Graphing distribution of expert opinion.

out onto graph paper. On reflection, the manager decides that there is a little too much emphasis being placed on the right tail and draws out a more realistic shape. The revised curve can then be converted to a relative distribution and entered into the model. Crosses are placed at strategic points along the curve so that drawing straight lines between these crosses will produce a reasonable approximation of the distribution. Then the x- and y-axis values are read off for each point and noted. Finally, the manager is asked to sign and date the figure for the records.

The above technique is flexible, quite accurate and reassuringly transparent to the expert being questioned. This technique can now also be done without the need for pen and paper, using RISKview software.

Figure 14.19 illustrates the same example using RISKview. The PERT(5, 7, 10) distribution (top panel) is moved to the Distribution Artist facility of RISKview and automatically converted into a relative distribution (bottom panel) with a user-defined number of points (10 in this example). This distribution can now be modified to better reflect the expert's opinion by sliding the points up and down. The modified distribution can also immediately be viewed as an ascending or descending cumulative frequency plot to allow the expert to see if the cumulative percentiles also make sense. When the final distribution has been settled on, it can be directly inserted into a spreadsheet model at the click of an icon.

14.6.2 Subjective estimation of discrete probabilities

Experts will sometimes be called upon to provide an estimate of the probability of occurrence of a discrete event. This is a difficult task for experts. It requires that they have some feel for probabilities that is both difficult for them to acquire and to calibrate. If the discrete event in question has occurred in the past, the analyst can assist by presenting the data and a beta distribution of the probabilities possible from that data (see Section 8.2.3). The experts can then give their opinion based on the amount of information available.

However, it is quite usual that past information has no relevance to the problem at hand. For example, political analysts cannot look to past general election results for guidance in estimating whether the Labour Party will win the next general election. They will have to rely on their gut feeling based on their understanding of the current political climate. In effect, they will be asked to pick a probability out of the air – a daunting task, complicated by the difficulty of having to visualise the difference between, say, 60 and 70 %. A possible way to avoid this problem is to offer experts a list of probability phrases, for example:

- almost certain;
- very likely;
- highly likely;
- reasonably likely;
- fairly likely;
- even chance;
- fairly unlikely;
- reasonably unlikely;
- highly unlikely;
- very unlikely;
- almost impossible.

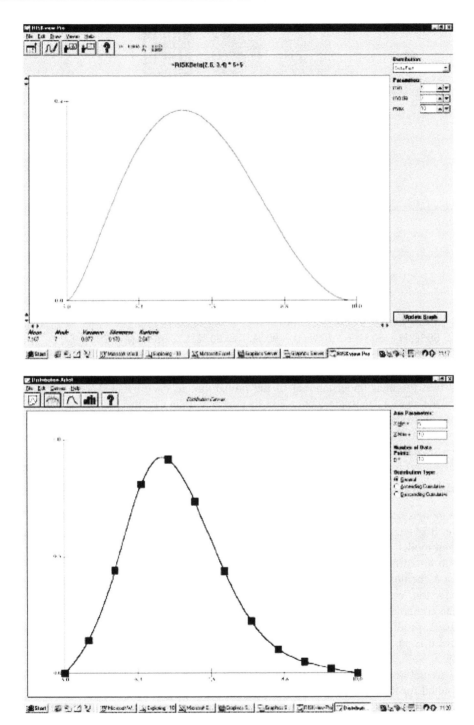

Figure 14.19 Using the RISKview software to model expert opinion.

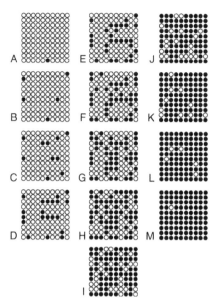

Figure 14.20 Visual aid for estimating probabilities: A = 1 %, B = 5 %, C = 10 %, D = 20 %, E = 30 %, F = 40 %, G = 50 %, H = 60 %, I = 70 %, J = 80 %, K = 90 %, L = 95 %, M = 99 %.

The phrases are ranked in order and the experts are told of this ranking. They are then asked to select a phrase that best fits their understanding of the probability of each event that has to be considered. At the end of the session, they are also asked to match as many of the phrases as possible to visual representations of probability. For example, matching a phrase to the probability of picking out a black ball at random from the trays of Figure 14.20. Since we know the percentage of black balls in each tray, we can associate a probability with each phrase and thus with each estimated event.

14.6.3 Subjective estimation of very low and very high probabilities

Risk analysis models occasionally incorporate very unlikely events, i.e. those with a very low probability of occurrence. It is recommended that readers review Section 4.5.1 before deciding to incorporate rare events into their model. The risk of the rare event is usually modelled as the probability of its occurrence combined with a distribution of its impact should it occur. An example might be the risk of a large earthquake on a chemical plant. The distribution of impact on the chemical plant (in terms of damage and lost production, etc.) can be reasonably estimated since there is a basis on which to make the estimation (the components most at risk in an earthquake, the cost of replacement, the time required to effect the repairs, production rates, etc.). However, the probability of an earthquake is far less easy to estimate. Since it is so rare, there will be very few recorded occurrences on which to base the estimate of probability.

When data are not available to determine estimates of probability of very unlikely events, experts will often be consulted for their opinion. Such consultation is fraught with difficulties. Experts, like the rest of us, are very unlikely to have any feel whatsoever for low probabilities unless there is a reasonable amount of data on which to base their estimates (in which case they can offer their opinion based around the frequency of observed occurrences). The best that the experts can do is to make some comparison with the frequency of other low-probability events whose probabilities are well defined. Figure 14.21

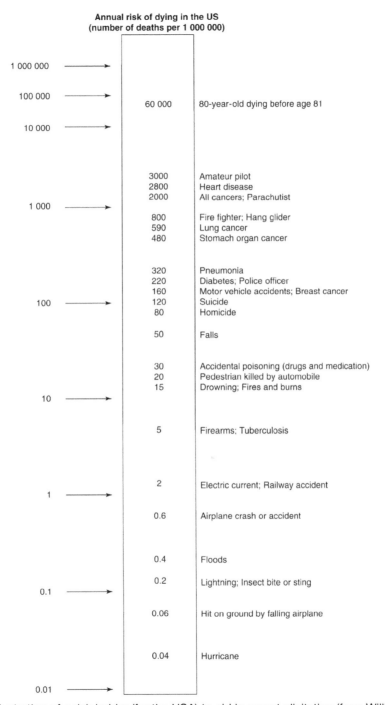

Figure 14.21   Illustration of a risk ladder (for the USA) to aid in expert elicitation (from Williams, 1999, with the author's permission).

offers a list of well-determined low probabilities in a graphical format that the reader may find helpful in this regard.

This inaccuracy in estimating the probability of a rare event will have a very large impact on a risk analysis. Consider two experts estimating the expected cost of the risk of a gas turbine failing. They agree that it would cost the company about £600 000 ± £200 000 should it fail. However, the first expert estimates the probability of the event as 1:1000/year and the second as 1:5000/year. Both see the probability as very low, but the expected cost for the first estimate is 5 times that of the second, i.e. £600 000 * 1/1000 = £600 compared with 600 000 * 1/5000 = £120.

An estimate of the probability of a rare event can sometimes be broken down into a series of consecutive events that are easier to determine. For example, the failure of the cooling system of a nuclear power plant would require a number of safety mechanisms all to fail at the same time. The probability of failure of the cooling system is then the product of the probability of failure of each safety mechanism, each of which is usually easier to estimate than the total probability of the event. As another example, this technique is also enjoying increasing popularity in epidemiology for the assessment of the risks of introducing exotic diseases to a country through imports. The imported entity (animal, vegetable or product of either) must first have the disease. Then it must slip through any quality checks in its country of origin. After that, it must still slip through quarantine checks in the importing country, and finally it has to infect a potential host. Each step has a probability (which may often be broken down even further) which is estimated, and these probabilities are then multiplied together to determine the final probability of the introduction of the disease from one animal.

Chapter 15

Testing and modelling causal relationships

Testing and modelling causal relationships is the subject of plenty of books. I recommend Pearl (2000), Neapolitan (2004) and Shipley (2002) because they are thorough, fairly readable if you're good at mathematics and take a practical viewpoint. The technical details of causal inference lie very firmly in the domain of statistics, so I'll leave it to these books to explain them. In this chapter I want to look at some practical issues of causality from a risk analysis perspective. The main impetus to including this as a separate topic is to help you avoid some of the nonsense that I have come across over the years while reviewing models and scientific papers, battling in court as an expert witness or just watching the news on TV. There are a few simple, very practical and intuitive rules that will help you test a hypothesised causal relationship.

Causal inference is mostly applied to health issues, although the thinking has potential applications in other areas such as econometrics (in his book, Pearl laments the lack of rigorous causal thinking in current econometric practices), so I am going to use health issues as examples in this chapter. We can attempt to use a causal model to answer three different types of question:

- *Predictions* – what will happen given a certain set of conditions?
- *Interventions* – what would be the effect of controlling one or more conditions?
- *Counterfactuals* – what would have happened differently if one or more conditions had been different?

In a deterministic (non-random) world there is a straightforward interpretation to causality. *CSI Miami* and derivatives, and all those medical dramas, are such fun programmes because we viewers try to figure out what really happened – what caused this week's murder(s), and of course the programme always finishes with a satisfyingly unequivocal solution. I was once stranded in a US airport hotel in which a real-world CSI conference was taking place, and they were keen to tell me how their reality was rather different. They don't have the flashy cars, cool clothes, ultrasophisticated equipment or trendy offices bathed in moody light. More importantly, when they search a database of fingerprints, it comes up with a list, if they're lucky, of a dozen or so *possible* candidates, probably with "whereabouts unknown". For them, the truth is far more elusive.

In the risk analysis world we have to work with causal relationships that are usually probabilistic in nature, for example:

- the probability of having lung cancer within your life is x if you smoke;
- the probability of having lung cancer within your life is y if you don't smoke.

We all know that $x > y$, which makes being a smoker a risk factor. But life is more complicated than that: there is a biological gradient, meaning in this case the more you smoke, the more likely the cancer. If we were to do a study designed to determine the causal relationship between smoking and cancer, we should look not just at whether people smoked at all, but at how much a person has smoked, for how long and in what way (cigars, cigarettes with or without filters, pipes, little puffs or deep inhaling, brand, etc). Things are further complicated because people can change their smoking habits over time. How about:

- the probability of having lung cancer within your life is a if you carry matches;
- the probability of having lung cancer within your life is b if you don't carry matches.

I haven't done the study, but I bet $a > b$, although carrying matches should not be a risk factor. A correct statistical analysis will determine the high correlation between carrying matches (or lighters) and using tobacco products. A sensible statistician would figure out that matches should be removed from the analysis. An uncontrolled statistical analysis can produce some silly results (imagine we had no idea that tobacco could be related to cancer and didn't collect any tobacco-related data), so we should always apply some disciplined thinking to how we structure and interpret a statistical model. We need a few definitions to begin:

- A *risk factor* is an aspect of personal behaviour or lifestyle, environment or characteristic thought to be associated positively or negatively with a particular adverse condition.

- A *counterfactual world* is an epidemiological hypothetical idea of a world similar to our own in all ways but for which the exposure to the hazard, or people's behaviour or characteristics, or some other change that affects exposure, has been changed in some way.

- The *population attributable risk* (PAR) (aka *population aetiological fraction*, among many others) is the proportion of the incidence in the population attributable to exposure to a risk factor. It represents the fraction by which the incidence in the population would have reduced in a counterfactual world where the effect associated with that risk factor was not present.

These concepts are often used to help model what the future might look like if we were to eliminate a risk factor, but we need to be careful as they technically only refer to the comparison of an observed world and a counterfactual parallel world in which the risk factor does not appear – making predictions of the future means that we have to assume that the future world would look just like that counterfactual one.

In figuring out the PAR, we may well have to consider interactions between risk factors. Consider the situation where the presence of either of two risk factors gives an extremely high probability of the risk of interest, and where a significant fraction of the population is exposed to both risk factors. In this case there is a lot of overlap and an individual risk factor has less impact because the other risk factor is competing for the same victims. On the other hand, exposure to two chemicals at the same time might produce a far greater effect than either chemical alone. We talk about synergism and antagonism when the risk factors work together or against each other respectively. Synergism is more common, so the PAR for the combination of two or more risk factors is usually less than the sum of their individual PARs.

15.1 *Campylobacter* Example

A large survey conducted by CDC (the highly reputable Center for Disease Control and Prevention) in the United States looked at why people end up getting a certain type of food poisoning (campylobacteriosis). You get campylobacteriosis when bacteria called *Campylobacter* enter your intestine, find a suitably protected location and multiply (form a colony). Thus, the sequence of events resulting in campylobacteriosis must include some exposure to the bacteria, then survival of those bacteria through the stomach (the acid can kill them), then setting up a colony. In order for us to observe the infection, that person has to become ill. In order to identify the disease as campylobacteriosis, a doctor has to ask for a stool sample, it has to be provided, the stool sample has to be cultured and the *Campylobacter* have to be isolated and identified. Campylobacteriosis will usually resolve itself after a week or so of unpleasantness, so many more people therefore have campylobacteriosis than a healthcare provider will observe.

The US survey looked at behaviour patterns of people with confirmed cases, tried to match them with others of the same sex, age, etc., known *not* to have suffered from a foodborne illness and looked for patterns of differences. This is called a case-control study. Some of the key factors were as follows (+ meaning positively associated with illness, − meaning negatively associated):

1. Ate barbecued chicken (+).
2. Ate in a restaurant (+).
3. Were male and young (+).
4. Had healthcare insurance (+).
5. Are in a low socioeconomic band (+).
6. There was another member of the family with an illness (+).
7. The person was old (+).
8. Regularly ate chicken at home (−).
9. Had a dog or cat (+).
10. Worked on a farm (+).

Let's see whether this matches our understanding of the world:

- Factor 1 makes sense since *Campylobacter* naturally occur in chicken and are very frequently to be found in chicken meat. People are also somewhat less careful with their hygiene and the cooking is less controlled at a barbecue (healthcare tip: when you've cooked a piece of meat, place it on a different plate than the one used to bring the raw meat to the barbecue).

- Factor 2 makes sense because of cross-contamination in the restaurant kitchen, so you might eat a veggie burger but still have consumed *Campylobacter* originating from a chicken.

- Factor 3 makes sense because we guys tend not to pay much attention to kitchen practices when we're young and start off rather hopeless when we first leave home.

- Factor 4 makes sense in that, in the USA, visiting a doctor is expensive, and that is the only way the healthcare will observe the infection.

- Factor 5 maybe seems right because poorer people will eat cheaper-quality food and will visit restaurants with higher capacity and lower standards (related to factor 2).

- Factor 6 is obvious since faecal−oral transmission is a known route (healthcare tip: wash your hands very well, particularly when you are ill).

- Factor 7 makes sense because older people have a less robust immune system, but maybe they also eat in restaurants more (less?) often, maybe they like chicken more, etc.

- Factor 8 seems strange. It appears from a number of studies that if you eat chicken at home you are less likely to get ill. Maybe that is because it displaces eating chicken at a restaurant, maybe it's because people who cook are wealthier or care more about their food or maybe (the current theory) it is because these people get regular small exposures to *Campylobacter* that boosts their immune system.

- Factor 9 is trickier. Perhaps pet food contains *Campylobacter*, perhaps the animal gets uncooked scraps, then cross-infects the family.

- Factor 10 makes sense. People working in chicken farms are obviously more at risk, but a farm will often have just a few chickens, or will buy in manure as fertiliser or used chicken bedding as cattle feed. Other animals also carry *Campylobacter*.

Each of the above is a demonstrable *risk factor* because each passed a test of statistical significance in this study (and others) and one can find a possible rational explanation. Of course, the possible rational explanation is often to be expected because the survey was put together with questions that were designed to test suspected risk factors, not the ones that weren't thought of. Note that the causal arguments are often interlinked in some way, making it difficult to figure out the importance of each factor in isolation. Statistical software can deal with this given the appropriate control.

15.2 Types of Model to Analyse Data

Data can be analysed in several different ways in an attempt to determine the magnitude of hypothesised causal relationships between variables (possible risk factors). Note, these models will not ever *prove* a causal relationship, just as it is not possible to prove a theory, only disprove it.

- **Neural nets** – look for patterns within datasets between several variables associated with a set of individuals. They can find correlations within datasets, and make predictions of where a new observation might lie on the basis of values for the conditioning variables, but they do not have a causal interpretation and tend to be rather black box in nature. Neural nets are used a lot in profiling. For example, they are used to estimate the level of credit risk associated with a credit card or mortgage applicant, or identify a possible terrorist or smuggler at an airport. They don't seek to determine *why* a person might be a poor credit risk, for example, just match the typical behaviour or history of someone who fails to pay their bills – things like having defaulted before, changing jobs frequently, not owning a home.

- **Classification trees** – can be used to break down case-control data to list from the top down the most important factors influencing the outcome of interest. This is done by looking at the difference in fraction of cases and controls that have the outcome of interest (e.g. disease) when they are split by each possible explanatory variable. So, for example, having a case-control study of lung cancer, one might find the fraction of people with lung cancer is much larger among smokers than among non-smokers, which forms the first fork in the tree. Looking then at the non-smokers only, one might find that the fraction of people with lung cancer is much higher for those who worked in a smoky environment compared with those who did not. One continually breaks down the population splits, figuring out which variable is the next most correlated with a difference in the risk until you run out of variables or statistical significance.

- **Regression models** – logistic regression is used a lot to determine whether there is a possible relationship between variables in a dataset and the variable to be predicted. The probability of a "success" (e.g. exhibiting the disease) of a dichotomous (two-possible-outcome) variable we wish to predict, p_i, is related to the various possible influencing variables by regression equations; for example

$$p_i = \cfrac{1}{1 + \exp\left[\sum_{j=1}^{k} \beta_j x_{j,i} + \text{Normal}(0, \sigma)_i\right]}$$

where subscript i refers to each observation, and subscript j refers to each possible explanatory variable in the dataset, of which there are k in total. Stepwise regression is used in two forms: forward selection starts off with no predictive variables and sequentially adds them until there is no statistically significant improvement in matching the data; backward selection has all variables in the pot and keeps taking away the least significant variable until the model's statistical predictive capability begins to suffer. Logistic regression can take account of important correlations between possible risk factors by including covariance terms. Like neural nets, it has no in-built causal thinking.

- **Bayesian belief networks** (aka directed acyclic graphs) – visually, these are networks of nodes (observed variables) connected together by arcs (probabilistic relationships). They offer the closest connection to causal inference thinking. In principle you could let DAG software run on a set of data and come up with a set of conditional probabilities – it sounds appealing and objectively hands off, but the networks need the benefit of human experience to know the direction in which these arcs should go, i.e. what the directions of influence really are (and if they exist at all). I'm a firm believer in assigning some constraints to what the model should test, but make sure you know why you are applying those constraints. To quote Judea Pearl (Pearl, 2000): "[C]ompliance with human intuition has been the ultimate criterion of adequacy in every philosophical study of causation, and the proper incorporation of background information into statistical studies likewise relies on accurate interpretation of causal judgment".

Commercial software are available for each of these methods. The algorithms they use are often proprietary and can give different results on the same datasets, which is rather frustrating and presents some opportunities to those who are looking for a particular answer (don't do that). In all of the above techniques, it is important to split your data up into a training set and a validation set to test whether the relationships that the software find in the training set will let you reasonably accurately (i.e. at the decision-maker's required accuracy) predict the outcome observations in the validation dataset. Best practice involves repeated random splitting of your data into training and validation sets.

15.3 From Risk Factors to Causes

Let's say that you have completed a statistical analysis of your data and your software has come up with a list of risk factors. The numerical outputs of your statistical analysis will allow you to calculate PAR for each factor, and here you should apply a little common sense because PAR relates to the decision question you are answering.

Let me take the campylobacteriosis study as an example. You first need to know a couple of things about *Campylobacter*. It does not survive long outside its natural host (animals like chickens, ducks and pigs where it causes no illness) and so it does not establish reservoirs in the ground, in water, etc. It also does not generally stay long in a human gut, although many people could be harbouring the bacteria unknowingly. This means that, if we were to eliminate all the *Campylobacter* at their animal sources, we would no longer have human campylobacteriosis cases (ignoring infections from travelling). I was lead risk analyst for the US FDA where we wanted to estimate the number of people who are infected with fluoroquinolone-resistant *Campylobacter* from poultry – fluoroquinolone is used to treat poultry (particularly chickens) with the respiratory disease they get from living in sheds with poor ventilation so the ammonia from their urine strips out the lining of their lungs. We reasoned: if say 100 000 people were getting campylobacteriosis from poultry, and say 10 % of the poultry *Campylobacter* were fluoroquinolone resistant, then about 10 000 were suffering campylobacteriosis that would not be treatable by administering fluoroquinolone (the antimicrobial is also often used to treat suspected cases of food poisoning). We used the CDC study and their PAR estimates. The case ended up going to court, and a risk analyst hired by the opposing side (the drug sponsor, who sold a lot more of their antimicrobial to chicken farms than to humans) got the CDC data under the Freedom of Information Act and did a variety of statistical analyses using various tools. He concluded: "A more realistic assessment based on the CDC case-control data is that the chicken-attributable fraction for [the pathogen] is between −11.6 % (protective effect) and 0.72 % (not statistically significantly different from zero) depending on how missing data values are treated". In other words, he is saying with this −11.6 % attributable fraction figure that chicken is protective, so in a counterfactual world without chicken contaminated with *Campylobacter* there would be *more* campylobacteriosis, i.e. if we could remove the largest source of exposure we have to *Campylobacter* (poultry), more people would get ill. Put another way, he believes that the *Campylobacter* on poultry are protective, but the *Campylobacter* from other sources are not.

Using classification trees, for example, he determined that the major risk factors were, in descending order of importance: visiting a farm, travelling, having a pet, drinking unprocessed water, being male (then eating ground beef at home, eating pink hamburgers and buying raw chicken) or being female (and then having no health insurance, eating high levels of fast food, eating hamburgers at home ... and finally, eating fried chicken at home). Note that chicken is at the bottom of both sequences.

So how did this risk analyst manage to justify his claim that eating chicken was actually protective – it did not pose a threat of campylobacteriosis? He did so by misinterpreting the risk factors. There is really no sense in considering a counterfactual world where people are all neuter (neither male nor female) – and anyway, since we don't have any of those, we have no idea how their behaviour will be different from males or females. Should we really be including whether people have insurance as a risk factor to which we assign a PAR? I think not. It is perhaps true that all these factors are *associated* with the risk – meaning that the probability of campylobacteriosis is correlated with each factor, but they are not risk factors within the context of the decision question. I don't think that by paying people's health insurance we would likely change the number of illnesses, although we would of course change the number reported and treated. What we hope to achieve is an understanding of how much disease is caused by *Campylobacter* from chicken, so the level of total human illness needs to be distributed among the sources of *Campylobacter*. That brings some focus to the PAR calculations: dining in a restaurant is only a risk factor because *Campylobacter* is in the restaurant kitchen. How did it get there? Probably chickens mostly, but also ducks and other poultry, although the US eat those in far lower volumes. It could also sometimes be a kitchen worker with poor hygiene unknowingly carrying *Campylobacter*, but where did that worker originally get the infection? Most probably from chicken. The sex[1] of a person is no longer relevant. Having a pet (it was mostly puppies) is a debatable point, since the puppy probably became infected from contaminated meat rather than being a natural carrier itself.

---

[1] Not "gender", which I found out one day listening to a debate in the UK House of Lords is what one feels oneself to be, while "sex" is defined by the reproductive equipment with which we are born.

Looking just at *Campylobacter* sources, we get a better picture, and, although regular small amounts of exposure (eating at home) may be protective, this is protecting against other mostly chicken-derived *Campylobacter* exposure and we end up with the same risk attribution that CDC determined from its own survey data.

We won the court case, and the other risk analyst's testimony was, very unusually, rejected as being unreliable – in no small part because of his selective and doctored quoting of papers.

15.4 Evaluating Evidence

The first test of causality you should make is to consider whether there is a known or possible causal mechanism that can connect two variables together. For this, you may need to think out of the box: the history of science is full of examples where people considered something impossible, in spite of an enormous amount of evidence to the contrary, because they were so firmly attached to their pet theory.

The second test is temporal ordering: if a change in variable A has an effect on variable B, then the change in A should occur before the resultant change in B. If a person dies of radiation poisoning (B) then that person must have received a large dose of radiation (A) at some previous time. We can often test for temporal ordering with statistics, usually some form of regression. But be careful, temporal ordering doesn't imply a causal relationship. Imagine you have a variable X that affects variables A and B, but B responds faster than A. If X is unobserved, all we see is that A exhibits some behaviour that strongly correlates in some way with the previous behaviour of B.

The third test is to determine in some way the size of the possible causal effect. That's where statistics comes in. From a risk analysis perspective, we are usually interested in what we can change about the world. That ultimately implies that we are only really interested in determining the magnitude of the causal relationships between variables we can control and those in which we are interested. Risk analysts are not scientists – our job is not to devise new theories but to adapt the current scientific (or financial, engineering, etc.) knowledge to help decision-makers make probabilistic decisions. However, as a breed, I like to think that we are quite adept at stepping back and asking whether a tightly held belief is correct, and then posing the awkward questions. It's quite possible that we can come up with an alternative explanation of the world supported by the available evidence, which is fine, but that explanation has to be presented back to the scientific community for their blessing before we can rely on it to give decision-making advice.

15.5 The Limits of Causal Arguments

My son is just starting his "Why?" phase. I can see the interminable conversations we will have: "Papa, why does a plane stay in the air". "Because it has wings". "Why?". "Because the wings hold it up". "Why?". "Because when an airplane goes fast the wind pushes the wings up". "Why?". Dim memories of Bernoulli's equation won't be of much help. "I don't know" is the inevitable end to the conversation. I can see why kids love this game – once we get to three or four answers, we parents reach the limit of our understanding. He's soon going to find out I don't know everything after all, and I'll plummet from my pedestal (he's already realised that I can't mend everything he breaks).

Causal thinking is the same. At some point we are going to have to accept the existence of the causal relationships we are using without really knowing why. If we're lucky, the causal link will be supported by a statistical analysis of good data, some experiential knowledge and a feeling that it makes sense. If we go back far enough, all that we believe we know is based on assumptions. My point is that, when you have completed your causal analysis, try to be aware that the analysis will always be based on some assumptions, so sometimes a simple analysis is all you need to get the necessary guidance to your problem.

15.6 An Example of a Qualitative Causal Analysis

Our company does a lot of work in the field of animal health, where we help determine the risk of introducing or exacerbating animal and human disease by moving animals or their products around the world. This is a very well-developed area of risk analysis, and a lot of models and guidelines have been written to help ensure that there is a scientifically based rationale for accepting, rejecting and controlling such risks. Chapter 22 discusses animal health risk analysis. I present a risk analysis below as an illustration of the need for a healthy cynicism when reviewing scientific literature and official reports, and as an example of a causal analysis that I performed with absolutely no quantitative data for an issue for which we do not yet have a complete understanding.

15.6.1 The problem

A year ago I was asked to perform a risk analysis on a particularly curious problem with pigs. Post-weaning multisystemic wasting syndrome (PMWS) affects pigs after they have finished suckling. I had had some dealings with this problem before in another court case. The "syndrome" part of the name means a pattern of symptoms, which is the closest veterinarians can come to defining the disease since nobody knows for sure what the pathogen is that creates the problem. Until recently there hasn't even been an agreed definition of what the pattern of symptoms actually is. A herd case definition for PMWS was recently agreed by an EU-funded consortium (EU, 2005) led by Belfast University. The PMWS case definition on herd level is based on two elements – (1) the clinical appearance in the herd and (2) laboratory examination of necropsied (autopsy for animals) pigs suffering from wasting.

1. **Clinical appearance on herd level**

    The occurrence of PMWS is characterised by an excessive increase in mortality and wasting post weaning compared with the historical level in the herd. There are two options for recognising this increase, of which 1a should be used whenever possible:

    1a. If the mortality has been recorded in the herd, then the increase in mortality may be recognised in either of two ways:

    1. Current mortality $\geq$ mean of historical levels in previous periods $+1.66$ standard deviations.
    2. Statistical testing of whether or not the mortality in the current period is higher than in the previous periods by the chi-square test.

    In this context, mortality is defined as the prevalence of dead pigs within a specific period of time. The current time period is typically 1 or 2 months. The historical reference period should be at least 3 months.

    1b. If there are no records of the mortality in the herd, an increase in mortality exceeding the national or regional level by 50% is considered indicative of PMWS.

2. **Pathological and histopathological diagnosis of PMWS**

    Autopsy should be performed on at least five pigs per herd. A herd is considered positive for PMWS when the pathological and histopathological findings, indicative for PMWS, are all present at the same time in at least one of the autopsied pigs. The pathological and histopathological findings are:

1. Clinical signs including growth retardation and wasting. Enlargement of inguinal lymph nodes, dyspnoea, diarrhoea and jaundice may be seen sporadically.

2. Presence of characteristic histopathological lesions in lymphoid tissues: lymphocyte depletion together with histiocytic infiltration and/or inclusion bodies and/or giant cells.

3. Detection of PCV2 in moderate to massive quantity within the lesions in lymphoid tissues of affected pigs (basically using antigen detection in tissue by immunostaining or *in situ* hybridisation).

Other relevant diagnostic procedures must be carried out to exclude other obvious reasons for high mortality (e.g. *E. coli* post-weaning diarrhoea or acute pleuropneumonia).

The herd case definition is highly unusual: a result of the lack of identification of the pathogenic organism. It will need revision when more is known about the syndrome. The definition is also vulnerable from a statistical viewpoint. To begin with, the definition acknowledges the wasting symptom in PMWS, but the definitions only apply to mortality. PMWS can only be defined at a herd level because one has statistically to differentiate the increase in rate of mortality and wasting post weaning from historical levels in the herd or from other unaffected herds. Thus, for example, PMWS can never be diagnosed for a backyard pig using this definition.

The chi-square test quoted above is based on making a normal approximation to a binomial variable. The approximation is only good if one has a sufficiently large number of animals n in a herd and a sufficiently high prevalence p of mortality or wasting in both unaffected and affected herds. Thus, it becomes progressively more difficult to differentiate an affected from an unaffected herd where the herd is small. The alternative requirement of prevalence at >1.66 standard deviations above previous levels and the chi-square table provided in this definition are determined by assuming that one should only diagnose that a herd has PMWS when one is at least 95 % confident that the observed prevalence is greater than normal. This means that one can choose to declare a herd as PMWS positive when one is only 95 % confident that the fraction of animals dying or wasting is greater than usual. While one needs to set a standard confidence for consistency, this is illustrative of the difference in approach between statistics and risk analysis: in risk analysis one balances the cost associated with correct and incorrect diagnosis and chooses a confidence level that minimises losses.

The definition has other statistical issues; for example, the use of prevalence assumes that a population is static (all in, all out) within a herd, rather than a continuous flow. It also does not take into account the possible effects of a deteriorated farm management that would raise the mortality and wasting rates, nor of an improved farm management whose improvements would balance against, and therefore mask, the increased mortality and wasting due to PMWS.

Other definitions of PMWS have been used. New Zealand, for example, made their PMWS diagnosis on the basis of at least a 15 % post-weaning mortality rate together with characteristic histopathological lesions and the demonstration of PCV2 antigen in tissues. Denmark diagnoses the disease in a herd on the basis of histopathology and demonstration of PCV2 antigen in pigs with or without clinical signs indicative of PMWS and regardless of the number of animals.

15.6.2 Collecting information

PMWS is a worldwide problem among domestic pig populations. It is very difficult to compare experiences in different countries because there hasn't been a single agreed definition until recently, and there are different motivations involved for reporting the problem. In one country I investigated, farmers were declaring they had PMWS with, it seemed, completely new symptoms – but when I talked confidentially to people "on the ground" I found out that, if the problem were declared to be PMWS, the farmers would be completely compensated by their government, whereas if it were another, more obvious issue they would not. Another country I investigated declared that it was completely free of PMWS, which seemed extraordinary given the ubiquitous nature of the problem and that genetically indistinguishable PCV2 had been detected at similar levels to other countries battling with PMWS. But the pig industry of this country wanted to keep out pork imports and their freedom from the ubiquitous PMWS was a good reason justified under international trading law. The country used a different (unpublished) definition of PMWS that included the necessity of observing an increased wasting rate, and I was told that in their one suspected herd the pigs that were wasting were destroyed prior to the government assessment, with the result that the required wasting rate was not observed.

The essence of my risk analysis was to try to determine which, if any, of the various causal theories could be true and then determine whether one could find a way to control the import risk for our clients given the set of plausible theories. The main impediment to doing so was that it seemed every scientist investigating the problem had their own pet theory and completely dismissed the others. Moreover, they conducted experiments designed to affirm their theory, rather than refute it. I distilled the various theories into the following components:

- *Theory 1.* PCV2 is the causal agent of PMWS in concert with a modulation of the pig's immune system.
- *Theory 2.* A mutation (or mutations) of PCV2 is the causal agent (sometimes called PCV2A).
- *Theory 3.* PCV2 is the causal agent, but only for pigs that are genetically more susceptible to the virus.
- *Theory 4.* An unidentified pathogen is the causal agent (sometimes called Agent X).
- *Theory 5.* PMWS does not actually exist as a unique disease but is the combination of other clinical infections.

Note that the five theories are not all mutually exclusive – one theory being true does not necessarily imply that the other theories are false. Theory 1 could be true together with theories 2 or 3 or both. Theories 2 and 3 are true only if theory 1 is true, and theories 4 and 5 eliminate the possibility of all other theories. A theory of causality can never be proved, only disproved – an absence of observation of a causal relationship cannot eliminate the possibility of that relationship. The five theories with their partial overlap were structured to provide the most flexible means for evaluating the cause of PMWS. I did a review of all (15) pieces of meaningful evidence I could find and categorised the level of support that each gave to the five theories as follows:

- **conflicts (C)**, meaning that the observations in this evidence would not realistically have occurred if the theory being tested was correct;
- **neutral (N)**, meaning that the observations in this evidence provide no information about the theory being tested;
- **partially supports (P)**, meaning that the observations in this evidence could have occurred if the theory being tested was correct, but other theories could also account for the observations;
- **supports (S)**, meaning that the observations in this evidence could only have occurred if the theory being tested was correct.

15.6.3 Results and conclusions

The results are presented in Table 15.1.

- *Theory 1 (PCV2 + immune system modulation causes PMWS)*. This theory is well supported by the available evidence. It explains the onset of PMWS post weaning and the presence of other infections, or vaccines, stimulating the immune system as being cofactors. It explains how the use of more stringent sanitary measures in a farm can help contain and avoid PMWS. On its own it does not explain the radially spreading epidemic observed in some countries, nor the difference in susceptibility observed between pigs and pig breeds.

- *Theory 2 (PCV2A)*. This theory is also well supported by the available evidence. It explains the radially spreading epidemic observed in some countries but does not explain the difference in susceptibility observed between pigs and between pig breeds.

- *Theory 3 (PCV2 + genetic susceptibility)*. This theory is supported by the small amount of data available. It could explain the targeting of certain herds over others and the difference in attack rates between pigs breeds.

- *Theory 4 (Agent X)*. This theory is unanimously contradicted by all the available evidence that could be used to test it.

- *Theory 5 (PMWS does not actually exist)*. This theory is unanimously contradicted by all the available evidence that could be used to test it.

As a result, I concluded (rightly, or wrongly, at the time of writing we still don't know the truth) that it appears from the available evidence that PMWS requires at least two components to be established:

1. *A mutated PCV2 that is more pathogenic than the ubiquitous strain(s)*. There may well be several different localised mutations of PCV2 in the world's pig population that have varying levels of pathogenicity. This would in part explain the high variance in attack rates in different countries, although farm practices, pig genetics and other disease levels will be confounders.

Table 15.1   Comparison of theories on the relationship between PCV2 and PMWS and the available evidence (S = supports; P = partially supports; N = neutral; C = conflicts).

Evidence	Theory 1	Theory 2	Theory 3	Theory 4	Theory 5
1	P	P	N	N	C
2	P	P	N	N	C
3	N	N	N	N	C
4	N	N	N	N	N
5	S	N	N	C	C
6	P	S	N	C	C
7	S	N	N	C	C
8	N	N	N	N	N
9	S	N	N	N	C
10	N	N	P	N	C
11	S	S	N	N	C
12	P	P	P	C	C
13	N	S	N	C	C
14	N	P	N	C	C
15	S	N	S	C	C

2. *Some immune response modulation, due either to another disease, stress, a live vaccine, etc.* The theory that PMWS requires an immune system modulation is particularly well supported by the data, both in *in vitro* and *in vivo* experiments, and from field observations that co-infection and stress are major risk factors.

There is also some limited, but very convincing, evidence (Evidence 15) from Ghent University (by coincidence the town I live in) that the onset of PMWS is related to a third factor:

1. *Susceptibility of individual pigs to the mutated virus.* The evidence collected for this report suggests that the variation in susceptibility, while genetic in nature, is not obviously linked to the parents of a pig. The apparent variation in susceptibility owing to race may mean that susceptibility can be inherited over many generations, i.e. that there will be a statistically significant difference over many generations, but the variation between individuals in a single litter would exceed the generational inherited variation.

15.7 Is Causal Analysis Essential?

In human and animal health risk assessment, we attempt to determine the causal agent(s) of a health impact. Once determined, one then attempts to apportion that risk among the various sources of the causal agent(s), if there is more than one source. Some risk analysts, particularly in the area of human health, argue that a causal analysis is essential to performing a correct risk analysis.

The US Environmental Protection Agency, for example, in its guidelines on hazard identification, discusses the first step in their risk analysis process: "The objective of hazard identification is to determine whether the available scientific data describe a causal relationship between an environmental agent and demonstrated injury to human health or the environment". Their approach is understandable. It is extremely difficult to establish any causal relationship between a chemical and any human effect that can arise owing to chronic exposure to that chemical (e.g. a carcinogen), since many chemicals can precipitate the onset of cancer and that may only eventuate after many years of exposure, probably to many different carcinogens. We can't start by assuming that all chemicals can cause cancer. On the other hand, we may fail to identify many carcinogens because the data and scientific understanding are not there. If we are to protect the population and environment, we have to rely on suspicion that a chemical may be carcinogenic because of similarities with other known carcinogens and act cautiously until we have the evidence that eliminates that suspicion.

In microbial risk assessment, the problem is simpler either because an exposure to bacteria will immediately result in infection or because the bacteria will pass through the human gut without effect, and cultures of stools or blood analyses will usually tell us which bacterium has caused the infection. By definition, *Campylobacter* causes campylobacteriosis, for example, so that the risk of campylobacteriosis must logically be distributed among the sources of *Campylobacter*, because if all sources of *Campylobacter* were removed in a counterfactual world there would be no more campylobacteriosis.

I am of the view that we should definitely take the first step of hazard identification and attempt to amass causal evidence, but the lack of evidence should not lead us to dismiss a suspected hazard from concern, although clear evidence of a lack of causality should. We should also perform broad causal studies with an open mind because, although a strong though unsuspected statistical inference does not prove a causal relationship, finding one may nevertheless offer some lines of investigation leading to discovery of previously unidentified hazards.

Chapter 16

Optimisation in risk analysis

by Dr Francisco Zagmutt, Vose Consulting US

16.1 Introduction

Analysts are often faced with the question of how to find a combination of values for interrelated decision variables (i.e. variables that one can control) that will provide an optimal result. For example, a bakery may want to know the best combination of materials to make good bread at a minimum price; a portfolio manager may want to find the asset allocation that yields the highest returns for a certain level of risk; or a medical researcher may want to design a battery of tests that will provide the most accurate results.

The purpose of this chapter is to introduce the reader to the basic principles of optimisation methods and their application in risk analysis. For more exhaustive treatments of different optimisation methods, the readers are directed to specialised books on the subject, such as Randin (1997), Dantzig and Thapa (1997, 2003) and Bazaraa *et al.* (2004, 2006).

Optimisation methods aim to find the values of a set of related variable(s) in the *objective function* that will produce the minimum or maximum value as required. There are two types of objective function: deterministic and stochastic. When the objective function is a calculated value in the model (deterministic), we simply find the combination of parameter values that optimise this calculated value. When the objective function is a simulated random variable, we need to decide on some statistical measure associated with that variable that should be optimised (e.g. its mean, it 95th percentile or perhaps the ratio of standard deviation to mean). Then the optimising algorithm must run a simulation for each set of decision variables values and record the statistic. If one wanted, for example, to minimise the 0.1th percentile, it would be necessary to run thousands of iterations, for each set of decision variable values tested, to have a reasonable level of accuracy – and that can make optimising under uncertainty very time consuming. As a general rule, we strongly advise that you try to find some means to calculate the objective function if at all possible. ModelRisk, for example, has many functions that return statistical measures for certain types of model, and the relationships between stochastic models discussed in Chapter 8 can help greatly simplify a model.

Let's start by introducing an example.

When a pet food manufacturer wants to make an economically optimal allocation of ingredients for a dog formula, he may have the choice to use different commodities (i.e. corn or wheat as the main source of carbohydrates), but the company will want to use the combination of components that will minimise the cost of manufacturing, without losing nutritional quality. Since the price of commodities fluctuates over short periods of time, the feed inputs will have to be optimised every time a new contract for commodities is placed. Hence, an optimal feed would be the one that minimises the ration cost but also maintains the nutritional value of the feed (i.e. required carbohydrate, protein and fat contents in a dog's healthy diet).

With this example we have introduced the reader to the concept of *constrained optimisation*, where the objective is still to minimise or maximise the output from a function by varying the input variables, but now the values of some input variables are *constrained* to only feasible values of those variables (the nutritional requirements). Going back to the dog feed example, if we know that adult dogs require a minimum of 18 % of protein (as % of dry matter), then the model solution should be constrained to the combination of ingredients that will minimise the cost while still providing at least 18 % of protein. An input can take more than one constraint; for example, dogs may also have a maximum protein requirement (to avoid certain metabolic diseases) which can also be constrained into the model.

The optimal blending of diets is in fact a classical application of linear programming, an area of optimisation that will be revisited later in this chapter.

Optimisation requires three basic elements:

- The objective function f and its goal (minimisation or maximisation). This is a function that expresses the relationship among the model variables. The outputs from the objective function are called responses, performance measures or criteria.

- Input variable(s), also called decision variables, factors, parameter settings and design variables, among many other names. These are the variables whose values we want to experiment with using the optimisation procedure, and that we can change or control (make a decision about, hence the name decision variable).

- Constraints (if needed), which are conditions that a solution to an optimisation problem must satisfy to be satisfactory. For example, when only limited resources are available, that constraint should be explicit in the optimisation model. Variable bounds represent a special case of constraints. For example, diet components can only take positive values; hence they are bounded to zero.

Throughout this chapter we will review how these elements combine to create an optimisation model. The field of optimisation is vast, and there are literally hundreds of techniques that can be used to solve different problems. However, in practical terms the main differences between methods reside in whether the objective function and constraints are linear or non-linear, whether the parameters are fixed or include variability and/or uncertainty and whether all or some parameters are continuous or integers. The following sections give the background to basic optimisation methods, and then present practical examples

16.2 Optimisation Methods

There are many optimisation methods available in the literature and implemented in commercial software. In this section we introduce some of the most used methods in risk analysis.

16.2.1 Linear and non-linear methods

In Section 16.1 we presented a diet blend model and mentioned it was a typical linear programming application. This model is linear since the objective function and constraints are linear. The general form of a linear objective function can be expressed as:

$$\max / \min f(x_1, x_2, \ldots, x_n) = a_1 x_1 + a_2 x_2 + \cdots + a_n x_n \tag{16.1}$$

where f is the objective function to be minimised or maximised, and x and a are input variables and their respective coefficients.

The objective function can be subject to constraints in the form

$$c_{i1}x_1 + c_{i2}x_2 + \cdots + c_{in}x_n \begin{pmatrix} \leq \\ = \\ \geq \end{pmatrix} b_i, \quad i = 1, \ldots, m \tag{16.2}$$

Equation (16.1) shows that the constraints imposed on the optimisation problem must also be linear to be considered a valid linear optimisation problem.

From Equations (16.1) and (16.2) we can deduce two important assumptions of linear optimisation: *additivity* and *proportionality*:

- *Additivity* entails that the values from the objective function are the result of the sum of all the variables multiplied by their coefficients, independently. In other words, the increase in the results of the objective function will be the same whether a certain variable increases from 10 to 11 or from 50 to 51.
- *Proportionality* requires that the value of a term in the linear function is directly proportional to the amount of that variable in the term. For example, if we are optimising a diet blend, the total cost of corn in the blend is directly related to the amount of corn used in the blend. Hence, for example, the concept of economies of scales would violate the assumption of proportionality since the marginal cost decreases as we increase production.

The most common methodology to solve linear programming problems is called the simplex algorithm, which was invented by George Dantzig in 1947 and is still used to solve purely linear optimisation problems. For a good explanation of the simplex methodology the reader is directed to the excellent book by Dantzig and Thapa (1997).

We cannot apply linear programming if our objective function includes a multiplicative term such as $f(x_1, x_2) = a_1x_1 * a_2x_2$ because we would be violating the additivity assumption. Recall that we mentioned that a unit increase in a decision variable will have the same impact on the results of the objective function, regardless of the current absolute value of the variable. We can't make this assumption with our multiplicative example, since now the impact that a change in a variable has in the objective function will depend on the size of the other variable by which it is multiplied. For example, in a simple function $f(x) = ax^2$, with $a = 5$, if we increase x from 1 to 2, the results will change by 15 units $(5 * 2^2 - 5 * 1^2)$, whereas if x increases from, say, 6 to 7, the function will change by 65 units $(5 * 7^2 - 5 * 6^2)$.

Non-linear problems impose an extra challenge in optimisation, since they may present more than one minimum or maximum depending on the domain being evaluated. Optimisation methods aiming and finding the absolute largest (or smallest) value of the objective function in the domain observed are called global optimisation methods. We will discuss different approaches to global optimisation in Section 16.3.

The final function to consider is where the relationships in a function are not only non-linear but also non-smooth. For example, the relationships among some variables in the model use Boolean logic (i.e. IF, VLOOKUP, INDEX, CHOOSE) with the effect that the function will present sudden changes, e.g. drastic jumps or drops, making it uneven or "jumpy". These functions are particularly hard to solve using standard non-linear programming methods and hence require special techniques to find reasonable solutions.

16.2.2 Stochastic optimisation

Stochastic optimisation has received a great deal of attention in recent years. One of the reasons for this growth is that many applied optimisation problems are too complex to be solved mathematically (i.e. using the linear and non-linear mathematical methods described in the previous section). Stochastic optimisation is the preferred methodology when problems include many complex combinations of options and/or relationships that are highly non-linear, since such problems either are impossible to solve mathematically or cannot feasibly be solved within a realistic timeframe.

Simulation optimisation is also essential if the parameters of the model are random or include uncertainty, which is usually the case in many of the models applied to real-world situations in risk analysis.

Fu (2002) presents a summary of current methodologies in stochastic optimisation, and some of the applications of this method. Most commercial stochastic optimisation software use *metaheuristics* to find the optimal solutions. In this method, the simulation model is treated as a black-box function evaluator, where the optimiser has no knowledge of the detailed structure of the model. Instead, combinations of the decision variables that achieve desirable results (i.e. minimise the objective function more than other combinations) are stored and recombined by the optimiser into updated combinations, which should eventually find better solutions. The main advantage of this method is that it does not get "stuck" in local minima or maxima. Some software vendors claim that this methodology also finds optimal values relatively faster than other methods, but this is not necessarily true, especially when the optimisation problem can be quickly solved with well-formulated mathematical functions.

Usually, three steps are taken at each iteration of the stochastic optimisation:

- Possible solutions for the variables are found.
- The solutions found in the previous step are applied to the objective function.
- If the stopping criterion is not accomplished, a new set of solutions is calculated after the results of the previous combinations are evaluated. Otherwise, stop.

Although the above process is conceptually simple, the key to a successful stochastic optimisation resides in the last step, because trying all the combinations of values from different random variables becomes unfeasible (especially when the model includes continuous variables). For this reason, most implementations of stochastic optimisation focus their efforts on how to narrow the potential solutions based on the solutions already known. Some of the methods used for this purpose include genetic algorithms, evolutionary algorithms, simulated annealing, path relinking, scatter search and tabu search, to name a few. It is beyond the objective of this chapter to review these methodologies, but interested readers are directed to the chapter on metaheuristics in Pardalos and Resende (2002), and to the work by Goldberg (1989) and by Glover, Laguna and Martí (2000).

Most commercial Excel add-ins include metaheuristic-based stochastic optimisation algorithms. Some of the most popular include OptQuest® for Crystal Ball®, RISKOptimiser® for @Risk® and very recently Risk Solver®. Similar tools are also available for discrete-event simulation suites. There is also a myriad of statistical and mathematical packages such as R®, SAS® and Mathematica® that allow for complicated optimisation algorithms. In Vose Consulting we rely quite heavily on these applications (particularly R®) when developing advanced models, but we will stick to Excel-based optimisers here to avoid having to explain their syntax structure.

16.3 Risk Analysis Modelling and Optimisation

In this section we introduce the reader to some applied principles to implement optimisation models in a spreadsheet environment, and then briefly explain the use of the different possible settings in Solver, the default optimisation tool in Excel.

16.3.1 Global optimisation

In the previous section we discussed some of the limitations of linear programming, including the problem with local minima and maxima depending on the starting values. Figure 16.1 shows a simple function in the form

$$f(x) = \sin\left(\cos(x)\exp\left(\frac{-x}{4}\right)\right)$$

The function has several peaks (maxima) and valleys (minima) within the plotted range. A function like this is called non-linear (changes in $f(x)$ are not monotonically increasing with x), and also non-convex (i.e. line segments drawn from any point to another point can lie above or below the graph of $f(x)$, depending on the region of the function domain).

Optimisation software like Excel's Solver and other linear and non-linear constrained optimisation software follow a path from the starting values to the final solution values, using as guide the direction and curvature of the objective function (and constraints). The algorithm will usually stop at the minimum or maximum closest to the initial values provided, making the optimiser output quite sensitive to the starting values.

For example, if the function in Figure 16.1 is to be maximised and a starting value is close to the smaller peak (Max 1), the "best" solution the software will find will be Max 1, when in fact the *global* peak for this particular function is located at Max 2.

Evidently, in most risk analysis applications the desirable solution will be the highest (or the lowest) peak and not a local one. In other words, we always want to make sure that the optimisation is *global* rather than local. Depending on the software used, there are several ways to make sure we can obtain a global optimisation.

Excel's Solver is among the most broadly used optimisation software, as it is part of the popular spreadsheet bundle, and its algorithms are very sensitive to the initial values provided by the analyst. Thus, when possible, the entire feasible range of the objective function should be plotted to identify the global peak or valleys. From evaluating the graph, a rough estimate can then be used as an initial value.

Consider the model shown in Figure 16.2. The objective function is again

$$f(x) = \sin\left(\cos(x)\exp\left(\frac{-x}{4}\right)\right)$$

and is unconstrained within the boundaries shown (-4.2 to 8). When plotting the function, we know the global maximum is somewhere close to -0.02, so we will use this value in Solver.

To do so, we first enter the value -0.02 into cell x (C2), and then we select Tools $\rightarrow$ Add-Ins and check the Solver Add-In box and click the OK button. Then go back to Excel and select Tools $\rightarrow$ Solver to obtain the menu shown in Figure 16.3.

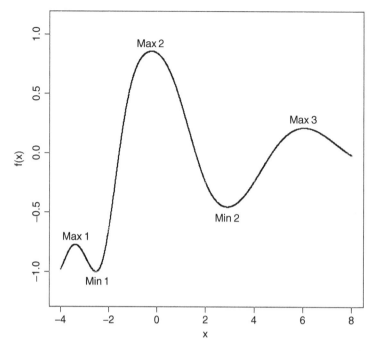

Figure 16.1 A non-linear function presenting multiple maxima and minima.

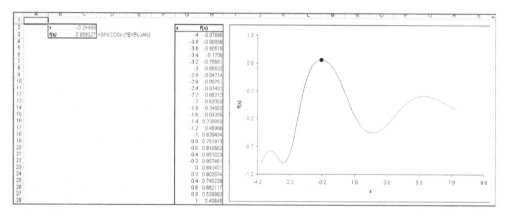

Figure 16.2 Sensitivity of Excel's Solver to local conditions. The dot represents the optimal solution found by Solver.

Under "Set Target Cell" we add a reference to the named cell fx (C3), then, since in this example we want to minimise the function, we select "Equal To" Max and we finally add a reference to named cell x (C2) under the "By Changing Cells" box. Now that we are ready to run the optimisation procedure (we will see more about the Solver menus and options later in this chapter, now we will use the default settings), we click the "Solve" button and after a very short period we should see a form stating that a

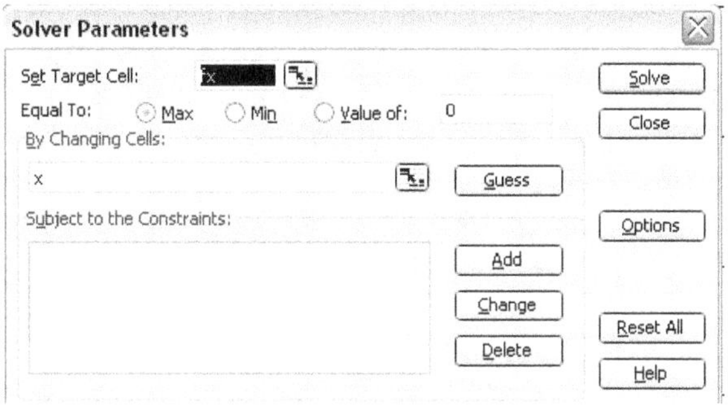

Figure 16.3 Excel's Solver main menu.

solution has been found. Select the "Keep Solver Solution" option and click the "OK" button. We can see that Solver successfully found the global maxima since we provided a good initial value.

What would happen if we didn't provide a reasonable initial value? If we repeated the same procedure but started with, say, -3 in cell x, we would obtain a maximum of -3.38, which turns out to be the first peak (Max 1 in Figure 16.1). If we started with a larger value, i.e. 4, Solver would find 6.04 as the optimal maximum, which is Max 3 in Figure 16.1. The reader can use the supplied model and try initial values to look for minima and maxima and explore how the optimisation algorithm behaves, particularly to notice the model behaviour when the Solver options (e.g. linearity assumption, quadratic estimates) are changed.

An alternative for dealing with local minima and maxima is to restrict the domain to be evaluated. We have already limited the domain by exploring only a limited section of our objective function (-4 to 8). However, the domain still contained several peaks and valleys. In contrast, if the domain observed contains only one peak or valley (i.e. -2, 2), the function becomes concave (or convex) which can be solved with a variety of fast and reliable techniques such as the interior point methods readily implemented in Solver. Since we know the global peak resides somewhere around zero, we can restrict the domain of the objective function to (-2, 2) using the constraint feature in Solver. First enter -2 in cell C6 and 2 in cell C7. Then name the cells "Min" and "Max" respectively. After that, open Solver and click on the Add button. Type "x" under cell reference, select $<=$ and then type "=Max" in the Constraint box. Once that is completed, click the Add button, and, following the same procedure, add the second constraint, $x >=$ Min. Once both constraints are added, click OK and then Solve. Solver should find an optimal x close to -0.25 which is the global maximum, so, even though the function has many local optimal values, now we have successfully restricted the domain enough so the numerical method can easily find the optimal values. Even if an aberrant number is entered (e.g. 1000) as the initial value, the domain is so narrow now that the algorithm will still find the optimal value. Try it!

When the function is not tractable (e.g. complex simulation models), plotting is not an option since the figure could be k-dimensional (and we all have a hard time interpreting elements with more than three dimensions). Hence, for this case, if the user plans on using Solver, he or she should attempt different initial values manually, based on the knowledge of the system being modelled. Another more automated option is to use more sophisticated applications that rely on metaheuristic methods, as explained in Section 16.2.2. Later in this chapter we present the solution to a problem where the function not only is intractable but also is highly non-linear and non-smooth and contains a series of integer decision variables and complex constraints.

Commercial optimisation software use different methods to make sure only global optimal solutions are found. As already discussed, metaheuristic methods can be very efficient in finding global optimal solutions. Other commercial software rely upon *multistart* methods for global optimisation, which automatically try different starting values until a global solution is found. Although they are reasonably effective, such methodologies can be quite time consuming when solving highly non-linear and non-smooth functions, or when little is known about the parameters to optimise (uninformed starting values).

16.3.2 A few notes on using Excel's Solver

We have already mentioned that Excel's Solver is an optimisation tool built into Microsoft's Excel and dispatched with all copies of Excel. Although the tool has limitations, it can be used in a variety of situations when stochastic simulation is not required. Solver implements a variety of algorithms to solve linear and non-linear problems. It uses the generalised reduced gradient (GRG) algorithm to solve non-linear programming methods, and, when the correct settings are used, it can use the simplex method, a well known and robust method for solving linear optimisation problems.

The mysterious Options menu in Solver

It is likely that many readers have used or tried to use Solver in the past and have managed fairly well. It is also likely that the reader has clicked on the Options button and didn't quite understand the meaning of all the settings. Furthermore, many readers may have found the explanations in the help file to be rather cryptic, so we will explain the various options.

We have already explained in previous sections how to use the general Solver menu. Now we will focus on the menus that appear under the Options buttons. To get there, select Tools → Solver and then click the Options button. The menu in Figure 16.4 should be displayed.

We briefly describe the meaning of each option below:

- The **Load Model** and **Save Model** buttons enable the user to recall and retain model settings so they don't need to be re-entered every time the optimisation is run.

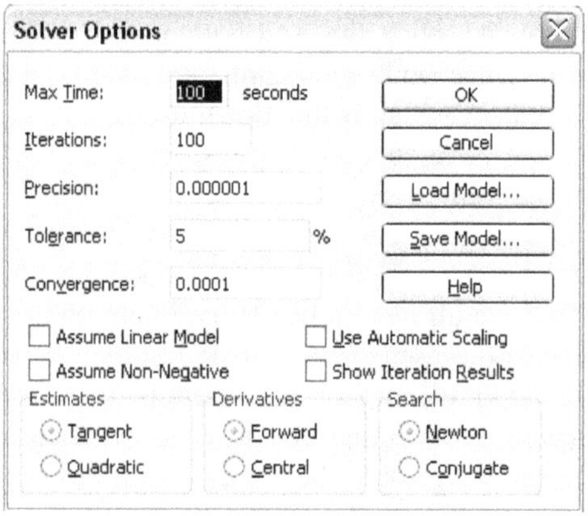

Figure 16.4   The Options menu in Excel's Solver.

- **Max Time** limits the time taken to find the solution (in seconds). The default 100 seconds should be appropriate for standard linear problems.

- **Iterations** restricts the number of iterations the algorithm can use to find a solution.

- **Precision** is used to determine the accuracy with which the value of a constraint meets a target value. A fractional number between 0 and 1. The higher the precision, the smaller the number (i.e. 0.01 is less precise than 0.0001)

- **Tolerance** applies only to integer constraints and is used to estimate the level of tolerance (as a percentage) by which the solution satisfying the constraints can differ from the true optimal value and still be considered acceptable. In other words, the lower the tolerance level, the longer it will take for the solutions to be acceptable.

- **Convergence** applies only to non-linear models and is a fractional number between 0 and 1. If after five iterations the relative change in the objective function is less than the convergence specified, Solver stops. As with precision and tolerance, the smaller the convergence number, the longer it will take to find a solution (up to Max Time that is).

Lowering precision, tolerance and convergence values will slow down the optimisation, but it may help the algorithm to find a solution. In general, these defaults should be changed if Solver is experiencing problems finding an optimal solution.

- **Assume Linear Model** is a very important choice. If the optimisation problem is truly linear, then this option should be chosen because Solver will use the simplex method, which should find a solution faster and be more robust than the default optimisation method. However, the function has to be truly linear for this option to be used. Solver has a built-in algorithm that checks for linearity conditions, but the analyst should not rely solely on this to assess the model structure.

- When the option **Show Iteration Results** is selected, Solver will pause to show the result of each iteration, and will require user input to reinitiate the next iteration. This option is certainly not recommended for computing intensive optimisation.

- When selected, **Use Automatic Scaling** will rescale the variable in cases where variables and results have large differences in magnitude

- **Assume Non-Negative** will bound to zero all the decision variables that have not been explicitly constrained. It is preferable, however, to specify explicitly the variables boundaries in the model.

- The **Estimates** section allows one to use either a **Tangent** method or a **Quadratic** method to estimate the optimal solution. The tangent method extrapolates from a tangent vector, whereas quadratic is the method of choice for highly non-linear problems.

- The **Derivatives** section specifies the differencing method used to estimate partial derivatives of objective and constraint functions (when differentiable, of course). In general, **Forward** should be used for most problems where the constraint values change slowly, whereas the **Central** method should be used when the constraints change more dynamically. The central method can be chosen when solver cannot find improving solutions.

- Finally, the **Search** section allows one to specify the algorithm used to determine the direction to search at each iteration. The options are **Newton**, which is a quasi-Newton method to be used when speed is an issue and computer power is a limiting factor, and **Conjugate**, which is the preferred method when memory is an issue, but speed can be slightly compromised.

Automating Solver with Visual Basic for Excel®

One of the most powerful tools in Excel is the integration with Visual Basic for Applications (VBA). This integration can also be extended to optimisation models with Solver. We will use the model presented in section 16.3.1 to show how to automate solver in Excel. The steps are:

1. Record a macro using Tools → Macro → Record New Macro and name the macro accordingly (e.g. "SolverRun").

2. Open the Solver form as previously explained and press Reset All to clear existing settings.

3. Repeat the steps followed to optimise the model (e.g. set objective function, decision variables and constraints and click the Solver button).

4. Once Solver has found a solution, stop recording the macro by clicking on the small red square in the macro toolbar, or by using Tools → Macro → Stop Recording.

5. Use the Forms Toolbar to add a button to the sheet.

6. Then assign the macro (e.g. "SolverRun") to the button by double clicking on it while in Design Mode and typing "Call SolverRun" in the procedure. For example, assuming the button is called CommandButton1, the VBA procedure should look as follows:

```
Private Sub CommandButton1_Click()
    Call SolverRun
    End Sub
```

7. Add a reference to Solver in Visual Basic by pressing Alt+F11, and then in the Visual Basic menu select Tools → References and make sure the box next to "Solver" is selected.

8. The VBA code for the recorded macro should look similar to the example below:

```
Sub SolverRun()
'This macro runs solver automatically
SolverOk SetCell:="$C$3", MaxMinVal:=1, ValueOf:="0", ByChange:="$C$2"
SolverAdd CellRef:="$C$2", Relation:=1, FormulaText:="Max"
SolverAdd CellRef:="$C$2", Relation:=3, FormulaText:="Min"
SolverOk SetCell:="$C$3", MaxMinVal:=1, ValueOf:="0", ByChange:="$C$2"
    SolverSolve userFinish:= True
        End Sub
```

Notice we have added an extra line "SolverSolve userFinish:=True" which suppresses the optimisation results from being shown at the end of each iteration. Now everything should be ready to use the macro. Make sure to exit the Design Mode and click on the button. The resulting model is not shown here but is provided for the user to explore.

16.4 Working Example: Optimal Allocation of Mineral Pots

This exercise is based on a simplified version of a real-life example taken from our consulting work.

A metallurgic company processes metal into 14 small containers called *pots*. The contents of the pots are then split among four larger *tubs* which are then used to create the final metal product that is sold. The resulting product receives a premium based on its level of purity (lack of unwanted minerals).

Since the input ore is different from batch to batch, the impurity levels will likely be different. It is then economically important to achieve certain purity level among batches while avoiding "bad" levels. The goal of the model is to optimise the allocation of pot metal contents into tubs in order to achieve a certain purity level in the final product.[1]

Note that, in reality, since the impurity level is estimated with samples, there is uncertainty about the actual impurity level of each batch. The client required that one was, say, 90 % confident that the concentration of each impurity in a tub was less than a certain threshold. Since speed was an important issue for the client, we avoided simulation by using classical statistics estimates of a mean (Chapter 9) to determine the 10th percentile of the uncertainty distribution for the true concentration in a tub.

For each pot, the variables are:

- purity of metal A (in percentage of total weight);
- purity of metal B (in percentage of total weight);
- weight (in pounds).

As the reader may imagine, the plant's operations present several constraints to be modelled, which are listed below:

1. A minimum of 1000 lb should be taken per pot.
2. The quantities taken from the pots are measured in discrete increments of 20 lb.
3. A maximum of five pots can be allocated to a given tub.
4. Pots can be only split in two parts (i.e. the contents of a pot cannot be split into three or four different tubs).
5. The maximum metal tonnage taken from a pot is equal to the pot weight (obvious, but this needs to be explicit in the model).
6. Every pot should be allocated into at least one tub (no "leftover" pots).
7. The maximum and minimum weights contained per tub are constrained (by certain values, for this example assumed to be a minimum of 5000 lb and a maximum of 10 000 lb).

Given the number of constraints and possible combinations to be optimised, this model would be quite complex to define in mathematical terms (especially when considering parameter uncertainty), and hence a more practical approach is to use optimisation. For this particular example, we employed OptQuest with Crystal Ball for its ease of use and connection with Excel, but other commercial spreadsheet add-ins could be used to achieve similar results. OptQuest is used here for a deterministic model but handles stochastic optimisation equally well.

One powerful feature of simulation optimisation is that complex constraints such as those imposed in this model can be specified by removing those scenarios rather than including them explicitly in the objective function. Such constraints are sometimes called simulation *requirements*. Although this approach can be slower than incorporating the constraint directly in the model, it allows for very complex interactions in the model. Also, the models can be significantly sped up by compiling many input variables into only one requirement variable. Figure 16.5 shows the general structure of the model.

Cells with a grey background represent input variables (variables that are changed during the optimisation process), and cells with a black background are requirements that are used to set the model

---

[1] Another goal was to optimise for several purity levels by their dollar premiums, but that is omitted here for simplicity.

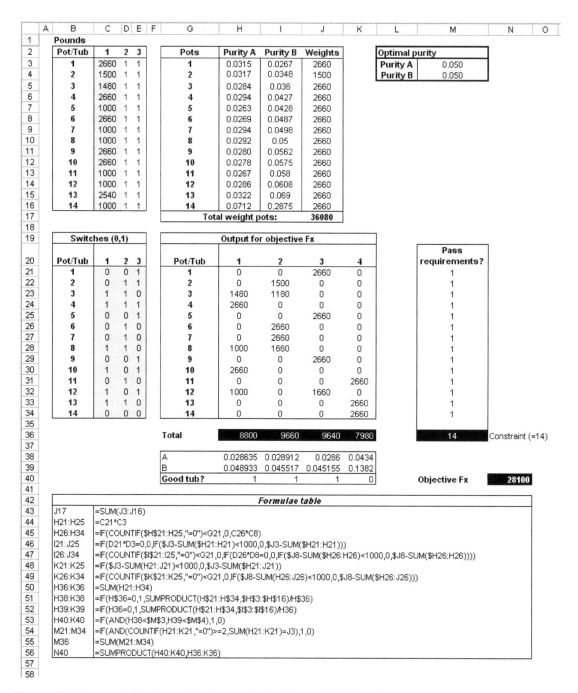

The following is a text reconstruction of the spreadsheet shown:

	A	B	C	D	E	F	G	H	I	J	K	L	M	N	O
1		**Pounds**													
2		Pot/Tub	1	2	3		Pots	Purity A	Purity B	Weights		**Optimal purity**			
3		1	2660	1	1		1	0.0315	0.0267	2660		Purity A	0.050		
4		2	1500	1	1		2	0.0317	0.0348	1500		Purity B	0.050		
5		3	1480	1	1		3	0.0284	0.036	2660					
6		4	2660	1	1		4	0.0294	0.0427	2660					
7		5	1000	1	1		5	0.0263	0.0428	2660					
8		6	2660	1	1		6	0.0269	0.0487	2660					
9		7	1000	1	1		7	0.0294	0.0498	2660					
10		8	1000	1	1		8	0.0292	0.05	2660					
11		9	2660	1	1		9	0.0280	0.0562	2660					
12		10	2660	1	1		10	0.0278	0.0575	2660					
13		11	1000	1	1		11	0.0267	0.058	2660					
14		12	1000	1	1		12	0.0286	0.0608	2660					
15		13	2540	1	1		13	0.0322	0.069	2660					
16		14	1000	1	1		14	0.0712	0.2875	2660					
17								Total weight pots:		36080					
19		**Switches (0,1)**					**Output for objective Fx**								
20		Pot/Tub	1	2	3		Pot/Tub	1	2	3	4	**Pass requirements?**			
21		1	0	0	1		1	0	0	2660	0	1			
22		2	0	1	1		2	0	1500	0	0	1			
23		3	1	1	0		3	1480	1180	0	0	1			
24		4	1	1	1		4	2660	0	0	0	1			
25		5	0	0	1		5	0	0	2660	0	1			
26		6	0	1	0		6	0	2660	0	0	1			
27		7	0	1	0		7	0	2660	0	0	1			
28		8	1	1	0		8	1000	1660	0	0	1			
29		9	0	0	1		9	0	0	2660	0	1			
30		10	1	0	1		10	2660	0	0	0	1			
31		11	0	1	0		11	0	0	0	2660	1			
32		12	1	0	1		12	1000	0	1660	0	1			
33		13	1	1	0		13	0	0	0	2660	1			
34		14	0	0	0		14	0	0	0	2660	1			
36							Total	8800	9660	9640	7980		14		Constraint (=14)
38							A	0.028635	0.028912	0.0286	0.0434				
39							B	0.048933	0.045517	0.045155	0.1382				
40							Good tub?	1	1	1	0		**Objective Fx**		28100

Formulae table

J17	=SUM(J3:J16)
H21:H25	=C21*C3
H26:H34	=IF(COUNTIF($H$21:H25,"=0")<G21,0,C26*C8)
I21:J25	=IF(D21*D3=0,0,IF($J3-SUM($H21:H21)<1000,0,$J3-SUM($H21:H21)))
I26:J34	=IF(COUNTIF($I$21:I25,"=0")<G21,0,IF(D26*D8=0,0,IF($J8-SUM($H26:H26)<1000,0,$J8-SUM($H26:H26))))
K21:K25	=IF($J3-SUM(H21:J21)<1000,0,$J3-SUM($H21:J21))
K26:K34	=IF(COUNTIF($K$21:K25,"=0")<G21,0,IF($J8-SUM(H26:J26)<1000,0,$J8-SUM($H26:J26)))
H36:K36	=SUM(H21:H34)
H38:K38	=IF(H$36=0,1,SUMPRODUCT(H$21:H$34,$H$3:$H$16)/H36)
H39:K39	=IF(H36=0,1,SUMPRODUCT(H$21:H$34,$I$3:$I$16)/H36)
H40:K40	=IF(AND(H38<$M$3,H39<$M$4),1,0)
M21:M34	=IF(AND(COUNTIF(H21:K21,"=0")>=2,SUM(H21:K21)=J3),1,0)
M36	=SUM(M21:M34)
N40	=SUMPRODUCT(H40:K40,H36:K36)

Figure 16.5 The metallurgic optimisation model implemented in Excel.

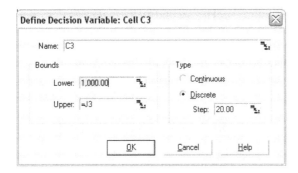

Figure 16.6 Dialogue to create decision variables in OptQuest with Crystal Ball.

constraints and define the objective function. The larger table in range G2:J17 contains the purity levels for both minerals and weight for each pot. The small table on the right contains the target purity levels that the model will optimise for.

The "Pounds" table (range B2:E16) contains input variables that are modified during the optimisation.

By selecting Define → Define Decision in Crystal Ball's menu, the user will see the form shown in Figure 16.6 with the settings for cell C3. The variables are discrete and can only increment in steps of 20 pounds (constraint 2), and are constrained to a fixed minimum of 1000 lb (constraint 1) and a maximum equal to the total content in the pot, which will vary depending on the batch; hence, the maximum value is linked to cell J3[2] which contains the pot weight. Similar variables are created for each combination of pots in tub 1, the only difference being the cell reference to their maximum weight. Decision variables are only needed for the first tub since the allocation for the other tubs is calculated on the basis of the initial allocation to the first tub. Thus, the remaining cells in the "Pounds" matrix are left empty or with a constant value of 1.

The "Switches" matrix (range B19:E34) contains input variables that can only take values of 0 or 1. The set of input variables from the "Pounds" matrix is multiplied by the variables in the "Switches" matrix to generate the output matrix "Output for objective Fx". Notice that, for the "Switch" variables, input variables are only needed for the first three tubs, because the fourth tub can be filled with what is left in the pots after their content has been allocated to the other three.

The remaining components in the model are the constraints and objective function. As previously mentioned, for this model some constraints are built into the simulation model, whereas others are set as scenarios that cannot be included in the optimal solution. Hence, anything that does not meet certain requirements is "tossed" from the set of possible options. The equation from pot 6, tub 1, in the output matrix incorporates constraint 3 as follows:

$$= \text{IF(COUNTIF(\$H\$21 : H25, " = 0")} < \text{G21}, 0, \text{C26} * \text{C8})$$

which summarises into "if 5 pots have been allocated to tub 1, then do not allocate the product from pot 6 into tub 1, otherwise, allocate the content defined in cell C8 (which is a decision variable as in Figure 16.6) multiplied by cell C26". The first part of this equation limits a maximum of five pots to

---

[2] For some reason unknown to this author, sometimes the cell reference in the decision variables may be lost after opening OptQuest, and will be replaced by the last number in the cell, e.g. the maximum weight entered for the pot (we are using OptQuest with Crystal Ball V. 7.3, Build 7.3.814). Readers should be aware of this issue when using this and other models with dynamic referencing on decision variable parameters.

be allocated to the tub (constraint 3). The second part (multiplication of two cells) is used to make sure that there is no bias in the order of the allocation of the pots to tubs (by using the binary decision variables in the "Switch" matrix). The same logic is used for pots 7 to 14 in tub 1.

For tubs 2 and 3, the equation for pot 6 is modified so that we add "if the remaining weight left in the pot is less than 1000 pounds, do not allocate any metal to this tub (constraint 1), otherwise, allocate the remaining material from pot 6 into this tub". The subtraction from the total pot weight satisfies constraint 5.

The reader will notice that, since we can only allocate one pot to one or two tubs (constraint 4), there is no need for an input variable in columns D and E since the material allocated to tubs 2 to 4 is dependent on whether tub 1 received material from a given pot. Thus, the pot/tub combinations for tubs 2 to 3 in the "Pounds" matrix contains only 1s, so a 1 is returned when multiplied by 1s from the "Switch" matrix.

Finally, metal from the pot that has not been allocated to tubs 1 to 3 (and that is at least 1000 pounds) is allocated to tub 4. As for the other tubs, formulas from pot 6 onwards are constrained, so no more than 5 pots can be allocated to one tub.

We cannot waste any remaining material in a pot, of course, so another exogenous constraint (*requirement*) that we add is that the sum of the pounds allocated from a pot should be exactly the same as the total weight in that pot. In addition, we can include constraint 6 into the same requirement to speed up the optimisation. The resulting formula (cell M21 shown, same for all pots) is

$$= \text{IF(AND(COUNTIF(H21 : K21, " = 0")} >= 2, \text{SUM(H21 : K21)} = \text{J3}), 1, 0)$$

In other words, if the pot has not been allocated to more than two tubs, and the sum of the weights allocated is equal to the weight of the pot, then return a 1, otherwise a 0. The same test is applied to each pot. Therefore, to meet the conditions, the sum of cells M21:M34 (cell M36) should be exactly 14 because, if all pots "pass the test", each individual pot test should return a 1.

Some readers may wonder why constraint 6 was added into this formula although it was already mentioned that, if nothing is allocated to tubs 1 to 3, the total weight is allocated to tub 4. In reality, the constraint is not necessary but is left in the equation to exemplify how to combine several constraints into one formula, making the model computations significantly faster. Also, when a model is going to be continuously modified, it is always good to have logical checks to make sure the algorithm is working the way it is supposed to.

Before we include the final values in the objective function, we need to identify which tubs are lower than the desired threshold of purity for minerals A and B. The formula we use for this is (cell H40:K40, H40 shown):

$$= \text{IF(AND(H38} < \text{Opt\_A, H39} < \text{Opt\_B}), 1, 0)$$

where Opt_A and Opt_B are the optimal purity levels for metals A and B respectively.

This formula returns a 1 when the requirements are met. Finally, the objective function is contained in cell N40 and is the sum of the total weights per tub, multiplied by the "Good tub" indicator. The optimisation model will try to maximise the value of this objective function (the total weight of "good" metal in tubs).

Once the variables, constraints and objective functions are defined, the last step left is to use OptQuest to set up and then run the optimisation procedure. To do so, in the Crystal Ball menu, select Run → OptQuest → and open a new optimisation file. All variables in the Decision Variables form should be selected. In the Forecast Selection form the inputs should be selected as in Figure 16.7 below.

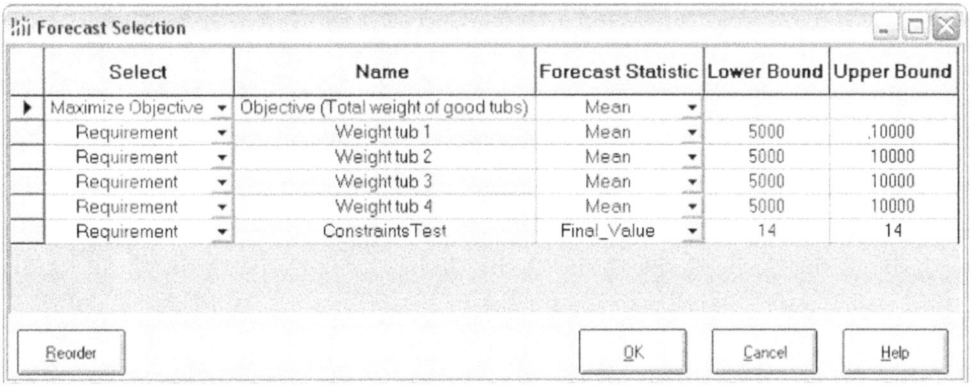

Forecast Selection

Select	Name	Forecast Statistic	Lower Bound	Upper Bound
Maximize Objective	Objective (Total weight of good tubs)	Mean		
Requirement	Weight tub 1	Mean	5000	10000
Requirement	Weight tub 2	Mean	5000	10000
Requirement	Weight tub 3	Mean	5000	10000
Requirement	Weight tub 4	Mean	5000	10000
Requirement	ConstraintsTest	Final_Value	14	14

Figure 16.7 Forecast selection menu in OptQuest for the metallurgic optimisation model.

The objective function is maximised (we want to have the maximum amount of pure metal), the constraint tests should be equal to 14 and the minimum and maximum contents of the tubs should be 5000 and 10 000 lb respectively (constraint 7). The software will discard any scenario that does not meet the requirements, and the objective function will be maximised by finding the best combination of input variables.

Provided the initial values are reasonable, an optimal solution takes less than an hour to run on a modern PC, which is important because the production line has to run this model twice a day.

16.4.1 Uncertainty in the model

In the actual model for our client we included the uncertainty about the impurity concentrations. The user set a required confidence level *CL* (e.g. 90 %), and the model optimised to produce "tubs" that had less than the specified impurity level with this confidence. The amount of impurity is determined by

$$\text{Weight of pot} * \text{Impurity concentration}$$

The source of the uncertainty came from the uncertainty of the weight of a pot (mean μ_P and standard deviation σ_P, lbs) and from the uncertainty of the impurity concentrations (mean μ_A and standard deviation σ_A for impurity A, for example). The mean and standard deviation of the distribution of the product (μ_P, σ_P) of these two random variables is given by

$$\mu_P = \mu_A \mu_B$$
$$\sigma_P = \sqrt{(\mu_A \sigma_B)^2 + (\mu_B \sigma_A)^2 + (\sigma_A \sigma_B)^2}$$

In order to calculate the impurity level at the required confidence, we use Excel's NORMINV(*CL*, μ_P, σ_P) function. The normal approximation is a reasonable approximation in this case because the uncertainty of the concentration was close to a normal distribution and was greater than the weight uncertainty so dominated the shape of the product. As mentioned before, finding a way of avoiding having to optimise a simulation model (rather than the calculation model here) is very helpful because it speeds up the optimisation time hugely: one calculation replaces a simulation of, say, 1000 iterations to be sure of the required confidence level value.

Chapter 17

Checking and validating a model

In this chapter I describe various methods that can be used to help validate the quality and predictive capabilities of a model. Some techniques can be carried out during a model's construction, which will help ensure that the finished model is as free from errors and as accurate and useful as possible. Other techniques can only be executed at a future time when some of the model's predictions can be compared against what actually happened, but one may nonetheless devise a plan to help facilitate that comparison.

Key points to consider are:

- Does the model meet management needs?
- Is the model free from errors?
- Are the model's predictions robust?

The following topics describe the methods we use to help answer these questions:

- Ensuring the model meets the decision-makers' requirements.
- Comparing predictions against reality.
- Informal auditing.
- Checking units propagate correctly.
- Checking model behaviour.
- Comparing results of alternative models.

17.1 Spreadsheet Model Errors

Your company may have hundreds or thousands of spreadsheet models in use. If even 1 % of these have errors, you could be making many decisions based on quite inaccurate information. If you now introduce risk analysis models using Monte Carlo simulation, which is more difficult to write (because we have to write models that work dynamically) and to check (because the numbers change with each iteration), the problem could get much worse.

Errors come in several forms:

- **Syntax errors** where a formula is incorrectly put together. For example, you mismatch brackets, forget to make a formula into an array formula (by entering with Ctrl + Shift + Enter instead of Enter), use the wrong function, etc.
- **Mechanical errors** which are hitting the wrong key, pointing to the wrong cell, etc. About 1 % of spreadsheet cells contain such errors.
- **Logical errors** which are incorrect formulae due to mistaken reasoning, misunderstanding of a function or the appropriate use of probability mathematics. These errors are more difficult to detect than mechanical errors and occur in about 4 % of spreadsheet cells in normal (unrisked) models.

- **Application errors** where the spreadsheet function does not perform as it should. Excel generates incorrect results for some statistical functions: GAMMADIST and BINOMDIST are awful, for example. Some versions of Excel also don't automatically update all formulae correctly – use Ctrl + Alt + F9 instead of F9 to be sure it updates correctly. Random number generation for certain distributions is quite numerically difficult, so you will see artificial limits to the parameters allowed for distributions in a lot of software: @RISK, for example, allows a maximum of 32 767 trials in a binomial distribution and for a hypergeometric population, while Crystal Ball allows a maximum of 1000 for a Poisson mean and parameters for the beta distribution must lie on [0.3, 1000]. It is frustrating, of course, to have to work around such limits, and often you'll only find them because the model didn't work for some iterations, so we have designed ModelRisk to have no such issues.

- **Omission errors** where a necessary component of the model has been forgotten. These are the most difficult errors to detect.

- **Administrative errors**, for example using an old version of a spreadsheet or graph, failing to update a model with new data, failing to get the spreadsheet to recalculate after changes, importing data from another application incorrectly, etc.

We have tried to help reduce the frequency of these types of error with ModelRisk. Each function returns an informative error message when inappropriate parameter values are entered. For example:

- = VoseNormal(100, −10) returns "Error: sigma must be $>= 0$" because a standard deviation cannot be negative.

- = VoseHypergeo(20, 30, 10) returns "Error: n must be $<= M$" because one cannot take more samples without replacement ($n = 20$) than there are individuals in the population ($M = 10$).

- {= VoseAggregateMoments(VosePoissonObject(10), VoseLognormal(10, 3))} returns "Error: Severity distribution not valid" because the severity distribution needs to be an object, e.g. VoseLognormalObject(10, 3)

If you write any user-defined functions, for which the Excel user will be less familiar, please consider doing the same.

In ModelRisk we have also chosen to return pedantically correct answers for probability calculations, for example:

- = VoseHypergeoProb(2, 10, 25, 30, 0) returns 0: this is the probability of observing exactly two successes where the minimum possible is 5. If it's impossible, the probability is zero.

- = VoseBinomialProb(50, 10, 0.5, 1) returns 1: the probability of observing less than or equal to 50 successes when there are only 10 trials.

This means that you don't have to write special code to get around the function giving errors. For example, the Excel equivalent formulae are:

$$= \text{HYPGEOMDIST}(2, 10, 25, 30) \text{ returns \#NUM!}$$

$$= \text{BINOMDIST}(50, 10, 0.5, 1) \text{ returns \#NUM!}$$

You also need to check how your Monte Carlo simulation software handles special cases for particular values. Poisson(0), for example, means that the variable can only be zero. In a simulation model, it would be perfectly reasonable for a cell simulating a concentration to produce a zero value that fed into a Poisson distribution. However, software will handle this differently:

@RISK: = RiskPoisson(0) returns #VALUE!

Crystal Ball: = CB.Poisson (0) returns #NUM!

ModelRisk: = VosePoisson(0) returns 0

Perhaps the most useful error-reducing feature in ModelRisk is that we have interfaces that give a visual explanation and check of most ModelRisk features. For example, a cell containing the formula = VoseGammaProb(C3:C7, 2, 3, 0) returns the joint probability of the values in cells C3:C7 being randomly generated from a Gamma(2, 3) distribution. Selecting the cell with this formula and then clicking ModelRisk's View Function icon pulls up the interface shown in Figure 17.1.

Crystal Ball and @RISK both have very good interfaces, although these are limited to input distributions only.

A quick Internet search for "spreadsheet model errors" will provide you with a wealth of individuals and organisations who research into the source and control of spreadsheet errors. For example, the European Spreadsheet Risks Interest Group is dedicated to the topic. Raymond Panko from the University

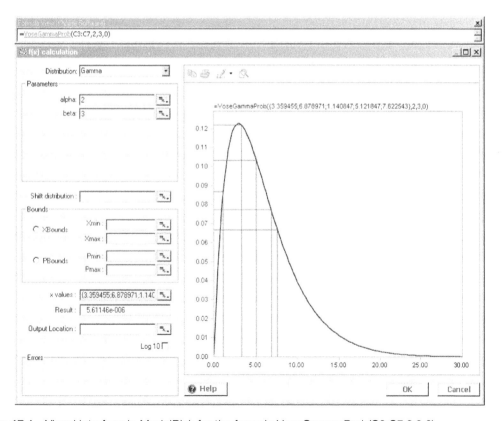

Figure 17.1 Visual interface in ModelRisk for the formula VoseGammaProb(C3:C7,2,3,0).

of Hawaii is a leader in the field and provides an interesting summary of spreadsheet error rates and reasons at http://panko.shidler.hawaii.edu/SSR/index.htm.

Looking at the error percentages, for large models the question is not "Are there any errors?" but "How many errors are there?". A company can help minimise model errors by establishing and enforcing a policy for model development and for model auditing. Dr Panko reports the recommendations of professional model auditors that one should spend 1/3 of the development time in checking the model.

17.1.1 Informal auditing

Studies have shown that the original builder of a spreadsheet model has a lower rate of error detection than an equivalently skilled coworker. It's not so surprising, of course, since we are more inclined than a reviewer to repeat the same logical, omission and administrative errors.

At Vose Consulting we do a lot of internal auditing. An important part of the process is sitting down and explaining to another analyst the decision question(s) and the model structure with pen and paper and then how we've executed it in a spreadsheet. Just the process of providing an explanation will often lead to finding errors in your logic, or to finding simpler ways to write the model.

Get another analyst to go through your code with the objective of finding your errors, so that a successful exercise is one that finds errors rather than one that pronounces your model to be error free. Having several analysts look at your model is even better, of course – it is interesting how people find different errors. For example, in writing our software, some of our team are just great at finding numerical bugs, others at wrong formulae, others still at finding inconsistencies in structure or presentation. Different things jump out at different people.

17.1.2 Checking units propagate correctly

I studied physics at university, and one of the first things you learn to do is a "dimensional analysis" of formulae. For example, there exists an equation relating initial speed u and final speed v to the distance s over which a body has constant acceleration a:

$$v^2 = u^2 + 2 * a * s$$

The dimensions involved are length L (in metres, for example) and time T (in seconds, for example). Distance has units L, speed has units L/T, and acceleration has units L/T^2. Replacing the elements in the above formulae with their dimensions gives

$$\left(\frac{L}{T}\right)^2 = \left(\frac{L}{T}\right)^2 + \left(\frac{L}{T^2}\right) * L$$

You can see that the left- and right-hand sides of the equation have the same units and that, when we add two things together, they have the same units too (so we are not adding "apples and oranges"). In a spreadsheet model we can use the same logic to help make sure our model is constructed properly.

It is good practice to label cells containing a number or formula with some explanation of what that value represents, but including units makes the logic of the model even clearer; for example, noting the currency when there is more than one in your model, or, if it is a rate, then noting the denominator, e.g. "$US/ticket", or "cases/outbreak". Then checking that the units flow through the model using dimensional analysis will often reveal errors.

Checking that the same units are used for a dimension (length, mass, etc.) is also important. We commonly come across two problems in this category in our auditing activities that are easily avoided:

- *Fractions*. The first is the use of a fraction, where the modeller might label a cell "Interest rate (%)" and then write a value like "6.5". Of course, to apply that interest rate, s/he will have to remember to divide by 100 to get to a percentage, and we've found that this is sometimes forgotten. Better by far, in our view, is to label a cell "Interest rate" and input the value "6.5 %" which will show on screen as 6.5 % but will be interpreted by Excel as 0.065 and can therefore be used directly.

- *Thousands, millions, etc*. In large investment analyses, for example, one is often dealing with very large numbers, so the modeller finds it more convenient to use units of thousands or millions. This would not present a problem if the entire spreadsheet used the same units, but very commonly there will be certain elements that do not; for example, cost/unit or price/unit for a manufacturer or retailer of high-volume products. The danger is that in summary calculations that evaluate cashflow streams, the modeller may forget to divide by 1000 or 1 000 000, in keeping with other currency cells. Even if it is all done correctly, it is more difficult to follow formulae where "/1000" and "* 1 000 000" appear without explanation.

Our preference is that the model be kept in the same units throughout, a base currency unit, for example, like $, € or £. Admittedly this can be tricky if you're converting from values you know in thousands or millions – we can easily get all those zeros mixed up. A convenient way to get around this in Excel is to use special number formatting. We use a few formats in particular, employing Excel's Format|Cells|Custom feature:

$$ \text{\_-"£" * \#,\#\#\#.0,, "M"; -"£" * \#,\#\#\#.0,, "M"; \_-"£" * 0.0"M"; \_-@\_)} $$

which will display 1234567890 as £1, 234.6M

$$ \text{\_-"£" * \#,\#\#\#.0,, "M"; [Red]-"£" * \#,\#\#\#.0,, "M"; \_-"£" * 0.0"M"; \_-@\_)} $$

which will display 1234567890 as £123.6M as above, but will display negative values in red

$$ \text{\_-"£"\#,\#\#\#.0,, "M"; [Red]-"£" \#,\#\#\#.0,, "M"; \_-"£"0.0"M"; \_-@\_)} $$

which does the same as the second option but has the "£" next to the numbers rather than left justified

$$ \text{\_-"£" * \#,\#\#\#.0, "k"; -"£" * \#,\#\#\#.0, "k"; \_-"£" * 0.0"k"; \_-@\_)} $$

which will display 1234567890 as £1, 234,567.9k

You can, of course, substitute a different currency symbol.

17.2 Checking Model Behaviour

Excel spreadsheet models have to be constructed so that they will work for all generated scenarios in which we are interested.[1] There are various ways to check that the model behaves the way it should:

- viewing random scenarios on screen and checking for credibility;
- splitting up complex formulae (megaformulae);
- comparing with known answers;
- analysing outputs;
- stressing parameter values;
- comparing results from alternative models.

These are discussed in turn below:

17.2.1 Viewing random scenarios on screen and checking for credibility

In ModelRisk all simulation functions return random values inside Excel. Thus, by repeatedly hitting the F9 (spreadsheet recalculation) key, you will see how the model behaves on screen when random scenarios are being generated. The same applies to @RISK. With Crystal Ball you click the Step icon. You can often make your review more effective by adding some test cells; for example, setting up a cell that calculates the maximum (or minimum, etc.) of an array to make sure no cell in that array produces any crazy numbers.

Imbedded graphs

We have found imbedding graphs of time series forecasts to be a particularly effective way to demonstrate that the model is producing reasonable numbers. Randomly recalculating the spreadsheet shows any trend, seasonality, range, etc., so the client may not understand all the technical detail behind the formulae, but s/he can readily appreciate the result. You should have an imbedded chart with a fixed scale if possible so that the viewer can visually compare each generated scenario.

The remaining difficulty is that viewing one scenario at a time doesn't help you really appreciate the full behaviour of a time series. The ModelRisk interface lets you view many possible pathways together for its time series, as shown in Figure 17.2. This gives a much better sense of what the modelled variable is likely to do over time. Hovering over any particular line will fade out the others so you can see the type of path the variable might take.

17.2.2 Splitting up complex formulae (megaformulae)

It is probably a good idea to avoid complex formulae (megaformulae) in risk analysis models unless you can thoroughly test them. Megaformulae, especially those performing array calculations, can certainly make a model run faster and keep its size much smaller, but they introduce an extra risk of error, and they are difficult for other reviewers and users to check. If you do use a megaformula, try first putting together a separate spreadsheet with each subcalculation so that you can check your logic, and make

---

[1] Not necessarily all possible scenarios, because sometimes you might want errors to be generated for the outputs for scenarios in which you are not interested, which means they will not appear in the output graphs and statistics of your simulation software.

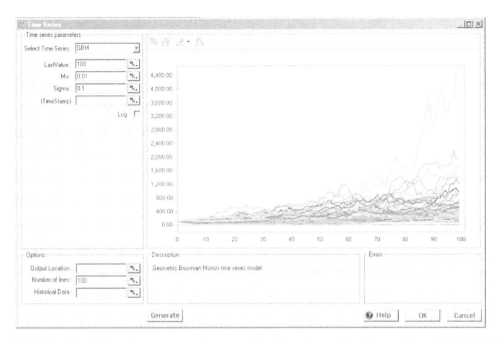

Figure 17.2   Viewing 100 random passes of a geometric Brownian motion time series with ModelRisk.

reference to it in your reporting so that others can retrace your steps. If the megaformula performs a function that you need often, consider creating a custom function using Visual Basic for Applications, which can be documented and need then only be thoroughly tested the once.

17.2.3 Comparing with known answers

You may well know the output you should get when the parameters are set to certain values, which you can then check. Similarly, you may logically know what the change in your output should be by changing an input parameter (e.g. double parameter X and the output mean should double). This will also often apply when you've integrated an extension to your model, and can set some parameter values so your model is equivalent to the previous version. Another technique is to set some parameters to particular values (most common would be setting some probability or rate to zero) that will render a part of your model irrelevant, and then check that the model is indeed not affected by the part that should now be irrelevant.

17.2.4 Analysing outputs

Certain graphical and statistical outputs are particularly helpful in checking that uncertain input parameters are having the expected influence on the model's outputs. Key among these are:

- scatter plots;
- tornado charts;
- spider plots;

- time series summary plots;
- correlation and regression statistics.

They are discussed at length in Chapter 5.

17.2.5 Stressing parameter values

A very useful, simple and powerful way of checking your model is to look at the effect of changing the model parameters. We use two different methods.

Propagate an error

In order to check quickly what elements of your model are affected by a particular spreadsheet cell, you can replace the cell contents with the Excel formula: =NA(). This will show the warning script "#N/A" (meaning data not available) in that cell and any other cell that relies on it (except where the ISNA() or ISERROR() functions are used). Imbedded Excel charts will simply leave the cell out. I like this method very much because it is quicker than using the Excel audit toolbar to trace dependents and it also works when you have VBA macros that pick up values from cells within the code, i.e. when the cells aren't inputs to the macro function the Trace Dependents function in Excel won't work in that situation.

Set parameter values to extremes

It is difficult to see whether your Monte Carlo simulation model is performing correctly for low-probability outcomes because generating scenarios on screen will obviously only rarely show those low-probability scenarios. However, there are a couple of techniques for concentrating on these low-probability events by temporarily altering the input distributions. We suggest that you first resave your model with another name (e.g. append "test" to the file name) to avoid accidentally leaving the model with the altered distributions. You can generate model extremes as follows:

(a) *Set a discrete variable to an extreme instead of its distribution*. The theoretical minimum and maximum of discrete bounded distributions are provided in the formulae pages for each distribution in Appendix III. Many distributions have a zero minimum, but only a few distributions have a maximum value (e.g. binomial). In general, it is not a good idea to stress a continuous variable with its minimum or maximum, however, because such values have a zero probability of occurrence and so the scenario is meaningless.

(b) *Modify the distribution to generate values only from an extreme range*. This is particularly useful for continuous distributions, and for discrete distributions where there is no defined minimum and/or maximum. Monte Carlo Excel add-ins normally offer the ability to bound a distribution. For example, in ModelRisk we can write the following to constrain a lognormal distribution:

$$\text{Only values above } 30: = \text{VoseLognormal}(10, 5,, \text{VoseXBounds}(30,))$$

$$\text{Only values below } 5: = \text{VoseLognormal}(10, 5,, \text{VoseXBounds}(, 5))$$

$$\text{Values between } 10 \text{ and } 11: = \text{VoseLognormal}(10, 5,, \text{VoseXBounds}(10, 11))$$

In @RISK, this would be

$$= \text{RiskLognorm}(0, 5, \text{RiskTruncate}(30,)), \text{etc.}$$

In Crystal Ball you apply bounds in the visual interface. Note that occasionally a model will have an acute response to a variable that is within a small range. For example, a model of the amplitude of vibrations of a car may have a very acute (highly non-linear) response to an input variable modelling the frequency of an external vibrating force, like the bounce from driving over a slatted bridge, when that frequency approaches the natural frequency of the car. In that case, the rare event that needs to be tested is not necessarily an extreme of the input variable but is the scenario that produces the extreme response in the rest of the model.

(c) *Modify the Probability of a Risk Occurring.* Often in a risk analysis model we have one or more risk events. We can simulate them occurring (with some probability) or not in a variety of ways. We can stress the model to see the effect of an individual risk occurring, or a combination of risks, by increasing their probability during the test. For example, setting a risk to have 50 % probability (where perhaps we actually believe it to have 10 % probability) and generating on-screen scenarios allows us comfortably to watch how the model behaves with and without the risk occurring. Setting two risks each to a 70 % probability will show both risks occurring at the same time in about 50 % of the scenarios, etc.

17.2.6 Comparing results of alternative models

There are often several ways that one could construct a Monte Carlo model to tackle the same problem. Each method should give you the same answer, of course. So, if you are unsure about one way of manipulating distributions, then try it another (perhaps less efficient) way and see if the answers are the same.

The more difficult area is where you may feel that there are two or more completely different stochastic processes that could explain the problem at hand. Ideally, one would like to be able to construct both models and see whether they come up with similar answers. But what do we mean by similar? In fact, from a decision analysis point of view we don't actually mean that they come up with the same numbers or distributions: we mean that, if presented with either result, the decision-maker would make the same decision. If we do have the luxury of being able to construct two completely different model interpretations of the world, we may be able to use a technique called Bayesian model averaging that weights the likelihood of each model on the basis of how probable they would make our observations.

We nearly always will not have the luxury of being able to model two or more different approaches to the same problem because of time and resource constraints. If you are going to have to put all your efforts into one model, try to make sure that your peers agree with your approach, and that the decision-maker will be comfortable with making a decision based on the model's assumptions. The decision-maker could prefer you to construct a model that may not be the most likely explanation for your problem, but that offers the most conservative guidance for managing it.

Finally, simple "back-of-the-envelope" checks can also be useful. Managers will often look at the results of a risk analysis and compare with their gut feeling and/or a simple calculation. It is surprising how often a modeller can get too involved in the modelling and pay too little attention to the numbers that come out at the end.

17.3 Comparing Predictions Against Reality

In many cases, this might be akin to "shutting the stable door after the horse has bolted". Clearly, if you have made an irreversible decision on the basis of a risk assessment, this exercise may be of limited value. However, even when that is true, analysing which parts of the model turned out to be the most inaccurate will help you focus in on how you might improve your risk models for the next decision, or prepare you for how badly you will have got it wrong.

Perhaps it is possible to structure a decision into a series of steps, each informed by risk analysis, so that at each step in the series of decisions the risk analysis predictions can be compared against what has happened so far. For example, setting up an investment that started with a pilot roll-out in a test market would let a company limit the risks and at the same time evaluate how well it had been able to predict the initial level of success.

Project risk analysis models, in which the cost and duration of the elements of a project are estimated, are an excellent example of where predictions can be continuously compared with reality. The uncertainty of the cost and time elements can be updated as each task is being completed to estimate the remaining duration and costs, while a review of each task estimate against what actually happened can give you a feel for whether your estimators have been systematically pessimistic or optimistic. Chapter 13 gives a number of techniques for monitoring and calibrating expert estimates.

Chapter 18

Discounted cashflow modelling

A typical discounted cashflow model for a potential investment makes forecasts of costs and revenues over the life of the project and discounts those revenues back to a present value. Most analysts start with a "base case" model and add uncertainty to the important elements of the model. Happily, the mathematics involved in adding risk to these types of model is quite simple. In this chapter, I will assume that you can build a base case cashflow model that will look something like Figure 18.2 and I will focus on the input modelling elements of Figure 18.1 and some financial outputs.

There are a number of topics that are already well covered in this book:

- *Expert estimates.* In capital investment models we rely a great deal on expert judgement to estimate variables like costs, time to market, sales volumes, discount levels, etc. Chapter 14 discusses how to elicit estimates from subject matter experts.

- *Fitting distributions to data.* We don't usually have a great deal of historic data to work with in capital investment projects because the investment is new. I have worked with a very successful retail company that investigates levels of pedestrian traffic at different locations in a town where it is considering locating a new outlet. It has excellent regional data on how that traffic converts to till receipts. That is quite typical of the type of data one might have for a cashflow analysis, and I will go through such a model later in this chapter. Hydrocarbon and mineral exploration will generally have improving levels of data about the reserves, but have specialised methods (e.g. Krieging) for statistically analysing their data, so I won't consider them further here. Otherwise, Chapter 10 discusses distribution fitting in some detail.

- *Correlation.* Simple forms of correlation modelling – recognising that two or more variables are likely to be linked in some way – are very important in cashflow models. The correlation techniques described in Sections 13.4 and 13.5 are particularly useful in cashflow models.

- *Time series.* Chapter 12 deals with many different technical time series models. GBM, seasonal and autoregressive models are useful for modelling inflation, exchange and interest rates over time in a cashflow model. Lead indicators can help predict market size a short time into the future. In this chapter I consider variables such as demand for products and sales volumes that are generally built on a more intuitive basis.

- *Common errors.* Risk analysis cashflow models are not generally that technically complicated, but our reviews show that the types of error described in Section 7.4 appear very frequently, so I very much encourage you to read that section carefully. The rest of Chapter 7 offers some ideas on model building that are very applicable to cashflow models.

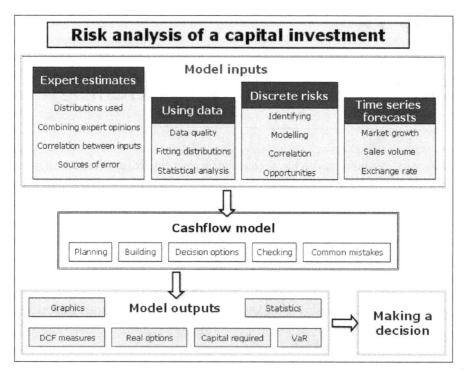

Figure 18.1 Modelling elements in a capital investment discounted cashflow model.

	A	B	C	D	E	F	G	H	I	J	K	L	M
1		NPV (10%)	$110,795.07										
2													
3		Year	2008	2009	2010	2011	2012	2013	2014	2015	2016	2017	
4													
5						Cash Flow							
6		Total Revenue	$ -	$ -	$ 208,388	$ 205,723	$ 216,537	$ 239,116	$ 317,872	$ 363,047	$ 423,458	$ 500,403	
7		Cost of Goods Sold	$ -	$ -	$ 86,234	$ 85,132	$ 89,606	$ 98,950	$ 131,540	$ 150,235	$ 175,234	$ 207,075	
8		Gross Margin	$ -	$ -	$ 122,154	$ 120,592	$ 126,930	$ 140,166	$ 186,331	$ 212,812	$ 248,224	$ 293,328	
9		Operating Expenses	$ 172,603	$ 174,041	$ 84,521	$ 55,000	$ 20,000	$ 20,000	$ 20,000	$ 25,000	$ 25,000	$ 25,000	
10		Earnings Before Taxes	$ (172,603)	$ (174,041)	$ 37,633	$ 65,592	$ 106,930	$ 120,166	$ 166,331	$ 187,812	$ 223,224	$ 268,328	
11		Tax Basis	$ (172,603)	$ (346,644)	$ (309,011)	$ (243,419)	$ (136,489)	$ (16,323)	$ 150,008	$ 187,812	$ 223,224	$ 268,328	
12		Income Tax	$ -	$ -	$ -	$ -	$ -	$ -	$ 69,004	$ 86,394	$ 102,683	$ 123,431	
13		Net Income	$ (172,603)	$ (174,041)	$ 37,633	$ 65,592	$ 106,930	$ 120,166	$ 97,328	$ 101,419	$ 120,541	$ 144,897	
14													
15						Market Conditions							
16		Number of Competitors	0	0	1	1	1	1	1	2	2	2	
17		Unit Cost			$23	$24	$25	$27	$28	$30	$32	$34	
18		Inflation Rate				4.7%	4.7%	5.5%	5.8%	6.0%	6.1%	5.8%	
19		Tax Rate	46%	46%	46%	46%	46%	46%	46%	46%	46%	46%	
20													
21						Sales Activity							
22		Sales Price			$56	$58	$61	$64	$68	$72	$77	$81	
23		Market volume			3,738	4,697	5,903	7,419	9,323	11,716	14,724	18,504	
24		Sales Volume			3,738	3,523	3,542	3,709	4,662	5,021	5,522	6,168	
25													
26						Production Expense							
27		Product Development	$ 47,603	$ 19,041	$ 9,521	$ -	$ -	$ -	$ -	$ -	$ -	$ -	
28		Capital Expenses	$ 125,000	$ 145,000	$ 55,000	$ 35,000	$ -	$ -	$ -	$ -	$ -	$ -	
29		Overhead	$ -	$ 10,000	$ 20,000	$ 20,000	$ 20,000	$ 20,000	$ 20,000	$ 25,000	$ 25,000	$ 25,000	
30		Total Expenses	$ 172,603	$ 174,041	$ 84,521	$ 55,000	$ 20,000	$ 20,000	$ 20,000	$ 25,000	$ 25,000	$ 25,000	
31													

Figure 18.2 A typical, if somewhat reduced, discounted cashflow model.

18.1 Useful Time Series Models of Sales and Market Size

18.1.1 Effect of an intervention at some uncertain point in time

Time series variables are often affected by single identifiable "shocks", like elections, changes to a law, the introduction of a competitor, the start or finish of a war, a scandal, etc. The modelling of the occurrence of a shock and its effects may need to take into account several elements:

- when the shock may occur (this could be random);
- whether this changes the probability or impact of other possible shocks;
- the effect of the shock – magnitude and duration.

Consider the following problem. People are purchasing your product at a current rate of 88/month, and the rate appears to be increasing by 1.3 sales/month with each month. However, we are 80 % sure that a competitor is going to enter the market and will do so between 20 and 50 months from now. If the competitor enters the market, they will take about 30 % of your sales. Forecast the number of sales there will be for the next 100 months.

Two typical pathways for this problem are shown in Figure 18.3, and the model that created them is shown in Figure 18.4. The Bernoulli variable returns a 1 with 80 % probability, otherwise a 0. It is used as a "flag", the 1 representing a competitor entry, the 0 representing no competitor. Other cells use conditional logic to adapt to the scenario. You can use a Binomial(1, 80 %) if your software does not have a Bernoulli distribution. In Crystal Ball this is also called a Yes:No distribution. The StepUniform generates integer values between 20 and 50, and cell E4 returns the month 1000 if the competitor does not enter the market, i.e. a time beyond the modelled period. It is a good idea if you use this type of technique to make such a number very far from the range of the modelled period in case someone decides to extend the period analysed. A Poisson distribution is used to model the number of sales reflecting that the sales are independent of each other and randomly distributed in time. The nice thing about a Poisson distribution is that it takes just one parameter – its mean, so you don't have to think about variation about that mean separately (e.g. determine a standard deviation).

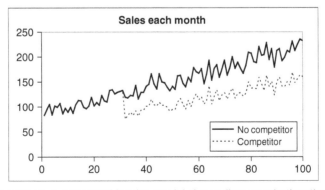

Figure 18.3 Possible pathways generated by the model depending on whether the competitor enters the market.

	A	B	C	D	E	F
1						
2		Probability competitor enters the market			80%	
3		Competitor entry flag			1	
4		Competitor entry time			28	
5		Expected fraction of sales that would be lost			30%	
6		Current sales/month			88.00	
7		Expected growth per month			1.30	
8						
9		Month	Expected sales	Sales fraction lost	Sales	
10		1	89.30	0	79	
11		2	90.60	0	111	
12		3	91.90	0	85	
13		4	93.20	0	103	
14		5	94.50	0	99	
15		6	95.80	0	97	
108		99	216.70	0.3	159	
109		100	218.00	0.3	153	
110						
111			*Formulae table*			
112	E3		=VoseBernoulli(E2)			
113	E4		=IF(E3=1,VoseStepUniform(20,50),1000)			
114	C10:C109		=B10*$E$7+$E$6			
115	D10:D109		=IF(B10<$E$4,0,$E$5)			
116	E10:E109		=VosePoisson(C10*(1-D10))			
117						

Figure 18.4 Model of Poisson sales affected by the possible entry of a competitor.

18.1.2 Distributing market share

When competitors enter an established market they have to establish the reputation of their product and fight for market share with others that are already established. This takes time, so it is more realistic to model a gradual loss of market share to competitors.

Consider the following problem. Market volume for your product is expected to grow each year by (10%, 20%, 40%) beginning next year at (2500, 3000, 5000) up to a maximum of 20 000 units. You expect one competitor to emerge as soon as the market volume reaches 3500 units in the previous year. A second will appear at 8500 units. Your competitors' shares of the market will grow linearly until you all have equal market share after 3 years. Model the sales you will make.

Figure 18.5 shows the model. It is mostly self-explanatory. The interesting component lies in cells F10:L10, which divides the forecast market for your product among the average of the number of competitors over the last 3 years and yourself (the "1" in the equation). Averaging over 3 years is a neat way of allocating an emerging competitor 1/3 of your market strength in the first year, 2/3 in the second and equal strength from the third year on – meaning that they will then sell as many units as you. What is so helpful about this little trick is that it automatically takes into account each new competitor and when they entered the market, which is rather difficult to do otherwise. Note that we need three zeros in cells C8:E8 to initialise the model.

	A	B	C	D	E	F	G	H	I	J	K	L
1												
2		Market size trigger										
3		1 competitor	3500									
4		2 competitors	8500									
5		Market growth	24%									
6												
7		**Year from now**			**0**	**1**	**2**	**3**	**4**	**5**	**6**	**7**
8		Number of Competitors	0	0	0	0	0	1	1	1	1	2
9		Market volume			2,775	3,449	4,286	5,326	6,619	8,225	10,221	12,702
10		Sales Volume			2,775	3,449	4,286	3,995	3,971	4,112	5,111	5,444
11												
12		*Formulae table*										
13		C5	=VosePERT(10%,20%,40%)									
14		C8:E8	{0,0,0}									
15		F8:L8	=IF(E9>$C$4,2,IF(E9>$C$3,1,0))									
16		E9	=VosePERT(2500,3000,5000)									
17		F9:L9	=MIN(20000,E9*(1+$C$5))									
18		F10:L10 (output)	=ROUND(E9/(AVERAGE(C8:E8)+1),0)									
19												

Figure 18.5 Model of sales where the total market is shared with new-entry competitors.

18.1.3 Reduced sales over time to a finite market

Some products are essentially a once-in-a-lifetime purchase, e.g. a life insurance, big flat-screen TV, a new guttering system or a pet identification chip. If we are initially quite successful in selling the product into the potential market, the remaining market size decreases, although this can be compensated for to some degree by new potential consumers. Consider the following problem: There are currently PERT(50 000, 55 000, 60 000) possible purchasers of your product. Each year there will be about a 10 % turnover (meaning 10 % more possible purchasers will appear). The probability that you will sell to any particular purchaser in a year is PERT(10 %, 20 %, 35 %). Forecast sales for the next 10 years.

Figure 18.6 shows the model for this problem. Note that C8:C16 is subtracting sales already made from the previous year's market size but also adding in a regenerated market element. The binomial distribution then converts the current market size to sales. In the particular scenario shown in Figure 18.6, the probability of selling is high (26 %), so sales start off high and drop off quickly as the regeneration rate is so much lower (10 %). Note that some Monte Carlo software cannot handle large numbers of trials in their binomial distribution, in which case you will need to use a Poisson or normal approximation (Section III.9.1).

18.1.4 Growth of sales over time up to a maximum as a function of marketing effort

Sometimes we might find it easier to estimate what our annual sales will be when stabilised, but be unsure of how quickly we will be able to achieve that stability. In this sort of situation it can be easier to model a theoretical maximum sales and match it to some ramping function. A typical form of such

	A	B	C	D	E	F
1						
2		Current market size			54613	
3		Turnover rate			10%	
4		Probability selling to an individual			26.0%	
5						
6		Year	Market size	Sales		
7		1	54,613	14,219		
8		2	45,855	11,834		
9		3	39,482	10,212		
10		4	34,731	9,153		
11		5	31,039	8,094		
12		6	28,406	7,443		
13		7	26,424	6,862		
14		8	25,023	6,564		
15		9	23,920	6,201		
16		10	23,180	6,005		
17						
18			*Formulae table*			
19		E2	=VosePERT(50000,55000,60000)			
20		E4	=VosePERT(10%,20%,35%)			
21		C7	=ROUND(E2,0)			
22		C8:C16	=ROUND(C7–D7+$E$2*$E$3,0)			
23		D7:D16	=VoseBinomial(C7,$E$4)			
24						

Figure 18.6 Model forecasting sales over time to a finite market.

a ramping function $r(t)$ is

$$r(t) = 1 - 0.5^{\wedge} \frac{t}{t_{1/2}}$$

which will produce a curve that starts at 0 for $t = 0$ and asymptotically reaches 1 at an infinite value of t, but reaches 0.5 at $t = t_{1/2}$. Consider the following problem: you expect a final sales rate of PERT(1800, 2300, 3600) and expect to achieve half that in the next PERT(3.5, 4, 5) years. Produce a sales forecast for the next 10 years.

Figure 18.7 provides a solution.

18.2 Summing Random Variables

Perhaps the most common errors in cashflow modelling occur when one wishes to sum a number of random costs, sales or revenues. For example, imagine that you expect to have Lognormal(100 000, 25 000) customers enter your store per year and they will spend \$Lognormal(55, 12) each – how would you estimate the total revenue? People generally write something like

$$= \text{ROUND}(\text{Lognormal}(100\,000, 25\,000), 0) * \text{Lognormal}(55, 12) \tag{18.1}$$

using the ROUND function in Excel to recognise that the number of people must be discrete. But let's think what happens when the software starts simulating. It will pick a random value from each

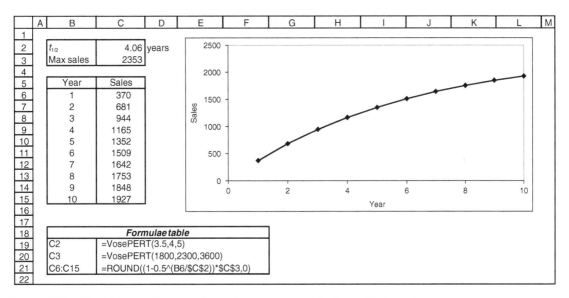

Figure 18.7 Model forecasting ramping sales to an uncertain theoretical maximum.

distribution and multiply them together. Picking a reasonably high till receipt, the probability that a random customer will spend more than \$70, for example, is

$$= 1 - \text{VoseLognormalProb}(70, 55, 12, 1) = 0.11\%$$

The probability that two people will do the same is $11\% * 11\% = 1.2\%$, and the probability that thousands of people will spend that much is infinitesimally small. However, Equation (18.1) will assign a 11 % probability that all customers will spend over \$70 no matter how many there are. The equation is wrong because it should have summed ROUND(Lognormal(100 000, 25 000), 0) *separate* Lognormal(55, 12) distributions. That's a big, slow model, so we use a variety of techniques to shortcut to the answer, which is the topic of Chapter 11.

18.3 Summing Variable Margins on Variable Revenues

A common situation is that we have a large random number of revenue items that follow the same probability distribution but that are independent of each other, and we have independent profit margins that follow another distribution that must be applied to each revenue item. This type of model quickly becomes extremely cumbersome to implement because for each revenue item we need two distributions, one for revenue and another for the profit margin, and we may have large numbers of revenue items. It is such a common problem that we designed a function in ModelRisk to handle this, allowing you to keep the model to a manageable size, speeding up simulation time and making the model far simpler to review. Perhaps most importantly, it allows you to avoid a lot of conditional logic that it is easy to get wrong.[1] Consider the following problem. A capital venture company is considering investing in

---

[1] I apologise if this comes across as a sales pitch for ModelRisk, but it is designed with finance people in mind.

a company that makes TV shows. They expect to make PERT(28, 32, 39) pilots next year which will generate a revenue of $PERT(120, 150, 250)k each independently and from which the profit margin is PERT(1%, 5%, 12%). There is a 30% chance that each pilot is made into a TV show in that country running for Discrete({1, 2, 3, 4, 5},{0.4, 0.25, 0.2, 0.1, 0.05}) series, where each season of each series generates $PERT(120, 150, 250)k with margins of PERT(15%, 25%, 45%). There is a 20% chance that these local series will be sold to the US, generating $PERT(240, 550, 1350)k per season sold, of which the profit margin is PERT(65%, 70%, 85%). What is the total profit generated from next year's pilots?

The problem is not technically difficult, but the scale of the modelling explodes very quickly. We worked on the model for a real investment of this type and it had many more layers: pilots in several countries, merchandising of various types, repeats, etc., and it took a lot of effort to manage. Figure 18.8 shows a surprisingly succinct model: rows 2 to 11 are the input data, rows 14 to 16 are the actual calculations.

There are a few things to point out. In cell F2, 1/2 is subtracted and added to the minimum and maximum estimates respectively of the number of pilots to give a more realistic chance of their occurrence after rounding. Distributions are input as ModelRisk objects in cells F3, F4, F6, F7, F8, F10 and F11 because we want to use these distributions many times. Cell C16, and elsewhere, uses the Vose Sum Product function to add together revenue * margin for each pilot, where the revenue and

	A	B	C	D	E	F	G
1						*Values in $000*	
2		Number of new pilots				33	
3		Pilot revenue				VosePERT(120,150,250)	
4		Pilot profitability as fraction of revenue				VosePERT(0.01,0.05,0.12)	
5		Probability pilot converts to local series				35%	
6		Number of seasons in a series				VoseDiscrete({1,2,3,4,5},{0.4,0.25,0.2,0.1,0.05})	
7		Revenue for a season for a local series				VosePERT(120,150,250)	
8		Local profitability as fraction of revenue				VosePERT(0.15,0.25,0.45)	
9		Probability local series sold to US				20%	
10		Revenue from US for a season				VosePERT(240,550,1350)	
11		US profitability as fraction of revenue				VosePERT(0.65,0.7,0.85)	
12							
13			Pilots made	Local only series	Local & US series	Total	
14		Series made	NA	8	3	11	
15		Seasons made	NA	15	9		
16		Profit	295	681	3933	**4909**	
17							
18					*Formulae table*		
19		F2		=ROUND(VosePERT(8-0.5,11,17+0.5),0)			
20		F3 (F4, F7, F10, F11 similar)		=VosePERTObject(120,150,250)			
21		F6		=VoseDiscreteObject({1,2,3,4,5},{0.4,0.25,0.2,0.1,0.05})			
22		F14		=VoseBinomial(F2,F5)			
23		E14		=VoseBinomial(F14,F9)			
24		D14		=F14-E14			
25		D15:E15		=VoseAggregateMC(D14,$F$6)			
26		C16		=VoseSumProduct(F2,F3,F4)			
27		D16		=VoseSumProduct(D15,F7,F8)			
28		E16		=VoseSumProduct(E15,F7,F8)+VoseSumProduct(E15,F10,F11)			
29		F16 (output)		=SUM(C16:E16)			
30							

Figure 18.8 Model forecasting profits from TV series.

margin distributions are defined by the distribution objects in cells F3 and F4 respectively. Cell F14 simulates the number of pilots that made it to become series, from which the model determines how many of those become series also sold into the US in cell E14, the difference being the number of pilots that only became local series in cell D14. Setting up the logic this way ensures that we have a consistent model: the local only and the US and local series always add up to the total series produced. Cells D15 and E15 use the VoseAggregate(x, y) function to simulate the sum of x random variables all taking the same distribution y defined as an object.

18.4 Financial Measures in Risk Analysis

The two main measures of profitability in DCF models are *net present value* (NPV) and *internal rate of return* (IRR). The two main measures of financial exposure are value at risk (VAR) and expected shortfall. Their pros and cons are discussed in Section 20.5.

18.4.1 Net present value

Net present value (NPV) attempts to determine the *present value* of a series of cashflows from a project that stretches out into the future. This present value is a measure of how much the company is gaining at today's money by undertaking the project: in other words, how much more the company itself will be worth by accepting the project.

An NPV calculation discounts future cashflows at a specified discount rate r that takes account of:

1. The time value of money (e.g. if inflation is running at 4%, £1.04 in a year's time is only worth £1.00 today).

2. The interest that could have been earned over inflation by investing instead in a guaranteed investment.

3. The extra return that is required over parts 1 and 2 to compensate for the degree of risk that is being accepted in this project.

Parts 1 and 2 are combined to produce the risk-free interest rate, r_f. This is typically determined as the interest paid by guaranteed fixed-payment investments like government bonds with a term roughly equivalent to the duration of the project.

The extra interest r^* over r_f needed for part 3 is determined by looking at the uncertainty of the project. In risk analysis models, this uncertainty is represented by the spread of the distributions of cashflow for each period. The sum of r^* and r_f is called the risk-adjusted discount rate r.

The most commonly used calculation for the NPV of a cashflow series over n periods is as follows:

$$\text{NPV}(r) = \sum_{i=1}^{n} \frac{\overline{C}_i}{(1+r)^i}$$

where $\overline{C}_i$ are the expected (i.e. average) values of the cashflows in each period and r is the risk-adjusted discount rate.

NPV calculations performed in a risk analysis spreadsheet model are usually presented as a distribution of NPVs because the cashflow values selected in the NPV calculations are their distributions rather than their expected values. *Theoretically*, this is incorrect. Since an NPV is the net *present* value, it can have no uncertainty. It is the amount of money at which the company values the project today. The problem is that we have double-counted our risk by first discounting at the risk-adjusted discounted rate r and then showing the NPV as a distribution (i.e. it is uncertain).

Two theoretically correct methods for calculating an NPV in risk analysis are discussed below, along with a more practical, but strictly speaking incorrect, alternative:

- *Theoretical approach 1: Discount the cashflow distributions at the risk-free rate*. This produces a distribution of NPVs at r_f and ensures that the risk is not double-counted. However, such a distribution is not at all easy to interpret since decision-makers will almost certainly never have dealt with risk-free rate NPVs and therefore have nothing to compare the model output against.

- *Theoretical approach 2: Discount the expected value of each cashflow at the risk-adjusted discount rate*. This is the application of the above formula. It results in a single figure for the NPV of the project. A risk analysis is run to determine the expected value and spread of the cashflows in each period. The discount rate is usually determined by comparing the riskiness associated with the project's cashflows against the riskiness of other projects in the company's portfolio. The company can then assign a discount rate above or below its usual discount rate, depending on whether the project being analysed exhibits more or less risk than the average. Some companies determine a range of discount rates (three or so) to be used against projects of different riskiness.

The major problems of this method are that it assumes the cashflow distributions are symmetric and that no correlation exists between cashflows. Distributions of costs and returns almost always exhibit some form of asymmetry, and in a typical investment project there is also always some form of correlation between cashflow periods. For example, sales in one period will be affected by previous sales, a capital injection in one period often means that it doesn't occur in the next one (e.g. expansion of a factory) or the model may include an autocorrelated time series forecast of prices, production rates or sales volume. If there is a strong positive correlation between cashflows, this method will overestimate the NPV. Conversely, a strong negative correlation between cashflows will result in the NPV being underestimated. The correlation between cashflows may take any number of, often complex, forms. I am not aware of any financial theory that provides a practical method for adjusting the NPV to take account of these correlations.

In practice, it is easier to apply the risk-adjusted discount rate r to the cashflow distributions to produce a distribution of NPVs. This method incorporates correlation between distributions automatically and enables the decision-maker to compare directly with past NPV analyses.

As I have already explained, the problem associated with this technique is that it will double-count the risk: firstly in the discount rate and then by representing the NPV as a distribution. However, if one is aware of this shortfall, the result is very useful in determining the probability of achieving the required discount rate (i.e. the probability of a positive NPV). The actual NPV to quote in a report would be the expected value of the NPV distribution.

18.4.2 Internal rate of return

The internal rate of return (IRR) of a project is the discount rate applied to its future cashflows such that it produces a zero NPV. In other words, it is the discount rate that exactly balances the value of all costs and revenues of the project. If the cashflows are uncertain, the IRR will also be uncertain and therefore have a distribution associated with it.

A distribution of the possible IRRs is useful to determine the probability of achieving any specific discount rate, and this can be compared with the probability other projects offer of achieving the target discount rate. It is not recommended that the distribution and associated statistics of possible IRRs be used for comparing projects because of the properties of IRRs discussed below.

Unlike the NPV calculation, there is no exact formula for calculating the IRR of a cashflow series. Instead, a first guess is usually required, from which the computer will make progressively more accurate estimates until it finds a value that produces an NPV as near to zero as required.

If the cumulative cashflow position of the project passes through zero more than once, there is more than one valid solution to the IRR inequality. This is not normally a problem with deterministic models because the cumulative cashflow position can easily be monitored and the smallest of any IRR solutions selected. However, a risk analysis model is dynamic, making it difficult to appreciate its exact behaviour. Thus, the cumulative cashflow position may pass through zero and back in some of the risk analysis iterations and not be spotted. This can produce quite inaccurate distributions of possible IRRs. In order to avoid this problem, it may be worth including a couple of lines in your model that calculate the cumulative cashflow position and the number of times it passes through zero. If this is selected as a model output, you will be able to determine whether this is a statistically significant problem and alter the first guess to compensate for it.

IRRs cannot be calculated for only positive or only negative cashflows. IRRs are therefore not useful for comparing between two purely negative or positive cashflow options, e.g. between hiring or buying a piece of equipment.

It is difficult to compare distributions of IRR between two options unless the difference is very large. Stochastic dominance tests (Section 5.4.5) will certainly be of little direct use. This is because a percentage increase in an IRR at low returns (e.g. from 3 to 4 %) is of much greater real value than a percentage increase at high returns (e.g. from 30 to 31 %). Consider the following illustration. I am offered payments of £20 a year for 10 years (i.e. £200 total) in return for a single payment now. I am asked to pay £200 – obviously a bad investment giving an IRR of 0 %. I negotiate to drop the price and thereby produce a positive IRR. Figure 18.9 illustrates the relationship between the reduction in price I achieve and the resulting IRR. The reduction in price I achieve is directly equivalent to the increase in the present value of the investment, so the graph relates real value to IRR. As the saving I make

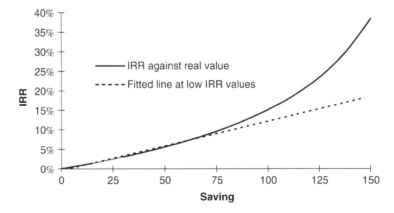

Figure 18.9 An example of the non-linear relationship between IRR and real (or present) value.

approaches £200, the IRR approaches infinity. Clearly there is no straight-line relationship between IRR and true value. It is therefore *very* difficult to compare the value of two projects in terms of the IRR distributions they offer. One project may offer a long right-hand tail that can easily increase the expected IRR, but in real-value terms this could easily be outweighed by a comparatively small diminishing of the left-hand tail of the other option.

Chapter 19

Project risk analysis

Project risk analysis is concerned with the assessment of the risks and uncertainties that threaten a project. A "project" consists of a number of interrelated tasks whose aim is to produce a specific result or results. Typically, a project risk analysis consists of analysing schedule and cost risk, although other aspects like the quality of the final product are sometimes included. There will also often be an analysis of the cashflow of the project, especially at the conception and bidding stages, but these are not discussed here as a cashflow model is fairly simple to produce.

A cost risk analysis consists of looking at the various costs associated with a project, their uncertainties and any risks or opportunities that may affect these costs. Risks and opportunities are defined as discrete possible events that will increase and decrease the project costs respectively. They are both characterised by estimates of their probability of occurrence and the magnitude of their impact. The distributions of cost are then added up in a risk analysis to determine the uncertainty in the total cost of the project.

A schedule risk analysis looks at the time required to complete the various tasks associated with a project, and the interrelationship between these tasks. Risks and opportunities are identified for each task and an analysis is performed to determine the total duration of the project and, usually, the durations until specific milestones within the project are achieved. A schedule risk analysis is generally more complex to perform than a cost risk analysis because the logical connections between the tasks have to be modelled in order to determine the critical path. For this reason, we will look at the elements of a cost risk analysis first.

A project's cost and duration are, in reality, linked together. Tasks in a project are often quantified by, among other things, the number of person-weeks (amount of work) needed to complete them. The duration of the task is then equal to the person-weeks/people on the job, and the cost equals [person-weeks] * [labour rate]. Costs and durations are also linked if the model includes a penalty clause for exceeding a deadline.

Cost elements and, particularly, schedule durations are also often correlated. Correlation, or dependency, modelling has been described in detail in Chapter 12 and will not be repeated here. However, it is important to be aware that dependencies often exist in a risk analysis model, and failure to include them in an analysis will generally underestimate the risk.

In this chapter, we will assume that a preliminary exercise has already been carried out to identify the various risks associated with the project. We will assume that a risk register has been drawn up (see Section 1.6) and that sufficient information has been gathered to be able adequately to quantify the probabilities associated with each risk and the size of potential impact on the tasks of the project.

A project risk analysis is often completed after a more rudimentary (deterministic) analysis that uses single-point estimates for each task duration and cost. A comparison of the results of this deterministic analysis with those of the risk analysis, where distributions have been used to model uncertainty components, often surprises people. Somehow, one expects that a deterministic analysis based on values one thinks most likely to occur should produce results that equate to the mode of the risk analysis output distribution. In fact, it turns out that a risk analysis model will provide a mode and mean that are nearly always greater than the deterministic model result. Sometimes the risk analysis output distribution will not even include the deterministic result! The main reason for this is that the distributions one assigns to uncertainty components are nearly always right skewed, i.e. they have a longer tail to the right than to the left. This is because there are many more things that can go wrong than go right, and because we are always trying to place emphasis on doing the job as quickly and cheaply as possible. Thus, the model distributions nearly always have more probability to the right of the mode than to the left, which means that, in the aggregate, for most models one is much more likely to have a scenario that exceeds the deterministic scenario. A schedule risk analysis will diverge even more from its deterministic equivalent than a cost model because any task whose commencement depends on the finish of two or more other tasks begins at the maximum of the samples from the distributions of finish dates of the other tasks, not the maximum of their modes.

19.1 Cost Risk Analysis

A cost risk analysis is usually developed from a work breakdown structure (WBS) which is a document that details, from the top down, the various work packages (WPs) comprising the project. Each WP may then be subdivided into a bill of quantities and estimates of the labour required to complete them.

There will usually be a number of cost items associated with each WP that have an element of uncertainty. In addition, there may be discrete events (risks or opportunities) that could change the size of these costs. The normal uncertainties in the cost items are modelled by continuous distributions like the PERT or triangular distribution. I will use the triangular distribution for the rest of this chapter for simplicity, but the reader should by now be aware (see Section 14.3.2) of the misgivings I have about this distribution. The impact of the risks and opportunities will similarly be modelled by continuous distributions, but whether they occur or not is modelled with a discrete distribution. To illustrate this, consider the following example.

Example 19.1

A new office block has been designed to be roofed with corrugated galvanised steel at a cost of between £165 000 and £173 000, but most probably £167 000. However, the council's planning department has received a number of objections from local residents. The architect thinks there is about a 30 % chance that the building will have to be roofed with slate at a cost of between £193 000 and £208 000, but most likely about £198 000.

Figure 19.1 shows how to model the roofing's cost using triangular distributions. The model selects a steel roof (cell C5) for 70 % of the scenarios and a slate roof (cell C6) for the remaining 30 % to produce a combined uncertainty in cell C8. ♦

Many of the cost items for the project will be in the form of: x items @ £y/item, where x and y are both uncertain quantities. At first sight it seems logical simply to multiply these two variables together to get the cost, i.e. cost $= x \cdot y$. However, there is a potential problem with this approach (determining the sum of random variables is discussed in detail in Chapter 11). Consider the following two examples.

Example 19.2

A ship's hull consists of 562 plates, each of which has to be riveted in place. Each plate is riveted by one worker. The supervisor, reflecting on the efficiency of her workforce, considers that the best her riveters have ever done is put up a plate in 3 h 45 min. On the other hand, the longest they have taken

	A	B	C	D	E	F	G	H
1								
2		**Model of the cost of the roof of the new office block**						
3								
4			Distribution	Minimum	Most likely	Maximum	Probability	
5		Galvanised steel roof	168,333	£ 165,000	£ 167,000	£ 173,000	70%	
6		Slate roof	198,000	£ 193,000	£ 198,000	£ 203,000	30%	
7								
8		**Combined estimate**	168,333					
9								
10		*Formulae table*						
11		C5:C6	=VoseTriangle(D5,E5,F5)					
12		C8 (output)	=VoseDiscrete(C5:C6,G5:G6)					
13								

Figure 19.1   Cost model for Example 19.1.

is about 5 h 30 min, and it is far more likely that a plate would be riveted in about 4 h 15 min. Each riveter is paid £7.50 an hour. What is the total labour cost for riveting? One's first thought might be to model the total cost as follows:

$$\text{Cost} = 562 * \text{Triangle}(3.75, 4.25, 5.5) * £7.50$$

What happens if we run a simulation on this formula? In some iterations we will produce values close to 3.75 from the triangular distribution. This is saying that all of the plates could have been riveted in record time – clearly not a realistic scenario. Similarly, some iterations will generate values close to 5.5 from the triangular distribution – the scenario that the workforce took as long to put up *every* plate on the ship as it took them to do the trickiest plate in memory.

The problem lies in the fact that the triangular distribution is modelling the uncertainty of an *individual* plate but we are using it as if it were the distribution of the *average* time for 562 plates.

There are several approaches (Chapter 11) to the correct modelling of this problem. The easiest is to model each plate separately, i.e. set up a column of 562 Triangle(3.75, 4.25, 5.5) distributions, add them up and multiply the sum by £7.50. While this is quite correct, it is obviously impractical to use a spreadsheet model of 562 cells just for this one cost item, so the technique is only really useful if there are just a few items to be summed, or one could use VoseAggregateMC(562, VoseTriangleObject(3.75, 4.25, 5.5)).

Another option is to apply the central limit theorem (see Section 6.3.3). The mean μ and standard deviation σ of a Triangle(3.75, 4.25, 5.5) distribution are

$$\mu = 4.5$$

$$\sigma = 0.368$$

Since there are 562 items, the distribution of the total person-hours for the job is given by

$$\text{Total person-hours} = \text{Normal}(4.5 \times 562, 0.368 \times \sqrt{562}) = \text{Normal}(2529, 8.724)$$

Then, the total labour cost for riveting is estimated as

$$\text{Cost} = \text{Normal}(2529, 8.724) \times £7.50 \; \blacklozenge$$

Once each cost item for the project has been identified, along with any associated risks and uncertainties, a model can be produced to estimate the total project cost. Figure 19.2 illustrates the sort of model structure that could be used. In this example, each item is clearly defined, along with the assumptions that are used in its estimation and the impacts and probabilities of any risks.

The results from a simulation of the total project cost can be represented in a number of ways, as described in Chapter 5. An analysis of the project's costs will generally be used to produce figures for the budget and contingency and, if the project is being commissioned by another organisation, a bid price. Section 15.3.2 describes how these are determined.

One question that management will often ask is how the budget and contingency are distributed back among the cost items. This knowledge will help the project manager to keep an eye on how the project is progressing. My approach is to distribute back the budget and contingency costs so that the figures associated with each cost item have the same probability of being exceeded. Using this approach will give each cost item the same chance of coming in within its budget figure or its (budget + contingency) figure and will avoid controllers of some cost items being given almost impossible targets to meet and others easy targets. This method of distributing budget and contingency costs among cost items is demonstrated in the following example, using the cost model from Figure 19.2.

A	B	C	D	E	F	G	H	I
		Cost model for the new bridge						
			Distribution	Minimum	Most likely	Maximum	Probability	
	WP1	Planning	£ 17,267	£ 15,500	£ 17,200	£ 19,100	0.6	
	R1	Initial application refused	£ 19,767	£ 18,400	£ 19,700	£ 21,200	0.4	
		WP1 total	£ 17,267					
	WP	Earthworks	£ 76,667	£ 72,000	£ 74,500	£ 83,500	0.8	
	R2	Water table problem	£ 85,400	£ 81,300	£ 84,600	£ 90,300	0.2	
		WP2 total	£ 76,667					
	WP3	Steel	£ 57,533	£ 56,300	£ 57,200	£ 59,100		
	WP4	Concrete	£ 47,533	£ 44,300	£ 46,700	£ 51,600		
	WP5	Labour	£ 34,200	£ 32,300	£ 33,500	£ 36,800	0.75	
	R3	First choice contractor not available	£ 41,200	£ 38,300	£ 41,200	£ 44,100	0.25	
		WP5 total	£ 34,200					
	WP6	Plant hire	£ 31,633	£ 29,600	£ 31,200	£ 34,100		
	WP7	Road surfacing	£ 22,933	£ 22,000	£ 22,700	£ 24,100		
	WP8		£ 11,633	£ 11,000	£ 11,500	£ 12,400		
		Total cost	£ 299,400					
		Formulae table						
		D5,D6,D9,D10,D13:D18,D21:D25	=VoseTriangle(E5,F5,G5)					
		D7,D11,D19	=VoseDiscrete(D5:D6,H5:H6)					
		D27	=D7+D11+D13+D15+SUM(D19:D25)					

Figure 19.2 Example of a project cost model structure.

Example 19.3

Figure 19.3 shows the cumulative distribution of the project's total cost. The mean of the generated values, £303 856, is selected as the budget, and the (80th percentile − budget), i.e. £308 588 − £303 856 = £4732, is selected as the risk contingency. The budget is then the cost that the organisation will realistically try to achieve or better, and the contingency is the additional amount put aside should the need arise. If the cost risk model is accurate, there is a 53 % chance that the budget will be sufficient and an 80 % chance that the project's costs will not exceed the budget + contingency.

In order to be able to distribute the budget and contingency back among the cost items, each cost item must be nominated as an output of the model. The generated data points from each cost item are then output to a spreadsheet, and each column of values is then ranked separately in ascending order (Figure 19.4). Then, the costs generated for all items in each row are summed to give a total project cost.

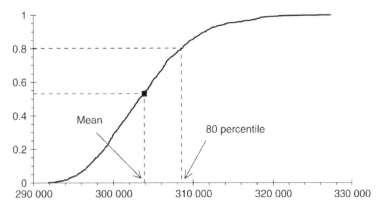

Figure 19.3   The cumulative distribution of total project cost for the model in Figure 19.2.

Iteration	WP1	WP2	WP3	WP4	WP5	WP6	WP7	WP8	WPi
1	15567	72193	56321	44410	32400	29660	22030	11028	283609
2	15647	72328	56389	44536	32442	29737	22061	11049	284189
..	..	..	Work package budgets				..	..	..
..	..	..					..	..	..
294	18634	78294	57617	47759	34975	31776	22998	11678	303732
295	*18682*	*78327*	*57623*	*47763*	*34984*	*31784*	*23001*	*11681*	*303845*
296	18688	78343	57626	47777	34989	31788	23004	11681	303895
..	..	..	Work package budgets + contingencies				..	..	..
..	..	..					..	..	..
352	19307	..	57841	48342	35781	32134	23167	11787	228360
353	*19315*	*80180*	*57846*	*48347*	*35840*	*32141*	*23168*	*11790*	*308628*
354	19333	80198	57850	48368	35849	32141	23173	11792	308703
..	..	..							

Project budget

Project budget + contingency

Cost values for the work packages are ranked in ascending order in each column....

...and their totals are calculated for each row

Figure 19.4   Distributing the budget and (budget + contingency) values back among the project's individual cost items for Example 19.3.

Next, the budget and (budget + contingency) values are looked up in the column of summed costs and the values most precisely equating to the calculated budget and (budget + contingency) figures are determined. The values that appear in the same row for each cost item are then nominated as the budgets and (budget and contingency) values for the cost items. Figure 19.4 illustrates this process. More iterations would allow item budget and (budget + contingency) values to be determined more precisely. ◆

19.2 Schedule Risk Analysis

Schedule risk analysis uses the same principles as cost risk analysis for modelling general uncertainty and risks and opportunities. However, it must also cope with the added complexity of modelling the interrelationships between the various tasks of a project. This section looks at the simple building blocks that typically make up a schedule risk analysis and then shows how these elements are combined to produce a realistic model.

A number of software tools allow the user to run Monte Carlo simulations on standard project planning applications like Microsoft Project and Open Plan. However, these products do not have the flexibility to model discrete risks and feedback loops, described below, which are common features of a real project. For now, the most flexible environment for project schedule modelling remains the spreadsheet, and all of the examples below are illustrated in this format.

A project plan consists of a number of individual tasks. The start and finish dates of these tasks can be related in a number of ways:

1. One task cannot start until another has finished (the link is called finish–start or F–S). This is the most common type of linking in project planning models.
2. One task cannot start until another task has started (start–start or S–S).
3. One task cannot start until another has been partially completed (start–start + lag or S–S +x).
4. One task cannot finish until another has finished (finish–finish or F–F).
5. One task cannot finish until another is a certain way from finishing too (finish–finish–lag or F–F–x).

Figure 19.5 shows how these interrelationships are represented diagrammatically. In the rest of this chapter we will use the notation "(a, b, c)" to denote a Triangle(a, b, c) distribution. So: Lag(5, 6, 7) weeks is a lag modelled by a Triangle(5, 6, 7) distribution in units of weeks, etc.

It is essential that a schedule risk model is set up to be as clear as possible, because it can easily become rather complex. Figure 19.6 illustrates a useful format, where all of the assumptions are immediately apparent.

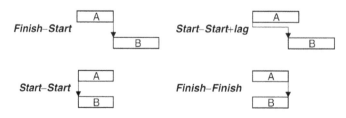

Figure 19.5 Diagrammatic representation of the common types of task linking in project planning.

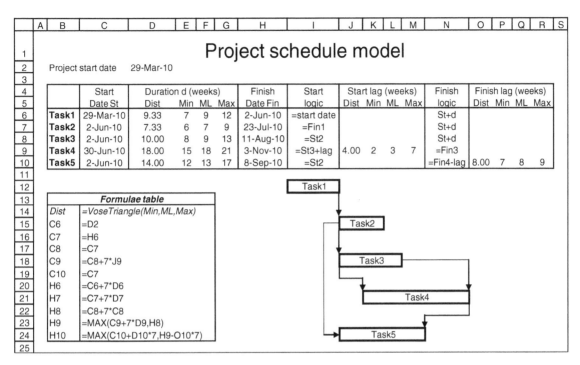

Figure 19.6 Example of a project schedule model structure.

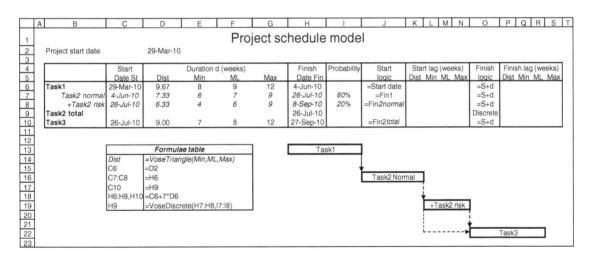

Figure 19.7 Modelling schedule risk as *additional* duration.

More complex relationships involving several tasks can now be constructed. So far, bold lines have been used to indicate the links between tasks. Dashed lines are now introduced to illustrate links that may or may not occur (i.e. risks and opportunities). Risks and opportunities can be modelled in two ways: by modelling the additional impact on the task's duration should the risk occur, as shown in Figure 19.7, or by separately modelling the total durations of the task should the risk occur or not occur, as shown in

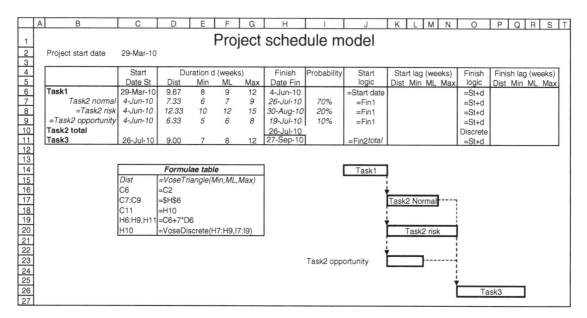

Figure 19.8 Modelling schedule risk as *alternative* durations.

Figure 19.8. In the example of Figure 19.7, task 2 is expected to take $(6, 7, 9)$ weeks, but there is a 20 % chance of a problem occurring that would extend the task's duration by $(4, 6, 9)$ weeks. In Figure 19.8, task 2 is estimated to take $(6, 7, 9)$ weeks, but there is a 20 % chance that a particular risk will increase its duration to $(10, 12, 15)$; there is also an opportunity, with about a 10 % chance of occurring, that would reduce the duration to $(5, 6, 8)$. The start of task 3 is equal to a discrete distribution of the finish dates of task 2's possible scenarios.

The most common multiple relationship between tasks in a project schedule is where one task cannot start until several others have finished, which is modelled using the MAX function. This completes our look at all of the basic building blocks of a schedule risk model. Figures 19.9 and 19.10 illustrate all of these building blocks being used together to model Example 19.4.

Example 19.4

A new building is to be constructed by a consortium for a client. The project can be divided into seven sections, as described below. The client wishes to see a risk analysis of the schedule and cost risks and how these relate to each other.

Design

The detailed design will take $(14, 16, 21)$ weeks, but the architect thinks there is about a 20 % chance that the client will require some rework on the design that will mean an additional $(3, 4, 6)$ weeks. The architect team will charge a £160 000 flat fee but will require £12 000 per week for any rework.

Earthworks

The site will have to be levelled. These earthworks can begin immediately on award of the contract. The earthworks will take $(3, 4, 7)$ weeks at a cost of $(£4200, £4500, £4700)$ a week. There is a risk that

Project schedule model

Udesign	0.6565
Ubrown	0.2125

Contract award date   29-Mar-10

	Start Date St	Duration d (weeks)				Finish Date Fin	Probability	Start logic	Start lag (weeks)				Finish logic	Finish lag (weeks)			
		Dist	Min	ML	Max				Dist	Min	ML	Max		Dist	Min	ML	Max
DESIGN (Task1)																	
Detail (a)	29-Mar-10	17.7	12	16	25	30-Jul-10	80%	=Start date					St+d				
Rework risk (b)	30-Jul-10	4.3	3	4	6	30-Aug-10	20%	Fin Detail					St+d				
Total (c)						30-Jul-10							Discrete				
EARTHWORKS (Task2)																	
Normal (a)	29-Mar-10	4.7	3	4	7	30-Apr-10	70%	=Start date					St+d				
Archaeo risk (b)	30-Apr-10	10.7	8	10	14	14-Jul-10	30%	Fin2a					St+d				
Total (c)						30-Apr-10							Discrete				
FOUNDATIONS (Task3)																	
	30-Apr-10	7.0	6	7	8	18-Jun-10		Fin2c					St+d				
STRUCTURE (Task4)																	
Floor1 (a)	6-Aug-10	4.8	4	4.5	6	9-Sep-10		Fin3+lag	7.0	6	7	8	St+d				
Floor2 (b)	9-Sep-10	4.8	4	4.5	6	13-Oct-10		Fin4a					St+d				
Floor3 (c)	13-Oct-10	4.8	4	4.5	6	16-Nov-10		Fin4b					St+d				
Roofing (d)	16-Nov-10	8.3	7	8	10	13-Jan-11							St+d				
ENVELOPE (Task5)																	
Brown Bros							90%										
Floor1 (a)	30-Sep-10	8.0	7	8	9	25-Nov-10		Fin4a+lag		3	3		St+d				
Floor2 (b)	25-Nov-10	8.0	7	8	9	20-Jan-11		Fin5a					St+d				
Floor3 (c)	20-Jan-11	8.0	7	8	9	17-Mar-11		Fin5b					St+d				
Redd&Greene							10%										
Floor1 (d)	30-Sep-10	8.3	6	8	11	27-Nov-10		Fin4a+lag		3	3		St+d				
Floor2 (e)	27-Nov-10	8.3	6	8	11	25-Jan-11		Fin5d					St+d				
Floor3 (f)	25-Jan-11	8.3	6	8	11	24-Mar-11		Fin5e					St+d				
Totals Brown Bros						17-Mar-11	90%										
Redd&Greene						24-Mar-11	10%										
(g) Combined						17-Mar-11							Discrete				
SERVICES AND FINISHINGS (Task6)																	
Services																	
Floor1 (a)	17-Mar-11	10.3	8	10	13	28-May-11		Fin5g					St+d				
Floor2 (b)	28-May-11	10.3	8	10	13	9-Aug-11		Fin6a					St+d				
Floor3 (c)	9-Aug-11	10.3	8	10	13	20-Oct-11		Fin6b					St+d				
Finishings																	
Floor1 (d)	28-May-11	11.0	9	11	13	13-Aug-11		Fin6a					St+d				
Floor2 (e)	9-Aug-11	11.0	9	11	13	25-Oct-11		Fin6b					St+d				
Floor3 (f)	20-Oct-11	11.0	9	11	13	5-Jan-12		Fin6c					Max	3	2	3	4
COMMISSIONING (Task7)																	
Tidy up site (a)	5-Jan-12	2.0		2		19-Jan-12	55%	Fin6f					St+d				
1st call back (b)	19-Jan-12	2.5	0.5	2	5	6-Feb-12	40%	Fin7a					St+d				
2nd call back (c)	6-Feb-12	1.0	0.5	1	1.5	13-Feb-12	5%	Fin7b					St+d				
Total						19-Jan-12							Discrete				

FINISH DATE   13-Feb-12

Formulae table

I1 (Udesign)	=VoseUniform(0,1)	I2	=VoseUniform(0,1)	H36	=VoseDiscrete(H34:H35,I34:I35,Ubrown)
C7	=C2	C23	=H22	C40	=H36
C8	=H7	C27	=H20+7*K27	C41	=H40
H9	=VoseDiscrete(H7:H8,I7:I8,Udesign)	C28	=H27	C42	=H41
C12	=C2	C29	=H28	C44	=H40
C13	=H12	C31	=H20+7*K31	C45	=H41
H14	=Discrete(H12:H13,I12:I13)	C32:C33	=H31	C46	=H42
C17	=H14	H34	=H29	H46	=MAX(C46+7*D46,H42+7*P46)
C20	=H17+7*K20	H35	=H33	C50	=H49
C21	=H20	I34	=I26	C51	=H50
C22	=H21	I35	=I30	H52	=VoseDiscrete(H49:H51,I49:I51)
D7,D8,D12,D13,D17,D20:D23,D27:D29,D31:D33,D40:D42,D44:D46,D49:D51	=VoseTriangle(E7,F7,G7)			C54	=MAX(H7:H52)
H7,H8,H12,H13,H17,H20:H23,H27:H29,H31:H33,H40:H42,H44:H46,H49:H51	=C7+D7*7				

Figure 19.9   Schedule model layout for Example 19.4.

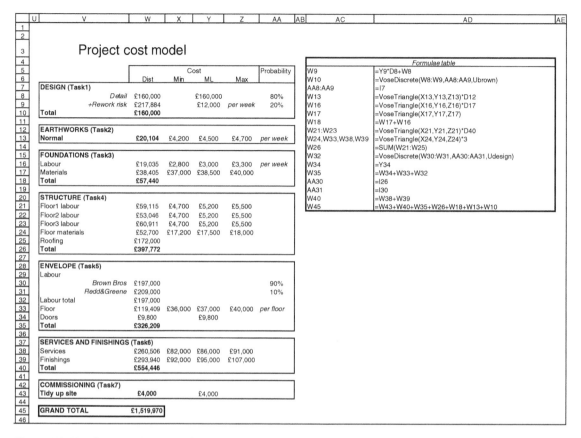

Figure 19.10 Cost model layout for Example 19.4.

the earthworks will reveal artefacts that will require an archaeological survey to be carried out before any building work can proceed. Local knowledge suggests that there is about a 30 % chance of finding any significant artefacts and that the surveying would then take (8, 10, 14) weeks.

Foundations

The foundations can be started when the earthworks are complete, and will take (6, 7, 8) weeks. The costs will be (£2800, £3000, £3300) per week for labour, plus (£37 000, £38 500, £40 000) for materials.

Structure

The building's structural components (floors, pillars, roofing, etc.) can be started (3, 4, 6) weeks after the foundation work is completed, depending on the weather. There are three floors, all exactly the same, and the building contractor believes each floor can be constructed in (4, 4.5, 6) weeks depending mostly on the weather. Each floor will cost (£4700, £5200, £5500) per week for labour and (£17 200, £17 500, £18 000) for materials, depending on the exact final design. The roofing will take (7, 8, 10) weeks for a fixed price of £172 000.

Envelope

The envelope (walls, windows, external doors) work can be started 3 weeks after the first floor is completed. The materials will cost (£36 000, £37 000, £40 000) per floor, depending on the final architect design. The ground floor will require high-security doors at a cost of £9800. The envelope work labour will be provided by Brown Bros Ltd, at a quoted price of £197 000, who estimate that each floor will take (7, 8, 9) weeks to complete, depending on the weather. However, Brown Bros Ltd are being taken over by another firm, and the Managing Director thinks there is about a 10 % chance that, under the new owners, they will not be allowed to accept the work. The next alternative is Redd and Greene Ltd who have quoted £209 000 for the labour. They estimate it would take them (6, 8, 11) weeks to complete each floor, again depending on the weather.

Services and finishings

The services (plumbing, electricity, computer cabling, etc.) and finishings (internal partitioning, decorations, etc.) can be started when each floor is completed. Services will cost (£82 000, £86 000, £91 000) for each floor, and finishings will cost (£92 000, £95 000, £107 000) for each floor.

Commissioning

Two weeks are needed after all work has been completed to tidy up the site and test all of the facilities, at a cost of £4000. It is thought that there is a 40 % chance that the services contractor will be called back to fix problems, resulting in a delay of (0.5, 2, 5) weeks, and a 5 % chance they could be called back again, resulting in a further delay of (0.5, 1, 1.5) weeks.

Figure 19.9 illustrates a spreadsheet model of the project plan for this example, using the expected value of each uncertain task duration. Figure 19.10 illustrates the cost model for this example. Note that the two models actually reside within the same spreadsheet to allow linking between them. Also note that a Uniform(0, 1) distribution at cell I1 is being used to control the generation of values from distributions in cells H9 and W10 which will ensure they have a 100 % correlation. The same applies with a Uniform(0,1) distribution at cell I2 which will generate a 100% correlation between cells H36 and W32. This is equivalent to using a 100 % rank order correlation between the variables.

The distributions of schedule and cost for this model are shown in Figures 19.11 and 19.12. Their interrelationship is illustrated in the scatter plot of Figure 19.13 which shows that the cost of the project is not strongly influenced by the amount of time it will take to complete. ♦

19.2.1 Critical path analysis

In traditional project planning, the duration of each task is given a single-point estimate and an analysis is performed to determine the critical path, i.e. the tasks that are directly determining the duration of the project. In a project schedule risk analysis, the critical path will not usually run through the same line of tasks in every iteration of the model. It is therefore necessary to introduce a new concept: the critical index. The *critical index* is calculated for each task and gives the percentage of the iterations for which that task lies on the critical path.

The critical index is determined by assigning a function to each task in the risk analysis model that generates a "1" if the task is on the critical path and a "0" if it is not. This function is nominated as an output and the mean of its result is then the critical index. It is often not necessary to calculate the critical index for every task. The structure of the schedule will usually mean that, if one task is on the

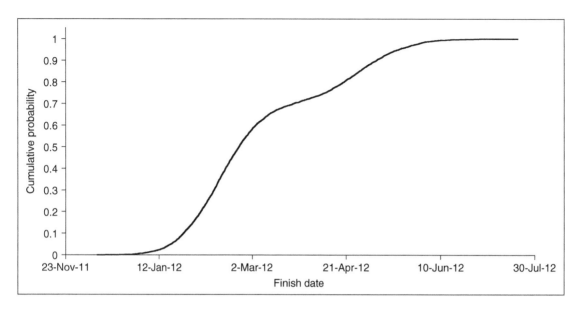

Figure 19.11   Cumulative distribution of finish date for Example 19.4.

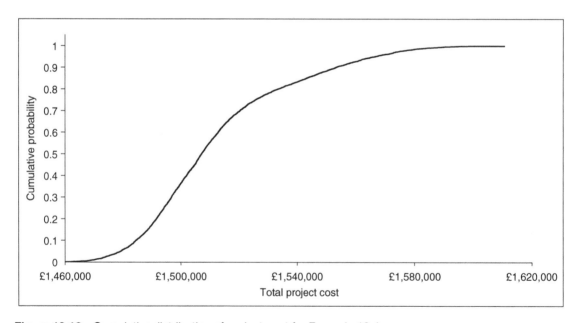

Figure 19.12   Cumulative distribution of project cost for Example 19.4.

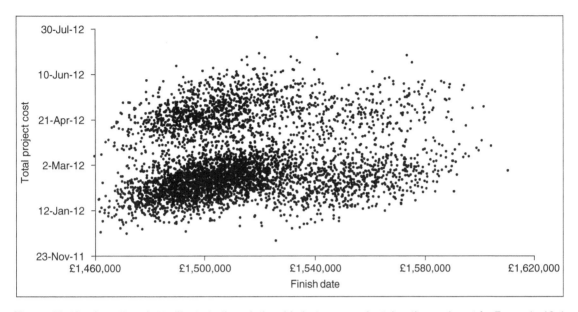

Figure 19.13 A scatter plot to illustrate the relationship between project duration and cost for Example 19.4.

critical path, several others will be too, or that the critical index in one branch is 1 minus the critical index of another.

Example 19.5

Figure 19.14 illustrates the sort of logic that one can usually apply quickly to determine critical indices. In this example, tasks A and J are always on the critical path, therefore $CI(A) = CI(J) = 1$:

$$\text{If } CI(B) = p, \quad CI(G) = CI(H) = CI(I) = 1 - p \text{ and } CI(F) = p$$
$$\text{If } CI(E) = q, \qquad CI(C) = CI(D) = p - q$$

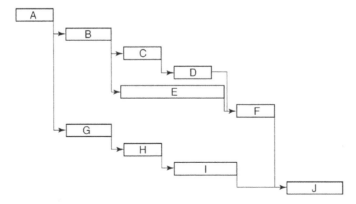

Figure 19.14 Task linking to determine critical index logic for Example 19.5.

i.e. for this example it is only necessary to determine p and q, and all of the other critical indices can be deduced.

Index p can be determined by writing the following function:

$$f(p) = \text{IF (start\_of\_J} = \text{finish\_of\_F}, 1, 0)$$

i.e. if the start of task J equals the end of task F, return a "1", otherwise return a "0".

Index q can be determined by the following function:

$$f(q) = f(p) * \text{IF (start\_of\_F} = \text{finish\_of\_E}, 1, 0)$$

i.e. if the start of task F equals the end of task E and the start of task J equals the end of task F, return a "1", otherwise return a "0". ◆

If the critical index is close to zero, reduction in the duration of the task is very unlikely to affect the project's duration. On the other hand, progressively larger values of the critical index indicate increasing influence over a project's duration. The index can therefore help the project manager target those tasks for which she should attempt to reduce the duration, or reschedule within the project plan in a way that removes them from the critical path.

If the individual task durations are nominated as outputs, along with the critical index functions, the analyst can look at the raw generated data and analyse in which situations each task is on the critical path. A conditional median analysis (Chapter 15) can be carried out, comparing the data subsets for the duration of each task from the iterations when the task is on the critical path against the entire dataset of generated durations for that task. The higher the value of conditional median analysis index α associated with a task, the greater the influence that task is having on extending the project's duration.

19.3 Portfolios of risks

A large project may have many risks listed in its risk register – sometimes a thousand or more! For most practical purposes that is an awful lot to put into a simulation model where each one is of the form

$$= \text{VoseBinomial}(1, p) * \text{VosePERT}(Min, Mode, Max)$$

or

$$= \text{VoseRiskEvent}(p, \text{VosePERTObject}(Min, Mode, Max))$$

where p is the probability of occurrence and the PERT distribution reflects the size of the impact should it occur. The VoseRiskEvent function in ModelRisk allows you to simulate a risk event as one variable, rather than the usual two (Binomial(1, p) or Bernoulli(p) and impact distribution) which lets you perform a correct sensitivity analysis.

There is a faster way to model the aggregate risk if each risk represents a potential impact on the cost of the project, and there are no cascading effects, meaning that one risk's occurrence does not change the probability or impact size of any other risk.

Let μ_I and V_I be the mean and variance of the impact distribution should the risk occur. Then the mean and variance of the risk as a whole are given by

$$\mu_R = p\mu_I$$

$$V_R = pV_I + \mu_I^2 p(1 - p)$$

If the risks are independent, then we can estimate the total impact by simply summing the means and variances, i.e.

$$\mu_{TOTAL} = \sum_{i=1}^{n} p_i \mu_{Ii}$$

$$V_{TOTAL} = \sum_{i=1}^{n} p_i V_{Ii} + \mu_{Ii}^2 p_i (1 - p_i)$$

Appendix III gives the formulae for the mean and variance for many distributions – certainly all the ones I would expect you would use to model a risk impact. You can also get the moments directly in ModelRisk by using special functions, e.g.

$\quad =$ VoseMean(VosePERTObject(2, 3, 6)) returns the mean of a PERT(2, 3, 6) distribution

$\quad =$ VoseVariance(VoseTriangleObject(D8, E8, F8)) returns the variance of a

$\quad\quad$ Triangle(D8, E8, F8) distribution

These functions make life a lot easier if you are using several different distribution types for modelling the impact. If you have a large number of risks – some risk registers have thousands of risks – it is often a reasonable approximation to model the aggregate impact as a Normal(μ_{TOTAL}, $\sqrt{V_{TOTAL}}$) distribution. ModelRisk has several other functions relating to a portfolio of risks that will simulate the aggregate distribution in one cell (speeding up the simulation a great deal by running it all in C++), identify the risks of greatest impact to the total mean or variance and fit certain distributions like the normal, or skewed and shifted distributions based on matching the mean and variance of the aggregate risk portfolio – the last feature will speed up a simulation enormously if used as a surrogate.

19.4 Cascading Risks

We have just had a postal strike in Gent where I live that lasted, I think, 12 days. The post office lost a fair bit of money on that strike, I imagine, and perhaps the employees too. Belgium is a country of contrasts – we don't have cheques any more, so everyone pays electronically, yet invoices and a vast array of perplexing official administration always come in the mail. So for 12 days my office didn't receive any bills, and for the next 2 weeks the post office was dealing with the backlog, so we got bank statements too late to close the books properly, etc. I wonder what the reaction will be. We bought a rather high-end computer in that period from a small shop that can build fancy custom PCs and they needed paying quickly, so unusually they emailed the invoice and it was paid 10 minutes later. My son's birthday presents arrived late, printed invitations for an exhibition that was being held in my house only arrived the morning before the exhibition, etc., etc. Multiply that irritation by a couple of hundred thousand households and I think the post office will find a considerable impact on their future because people will look at ways of avoiding using the post office. The impact goes far beyond managing 12 days of backlog. How about the risk of being forced to privatise – maybe that is now higher. Or the risk that a competitor will enter the market, or that Belgacom or Telenet, who offer Internet services here, will capitalise on the strike with some highly amusing advert and get people to think about moving to electronic mail more.

Ideally, we would like to be able to capture the complete potential impact of a risk to be able to understand the level of attention it should receive. Maybe some risk occurring in a project has a relatively minor impact directly, but it increases the chances of another, much larger risk. We can think of lots of reasons why: management are focused on handling the effects of small risk A so nobody is paying attention to a looming big risk B; little risk A occurs, blame is passed liberally around, people stop communicating and helping each other and those who can see big risk B coming along think "It's not *my* problem". The biggest risks in projects are, after all, driven by people issues. I think that the occurrence of a lot of big risks comes at the end of a chain of small risks occurring that were perhaps much easier and less costly to deal with.

Let's look, therefore, at a couple of simple ways of modelling a cascading set of risks in a project. We want to model the probability of a risk occurring, and perhaps the size of its impact too, as being to some degree influenced by whether other risks have occurred. Figure 19.15 gives an example.

	A	B	C	D	E	F	G	H
1				Impact				
2		Risk	Min	Most likely	Max	Probability	Risk simulation	
3		A	7	10	15	30%	11.0995156	
4		B	9.8	12	18	20%	0	
5		C	10.4	13	19.5	10%	0	
6		D	11.2	14	21	50%	11.94230625	
7		E	6.4	8	12	45%	7.891018621	
8		F	4.8	6	9	12%	0	
9		G	6.4	8	12	7%	0	
10		H	9.6	12	18	5%	0	
11		I	8.8	11	16.5	19%	0	
12		J	11.2	14	21	23%	0	
13		Sum				Total risk impact:	30.93284047	
14								
15				Formulae table				
16	C3:C12	=D3*0.8						
17	E3:E12	=D3*1.5						
18	F3:F12	=VosePERT(C3,D3,E3)						
19	F6	=IF(OR(G3,G5),50%,15%)						
20	F7	=IF(OR(G3,G6),45%,22%)						
21	F10	=IF(AND(G4,G5,G7,G8),13%,5%)						
22	G3:G9, G11:G12	=VoseRiskEvent(F3,VosePERTObject(C3,D3,E3))						
23	G10	=IF(AND(G4,G5,G7,G8),3.2,1)*VoseRiskEvent(F10,VosePERTObject(C10,D10,E10))						
24	G13	=SUM(G3:G12)						
25								

Figure 19.15 Model of correlated (cascading) risks.

The model uses the ModelRisk function VoseRiskEvent because it has certain advantages, as we'll see in a minute, but otherwise just replace formulae of the type

$$= \text{VoseRiskEvent}(F3, \text{VosePERTObject}(C3, D3, E3))$$

with

$$= \text{VoseBinomial}(1, F3) * \text{VosePERT}(C3, D3, E3)$$

The interesting parts of this model reside in shaded cells F6, F7, F10 and G10, where I have used IF statements to change either the probability or impact of a risk depending on whether other risks or a combination of risks have occurred: if Risk A occurs, it increases the probability of risks D and E occurring; and if risks B, C, E and F all occur, then both the probability of occurrence and the size of impact of risk H increase.

Let's now look at the influence each risk has on the output sum in cell G13. Most Monte Carlo add-ins have the ability to plot tornado charts (see Section 5.3.7) automatically by saving the values generated from their distributions during a simulation. Depending on your host Monte Carlo add-in, you can force it to save values from a cell as if they were generated by that software's own distribution. We want to see the effect of risk A, so we make cell G3 the input to, say, a Normal(C3, 0) or a DUniform(C3). Applying this method and running a simulation, I can generate plots like the ones in Figure 19.16.

The left-hand pane of Figure 19.16 shows that, with correlation added to the model, risk D is most rank order correlated with the total, which sort of makes sense because it has about a 20 % chance of occurring (the variance introduced by a risk has a component that is proportional to $p * (1 - p)$, where p is the probability of occurrence, so, the closer p is to 0.5, the more uncertainty the risk adds) and a wide impact distribution. The right-hand pane shows that, with no correlation in the model, risk D drops to second place. That may seem strange because risk D wasn't influencing any other risks, so why should it lose first place? The answer lies in the fact that in the left pane risk D is being influenced

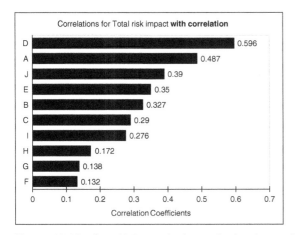
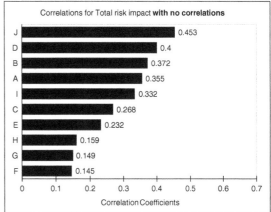

Figure 19.16 Sensitivity analysis results for the model of Figure 19.15. Left pane – with correlations; right pane – without.

by risk A, which also influences risk E. These three risks will therefore all be correlated to some degree and thus their rank correlation with the output goes up as it gets "credited" for the output correlation with risks A and E. It is important not to read these types of graphs in a vacuum – one should also consider any causal direction. Comparing the two plots, you'll see that risks A and E have moved up two and three places respectively, which aligns with the correlation we've built in.

Finally, since tornado charts remain a little confusing, let's redo the sensitivity analysis using spider plots (Section 5.3.8). To achieve this, we have to be able to control the sampling of the RiskEvent distributions, which we do via its optional U-parameter. For example

$$= \text{VoseRiskEvent(F3, VosePERTObject(C3, D3, E3))}$$

generates random values from the distribution of possible values of the risk, while adding a U-parameter of 0.9

$$= \text{VoseRiskEvent(F3, VosePERTObject(C3, D3, E3), 0.9)}$$

yields the 90th percentile of the distribution. The spider plot for this model (Figure 19.17) can be plotted by starting at each risk event's 50th percentile, since none of the risks has greater than a 50 % chance of occurring, so their 50th percentiles and below are zero.

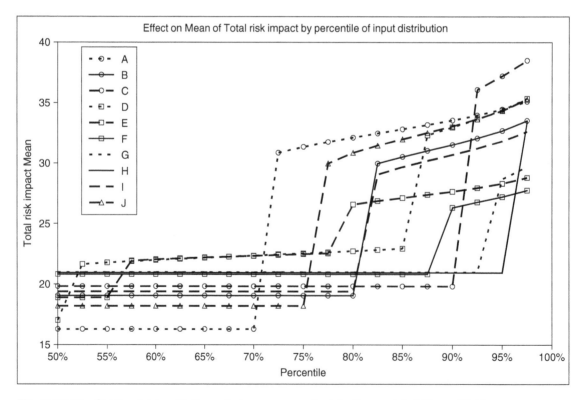

Figure 19.17 Spider plot sensitivity analysis on mean output for the model of Figure 19.15.

Spider plots are easy to read when the variables are all continuous and not so easy to read when they are a discrete–continuous (combined) distribution, but with a little practice they can reveal a lot. Let's take the line for risk A, which starts at the lowest y value on the left and jumps after the 70 % mark: that's because the risk has a 30 % $(1 - 70\%)$ chance of occurring. The minimum value of the impact of risk A is 7, yet, when the line kicks, it jumps up by about 14.6 units. That's because risk D (with a mean of 14.7) increases from 15 to 50 % and risk E (with a mean of 8.4) increases from 22 to 45 %. That gives an expected increase of $(50\% - 15\%) \ast 14.7 + (45\% - 22\%) \ast 8.4 = 7.1$. Here, $7 + 7.1$ gives us almost the jump we see – the extra bit is because the first plotted point above $x = 70\% is = 72.5\%$, which is the $2.5\%/30\% = 8.3$ percentile of the PERT, not its minimum.

You can probably make out that risks D and E have two kicks: D somewhere in [50 %, 52.5 %], and again in [85 %, 87.5 %]. That's because D has either a 15 % or a 50 % chance of occurring, depending on the occurrence or risks A and C. The same thinking applies to risk E. The vertical range that each line takes tells us the variation that the output mean can take depending on each risk event's value. The range is largest for risks A and C, but risk C jumps at a much higher x-axis percentile than risk A, so has less influence in terms of correlation, although more in terms of extreme values for the output mean.

Chapter 20

Insurance and finance risk analysis modelling

In this chapter I introduce some techniques that have been developed in insurance and finance risk modelling. Even if insurance and finance are not your fields, you might still find some interesting ideas in here. Insurance and finance analysts have placed a lot of emphasis on finding numerical solutions to stochastic problems – something that is highly desirable because it gives more immediate and accurate answers than Monte Carlo simulation. In this chapter I dash about showing some modelling techniques to give you a flavour of what can be done. For those of you involved in insurance and finance, I hope it will also have piqued your curiosity about the ModelRisk software, which is described in Appendix II. Sections 20.1 to 20.5 explain some techniques from the finance field, and Section 20.6 onwards looks at some insurance ideas. You will notice that they frequently share some common principles.

20.1 Operational Risk Modelling

Operational risk is defined in the Basel II capital accord as "The risk of loss resulting from inadequate or failed internal processes, people and systems or from external events". It includes: internal and external fraud; workers' discrimination and health and safety; antitrust, trading and accounting violations; natural disasters and terrorism; computer systems failure; data errors; failed mandatory reporting (e.g. sending out statements or policy documents within a required time); and negligent loss of clients' assets. However, it excludes strategic risk and reputation risk, although the latter can be affected by the occurrence of a high-visibility operational risk. Basel II and various corporate scandals have brought operational risk into particular focus in the banking sector, where operational risks are required to be closely and transparently monitored and reported. Sufficient capital must be held in reserve to cover operational risk at a high level of certainty to achieve the highest rating under Basel II. Under Basel II's "Advanced Measurement Approach", which will usually be the least onerous on a bank provided they have the necessary reporting systems in place, operational risk can be modelled as an aggregate portfolio problem similar to insurance risk. The model of Figure 20.1 uses an FFT method to calculate the capital required to cover a bank's risks at the 99.9th percentile level. Basel II allows a bank to use Monte Carlo simulation to determine the 99.9th percentile, but the use of FFT methods is to be preferred over simulation because such a high loss distribution percentile requires a very large number of iterations to determine its value with any precision. The difference between the 99.9th percentile and the expected loss is called the "unexpected loss" and equates to the capital charge that the bank must set aside to cover operational risk.

The model has assumed that each risk is independent (making a Poisson distribution appropriate to model the frequency, although a Pólya or Delaporte may well be better – see Section 8.3.7) and that

Risk category	Process	Sub process	Expected frequency	Severity mean	Severity Stdev	Frequency distribution	Severity distribution
Type 1	A	1	22.7	9.1	5.2	VosePoisson($E$3)	VoseLognormal($F$3,$G$3)
		2	2.5	8.1	5.3	VosePoisson($E$4)	VoseLognormal($F$4,$G$4)
		3	4.9	7.1	8.1	VosePoisson($E$5)	VoseLognormal($F$5,$G$5)
		4	21.9	12.5	9.2	VosePoisson($E$6)	VoseLognormal($F$6,$G$6)
		5	8.8	2.7	1.6	VosePoisson($E$7)	VoseLognormal($F$7,$G$7)
	B	1	32.6	23.2	3.2	VosePoisson($E$8)	VoseLognormal($F$8,$G$8)
		2	22.6	13.5	35.9	VosePoisson($E$9)	VoseLognormal($F$9,$G$9)
		3	7.7	13.8	24.1	VosePoisson($E$10)	VoseLognormal($F$10,$G$10)
		4	11.1	16.8	2.4	VosePoisson($E$11)	VoseLognormal($F$11,$G$11)
		5	8.3	8.1	14.6	VosePoisson($E$12)	VoseLognormal($F$12,$G$12)
	C	1	38.6	4.8	7.4	VosePoisson($E$13)	VoseLognormal($F$13,$G$13)
		2	11.5	9.5	12.3	VosePoisson($E$14)	VoseLognormal($F$14,$G$14)
	B	4	12.3	16.1	10.1	VosePoisson($E$41)	VoseLognormal($F$41,$G$41)
		5	24	15.2	38.4	VosePoisson($E$42)	VoseLognormal($F$42,$G$42)
Type 3	C	1	17.3	56.6	38.2	VosePoisson($E$43)	VoseLognormal($F$43,$G$43)
		2	12.1	18.2	11.6	VosePoisson($E$44)	VoseLognormal($F$44,$G$44)
		3	10.1	1.2	0.7	VosePoisson($E$45)	VoseLognormal($F$45,$G$45)
		4	11.4	13	19	VosePoisson($E$46)	VoseLognormal($F$46,$G$46)
		5	5.7	22.8	17.4	VosePoisson($E$47)	VoseLognormal($F$47,$G$47)

Required percentile	99.9%
Expected cost	8289.65
Capital charge	2415.574

Formulae table

H3:H47	=VosePoissonObject(E3)
I3:I47	=VoseLognormalObject(F3,G3)
M4 (output)	=SUMPRODUCT(E3:E47,F3:F47)
M5 (output)	=VoseAggregateMultiFFT($H$3:$H$47,$I$3:$I$47,M3)-M4

Figure 20.1 Model to determine a financial institution's capital allocation to cover operational risk under Basel II.

the impacts all follow a lognormal distribution. In this model one could have used fitted distribution objects (e.g. VoseLognormalFitObject(*data*)) that were linked to the available data. The chief difficulty in performing an operational risk calculation is the acquisition of relevant data that could be used to determine the parameters of the distributions. Operational risks, especially those with a large impact, occur very infrequently, so there is often an absence of any data at all within an individual bank. However, one can base the frequency and severity distributions on general banking industry databases, and use credibility theory (for example, using the Bühlmann credibility factor (Klugman *et al.*, 1998)) gradually to assign more weight over time to the individual bank's experience against the industry as a whole. Credibility theory is often used in the insurance industry when one offers a new policy hoping to attract a particular sector of the population with a known risk level: as a history of claims emerges, one migrates from the expected claim frequency and severity to that actually observed.

20.2 Credit Risk

Credit risk is the risk of loss due to a debtor's failure or partial failure to repay a loan or other credit instrument (bonds). We need three components to assess the credit risk of an individual obligor:

1. Default probability.
2. Exposure distribution.
3. Loss given default as a fraction of the exposure.

Components 2 and 3 can sometimes be replaced with a single distribution of loss given default.

Chapter 10 describes how to fit probability distributions to data which are used to estimate 2 and 3 above. Section 9.1.4 describes how to estimate the binomial probability needed for the probability of default. There are a number of methods we can use to determine the aggregate distribution, the bases of which are described in Chapter 11.

20.2.1 Single portfolio example

Figure 20.2 shows a credit risk model for a single portfolio of independent, lognormally distributed random individual loss distributions where there are 2 135 debtors each with the same 8.3 % probability of default.

In this model the VoseAggregateMC function in cell C11 is randomly sampling n Lognormal(55, 12) distributions and summing them together, where n is itself a Binomial(2135, 8.3 %) distribution. This is the "brute-force" Monte Carlo approach to summing random variables, but with the advantage that the simulation is all done within C++ (which is faster) and the final random sum is returned back to Excel. Figure 20.3 shows the equivalent model performed in Excel. The model takes up a lot more space (note the number of hidden rows) and runs many times slower, but, more importantly, it needs resizing if we change the number of obligors or the probability of default.

Since the model of Figure 20.2 is estimating a distribution of loss, the value at risk (VaR) (see Section 20.5.1) at the 95th confidence level is simply the 95th percentile of the output distribution, which is returned directly into the spreadsheet at cell E11 at the end of a simulation. In this example, running 1 000 000 iterations produces a VaR of 10 943.62. We can take a different approach by constructing the aggregate distribution using fast Fourier transforms (here using VoseAggregateFFT). Cell C13 generates random values from this distribution, while cell E13 employs the U-parameter (see Appendix II) to return the 95th percentile of the aggregate distribution directly without any simulation. The ModelRisk screen capture of Figure 20.4 shows this second use of the function.

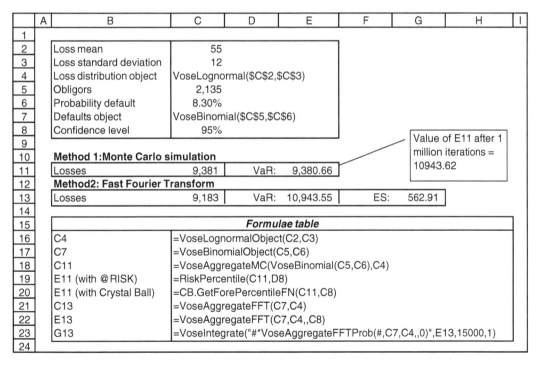

Figure 20.2 Credit risk model for a single portfolio.

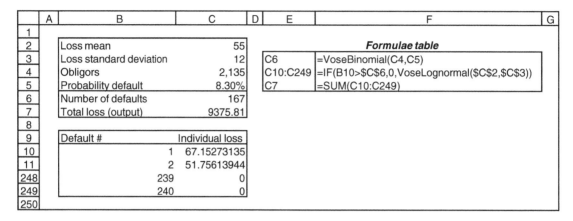

Figure 20.3 Monte Carlo simulation performed in Excel.

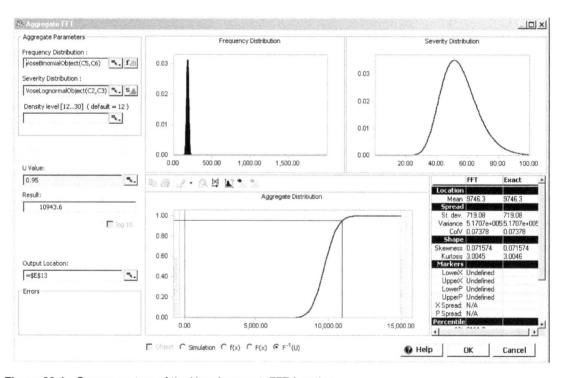

Figure 20.4 Screen capture of the VoseAggregateFFT function.

In cell G13 the formula:

$$=\text{VoseIntegrate}("\#{}^{*}\text{VoseAggregateFFTProb}(\#, C7, C4, , 0)", E13, 15\,000, 1)$$

calculates the integral to determine the expected shortfall (see Section 20.5.2):

$$\int_{E13}^{15\,000} x f(x)\, dx$$

where E13 is the defined threshold, x is the value of the aggregate loss distribution, $f(x)$ is the density function for the aggregate loss distribution (determined by the function VoseAggregateFFTProb($\ldots$)) and 15 000 is a sufficiently large value to be used as a maximum for the integral, as shown in the screen capture of Figure 20.5.

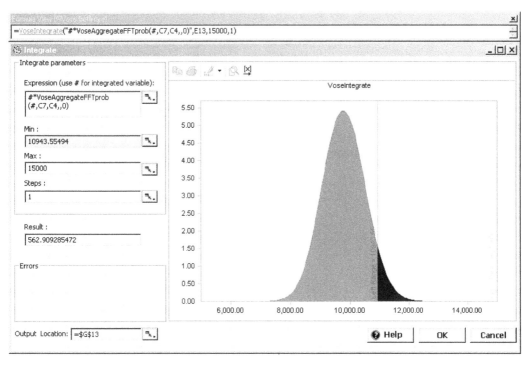

Figure 20.5 Integration to determine the expected shortfall of a credit portfolio. The "Steps" parameter is an optional integer used to determine how many subintervals are made within each interval approximation as the function iterates to optimised precision.

20.2.2 Single portfolio example with separate exposure and loss given default distributions

At the beginning of this section I pointed out that one may generally have separate distributions for the amount of exposure a debt holder has, and the fraction of that exposure that is realised as a loss. This means that we need to determine the sum

$$\sum_{i=1}^{\# \text{ defaults}} \text{Exposure}_i * \text{LossFraction}_i$$

This is easily done with Monte Carlo simulation in a manner similar to the model of Figure 20.3 but replacing the lognormal variable with the product of two variables. Alternatively, with ModelRisk you can use the VoseSumProduct function to return the aggregate distribution with one cell formula. Both methods are shown in Figure 20.6.

The VoseSimulate function simply generates random values from its object distribution parameter, which allows the user to keep the distribution in one place in the spreadsheet rather than many. The VoseSumProduct($n, a, b, c \ldots$) adds n variables together where each variable is $a * b * c * \ldots$, where a, b, c, etc., are distribution objects, so an independent sample is taken from each variable, $a, b, c \ldots$ for each of the n variables.

We can also construct the density function $f_L(x)$ for the individual loss distribution as follows:

$$f_L(x) = \int_0^1 f_F(y) . f_E\left(\frac{x}{y}\right) dy$$

	A	B	C	D	E
1					
2		Exposure distribution	VoseLognormal(100,10)		
3		Loss fraction	VoseBeta(13,43)		
4		Obligors	5384		
5		Probability of default	2.30%		
6		Number of defaults	132		
7					
8		**Method 1: SumProduct**			
9		Total loss (output)	3098.42		
10		**Method 2: Pure simulation**			
11		Total loss (output)	3082.48		
12					
13		Number of defaults	Individual loss		
14		1	18.30		
15		2	20.10		
192		179	0.00		
193		180	0.00		
194					
195			*Formulae table*		
196		C2	=VoseLognormalObject(100,10)		
197		C3	=VoseBetaObject(13,43)		
198		C6	=VoseBinomial(C4,C5)		
199		C9	=VoseSumProduct(C6,C2,C3)		
200		C14:C193	=IF(B12>$C$6,0,VoseLognormal(100,10)*VoseVoseBeta(13,43))		
201		C14:C193 (alternative)	=IF(B12>$C$6,0,VoseSimulate($C$2)*VoseSimulate($C$3))		
202		C11	=SUM(C14:C193)		
203					

Figure 20.6   Credit risk model with separate exposure and loss fraction components.

where $f_F()$ is the density function for the loss fraction distribution and $f_E()$ is the density function for the exposure distribution. Then the loss given default distribution can be constructed and used in an FFT calculation. The ModelRisk function VoseAggregateProduct performs this routine, so we can write

$$=\text{VoseAggregateProduct}(\text{VosePoissonObject}(1000), \text{VoseLognormalObject}(100, 10),$$
$$\text{VoseBetaObject}(11, 35))$$

20.2.3 Default probability as a variable

Default probabilities can perhaps be considered constant over a short period, but over a longer period or where the market is very volatile they should also be modelled as functions of the condition of the economy and, for corporate credit risk, as functions of the state of the regional business sector too. The same may apply for the loss given default variable, as the debt holder may recover a smaller fraction of the exposure in more stressing times. This means that we must construct credit portfolios that are disaggregated at an appropriate level and sum their cashflows. Failure to model these correlations will underestimate the risk of losses. For example, we might produce a model that varies the probability of default (PD) as a function of changes in GDP growth (GDP), interest rate (IR) and inflation (I) using an equation of the form

$$\text{PD}_t = \text{PD}_0\,{}^* \exp[\text{Normal}(1 + a\,{}^*\,(\text{GDP}_t - \text{GDP}_0) + b\,{}^*\,(\text{IR}_t - \text{IR}_0) - c\,{}^*\,(\text{I}_t - \text{I}_0), \sigma)]$$

where a, b and c are constants, t is some time in the future, σ is a residual volatility and X_0 means the value of the variable X now.

20.3 Credit Ratings and Markov Chain Models

Markov chains are often used in finance to model the variation in corporations' credit ratings over time. Rating agencies like Standard & Poor's and Moody's publish transition probability matrices that are based on how frequently a company that started with, say, an AA rating at some point in time has dropped to a BBB rating after a year. Provided we have faith in their applicability to the future, we can use these tables to forecast what the credit rating of a company, or a portfolio of companies, might look like at some future time using matrix algebra.

Let's imagine that there are just three ratings, A, B and default, with a probability transition matrix for one year as shown in Table 20.1.

We interpret this table as saying that a random A-rated company has an 81 % probability of remaining A-rated, an 18 % probability of dropping to a B rating, and a 1 % chance of defaulting on their loans. Each row must sum to 100 %. Note the matrix assigns a 100 % probability of remaining in default once

Table 20.1 Transition matrix example.

		Finish		
		A	**B**	**Default**
Start	**A**	81%	18%	1%
	B	17%	77%	6%
	Default	0%	0%	100%

Table 20.2 Transition scenarios and their probabilities for a 2 year period for a company with rating B.

Rating in 1 year (transition probability)	Rating in 2 years (transition probability)	Combined probability
A (0.17)	A (0.81)	0.1377
A (0.17)	B (0.18)	0.0306
A (0.17)	Default (0.01)	0.0017
B (0.77)	A (0.17)	0.1309
B (0.77)	B (0.77)	0.5929
B (0.77)	Default (0.06)	0.0462
Default (0.06)	A (0.0)	0.0
Default (0.06)	B (0.0)	0.0
Default (0.06)	Default (1.0)	0.06

one is there (called an absorption state). In reality, companies sometimes come out of default, but I'm keeping my example simple to focus on a few features of Markov chains.

Now let's imagine that a company starts with rating B and we want to determine the probability it has of being in each of the three states in 2 years. The possible transitions are shown in Table 20.2.

Thus, the probability that the currently B-rated company will have each rating after 2 years is

$$P(\text{A rating}) = 0.1377 + 0.1309 + 0.0 = 0.2686$$

$$P(\text{B rating}) = 0.306 + 0.5929 + 0.0 = 0.6235$$

$$P(\text{default}) = 0.0017 + 0.0462 + 0.06 = 0.1079$$

The calculations get rather more tiresome when there are many possible states (not the three we have here), but fortunately we are simply performing a matrix multiplication. Excel's MMULT array function can do this for us quickly, as shown in Figure 20.7: cells D11:F11 give the above calculated probabilities and the table D10:F12 gives the probabilities for a company starting in any other state.

Now let's imagine that we have a portfolio of 27 companies with an A rating and 39 companies with a B rating, and we would like to forecast what the portfolio might look like in 2 years. Figure 20.8 models the portfolio in three ways: using just binomial distributions if that is all your simulation software has, using the multinomial distribution and using ModelRisk's VoseMarkovSample function.

Methods 1 and 2 in this model have two limitations. The first is that the model can become very large if we want to forecast out many periods because we would have to repeat the MMULT calculation many times. The second, more important, limitation is that the model can only handle integer time steps. So, for example, our transition matrix may be for a year, but we might want to forecast out just 10 days ($t = 10/365 = 0.027397$). The VoseMarkovSample function removes these obstacles: if the transition matrix is positive definite, we can replace the value 2 in the function at cells F19:F21 with any non-negative value, as illustrated with the formula in cells L19:L21.

I mentioned that in this model "Default" is assumed to be an absorption state. This means that, if a path exists from any other state (A rating, B rating) to the default state, then eventually all individuals will end up in default. The model of Figure 20.9 shows the transition matrix for $t = 1$, 10, 50 and 200. You can see that for $t = 50$ years there is about an 81 % probability that an A-rated company will

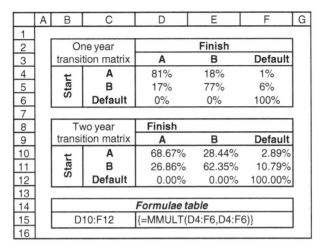

Figure 20.7 Calculation of a 2 year transition matrix.

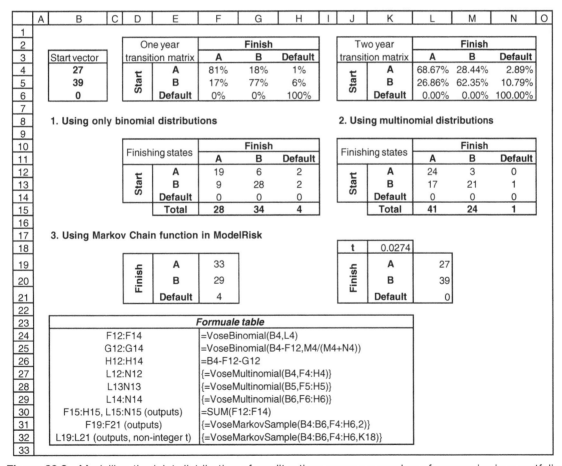

Figure 20.8 Modelling the joint distribution of credit ratings among a number of companies in a portfolio after 2 years.

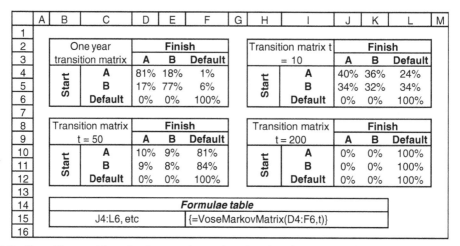

Figure 20.9 Transition matrices for large values of t, showing the progressive dominance of the default absorption state.

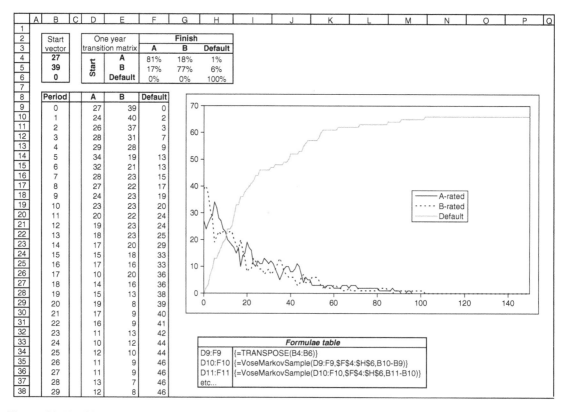

Figure 20.10 Markov chain time series showing the progressive dominance of the default state.

already have defaulted, and about an 84 % chance for a B-rated company. By 200 years there is almost a 100 % chance that any company will have already defaulted. Figure 20.10 shows this effect as a time series model. If this Markov chain model is a reasonable reflection of reality, one might wonder how it is that we have so many companies left. A crude but helpfully economic theory of business rating dynamics assumes that, if a company loses its rating position within a business sector, a competitor will take its place (either a new company or an existing company changing its rating), so we have a stable population distribution of rated companies.

20.4 Other Areas of Financial Risk

Market risk concerns equity, interest rate, currency and commodity risks. The returns or values of a portfolio of assets are subject to individual-level uncertainty but are also subject to various correlations at two levels: specific risks apply to a small number of assets that are subject to a common acute driver; and systematic risks apply more generally to a market sector (e.g. the price of natural gas affects methanol producers) or the market as a whole (e.g. exchange rate). Correctly recognising the effects of market risk allows an investor to manage its portfolio of assets by mixing negatively correlated assets to offset specific risks (e.g. investing in both a methanol and an oil company) and systematic risks (investing in assets in different countries). The quality of market risk analysis is highly dependent on accurate modelling of correlation. Copulas (Section 13.3) are particularly helpful in this regard because they offer considerable flexibility in representing and fitting the structure of any correlation.

Liquidity risk concerns a party who is an owner, or is considering becoming an owner, of an asset, and is unable to trade the asset at its proper value (or at all) because nobody in the market is interested. Liquidity risk arises when the party needs to raise cash at short notice, so it is intimately linked to the cash position of the party. The problem mostly concerns emerging or low-volume markets when the assets are stocks, etc. When the asset is an entire company and there are few potential buyers, the buyer may take advantage of the urgency to sell.

20.5 Measures of Risk

20.5.1 Value at risk

Value at risk (VaR) is defined as the amount that, over a predefined amount of time, losses won't exceed at a specified confidence level. As such, VaR represents a worst-case scenario at a particular confidence level. It does not include the time value of money, as there is no discount rate applied to each period's cashflows. VaR is very often used at banks and insurance companies to give some feel for the riskiness of an investment strategy. In that case, the time horizon should be the time required to be able to liquidate the investments in an orderly fashion.

VaR is very easy to calculate using Monte Carlo simulation on a cashflow model. You set up a cell to sum the cashflows over the period of interest, say in cell A1. Then, in another cell, to get the VaR at the 95 % confidence level, you write

$$= -\text{RiskPercentile}(\text{A1}, 5\,\%) \qquad \text{in @RISK}$$

$$= -\text{CB.GetForePercentileFN}(\text{A1}, 5\,\%) \qquad \text{in Crystal Ball}$$

which will return the VaR directly into the spreadsheet cell at the end of the simulation. Otherwise, just run a simulation with A1 as an output, read off the 5th percentile and put a minus sign in front of it. I gave an example of a VaR calculation in Figure 20.2.

The main problem with VaR is that it is not *subadditive* (Embrechts, 2000), meaning that it is possible to design two portfolios, X and Y, in such a way that $VaR(X + Y) > VaR(X) + VaR(Y)$. That is counterintuitive because we would normally consider that, by investing in independent portfolios, we have reduced risk.

For example, consider a defaultable corporate bond. A bond is a contract of debt: the corporation owes to the bond holder an amount called the face value of the bond and has to pay at a certain time – unless they go bust, in which case they default and the bond holder gets nothing. Let's say that the probability of default is 1 %, the face value is $100 and the current price of the bond is $98.5. If you buy this bond, the total cashflow at exercise can be modelled as

$$\text{Bernoulli}(99\,\%) * \$100 - \$98.5$$

i.e. a 1 % chance of −$98.5 and a 99 % chance of $1.50: a mean of $0.50.

You could buy 50 such bonds for the same company, which means that you will either get 50 * $100 or nothing, i.e. a cashflow of

$$(\text{Bernoulli}(99\,\%) * \$100 - \$98.5) * 50$$

with a mean of $25. Alternatively, perhaps you could buy 50 bonds with the same face value and default probability but each with different companies that have no connection between them so the default events are completely independent, in which case your cashflow is

$$\text{Binomial}(50, 99\,\%) * \$100 - \$98.5 * 50$$

but has the same mean of $25. Obviously the latter is less risky since one would expect most bonds to be honoured. Figure 20.11 plots the two cumulative distributions of revenue together.

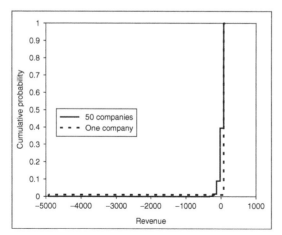 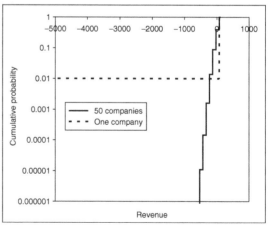

Figure 20.11 Cumulative distributions for the two bond portfolios. The probability scale is in logs in the right pane to show details at low probability.

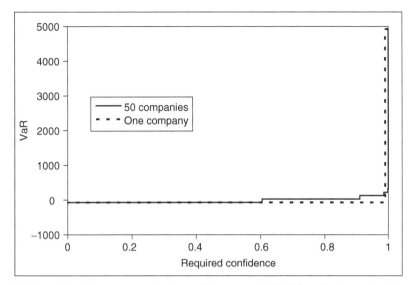

Figure 20.12 Relationship between required confidence and VaR for the two bond portfolios in the example.

The relationship between required confidence and VaR for these two portfolios is shown in Figure 20.12.

In this example the VaR is *larger* for the diversified portfolio (the 50 bonds) until the required confidence is greater than (1 – default probability). For models of more traditional investments, where revenues can be considered approximately normal or t-distributed (elliptical portfolios), this was not a problem even with correlations. However, financial instruments like derivatives and bonds are now traded very heavily, and these are either discrete variables or a discrete–continuous mix, and non-subadditivity then applies. For example, if analysts use optimising software (as is often done) to find a portfolio that minimises the ratio of VaR to mean return, they can inadvertently end up with a highly risky portfolio. The expected shortfall method of valuing risk discussed next avoids this problem.

20.5.2 Expected shortfall

Expected shortfall (ES) is superior to VaR because it satisfies all the requirements for a coherent risk measure (Artzner *et al.*, 1997), including subadditivity. It is simply negative the mean of the loss returns in the distribution with a greater loss than specified by the confidence interval. For example, the 99 % ES is negative the mean of the returns under the remaining 1 % of the distribution. The 100 % ES is just negative the mean of the revenue distribution. Figure 20.13 shows the ES for the two bond portfolios.

You can see that the 50-company-bond portfolio has a lower ES until the required confidence exceeds (1 – default probability), in which case they match. The chance that none of the 50 different bonds defaults is 99 %^50 = 60.5 %, so once we pass the 39.5 % confidence level the ES returns negative the portfolio expected value of 25. For the portfolio of the same bonds with one company we are only 99 % confident of no default and thus receiving payment to give us the portfolio expected value.

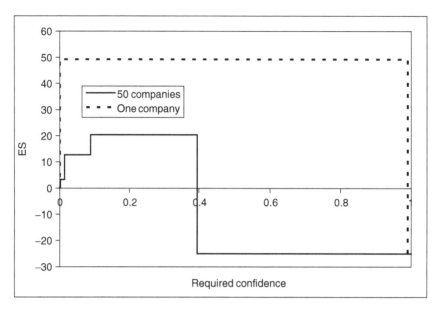

Figure 20.13 Relationship between required confidence and ES for the two bond portfolios in the example.

20.6 Term Life Insurance

In term life insurance, cover is purchased that will pay a certain sum if the insured person dies within the term of the contract (usually a year, but it could be 5, 10, 15, etc., years). Since the insured are generally healthy, the insurer has a very low probability (maybe as low as 1%) of paying out, which means that the insured can obtain cover for a low premium. The major downside for the insured party is that there is no obligation to renew cover beyond the original term, so a person acquiring a terminal illness within the term of the cover won't be able to obtain a renewal.

The insurance contract generally provides for a fixed benefit B in the event of death. Thus the payout P can be modelled as

$$P = \text{Binomial}(1, q) * B$$

where q is the probability that the individual will die within the contract term. Actuaries determine the value of q from mortality tables (aka life tables). These tables determine the probability of death in the next year given that one is currently a certain age combined with other factors like whether one smokes, or has smoked, whether one is a diabetic, etc.

An insurer offering term life insurance will have a portfolio of people with different q values and different benefit levels B. One could calculate the distribution of total payout for n insured persons by summing each of k different payout amounts:

$$P_n = \sum_{k=1}^{n} \text{Binomial}(1, q_k) * B_k$$

This is often called the *individual life model.* It is rather laborious to determine for large n. An alternative is to group insured people into the number n_{ij} who have similar probabilities q_j of death and similar benefit levels B_i:

$$P_n = \sum_{j=1}^{J} \sum_{i=1}^{I} \text{Binomial}(n_{ij}, q_j) * B_i$$

where

$$n = \sum_{j=1}^{J} \sum_{i=1}^{I} n_{ij}$$

De Pril (1986, 1989) determined a recursive formula that allows the exact computation of the aggregate claim distribution under the assumption that the benefits are fixed values rather than random variables and take integer multiples of some convenient base (e.g. \$1000) with a maximum value $M * base$, i.e. $B_i = \{1 \ldots M\}* base$. Let n_{ij} be the number of policies with benefit B_i and probability of claim q_j. Then De Pril demonstrates that the probability $p(x)$ that the aggregate benefit payout X will be equal to $x * base$ is given by the recursive formula

$$p(x) = \frac{1}{x} \sum_{i=1}^{\min[x,M]} \sum_{k=1}^{\lfloor x/i \rfloor} p(x - ik)h(i, k) \quad \text{for } x = 1, 2, 3, \ldots$$

and

$$p(0) = \prod_{i=1}^{M} \prod_{j=1}^{J} (1 - q_j)^{n_{ij}}$$

where

$$h(i, k) = i(-1)^{k-1} \sum_{j=1}^{J} n_{ij} \left(\frac{q_j}{1 - q_j}\right)^k$$

The formula has the benefit of being exact, but it is very computationally intensive. However, the number of computations can usually be significantly reduced if one accepts ignoring small aggregate costs to the insurer. Let K be a positive integer. Then the recursive formulae above are modified as follows:

$$p_K(0) = p(0)$$

$$p_K(x) = \frac{1}{x} \sum_{i=1}^{\min[x,M]} \sum_{k=1}^{\min[K,x/i]} p_K(x - ik)h(i, k)$$

Dickson (2005) recommends using a value of 4 for K. The De Pril method can be seen as the counterpart to Panjer's recursive method for the collective model. ModelRisk offers a set of functions for implementing De Pril's method.

20.6.1 Compound Poisson approximation

The compound Poisson approximation assumes that the probability of payout for an individual policy is fairly small – which is usually true, but has the advantage over the De Pril method in allowing that the payout distribution is a random variable rather than a fixed amount.

Let n_j be the number of policies with probability of claim q_j. The number of payouts in this stratum is therefore Binomial(n_j, q_j). If n_j is large and q_j is small, the binomial is well approximated by a Poisson $(n_j * q_j) = $ Poisson(λ_i) distribution $(n^{0.31}q < 0.47$ is a good rule) where $\lambda_i = n_j * q_j$. The additive property of the Poisson distribution tells us that the expected frequency for payouts over all groups of lines of insurance is given by

$$\lambda_{\text{all}} = \sum_{i=1}^{k} \lambda_i = \sum_{i=1}^{k} n_i q_i$$

and the total number of claims $= $ Poisson(λ_{all}). The probability that one of these claims, randomly selected, comes from stratum j is given by

$$P(j) = \frac{\lambda_j}{\sum_{i=1}^{k} \lambda_i}$$

Let $F_j(x)$ be the cumulative distribution function for the claim size of stratum j. The probability that a random claim is less than or equal to some value x is therefore

$$F(x) = \frac{\sum_{j=1}^{k} F_j(x)\lambda_j}{\sum_{i=1}^{k} \lambda_i}$$

Thus, we can consider the aggregate distribution for the total claims to have a frequency distribution equal to Poisson(λ_{all}) and a severity distribution given by $F(x)$. ModelRisk offers several functions related to this method that use Panjer recursive or FFT methods to determine the aggregate distribution or descriptive statistics such as moments and percentiles.

20.6.2 Permanent life insurance

Here, the insured are covered for their entire life, providing the premiums continue to be paid, so a payment will always be made and the policy accrues value over time. Some policies also allow the flexibility of withdrawing cash from the policy. Thus, permanent life insurance is more of an investment instrument for the policyholder with a final payout determined by the death of the insured. Determining premiums requires simulating the possible lifetime of the insured and applying a discounted cashflow calculation to the income (annual premiums) and costs (payment at death and administration costs over the life of the policy).

20.7 Accident Insurance

An insurance company will provide cover for financial loss associated with accidents for a fixed period, usually a year (for example: car, house, boat and fire insurance). The amount the insurer pays out is a function of the number of accidents that will occur and the cost to the insurer of each accident. The starting point is to assume that, for a given insured party, the accidents are unconnected to each other and occur randomly in time, which satisfies the assumptions underpinning a Poisson process. The frequency of accidents is then characterised by the expected frequency λ over the insured period.

Insurance companies nearly always apply a retention or deductible D. This means that the insured party pays the first part of the cost in an insured event up to D and the insurance company pays (cost $- D$) thereafter, so a cost x and claim size y are related as follows:

$$y = \text{MAX}(x - D, 0)$$

Most insurance policies also apply a maximum limit L, so that, if the cost of the risk event is greater than $L + D$, the policy only pays out L. Then we have

$$y = \text{IF}(x - D < 0, 0, \text{IF}(x - D > L, L, x - D)) \tag{20.1}$$

So, for example, if $x = \text{Lognormal}(10, 7)$, $D = 5$ and $L = 25$, we get the claim distribution shown in Figure 20.14.

Determining an aggregate distribution of claim sizes is simulation intensive, especially if the number of claims can be large, but there are a couple of ways to speed up the simulation. Consider the following problem. Historically we have observed 0.21 claims per insured party per year when the deductible was 8, and we wish to model the aggregate loss distribution for 3500 insured parties over a year with a new deductible of 5.

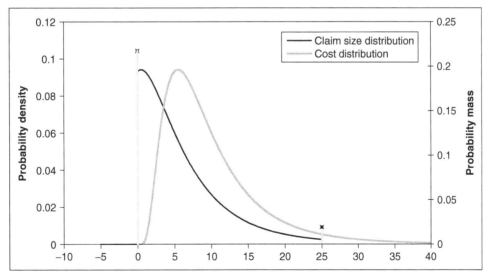

Figure 20.14 Comparison of claim size vs risk event cost distribution. Vertical lines with markers represent a probability mass.

The claims data we had were truncated (Section 10.3.3 describes how to fit a distribution to truncated data). We'll assume that we were able to estimate the underlying risk event cost distribution to be the Lognormal(10, 7) from above. Thus, the expected rate of risk events was $1/(1 - F(8))$ times the rate of claims, where $F(x)$ is the cumulative probability for a Lognormal(10, 7). The fraction of these events that will incur a claim is now $(1 - F(5))$, so the new frequency of claims per insured party per year will be $0.21 * (1 - F(5))/(1 - F(8))$. From Figure 20.14 you can see that the claim size distribution excluding zero is a lognormal distribution truncated at 5 and 30 and then shifted -5 units, i.e.

$$=\text{VoseLognormal}(10, 7, , \text{VoseXBounds}(5, 30), \text{VoseShift}(-5)) \qquad \text{in ModelRisk}$$

$$=\text{RiskLognorm}(10, 7, \text{RiskTrunc}(5, 30), \text{RiskShift}(-5)) \qquad \text{in @RISK}$$

We can use this distribution to simulate only claims rather than the entire risk event cost. ModelRisk has a range of special functions that convert a distribution object into another object of the form of Figure 20.14. For example

$$=\text{VoseDeductObject}(\text{CostDistributionObject}, \text{deductible}, \text{maxlimit}, \text{zeros})$$

The zero parameter is either TRUE or FALSE (or omitted). If FALSE, the DeductObject has no probability mass at zero, i.e. it is the distribution of a claim size given that a claim has occurred. If TRUE, the DeductObject has probability mass at zero, i.e. it is the distribution of a claim size given that a risk event has occurred. The DeductObject can be used in all the usual ways, e.g. if we start with the Lognormal(10, 7) distribution from above and apply a deductible and limit:

$$\text{A1: } = \text{VoseLognormalObject}(10, 7)$$

$$\text{A2: } = \text{VoseDeductObject}(\text{A1}, 5, 25, \text{TRUE})$$

The object in cell A2 can then be used in recursive and FFT aggregate methods, since these methods discretise the individual loss distribution and can therefore take care of a discrete–continuous mixture. Thus, we can use, for example

$$=\text{VoseAggregateFFT}(\text{VosePoissonObject}(2700), \text{A2})$$

to simulate the cost of Poisson(2700) random claims, and

$$=\text{VoseAggregateFFT}(\text{VosePoissonObject}(2700), \text{A2}, 0.99)$$

to calculate the 99th percentile of the aggregate cost of Poisson(2700) random claims.

20.7.1 Non-standard insurance policies

Insurance policies are becoming ever more flexible in their terms, and more complex to model as a result. For example, we might have a policy with a deductible of 5, and a limit of 20 beyond which the insurer pays only half the damages. Using a cost distribution of Lognormal(31, 23) and an accident frequency distribution of Delaporte(3, 5, 40), we can model this as follows:

$$A1: = \text{VoseLognormalObject}(31, 23)$$

$$A2: = \text{VoseExpression}("\text{IF}(\#1 > 20, (\#1 - 25)/2, \text{IF}(\#1 < 5, 0, \#1))", A1)$$

$$A3 \text{ (output)}: = \text{VoseAggregateMC}(\text{VoseDelaporte}(3, 5, 40), A2)$$

The VoseExpression function allows one a great deal of flexibility. The "#1" refers to the distribution linked to cell A1. Each time the VoseExpression function is called, it will generate a new value from the lognormal distribution and perform the calculation replacing "#1" with the generated value. The Delaporte function will generate a value (call it n) from this distribution, and the AggregateMC function will then call the VoseExpression function n times, adding as it goes along and returning the sum into the spreadsheet.

The VoseExpression allows several random variables to take part in the calculation. For example

$$=\text{VoseExpression}("\#1 * \#2", \text{VoseBernoulliObject}(0.3), \text{VoseLognormalObject}(20, 7))$$

will model a cost that follows a Lognormal(20, 7) distribution with 30 % probability and zero with 70 % probability, while

$$=\text{VoseExpression}("\#1 * (\#2 + \#3)", \text{VoseBernoulliObject}(0.3),$$

$$\text{VoseLognormalObject}(20, 7), \text{VoseParetoObject}(4, 7))$$

will model a cost that follows a (Lognormal(20, 7) + VosePareto(4, 7)) distribution with 30 % probability and zero with 70 % probability.

20.8 Modelling a Correlated Insurance Portfolio

Imagine that you are an insurance company with several different policies. For each policy you have the number of policy holders, the expected number of accidents per policy per year and the mean and standard deviation of the cost of each accident, and each policy has its own deductible and limit. It is a simple, though perhaps laborious, exercise to model the total payout associated with one policy and to sum the aggregate payout using simulation. Now imagine that you feel there is likely to be some correlation between these aggregate payouts: perhaps historic data have shown this to be the case. Using simulation, we cannot correlate the aggregate payout distributions. However, we can include a correlation if we use FFT methods to construct the aggregate loss distribution. The model of Figure 20.15 shows the aggregate loss distribution of five different policies being correlated together via a Clayton(10) copula (Section 13.3.1). Note that the equations used in cells C10:C14 use 1 minus the Clayton copula values, which will make the large aggregate claim values correlate more tightly than at the low end.

	A	B	C	D	E	F	G	H	I
1						Event cost data $000			
2		Policy	Policy holders	Expected events/yr/policy	Damage mean	Damage stdev	Deductible	Limit	
3		A	464	0.245	2.4	0.9	1.5	5	
4		B	852	0.118	3.56	1.82	1.5	5	
5		C	396	0.326	0.82	1.26	0.25	4	
6		D	144	0.089	8.25	11.37	1	25	
7		E	366	0.412	0.63	1.28	0.1	1.8	
8									
9			Aggregate claim $000	Copula	Frequency distribution		Claim size distribution		
10			$ 128	0.18887942	VosePoisson(113.68)	VoseDeduct(VoseLognormalObject($E$3,$F$3),$G$3,$H$3,1)			
11			$ 202	0.212641231	VosePoisson(100.536)	VoseDeduct(VoseLognormalObject($E$4,$F$4),$G$4,$H$4,1)			
12			$ 92	0.185912101	VosePoisson(129.096)	VoseDeduct(VoseLognormalObject($E$5,$F$5),$G$5,$H$5,1)			
13			$ 93	0.235597851	VosePoisson(12.816)	VoseDeduct(VoseLognormalObject($E$6,$F$6),$G$6,$H$6,1)			
14			$ 57	0.250565481	VosePoisson(150.792)	VoseDeduct(VoseLognormalObject($E$7,$F$7),$G$7,$H$7,1)			
15									
16		Total $000	$ 572						
17									
18				Formulae table					
19		C10:C14	=VoseAggregateFFT(E10,F10,,1-D10)						
20		D10:D14	{=VoseCopulaMultiClayton(10)}						
21		E10:E14	=VosePoissonObject(C3*D3)						
22		F10:F14	=VoseDeductObject(VoseLognormalObject(E3,F3),G3,H3,TRUE)						
23		C16 (output)	=SUM(C10:C14)						
24									

Figure 20.15 Simulating the loss distribution for a number of policies where the aggregate loss distribution for policies is correlated in some fashion.

20.9 Modelling Extremes

Imagine that we have a reasonably large dataset of the impacts of natural disasters that an insurance or reinsurance company covers. It is quite common to fit such a dataset, or at least the high-end tail values, to a Pareto distribution, because this has a longer tail than any other distribution (excepting curiosities like the Cauchy, slash and Lévy, which have infinite tails but are symmetric). An insurance company will often run a stress test of a "worst-case" scenario where several really high impacts hit the company within a certain period. So, for example, we might ask what could be the size of the largest of 10 000 impacts drawn from a fitted Pareto(5, 2) distribution modelling the impact of a risk in $billion.

Order statistics tells us that the cumulative probability U of the largest of n samples drawn from a continuous distribution will follow a Beta(n, 1) distribution (see Section 10.2.2). We can use this U value to invert the cdf of the Pareto distribution. A Pareto(θ, a) distribution has cdf

$$F(x) = 1 - \left(\frac{a}{x}\right)^{\theta}$$

giving

$$x = \frac{a}{\sqrt[\theta]{1-U}}$$

Thus, we can directly generate what the value of the largest of 10 000 values drawn from this distribution might be in $billion as follows:

$$= 2/(1 - \text{VoseBeta}(10\,000, 1))^{\wedge}(1/5)$$

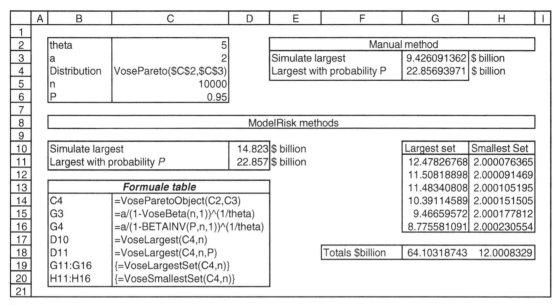

Figure 20.16 Determination of extreme values for 10 000 independent random variables drawn from a Pareto(5, 2) distribution.

One can also determine, for example, the value we are 95 % sure the largest of 10 000 risk impacts will not exceed by simply finding the 95th percentile of the beta distribution and use that in the above equation instead:

$$= 2/(1 - \text{BETAINV}(0.95, 10\,000, 1))^\wedge(1/5)$$

The same method can be applied to any distribution for which we have the inverse to the cdf. The principle can also be extended to model the largest *set* of values, or smallest, as shown in the model of Figure 20.16 which allows you to simulate the sum of the largest several possible values (in this case six, since the array function has been input to cover six cells). ModelRisk can perform these extreme calculations for all of its 70+ univariate distributions (Figure 20.17).

20.10 Premium Calculations

Imagine that we are insuring a policy holder against the total damage X that might be accrued in automobile accidents over a year. The number of accidents the policyholder might have is modelled as Pólya(0.26, 0.73). The damages incurred in any one accident are $Lognormal(300, 50). The insurer has to determine the premium to be charged.

The premium must be at least greater than the expected payout $E[X]$, otherwise, according to the law of large numbers, in the long run the insurer will be ruined. The expected payout is the product of the expected values of the Pólya and lognormal distributions, in this case $= 0.1898 * \$300 = \$56.94$. The question is then: how much more should the premium be over the expected value? Actuaries

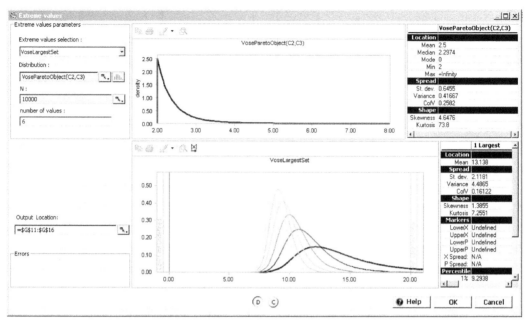

Figure 20.17 ModelRisk screen capture of the Function View for the VoseLargest array function in cells G11:G16 from the model in Figure 20.16, showing the relationships between the marginal distributions for the six largest-value variables.

have a variety of methods to determine the premium. Four of the most common methods, shown in Figure 20.18, are:

1. *Expected value principle.* This calculates the premium in excess of $E[X]$ as some fraction θ of $E[X]$:

$$\text{Premium} = (1 + \theta)E[X], \theta > 0$$

Ignoring administration costs, θ represents the return the insurer is getting over the expected capital required, $E[X]$, to cover the risk.

2. *The Standard deviation principle.* This calculates the premium in excess of $E[X]$ as some multiple α of the standard deviation of X:

$$\text{Premium} = E[X] + \alpha\sigma[X], \alpha > 0$$

The problem with this principle is that, at an individual level, there is no consistency in the level of risk the insurer is taking for the expected profit $\alpha\sigma[X]$, since σ has no consistent probabilistic interpretation.

3. *Esscher principle.* The Esscher method calculates the ratio of the expected values of $X\,\mathrm{e}^{hX}$ to e^{hX}:

$$\text{Premium} = \frac{E[X\mathrm{e}^{hX}]}{E[\mathrm{e}^{hX}]}, h > 0$$

	A	B	C	D	E	F	G
1					\multicolumn{2}{c}{Aggregate moments}		
2		Frequency:	VosePolya(0.26,0.73)		Mean	56.94	
3		Severity:	VoseLognormal(300,50)		Variance	30026.36	
4					Skewness	4.335965956	
5					Kurtosis	29.55131718	
6							
7		\multicolumn{2}{c}{Expected value method:}			\multicolumn{2}{c}{Standard deviation method:}	
8		theta	0.03		alpha	0.01	
9		Premium	58.648		Premium	58.673	
10							
11		\multicolumn{2}{c}{Esscher method:}			\multicolumn{2}{c}{Risk adjusted method:}	
12		h	0.00012		rho	1.04	
13		Premium	60.195		Premium	62.534	
14							
15		\multicolumn{3}{c}{Formulae table}				
16		C2	=VosePolyaObject(0.26,0.73)				
17		C3	=VoseLognormalObject(300,50)				
18		E2:F5	{=VoseAggregateMoments(C2,C3)}				
19		C9 (output)	=VosePrincipleEV(C2,C3,C8)				
20		F9 (output)	=VosePrincipleStdev(C2,C3,F8)				
21		C13 (output)	=VosePrincipleEsscher(C2,C3,C12)				
22		F13 (output)	=VosePrincipleRA(C2,C3,F12)				
23							

Figure 20.18 Calculation of premiums under four different principles. The mean and variance of the aggregate distribution, shown with a grey background, provide a reference point (e.g. the premiums must exceed the mean of 56.94).

The principle gets its name from the Esscher transform which converts a density function from $f(x)$ to $a * f(x) * \exp[b * x]$, where a and b are constants. It was introduced by Bühlmann (1980) in an attempt to acknowledge that the premium price for an insurance policy is a function of the market conditions in addition to the level of risk being covered. Wang (2003) gives a nice review.

4. *Risk adjusted or PH principle.* This is a special case of the proportional hazards premium principle based on coherent risk measures (see, for example, Wang, 1996). The survival function $(1 - F(x))$ of the aggregate distribution which lies on [0, 1] is transformed into another variable that also lies on [0, 1]:

$$\text{Premium} = \int_{\min}^{\max} [1 - F(x)]^{1/\rho} \, dx, \rho > 1$$

where $F(x)$ is the cumulative distribution function from the aggregate distribution.

Chapter 21

Microbial food safety risk assessment

In the field of microbial risk, modelling is called "risk assessment" rather than risk analysis, and I'll follow that terminology in this chapter. Microbial risk assessment attempts to assess the human health impact of the presence of bacteria on food. It is a big problem: I'm sure you, or someone close to you, will have experienced food poisoning at some time. The usual effect is 2–10 days of vomit, cramps, fever and/or diarrhoea, but it can be a lot more serious, from hospitalisation to permanent disability and death. A considerable part of our company's work has been in microbial risk assessment. We teach an advanced two-week course on modelling methods, and I have coauthored or edited a number of national and international guidelines on microbial risk assessment.

Microbial risk assessment has been undertaken since the mid-1990s and built initially (with limited success) on the development of nuclear and toxicological human health risk assessments. The modelling techniques that are available now are reasonably advanced and generally based around some form of Monte Carlo model. The major problems faced by a risk assessor are the availability of recent, targeted data and adequately capturing the complexity of the real-world problem. The goal of the modelling is to evaluate the health impact of changes to the system (and perhaps minimise the effect): e.g. more control of animal waste, a new product entering the market, changing the regulatory requirements on testing farms, food or animal food, changes to farm practices, educating people to be more careful with their food, etc. The most common approach to microbial food safety has been to try to model the pathways that bacteria take from the farm to the human ingestion event, figuring out along the way how many bacteria there might be (probability distributions). The numbers of bacteria ingested are then translated into a probability of infection, illness, severe illness and/or mortality through a dose–response model. Put it all together and we get an estimate of the human impact of the bacterium.

To illustrate the level of complexity, consider the biggest foodborne illness risk in the developed world – non-typhoidal salmonellosis, which you get from exposure to a group of bacteria known as *Salmonella* (named after its discoverer Dr Daniel Salmon). For a random person to contract salmonellosis, he or she must have ingested (ate, drank, breathed in) one of these bacteria that then found a suitable place in the body (the lower intestine) to set up home and multiply (colonise), which is the infection. You need just one bacterium to become infected because it then multiplies in the human gut, but if you eat something with thousands of bacteria on it you obviously have more chance of infection. Usually an infected person will experience diarrhoea, fever and cramps which stop on their own after 6 days or so, but in severe cases a person can be hospitalised and can develop Reiter's syndrome, which is really unpleasant and can last for years, or, if the infection spreads from the gut into the bloodstream, it can attack the body's organs and result in death.

These bacteria grow naturally without effect in the intestines of animals, many of which we eat. The major sources of human exposure are food related: eggs are generally the biggest one (*Salmonella enteritidis*), but also chicken, beef, pork and related products. However, you can find it in vegetables (think fertiliser), recreational waterways (think ducks) and household pets (don't give your dog uncooked chicken). The bacteria are killed by heating them sufficiently – so well-cooked chicken meat can be less risky than raw vegetables. In order for us to model a nation's exposure to *Salmonella*, we need to model the number of bacteria from each source and how many survive to get into our gut. Let's just take commercially raised chicken: eggs are produced by layer flocks and sent to farms that hatch the chicks which are then sent to farms that raise the birds in flocks that are kept in sheds protected from the outside world. In some countries the bedding is not changed through the life of the flock. *Salmonella* can enter from infected hatching farms, wild birds or rodents entering the shed, infected feed, visitors, etc. At a certain age (you don't want to know just how young) the flock is sent en masse to a slaughter plant in trucks (which may be clean, but may not be). The chickens get nervous (they've never left the shed before), the acidity in their stomach changes and the *Salmonella* multiply many times. The chickens are then converted into supermarket-ready neat packages in a messy process that involves considerable redistribution of bacteria between carcasses in a flock, and from one flock following another in the slaughter plant. Then these neat packages take many forms: wings, breast, oven ready, chilled or frozen, TV dinners. Scraps that don't make neat supermarket packages are converted into sausages and burgers. They are sent to warehouses where they are redistributed. Freezing kills some bacteria (we say "are attenuated") as a function of time and temperature, as does cooking. Some bacteria become dormant, so when we test them we think they are dead (they won't grow), but they can revive over time and start multiplying again, so there is some uncertainty about how to interpret the data for attenuation experiments.

How about the bedding the flock lived on? We eat a *lot* of chickens and they produce a lot of waste that the poultry farmer has to get rid of somehow. It gets cleaned out after the chickens have left and used as fertiliser (at current prices, it would be worth about $30 per ton as a commercial fertiliser equivalent). However, it can be worth a lot more – in some countries (the USA included) it is fed to cattle as it is as nutritious as alfalfa hay (sceptical? – try googling "poultry litter cattle feed"). Apparently, however, it is not as palatable to the cow (which is not hard to believe), so they take some time to get used to it. The bacteria in the litter are (hopefully) killed by deep stacking the litter and leaving it until it reaches 54 Celsius.

Measuring the number of bacteria in food is a tricky problem. The bacteria tend to grow very fast (doubling every 20 minutes in good conditions is common) so they tend to be in small locations of large numbers. The food doesn't smell or look bad, so we have to rely on random samples, which are a very hit and miss affair. We count the bacteria in logs because that is the only way to make sense of the huge variation in numbers one sees. Perhaps the most difficult part of the farm-to-fork sequence (you may prefer the term "moo-to-loo") is the contribution played out in the domestic and commercial kitchens that prepare the chicken. The chicken itself may be well cooked, but the fat and liquids that come off the uncooked carcass can spread around and cross-contaminate other foods via hands, knives, chopping boards, etc. Some researchers have produced mocked-up sterile kitchens and invited people to prepare a meal, then investigated the contamination that occurs. It can be a lot – I used to have a kitchen with a black granite top that showed the slightest grease spot – bad choice for a kitchen perhaps, but it looked beautiful and provided an excellent demonstration of just how difficult it is to completely clean a surface. Imagine trying to clean a porous wooden chopping board instead. Think about how hard it is to wash raw chicken fat off your hands. Maybe, like me, you wipe your hands frequently on an apron or towel (or your clothes) while you are cooking, offering another cross-contamination route. I am sure that you can see that there are many possible exposure pathways and there is a lot of difficulty in counting bacteria.

The exposure assessment portion of a microbial risk assessment requires development of a model to represent the various pathways or scenarios that can occur as product moves through the farm to consumer continuum. The possibilities are nearly endless. Modelling the myriad pathways through which a product can move is complex, and models must necessarily be simplified yet still adequately represent reality. Generally, the different pathways are modelled in a summary form by using frequency distributions to represent the possible scenarios.

The primary difficulty in aggregating the scenarios, however, is determining what proportion of the real world each scenario should represent. The number of possible post-processing scenarios for even a single product pathogen pair is large. If we include cross-contamination of other products, the effort could become intractable. In spite of best efforts adequately to represent the scenarios in the model, there can be other important scenarios that are missed simply because they haven't been imagined by the risk managers or risk assessors.

There are two components in a microbial risk assessment that are rather particular to the field: growth and attenuation models, which predict the changing numbers of bacteria as a function of environmental conditions, and dose–response models, which translate the number of bacteria ingested into a probability of illness. I'll explain them here because the thinking is quite interesting, even if you are not a food safety specialist (and I promise there won't be anything else that puts you off your food). Then I recommend you go to www.foodrisk.org/risk_assessments.cfm, which gives you access to many risk assessments that use these and other ideas. At WHO and FAO's websites you can also find far more detailed explanations of these ideas, together with the data issues one faces.

21.1 Growth and Attenuation Models

In microbial food safety the dose measure is assigned a probability distribution to reflect the variation in dose between exposure events. The probability distribution of a non-zero dose in microbial risk assessment is usually modelled as being lognormal for a number of reasons:

- Changes in microorganism concentrations across various processes in the farm-to-fork chain are measured in log differences.

- Processes are considered generally to have a multiplicative effect on the microorganism number or concentration.

- There are very many (even if perhaps not individually identified) events and factors contributing to the growth and attenuation of microorganism numbers.

- The central limit theorem states that, if we multiply a large number of positive random variables together with no process dominant, the result is asymptotically lognormal.

For convenience and ease of interpretation, risk assessors work in log base 10, so the exposure dose is of the form

$$\log[dose] = \text{Normal}(\mu_{10}, \sigma_{10})$$

The most common growth and attenuation models in current use are the exponential, square-root, Bělehrádek, logistic, modified Gompertz and Baranyi–Roberts models. These models can be divided into two mathematical groups: those that have memory and those that do not. "Memory" means that the predicted growth in any time interval depends on the growth history that has already occurred. In microbial food safety models we often encounter the situation where bacteria move in and out of conditions (usually temperature) that are conducive to growth, and therefore we need to estimate the effect of growth across the entire history.

The most common way to estimate the parameters of growth and attenuation models is through controlled laboratory experiments that grow an organism in a specific medium and under specific environmental conditions. The number of microorganisms is recorded over time, and the various models are fit to these data to derive the parameter values for this combination of microorganism/growth medium/environmental conditions. Growth experiments essentially start with a medium naïve to the organism and then monitor the gradual colonisation of that medium to saturation point. The log number of organisms thus tends to follow an S-shaped (sigmoidal) function of time (Figure 21.1). The sigmoidal curve has a gradient (rate of increase in log bacteria numbers) that is a function of time or, equivalently, of the number of bacteria already present once the lag phase is complete.

Interpretation of these curves requires some care. We can to some extent eliminate the difficulty of scaling of the amount of the medium in which the bacteria are grown by considering surface density instead of absolute numbers. However, by using these fitted growth models in risk assessments where there is more than one opportunity for growth, we are effectively resetting the food medium to be naïve of bacteria at each growth event and resetting the pathogen to have no memory of previous growth. Thus, in order to be able to use sequential growth models, we either need some corrective mechanism to compensate for already being part of the way along a growth curve or we need to accept a simpler method with fewer assumptions.

21.1.1 Empirical data

Empirical data are often used in microbial food safety to model the effect of current operations on pathogen numbers. For example, one might estimate the number of pathogenic organisms in the gut of poultry before and after transportation from shed to slaughter plant to determine any amplification (see, for example, Stern *et al.*, 1995) or track pathogen levels through a slaughter plant (see, for example, the data tabulated for *Salmonella* in poultry in Section 4.4 of FAO/WHO (2000)).

Experiments to enumerate levels of pathogenic organisms at farms and in slaughter plants struggle with a variety of problems: the detection threshold of the test; the transfer rate to swabs or rinse

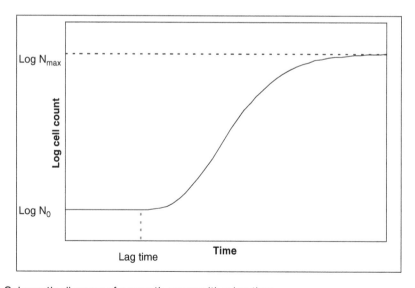

Figure 21.1 Schematic diagram of a growth curve with a lag time.

solution; the most probable number (MPN) algorithm used to interpret the observed counts; and the representativeness of samples like swabs from skin, faecal samples, etc. Perhaps the greatest difficulties in obtaining representative results are caused by the heterogeneity of pathogen distribution between animals and over carcass surfaces and the several orders of magnitude of variability observed.

Slaughter plant processes that redistribute and attenuate pathogen load are highly complex and make data collection and modelling extremely difficult. For example, Stern and Robach (2003) conducted poultry slaughter plant experiments, enumerating for individual birds the levels in their faeces preslaughter and on their fully processed carcasses, and found no correlation between the two.

21.1.2 Growth and attenuation models without memory

Exponential growth model

Growth models for replicating microorganisms are based on the idea that each organism grows independently by division at a rate controlled by its environment. For environment-independent growth we can write

$$\frac{\partial N}{\partial t} = kN$$

which gives the exponential growth model

$$N_t = N_0 \exp(kt)$$

where N_0 and N_t are the number (or density) of microorganisms at times zero and t respectively, and k is some non-negative constant reflecting the performance of a particular microorganism under particular stable environmental conditions. This equation produces a growth curve of the form shown in Figure 21.2.

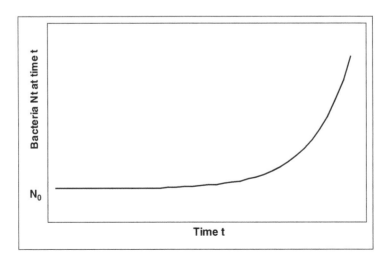

Figure 21.2 Exponential growth.

In fact, this model only describes the expected value for N_t. The stochastic model is known as the Yule model (Taylor and Karlin, 1998), which has not yet been adopted in food safety modelling:

$$N_t = \text{NB}(N_0, \exp(-kt)) + N_0$$

where NB is a negative binomial distribution with probability mass function

$$f(x) = \binom{N_0 + x - 1}{x} (\exp(-kt))^{N_0} (1 - \exp(-kt))^x$$

ModelRisk has functions that will fit a Yule time series to data and/or make a projection. There are also options for doing the analysis in $\log_{10}$.

N_t has mean μ and variance V given by

$$\mu = N_0 \exp(kt)$$
$$V = N_0(1 - \exp(-kt)) \exp(2kt)$$

Bělehrádek growth model

Extensions to the exponential model can account for different environments. The full temperature Bělehrádek environment-dependent growth model modifies k to be a function of temperature:

$$\sqrt{k} = (b\{T - T_{min}\}\{1 - \exp[c(T - T_{max})]\})$$

where b and c are fitting constants, T is temperature and T_{min} and T_{max} are the minimum and maximum temperature at which growth can occur respectively. It is sometimes known as the square-root model and leads to

$$N_t = N_0 \exp[t\,(b\{T - T_{min}\}\{1 - \exp[c(T - T_{max})]\})^2] \qquad (21.1)$$

Other versions take into account environmental factors such as pH and water activity. In general, these models take the form

$$N_t = N_0 \exp(t.f(conditions))$$

Taking logs, we have

$$\log[N_t] = \log[N_0] + t.f(conditions)/\ln[10]$$

So, for example, taking logs of Equation (21.1) gives

$$\log[N_t] = \log[N_0] + [t\,(b\{T - T_{min}\}\{1 - \exp[c(T - T_{max})]\})^2]/\ln[10]$$

Parameter b can be rescaled to be appropriate to a $\log_{10}$ model:

$$\log[N_t] = \log[N_0] + [t\,(b_{10}\{T - T_{min}\}\{1 - \exp[c(T - T_{max})]\})^2]$$

The exponential and Bělehrádek models are memoryless, meaning that they take no account of how long the microorganisms have already been growing, only how many there are at time $t = 0$. Thus, we can break down t into two or more separate divisions and get the same result. For example, let

$$t = t_1 + t_2$$

The number of bacteria at time t_1 is given by

$$\log[N_{t1}] = \log[N_0] + t_1 . f\,(conditions)/\ln[10]$$

and the number of bacteria at time t_2 is then given by

$$\begin{aligned}
\log[N_{t2}] &= \log[N_1] + t_2 . f\,(conditions)/\ln[10]\\
&= \log[N_0] + t_1 . f\,(conditions)/\ln[10] + t_2 . f\,(conditions)/\ln[10]\\
&= \log[N_0] + (t_1 + t_2) . f\,(conditions)/\ln[10]\\
&= \log[N_0] + t . f\,(conditions)/\ln[10]
\end{aligned}$$

which is the same result as performing the model on t directly.

Attenuation models

Attenuation models for microorganisms are based on the idea (Stumbo, 1973) that each organism dies or is inactivated independently and that the event follows a Poisson process whose rate is controlled by the environmental conditions, which leads to the general exponential attenuation equation

$$E[N_t] = N_0 \exp(-kt)$$

where $E[N_t]$ is the expected number of CFU (colony-forming units, i.e. microorganisms that are capable of multiplying to form a colony) at time t and N_0 is the initial number of CFU prior to growth, and k is a fixed positive value or a function of the environmental conditions; k^{-1} is then the average life of the pathogen in this environment. Taking logs, we have

$$\log[E[N_t]] = \log[N_0] - \frac{k}{\ln[10]}t$$

This model only describes the expected value for N_t. The stochastic model is known as the "pure death" model (Taylor and Karlin, 1998) which can be written as

$$N_t = \text{Binomial}(N_0, \exp(-kt))$$

ModelRisk has functions that will fit a "pure death" time series to data and/or make a projection. There are also options for doing the analysis in $\log_{10}$.

The distribution of N at any moment t has mean μ and variance V given by

$$\mu = N_0 \exp(-kt)$$

$$V = N_0 \exp(-kt)(1 - \exp(-kt))$$

These equations give us a probabilistic way of analysing data on attenuation and death. Imagine that, on average, a process decreases pathogen load by r logs:

$$E[\log[N_t]] = \log[N_0] - r$$

Then the distribution for $\log[N_t]$ will be approximately[1]

$$\log[N_t] = \text{Normal}(\log[N_0] - r, \sqrt{r})$$

By the pivotal method of classical statistics and the principle of a sufficient statistic, if we have observed a log reduction of x, i.e.

$$\log[N_{t(\text{observed})}] = \log[N_{0(\text{observed})}] - x$$

then we can estimate r to be

$$\hat{r} = \text{Normal}(x, \sqrt{x})$$

The probability that all the pathogenic organisms will be killed by time t is the binomial probability that $N_t = 0$, i.e.

$$P(N_t = 0) = [1 - \exp(-kt)]^{N_0}$$

and the time until all the pathogenic organisms are killed or attenuated is, from Poisson theory, the random variable

$$t(N_t = 0) = \text{Gamma}\left(N_0, \frac{1}{k}\right) \tag{21.2}$$

Gamma distributions are difficult to generate for large N_t, so we can use the normal distribution approximation to Equation (21.2):[2]

$$t(N_t = 0) = \frac{1}{k}\text{Normal}(N_0, \sqrt{N_0})$$

As with exponential growth models, other versions take into account environmental factors such as pH and water activity. For example, the Arrhenius–Davey environment-dependent inactivation model has the following equation:

$$N_t = N_0 \exp\left(-t.\exp\left(a + \frac{b}{T} + \frac{c}{pH} + \frac{d}{pH^2}\right)\right)$$

where a, b, c and d are constants, T is temperature and pH is the pH of the environment.

In general, these models take the form

$$N_t = N_0 \exp(-t.f(conditions))$$

---

[1] Using the normal approximation to the binomial: Binomial$(n, p) \approx \text{Normal}(np, \sqrt{np(1-p)})$

[2] Using the normal approximation to the gamma: Gamma$(\alpha, \beta) \approx \text{Normal}(\alpha\beta, \sqrt{\alpha}\beta)$, accurate to within at most 0.7 % for $\alpha > 50$.

21.1.3 Growth and attenuation models with memory

Logistic growth and attenuation model

The logistic[3] model dampens the rate of growth by using

$$\frac{\partial N}{\partial t} = kN \left(1 - \frac{N}{N_\infty} \right)$$

where N_∞ is the population size at $t = \infty$. The concept behind this equation is that a population naturally stabilises after time to its maximum sustainable size N_∞ which will be a function of the resources available to the population. The differential equation is a simple form of the Bernoulli equation (Kreyszig, 1993) which, by setting $N = N_0$ when $t = 0$, integrates to give

$$N_t = \frac{N_0 N_\infty}{N_0 + (N_\infty - N_0) \exp(-kt)} \tag{21.3}$$

or a more intuitive form of the equation

$$\frac{N_0}{N_t} = \frac{N_0}{N_\infty} + \left(1 - \frac{N_0}{N_\infty} \right) \exp(-kt)$$

The equation can be fitted to data from laboratory growth studies that give estimates of k and the maximum microorganism number (or density) N_∞ for the particular environment and organism. The function takes three forms: if $k = 0$ there is no change in N with time; if $N_0 > N_\infty$, then N_t will decrease (attenuation model) in a sigmoidal fashion towards N_∞; and, of most relevance to microbial food safety, if $N_0 < N_\infty$, then N_t will increase (growth model) in a sigmoidal fashion towards N_∞.

A problem in using Equation (21.3) in microbial risk assessment is the non-linear appearance of N_0. This means that, if we split time into two components, we will not get the same answer, i.e.

$$N_t = \frac{N_0 N_\infty}{N_0 + (N_\infty - N_0) \exp(-kt)} \neq \frac{N_{t1} N_\infty}{N_{t1} + (N_\infty - N_{t1}) \exp(-kt_2)}$$

where

$$N_{t1} = \frac{N_0 N_\infty}{N_0 + (N_\infty - N_0) \exp(-kt_1)}$$

$$t = t_1 + t_2$$

The reason for this is that the equation assumes that the starting position ($t = 0$) equates to the beginning of the sigmoidal curve. It is therefore inappropriate to use Equation (21.3) if one is at some point in time significantly into the growth (or attenuation) period.

---

[3] The term logistic has no relation to logistic regression. In human population modelling it is called the Verhulst model after the nineteenth-century Belgian mathematician Pierre Verhulst. In 1840 he predicted what the US population would be in 1940 and was less than 1 % off, and did just as well with estimating the 1994 Belgian population (excluding immigration). However, his success with human populations is no comfort to the predictive microbiologist, as Verhulst was dealing with a single environment (a country) and could derive a logistic growth curve to match historic population data and thus predict future population size. In predictive microbiology we are modelling growth on a contaminated food, and we don't have the historic data to know where on the logistic growth curve we are.

The same problem applies to almost all sigmoidal growth models, which include the Gompertz, modified Gompertz and Baranyi–Roberts models which are in frequent use in food safety risk assessments. The van Boekel attenuation model is an exception.

Van Boekel attenuation model

Van Boekel (2002) proposed an environment-independent Weibull attenuation model that has memory of the following form

$$S(t) = \exp\left(-\left(\frac{t}{\beta}\right)^{\alpha}\right)$$

where $S(t)$ is the Weibull probability of surviving after time t, and α and β are fitting parameters to which he gives some loose physical interpretation.

The model can be restated as

$$N_t = N_0 \exp\left(-\left(\frac{t}{\beta}\right)^{\alpha}\right) \tag{21.4}$$

or, more precisely, as a binomial variable:

$$N_t = \text{Binomial}\left(N_0, \exp\left(-\left(\frac{t}{\beta}\right)^{\alpha}\right)\right)$$

He fitted his model to a large number of datasets which performed better than the simpler $N_t = N_0 \exp(-kt)$. Equation (21.4) is linear in N_0, which means that, with some elementary algebra, time can be divided into two or more intervals and the results still hold:

$$N_t = N_0 \exp\left(-\left(\frac{t}{\beta}\right)^{\alpha}\right) = N_{t1} \exp\left(\frac{t_1^{\alpha} - (t_1 + t_2)^{\alpha}}{\beta^{\alpha}}\right)$$

Thus, although this model has memory of previous attenuation, it can still be used for subsequent attenuation events.

N_t has mean μ and variance V given by

$$\mu = N_0 \exp\left(-\left(\frac{t}{\beta}\right)^{\alpha}\right)$$

$$V = N_0 \exp\left(-\left(\frac{t}{\beta}\right)^{\alpha}\right)\left(1 - \exp\left(-\left(\frac{t}{\beta}\right)^{\alpha}\right)\right)$$

The probability that all the pathogenic organisms will be killed by time t is the binomial probability that $N_t = 0$, i.e.

$$P(N_t = 0) = \left[1 - \exp\left(-\left(\frac{t}{\beta}\right)^{\alpha}\right)\right]^{N_0} \tag{21.5}$$

Equation (21.5) can be rearranged to generate values for the distribution of time until all pathogenic organisms are killed:

$$t(N_t = 0) = \alpha \sqrt[\beta]{-\ln[1 - \sqrt[N_t]{U}]}$$

where U is a Uniform(0, 1) random variable.

21.2 Dose–Response Models

There are four dose–response equations in common use that are based on theory conforming to WHO guidelines (FAO/WHO, 2003) of no threshold (i.e. it only takes one organism to cause an infection) and are given in Table 21.1.

The first three of these models can be viewed as stemming from a simple binomial equation for the probability of infection:

$$P(\inf|D) = 1 - (1 - p)^D \qquad (21.6)$$

where p is the probability that a single pathogenic organism causes infection, and D is the number of pathogenic organisms in the exposure event. Thus, the equation for $P(\inf)$ is the binomial probability that at least one of the D pathogenic organisms succeeds in infecting the exposed person, i.e. 1 minus the probability that zero organisms will succeed in infecting. Implicit in this equation are two important assumptions:

- The exposure to the D organisms occurs in a single event.
- The organisms all have the same probability of causing infection independently of the number of organisms D.

21.2.1 The exponential model

The exponential dose–response model assumes that the received dose is Poisson distributed with mean λ i.e.

$$P(\inf|\lambda) = 1 - (1 - p)^{\text{Poisson}(\lambda)}$$

Table 21.1 The four most common microbial dose–response models.

D–R model	Dose measure	P(effect)
Exponential	Mean dose λ	$= 1 - \exp(-\lambda p)$
Beta–Poisson	Mean dose λ	$\approx 1 - \left(1 + \dfrac{\lambda}{\beta}\right)^{-\alpha}$
Beta–binomial	Actual dose D	$= 1 - \dfrac{\Gamma(D + \beta)\Gamma(\alpha + \beta)}{\Gamma(\alpha + \beta + D)\Gamma(\beta)}$
Weibull–gamma	Actual dose D	$= 1 - \left(1 + \dfrac{D^b}{\beta}\right)^{-\alpha}$

which simplifies to

$$P(\text{inf}|\lambda) = 1 - \exp(-\lambda p) \tag{21.7}$$

We can think of λp as the expected number of infections a person will have from exposure to this dose, and the equation for $P(\text{inf}|\lambda)$ is then just the Poisson probability of at least one infection. The assumption of a Poisson-distributed dose is quite appropriate for modelling bacteria, viruses and cysts in water, for example, if we can accept that these organisms don't clump together.

Some authors have reinterpreted Equation (21.7) to be

$$P(\text{inf}|D) = 1 - \exp(-rD) \tag{21.8}$$

where r is the same probability p but the Poisson mean λ has been replaced by the actual dose D received, which is inconsistent with the underlying theory. The potential problem is that Equation (21.8) will add additional randomness to the dose by wrapping a Poisson distribution around D, which is inappropriate if D has been determined as an actual dose received. A Poisson λ distribution has mean λ and standard deviation $\sqrt{\lambda}$. Thus, for a Poisson-distributed dose with large λ the actual dose received will be very close to λ; for example, for $\lambda = 1E6$ organisms the actual dose received lies with $>99\%$ probability between 0.9997E6 and 1.0003E6 (Figure 21.3), and using the approximation of Equation (21.8) adds little additional randomness.

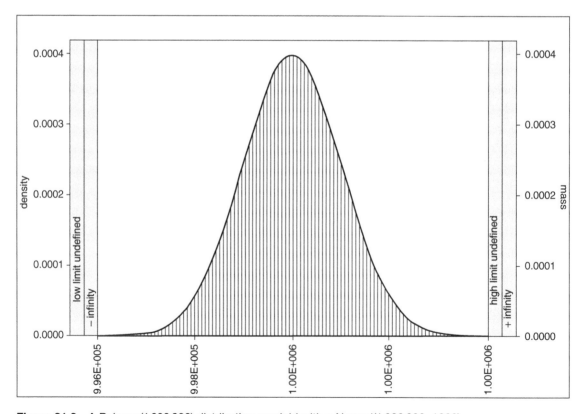

Figure 21.3   A Poisson(1 000 000) distribution overlaid with a Normal(1 000 000, 1000).

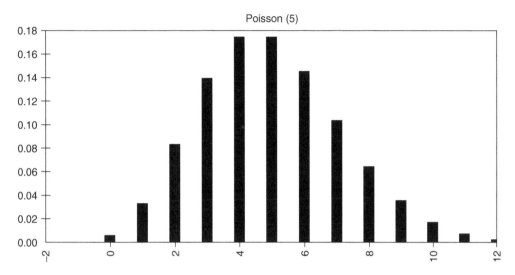

Figure 21.4 A Poisson(5) distribution.

However, for low values of D this is not the case. For example, if $D = 5$ organisms, Equation (21.7) adds a probability distribution around that value with a 99 % probability range of $1-11$ organisms, and includes a 0.7 % probability that the dose is actually zero (Figure 21.4).

21.2.2 The beta–Poisson model

The beta–Poisson dose–response model assumes that the received dose is Poisson distributed and the probability of an organism infecting an individual is beta distributed:

$$p = \text{Beta}(\alpha, \beta)$$

$$D = \text{Poisson}(\lambda)$$

i.e.

$$P(\text{inf}|\lambda) = 1 - (1 - \text{Beta}(\alpha, \beta))^{\text{Poisson}(\lambda)}$$

Using the same principle as Equation (21.7), this can be rewritten as

$$P(\text{inf}|\lambda) = 1 - \exp(-\text{Beta}(\alpha, \beta) * \lambda) \qquad (21.9)$$

The beta distribution has a mean of

$$\overline{p} = \frac{\alpha}{\alpha + \beta} \qquad (21.10)$$

Integrating out the effect of the beta random variable in Equation (21.9) produces an equation for $P(\text{inf}|\lambda)$ that involves the Kummer confluent hypergeometric function which is difficult to evaluate numerically. However, there is a good approximation available for Equation (21.9) if p is small that, from Equation (21.10), gives the restriction that $\alpha \ll \beta$ (Furumoto and Mickey, 1967; Teunis and Havelaar, 2000):

$$P(\text{inf}|\lambda) \approx 1 - \left(1 + \frac{\lambda}{\beta}\right)^{-\alpha} \tag{21.11}$$

There is some confusion about what variation is being modelled by the Beta(α, β) distribution. Equation (21.9) illustrates that to calculate $P(\text{inf}|\lambda)$ we must first select a random value p from the beta distribution and another value D from the Poisson distribution and perform the calculation $1 - (1 - p)^D$. The scenario being modelled is that in a random exposure event one particular value of p applies, i.e. that each of the D organisms has the same probability p of causing infection to the human involved in this exposure event. Allowing p to vary with the beta distribution means that we are acknowledging that some people will be more susceptible (higher p) than others to infection and/or that some doses will consist of organisms that are more infective than others. The model does not include the possibility that the dose will consist of organisms of varying infectiveness. It also cannot distinguish between variations in human susceptibility and organism infectiveness.

The beta–Poisson model is frequently fitted to feeding trial data. In these trials, doses are prepared by making suspensions of a pathogenic organism at varying concentrations, and samples of precisely measured volumes drawn from these suspensions are administered to the participants. Thus, it is reasonable to assume that the dose given to each participant will be Poisson distributed. However, each suspension is usually produced by first growing a batch of organisms from one colony, which means that there is little or no variation in the infectiveness across the population of organisms in the doses administered. The participants in feeding trials are generally healthy young males, and certainly never knowingly include anyone pregnant, sick or immuno-compromised. Therefore, the α and β beta–Poisson parameters fitted to the results of a feeding trial can only hope to describe the effect of the variation in susceptibility of healthy young individuals on the variation in p, and for organisms drawn from a single colony. Use of the estimated values for α and β in risk assessments means that one must accept the extrapolation to the much more widely varying human and pathogen populations.

21.2.3 The beta–binomial model

The beta–binomial dose–response model assumes, like the beta–Poisson model, that the probability of an organism infecting an individual is beta distributed but, unlike the beta–Poisson model, that the received dose is known, i.e.

$$P(\text{inf}|D) = 1 - (1 - \text{Beta}(\alpha, \beta))^D \tag{21.12}$$

There exists a beta–binomial distribution (Section III.7.1) that parallels this model:

$$\text{Beta–Binomial}(D, \alpha, \beta) = \text{Binomial}(D, \text{Beta}(\alpha, \beta))$$

The beta–binomial distribution has the probability mass function

$$f(x) = \binom{D}{x} \frac{\Gamma(\alpha + x)\Gamma(D + \beta - x)\Gamma(\alpha + \beta)}{\Gamma(\alpha + \beta + D)\Gamma(\alpha)\Gamma(\beta)}$$

where $\Gamma(\cdot)$ is a gamma function. Following the same thinking as behind Equation (21.6), the probability of infection is

$$P(\inf|D) = 1 - f(0) = 1 - \frac{\Gamma(D+\beta)\Gamma(\alpha+\beta)}{\Gamma(\alpha+\beta+D)\Gamma(\beta)} \qquad (21.13)$$

Some of the gamma function values can extend beyond the range a computer can handle, and mathematical programs often offer the facility to calculate the natural log of a gamma function, so the following formula is more useful in practice:

$$P(\inf|D) = 1 - \exp[\ln\Gamma(D+\beta) + \ln\Gamma(\alpha+\beta) - \ln\Gamma(\alpha+\beta+D) - \ln\Gamma(\beta)]$$

The beta–binomial model uses the same parameters α and β as the beta–Poisson model. If a beta–Poisson model has been fitted to data (usually feeding trial data) for a risk assessment, and the risk assessment model is calculating (simulating) the actual exposure dose rather than the mean of a Poisson-distributed dose, then the beta–binomial model is the most appropriate to use with the α and β values of the fitted beta–Poisson model.

21.2.4 The Weibull–gamma model

The Weibull–gamma dose–response model begins by assuming that the probability of an organism infecting an individual can be described by the cumulative distribution function of a Weibull distribution:

$$P(\inf|D) = 1 - \exp(-aD^b) \qquad (21.14)$$

A Weibull distribution is commonly used in reliability theory to describe the time until a machine or component fails, where the instantaneous failure rate $z(t)$ (the probability of failure in some small increment of time given survival up to that moment) is a function of time of the form

$$z(t) = abt^{b-1} \qquad (21.15)$$

Equation (21.15) describes a system with memory, meaning that the instantaneous failure rate changes over the lifetime of the machine. The parameter b is commonly greater than 1 in reliability modelling, signalling that a component "wears out" over time, i.e. the component becomes more likely to fail. If $b = 1$, the formula reduces to

$$z(t) = a$$

so $z(t)$ becomes independent of time. In other words, the system becomes memoryless – the component has no greater probability of failing at any increment of time, given it has not already failed, than at any other. The parameter a effectively becomes the probability that the system will fail in an incremental unit of time.

In the dose–response model, time t is replaced by the dose D and the failure of a component becomes the failure of the immune system to combat the exposure. If we think of the organisms in a dose D arriving sequentially, then $P(\inf|D)$ is the probability of a person not getting infected until the Dth organism arrives. The parameter a becomes, to a first approximation, the probability that an organism will independently infect a person. The parameter b can now be thought of as describing how rapidly the immune system is "wearing out". The larger the value of b, the quicker the immune system is overcome: $b = 1$ would mean that the immune system is "memoryless", in other words it is equally capable of coping with the last organism in the dose as it is of coping with the first; values of b less than 1 mean that the system becomes progressively more capable of coping with the organisms as they arrive. We can also switch round the interpretation to say that if $b > 1$ the organisms "work together", if $b < 1$ they work against each other and if $b = 1$ they work independently.

In the Weibull–gamma model, the parameter a is replaced by a variable Gamma(α, β) to describe the variation in host susceptibility and organism infectiveness, in a similar fashion to the beta distribution for the beta–Poisson and beta–binomial models. Thus, Equation (21.14) becomes

$$P(\text{inf}|D) = 1 - \exp(-\text{Gamma}(\alpha, \beta) * D^b)$$

which, after integrating over the gamma density, simplifies to

$$P(\text{inf}|D) = 1 - \left(1 + \frac{D^b}{\beta}\right)^{-\alpha} \tag{21.16}$$

The Weibull–gamma dose–response model has three parameters, which gives it greater flexibility to fit data, but at the expense of greater uncertainty. Equation (21.11) for the beta–Poisson model and Equation (21.16) for the Weibull–gamma model take similar forms, although the conceptual models behind them are quite different. It is often stated that if $b = 1$ the Weibull–gamma reduces to the beta-Poisson approximation model of Equation (21.11). This isn't strictly true unless λ is large enough that one can ignore the approximation of setting $\lambda = D$ discussed above.

21.3 Is Monte Carlo Simulation the Right Approach?

The key tool of the microbial risk assessor in constructing foodborne pathogen risk assessment models is Monte Carlo simulation (MC), using products like Analytica, Crystal Ball, @RISK, Simul8 and bespoke Visual Basic applications, among others. MC is an excellent tool for constructing a probabilistic model of almost any desired complexity. It requires relatively little probability mathematics and the models can be presented in an intuitive manner. It has one major drawback, however. MC requires that all the parameters be quantitatively determined (with uncertainty if applicable) first, and then the model is run to make a projection of possible observations. This means that, for example, we must construct a model to predict the number of human illnesses in the population on the basis of contamination prevalence and load, tracked through the food production-to-consumption chain, and then convert to a human health impact through some dose–response model. However, we will often also have some estimate of what that human health impact currently actually is from data from healthcare providers. In Monte Carlo simulation, if these two estimates do not match we are somewhat stuck, and the usual approach is to adjust the dose–response function to make them match. This is not a statistically rigorous approach. A superior method is to construct a Markov chain Monte Carlo (MCMC) model; currently the most commonly used environment for this purpose is the freeware WinBUGS.

MCMC models can be constructed in a similar fashion to Monte Carlo models but offer the advantage that any data available at a stochastic node of the model can be incorporated into the model. The model then produces a Bayesian revision of the system parameter estimates. Models of possible interventions can be run in parallel that then estimate the effect of these changes. The great advantage is the ability to incorporate all available information in a statistically consistent fashion. The major problems in implementing an MCMC approach are: there aren't any commercial MCMC software available – WinBUGS is great but it is pretty difficult to use; and the computational intensity needed for MCMC modelling means that we could not use models of the level of complexity that is currently standard.

I have often found that the results and behaviour of a complex model can frequently be predicted to match a far simpler model, and that in turn means that we could use the MCMC method to write the model and estimate its parameters. In the next section I present some simplifications.

21.4 Some Model Simplifications

21.4.1 Sporadic illnesses

If a population is consuming V units of food items (servings) of which a fraction p are contaminated with some distribution with probability mass function $f(D)$ of the number of pathogenic organisms D of concern at the moment of exposure, the expected number of infections λ can be estimated as

$$\lambda_{\text{inf}} \approx V p P(\text{inf} \,|\, \text{exposure}) \tag{21.17}$$

where

$$P(\text{inf} \,|\, \text{exposure}) = \sum_{D=1}^{\infty} P(D) P(\text{inf} \,|\, \text{D})$$

If the infections are sporadic, i.e. they occur independently of each other, and the dose distribution and the distribution of levels of susceptibility are constant across the exposed population, then $P(\text{inf} \,|\, \text{exposure})$ can be considered as constant and the actual number of infections will be Poisson distributed:

$$\text{Infections} = \text{Poisson}(\lambda_{\text{inf}})$$

If the probability τ of illness of a certain type, or death (given infection has occurred), is independent of the initial dose (WHO's recommended default) (FAO/WHO, 2003), then Equation (21.17) becomes

$$\lambda_{\text{ill}} = \tau V p P(\text{inf} \,|\, \text{exposure}) \tag{21.18}$$

If the exposure events are independent, and we assume that just one person becomes ill per incident, then λ can again be interpreted as the mean for a Poisson distribution:

$$\text{Illnesses} = \text{Poisson}(\lambda_{\text{ill}})$$

Hald *et al.* (2004) used a WinBUGS model employing this method to determine the fraction of salmonellosis cases that could be attributed to various food sources.

21.4.2 Reduced prevalence

If contamination prevalence were to be reduced from p to q and the contaminated dose distribution were to remain constant for those food items still contaminated (perhaps by reducing the number of farms, herds, flocks or sheds that were infected), we could say the human health benefit was

$$\text{Infections avoided} \approx \text{Poisson}[V(p - q)P(\text{inf}|\text{exposure})]$$

If we already had a good estimate of the current human infections, and thus λ_{inf}, we could say

$$\text{Infections saved} = \text{Poisson}\left[\left(1 - \frac{q}{p}\right)\lambda_{\text{inf}}\right] \tag{21.19}$$

Elimination of the $P(\text{inf}|\text{exposure})$ means that we no longer need to have information on the dose distribution or the dose–response function. The same logic applies equally to illnesses. The Vose-FDA model (Bartholomew $et\ al.$, 2005) is an example of the use of this approach.

21.4.3 Low-infectivity dose

If the exposure pathways lead to pathogen numbers at exposure that $always$ have a small probability of infecting a person, then, no matter which dose–response function is used, the probability of infection will follow an approximately linear function of dose:

$$P(\text{inf}|D) \approx kD$$

If the probability τ of illness of a certain type, or death (given infection has occurred), is independent of the initial dose, then we get

$$P(\text{ill}|D) \approx kD\tau$$

For an exposure with dose distribution with probability mass function $f(D)$, we have

$$P(\text{ill}|\text{exposure}) \approx \sum_{D=1}^{\infty} f(D)kD\tau = k\overline{D}\tau$$

and for a volume V of product consumed that has a prevalence p of food items that are contaminated we can write

$$\lambda_{\text{ill}} \approx \tau V p k \overline{D} \tag{21.20}$$

again with the interpretation

$$\text{Illnesses} = \text{Poisson}(\lambda_{\text{ill}})$$

Thus, without loss of generality, for pathogens causing sporadic infections where the probability of infection is low for all exposures, we can state that the expected number of illnesses is a linear function of both the prevalence of contamination p and the mean dose on a contaminated item $\overline{D}$ or the total number of pathogenic organisms to which the population is exposed $p\overline{D}$.

I have used this approach to help model the effects of oyster and clam contamination with *Vibrio parahaemolyticus* when very few data were available.

The linearity of this model is not to be confused with the often criticised low-dose linear extrapolation used by the EPA (United States Environmental Protection Agency) in toxicological risk assessments. The EPA approach is to consider the lowest dose D at which a probability of an affect is observable P, then to extrapolate the dose–response curve with a straight line from (D, P) down to $(0, 0)$, which it is generally agreed gives an exaggeratedly high conservative estimate of low-dose probability of affect leading to very low tolerance of environmental exposure. The difference between these approaches lies in the problem of getting an observed affect in toxicological exposure: an unrealistically high dose (relative to real-world exposures) is needed to observe an affect in experimental exposures. Experiments are needed because, when a person is presented in the real world with some toxicological symptoms (e.g. cancer), it is rarely possible to attribute the case to exposure to a particular compound, or indeed the level of exposure which may be chronic and aggregated with exposure to other compounds. In microbial food safety we are largely relieved of this problem: the pathogenic organisms can often be cultured, the exposure is usually a single event rather than chronic and current wisdom suggests that microorganisms infect a person individually rather than through repeated exposure (chronic), allowing the use of binomial mathematics (Equation (21.6) above).

Chapter 22

Animal import risk assessment

This chapter and Chapter 21 have evolved from a course we have run many times in various forms entitled "Advanced Quantitative Risk Analysis for Animal Health and Food Safety Professionals". I very much enjoy teaching this particular course because the field requires that one models both uncertainty and variability explicitly. The problems that one faces in this area are very commonly modelled with combinations of binomial, Poisson and hypergeometric processes. It is therefore necessary that one has a good understanding of most of the material presented so far in this book in order to be able to perform a competent assessment of the risks in question. This chapter can therefore be seen as a good revision of the material I have discussed, and will also hopefully illustrate how many of the techniques presented can be used together. The rather mathematical basis for these assessments is in complete contrast to the analysis of projects in Chapter 19, and I hope that, between that chapter and this one, the reader will benefit from seeing two such diverse approaches to risk assessment.

Animal import risk assessments are concerned with the risk of introducing a disease into a country or state through the importation of animals or their products. Food safety risk assessments are concerned with the risk to a population or subpopulation of infection, morbidity (illness) or mortality from consuming a product contaminated with either some toxin or some microorganism. We will look at certain animal import problems first, and then consider a few problems associated with microbiological food safety.

Animal import risk assessment is becoming increasingly important with the removal of world trade barriers and the increasing volume of trade between countries. On the one hand, consumers have increased choice in the food that they consume and farmers have greater opportunity to improve their livestock through importing genetic material. On the other hand, the opening of a nation's borders to foreign produce brings with it an increased risk of disease introduction, usually to the livestock of that nation or the native fauna. The benefits of importing have to be balanced against the associated risks. This is not always easy to do, of course. Very often, the benefits accrue to certain people and the risks to others, which can lead to political conundrums. The World Trade Organisation (WTO) has encouraged nations to base their assessments on standards and guidelines developed by WTO member governments in other international organisations. These agencies are the Office International des Épizooties (OIE) for animal health and the International Plant Protection Convention (IPPC) for plant health. WTO nations have signed an agreement stating that they will open their borders to the produce of others and are committed to removing any trade barriers. The caveat in that agreement is that a nation is at liberty to ban the import of a product from another nation if that product presents a risk to the importing nation. Now, a product may present a risk to one nation but none to another. For example, importing pig meat on to some Pacific island may not present a risk if there are no live pigs on that island to catch any disease that is present in the meat. On the other hand, the same meat could easily present a significant risk to a country like Denmark that has pigs everywhere. Thus, a country that bans the importation of a product on the basis that it presents a significant risk must be prepared to demonstrate the rationale behind the ban. It could not, for example, allow in product A but not product B where product A logically presents a higher risk. In other words, the banning nation must be prepared to demonstrate consistency in its importing policies. Quantitative risk assessment can often provide such demonstration of consistency, and the OIE, Codex Alimentarius and IPPC continue to discuss and develop risk assessment techniques. The OIE has published (OIE, 2004) a handbook on quantitative import risk analysis that is largely drawn from the second edition of this book and the material from our courses, but also includes some more material.

The agricultural ministries of many nations are constantly being bombarded with requests to import products into the country. Many of the requests can be processed very quickly because the risk of disease introduction is, to the experienced regulator, very obviously too large to be acceptable or negligible. One can often quickly gauge the size of the risk by comparing the product with another similar product for which a full quantitative analysis has been done. For products whose risk lies somewhere between these two extremes, one may devise an import protocol that ensures the risk is reduced to an acceptable level at the minimum cost. Protocols usually involve a combination of plant and farm inspection, quarantining and testing for animal imports, and specifications of product source, quality controls and processing for animal product imports. Quantitative risk assessment provides a method for determining the remaining risk when adopting various protocols, and therefore which protocols are the least trade restrictive and most effective.

I have talked about the "risk" to an importing country in a very general way. A "risk" has been defined (Kaplan and Garrick, 1981) as the triplet {scenario, probability, impact}, where the "scenario" is the event or series of events that leads to the adverse effect, the "probability" is the likelihood of that adverse event occurring and the "impact" is the magnitude of the adverse event. At the moment, quantitative risk assessments in the animal import world mostly concern themselves with the first two of this triplet because of the political and economic pressures associated with any disease introduction, no matter how small the actual impact (number of infected animals, for example) on the importing country. This is a little unfortunate, since any truly rational management of risk must take into account both probability and impact.

Before proceeding any further, it will be helpful for the reader unfamiliar with this area to learn about a few basic concepts of animal diseases and their detection and a little bit of terminology. The reader familiar with this area will note that I have left out a number of terms for simplicity.

- *True prevalence, p.* The proportion of animals in a group or population that are infected with a particular disease.
- *Sensitivity, Se.* The probability that an animal will test positive given that it is infected. This conditional probability is a measure of the quality of the test: the closer the test sensitivity is to unity, the better the test.
- *Specificity, Sp.* The probability that an animal will test negative given that it is not infected. This conditional probability is also a measure of the quality of the test: the closer the test specificity is to unity, the better the test.
- *Pathogen.* The microorganism causing infection.
- *Infection.* The establishment of the microorganism in an animal.
- *Disease.* The physiological effect in the infected animal. The animal may be infected but not diseased, i.e. show no symptoms.
- *Morbidity.* Exhibiting disease.

22.1 Testing for an Infected Animal

This section looks at various different scenarios that frequently occur in animal import risk analyses and the questions that are posed. We start with the simplest cases and build up the complexity. Some formulae are specific to this field and are derived here for completeness and because the derivations show interesting, practical examples of the algebra of probability theory.

22.1.1 Testing a single animal

Problem 22.1: **An animal has been randomly selected from a herd or population with known (usually estimated) disease prevalence p. The animal is tested with a test having sensitivity Se and specificity Sp. (i) If the animal tests positive, what is the probability it is actually infected? (ii) If it tests negative, what is the probability it is actually infected?**

Solution: Figure 22.1 illustrates the four possible scenarios when testing an animal. (i) If the animal tests positive, either path A or path C must have occurred. Thus, from Bayes' theorem (see Section 6.3.5), the probability that the animal is infected, given it tested positive, is given by

$$P(\text{inf}|+) = \frac{P(A)}{P(A) + P(C)} = \frac{pSe}{pSe + (1-p)(1-Sp)}$$

(ii) Similarly, the probability that the animal is infected, given it tested negative, is given by

$$P(\text{inf}|-) = \frac{P(B)}{P(B) + P(D)} = \frac{p(1-Se)}{p(1-Se) + (1-p)Sp} \quad \blacklozenge$$

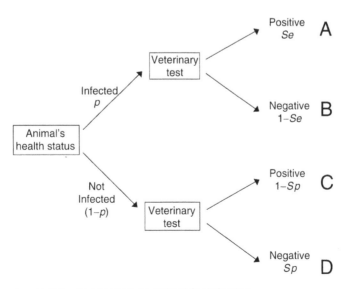

Figure 22.1 The four scenarios when testing an animal for infection.

22.1.2 Testing a group of animals

Usually, animals are imported in groups, rather than individually. Live animals, kept together during transportation or during quarantine, will often spread a pathogen among the group if one or more are infected, and the level of infection often reaches a stable percentage of the group if it is large enough.

Problem 22.2: **A group of n animals are to be imported, of which s are infected. All animals are tested with a test having sensitivity Se and specificity Sp. (i) How many will test positive? (ii) What is the probability that all animals will test negative?**

Solution: Of the s infected animals, Binomial(s, Se) will test positive. Similarly, of the $(n - s)$ animals not infected, Binomial$(n - s, 1 - Sp)$ will test positive. (i) The total number of positives is therefore Binomial$(s, Se) +$ Binomial$(n - s, 1 - Sp)$. (ii) The probability that all animals will test negative $P(all-)$ is the probability that all infected animals will test negative, i.e. $(1 - Se)^s$, multiplied by the probability that all animals not infected will test negative, i.e. $Sp^{(n-s)}$ Thus, $P(all-) = (1 - Se)^s Sp^{(n-s)}$.

A common error in this type of problem is to argue the following. Each of the n animals has a probability $p = s/n$ of being infected and a probability Se that it would then test positive. Similarly, each animal has a probability $(1 - p)$ of not being infected and a probability $(1 - Sp)$ that it would then test positive. The number of positives is thus Binomial$(n, pSe) +$ Binomial$(n, (1 - p)(1 - Sp))$. The calculation is incorrect since it assigns independence between the health status of each randomly selected animal as well as the distribution of the number of infected animals and the number of uninfected animals, where in fact they must always add up to n. A useful check is to look at the range of possible values this formula would generate: each of the binomial distributions has a maximum of n, so their sum gives a maximum of $2n$ positives – clearly not a possible scenario since there are only n animals. ◆

Problem 22.3: **A group of n animals are *all* tested with a test having sensitivity Se and specificity Sp. If s animals test positive, how many in the group are actually infected?**

Solution: This problem is looking from the opposite direction to Problem 22.2. In that problem, one was estimating how many positives there would be from a group with a certain rate of infection. Here we are estimating how many infected animals there were in the group given the observed number of positives.

There is actually a certain number x of animals that are truly infected in the group of n, we just don't know what that number is. Thus, we need to determine the distribution of our uncertainty about x. This problem lends itself to a Bayesian approach. With no better information, we can conservatively assume *a priori* that x is equally likely to be any whole number between 0 and n, then determine the likelihood function which is a combination of two binomial functions in the same way as Problem 22.2.

The solution to this problem is algebraically a little inelegant and is therefore more readily illustrated by assigning some numbers to the model parameters. Let $n = 50$, $Se = 0.8$, $Sp = 0.9$ and $s = 25$. Figure 22.2 illustrates the spreadsheet model that determines our uncertainty about x for these parameter values, and Figure 22.3 shows the posterior distribution for x.

It is rather interesting to see what happens if we change some of the parameter values. Figure 22.4 illustrates four examples: I leave as an exercise for you to work out why the graphs take the form they do for these parameter values.

As an aside, if $s = 0$ the data would lead us to question whether our parameter values were correct. The probability of observing no positives ($s = 0$) would be greatest if there were no infected animals in the group, in which case, using our original parameter values, the probability that $s = 0$ is given

	A	B	C	D	E	AB	AC	AD	AE	AF
1										
2		*n*	50							
3		*Se*	0.8							
4		*Sp*	0.9							
5		*s*	12							
6		Actually			Likelihood			*1.427*		
7		Infected			True positives			Posterior	Normalised	
8		*x*	Prior	*0*	*1*	*24*	*25*	distribution	posterior	
9		0	1	2.2E-03	0	0	0	2.2E-03	1.6E-03	
10		1	1	3.7E-04	4.3E-03	0	0	4.6E-03	3.2E-03	
58		49	1	0	0	0.0E+00	0.0E+00	7.9E-17	5.5E-17	
59		50	1	0	0	0	0.0E+00	2.3E-17	1.6E-17	
60										
61					Formulae table					
62		B9:B59	{0,1,2,...,49,50}							
63		D8:AC8	{0,1,2,...,24,25}							
64		D9:AC59	=IF(OR(D$8>$B9,D$8>s,n–$B9<s–D$8),0,BINOMDIST(D$8,$B9,Se,0)							
65			*BINOMDIST(s–D$8,n–$B9,1–Sp,0))							
66		AD9:AD59	=C9*SUM(D9:AC9)							
67		AD6	=SUM(AD9:AD59)							
68		AE9:AE59	=AD9/$AD$6							
69										

Figure 22.2 Spreadsheet model for Problem 22.3.

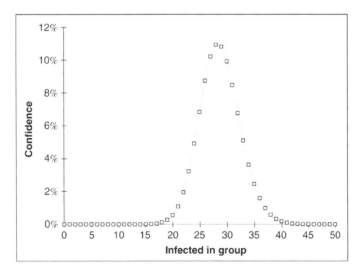

Figure 22.3 Confidence distribution for number infected for Problem 22.3.

by $(Sp)^n = 0.9^{50} = 5.15 \times 10^{-3}$ – not very high. One might reasonably conclude that the estimate of specificity Sp was too low. In hindsight, a better but still conservative estimate for Sp, given our data, would be Beta(51, 1), which has a mean of 0.981 – see Section 8.2.3. The same logic could have been applied to the sensitivity value if all tests had been positive. In that case, using the original value for $Se = 0.8$, if one assumed that all animals were actually infected, which would be the most feasible

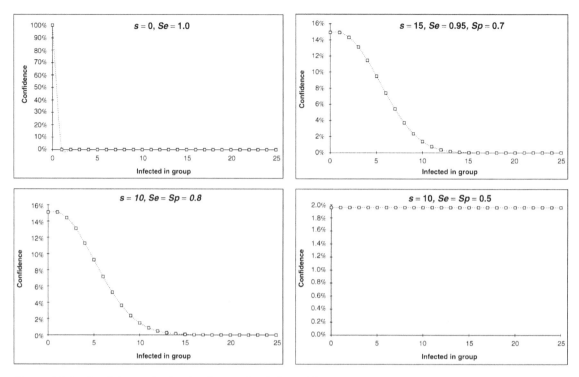

Figure 22.4 Confidence distribution for number infected for Problem 22.3 with various parameter values.

scenario, the probability of observing all tests positive $= Se^n = 0.8^{50} = 1.43 \times 10^{-5}$. Again, a better but still conservative estimate for Se would have been Beta(51, 1).

These beta distributions added to Se and Sp are hyperpriors, discussed in Section 9.2.1. If one has uncertainty distributions for parameters that are defining either the prior distribution or the likelihood function in a Bayesian calculation, the hyperprior needs to be integrated out of the calculation to determine the posterior distribution. This is most easily accomplished using Monte Carlo simulation. In the spreadsheet model of Figure 22.2, the uncertainty distributions for Se and Sp are input into cells C3 and C4 and a Monte Carlo simulation is run on the posterior distribution column (column AE). The mean of the values generated for each cell in that column equates to the posterior distribution after inclusion of the hyperpriors. ♦

Problem 22.4: **A group of n animals has been randomly selected from a herd or population with known disease prevalence p. All animals are tested with a test having sensitivity Se and specificity Sp. How many in the group will test positive?**

Solution: If we assume that the population from which the n animals are drawn is much larger than n, then p can be considered as the probability that any one animal is infected (this is the binomial approximation to the hypergeometric, discussed in Section III.9.3). Then each animal has the same probability $p.Se + (1 - p).(1 - Sp)$ of testing positive and the number of positives is given by Binomial(n, $pSe + (1 - p)(1 - Sp)$). We could have broken this problem down into parts, as shown in the spreadsheet of Figure 22.5. Here, we model the number of infected animals using $I = $ Binomial(n, p)

	A	B		C	D	E		F	G
1									
2		n		50		Truly infected (I)		32	
3		Se		0.8		True positives (TP)		26	
4		Sp		0.9		False positives (FP)		2	
5		p		0.7		**Total positives**		28	
6									
7				*Formulae table*					
8		F2		=VoseBinomial(n,p)					
9		F3		=VoseBinomial(F2,Se)					
10		F4		=VoseBinomial(n-F3,1-Sp)					
11		F5 (output)		=TP+FP					
12									

Figure 22.5   Spreadsheet model for Problem 22.4.

in cell F2, then use this as an input to determine the number of true positives *TP* in cell F3: $TP =$ Binomial(I, Se). The same logic is applied to the number of false positives in cell F4, and then all positives, true and false, are added up in the output, cell F5. ◆

Problem 22.5: **A group of *n* animals has been randomly selected from a herd or population with known (usually estimated) disease prevalence *p*. All animals are tested with a test having sensitivity *Se* and specificity *Sp*. If *s* animals test positive, how many in the group are actually infected?**

Solution: This is the same as Problem 22.3, except that we have some additional information with which to construct our prior distribution, namely that the prevalence of the population from which this group is drawn is *p*, so our prior distribution is now Binomial(n, p) in a similar way to Example 9.3. Figure 22.6 shows how this new prior affects the results of our uncertainty distribution. Since we have more information, and since the results of our testing did not contradict that information, we have a greater certainty (narrower distribution) than in Problem 22.3. However, if the number of positives had been very low or very high, so that the original information about prevalence was contradicted by our observations of positive tests, the uncertainty would have widened rather than narrowed. This is a

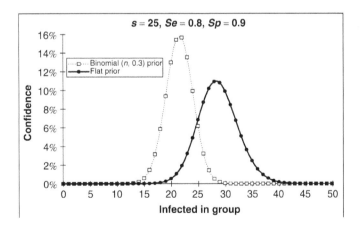

Figure 22.6   Change in the distribution of Figure 22.3 when the prior is changed.

good example of how Bayes' theorem can help us avoid overconfidence, rather than just narrowing our uncertainty. ◆

22.2 Estimating True Prevalence in a Population

Imagine we have a large population of animals (dairy cattle in the USA, for example) for which we wish to determine the prevalence of a certain disease. It is almost never practical to test every animal in a population or even a large portion of it. Instead, one may choose to take a (hopefully) random and therefore unbiased sample from that population, test that sample and then infer the population prevalence. There are often gold standard tests available that have extremely high sensitivity and specificity (these may involve converting the animal to be tested into very thin slices, the details of which we need not go into), but the tests are generally expensive. On the other hand, cheaper tests will have a greater chance of giving false results.

Problem 22.6: **There are 22 600 000 beef cattle in a certain country. 1000 animals are randomly sampled from that population and tested with a gold standard test, and 27 test positive. (i) What is the prevalence of infection? (ii) How many infected animals are there in the population?**

Solution: (i) Assuming we have no prior knowledge about the infection status of this population of cattle, or that we wish to ignore that prior knowledge and remain maximally conservative or non-committal (see Section 9.2.2), one can use the beta distribution to model the true prevalence = Beta(27 + 1, 1000 − 27 + 1) = Beta(28, 974). (ii) The number of beef cattle infected with this disease agent can thus be estimated as 22 600 000 * Beta(28, 974), and one can round up to the nearest whole animal if required by using ROUND(22 600 000 * Beta(28, 974), 0).

Note: a very common mistake is to estimate the number of diseased animals in the form Binomial(22 600 000, Beta(28, 974)). This is incorrect since the prevalence we are estimating is the proportion of animals that are infected. Using the binomial distribution would be interpreting the prevalence estimate as the constant probability of infection for each of the 22 600 000 individual animals. That would not be true since, each time we were to pick an infected animal, the probability that the next animal was infected would alter. Using the binomial distribution inappropriately here would have the effect of exaggerating our uncertainty about the number of infected animals. We could have modelled the distribution of uncertainty about the number infected in the population using a formal Bayesian approach with a uniform prior, i.e. $\pi(\theta)$ = constant with a hypergeometric probability likelihood function:

$$l(X|\theta) = \frac{\binom{\theta}{27}\binom{22\ 600\ 000 - \theta}{1000 - 27}}{\binom{22\ 600\ 000}{1000}} \propto \frac{\theta!(22\ 600\ 000 - \theta)!}{(\theta - 27)!(22\ 599\ 027 - \theta)!}$$

but the large numbers involved make this approach impractical, and no more accurate than using the beta distribution above directly. ◆

Problem 22.7: **There are 22 600 000 beef cattle in a certain country. 100 animals are randomly sampled from that population and tested with a test having sensitivity *Se* and specificity *Sp*. T^+ test positive. What is the prevalence of infection in the country's population?**

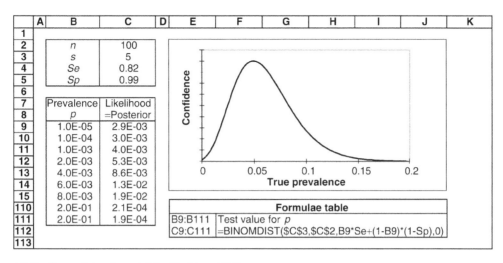

Figure 22.7 Spreadsheet model for Problem 22.7.

Solution: The sample of 100 animals is very much smaller than the population, so we can say that the number of infected in the sample will be Binomial(100, p) distributed, where p is the population prevalence. The spreadsheet of Figure 22.7 shows a Bayesian model to determine the uncertainty distribution for p. The probability that an animal will test positive is given by

$$P(T^+) = pSe + (1 - p)(1 - Sp)$$

i.e. the probability it is infected and gives a true positive plus the probability it is not infected and gives a false positive. The probability an animal tests negative is obviously $1 - P(T^+)$ or

$$P(T^-) = p(1 - Se) + (1 - p)Sp$$

so the probability of observing x positives $P(T^+ = x)$ in a sample of size n is given by

$$P(T^+ = x) = \binom{n}{x} (P(T^+))^x (1 - P(T^+))^{n-x}$$

or using the Excel function BINOMDIST($x, n, P(T^+), 0$). The spreadsheet model uses a uniform prior for p and the $P(T^+ = 5)$ likelihood function.

The graph in Figure 22.7 shows the result of this model when $Se = 0.82$ and $Sp = 0.99$. If Sp drops to 0.95 or below, the most likely prevalence is zero, i.e. that all positives were false positives. Also, if $Se = Sp = 0.5$, we can learn nothing more through doing the tests since our posterior distribution is the same as our prior. Finally, as Se and Sp approach 1, we get closer to the Beta($5 + 1$, $100 - 5 + 1$) = Beta(6, 96) distribution. ◆

22.2.1 Dealing with single-point information on *Se* and *Sp*

The problems above are quite easy because we have assumed that there is no uncertainty about the parameters for which we have data. Usually, of course, there will be – and perhaps we have some data that allowed us to estimate those parameters. For example, if we are lucky we may have found that the test sensitivity of 90 % quotes by the manufacturer was based on testing 10 deliberately infected animals

Table 22.1 Testing how many trials were completed to get a success rate of 0.83.

n	=ROUND(n * 0.83, 0)	=ROUND(n * 0.83, 0)/n
2	2	1.00
3	2	0.67
4	3	0.75
5	4	0.80
6	5	0.83
7	6	0.86
8	7	0.88
9	7	0.78
10	8	0.80
11	9	0.82
12	10	0.83
13	11	0.85
14	12	0.86
15	12	0.80
16	13	0.81

of which nine returned a positive result. In that case we could model test sensitivity as Beta$(9 + 1, 10 - 9 + 1) = $ Beta$(10, 2)$. However, I doubt you will often find such data. I am frequently frustrated by the reporting in journals that give just a single point, e.g. 0.83.

We cannot ignore the uncertainty because we don't have the number of trials and successes. However, you can write a simple spreadsheet that tests different possible values of trials $n\{2, 3, 4 \ldots\}$ and for each n calculates the number of successes s ($s = $ ROUND$(n * 0.83, 0)$ in this case), then calculate s/n and see if you get the same value to the number of quoted significant figures. Table 22.1 gives an example.

You can see from this table that the minimum number of trials consistent with the reported 0.83 success rate is 6, with five successes. Maybe the experimenters did 12, 18, etc., but we don't know so we have little choice (unless you want to contact them, which I encourage!) but to be maximally conservative about the knowledge level and model the true success rate uncertainty as Beta$(5 + 1, 6 - 5 + 1) = $ Beta$(6, 2)$.

Perhaps we also have a confidence interval too, e.g.

$$\text{Sensitivity} = 0.87 \text{ with } 95\text{CI} = [0.676, 0.953]$$

We cannot use a normal distribution to interpret the confidence interval above because it will extend above 1 (not really a problem if you have a tight confidence interval well away from 0 or 1, but we rarely do). We can, however, pinpoint the actual number of trials pretty well by extending the analysis of Table 12.1 as in Table 22.2.

Here we see that $n = 23$ and $s = 20$. You might not get such a perfect match with your confidence intervals because they depend on the statistical method used, but you will get close.

22.2.2 Incorporating uncertainty about *Se* and *Sp*

Let's now imagine that you have uncertainty for the test sensitivity and specificity and want to estimate a population prevalence. Adding distributions to the model in Figure 22.7 might seem like a reasonable method: you could take the mean of the values generated in column C at the end of a simulation. I actually use this technique in my classes as a way to show the effect of adding parameter uncertainty, but it isn't quite right. Let's take the example of that model where five out of 100 animals were infected

Table 22.2 Testing how many trials were completed to get a success rate of 0.87 and 95CI = [0.676, 0.953].

n	=ROUND ($n * 0.87$, 0)	=ROUND ($n * 0.83$, 0)/n	=BETAINV (0.025, $s + 1$, $n - s + 1$)	=BETAINV (0.975, $s + 1$, $n - s + 1$)
15	13	0.87	0.617	0.960
16	14	0.88	0.636	0.962
17	15	0.88	0.653	0.964
18	16	0.89	0.669	0.966
19	17	0.89	0.683	0.968
20	17	0.85	0.637	0.946
21	18	0.86	0.651	0.948
22	19	0.86	0.664	0.950
23	20	0.87	0.676	0.953
24	21	0.88	0.688	0.955
25	22	0.88	0.698	0.956
26	23	0.88	0.708	0.958
27	23	0.85	0.673	0.939
28	24	0.86	0.683	0.942
29	25	0.86	0.693	0.944

and we are not sure about the sensitivity and specificity. If the sample from our uncertainty distribution for sensitivity were very high (say close to 1), that would mean that we would very likely have detected all of the 100 animals that were infected in the group. For the prevalence to be, say, 10 % , we would have to have had a smaller number of infected animals in the group than expected (10), but it also means that the specificity would have had to be very high so we didn't get any false positives. In other words, the three uncertainty distributions for sensitivity, specificity and prevalence are all interlinked. We can't easily perform the analysis in a standard Monte Carlo package, but it is easy to do with Markov chain Monte Carlo using WinBUGS. The following WinBUGS script achieves this, where our initial uncertainty about *Se* and *Sp* are described by Beta(91, 11) and Beta(82, 13) respectively:

```
model
{

Positive ~ dbin(pr,Tested)
pr<- Prevalence*Se+(1-Prevalence)*(1-Sp)
Se~ dbeta(7,4)
Sp~ dbeta(6,2)
Prevalence~ dbeta(1,1)

}

Data
list(Positive = 5, Tested = 100)
```

After a decent burn-in period (100 000 iterations here), the model returns the prevalence estimate in Figure 22.8.

We also have revised estimates for the test sensitivity *Se* and specificity *Sp* (Figure 22.9).

You'll see that the *Se* estimate has not changed greatly because we had few positive test results, but the *Sp* estimate is significantly different: the *Se* estimate is about 0.7 which would suggest the

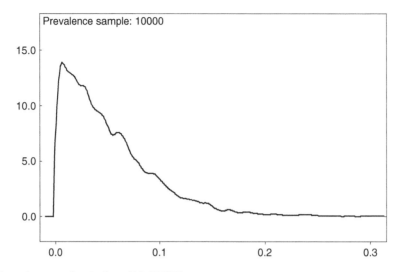

Figure 22.8   Prevalence estimate from WinBUGS.

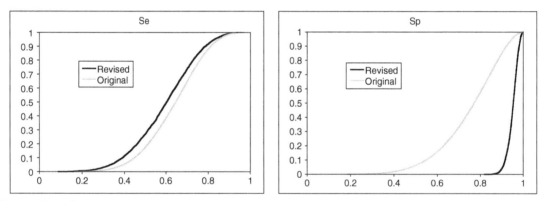

Figure 22.9   Cumulative distribution comparisons of prior (original) and posterior (revised) estimates of *Se* and *Sp* from the WinBUGS model.

prevalence is around 7 % at most (five positive/0.7 out of 100 animals) in which case at least around 90 of the animals tested were not infected. That means that the specificity must be high, or else we would have seen many more positive animals.

WinBUGS has grown enormously in popularity in the epidemiology fields in the last few years. You can do really interesting things with it, like estimate sensitivity and specificity by using the test on two or more populations of known prevalence. You can build models that include correlation between tests, that estimate prevalence in the absence of any gold standard, etc. Here's another example.

Example 22.1

Let's imagine that we have two tests to detect bacterial contamination of a food-producing animal, and we have three animal populations to which we apply the test. We are uncertain about the sensitivities and specificities of both tests as well as the prevalence of each population. We test 100 animals from each population with both tests. We record the results of each test by animal. We want to estimate *Se* and *Sp* of each test as well as the prevalence in each population. The resultant data and WinBUGS script are as follows:

Population 1
NegNeg = 77
NegPos = 7
PosNeg = 8
PosPos = 8

Population 2
NegNeg = 51
NegPos = 9
PosNeg = 11
PosPos = 29

Population 3
NegNeg = 86
NegPos = 6
PosNeg = 6
PosPos = 2

Model

```
{
r[1:4] ~ dmulti(pr[1:4],100)
pr[1]<- prev1*(1-se1)*(1-se2) + (1-prev1)*sp1*sp2 #NegNeg
pr[2]<- prev1*(1-se1)*se2 + (1-prev1)*sp1*(1-sp2) #NegPos
pr[3]<- prev1*se1*(1-se2) + (1-prev1)*(1-sp1)*sp2 #PosNeg
pr[4]<- prev1*se1*se2 + (1-prev1)*(1-sp1)*(1-sp2) #PosPos

s[1:4] ~ dmulti(ps[1:4],100)
ps[1]<- prev2*(1-se1)*(1-se2) + (1-prev2)*sp1*sp2
ps[2]<- prev2*(1-se1)*se2 + (1-prev2)*sp1*(1-sp2)
ps[3]<- prev2*se1*(1-se2) + (1-prev2)*(1-sp1)*sp2
ps[4]<- prev2*se1*se2 + (1-prev2)*(1-sp1)*(1-sp2)

t[1:4] ~ dmulti(pt[1:4],100)
pt[1]<- prev3*(1-se1)*(1-se2) + (1-prev3)*sp1*sp2
pt[2]<- prev3*(1-se1)*se2 + (1-prev3)*sp1*(1-sp2)
pt[3]<- prev3*se1*(1-se2) + (1-prev3)*(1-sp1)*sp2
pt[4]<- prev3*se1*se2 + (1-prev3)*(1-sp1)*(1-sp2)

prev1 ~ dbeta(1,1)
prev2 ~ dbeta(1,1)
prev3 ~ dbeta(1,1)
se1~ dbeta(1,1)
sp1~ dbeta(1,1)
se2~ dbeta(1,1)
sp2~ dbeta(1,1)
}
```

Data

```
list(r=c(77,7,8,8), s=c(51,9,11,29), t=c(86,6,6,2))
```

Initial values for two chains

```
list(prev1=0.5,prev2=0.5,prev3 = 0.5,se1=0.8,sp1=0.8,se2=0.8,sp2=0.8)
list(prev1=0.1,prev2=0.2,prev3=0.3,se1=0.9,sp1=0.9,se2=0.9,sp2=0.9)
```

The model above is specified for two chains, which means two versions of the model running in parallel, which helps figure out whether the model has stabilised. The `dmulti` function is a multinomial distribution. Note that all priors are Beta(1, 1), i.e. uniform distributions, meaning that we start with no knowledge about the model parameters. With no gold standard to compare against, we can nonetheless estimate the prevalence of each population and the test *Se* and *Sp*. The results are shown in Figure 22.10.

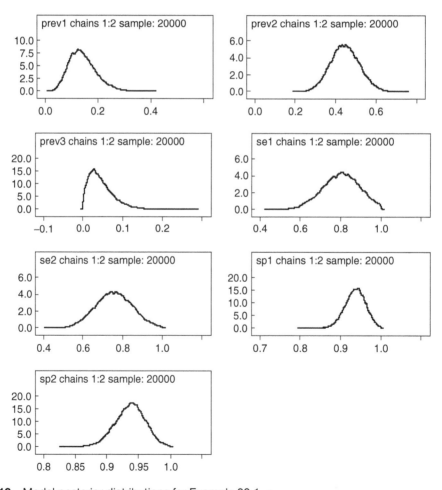

Figure 22.10   Model posterior distributions for Example 22.1 ♦.

WinBUGS is a powerful tool, but please do be careful: WinBUGS will find the posterior density for parameters estimated jointly from different datasets even when it is completely unrealistic that those two datasets could genuinely occur together. There is still plenty of room for common sense.

22.2.3 Some caveats about how we use *Se* and *Sp*

Diagnostic tests that we use to detect infections in animals (and in humans) react to the presence of some disease indicator like the pathogen in question or the antibodies that an animal produces. An individual animal will have different levels of antibodies, for example, depending on the part of the infectious cycle of the disease. If the animal was infected yesterday, the levels will probably be much lower than if it was infected last week (BSE is a strange case, where the prion level rises suddenly and exponentially at some indeterminable time). The more antibodies in the animal, the more likely it is that the test will react positively. That has a great deal of impact on the assumptions behind the mathematics that you'll find in this chapter.

First of all, put yourself in the place of a diagnostic test manufacturer. Let's look at two choices: we infect 20 robust animals today, test them tomorrow and report the fraction that were positive as our sensitivity; or we select a highly sensitive breed, pick 20 weaklings, infect them, wait until the animals are half-dead with disease and then test them. It would be unethical to do the latter, and commercial suicide to do the former. It's a competitive market, and there's a large grey area for the manufacturer to pick, and I am sure plenty of tricks they can apply (diet, stressing the animal, etc.). What worries me is that we tend just to look up the diagnostic performance measures and trust them. When I've done statistical analyses of test results, I've often seen that the reported performance is rather optimistic. Perhaps it was done perfectly well, but with cows or pigs, etc., from one particular country or blood line – assuming that the results can be translated across to another population is quite a leap of faith. That's why many countries with the resources at their disposal do their own testing.

What is test sensitivity really? In theory, the way we use it for our modelling, it is the probability that a randomly selected infected animal will test positive. The "randomly selected" bit is important. Ask a veterinarian what he or she will do when charged with testing a flock of sheep for some debilitating disease. Our mathematics assumes an animal is randomly selected, but a more practical method is to walk into the middle of the flock and start making a big noise. Then test the slowest to move away. Our mathematics will underpredict the veterinarian's probability of detecting the flock infection.

"Randomly selected" also means that we are picking an infected animal at random somewhere within its infectious cycle. Consider a consignment of animals being moved from one country to another. The animals are gathered together from around the country and put in a crate. They go on a ship for a week or so and arrive at the importing country where they are tested. Imagine that one animal in that group was infected at the voyage start. The animal is probably not showing any symptoms yet, of course, and also probably tested negative before embarking if that is part of the import protocol, which is usually the case. They are probably all infected by the time they reach their destination, but only recently so the probability of detecting the infection with a test may be quite far below the official sensitivity. Unless we hold the animals in quarantine, we run the risk of greatly overestimating the protection afforded by our import protocol.

There are some potential benefits we can get from recognising the relationship between the disease indicator and infectious cycle. For example, if there are two indicators that peak at different times in an infectious cycle, we could devise a protocol that gave the maximum probability of detection, e.g. by staggering the tests, and reduce testing costs (e.g. by using a cheaper test first). Figure 22.11 shows four different scenarios in testing an infected animal that we use to illustrate this point in our courses. The indicator for test 1 peaks early in the infectious cycle, the indicator for test 2 later. The length of the infectious cycle is a random variable, as are the indicator profiles reflecting interindividual variability between animals and day-to-day variability. The model is running the scenario that both tests are performed together. A white circle represents a positive test, a black circle is a negative test result and the dashed lines represent the test threshold. Running a simulation and counting up the fraction of iterations where at least one test is positive gives us the sensitivity for the two tests performed together. If one adds another component for an uninfected animal and assigns costs to testing, to failing to detect an infected animal and getting a false positive, one could vary the thresholds and test timing to optimise the performance:cost ratio.

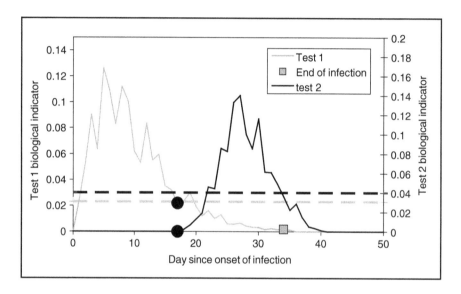

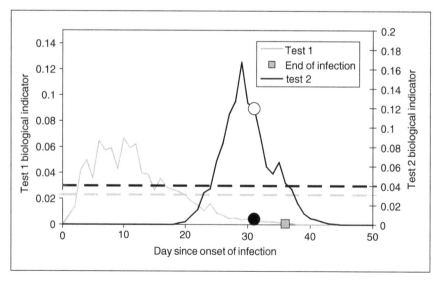

Figure 22.11 The four possible scenarios for testing an infected animal for two biological indicators.

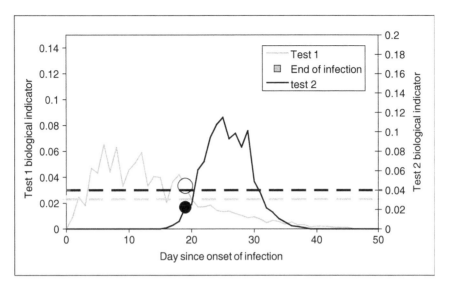

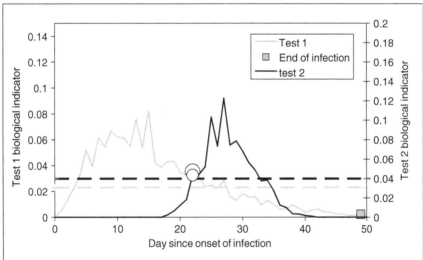

Figure 22.11 Continued.

22.3 Importing Problems

Agricultural regulating authorities are often concerned with the risk of introduction of a foreign disease agent through the importation of animals or animal products. Usually they are concerned with the probability that the disease agent will enter the country undetected, but they may also be interested in the number of entries too.

In order to estimate the magnitude of a risk, we must first of all define exactly what measure of risk we are going to use. It has to be a measure that is useful to the decision-maker, as well as something that we can actually calculate. The risk will be related to the quantity of the imports, so the measure of risk is related to some import volume measurement, for example {probability of agent entry; frequency of agent entry; distribution of cost, environmental impact, human health impact} per {metric tonne; year of import; consignment; average yearly per capita consumption}, etc.

Problem 22.8: **An animal population has prevalence p. You are to import a consignment of size n from this population (n is much smaller than the population size). (i) What is the probability that at least one animal will be infected? (ii) If all animals are tested with a test having sensitivity Se and specificity Sp, what is the probability that at least one infected animal will be allowed entry into the country if (a) one or more positive tests result in the rejection of the whole group and (b) positive tests result in the rejection of only those animals that tested positive.**

Solution: (i) Since n is much smaller than the population size, we can use the binomial approximation to the hypergeometric (Section III.9.3). The probability that an individual animal is not infected $= (1 - p)$. The probability that all n animals are not infected $= (1 - p)^n$, so the probability that at least one animal is infected $= 1 - (1 - p)^n$.

(ii,a) The rejection of the consignment has a probability related to the number of infected animals in the consignment: the more infected animals, the higher is its chance of being rejected. To get the required answer, we can consider the scenario of there being a specific number x of infected animals and none being detected, find the equation for the probability for such a scenario and then sum that equation for all possible values of x.

The probability that there will be x infected animals (where $0 \leq x \leq n$) is given by the binomial probability mass function

$$P(x) = \binom{n}{x} p^x (1 - p)^{(n-x)}$$

The probability that those n animals then all test negative is

$$P(-ve|x) = (1 - Se)^x Sp^{n-x}$$

The probability that there will be at least one infected animal in the group of size n, all of which test negative, is then the product of these two probabilities summed from $x = 1$ to $x = n$:

$$P(>0 \text{ infected} \cap \text{all} - \text{ve}) = \sum_{x=1}^{n} \binom{n}{x} (p(1 - Se))^x (Sp(1 - p))^{(n-x)}$$

$$= \sum_{x=0}^{n} \binom{n}{x} (p(1 - Se))^x (Sp(1 - p))^{(n-x)} - (Sp(1 - p))^n \quad (22.1)$$

Now, the binomial theorem (Section 6.3.4) states that

$$(A + B)^n = \sum_{x=0}^{n} \binom{n}{x} A^x B^{(n-x)}$$

Comparing this with Equation (22.1), we can see that Equation (22.1) can be simplified to

$$P(>0 \text{ infected} \cap \text{all} - \text{ve}) = (p(1 - Se) + Sp(1 - p))^n - (Sp(1 - p))^n$$

(ii,b) Each animal is accepted or rejected individually, so we can look at the fate of an individual animal first and then extrapolate to get the required answer. The probability that an animal is infected and escapes detection is $p(1 - Se)$. The probability that this does not happen (i.e. the probability that an animal is not infected or is infected but is detected) is then $\{1 - p(1 - Se)\}$. The probability that this happens to all animals is then $\{1 - p(1 - Se)\}^n$, and so, finally, the probability that at least one animal is infected but not detected and therefore not rejected is

$$1 - (1 - p(1 - Se))^n$$

We could also have arrived at the same equation by taking the summation approach of (ii,a).

The probability that there will be x infected animals (where $0 \leq x \leq n$) is given by the binomial probability mass function

$$P(x) = \binom{n}{x} p^x (1 - p)^{(n-x)}$$

The probability that one fails to detect *all* x animals is $1 - Se^x$, so the probability that there are one or more remaining infected animals in the consignment is

$$P(>0 \text{ infected} \cap \text{ all} - \text{ve}) = \sum_{x=1}^{n} \binom{n}{x} (1 - Se^x) p^x (1 - p)^{(n-x)}$$

$$= \sum_{x=1}^{n} \binom{n}{x} p^x (1 - p)^{(n-x)} - \sum_{x=1}^{n} \binom{n}{x} (pSe)^x (1 - p)^{(n-x)}$$

Again, using the binomial theorem, this reduces to

$$P(>0 \text{ infected} \cap \text{ all} - \text{ve}) = [1 - (1 - p)^n] - [(1 - p + pSe)^n - (1 - p)^n]$$
$$= 1 - (1 - p(1 - Se))^n$$

Clearly, the probability of at least one infected animal entering undetected in a consignment is greater if animals are rejected individually when they test positively than if the whole group is rejected when there is at least one positive test, because we have the opportunity of fortuitously rejecting an infected animal that has tested negative. Thus, $1 - (1 - p(1 - Se))^n > (1 - pSe)^n - (1 - p)^n$. Figure 22.12 illustrates the relationship between these two equations for $n = 20$ and varying prevalence p and sensitivity Se. By solving the following equation for p

$$\frac{\mathrm{d}}{\mathrm{d}p}((1 - pSe)^n - (1 - p)^n) = 0$$

we see that the probability that at least one animal will be infected in a group when the animals are rejected as a group is a maximum when the prevalence is given by

$$p = \frac{\sqrt[n-1]{Se} - 1}{\sqrt[n-1]{Se^n} - 1} \quad \blacklozenge$$

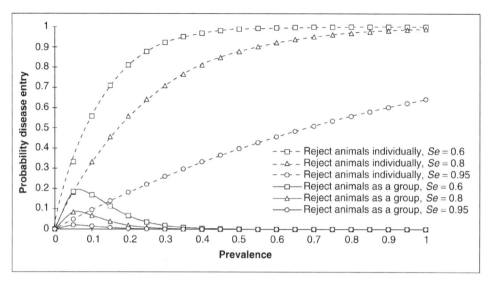

Figure 22.12   Relationship between probability of an infected group when the animals are rejected individually or as a group ($n = 20, p$ and Se varying).

An importing country is not usually worried about the infected consignments it rejects before importation, but is more concerned about the probability that a consignment that has been accepted is infected. This requires a simple Bayesian revision, as illustrated in the next problem.

Problem 22.9: **An animal population has prevalence p. You are to import consignments of size n from this population (n is much smaller than the population size). If all animals are tested with a test having sensitivity Se and specificity Sp, what is the probability that a consignment that has passed the test and therefore has been allowed entry into the country is infected if (a) one or more positive tests result in the rejection of the whole group and (b) positive tests result in the rejection of only those animals that tested positive.**

Solution: The reader is left to prove the following results:

$$\text{(a) } P(\text{infected}|\text{tested} - \text{ve}) = \frac{(p(1 - Se) + Sp(1 - p))^{n} - (Sp(1 - p))^{n}}{(p(1 - Se) + Sp(1 - p))^{n}}$$

$$\text{(b) } P(\text{infected}|\text{tested} - \text{ve}) = \frac{1 - (pSe + (1 - p))^{n}}{1 - (pSe + (1 - p)(1 - Sp))^{n}} \quad \blacklozenge$$

22.4 Confidence of Detecting an Infected Group

Veterinarians are often concerned with the number of animals in a group that need to be tested, given a certain test, in order to be reasonably certain that one will detect infection in the group if it is infected with the pathogen in question. Provided that we have a strong belief of what the prevalence within the group will be, if infected, we can determine the number of animals to test. We must first of all state what we mean by being "reasonably certain" that we will detect the infection by saying that there is probability α that we would fail to detect the infection (we have no positive tests) were it there. α is usually in the order of 0.1–5 %.

22.4.1 A perfect test with a very large group

A perfect test means that the test has Se and $Sp = 1$. If we know that the prevalence would be p, should the group be infected, then the probability of failing to detect the infection in sampling s animals is given by the binomial probability

$$\alpha = (1 - p)^s$$

where s is the number of animals tested. Rearranging this formula gives

$$s = \frac{\ln[\alpha]}{\ln[1 = p]}$$

For example, if $p = 30\%$ and $\alpha = 1\%$, then

$$\frac{\ln[\alpha]}{\ln[1 - p]} = \frac{\ln[0.01]}{\ln[0.7]} = 12.911$$

so we would have to test at least 13 animals to have 99 % probability of detecting any infection that was there.

22.4.2 A perfect test with a smaller group

Assuming we know the prevalence would be p, should the group be infected, and the group size is M, there will be pM infected animals. Then the probability of failing to detect the infection is given by the hypergeometric probability $p(0)$:

$$\alpha = \frac{\binom{M(1 - p)}{s}}{\binom{M}{s}}$$

This formula is hard to work out for large M and s. Section III.10 shows that a very good approximation is given by

$$\alpha \approx \sqrt{\frac{M(1 - p)(M - s)}{M(M - Mp - s)}} \; \frac{(M - Mp)^{M(1-p)}(M - s)^{(M-s)}}{(M - Mp - s)^{(M-Mp-s)} M^M}$$

where s is again the number of animals tested. The formula is too complicated to rearrange for s, but it can still be solved graphically. Figure 22.13 illustrates a spreadsheet where the number of tested animals is determined to be 14 when $\alpha = 5\%$, $p = 20\%$ and $M = 1000$. The formula can also be solved using a spreadsheet optimiser like Evolver, as shown at the bottom of the worksheet.

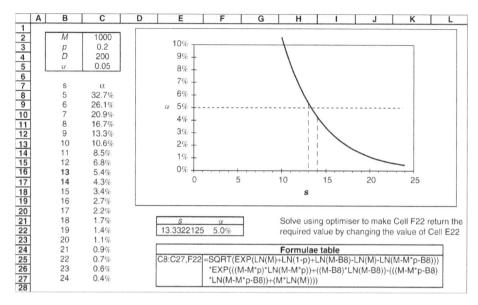

Figure 22.13 Interpolating model for Section 22.4.2.

A more convenient approximation to $p(0)$ is given by Cannon and Roe (1982), by expanding the factorials of $p(0)$ and taking the middle value of the numerator and denominator, which gives

$$\alpha \approx \left(1 - \frac{Mp}{M - (s - 1)/2}\right)^s$$

Again, this formula can be used graphically to find the required level of testing.

22.4.3 An imperfect test with a very large group

If we know that the prevalence would be p, should the group be infected, and that the test has sensitivity Se and specificity Sp, then the probability of observing zero positives in a test of size s is the combined probability that all infected animals test negative falsely (with probability $1 - Se$) and all uninfected animals test negative correctly (with probability Sp). Thus, we have

$$p(0) = \alpha = \sum_{x=0}^{s} \binom{s}{x} p^x (1 - p)^{s-x} (1 - Se)^x (Sp)^{s-x} = (p(1 - Se) + (1 - p)Sp)^s$$

from the binomial theorem (Section 6.3.4). Rearranging, we get

$$s = \frac{\ln[\alpha]}{\ln[p(1 - Se) + (1 - p)Sp]}$$

So, for example, if we have a test with $Se = 0.9$ and $Sp = 0.95$, and are fairly certain that the prevalence would be 0.2, the number of animals we would have to test to have a 90 % probability of detecting infection in the group is calculated by

$$s = \frac{\ln[0.1]}{\ln[0.2 \times 0.1 + 0.8 \times 0.95]} = 9.26$$

So we would have to test at least 10 animals.

22.4.4 An imperfect test with a smaller group

This problem requires that one use a hypergeometric sample with the probabilities of getting negative results from the previous problem, which gives

$$\alpha = p(0) = \sum_{x=0}^{s} \frac{\binom{pM}{x} \binom{(1-p)M}{s-x}}{\binom{M}{s}} (1 - Se)^x Sp^{s-x}$$

This equation is not easily rewritten to give a value of s for a given probability α, but s can still be reasonably easily determined by setting up a spreadsheet, using Stirling's approximation for large factorials and using the linear solver to get the required value of α. ModelRisk has several summation functions that are very helpful for these types of calculation: VosejSum (see below), VosejkSum (performs a two-dimensional sum) and VosejSumInf (calculates the sum of an infinite series providing it converges). For example, the equation above could be written with ModelRisk as

$$= \text{VosejSum}(''\text{VoseHypergeoProb}(j, j, D, M, 0) * ((1 - Se)^{\wedge}j) * (Sp^{\wedge}(s-j)'', 0, s)$$

The VosejSum function sums the expression within " " over integer values of j between 0 and s. The ModelRisk VoseHypergeoProb function in the expression has no problems with large factorials and, unlike Excel's HYPGEOMDIST, returns correct values across the parameter ranges, including returning a zero probability when a scenario is not possible instead of the #NUM! that HYPGEODIST returns. Now we can use Excel's Solver to vary s until the above formula returns the required value for α.

22.5 Miscellaneous Animal Health and Food Safety Problems

Problem 22.10: **I trap 100 Canada geese. Surveillance data show that the population has a 3 % prevalence of foaming beak disease (FBD). How many will have FBD? Canada geese also suffer from irritable feet syndrome (IFS), with a prevalence of 1 %. How many of my 100 geese will have at least one of these diseases? How many will have both?**

Solution: The number of geese with FBD can be modelled as Binomial(100, 3 %). The probability that a goose will have at least one of FBD and IFS is $1 - (1 - 3\%)(1 - 1\%) = 3.97\%$. The number of geese with at least one disease is therefore Binomial(100, 3.97 %).

The probability that a goose will have both FBD and IFS is $3\% * 1\% = 0.03\%$. The number of geese with both diseases is therefore Binomial(100, 0.03 %). These last two answers assume that the probabilities of a bird having IFS and of FBD are constant, whether they have the other disease or not. ♦

Problem 22.11: **Disease Y had a 25 % prevalence among the 120 bulls randomly tested from a country's population. Disease Y also had a 58 % prevalence among the 200 cows tested from that country's population. According to extensive experiments, a foetus has a 36 % probability of contracting the disease from an infected parent. If 100 foetuses are imported from this country and if it is assumed that each foetus has different parents, what is the distribution of the number of infected foetuses that will be imported?**

Solution: Uncertainty about prevalence among bulls p_B can be estimated as: Beta(31, 91). Uncertainty about prevalence among cows p_C can be estimated as: Beta(117, 85). One of four scenarios are possible with the parents: neither parent has the disease either one has or both have. They have the following probabilities:

$$
\begin{array}{ll}
\text{Neither:} & (1 - p_B)(1 - p_C) \\
\text{Bull only:} & p_B(1 - p_C) \\
\text{Cow only:} & (1 - p_B)p_C \\
\text{Both:} & p_B p_C
\end{array}
$$

Let p be the probability of infection of a foetus if one parent is infected ($= 36\%$). Then

Probability of foetus infection given neither parent is infected: 0

Probability of foetus infection given one parent is infected: p

Probability of foetus infection given both parents are infected: $1 - (1 - p)^2$

Thus, the probability that a foetus is infected

$$P(\text{inf}) = [p_B(1 - p_C) + (1 - p_B)p_C]p + p_B p_C[1 - (1 - p)^2]$$

and the number of infected foetuses is equal to Binomial(100, $P(\text{inf})$). ♦

Problem 22.12: **A large vat contains 10 million litres of milk. The milk is known to be contaminated with some virus, but the level of contamination is unknown. Fifty samples of 1 litre are taken from the vat and tested by an extremely reliable procedure. The test reports a positive on each of the samples if there are one or more virus particles in each sample. The results therefore do not distinguish how many virus particles there are in a positive sample. Estimate the concentration of virus particles if there were seven positive tests.**

It is known that one needs to consume some eight particles in a single dose of milk in order to have any chance of being infected. It is also considered that the people consume, at most, 10 litres of milk in a single helping. What is the probability P_{10} that somebody consuming a 10 litre volume of this milk will consume an infective dose?

Solution: We can use Bayesian inference to estimate the concentration of virus particles in the milk. Let us assume that the virus particles are perfectly mixed within the milk. This is probably a reasonable assumption as they are extremely small and will not settle to the bottom, but this does assume that there is no clumping. The total sample volume taken from the milk is very small compared with the volume in the vat, so we are safe to assume that our sampling has not materially altered the virus concentration in the vat. This would not be the case, for instance, if the vat were very small, say 10 litres, and we had sampled five of those litres with one positive result, since we could well have removed the only virus particle in the entire vat. ♦

Method 1. We can now see that the number of virus particles in a sample of milk will be Poisson(λt) distributed, where λ is the mean concentration per litre in the milk and t is the sample size in litres. If there were some clumping, we would probably use a Poisson distribution to describe the number of clumps in a sample, and some other distribution to describe the number of virus particles in each clump.

If λ is the concentration of virus particles per litre, the probability of having no virus particles in a sample of 1 litre is given by the Poisson probability mass function for $x = 0$, i.e. $p(0) = \exp[-\lambda]$. The probability of at least one virus particle in a litre sample is then $1 - \exp[-\lambda]$. The probability of having s infected samples out of n is given by the binomial probability function, since each sample is independent and has the same probability of being infected, i.e.

$$p(s;\ n,\ \lambda) = \binom{n}{s}\ (1 - \exp[-\lambda])^s(\exp[-\lambda])^{n-s}\ \propto\ (1 - \exp[-\lambda])^s(\exp[-\lambda])^{n-s}$$

Using an uninformed prior $p(\lambda) = 1/\lambda$ and the above equation with $n = 50$ and $s = 7$ as the likelihood function for λ, we can construct the posterior distribution. The points on this curve can then be entered into a relative distribution and used to calculate the probability P_{10} in the question using the Excel function POISSON as follows:

$$P_{10} = 1 - \text{POISSON}(7, 10\lambda, 1)\text{or VosePoissonProb}(7, 10\lambda, 1)$$

Method 2. In method 1 we looked at the Poisson process first, then at the binomial process. Now we start from the other end. We know that the 50 samples are all independent binomial trials and that we had seven successes, where a success is defined as an infected sample. Then we can estimate the probability of success p using the beta distribution:

$$p = \text{Beta}(7 + 1, 50 - 7 + 1) = \text{Beta}(8, 44)$$

From method 1 we also know that p equates to $1 - exp[-\lambda]$, so $\lambda = - \ln[1 - p] = - \ln[1 - \text{Beta}(8, 44)] = - \ln[\text{Beta}(44, 8)]$; the last identity occurs because switching the parameters for a beta distribution is equivalent to switching what we define to be successes and failures. In using the beta distribution in this fashion, we are assuming a Uniform(0, 1) prior for p. It is interesting to look at what this would equate to as a prior for λ, i.e. the distribution of λ when $\lambda = - \ln[\text{Uniform}(0, 1)]$. It turns out that this means λ has an Expon(1) distribution or, equivalently, a Gamma(1, 1) distribution. The reader can prove this by using the Jacobian transformation or, more simply, by making a comparison with the cumulative distribution function of the exponential distribution. The prior in method 1 gives $\pi(\lambda) \propto 1/\lambda$, whereas the prior for lambda in the second method is $\pi(\lambda) \propto \exp[-\lambda]$. These two priors are quite different, illustrating some of the difficulties in determining an uninformed prior. ♦

A prior where $\pi(\theta) \propto 1/\theta$ is very close to a Gamma(α, $1/\alpha$) distribution where α is very large. The gamma distribution is the conjugate prior for the Poisson likelihood function. In estimating the Poisson mean λ number of events per period, using a Gamma(α, β) prior and a Poisson likelihood function for S observations in n periods, we get (see Section 8.3.3) a posterior distribution for λ equal to a Gamma($\alpha + S$, $\beta/(1 + \beta n)$). Thus, using the Expon(1) = Gamma(1, 1) prior, one gets a posterior equal to

$$\lambda|\text{observations} = \text{Gamma}(S + 1, 1/(n + 1))$$

while using the $\pi(\theta) \propto 1/\theta$ prior yields roughly

$$\lambda|\text{observations} = \text{Gamma}(S, 1/n)$$

The difference in these two equations shows that it does not take too large a set of data for the importance of the form of the prior to be overpowered by the likelihood function (i.e. $S + 1 \approx S$ and $n + 1 \approx n$).

Problem 22.13: **1000 eggs, each of 60 ml, are mixed together. It is estimated that 100 of those eggs have *Salmonella*. After mixing, 60 ml of liquid egg is removed and consumed. If there are 100 *Salmonella* CFU/infected egg, how many CFU will be consumed in that 60 ml? What is the probability that at least 1 CFU will be consumed? How much liquid egg will need to be consumed to receive the minimum infectious dose of 12 CFU? [A CFU is a colony-forming unit – a surrogate measure for the number of individual virus particles.]**

Now, instead of a minimum infectious dose, we use the following dose–response model:

$$P_{\text{inf}}(x) = 1 - \exp(-x/5)$$

where x is the consumed dose. What is the probability of becoming infected from consuming a 60 ml volume of liquid egg?

Solution: One in every 10 eggs is infected, so the average *Salmonella* concentration will be 10 CFU/60 ml. Taking one egg's worth of liquid from the mass of 1000 eggs is a small amount, and, if the eggs are well mixed, we can assume that a sample will follow a Poisson distribution of CFU with the above average concentration. The number of CFU in one 60 ml sample will then take a Poisson(10) distribution. The probability of at least 1 CFU in that volume $= 1 - p(0) = 1 - \exp(-10) = 99.996\,\%$. The amount of egg that needs to be consumed for a dose of 12 CFU is Gamma(12, $\frac{1}{10}$).

Using the dose–response model, the probability of becoming infected P is the Poisson probability of consuming x CFU multiplied by $P_{\text{inf}}(x)$, summed over all possible values of x, i.e.

$$P = \sum_{x=1}^{\infty} \frac{\exp(-10) \times 10^x}{x!} \left(1 - \exp\left(\frac{-x}{5}\right)\right)$$

which has no closed form but can be evaluated quickly by summing an array in a worksheet or using ModelRisk:

$$= \text{VosejSum}(''\text{VosePoissonProb}(j, 10, 0) * (1 - \exp(-j/5)'', 1, 1000)$$

where 1000 is easily large enough, or more correctly

$$= \text{VosejSumInf}(''\text{VosePoissonProb}(j, 10, 0) * (1 - \exp(-j/5)'', 1, 0.000000001)$$

which will sum the expression over j from 1 onwards in integer steps until a value has been reached with a precision of 0.000000001.

The answer is 83.679 %. ◆

Problem 22.14: **Over the last 20 years there has been an average of four outbreaks of disease Z in rural swine herds owing to contact with feral pigs. If an outbreak usually infects Normal(100, 30) pigs and if an individual pig is worth \$Normal(120, 22), calculate the total cost of outbreaks for the next 5 years.**

Assuming there is a 5 % chance that contact of a rural swine herd with domestic pigs will result in an outbreak of disease Z, estimate how many actual contacts occur each year given that the average number of outbreaks per year is 5.

Solution: We can assume that each outbreak is independent of every other, in which case the outbreaks follow a Poisson process. With an average of four outbreaks per year, and assuming the rate of outbreaks is constant over the last 20 years, we can model the outbreaks in the next 5 years as Poisson(4 × 5) = Poisson(20).

The number of outbreaks is a variable, so we have to add up a sum of a varying number of Normal(100, 30) distributions to get the number of infected pigs. Then we have to add up a varying number of Normal(120, 22) distributions, depending on the number of infected pigs, to get the total cost over the next 5 years of these outbreaks. One might think the solution would be

$$\text{Total cost} = \text{Poisson}(20) \times \text{Normal}(100, 30) \times \text{Normal}(120, 22)$$

The answer seems at first glance to be quite intuitive, but fails on further inspection. Imagine that the Poisson distribution in a Monte Carlo simulation produces a value of 25, and the Normal(100, 30) distribution produces a value of 160. That is saying that, on average, the 25 outbreaks produce 160 infected pigs each. The 160 value is two standard deviations above the mean, and the probability of the 25 outbreaks all taking such high values is extremely small. We have forgotten to recognise that each of the 25 distributions (of the number of infected pigs in each of the 25 outbreaks) is independent. However, this can easily be accounted for by using the central limit theorem (see Section 6.3.3). The correct approach is shown in the spreadsheet of Figure 22.14. Figure 22.15 shows the difference between the results for the correct approach and the incorrect formula shown above. One can see that the incorrect approach, failing to recognise independence between the number of infected pigs in each outbreak and between the value of each infected pig, produces an exaggerated spread for the distribution of possible cost.

Note that it is a simple matter to use the central limit theorem in this problem, because the theorem works exactly when summing any number of normal distributions. However, if the number of infected pigs in an outbreak were Lognormal(70, 50) – a fairly skewed distribution – we would need to be adding together some 30 or so of these distributions to get a good approximation to a normal for the sum. Since the Poisson(20) distribution has a small probability of generating values above 30, we may be uncomfortable with using the shortcut of the central limit theorem. The spreadsheet of Figure 22.16 revisits the problem, using the lognormal distribution, where we are adding up a varying number of lognormal distributions depending on the value generated by the Poisson distribution. The VoseAggregateMC function is equivalent to the array model (see Sections 11.1 and 11.2.2).

In solving this problem, we have assumed exact knowledge of each parameter. However, undoubtedly there will be some uncertainty associated with these parameters, and it may be worth investigating

	A	B	C	D	E	F	G
1							
2		Number of outbreaks in 5 years			14		
3		Pigs infected			1,377		
4		Cost			166,917		
5							
6							
7			*Formulae table*				
8		F2	= VosePoisson(4*5)				
9		F3	= ROUND(VoseNormal(100*E2,30*SQRT(E2)),0)				
10		F4 (Output)	= VoseNormal(120*E3,22*SQRT(E3))				
11							

Figure 22.14 Spreadsheet model for Problem 22.14.

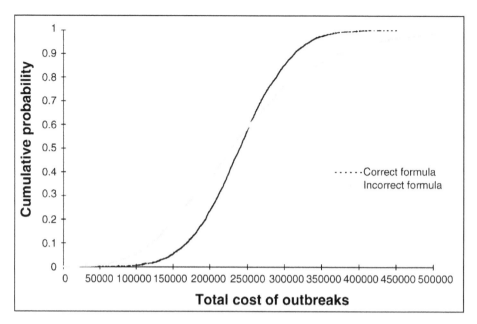

Figure 22.15 Distribution of difference between correct and incorrect approaches for Problem 22.14.

	A	B	C	D	E	F	G
1							
2		Number of outbreaks in 5 years		21			
3							
4		Outbreak	Pigs in outbreak				
5		1	53.79				
6		2	66.77				
7		3	52.74				
54		49	0				
55		50	0				
56							
57		Pigs infected	1,696				
58		Cost	203,870				
59							
60			*Formulae table*				
61		D2	=VosePoisson(4*5)				
62		C5:C55	=IF(B5>$D$2,0,VoseLognormal(70,50))				
63		C57	=ROUND(SUM(C5:C55),0)				
64		C58 (output)	=VoseNormal(120*C57,22*SQRT(C57))				
65		C58 (alternative)	=VoseAggregateMC(VosePoisson(4*5),VoseLognormalObject(70,50))				
66							

Figure 22.16 Spreadsheet model for Problem 22.14 using lognormal distributions.

exactly how well specified these parameters really are. The only parameter for which we can quantify the uncertainty in this problem is the mean number of outbreaks per year. To do this, we must still assume that the rate of outbreaks is constant over 20 years (which seems unlikely for most countries owing to changes in international trade and veterinary practices, for example), which may be our biggest

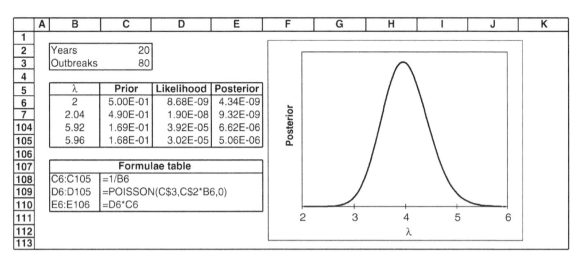

Figure 22.17 Spreadsheet model for the uncertainty in λ for Problem 22.14.

source of uncertainty. That aside, the uncertainty about the mean outbreaks per year λ can be readily quantified using Bayes' theorem. We can use an uninformed prior:

$$\pi(\lambda) = 1/\lambda$$

and a likelihood function

$$l(X|\lambda) = \frac{e^{-20\lambda}(20\lambda)^{80}}{80!}$$

since there were 80 outbreaks in the last 20 years. This is given by the Excel function POISSON(80, 20λ, 0). Figure 22.17 shows the spreadsheet calculation and resultant uncertainty distribution for λ which, unsurprisingly given the fairly large amount of data (see Section III.9.2), looks very close to being normally distributed. This distribution can be used to create a second-order model, separating uncertainty and variability, as described in Section 4.3.2. ♦

Problem 22.15: **100 turkeys, randomly selected from a population, were tested for infectious bursal disease (IBD). 17 were infected. Of these 17, six had infected kidneys. After freezing these infected kidneys for 10 days at −5°C, only half still had viable IBD virus particles.**

You are importing turkey kidneys from this population at a rate of 1600/year. What is your estimate of probability/year of importing at least one kidney with viable IBD virus? Note: it takes 12 days for the product to ship to your country and 2 days to clear customs. You, as the regulating authority, may set importing restrictions (i.e. storage temperatures) for the importer.

Solution: I leave this as an exercise, but with a hint: you should model the fact that each turkey has two kidneys, and that, if one kidney becomes infected, so will the other. In other words, the kidneys are being produced and exported two by two. The problem leaves a number of questions open, in that you need to make some assumptions. This is often the way with a risk analysis: once you get started, you realise that some additional information could be useful. ♦

Problem 22.16: **Over the last 6 years, the following numbers of outbreaks of disease *XYZ* in sheep have occurred in your area: 12, 10, 4, 8, 15, 9. It is thought that about 80 % of these outbreaks originate directly from attacks by wild dogs. It has further been estimated that contact with wild dogs has around a 20–50 % chance of resulting in an infection.**

Recent experiments have shown that putting llamas in with herds of sheep would halve the number of attacks by dogs. (Llamas apparently have an in-built hatred of dogs and head butt them on sight. Appearing to a dog to be a sheep on steroids, they also have an unpleasant habit of spitting.) Estimate the number of outbreaks next year if llamas were put to use in all flocks throughout your area.

Solution: This problem is a bit mean, in that I have added some irrelevant information. First of all, an uncertainty distribution for the mean number of outbreaks per year λ is determined in the same manner as Problem 22.14. After llamas have been installed there will only be 50 % of the 80 % of outbreaks due to dogs, plus the 20 % that are not, i.e. the new mean number of outbreaks per year would be 0.6λ and the number of outbreaks next year will follow a Poisson(0.6λ) distribution. ◆

Appendix I

Guide for lecturers

Risk analysis can be a fascinating topic to learn if the course focuses on the problem solving part, supported by plenty of examples. I tend to keep the theory to a minimum in my lectures and try to find visual methods to explain probability ideas rather than formulae. The type of person who is likely to be a successful risk analyst is more usually attracted by the problem solving side of the work and the practical application of mathematics and logic rather than the mathematics *per se*. I always start a course by getting people to say a little about themselves, and this helps me find examples that have the greatest resonance with the particular audience. In my classes I set lots of problems and ask people to work in pairs, for small problems, or groups of six or so for larger problems. This makes a course a lot more dynamic, gives people a sense of achievement when they solve a problem and really helps people understand better because they have to debate and defend or give up their ideas. I also keep a box of little chocolates on my desk and throw them to course participants when they make a good comment, are first to solve a problem, etc. It helps keep things fun and is surprisingly motivating.

At Vose Software we have an educational programme in which graduate and postgraduate students at accredited universities can obtain copies of ModelRisk for a nominal charge through a bulk order via their university. The software is a full version but time limited to 1 year. More information is available at www.vosesoftware.com/academic .htm. We have placed a lot of emphasis on user-friendly interfaces for as much of the functionality of ModelRisk as possible (see Appendix II), which makes it ideally suited as a teaching aid. Below I give some ideas on what to include in a risk analysis course for various disciplines.

Risk management

A major issue faced by risk analysts is that the management to whom they report don't fully understand what a risk analysis is, or how to use it. In my view it would be a great help if MBAs or similar business and public administration courses offered a basic introduction to risk analysis. I suggest the following:

- Chapters 1 to 5, to give a background on the purpose of risk analysis and how to use the results;
- Chapter 7, to explain how a simulation works;
- Chapter 17 on checking and validation.

Insurance and finance risk analysis

Insurance and finance risk modelling is probably the most technical area of risk. I suggest:

- Chapter 5, to illustrate how results can be expressed and used;
- Chapters 6, 8 to 13, 16 to 18 and 20 for an in-depth technical course.

Animal health

Animal health has quite an emphasis on modelling the probabilities of different pathways via which disease can spread. I would focus on:

- Chapters 1 to 5, to set the scene;

- Chapter 6 for the probability ideas;
- Chapters 8, 9 and 17 for the technical aspects of modelling;
- Chapter 22 for topic-specific ideas.

Business investment risk

Typical business investment problems involve deciding whether to invest in a new venture or expand on a proven venture. The analyses are usually performed using discounted cashflows. I recommend:

- Chapters 1 to 5, to set the scene;
- Chapter 7 on how to run a model;
- Chapters 9 and 10 for analysing data and fitting distributions;
- Chapter 11 on sums of random variables – this is an area in which people make lots of mistakes;
- Chapter 12 for forecasting time series;
- Chapter 13 on correlation, particularly the subjective modelling of correlation;
- Chapter 14 – perhaps the most important chapter in this area, since SMEs are often the source of most estimates in an investment analysis;
- Chapter 16 on optimisation, as this helps determine the best investment strategy, especially for things like staged investment;
- Chapter 18 for topic-specific ideas.

Inventory management and manufacturing

While not strictly risk analysis, we do a lot of this type of work because of the statistical analysis one can apply to historical inventory and demand data and production profiles. I recommend:

- Chapter 5, to explain how to present and interpret results;
- Chapters 6 to 10, 12 and 13 for technical material;
- Chapter 16 on optimisation;
- Chapter 17 on model validation.

Microbial food safety

There has been an over-emphasis in the past on rather abstract and complex models of microbial food safety. I recommend:

- Chapters 1 to 5, to set the scene and give some tools for the risk analyst to express the level of confidence one should have in the model's outputs;
- Chapters 8 to 11 and 17 for the technical aspects of modelling;
- Chapter 15 for causal thinking;
- Chapter 21 for topic-specific ideas.

Appendix II

About ModelRisk

ModelRisk™ is a comprehensive risk analysis software tool with many unique features that make risk modelling more accessible, easier and more transparent for novice and advanced users alike. The design concepts and features in ModelRisk are the result of struggling with available risk analysis software to solve our clients' problems. It is the tool that realises our view on how good and defensible risk analyses should be performed. It is our answer to those who argue that complex models are too vulnerable to errors and simple ones are a better alternative. With ModelRisk, complex models can be built as easily as simple ones, and in almost no time!

The main idea behind creating such a tool was to make the most advanced risk analysis techniques accessible to a wide range of users including those who do not have the programming capabilities required to build a complex model. We put a lot of effort into making the software user friendly and leaving as much of the complex mathematics as possible "behind the scenes" so that a modeller can be guided through the chosen method and be sure s/he is using it correctly. We think this feature alone should save about 70 % of the modeller's time, as it is a well-known fact that reviewing and debugging a model is more time consuming than developing it.

In search for an ideal tool for risk analysis modelling, we asked ourselves a few questions:

- What methods and theories are widely known in the industry?
- How are they currently used and what are the problems with their implementation?
- How can we make a tool both simple and intuitive to use and also flexible enough to make it possible to model any complex customised situation?
- How can we make it easy to present and explain a complex model to a decision-maker?

ModelRisk was the answer to all of these questions, providing the modeller with the following features:

- It is based on the most recent achievements in industry-specific risk analysis theory.
- It is Excel-based: a widely used Excel spreadsheet environment provides the best foundation for making risk analysis techniques available to a wide range of users.
- It is flexible enough to model any complex customised business case.
- It includes many building blocks (tools) that allow the creation of complex models within minutes.
- It offers immediate help and thorough explanations of all tools.
- It gives warnings of errors and suggestions for corrections during model development in order greatly to increase the speed of modelling and debugging.
- It provides excellent precision of outcomes that is comparable with leading non-Excel statistical packages.
- It provides a visual interface that is great both for a self-check when building a model and for presenting the thinking and results to a reviewer.
- If needed, it can be used outside Excel for integration with other applications.

ModelRisk and Excel

ModelRisk is an add-in to Microsoft Excel, and its tools fully comply with Excel function rules, which makes its use intuitive for those who are familiar with the Excel spreadsheet environment. Even though ModelRisk uses the English language for its tools, it can work seamlessly on any language platform, including different language versions of Windows, Excel and various simulation tools. ModelRisk can be called from any programming environment that can make direct calls to dynamic link libraries (DLLs), including VBA, VB, C++ and others.

ModelRisk runs seamlessly in Excel with any Monte Carlo spreadsheet simulation package. This means that you can combine ModelRisk with Crystal Ball, @RISK or any other Monte Carlo simulation Excel add-in, using these add-ins to control how you run simulations and present the results, as well as making full use of more sophisticated features like sensitivity analysis and optimisation.

ModelRisk is offered as an industry-specific package of analysis and modelling tools, and the first version has been developed for insurance and finance. The full list of existing and to-be-developed ModelRisk versions for other industries is reachable from www.vosesoftware.com.

Distribution functions

ModelRisk has more than 65 univariate distributions and the ability to calculate the probability density (or mass), cumulative probability and percentile for each of them. The functions take the following format (using a Normal(μ, σ) distribution as an example):

- VoseNormal(μ, σ, U) calculates the Uth percentile;
- VoseNormalProb$(\{x\}, \mu, \sigma, 0)$ calculates the joint probability of observing the array of values $\{x\}$;
- VoseNormalProb$(\{x\}, \mu, \sigma, 1)$ calculates the joint cumulative probability of observing $\{x\}$.

All probability calculations can also be done in $\log_{10}$ space, as joint probability calculations often result in numbers that are too small to be supported by Excel. ModelRisk then performs the internal calculations in log space for greatest precision. For example

$$\text{VoseNormalProb}10(\{x\}, \mu, \sigma, 0) = \text{LOG}10(\text{VoseNormalProb}(\{x\}, \mu, \sigma, 0))$$

U-parameter functions

Functions with a U-parameter (e.g. VoseNormal(μ, σ, U)) can also be used to generate random values from the distributions using the inversion method (Section 4.4.1). Since the U-parameter represents a distribution's Uth percentile (0–100 %), making U a random sample from a Uniform(0, 1) distribution will give a valid sample from a valid Normal(μ, σ) distribution. For example

$$\begin{array}{ll} \text{VoseNormal}(\mu, \sigma, \text{RAND}()) & \text{using Excel} \\ \text{VoseNormal}(\mu, \sigma, \text{RiskUniform}(0, 1)) & \text{using @RISK} \\ \text{VoseNormal}(\mu, \sigma, \text{CB.Uniform}(0, 1)) & \text{using Crystal Ball} \end{array}$$

The U-parameter in ModelRisk functions is always optional, and if omitted the function will return a random sample from the distribution by internally sampling from a Uniform(0, 1) using the Mersenne twister random number generator.[1]

---

[1] The Mersenne twister is a pseudorandom number generator developed in 1997 by Makoto Matsumoto (松本 眞) and Takuji Nishimura (西村 拓士) that is based on a matrix linear recurrence over a finite binary field F_2. It provides fast generation of very high-quality pseudorandom numbers, and was designed specifically to rectify many of the flaws found in older algorithms.

Because all ModelRisk univariate distributions have a consistent format and a U-parameter, it is very easy to correlate all of them using five different correlation methods available in ModelRisk (Copulas[2]). The ModelRisk copulas offer a variety of correlation patterns and provide a far better control over the correlation than the more usual rank order correlation. They can also be fitted to data and compared statistically. A k-dimension copula function returns k random samples from a Uniform(0, 1) distribution, which are correlated according to a certain copula pattern. Thus, if the copula-generated values are being used as U-parameters in ModelRisk distributions, those distributions will be correlated. For example

A1:B1 =VoseCopulaBiClayton(10, 1)	A two-cell array function generating values from a Clayton(10) copula
A2: =VoseLognormal(3, 1, A1)	A Lognormal(3, 1) distribution with the U-parameter referenced to the first copula value
B2: =VoseNormal(0, 1, B1)	A Normal(0, 1) distribution with the U-parameter referenced to the second copula value

A scatter plot of the values generated by the Clayton copula looks like this:

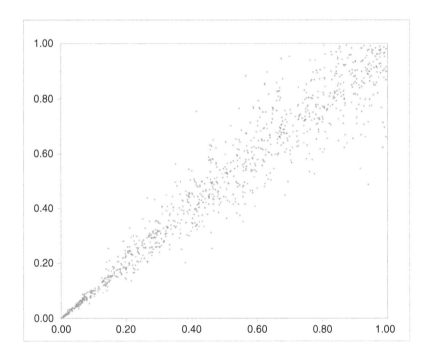

The correlation between the two parent (normal and lognormal) distributions will take the following pattern:

---

[2] In statistics, a copula is a multivariate joint distribution defined on the n-dimensional unit cube $[0, 1]^n$ such that every marginal distribution is uniform on the interval $[0, 1]$.

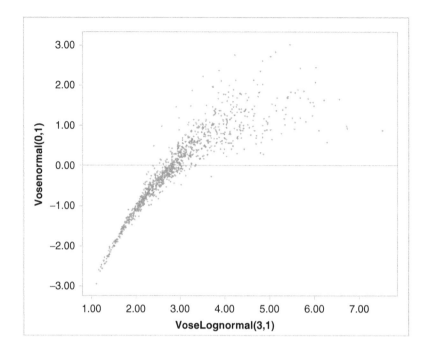

As shown above, Crystal Ball, @RISK, etc., can also provide the random number generator for ModelRisk distributions. This feature allows you to take advantage of Latin hypercube sampling (LHS) from ModelRisk distributions and other features like targeted sampling.

Using Crystal Ball or @RISK random number generators as engines for sampling from ModelRisk distributions also allows integration of ModelRisk simulation output statistics into Crystal Ball or @RISK output interfaces as well as advanced tools like sensitivity analysis. In other words, simulation with ModelRisk distributions is as easy as with native Crystal Ball or @RISK distributions.

Object functions

ModelRisk offers a unique approach to defining and manipulating random variables as objects, allowing unprecedented flexibility in modelling complex industry-related issues. For each univariate distribution, ModelRisk has an object function that takes the form

$$\text{VoseNormalObject}(\mu, \sigma)$$

$$\text{VosePoissonObject}(\lambda, \text{VoseShift}(3))$$

Modelling distributions as objects is a new concept in spreadsheet programming. It helps to overcome the limitations of Excel and adds flexibility that is available in high-end statistical packages. If the object function is put directly into a cell, it returns a text string, for example

$$\text{"VoseNormal(Mu, Sigma)"}$$

However, for ModelRisk this cell now represents a distribution, which can be used as a building block in many other tools. The user can use the reference to the object function to calculate a statistic or generate random numbers from the object's distribution. For example, if we write

$$\text{A1:} = \text{VoseNormalObject}(0, 1) \text{ the object function}$$

then the following formulae will access the Normal(0, 1) distribution defined in cell A1:

A2: =VoseSimulate(A1)	takes a random sample from the Normal(0, 1)
A3: =VoseSimulate(A1, 0.7)	calculates a 70%th percentile of the Normal(0, 1)
A4: =VoseProb(3, A1, 0)	calculates the density of Normal(0, 1) at $x = 3$
A5: =VoseProb(3, A1, 1)	calculates the cumulative density of Normal(0, 1) at $x = 3$
A6: =VoseMean(A1)	returns the mean of the Normal(0, 1)
A7: =VoseVariance(A1)	returns the variance of Normal(0, 1)
A8: =VoseSkewness(A1)	returns the skewness of Normal(0, 1)
A9: =VoseKurtosis(A1)	returns the kurtosis of Normal(0, 1)

The object functions are particularly useful in modelling combinations of distributions, for example

$$VoseSplice(VoseGammaObject(3, 0.8), VosePareto2Object(4, 6, VoseShift(1.5)), 3)$$

models a splice of two distributions. In the figure below, a Gamma(3, 0.8) on the left is being spliced onto a shifted Pareto2(4, 6) on the right at a splice point of 3. The figure shows a typical ModelRisk interface: with this constructed distribution one can select to insert a function into Excel that is an object, that simulates, that calculates a probability density (the option shown), that calculates a cumulative probability or that provides the inversion function.

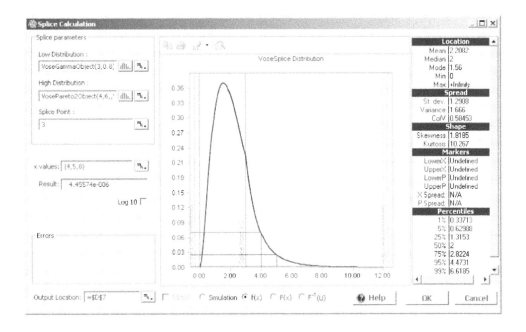

Objects are also used in modelling many other tools, such as aggregate distributions, for example

$$=VoseAggregateFFT(VosePoissonObject(50), VoseLognormalObject(10, 5))$$

This function uses the fast Fourier transformation method to construct the aggregate loss distribution, with the frequency of claims distributed as Poisson(50) and the severity of each claim as Lognormal(10, 5):

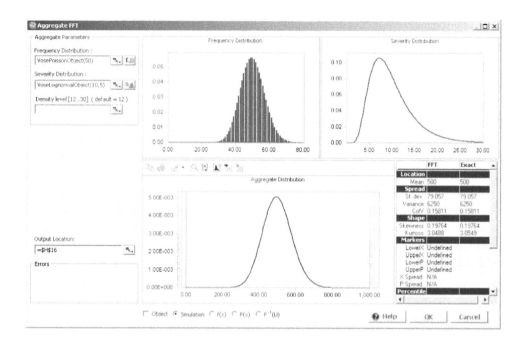

As mentioned earlier, the object functions can be used directly to calculate the moments of any object without performing simulation, for example

=VoseVariance(VoseAggregateFFTObject(VosePoissonObject(50), VoseLognormalObject(10, 5)))

=VoseKurtosis(VoseSpliceObject(VoseGammaObject(3, 0.8),

   VosePareto2Object(4, 6,, VoseShift(1.5)), 3))

Menu

Most of the ModelRisk tools can be accessed through the menu in Excel's menu bar:

The View Function tool on top of the menu brings up the ModelRisk Formula View window which is almost the same as Excel's Formula Bar but recognises ModelRisk functions and attaches hyperlinks to their corresponding interfaces:

The Formula View bar always stays on top so that the user can quickly browse through all ModelRisk tools in the current cell.

ModelRisk distributions are sorted into several industry-related categories to help the user identify the right distribution:

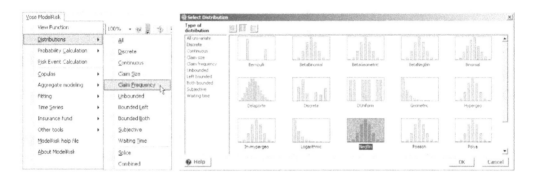

The Distribution category also has the Splice tool, which we've seen before, and the Combined tool, which allows the modelling of a combined distribution of several subjective opinions:

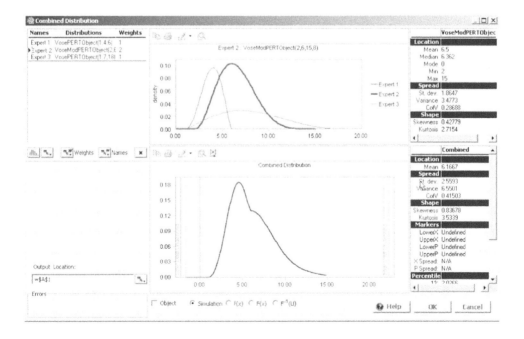

The Combined tool is typical of the ModelRisk approach. In risk analysis we often use subjective estimates of variables in our model, preferably having more than one expert providing an estimate for each variable. These estimates will not completely match, so we need to represent the resultant combined distribution correctly. The Combined tool does this automatically, allows you to weight each opinion and returns plots of the resultant distribution and statistics. The combined distribution can also be turned into an object and used as a building block for the other ModelRisk tools.

Risk events

A risk event calculation is another tool we devised in response to a genuine practical need. A risk event is an event that has a certain probability of occurring and, if it did occur, would have an impact following some distribution. In risk analysis modelling, we normally require two distributions to model this: a Bernoulli(p) multiplied by the impact distribution. The problem is that, in having two distributions, we cannot do a correct sensitivity analysis or perform other calculations like determining the variable's moments or percentiles. The Risk Event tool allows the modelling of a risk event as a single distribution:

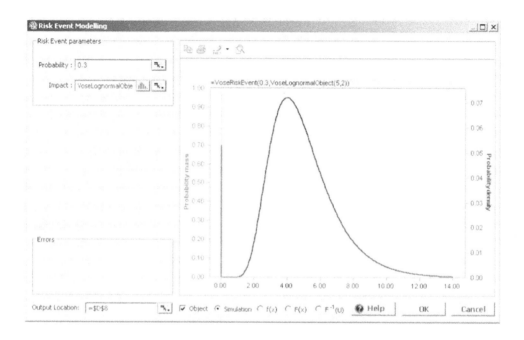

and, again, the risk event distribution can be converted into an object:

$$=\text{VoseRiskEventObject}(0.3, \text{VoseLognormalObject}(5, 2))$$

Copulas

ModelRisk has an interface for the bi- and multivariate copula tools showing scatter plots between the correlated variables:

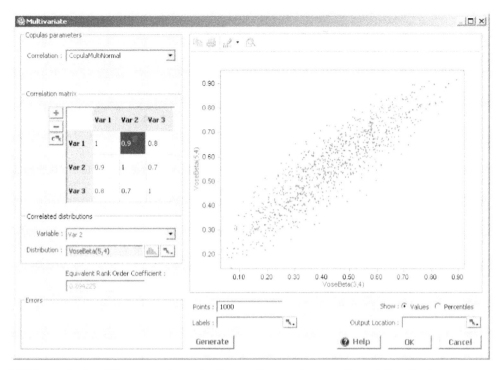

ModelRisk can fit the different copulas to the data and has another interface window for that:

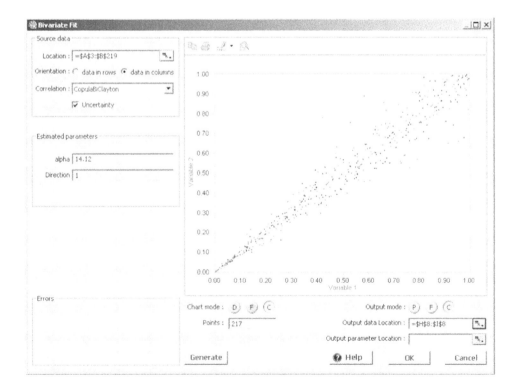

The screenshot above shows that the bivariate data (multivariate is also possible) are taken from location $A$3:$B$219 and shown as red (light) dots. ModelRisk estimates the fitted Clayton copula parameter alpha to be 14.12, and we get a visual verification of the fit by overlaying sampled values from Clayton(14.12) on the same chart as blue (dark) dots. Moreover, we can add uncertainty to our fitted parameter estimate by checking the corresponding option, and the sampled values in blue are now samples from the Clayton copula with an alpha that is an uncertainty distribution.

ModelRisk has some unique copula features. Bivariate copulas can be rotated to "pinch" in any quadrant, and we offer a multivariate empirical copula that will match to any observed pattern.

Aggregate modelling

ModelRisk has a large selection of aggregate modelling tools using sophisticated recursive and fast Fourier transformation (FFT) methods. The Panjer, de Pril and FFT tools allow the construction of an aggregate claim distribution based on the distributions of the frequency of claims and severity of each claim. It is highly laborious, and sometimes simply impossible, to do such calculations manually in a spreadsheet, while in ModelRisk it is only a one-cell expression. The Aggregate interface shows the frequency, severity and constructed aggregate plots, as well as a comparison of the constructed distribution's moments with their theoretical values, where they are available, so that the modeller can see how good the aggregate approximation is:

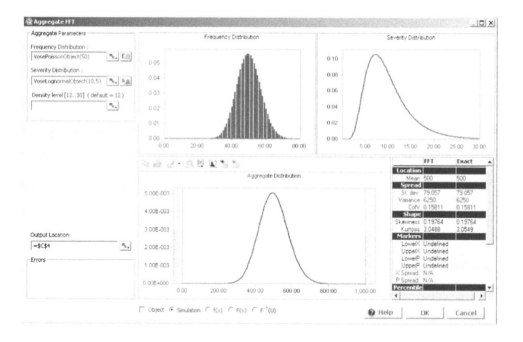

You can also fit a number of distributions to the calculated aggregate model by matching moments at the click of a button, which overlays the fitted distribution and compares statistics. The Aggregate pack of tools also allows modelling of the aggregate distribution of multiple frequency:severity aggregates using the FFT and brute-force (Monte Carlo) methods. An example of the latter is shown in the screenshot below, where the two risks have correlated frequency distributions equal to Poisson(50) and Pólya(10, 1), and corresponding severity distributions modelled as Lognormal(10, 5) and Lognormal(10, 2). The level of correlation between the two frequency distributions is described by a normal copula with a correlation parameter of 0.9:

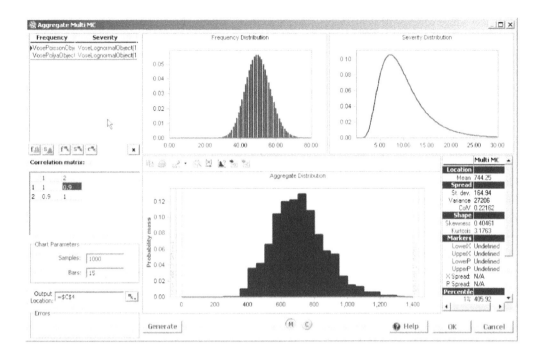

Time series

ModelRisk has a set of time series modelling functions, including variations of geometric Brownian motion (GBM) models with mean reversion, jump diffusion or both, seasonalised GBM, etc. Common financial time series are included, such as AR, MA, ARMA, ARCH, GARCH, APARCH, EGARCH and continuous-time Markov chain:

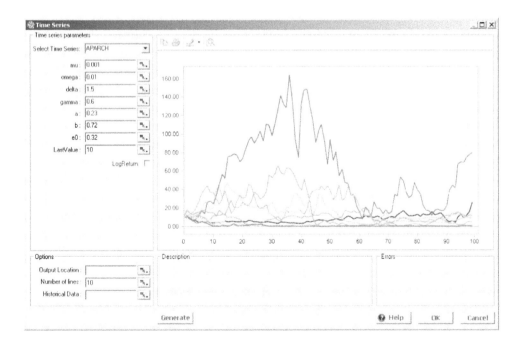

You can view a time series with as many possible paths as you wish and generate new sets of paths on screen, giving you a visual confirmation that the series is performing as you want. In addition to the ability to simulate the time series in a spreadsheet, ModelRisk has the tools to fit all of its time series to the data:

The above screen capture shows the original time series data on the left and the forecast sample from the fitted GBM model on the right. The Time Series Fit tool allows the inputting of the array of past time stamps (i.e. for certain time series it is not necessary that all observations are made at regular intervals, allowing, for example, missing observations) with which the historical data were collected and the future time stamps to specify the exact points of time for which the prediction values need to be modelled. Much like with the copula fit tool, the time series fit functions have an uncertainty parameter that switches the uncertainty about the fitted parameters on and off. With the uncertainty parameter off, the fit tool returns forecasts using the maximum likely estimates (MLEs).

Other features

Among many other tools, ModelRisk has the following highly technical features:

- distribution fitting of censored or truncated data and modelling of the uncertainty about the fitted parameters;
- goodness of fit of copulas, time series and distributions using three information criteria (Section 10.3.4);
- insurance fund ruin and depletion models, which model the inflows and outflows into the insurance fund and calculate the distributions of the chance of the ruin, the ruin time, etc.;
- a powerful, unique approach to extreme-value modelling, making it possible, for example, to calculate directly the probability that the largest of a million claims following a certain distribution will not exceed some value X with 95 % confidence;
- direct determination of insurance premiums using standard actuarial methods;
- one-click statistical analysis of data, including bootstrapping;

- multivariate stochastic dominance analysis;
- determination of a portfolio's efficient frontier;
- Wilkie time series models, which allow simulation of Wilkie time series in a spreadsheet;
- and many more.

Help file

In addition to all of the modelling tools described above, ModelRisk comes with a specialised version of ModelAssist™ for insurance and finance that shows how to use ModelRisk with hundreds of topics explaining any relevant theory, example Excel/ModelRisk model solutions, videos, a search engine and much more!

The help file is fully integrated into Excel and the ModelRisk interfaces, providing links to the help file from all the places you most need them.

Custom applications and macros

ModelRisk can also be used in any programming language that supports calls to DLLs, for example Visual Basic, C++ and Delphi. ModelRisk has a COM-object called "ModelRisk Library", which is automatically registered in a local system when ModelRisk is installed.

To access ModelRisk functions from Visual Basic, for example, one needs to register ModelRisk as a reference for the VB project as shown in the screenshot below:

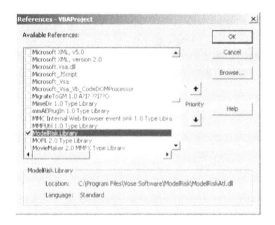

An example of a VB routine is given below:

```
Sub TestMR()

' Sample from the bounded Normal(0,1) distribution

Dim Sample As Double
Sample = ModelRisk.VoseNormal(0, 1, , VosePBounds(0.1, 0.9))


' Calculate the combined probability of observing
' the values 125, 112 and 94 from Poisson(100) distribution

Dim Prob as Double
```

```
Dim Values As Variant
Values = Array(125, 112, 94)
Prob = ModelRisk.VosePoissonProb(Values, 100, 0)


' Use Central Limit Theorem to sample from the
' distribution of the sum of 120 Normal(25, 3) distributions

Dim CLT As Double
CLT = ModelRisk.VoseCLTSum(120, 25, 3)


' Print the output values to the Debug console

Debug.Print Sample, Prob, CLT

End Sub
```

ModelRisk's COM Object offers a limited number of ModelRisk tools, such as distributions. The full set of ModelRisk tools is available to programmers in the ModelRisk SDK, which allows integrating the full power of ModelRisk into custom, non-spreadsheet stand-alone applications. An example of using ModelRisk SDK in C++ is shown in Exhibit 1. More information regarding the ModelRisk SDK is available at www.vosesoftware.com/ModelRisk SDK.htm.

Vose Software can also develop stand-alone or integrated ModelRisk-based risk analysis applications for you. We can create a user-friendly interface around the ModelRisk engine that addresses the client's requirements and leverages the efficiency of the final product by using our extensive expertise in developing risk analysis models. For more information regarding customised software development, please contact info@vosesoftware.com.

Exhibit 1. Using ModelRisk SDK in C++

ModelRisk SDK offers C++ developers a direct access to the ModelRisk Function library. The best way of doing it is using ≪ModelRisk_Core.h≫ and ≪ModelRisk_Core.lib≫ for access to the Core library – ≪ModelRisk_Core.dll≫. The ≪ModelRisk_Core.lib≫ file is compatible with ≪MS Visual C++ 2005≫. The following steps need to be taken to include ModelRisk library functions in your C++ project:

1. In MS Visual Studio, create an empty C++ project (skip this step for existing projects).
2. In the menu ≪Project≫, select ≪Add existing item... ≫.
3. At the bottom of the ≪Add existing item... ≫ window, change the ≪File of types≫ setting to ≪All files≫.
4. Use the ≪Add existing item... ≫ window explorer to change the current folder to the ModelRisk installation folder: ≪ ...Program Files\Vose Software\ModelRiskSDK\≫.
5. Using ≪Ctrl-Shift≫, select ≪ModelRisk_Core.h≫ and ≪ModelRisk_Core.lib≫ and click the ≪Add≫ button in the bottom-right corner of the ≪Add existing item... ≫ window.
6. Now you can directly call all ModelRisk functions declared in ≪ModelRisk_Core.h≫.

Common rules for using C++ Vosecore functions (VCFs) and error handling

1. All VCF types are ≪bool≫. They return ≪true≫ if the calculation finished without errors, or ≪false≫ if one or more options are invalid.
2. If a VCF returns ≪false≫, a developer can use VoseCoreError() to get an error string (it returns char* buffer address).

3. All VCFs return the result to one or more *first* argument(s). For example, if a VCF returns a single value (for example, ≪VoseNormal_Core≫), the result will be returned to the first parameter of type ≪&double≫. If the VCF returns a set of values (for example, ≪VoseTimeGBM≫), then the result is placed in the first two arguments of ≪double*≫ and ≪long≫ types (the first argument is an array, the second its length). Some of the VCFs return more than two outputs (such as VoseTimeGARCHFit – it calculates and returns four values of type ≪double≫).

4. *Memory allocation rule:* for all VCFs that return arrays of values, the output array must be allocated by the developer (statically or dynamically) and its length must be equal to the second argument.

Using distribution core functions

All VoseDistribution function declarations must be in the following format:

```
VoseDistribution_Core(double rc,           //the output
                      type1 arg1[,type2 arg2 ...],  //distribution arguments
                      double *pU,           //pointer to the percentile value
                      int *pBoundsMode,     //address of «Bound Mode» flag
                      double *pMin,         //pointer to the minimum limit value
                      double *pMax,         //pointer to the maximum limit value
                      double *pShiftValue   //pointer to the shift value
                      );
```

The parameters of VCF distributions are as follows.

rc	Output value (double).
type1 arg1[,type2 arg2 ...]	One or several distribution arguments.
*pU	A pointer to the percentile value, which must be in [0 ... 1]. If this pointer = 0, the percentile will be randomly generated using the inbuilt Mersenne twister random number generator.
*pBoundsMode	Address of ≪Bound Mode≫ flag – used for bounded distributions. If the first bit is 0, the *pMin is interpreted as a percentile, otherwise as a value. If the second bit is 0, the *pMax is interpreted as a percentile, otherwise as a value.
*pMin, *pMax	A pointer to the minimum and maximum limits
*pShiftValue	A pointer to the shift value

Example of using the Vosedistribution core function

```
void ExampleFunction()
{
    double x,U,Shift,max,min,BoundMode;
```

```
    // Example of a call to VoseNormal(0,1) distribution
    if ( !VoseNormal_Core( x,mu,sigma,0,0,0,0,0)){
          printf("%s",VoseCoreError());
    }else{
    printf("Normal(0,1)=%.10g", x);
}


// Example of a call to VoseNormal(0,1,0) distribution- with percentile = 0
U=0.0;
    if ( !VoseNormal_Core( x,mu,sigma,&U,0,0,0,0)){
          printf("%s",VoseCoreError());
}else{
    printf("Normal(0,1)=%.10g", x);
}

// Example of a call to VoseNormal(0,1,,VoseShift(10)) distribution- with percentile = 0;
    if ( !VoseNormal_Core( x,mu,sigma,0,0,0,0,&Shift)){
          printf("%s",VoseCoreError());
}else{
    printf("Normal(0,1)=%.10g", x);
}


// Example of a call to VoseNormal(0,1,,VosePBounds(0.3,0.8)) distribution- with random
// generated percentile and bounded using percentiles of maximum and minimum limits
BoundMode = 3; // set 1-st and 2-nd bits to = 1
min = 0.3;
max = 0.8;
    if ( !VoseNormal_Core( x,mu,sigma,0,& BoundMode,&min,&max,0)){
          printf("%s",VoseCoreError());
}else{
    printf("Normal(0,1)=%.10g", x);
}

}
```

Appendix III

A compendium of distributions

Compiled by Michael van Hauwermeiren

The precision of a risk analysis relies very heavily on the appropriate use of probability distributions to represent the uncertainty and variability of the problem accurately. In my experience, inappropriate use of probability distributions has proved to be a very common failure of risk analysis models. It stems, in part, from an inadequate understanding of the theory behind probability distribution functions and, in part, from failing to appreciate the knock-on effects of using inappropriate distributions. This appendix is intended to alleviate the misunderstanding by providing a practical insight into the various types of probability distribution in common use.

I decided in this third edition to place the compendium of distributions in an appendix because they are used in so many different places within the book. This appendix gives a very complete summary of the distributions used in risk analysis, an explanation of where and why they are used, some representative plots and the most useful descriptive formulae from a risk analysis viewpoint. The distributions are given in alphabetical order. The list comprises all the distributions that we have ever used at Vose Consulting (and have therefore included in ModelRisk), so I am pretty confident that you will find the one you are looking for. Distributions often have several different names depending on the application, so if you don't find the distribution you are searching for here, please refer to the index which may suggest an alternative name.

Most risk analysis and statistical software offer a wide variety of distributions, so the choice can be bewildering. I have therefore started this appendix with a list of different applications and the distributions that you might find most useful. Then I offer a little guide on how to read the probability equations that feature so prominently in this appendix: people's eyes tend to glaze over when they see probability equations, but with a few simple rules you will be able rapidly to "read" the relevant parts of an equation and ignore the rest, which can give you a much more intuitive feel for a distribution's behaviour.

III.1 Discrete and Continuous Distributions

The most basic distinguishing property between probability distributions is whether they are continuous or discrete.

III.1.1 Discrete distributions

A discrete distribution may take one of a set of identifiable values, each of which has a calculable probability of occurrence. Discrete distributions are used to model parameters like the number of bridges a roading scheme may need, the number of key personnel to be employed or the number of customers that will arrive at a service station in a hour. Clearly, variables such as these can only take specific values: one cannot build half a bridge, employ 2.7 people or serve 13.6 customers.

The vertical scale of a relative frequency plot of a discrete distribution is the actual probability of occurrence, sometimes called the *probability mass*. The sum of all these values must add up to 1.

Examples of discrete distributions are: binomial, geometric, hypergeometric, inverse hypergeometric, negative binomial, Poisson and, of course, the generalised discrete distribution. Figure III.1 illustrates a discrete distribution modelling the number of footbridges that are to be built across a planned stretch of motorway. There is a 30 %

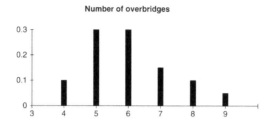

Figure III.1 Example of a discrete variable.

chance that six bridges will be built, a 10 % chance that eight bridges will be built, etc. The sum of these probabilities (10 % + 30 % + 30 % + 15 % + 10 % + 5%) must equal unity.

III.1.2 Continuous distributions

A continuous distribution is used to represent a variable that can take any value within a defined range (domain). For example, the height of an adult English male picked at random has a continuous distribution because the height of a person is essentially infinitely divisible. We could measure his height to the nearest centimetre, millimetre, tenth of a millimetre, etc. The scale can be repeatedly divided up, generating more and more possible values.

Properties like time, mass and distance that are infinitely divisible are modelled using continuous distributions. In practice, we also use continuous distributions to model variables that are, in truth, discrete but where the gap between allowable values is insignificant; for example, project cost (which is discrete with steps of one penny, one cent, etc.), exchange rate (which is only quoted to a few significant figures), number of employees in a large organisation, etc.

The vertical scale of a relative frequency plot of an input continuous probability distribution is the probability density. It does not represent the actual probability of the corresponding x-axis value since that probability is zero. Instead, it represents the probability per x-axis unit of generating a value within a very small range around the x-axis value.

In a continuous relative frequency distribution, the area under the curve must equal 1. This means that the vertical scale must change according to the units used for the horizontal scale. For example, the probability in Figure III.2(a) shows a theoretical distribution of the cost of a project using Normal(£4 200 000, £350 000). Since this is a continuous distribution, the cost of the project being precisely £4M is zero. The vertical scale reads a value of 9.7×10^{-7} (about one in a million). The x-axis units are £1, so this y-axis reading means that there is a one in a million chance that the project cost will be £4M plus or minus 50p (a range of £1). By comparison, Figure III.2(b) shows the same distribution but using million pounds as the scale, i.e. Normal(4.2, 0.35). The y-axis value at $x = $ £4 M is 0.97, 1 million times the above value. This does not, however, mean that there is a 97 % chance of being between £3.5M and £4.5M, because the probability density varies very considerably over this range. The logic used in interpreting the 9.7×10^{-7} value for Figure III.2(a) is an approximation that is valid there because the probability density is essentially constant over that range (£4M ± 50p).

III.2 Bounded and Unbounded Distributions

A distribution that is confined to lie between two determined values is said to be *bounded*. Examples of bounded distributions are: uniform – between minimum and maximum; triangular – between minimum and maximum; beta – between 0 and 1; and binomial – between 0 and n.

A distribution that is *unbounded* theoretically extends from minus infinity to plus infinity. Examples are: normal, logistic and extreme value.

A distribution that is constrained at either end is said to be *partially bounded*. Examples are: chi-square (>0), exponential (>0), Pareto ($>a$), Poisson (≥ 0) and Weibull (>0).

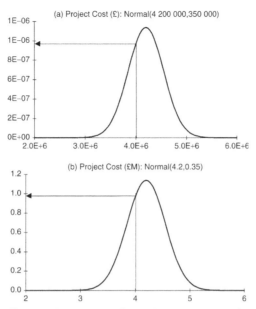

Figure III.2 Example of the effect on the *y* scale of a probability density function by changing the *x*-scale units: (a) units of £1; (b) units of £1M.

Unbounded and partially bounded distributions may, at times, need to be constrained to remove the tail of the distribution so that nonsensical values are avoided. For example, using a normal distribution to model sales volume opens up the chance of generating a negative value. If the probability of generating a negative value is significant, and we want to stick to using a normal distribution, we must constrain the model in some way to eliminate any negative sales volume figure being generated.

Monte Carlo simulation software usually provide truncated distributions for this purpose as well as filtering facilities. ModelRisk uses the XBounds or PBounds functions to bound a univariate distribution at either specified values or percentiles respectively. One can also build logic into the model that rejects nonsensical values. For example, using the IF function A2: $= \mathrm{IF}(\mathrm{A1} < 0, \mathrm{ERR}(), 0)$ only allows values into cell A2 from cell A1 that are ≥ 0 and produces an error in cell A2 otherwise. However, if there are several distributions being bounded this way, or you are using extreme bounds, you will lose a lot of the iterations in your simulation. If you are faced with the problem of needing to constrain the tail of a distribution, it is also worth questioning whether you are using the appropriate distribution in the first place.

III.3 Parametric and Non-Parametric Distributions

There is a very useful distinction to be made between model-based parametric and empirical non-parametric distributions. By "model-based" I mean a distribution whose shape is born of the mathematics describing a theoretical problem. For example: an exponential distribution is a waiting time distribution whose function is the direct result of assuming that there is a constant instantaneous probability of an event occurring; a lognormal distribution is derived from assuming that $\ln[x]$ is normally distributed, etc.

By "empirical distribution" I mean a distribution whose mathematics is defined by the shape that is required. For example: a triangular distribution is defined by its minimum, mode and maximum values; a histogram distribution is defined by its range, the number of classes and the height of each class. The defining parameters for general distributions are features of the graph shape. Empirical distributions include: cumulative, discrete, histogram, relative, triangular and uniform. Chapters 10 and 14 discussed the reasons for using these distinctions. They fall under the "empirical distribution" or non-parametric class and are intuitively easy to understand, extremely flexible and therefore very useful.

Model-based or parametric distributions require a greater knowledge of the underlying assumptions if they are to be used properly. Without that knowledge, analysts may find it very difficult to justify the use of the chosen distribution type and to gain peer confidence in their models. They will probably also find it difficult to make alterations should more information become available.

I am a keen advocate of using non-parametric distributions. I believe that parametric distributions should only be selected if: (a) the theory underpinning the distribution applies to the particular problem; (b) it is generally accepted that a particular distribution has proven to be very accurate for modelling a specific variable without actually having any theory to support the observation; (c) the distribution approximately fits the expert opinion being modelled and the required level of accuracy is not very high; (d) one wishes to use a distribution that has a long tail extending beyond the observed minimum or maximum. These issues are discussed in more detail in Chapter 10.

III.4 Univariate and Multivariate Distributions

Univariate distributions describe a single parameter or variable and are used to model a parameter or variable that is not probabilistically linked to any other in the model. Multivariate distributions describe several parameters or variables whose values are probabilistically linked in some way. In most cases, we create the probabilistic links via one of several correlation methods. However, there are a few multivariate distributions that have specific, very useful purposes and are therefore worth studying more.

III.5 Lists of Applications and the Most Useful Distributions

Bounded versus unbounded

The following tables organise distributions according to whether their limits are bounded. *Italics* indicate non-parametric distributions.

Univariate Distributions

	Continuous	*Discrete*
Unbounded	Cauchy Error function Error Hyperbolic secant JohnsonU Laplace Logistic Normal Student *t* F	
Left bounded	Bradford Burr Chi Chi-square Dagum	Beta–geometric Beta–negative binomial Delaporte Geometric Inverse hypergeometric

	Continuous	Discrete
	Erlang Exponential Extreme-value max Extreme-value min Fatigue life Fréchet Gamma Generalised logistic Inverse gaussian Loggamma Loglogistic LogLaplace Lognormal Lognormal (base E) Lognormal (base B) Pareto (first kind) Pareto (second kind) Pearson5 Pearson6 Rayleigh Weibull	Logarithmic Negative binomial Poisson Pólya
Left and right bounded	Beta Beta4 *Cumulative ascending* *Cumulative descending* *Histogram* JohnsonB Kumaraswamy Kumaraswamy4 *Modified PERT* Ogive *PERT* Reciprocal *Relative* *Split triangle* *Triangle* Uniform	Bernoulli Beta–binomial Binomial *Discrete* *Discrete uniform* Hypergeometric *Step uniform*

Multivariate Distributions

	Continuous	Discrete
Unbounded	Multivariate normal	
Left bounded		Negative multinomial 1 Negative multinomial 2
Left and right bounded	Dirichlet	Multinomial Multivariate hypergeometric Multivariate inverse hypergeometric 1 Multivariate inverse hypergeometric 2

Frequency distributions

The following distributions are often used to model events that are counted, like outbreaks, economic shocks, machine failures, deaths, etc.:

Bernoulli	Special case of binomial with one individual who may convert.
Binomial	Used when there is a group of individuals (trials) that may convert (succeed). For example, used in life insurance to answer how many policyholders will claim in a year.
Delaporte	Events occur randomly with a randomly varying risk level, the most flexible in modelling frequency patterns.
Logarithmic	Peaks at 1, looks exponential.
NegBin	Events occur randomly with a randomly varying risk level, more restrictive than the Pólya.
Poisson	Events occur randomly with constant risk level.
Pólya	Events occur randomly with a randomly varying risk level.

Risk impact

A risk is an event that may or may not occur, and the impact distribution describes the "cost" should it occur. For most applications, a continuous distribution that is right skewed and left bounded is most applicable. For situations like a foot and mouth disease outbreak, the number of sheep lost will of course be discrete, but such variables are usually modelled with continuous distributions anyway (and you can use ROUND(..., 0), of course:

Bradford	Looks exponential with min and max bounds.
Burr	Appealing because of its flexibility of shape.
Dagum	Lognormal looking with two shape parameters for more control, and a scale parameter.
Exponential	Ski-slope shape defined by its mean.
Ogive	Used to construct a distribution directly from data.
Loggamma	Can have a very long right tail.
Loglogistic	Impact is a function of several variables that are either correlated or one dominates.
Lognormal	Impact is a function of several uncorrelated variables.
Pareto (two kinds)	Ski-slope shape with the longest tail, so often used for conservative modelling of the extreme right tail.

Time or trials until . . .

Beta–geometric	Failures before one beta–binomial success.
Beta–negative binomial	Failures before s beta–binomial successes.
Erlang	Time until m Poisson counts.
Exponential	Time until one Poisson count.
Fatigue life	Time until gradual breakdown.
Geometric	Failures before one binomial success.

Gamma	Time until α Poisson counts, but used more generally.
Inverse hypergeometric	Failures before s hypergeometric successes.
Inverse gaussian	Theoretical waiting time use is esoteric, but the distribution has some flexibility through its parameters.
Lognormal	Time until an event that is the product of many variables. Used quite generally.
Negative binomial	Failures before s binomial successes.
Negative multinomial	Failures before s multinomial successes.
Rayleigh	A special case of the Weibull. Also distance to nearest, Poisson-distributed, neighbour.
Weibull	Time until an event where the instantaneous likelihood of the event occurring changes (usually increases) over time. Used a great deal in reliability engineering.

Variations in a financial market

We used to be happy to assume that random variations in a stock's return, an interest rate, were normally distributed. Normal distributions made the equations easier. Financial analysts now use simulation more so have become a bit more adventurous:

Cauchy	An extreme distribution a little like a normal but with infinite variance.
Extreme value (max, min)	Models the extreme movement, but tricky to use.
Generalised error (aka GED, error)	Very flexible distribution that will morph between a uniform, (nearly) a normal, Laplace, etc.
Inverse gaussian	Used in place of lognormal when it has a right tail that is too heavy.
Laplace	Defined by mean and variance like the normal, but takes a tent shape. Favoured because it gives longer tails.
Lévy	Appealing because it belongs to the "stable" family of distributions, gives fatter tails than a normal.
Logistic	Like a normal but more peaked.
Lognormal	Assumes that the market is randomly affected by very many multiplicative random elements.
Normal	Assumes that the market is randomly affected by very many additive random elements.
Poisson	Used to model the occurrence of jumps in the market.
Slash	A little like a normal, but with fatter tails, tending towards Cauchy tails.
Student	When rescaled and shifted, it is like the normal but with more kurtosis when v is small.

How large something is

How much milk a cow will produce, how big will a sale be, how big a wave, etc. We'll often have data and want to fit them to a distribution, but which one?

Bradford	Like a truncated Pareto. Used in advertising, but worth looking at.
Burr	Appealing because of its flexibility of shape.
Dagum	Flexible. Has been used to model aggregate fire losses.
Exponential	Ski-slope shape peaking at zero and defined by its mean.
Extreme value	Models extremes (min, max) of variables belonging to the exponential family of distributions. Difficult to use. VoseLargest and VoseSmallest are much more flexible and transparent.
Generalised error (aka GED, error)	Very flexible distribution that will morph between a uniform, (nearly) a normal, Laplace, etc.
Hyperbolic–secant	Like a normal but with narrower shoulders, so used to fit to data where a normal isn't quite right.
Inverse gaussian	Used in place of lognormal when it has a right tail that is too heavy.
Johnson bounded	Can have any combination of skewness and kurtosis, so pretty flexible at fitting to data, but rarely used.
Loggamma	If the variable is the product of a number of exponentially distributed variables, it may look loggamma distributed.
LogLaplace	The asymmetric logLaplace distribution takes a pretty strange shape, but has a history of being fitted to particle size data and similar.
Loglogistic	Has a history of being fitted to data for a fair few financial variables.
Lognormal	See central limit theorem. Size is a function of the product of a number of random variables. Classic example is oil reserves = area * thickness * porosity * gas:oil ratio * recovery rate.
Normal	See central limit theorem. Size is a function of the sum of a number of random variables, e.g. a cow's milk yield may be a function of genetics and farm care and mental well-being (it's been proven) and nutrition and …
Pareto	Ski-slope shape with the longest tail, so often used for conservative modelling of the extreme right tail, but generally fits the main body of data badly, so consider splicing (see VoseSplice function, for example).
Rayleigh	Wave heights, electromagnetic peak power or similar.
Student	If the variance of a normal distribution is also a random variable (specifically chi-square), the variable will take a Student distribution. So think about something that should be roughly normal with constant mean but where the standard deviation is not constant, e.g. errors in measurement with varying quality of instrument or operator.
Weibull	Much like the Rayleigh, including modelling wind speed.

Expert estimates

The following distributions are often used to model subject matter experts' estimates because they are intuitive, easy to control and/or flexible:

Bernoulli	Used to model a risk event occurring or not.
Beta4	A min, max and two shape parameters. Can be reparameterised (i.e. the PERT distribution). Shape parameters are difficult to use.
Bradford	A min, max and a ski-slope shape in between with controllable drop.
Combined	Allows you to combine correctly several SME estimates for the same parameter and weight them.
Cumulative (ascending and descending)	Good when expert thinks of a series of "probability P of being below x".
Discrete	Specify several possible outcomes with weights for each.
Johnson bounded	VISIFIT software available that will match to expert estimate.
Kumaraswamy	Controllable distribution, similar to Beta4.
Modified PERT	PERT distribution with extra control for spread.
PERT	A min, max and mode. Tends to place too little emphasis on tails if the distribution is quite skewed.
Relative	Allows you to construct your own shape.
Split triangle	Defined by low, medium and high percentiles. Splices two triangular distributions together. Intuitive.
Triangle	A min, mode and max. Some software also offer low and high percentiles as inputs. Tends to overemphasise tails.
Uniform	A min and max. Useful to flag when SME (see Section 14.4) has very little idea.

III.6 How to Read Probability Distribution Equations

The intention of this section is to help you better understand how to read and use the equations that describe distributions. For each distribution (except those with outrageously complicated moment formulae) in this appendix I give the following equations:

- probability mass function (for discrete distributions);
- probability density function (for continuous distributions);
- cumulative distribution function (where available);
- mean;
- mode;
- variance;
- skewness;
- kurtosis.

There are many other distribution properties (e.g. moment-generating functions, raw moments), but they are of little general use in risk analysis and would leave you facing yet more daunting pages of equations to wade through.

III.6.1 Location, scale and shape parameters

In this book, and in ModelRisk, we have parameterised distributions to reflect the most common usage, and where there are two or more common parameterisations we have used the one that is most useful to model risk. So I use, for example, mean and standard deviation a lot for consistency between distributions, or other parameters that most readily connect to the stochastic process to which the distribution is most commonly applied. Another way to describe parameters is to categorise them as location, scale and shape, which can disconnect the parameters from their usual meaning but is sometimes helpful in understanding how a distribution will change with variation in the parameter value.

A *location parameter* controls the position of the distribution on the x axis. It should therefore appear in the same way in the equations for the mode and mean – two measures of location. So, if a location parameter increases by 3 units, then the mean and mode should increase by 3 units. For example, the mean μ of a normal distribution is also the mode, and can be called a location parameter. The same applies for the Laplace, for example. A lot of distributions are extended by including a shift parameter (e.g. VoseShift), which has the effect of moving the distribution along the x axis and is a location parameter.

A *scale parameter* controls the spread of the distribution on the x axis. Its square should therefore appear in the equation for a distribution's variance. For example, β is the scale parameter for the gamma, Weibull and logistic distributions, σ for the normal and Laplace distributions, b for the ExtremeValueMax, ExtremeValueMin and Rayleigh distributions, etc.

A *shape parameter* controls the shape (e.g. skewness, kurtosis) of the distribution. It will appear in the pdf in a way that controls the manipulation of x in a non-linear fashion, usually as a coefficient of x. For example, the Pareto distribution has the pdf

$$f(x) \propto \frac{1}{x^{\theta+1}}$$

where θ is a shape parameter, as it changes the functional form of the relationship between $f(x)$ and x. Other examples you can look at are ν for a GED, Student and chi-square distribution, and α for a gamma distribution. A distribution may sometimes have two shape parameters, e.g. α_1 and α_2 for the beta distribution, and ν_1 and ν_2 for the F distribution.

If there is no shape parameter, the distribution always takes the same shape (like the Cauchy, exponential, extreme value, Laplace, logistic and normal).

III.6.2 Understanding distribution equations

Probability mass function (pmf) and probability density function (pdf)

The pmf or pdf is the most common equation used to define a distribution, for two reasons. The first is that it gives the shape of the density (or mass) curve, which is the easiest way to recognise and review a distribution. The second is that the pmf (or pdf) is always in a useful form, whereas the cdf frequently doesn't have a closed form (meaning a simple algebraic identity rather than expressed as an integral or summation).

The pmfs must sum to 1, and the pdfs must integrate to 1, in order to obey the basic probability rule that the sum of all probabilities equals 1. This means that a pmf or pdf equation has two parts: a function of x, the possible value of the parameter; and a normalising part that normalises the distribution to sum to unity. For example, the generalised error distribution pdf takes the (rather complicated) form

$$f(x) = \frac{K}{\beta} \exp\left[-\frac{1}{2} \left| \frac{x-\mu}{\beta} \right|^{\nu} \right] \tag{III.1}$$

where

$$K = \frac{\nu}{\Gamma\left(\frac{1}{\nu}\right) 2^{1+\frac{1}{\nu}}} \text{ and } \beta = \frac{\sigma}{2^{\frac{1}{\nu}}} \sqrt{\frac{\Gamma\left(\frac{1}{\nu}\right)}{\Gamma\left(\frac{3}{\nu}\right)}}$$

The part that varies with x is simply

$$\exp\left[-\frac{1}{2}\left|\frac{x-\mu}{\beta}\right|^{\nu}\right]$$

so we can write

$$f(x) \propto \exp\left[-\frac{1}{2}\left|\frac{x-\mu}{\beta}\right|^{\nu}\right] \tag{III.2}$$

The rest of Equation (III.1), i.e. K/β, is a normalising constant for a given set of parameters and ensures that the area under the curve equals unity. Equation (III.2) is sufficient to define or recognise the distribution and allows us to concentrate on how the distribution behaves with changes to the parameter values. In fact, probability mathematicians frequently work with just the component that is a function of x, keeping in the back of their mind that it will be normalised eventually.

For example, the $(x - \mu)$ part shows us that the distribution is shifted μ along the x axis (a location parameter), and the division by β means that the distribution is rescaled by this factor (a scale parameter). The parameter ν changes the functional form of the distribution. For example, for $\nu = 2$

$$f(x) \propto \exp\left[-\frac{1}{2}\left(\frac{x-\mu}{\beta}\right)^{2}\right]$$

Compare that with the normal distribution density function

$$f(x) \propto \exp\left[-\frac{1}{2}\left(\frac{x-\mu}{\sigma}\right)^{2}\right]$$

So we can say that, when $\nu = 2$, the GED is normally distributed with mean μ and standard deviation β. The functional form (the part in x) gives us sufficient information to say this, as we know that the multiplying constant must adjust to keep the area under the curve equal to unity.

Similarly, for $\nu = 1$ we have

$$f(x) \propto \exp\left[-\frac{1}{2}\left|\frac{x-\mu}{\beta}\right|\right]$$

which is the density function for the Laplace distribution.

So we can say that, when $\nu = 1$, the GED takes a Laplace(μ, β) distribution.

The same idea applies to discrete distributions. For example, the Logarithmic(θ) distribution has the pmf

$$f(x) = \frac{-\theta^{x}}{x \ln(1-\theta)} \propto \frac{-\theta^{x}}{x}$$

where $\frac{1}{\ln(1-\theta)}$ is the normalising part because it turns out that $\log(x)$ can be expressed as an infinite series so that

$$\sum_{x=1}^{\infty} \frac{-\theta^{x}}{x} = \ln(1-\theta)$$

Cumulative distribution function (cdf)

The cdf gives us the probability of being less than or equal to the variable value x. For discrete distributions this is simply the sum of the pmf up to x, so reviewing its equation is not more informative than the pmf equation. However, for continuous distributions the cdf can take a simpler form than the corresponding pdf. For example, for a Weibull distribution

$$f(x) = \alpha \beta^{-\alpha} x^{\alpha-1} \exp\left[-\left(\frac{x}{\beta}\right)^{\alpha}\right] \propto x^{\alpha-1} \exp\left[-\left(\frac{x}{\beta}\right)^{\alpha}\right]$$

$$f(x) = 1 - \exp\left[-\left(\frac{x}{\beta}\right)^{\alpha}\right] \tag{III.3}$$

The latter is simpler to envisage.

Many cdfs have a component that involves the exponential function (e.g. Weibull, exponential, extreme value, Laplace, logistic, Rayleigh). $\text{Exp}(-\infty) = 0$ and $\text{Exp}(0) = 1$, which is the range of $F(x)$, so you'll often see functions of the form

$$F(x) = \exp(-g(x))$$

or

$$F(x) = 1 - \exp(-g(x))$$

where $g(x)$ is some function of x that goes from zero to infinity or infinity to zero monotonically (meaning always increasing) with increasing x. For example, Equation (III.3) for the Weibull distribution shows us:

- The value β scales x.
- When $x = 0$, $F(x) = 1 - 1 = 0$, so the variable has a minimum of 0.
- When $x = \infty$, $F(x) = 1 - 0 = 1$, so the variable has a maximum of ∞.
- α makes the distribution shorter, because it "amplifies" x. For example (leaving $\beta = 1$), if $\alpha = 2$ and $x = 3$ it calculates $3^2 = 9$, whereas if $\alpha = 4$ it calculates $3^4 = 81$.

Mean μ

The mean of a probability distribution is useful to know for several reasons:

- It gives a sense of the location of the distribution.
- The central limit theorem (CLT) uses the mean.
- Knowing the equation of the mean can help us understand the distribution. For example, a Gamma(α, β) distribution can be used to model the time to wait to observe α independent events that occur randomly in time with a mean time to occurrence of β. It makes intuitive sense that, "on average", you need to wait, $\alpha * \beta$ which is the mean of the distribution.
- We sometimes want to approximate one distribution with another to make the mathematics easier. Knowing the equations for the mean and variance can help us find a distribution with these same moments.
- Because of CLT, the mean propagates through a model much more precisely than the mode or median. So, for example, if you replaced a distribution in a simulation model with its mean, the output mean value will usually be close to the output mean when the model includes that distribution. However, the same does not apply as well by replacing a distribution with its median, and often much worse still if one uses the mode.
- We can determine the mean and other moments of an aggregate distribution if we know the mean and other moments of the frequency and severity distributions.
- A distribution is often fitted to data by matching the data's mean and variance to the mean and variance equations of the distribution – a technique known as the method of moments.

When the pdf of a distribution is of the form $f(x) = g(x - z)$, where $g()$ is any function and z is a fixed value, the equation for the mean will be a linear function of z.

Mode

The mode is the location of the peak of a distribution and is the most intuitive parameter to consider – the "most likely value to occur".

If the mode has the same equation as the mean, it tells us the distribution is symmetric. If the mode is less than the mean (e.g. for the gamma distribution, mode $= (\alpha - 1)\beta$ and mean $= \alpha\beta$) we know the distribution is right skewed, if the mode is greater than the mean the distribution is left skewed. The mode is our "best guess", so it can be informative to see how the mode varies with the distribution's parameters. For example, the Beta(α, β) has a mode of

$$\frac{\alpha - 1}{\alpha + \beta - 2} \text{ if } \alpha > 1, \beta > 1$$

A Beta($s + 1, n - s + 1$) distribution is often used to estimate a binomial probability where we have observed s successes in n trials. This gives a mode of s/n: the fraction of our trials that were successes is our "best guess" at the true (long-run) probability, which makes intuitive sense.

Variance V

The variance gives a measure of the spread of a distribution. I give equations for the variance rather than the mean because it avoids having square-root signs all the time, and because probability mathematicians work in terms of variance rather than standard deviation. However, it can be useful to take the square root of the variance equation (i.e. the standard deviation σ) to help make more sense of it. For example, the Logistic(α, β) distribution has variance

$$V = \frac{\beta^2 \pi^2}{3}$$

so

$$\sigma = \sqrt{V} = \frac{\beta \pi}{\sqrt{3}}$$

which shows us that β is a scaling parameter: the distribution's spread is proportional to β. Another example – the Pareto(θ, a) distribution – has variance

$$V = \frac{a^2 \theta}{(\theta - 1)^2 (\theta - 2)}$$

so

$$\sigma = a \sqrt{\frac{\theta}{(\theta - 1)^2 (\theta - 2)}}$$

which shows us that a is a scaling parameter.

Skewness S

Skewness and kurtosis equations are not that important, so feel free to skip this bit. Skewness is the expected value of $(x - \mu)^3$ divided by $V^{3/2}$, so you'll often see a $\frac{...}{\sqrt{...}}$ or $\frac{...}{(...)^{3/2}}$ component. You can tell whether a distribution is left or right skewed and when by looking at this equation, bearing in mind the possible values of each parameter.

For example, the skewness equation for the negative binomial is

$$\frac{2 - p}{\sqrt{s(1 - p)}}$$

Since p lies on $(0, 1)$ and s is a positive integer, the skewness is always positive.

The beta distribution has skewness

$$2 \frac{(\beta - \alpha)}{(\alpha + \beta + 2)} \sqrt{\frac{\alpha + \beta + 1}{\alpha\beta}}$$

and, since α and β are > 0, this means because of the $(\beta - \alpha)$ term it has negative skewness when $\alpha > \beta$, positive skewness when $\alpha < \beta$ and zero skewness when $\alpha = \beta$.

An exponential distribution has a skewness of 2, which I find a helpful gauge against which to compare.

Kurtosis K

Kurtosis is the expected value of $(x - \mu)^4$ divided by V^2, so you'll often see a $\frac{\cdots}{(\ldots)^2}$ component.

The normal distribution has a kurtosis of 3, and that's what we usually compare against (the uniform distribution has a kurtosis of 1.8, and the Laplace a kurtosis of 6, which are two fairly extreme points of reference).

The Poisson(λ) distribution, for example, has a kurtosis of

$$3 + \frac{1}{\lambda}$$

which means, when taken together with the behaviour of other moments, the bigger the value of λ, the closer the distribution is to a normal.

The same story applies for the Student(ν) distribution, for example, which has a kurtosis of

$$3\left(\frac{\nu - 2}{\nu - 4}\right)$$

so the larger ν, the closer the kurtosis is to 3.

The kurtosis of a Lognormal(μ, σ) distribution is $z^4 + 2z^3 + 3z^2 - 3$, where

$$z = 1 + \frac{\mu}{\sigma}$$

What does that imply about when the lognormal will look normal?

III.7 The Distributions

III.7.1 Univariate distributions

# Bernoulli
VoseBernoulli(p)

Graphs

The Bernoulli distribution is a binomial distribution with $n = 1$. The Bernoulli distribution returns a 1 with probability p and a 0 otherwise.

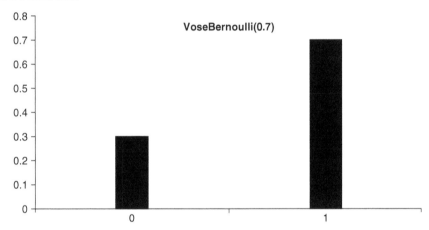

Uses

The Bernoulli distribution, named after Swiss scientist Jakob Bernoulli, is very useful for modelling a risk event that may or may not occur.

VoseBernoulli(0.2) * VoseLognormal(12, 72) models a risk event with a probability of occurring of 20 % and an impact, should it occur, equal to Lognormal(12, 72).

Equations

Probability mass function	$f(x) = p^x (1 - p)^{1-x}$
Cumulative distribution function	$F(0) = 1 - p, F(1) = 1$
Parameter restriction	$0 \le p \le 1$
Domain	$x = \{0, 1\}$
Mean	p
Mode	$\lfloor 2p \rfloor$
Variance	$p(1 - p)$
Skewness	$\dfrac{1 - 2p}{\sqrt{p(1 - p)}}$
Kurtosis	$\dfrac{1}{p(1 - p)} - 3$

# Beta
VoseBeta(α, β)

Graphs

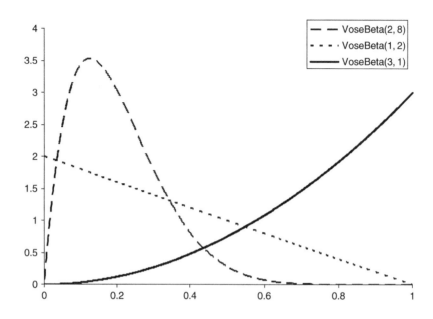

Uses

The beta distribution has two main uses:

- As the description of uncertainty or random variation of a probability, fraction or prevalence.
- As a useful distribution one can rescale and shift to create distributions with a wide range of shapes and over any finite range. As such, it is sometimes used to model expert opinion, for example in the form of the PERT distribution.

The beta distribution is the conjugate prior (meaning it has the same functional form, and is therefore also often called the "convenience prior") to the binomial likelihood function in Bayesian inference, and, as such, is often used to describe the uncertainty about a binomial probability, given a number of trials n have been made with a number of recorded successes s. In this situation, α is set to the value $(s + x)$ and β is set to $(n - s + y)$, where Beta(x, y) is the prior.

Equations

Probability density function	$f(x) = \dfrac{(x - \min)^{\alpha-1}(\max - x)^{\beta-1}}{B(\alpha, \beta)(\max - \min)^{\alpha+\beta-1}}$ where $B(\alpha, \beta)$ is a beta function
Cumulative distribution function	No closed form
Parameter restriction	$\alpha > 0, \beta > 0, \min < \max$
Domain	$\min \leq x \leq \max$
Mean	$\min + \dfrac{\alpha}{\alpha + \beta}(\max - \min)$

Mode	$\min + \dfrac{\alpha - 1}{\alpha + \beta - 2}(\max - \min)$ if $\alpha > 1, \beta > 1$ min, max if $\alpha < 1, \beta < 1$ min if $\alpha < 1, \beta \geq 1$ or if $\alpha = 1, \beta > 1$ max if $\alpha \geq 1, \beta < 1$ or if $\alpha > 1, \beta = 1$ does not uniquely exist if $\alpha = 1, \beta = 1$
Variance	$\dfrac{\alpha\beta}{(\alpha + \beta)^2(\alpha + \beta + 1)}(\max - \min)^2$
Skewness	$2\dfrac{\beta - \alpha}{\alpha + \beta + 2}\sqrt{\dfrac{\alpha + \beta + 1}{\alpha\beta}}$
Kurtosis	$3\dfrac{(\alpha + \beta + 1)\,(2\,(\alpha + \beta)^2 + \alpha\beta\,(\alpha + \beta - 6))}{\alpha\beta\,(\alpha + \beta + 2)(\alpha + \beta + 3)}$

# Beta4
VoseBeta4(α, β, min, max)

Graphs

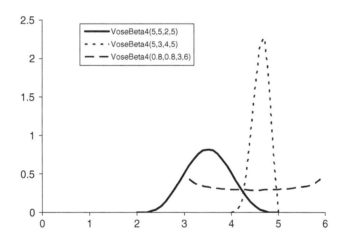

Uses

See the beta distribution

Equations

Probability density function	$f(x) = \dfrac{(x - \min)^{\alpha - 1}(\max - x)^{\beta - 1}}{B(\alpha, \beta)(\max - \min)^{\alpha + \beta - 1}}$ where $B(\alpha, \beta)$ is a beta function
Cumulative distribution function	No closed form
Parameter restriction	$\alpha > 0$, $\beta > 0$, min $<$ max
Domain	$\min \leq x \leq \max$

Mean	$\min + \dfrac{\alpha}{\alpha + \beta}(\max - \min)$
Mode	$\min + \dfrac{\alpha - 1}{\alpha + \beta - 2}(\max - \min)$ *if* $\alpha > 1, \beta > 1$ $\min, \max$ $\quad$ if $\alpha < 1, \beta < 1$ $\min$ $\quad$ if $\alpha < 1, \beta > 1$ or if $\alpha = 1, \beta > 1$ $\max$ $\quad$ if $\alpha \geq 1, \beta < 1$ or if $\alpha > 1, \beta = 1$ does not uniquely exist $\quad$ if $\alpha = 1, \beta = 1$
Variance	$\dfrac{\alpha\,\beta}{(\alpha + \beta)^2(\alpha + \beta + 1)}(\max - \min)^2$
Skewness	$2\,\dfrac{\beta - \alpha}{\alpha + \beta + 2}\sqrt{\dfrac{\alpha + \beta + 1}{\alpha\,\beta}}$
Kurtosis	$3\,\dfrac{(\alpha + \beta + 1)\,(2\,(\alpha + \beta)^2 + \alpha\,\beta\,(\alpha + \beta - 6))}{\alpha\,\beta\,(\alpha + \beta + 2)(\alpha + \beta + 3)}$

Beta–Binomial

VoseBetaBinomial(n, α, β)

Graphs

A beta–binomial distribution returns a discrete value between 0 and n. Examples of a Beta–Binomial(30, 10, 7) and a Beta–Binomial(20, 12, 10) distribution are given below.

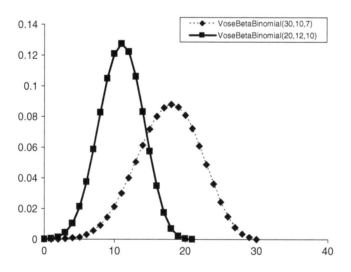

Uses

The beta–binomial distribution is used to model the number of successes in n binomial trials (usually $=$ Binomial(n, p)) but when the probability of success p is also a random variable and can be adequately described by a beta distribution.

The extreme flexibility of the shape of the beta distribution means that it is often a very fair representation of the randomness of p.

The probability of success varies randomly, but in any one scenario that probability applies to *all* trials. For example, you might consider using the beta–Binomial distribution to model:

- the number of cars that crash in a race of n cars, where the predominant factor is not the skill of the individual driver but the weather on the day;
- the number of bottles of wine from a producer that are bad, where the predominant factor is not how each bottle is treated but something to do with the batch as a whole;
- the number of people who get ill at a wedding from n invited, all having a taste of the delicious soufflé, unfortunately made with contaminated eggs, where their risk is dominated not by their individual immune system, or the amount they eat, but by the level of contamination of the shared meal.

Comments

The beta–binomial distribution is always more spread than its best-fitting binomial distribution, because the beta distribution adds extra randomness. Thus, when a binomial distribution does not match observations, because the observations exhibit too much spread, a beta–binomial distribution is often used instead.

Equations

Probability mass function	$f(x) = \binom{n}{x} \dfrac{\Gamma(\alpha + x)\Gamma(n + \beta - x)\Gamma(\alpha + \beta)}{\Gamma(\alpha + \beta + n)\Gamma(\alpha)\Gamma(\beta)}$
Cumulative distribution function	$F(x) = \displaystyle\sum_{i=0}^{x} \binom{n}{i} \dfrac{\Gamma(\alpha + i)\Gamma(n + \beta - i)\Gamma(\alpha + \beta)}{\Gamma(\alpha + \beta + n)\Gamma(\alpha)\Gamma(\beta)}$
Parameter restriction	$\alpha > 0;\ \beta > 0;\ n = \{0, 1, 2, \ldots\}$
Domain	$x = \{0, 1, 2, \ldots, n\}$
Mean	$n\dfrac{\alpha}{\alpha + \beta}$
Mode	$\begin{cases} \left[n\left(\dfrac{\alpha - 1}{\alpha + \beta - 2} + \dfrac{1}{2} \right) \right] & \text{if } \alpha > 1, \beta > 1 \\ 0, n & \text{if } \alpha < 1, \beta < 1 \\ 0 & \text{if } \alpha < 1, \beta \geq 1 \text{ or if } \alpha = 1, \beta > 1 \\ n & \text{if } \alpha \geq 1, \beta < 1 \text{ or if } \alpha > 1, \beta = 1 \\ \text{does not uniquely exist} & \text{if } \alpha = 1, \beta = 1 \end{cases}$
Variance	$n\dfrac{\alpha\beta(\alpha + \beta + n)}{(\alpha + \beta)^2(\alpha + \beta + 1)}$
Skewness	$(\alpha + \beta + 2n)\dfrac{(\beta - \alpha)}{(\alpha + \beta + 2)} \sqrt{\dfrac{(1 + \alpha + \beta)}{n\alpha\beta(n + \alpha + \beta)}}$

Kurotosis

$$\dfrac{(\alpha + \beta)^2(1 + \alpha + \beta)}{n\alpha\beta(\alpha + \beta + 2)(\alpha + \beta + 3)(\alpha + \beta + n)}$$
$$\left((\alpha + \beta)(\alpha + \beta - 1 + 6n) + 3\alpha\beta(n - 2) + 6n^2 - \dfrac{3\alpha\beta n(6 - n)}{\alpha + \beta} - \dfrac{18\alpha\beta n^2}{(\alpha + \beta)^2} \right)$$

# Beta–Geometric
VoseBetaGeometric(α, β)

Graphs

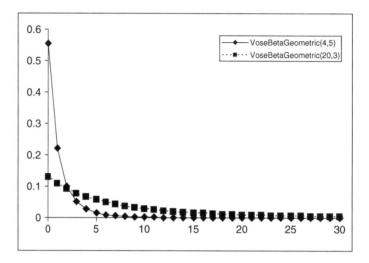

Uses

The BetaGeometric(a, b) distribution models the number of failures that will occur in a binomial process before the first success is observed and where the binomial probability p is itself a random variable taking a Beta(a, b) distribution.

Equations

Probability mass function	$f(x) = \dfrac{\beta \Gamma(\alpha + \beta)\Gamma(\alpha + x)}{\Gamma(\alpha)\Gamma(\alpha + \beta + x + 1)}$
Cumulative distribution function	$F(x) = \displaystyle\sum_{i=0}^{x} \dfrac{\beta \Gamma(\alpha + \beta)\Gamma(\alpha + i)}{\Gamma(\alpha)\Gamma(\alpha + \beta + i + 1)}$
Parameter restriction	$\alpha > 0, \beta > 0$
Domain	$x = \{0, 1, 2, \ldots\}$
Mean	$\dfrac{\alpha}{\beta - 1}$ for $\beta > 1$
Mode	0
Variance	$\dfrac{\alpha\beta(\alpha + \beta - 1)}{(\beta - 2)(\beta - 1)^2}$ for $\beta > 2$
Skewness	$\dfrac{1}{V^{3/2}} \dfrac{\alpha\beta(\alpha + \beta - 1)(2\alpha + \beta - 1)(\beta + 1)}{(\beta - 3)(\beta - 2)(\beta - 1)^3}$ for $\beta > 3$
Kurtosis	Complicated

Beta–Negative Binomial

VoseBetaNegBin(s, α, β)

Graphs

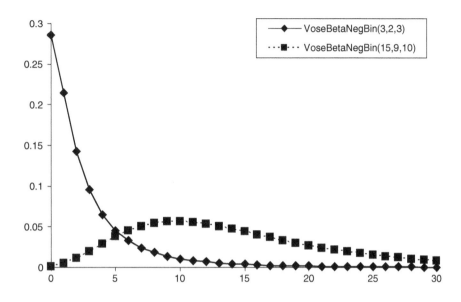

Uses

The Beta–Negative Binomial(s, α, β) distribution models the number of failures that will occur in a binomial process before s successes are observed and where the binomial probability p is itself a random variable taking a Beta(α, β) distribution.

Equations

Probability mass function	$f(x) = \dfrac{\Gamma(s+x)\,\Gamma(\alpha+\beta)\,\Gamma(\alpha+x)\,\Gamma(\beta+s)}{\Gamma(s)\,\Gamma(x+1)\,\Gamma(\alpha)\,\Gamma(\beta)\,\Gamma(\alpha+\beta+s+x)}$
Cumulative distribution function	$F(x) = \displaystyle\sum_{i=0}^{x} \dfrac{\Gamma(s+i)\,\Gamma(\alpha+\beta)\,\Gamma(\alpha+i)\,\Gamma(\beta+s)}{\Gamma(s)\,\Gamma(i+1)\,\Gamma(\alpha)\,\Gamma(\beta)\,\Gamma(\alpha+\beta+s+i)}$
Parameter restriction	$s > 0,\ \alpha > 0,\ \beta > 0$
Domain	$x = \{0, 1, 2, \ldots\}$
Mean	$\dfrac{s\,\alpha}{\beta-1}$ for $\beta > 1$
Variance	$\dfrac{s\,\alpha\,(s\,\alpha + s\,\beta - s + \beta^2 - 2\beta + \alpha\beta - \alpha + 1)}{(\beta-2)(\beta-1)^2} \equiv V$ for $\beta > 2$
Skewness	$\dfrac{1}{V^{3/2}} \dfrac{s\,\alpha\,(\alpha+\beta-1)\,(2\alpha+\beta-1)\,(s+\beta-1)\,(2s+\beta-1)}{(\beta-3)\,(\beta-2)\,(\beta-1)^3}$ for $\beta > 3$
Kurtosis	Complicated

# Binomial
VoseBinomial(n, p)

Graphs

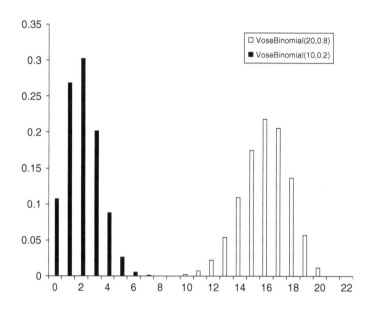

Uses

The binomial distribution models the number of successes from n independent trials where there is a probability p of success in each trial.

The binomial distribution has an enormous number of uses. Beyond simple binomial processes, many other stochastic processes can be usefully reduced to a binomial process to resolve problems. For example:

- Binomial process:
  - number of false starts of a car in n attempts;
  - number of faulty items in n from a production line;
  - number of n randomly selected people with some characteristic.
- Reduced to binomial:
  - number of machines that last longer than T hours of operation without failure;
  - blood samples that have 0 or >0 antibodies;
  - approximation to a hypergeometric distribution.

Comments

The binomial distribution makes the assumption that the probability p remains the same value no matter how many trials are performed. That would imply that my aim doesn't get better or worse. It wouldn't be a good estimator, for instance, if the chance of success improved with the number of trials.

Another example: the number of faulty computer chips in a 2000 volume batch where there is a 2 % probability that any one chip is faulty = Binomial(2000, 2 %).

Equations

Probability mass function	$f(x) = \binom{n}{x} p^x (1-p)^{n-x}$
Cumulative distribution function	$F(x) = \sum_{i=0}^{\lfloor x \rfloor} \binom{n}{i} p^i (1-p)^{n-i}$
Parameter restriction	$0 \le p \le 1; n = \{0, 1, 2, \ldots\}$
Domain	$x = \{0, 1, 2, \ldots, n\}$
Mean	np
Mode	$p(n+1)-1$ and $p(n+1)$ if $p(n+1)$ is an integer $p(n+1)$ otherwise
Variance	$np(1-p)$
Skewness	$\dfrac{1-2p}{\sqrt{np(1-p)}}$
Kurtosis	$\dfrac{1}{np(1-p)} + 3\left(1 - \dfrac{2}{n}\right)$

# Bradford
VoseBradford(θ, min, max)

Graphs

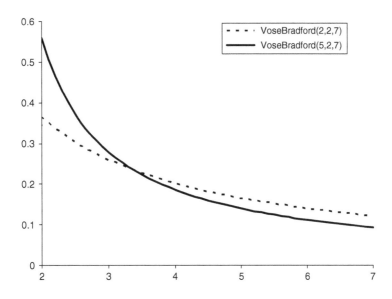

Comments

The Bradford distribution (also known as the "Bradford law of scattering") is similar to a Pareto distribution that has been truncated on the right. It is right skewed, peaking at its minimum. The greater the value of θ, the faster its density decreases as one moves away from the minimum. Its genesis is essentially empirical, and very similar to the idea behind the Pareto too. Samuel Clement Bradford originally developed data by studying the distribution of articles in journals in two scientific areas, applied geophysics and lubrication. He studied the rates at which articles relevant to each subject area appeared in journals in those areas. He identified all journals that published more than a certain number of articles in the test areas per year, as well as in other ranges of descending frequency. He wrote (Bradford, 1948, p. 116):

> *If scientific journals are arranged in order of decreasing productivity of articles on a given subject, they may be divided into a nucleus of periodicals more particularly devoted to the subject and several groups or zones containing the same number of articles as the nucleus, when the numbers of periodicals in the nucleus and succeeding zones will be as $1 : n : n^2 \ldots$*

Bradford only identified three zones. He found that the value of n was roughly 5. So, for example, if a study on a topic discovers that six journals contain one-third of the relevant articles found, then $6 \times 5 = 30$ journals will, among them, contain another third of all the relevant articles found, and the last third will be the most scattered of all, being spread out over $6 \times 5^2 = 300$ journals.

Bradford's observations are pretty robust. The theory has a lot of implications in researching and investment in periodicals; for example, how many journals an institute should subscribe to, or one should review in a study. It also gives a guide for advertising, by identifying the first third of journals that have the highest impact, helps determine whether journals on a new(ish) topic (or arena like e-journals) have reached a stabilised population and tests the efficiency of web browsers.

Equations

Probability density function	$f(x) = \dfrac{\theta}{(\theta(x - \min) + \max - \min) \log(\theta + 1)}$
Cumulative distribution function	$F(x) = \dfrac{\log\left(1 + \dfrac{\theta(x - \min)}{\max - \min}\right)}{\log(\theta + 1)}$
Parameter restriction	$0 < \theta$, $\min < \max$
Domain	$\min \leq x \leq \max$
Mean	$\dfrac{\theta(\max - \min) + k[\min(\theta + 1) - \max]}{\theta k}$ where $k = \log(\theta + 1)$
Mode	$\min$
Variance	$\dfrac{(\max - \min)^2[\theta(k - 2) + 2k]}{2\theta k^2}$
Skewness	$\dfrac{\sqrt{2}(12\theta^2 - 9k\theta(\theta + 2) + 2k^2(\theta(\theta + 3) + 3))}{\sqrt{\theta(\theta(k - 2) + 2k)}(3\theta(k - 2) + 6k)}$
Kurtosis	$\dfrac{\theta^3(k - 3)(k(3k - 16) + 24) + 12k\theta^2(k - 4)(k - 3) + 6\theta k^2(3k - 14) + 12k^3}{3\theta(\theta(k - 2) + 2k)^2} + 3$

# Burr
VoseBurr(a, b, c, d)

Graphs

The Burr distribution (type III of the list originally presented by Burr) is a right-skewed distribution bounded at a; b is a scale parameter, while c and d control its shape. Burr(0, 1, c, d) is a unit Burr distribution. Examples of the Burr distribution are given below.

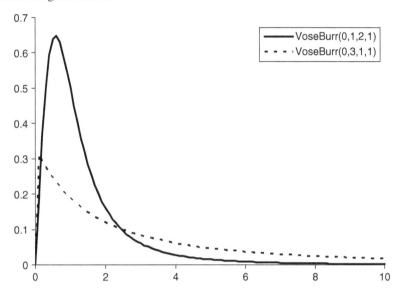

Uses

The Burr distribution has a flexible shape and controllable scale and location that make it appealing to fit to data. It has, for example, been found to fit tree trunk diameter data for the lumber industry. It is frequently used to model insurance claim sizes, and is sometimes considered as an alternative to a normal distribution when data show slight positive skewness.

Equations

Probability density function	$f(x) = \dfrac{cd}{bz^{c+1}(1 + z^{-c})^{d-1}}$ where $z = \left(\dfrac{x - a}{b}\right)$
Cumulative distribution function	$F(x) = \dfrac{1}{(1 + z^{-c})^d}$
Parameter restriction	$b > 0, c > 0, d > 0$
Domain	$x \geq a$
Mean	$a + \dfrac{b\Gamma\left(1 - \dfrac{1}{c}\right)\Gamma\left(d + \dfrac{1}{c}\right)}{\Gamma(d)}$
Mode	$a + b\left(\dfrac{cd - 1}{c + 1}\right)^{\frac{1}{c}}$ if $c > 1$ and $d > 1$ a otherwise

Variance	$\dfrac{b^2}{\Gamma^2(d)}k$ where $k = \Gamma(d)\Gamma\left(1 - \dfrac{2}{c}\right)\Gamma\left(d + \dfrac{2}{c}\right) - \Gamma^2\left(1 - \dfrac{1}{c}\right)\Gamma^2\left(d + \dfrac{1}{c}\right)$

Skewness

$$\frac{\Gamma^2(d)}{k^{3/2}}\left[\frac{2\Gamma^3\left(1 - \frac{1}{c}\right)\Gamma^3\left(\frac{1}{c} + d\right)}{\Gamma^2(d)} - \frac{3\Gamma\left(1 - \frac{2}{c}\right)\Gamma\left(1 - \frac{1}{c}\right)\Gamma\left(\frac{1}{c} + d\right)\Gamma\left(\frac{2}{c} + d\right)}{\Gamma(d)} + \Gamma\left(1 - \frac{3}{c}\right)\Gamma\left(\frac{3}{c} + d\right)\right]$$

Kurtosis

$$\frac{\Gamma^3(d)}{k^2}\left[\frac{6\Gamma\left(1 - \frac{2}{c}\right)\Gamma^2\left(1 - \frac{1}{c}\right)\Gamma^2\left(\frac{1}{c} + d\right)\Gamma\left(\frac{2}{c} + d\right)}{\Gamma^2(d)} - \frac{3\Gamma^4\left(1 - \frac{1}{c}\right)\Gamma^4\left(\frac{1}{c} + d\right)}{\Gamma^3(d)}\right.$$

$$\left. - \frac{4\Gamma\left(1 - \frac{3}{c}\right)\Gamma\left(1 - \frac{1}{c}\right)\Gamma\left(\frac{1}{c} + d\right)\Gamma\left(\frac{3}{c} + d\right)}{\Gamma(d)} + \Gamma\left(1 - \frac{4}{c}\right)\Gamma\left(\frac{4}{c} + d\right)\right]$$

Cauchy

VoseCauchy(a, b)

Graphs

The standard Cauchy distribution is derived from the ratio of two independent normal distributions, i.e. if X and Y are two independent Normal$(0, 1)$ distributions, then

$$X/Y = \text{Cauchy}(0, 1)$$

The Cauchy(a, b) is shifted to have a median at a, and to have b times the spread of a Cauchy$(0, 1)$. Examples of the Cauchy distribution are given below.

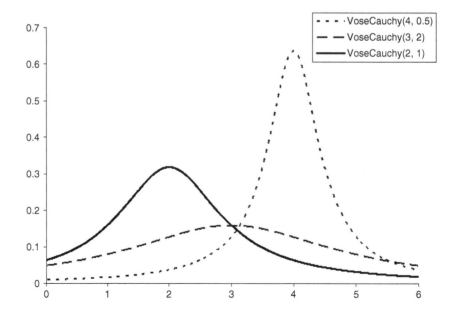

Uses

The Cauchy distribution is not often used in risk analysis. It is used in mechanical and electrical theory, physical anthropology and measurement and calibration problems. For example, in physics it is usually called a Lorentzian distribution, where it is the distribution of the energy of an unstable state in quantum mechanics. It is also used to model the points of impact of a fixed straight line of particles emitted from a point source.

The most common use of a Cauchy distribution is to show how "smart" you are by quoting it whenever someone generalises about how distributions are used, because it is the exception in many ways: in principle, it has no defined mean (although by symmetry this is usually accepted as being its median $= a$), and no other defined moments.

Comments

The distribution is symmetric about a and the spread of the distribution increases with increasing b. The Cauchy distribution is peculiar and most noted because none of its moments is well defined (i.e. mean, standard deviation, etc.), their determination being the difference between two integrals that both sum to infinity. Although it looks similar to the normal distribution, it has much heavier tails. From $X/Y = \text{Cauchy}(0, 1)$ above you'll appreciate that the reciprocal of a Cauchy distribution is another Cauchy distribution (it is just swapping the two normal distributions around). The range $a - b$ to $a + b$ contains 50 % of the probability area.

Equations

Probability density function	$f(x) = \left\{ \pi b \left[1 + \left(\frac{x-a}{b} \right)^2 \right] \right\}^{-1}$
Cumulative distribution function	$F(x) = \frac{1}{2} + \frac{1}{\pi} \tan^{-1} \left(\frac{x-a}{b} \right)$
Parameter restriction	$b > 0$
Domain	$-\infty < x < +\infty$
Mean	Does not exist
Mode	a
Variance	Does not exist
Skewness	Does not exist
Kurtosis	Does not exist

# Chi
VoseChi(v)

Graphs

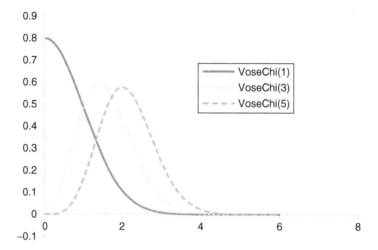

Uses and comments

The standardised chi distribution with v degrees of freedom is the distribution followed by the square root of a Chi-square(v) random variable:

$$\text{Chi}(v) = \sqrt{\text{ChiSq}(v)}$$

Chi(1) is known as a half-normal distribution, i.e.

$$\text{Chi}(0, 1, 1) = \sqrt{\text{ChiSq}(1)} = \sqrt{\text{Normal}(0, 1)^2} = |\text{Normal}(0, 1)|$$

The chi distribution usually appears as the length of a k-dimensional vector whose orthogonal components are independent and standard normally distributed. The length of the vector will then have a chi distribution with k degrees of freedom. For example, the Maxwell distribution of (normalised) molecular speeds is a Chi(3) distribution.

Equations

Probability density function	$f_v(x) = \dfrac{x^{v-1} \exp\left(-\dfrac{x^2}{2}\right)}{2^{\frac{v}{2}-1} \Gamma\left(\dfrac{v}{2}\right)}$
Cumulative distribution function	$F_v(x) = \dfrac{\gamma\left(\dfrac{v}{2}, \dfrac{x^2}{2}\right)}{\Gamma\left(\dfrac{v}{2}\right)}$ where γ is the lower incomplete gamma function: $\gamma(a, x) = \displaystyle\int_0^x t^{a-1}e^{-t}dt$
Parameter restriction	v is an integer

Domain	$x \geq 0$
Mean	$\dfrac{\sqrt{2}\Gamma\left(\dfrac{\nu+1}{2}\right)}{\Gamma\left(\dfrac{\nu}{2}\right)} \equiv \mu$
Mode	$\sqrt{\nu-1}$ for $\nu \geq 1$
Variance	$\nu - \mu^2 \equiv V$
Skewness	Complicated
Kurtosis	Complicated

Chi-squared

VoseChiSq(ν)

Graphs

The Chi-Squared distribution is a right-skewed distribution bounded at zero. ν is called the "degrees of freedom" from its use in statistics below.

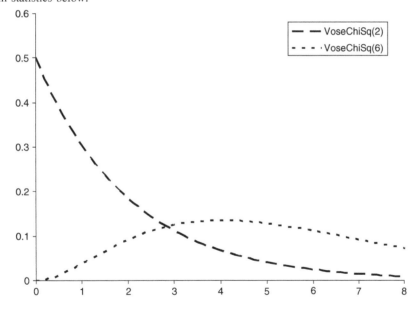

Uses

The sum of the squares of ν unit normal distributions (i.e. Normal(0, 1)^2) is a ChiSq(ν) distribution: so ChiSq(2) = Normal(0, 1)^2 + Normal(0, 1)^2, for example. It is this property that makes it very useful in statistics, particularly classical statistics.

In statistics we collect a set of observations and from calculating some sample statistics (the mean, variance, etc.) attempt to infer something about the stochastic process from which the data came. If the samples are from a normally distributed population, then the sample variance is a random variable that is a shifted, rescaled ChiSq distribution.

The chi-square distribution is also used to determine the goodness of fit (GOF) of a distribution to a histogram of the available data (a ChiSq test). The method attempts to make a ChiSq-distributed statistic by taking the sum of squared errors, normalising them to be N(0, 1).

In our view, the ChiSq tests and statistics get overused (especially the GOF statistic) because the normality assumption is often tenuous.

Comments

As v gets large, so it is the sum of a large number of [N(0, 10^2] distributions and, through the central limit theorem, approximates a normal distribution itself.

Sometimes written as $\chi^2(v)$. Also related to the gamma distribution: Chisq(v) = Gamma$(v/2, 2)$.

Equations

Probability density function	$f(x) = \dfrac{x^{\frac{v}{2}-1} \exp\left(-\dfrac{x}{2}\right)}{2^{\frac{v}{2}} \Gamma\left(\dfrac{v}{2}\right)}$
Cumulative distribution function	No closed form
Parameter restriction	$v > 0$, v is an integer
Domain	$x \geq 0$
Mean	v
Mode	$\begin{array}{ll} 0 & \text{if } v < 2 \\ v - 2 & \text{otherwise} \end{array}$
Variance	$2v$
Skewness	$\sqrt{\dfrac{8}{v}}$
Kurtosis	$3 + \dfrac{12}{v}$

Cumulative Ascending

VoseCumulA(min, max, $\{x_i\}$, $\{P_i\}$)

Graphs

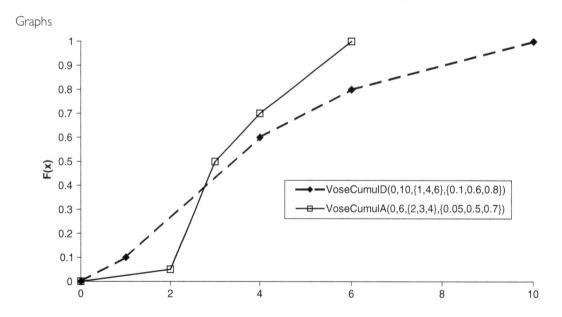

Uses

1. *Empirical distribution of data*. The cumulative distribution is very useful for converting a set of data values into a first- or second-order empirical distribution.

2. *Building a statistical confidence distribution*. The cumulative distribution can be used to construct uncertainty distributions when using some classical statistical methods. Examples: p in a binomial process with s observed suucesses in n trials ($F(x) = 1 - \text{VoseBinomialProb}(s, n, p, 1) + 0.5 * \text{VoseBinomialProb}(s, n, p, 0)$); and λ in a Poisson process with α events observed in some unit of exposure ($F(x) = 1 - \text{VosePoissonProb}(\alpha, \lambda, 1) + 0.5 * \text{VosePoissonProb}(\alpha, \lambda, 0)$).

3. *Modelling expert opinion*. The cumulative distribution is used in some texts to model expert opinion. The expert is asked for a minimum, maximum and a few percentiles (e.g. 25 %, 50 %, 75 %). However, we have found it largely unsatisfactory because of the insensitivity of its probability scale. A small change in the shape of the cumulative distribution that would pass unnoticed produces a radical change in the corresponding relative frequency plot that would not be acceptable.

The cumulative distribution *is* however very useful to model an expert's opinion of a variable whose range covers several orders of magnitude in some sort of exponential way. For example, the number of bacteria in a kg of meat will increase exponentially with time. The meat may contain 100 units of bacteria or 1 million. In such circumstances, it is fruitless to attempt to use a relative distribution directly.

Equations

Probability density function	$f(x) = \dfrac{P_{i+1} - P_i}{x_{i+1} - x_i}$ for $\begin{array}{l} x_i \leq x < x_{i+1} \\ i \in \{0, 1, \ldots, n\} \end{array}$ where $x_0 = \min,\quad x_{n+1} = \max,\quad P_0 = 0, P_{n+1} = 1$
Cumulative distribution function	$F(x) = \dfrac{x - x_i}{x_{i+1} - x_i}(P_{i+1} - P_i) + P_i$ for $\begin{array}{l} x_i \leq x < x_{i+1} \\ i \in \{0, 1, \ldots, n\} \end{array}$
Parameter restriction	$0 \leq P_i \leq 1,\quad P_i \leq P_{i+1},\quad x_i < x_{i+1},\quad n > 0$
Domain	$\min \leq x \leq \max$
Mean	$\displaystyle\sum_{i=0}^{n} \frac{f(x_i)}{2}(x_{i+1}^2 - x_i^2)$
Mode	No unique mode
Variance	Complicated
Skewness	Complicated
Kurtosis	Complicated

# Cumulative Descending
VoseCumulD(min, max, $\{x_i\}$, $\{P_i\}$)

Graphs

This is another form of the cumulative distribution, but here the list of cumulative probabilities are the probabilities of being greater than or equal to their corresponding x values.

Examples of the cumulative descending distribution are given below.

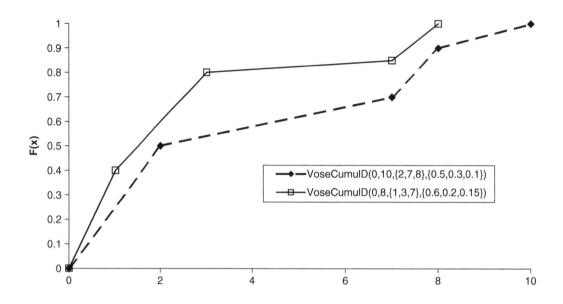

Uses and equations

See the cumulative ascending distribution (only here $P_{i+1} \leq P_i$, so the P_i values can be converted to those of the CumulA distribution by subtracting them from 1: $P_i' = 1 - P_i$.

Dagum

VoseDagum(a, b, p)

Graphs

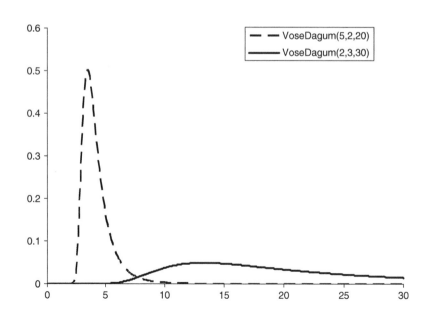

The Dagum distribution is often encountered in the actuarial literature or the income distribution literature. The distribution was originally derived by Dagum while studying the elasticity of the cdf of income. a and p are shape parameters and b is a scale parameter.

Uses

The Dagum distribution is sometimes used for fitting to aggregate fire losses.

Equations

Probability density function	$f(x) = \dfrac{ap\, x^{ap-1}}{b^{ap}\left[1+\left(\frac{x}{b}\right)^a\right]^{p+1}}$
Cumulative distribution function	$F(x) = \left[1+\left(\frac{x}{b}\right)^{-a}\right]^{-p}$
Parameter restriction	$a > 0,\, b > 0,\, p > 0$
Domain	$x \geq 0$
Mean	$\dfrac{b\,\Gamma\left(p+\frac{1}{a}\right)\,\Gamma\left(1-\frac{1}{a}\right)}{\Gamma(p)}$
Mode	$b\left(\dfrac{ap-1}{a+1}\right)^{\frac{1}{a}} \quad \text{if } ap > 1$ $0 \qquad\qquad\qquad \text{else}$
Variance	$\dfrac{b^2}{\Gamma^2(p)}\left[\Gamma(p)\,\Gamma\left(p+\frac{2}{a}\right)\Gamma\left(1-\frac{2}{a}\right) - \Gamma^2\left(p+\frac{1}{a}\right)\Gamma^2\left(1-\frac{1}{a}\right)\right]$
Skewness $\dfrac{b^3}{V^{3/2}\,\Gamma^3(p)}$	$\left[\begin{array}{l}\Gamma^2(p)\,\Gamma\left(p+\frac{3}{a}\right)\Gamma\left(1-\frac{3}{a}\right) - 3\Gamma(p)\Gamma\left(p+\frac{2}{a}\right)\Gamma\left(1-\frac{2}{a}\right)\Gamma\left(p+\frac{1}{a}\right)\Gamma\left(1-\frac{1}{a}\right) \\ +2\Gamma^3\left(p+\frac{1}{a}\right)\Gamma^3\left(1-\frac{1}{a}\right)\end{array}\right]$
Kurtosis: $\dfrac{b^4}{V^2\,\Gamma^4(p)}$	$\left[\begin{array}{l}\Gamma^3(p)\Gamma\left(p+\frac{4}{a}\right)\Gamma\left(1-\frac{4}{a}\right) - 4\Gamma^2(p)\Gamma\left(p+\frac{3}{a}\right)\Gamma\left(1-\frac{3}{a}\right)\Gamma\left(p+\frac{1}{a}\right)\Gamma\left(1-\frac{1}{a}\right) \\ +6\Gamma(p)\Gamma\left(p+\frac{2}{a}\right)\Gamma\left(1-\frac{2}{a}\right)\Gamma^2\left(p+\frac{1}{a}\right)\Gamma^2\left(1-\frac{1}{a}\right) - 3\Gamma^4\left(p+\frac{1}{a}\right)\Gamma^4\left(1-\frac{1}{a}\right)\end{array}\right]$

Notes

The Dagum distribution is also called the *inverse Burr distribution* or the *kappa distribution*.
When $a = p$, the distribution is also called the *inverse paralogistic distribution*.

Delaporte

VoseDelaporte(α, β, λ)

Graphs

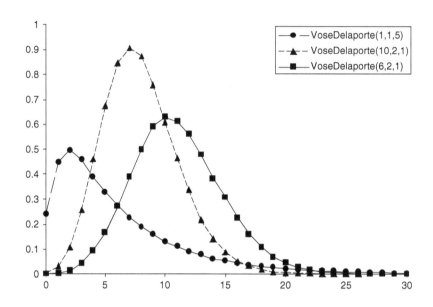

Uses

A very common starting point for modelling the numbers of events that occur randomly distributed in time and/or space (e.g. the number of claims that will be received by an insurance company) is the Poisson distribution:

$$\text{Events} = \text{Poisson}(\lambda)$$

where λ is the expected number of events during the period of interest. The Poisson distribution has a mean and variance equal to λ, and one often sees historic data (e.g. frequency of insurance claims) with a variance greater than the mean so that the Poisson model underestimates the level of randomness. A standard method to incorporate greater variance is to assume that λ is itself a random variable (and the resultant frequency distribution is called a mixed Poisson model). A Gamma(α, β) distribution is most commonly used to describe the random variation of λ between periods, so

$$\text{Events} = \text{Poisson}(\text{Gamma}(\alpha, \beta)) \tag{1}$$

This is the Pólya(α, β) distribution.

Alternatively, one might consider that some part of the Poisson intensity is constant and has an additional component that is random, following a gamma distribution:

$$\text{Events} = \text{Poisson}(\lambda + \text{Gamma}(\alpha, \beta)) \tag{2}$$

This is the Delaporte distribution, i.e.

$$\text{Poisson}(\lambda + \text{Gamma}(\alpha, \beta)) = \text{Delaporte}(\alpha, \beta, \lambda)$$

We can split this equation up:

$$\text{Poisson}(\lambda + \text{Gamma}(\alpha, \beta)) = \text{Poisson}(\lambda) + \text{Poisson}(\text{Gamma}(\alpha, \beta))$$
$$= \text{Poisson}(\lambda) + \text{Pólya}(\alpha, \beta)$$

Special cases of the Delaporte distribution:

$$\text{Delaporte}(\lambda, \alpha, 0) = \text{Poisson}(\lambda)$$
$$\text{Delaporte}(0, \alpha, \beta) = \text{Pólya}(\alpha, \beta)$$
$$\text{Delaporte}(0, 1, \beta) = \text{Geometric}(1/(1 + \beta))$$

Equations

Probability density function	$f(x) = \displaystyle\sum_{i=0}^{x} \frac{\Gamma(\alpha + i)\beta^i \lambda^{x-i} e^{-\lambda}}{\Gamma(\alpha)i!(1 + \beta)^{\alpha+i}(x - i)!}$
Cumulative distribution function	$F(x) = \displaystyle\sum_{j=0}^{x}\sum_{i=0}^{j} \frac{\Gamma(\alpha + i)\beta^i \lambda^{j-i} e^{-\lambda}}{\Gamma(\alpha)i!(1 + \beta)^{\alpha+i}(j - i)!}$
Parameter restriction :	$\alpha > 0,\ \beta > 0,\ \lambda > 0$
Domain	$x = \{0, 1, 2, \ldots\}$
Mean	$\lambda + \alpha\beta$
Mode	$z, z + 1$ if z is an integer where $z = (\alpha - 1)\beta + \lambda$ $\lfloor z \rfloor$ else
Variance	$\lambda + \alpha\beta(\beta + 1)$
Skewness	$\dfrac{\lambda + \alpha\beta(1 + 3\beta + 2\beta^2)}{(\lambda + \alpha\beta(1 + \beta))^{3/2}}$
Kurtosis	$\dfrac{\lambda + 3\lambda^2 + \alpha\beta(1 + 6\lambda + 6\lambda\beta + 7\beta + 12\beta^2 + 6\beta^3 + 3\alpha\beta + 6\alpha\beta^2 + 3\alpha\beta^3)}{(\lambda + \alpha\beta(1 + \beta))^2}$

# Discrete
VoseDiscrete($\{x_i\}, \{p_i\}$)

Graphs

The discrete distribution is a general type of function used to describe a variable that can take one of several explicit discrete values $\{x_i\}$ and where a probability weight $\{p_i\}$ is assigned to each value; for example, the number of bridges to be built over a motorway extension or the number of times a software module will have to be recoded after testing. An example of the discrete distribution is shown below.

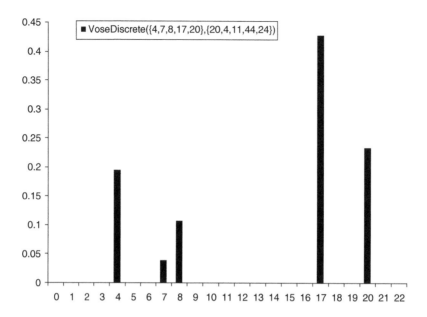

Uses

1. *Probability branching.* A discrete distribution is also particularly useful to describe probabilistic branching. For example, a firm estimates that it will sell Normal(120, 10) tonnes of weed killer next year unless a rival firm comes out with a competing product, in which case it estimates its sales will drop to Normal(85, 9) tonnes. It also estimates that there is a 30 % chance of the competing product appearing. This could be modelled by

$$Sales = VoseDiscrete(A1:A2, B1:B2)$$

where the cells A1:B2 contain the formulae

$$A1: = VoseNormal(120, 10)$$

$$A2: = VoseNormal(85, 9)$$

$$B1:70\%$$

$$B2:30\%$$

2. *Combining expert opinion.* A discrete distribution can also be used to combine two or more conflicting expert opinions.

Equations

Probability mass function	$f(x_i) = p_i$
Cumulative distribution function	$F(x) = \sum_{j=1}^{i} p_j \qquad \text{if } x_i \leq x < x_{i+1}$ assuming the x_is are in ascending order
Parameter restriction	$p_i > 0 , n > 0 , \sum_{i=1}^{n} p_i > 0$

Domain	$x = \{x_1, x_2, \ldots, x_n\}$
Mean	No unique mean
Mode	The x_i with the greatest p_i
Variance	$\sum_{i=1}^{n} (x_i - \bar{x})^2 p_i \equiv V$
Skewness	$\frac{1}{V^{3/2}} \sum_{i=1}^{n} (x_i - \bar{x})^3 p_i$
Kurtosis	$\frac{1}{V^2} \sum_{i=1}^{n} (x_i - \bar{x})^4 p_i$

# Discrete Uniform
VoseDUniform($\{x_i\}$)

Graph

The discrete uniform distribution describes a variable that can take one of several explicit discrete values with equal probabilities of taking any particular value.

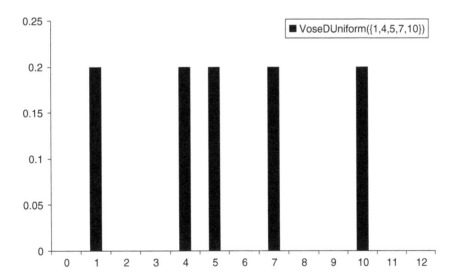

Uses

It is not often that we come across a variable that can take one of several values each with equal probability. However, there are a couple of modelling techniques that require that capability:

- *Bootstrap*. Resampling in univariate non-parametric bootstrap.
- *Fitting empirical distribution to data*. Creating an empirical distribution directly from a dataset, i.e. where we believe that the list of data values is a good representation of the randomness of the variable.

Equations

Probability mass function	$f(x_i) = \frac{1}{n}, i = 1, \ldots, n$
Cumulative distribution function	$F(x) = \dfrac{i}{n}$ if $x_i \le x < x_{i+1}$ assuming the x_is are in ascending order
Parameter restriction	$n > 0$
Domain	$x = \{x_1, x_2, \ldots, x_n\}$
Mean	$\dfrac{1}{n} \sum\limits_{i=1}^{n} x_i$
Mode	Not uniquely defined
Variance	$\dfrac{1}{n} \sum\limits_{i=1}^{n} (x_i - \mu)^2 \equiv V$
Skewness	$\dfrac{1}{nV^{3/2}} \sum\limits_{i=1}^{n} (x_i - \mu)^3$
Kurtosis	$\dfrac{1}{nV^2} \sum\limits_{i=1}^{n} (x_i - \mu)^4$

# Error Function
VoseErf(h)

Graphs

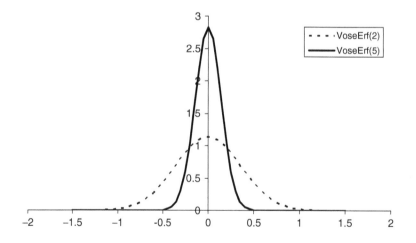

Uses

The error function distribution is derived from a normal distribution by setting $\mu = 0$ and $\sigma = \dfrac{1}{h\sqrt{2}}$. Therefore, the uses are the same as those of the normal distribution.

Equations

Probability density function	$f(x) = \frac{h}{\sqrt{\pi}} \exp(-(hx)^2)$
Cumulative distribution function	$F(x) = \Phi(\sqrt{2}hx)$ Φ: error function
Parameter restriction	$h > 0$
Domain	$-\infty < x < +\infty$
Mean	0
Mode	0
Variance	$\frac{1}{2h^2}$
Skewness	0
Kurtosis	3

# Erlang
VoseErlang(m,β)

Graphs

The Erlang distribution (or m-Erlang distribution) is a probability distribution developed by A. K. Erlang. It is a special case of the gamma distribution. A Gamma(m, β) distribution is equal to an Erlang(m, β) distribution when m is an integer.

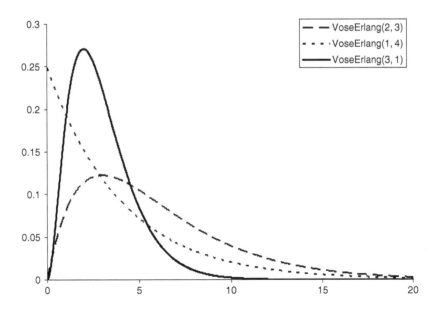

Uses

The Erlang distribution is used to predict waiting times in queuing systems, etc., where a Poisson process is in operation, in the same way as a gamma distribution.

Comments

A. K. Erlang worked a lot in traffic modelling. There are thus two other Erlang distributions, both used in modelling traffic:

- Erlang B distribution: this is the easier of the two, and can be used, for example, in a call centre to calculate the number of trunks one needs to carry a certain amount of phone traffic with a certain "target service".
- Erlang C distribution: this formula is much more difficult and is often used, for example, to calculate how long callers will have to wait before being connected to a human in a call centre or similar situation.

Equations

Probability density function	$f(x) = \dfrac{\beta^{-m} x^{m-1} \exp\left(-\dfrac{x}{\beta}\right)}{(m-1)!}$
Cumulative distribution function	No closed form
Parameter restriction	$m > 0$, $\beta > 0$
Domain	$x > 0$
Mean	$m\beta$
Mode	$\beta(m-1)$
Variance	$m\beta^2$
Skewness	$\dfrac{2}{\sqrt{m}}$
Kurtosis	$3 + \dfrac{6}{m}$

Error
$$\text{VoseError}(\mu, \sigma, \nu)$$

Graphs

The error distribution goes by the names "exponential power distribution" and "generalised error distribution".

This three-parameter distribution offers a variety of symmetric shapes, as shown in the figures below. The first pane shows the effect on the distribution's shape of varying parameter ν. Note that $\nu = 2$ is a normal distribution, $\nu = 1$ is a Laplace distribution and the distribution approaches a uniform as ν approaches infinity. The second pane shows the change in the distribution's spread by varying parameter σ, its standard deviation. Parameter μ is simply the location of the distribution's peak, and the distribution's mean.

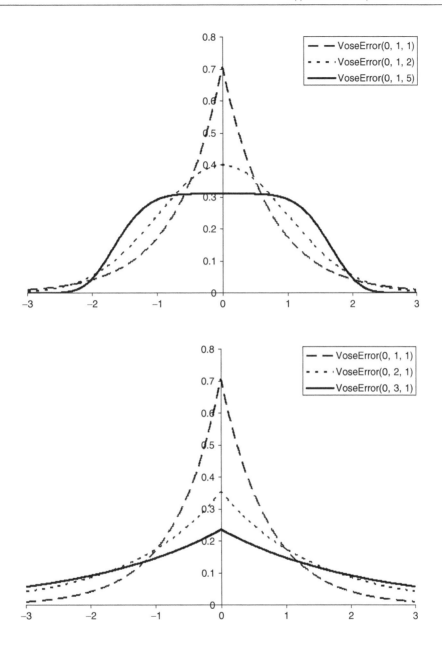

Uses

The error distribution finds quite a lot of use as a prior distribution in Bayesian inference because it has greater flexibility than a normal prior, in that the error distribution is flatter than a normal (platykurtic) when $v > 2$, and more peaked than a normal distribution (leptokurtic) when $v < 2$. Thus, using the GED allows one to maintain the same mean and variance, but vary the distribution's shape (via the parameter v) as required.

We have also seen the error distribution being used to model variations in historic UK property market returns.

Equations

Probability density function	$f(x) = c_1\sigma^{-1}\exp[-\|c_0^{1/2}\sigma^{-1}(x-\mu)\|^{\nu}]$ where $c_0 = \dfrac{\Gamma\left(\dfrac{3}{\nu}\right)}{\Gamma\left(\dfrac{1}{\nu}\right)}$ and $c_1 = \dfrac{2c_0^{1/2}}{\nu\Gamma\left(\dfrac{1}{\nu}\right)}$
Cumulative distribution function	No closed form
Parameter restriction	$-\infty < \mu < +\infty$, $\sigma > 0$, $\nu > 0$
Domain	$-\infty < x < +\infty$
Mean	μ
Mode	μ
Variance	σ^2
Skewness	0
Kurtosis	$\dfrac{\Gamma\left(\dfrac{5}{\nu}\right)\Gamma\left(\dfrac{1}{\nu}\right)}{\Gamma\left(\dfrac{3}{\nu}\right)^2}$

# Exponential
VoseExpon(β)

Graphs

The Expon(β) is a right-skewed distribution bounded at zero with a mean of β. It only has one shape. Examples of the exponential distribution are given below.

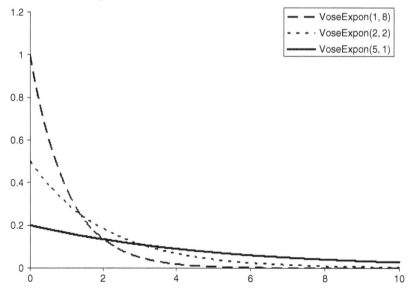

Uses

The Expon(β) models the time until the occurrence of a first event in a Poisson process. For example:

- the time until the next earthquake;
- the decay of a particle in a mass of radioactive material;
- the length of telephone conversations.

The parameter β is the mean time until the occurrence of the next event.

Example

An electronic circuit could be considered to have a constant instantaneous failure rate, meaning that at a small interval of time it has the same probability of failing, given it has survived so far. Destructive tests show that the circuit lasts on average 5200 hours of operation. The time until failure of any single circuit can be modelled as Expon(5200) hours. Interestingly, if it conforms to a true Poisson process, this estimate will be independent of how many hours of operation, if any, the circuit has already survived.

Equations

Probability density function	$f(x) = \dfrac{\exp\left(-\dfrac{x}{\beta}\right)}{\beta}$
Cumulative distribution function	$F(x) = 1 - \exp\left(-\dfrac{x}{\beta}\right)$
Parameter restriction	$\beta > 0$
Domain	$x > 0$
Mean	β
Mode	0
Variance	β^2
Skewness	2
Kurtosis	9

# Extreme Value Maximum
VoseExtValueMax(a, b)

Graph

The extreme value maximum models the maximum of a set of random variables that have an underlying distribution belonging to the exponential family, e.g. exponential, gamma, Weibull, normal, lognormal, logistic and itself.

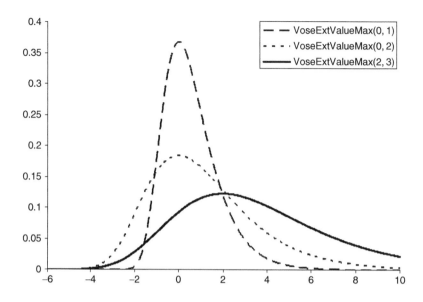

Uses

Engineers are often interested in extreme values of a parameter (like minimum strength, maximum impinging force) because they are the values that determine whether a system will potentially fail. For example: wind strengths impinging on a building – it must be designed to sustain the largest wind with minimum damage within the bounds of the finances available to build it; maximum wave height for designing offshore platforms, breakwaters and dikes; pollution emissions for a factory to ensure that, at its maximum, it will fall below the legal limit; determining the strength of a chain, since it is equal to the strength of its weakest link; modelling the extremes of meteorological events since these cause the greatest impact.

Equations

Probability density function	$f(x) = \left(\dfrac{1}{b}\right) \exp\left(-\dfrac{x-a}{b}\right) \exp\left[-\exp\left(-\dfrac{x-a}{b}\right)\right]$
Cumulative distribution function	$F(x) = \exp\left[-\exp\left(-\dfrac{x-a}{b}\right)\right]$
Parameter restriction	$b > 0$
Domain	$-\infty < x < +\infty$
Mean	$a - b\Gamma'(1)$ where $\Gamma'(1) \cong -0.577216$
Mode	a
Variance	$\dfrac{b^2\pi^2}{6}$
Skewness	1.139547
Kurtosis	5.4

# Extreme Value Minimum
VoseExtValueMin(a, b)

Graph

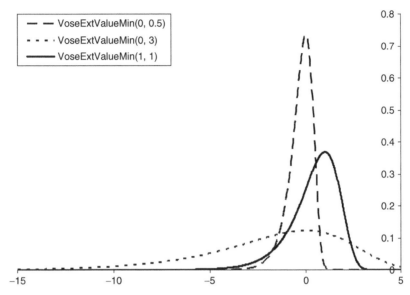

The extreme value minimum models the minimum of a set of random variables that have an underlying distribution belonging to the exponential family, e.g. exponential, gamma, Weibull, normal, lognormal, logistic and itself.

Uses

Engineers are often interested in extreme values of a parameter (like minimum strength, maximum impinging force) because they are the values that determine whether a system will potentially fail. For example: wind strengths impinging on a building – it must be designed to sustain the largest wind with minimum damage within the bounds of the finances available to build it; maximum wave height for designing offshore platforms, breakwaters and dikes; pollution emissions for a factory to ensure that, at its maximum, it will fall below the legal limit; determining the strength of a chain, since it is equal to the strength of its weakest link; modelling the extremes of meteorological events since these cause the greatest impact.

Equations

Probability density function	$f(x) = \left(\dfrac{1}{b}\right) \exp\left(\dfrac{x-a}{b}\right) \exp\left[-\exp\left(\dfrac{x-a}{b}\right)\right]$
Cumulative distribution function	$F(x) = 1 - \exp\left[-\exp\left(\dfrac{x-a}{b}\right)\right]$
Parameter restriction	$b > 0$
Domain	$-\infty < x < +\infty$
Mean	$a + b\Gamma'(1)$ where $\Gamma'(1) \cong -0.577216$
Mode	a

Variance	$\dfrac{b^2 \pi^2}{6}$
Skewness	-1.139547
Kurtosis	5.4

F

$$\text{VoseF}(\nu_1, \nu_2)$$

Graphs

The F distribution (sometimes known as the Fisher–Snedecor distribution, and taking Fisher's initial) is commonly used in a variety of statistical tests. It is derived from the ratio of two normalised chi-square distributions with ν_1 and ν_2 degrees of freedom as follows:

$$F(\nu_1, \nu_2) = (\text{ChiSq}(\nu_1)/\nu_1)/(\text{ChiSq}(\nu_2)/\nu_2)$$

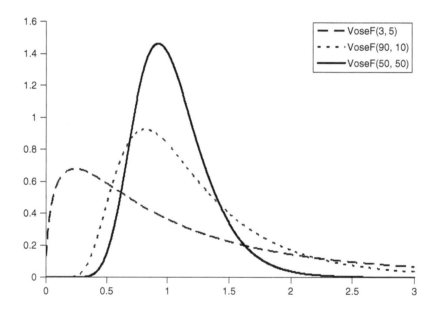

Uses

The most common use of the F distribution you'll see in statistics textbooks is to compare the variance between two (assumed normally distributed) populations. From a risk analysis perspective, it is very infrequent that we would wish to model the ratio of two estimated variances (which is essentially the F-test in this circumstance), so the F distribution is not particularly useful to us.

Equations

Probability density function	$f(x) =$ $\dfrac{\Gamma\left(\dfrac{\nu_1 + \nu_2}{2}\right)}{\Gamma\left(\dfrac{\nu_1}{2}\right)\Gamma\left(\dfrac{\nu_2}{2}\right)} \left(\dfrac{\nu_1}{\nu_2}\right)^{\frac{\nu_1}{2}} x^{\frac{\nu_1}{2}-1} \left(1 + \left(\dfrac{\nu_1}{\nu_2}\right)x\right)^{-\left(\frac{\nu_1+\nu_2}{2}\right)}$

Cumulative distribution function	No closed form
Parameter restriction	$v_1 > 0, v_2 > 0$
Domain	$x > 0$
Mean	$\dfrac{v_2}{v_2 - 2}$ for $v_2 > 2$
Mode	$\dfrac{v_2(v_1 - 2)}{v_1(v_2 + 2)}$ if $v_1 > 2$ 0 if $v_1 = 2$
Variance	$\dfrac{2v_2^2(v_1 + v_2 - 2)}{v_1(v_2 - 2)^2(v_2 - 4)}$ if $v_2 > 4$
Skewness	$\dfrac{(2v_1 + v_2 - 2)\sqrt{8(v_2 - 4)}}{(v_2 - 6)\sqrt{v_1(v_1 + v_2 - 2)}}$ if $v_2 > 6$
Kurtosis	$\dfrac{12(20v_2 - 8v_2^2 + v_2^3 + 44v_1 - 32v_1 v_2 + 5v_2^2 v_1 - 22v_1^2 + 5v_2 v_1^2 - 16)}{(v_1(v_2 - 6)(v_2 - 8)(v_1 + v_2 - 2))} + 3$ if $v_2 > 8$

Fatigue Life

VoseFatigue(α, β, γ)

Graphs

The fatigue life distribution is a right-skewed distribution bounded at α. β is a scale parameter, while γ controls its shape. Examples of the fatigue life distribution are given below.

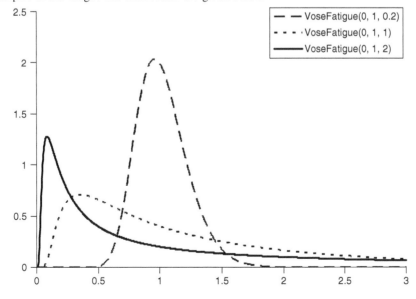

Uses

The fatigue life distribution was originally derived in Birnbaum and Saunders (1969) as the failure of a structure owing to the growth of cracks. The conceptual model had a single dominant crack appear and grow as the structure experiences repeated shock patterns up to the point that the crack is sufficiently long to cause failure. Assuming that the incremental growth of a crack with each shock follows the same distribution, that each incremental growth is an independent sample from that distribution and that there are a large number of these small increases in length before failure, the total crack length will follow a normal distribution from the central limit theorem. Birnbaum and Saunders determined the distribution of the number of these cycles necessary to cause failure. If the shocks occur more or less regularly in time, we can replace the probability that the structure will fail by a certain number of shocks with the probability that it fails within a certain amount of time.

Thus, the fatigue life distribution is used a great deal to model the lifetime of a device suffering from fatigue. Other distributions in common use to model the lifetime of a devise are the lognormal, exponential and Weibull.

Big assumptions, so be careful in using this distribution regardless of its popularity. If the growth is likely to be proportional to the crack size, the lognormal distribution is more appropriate.

Equations

Probability density function	$f(x) = \dfrac{z + \frac{1}{z}}{2\beta\gamma z^2} \varphi\left(\dfrac{z - \frac{1}{z}}{\gamma}\right)$ where $z = \sqrt{\frac{x-\alpha}{\beta}}$ and φ = unit normal density
Cumulative distribution function	$F(x) = \Phi\left(\dfrac{z - \frac{1}{z}}{\gamma}\right)$ where Φ = unit normal cdf
Parameter restriction	$\beta > 0, \gamma > 0$
Domain	$x > \alpha$
Mean	$\alpha + \beta\left(1 + \frac{\gamma^2}{2}\right)$
Mode	Complicated
Variance	$\beta^2\gamma^2\left(1 + \frac{5\gamma^2}{4}\right)$
Skewness	$\dfrac{4\gamma^2(11\gamma^2 + 6)}{(4 + 5\gamma^2)\sqrt{\gamma^2(4 + 5\gamma^2)}}$
Kurtosis	$\dfrac{3(211\gamma^4 + 120\gamma^2 + 16)}{(4 + 5\gamma^2)^2}$

Gamma
VoseGamma(α, β)

Graphs

The gamma distribution is right skewed and bounded at zero. It is a parametric distribution based on Poisson mathematics. Examples of the gamma distribution are given below.

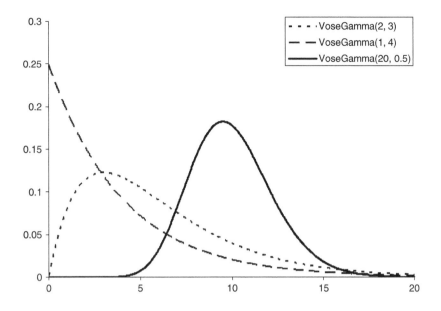

Uses

The gamma distribution is extremely important in risk analysis modelling, with a number of different uses:

1. *Poisson waiting time.* The Gamma(α, β) distribution models the time required for α events to occur, given that the events occur randomly in a Poisson process with a mean time between events of β. For example, if we know that major flooding occurs in a town on average every 6 years, Gamma(4, 6) models how many years it will take before the next four floods have occurred.

2. *Random variation of a Poisson intensity* λ The gamma distribution is used for its convenience as a description of random variability of λ in a Poisson process. It is convenient because of the identity

$$\text{Poisson(Gamma}(\alpha, \beta)) = \text{Pólya}(\alpha, \beta)$$

    The gamma distribution can take a variety of shapes, from an exponential to a normal, so random variations in λ for a Poisson can often be well approximated by some gamma, in which case the NegBin distribution becomes a neat combination of the two.

3. *Conjugate prior distribution in Bayesian inference.* In Bayesian inference, the Gamma(α, β) distribution is the *conjugate* to the Poisson likelihood function, which makes it a useful distribution to describe the uncertainty about the Poisson mean λ.

4. *Prior distribution for normal Bayesian inference.* If X is Gamma(α, β) distributed, then $Y = X^{\wedge}(-1/2)$ is an inverted gamma distribution (InvGamma(α, β)) which is sometimes used as a Bayesian prior for σ for a normal distribution.

Equations

Probability density function	$f(x) = \dfrac{\beta^{-\alpha} x^{\alpha-1} \exp\left(-\dfrac{x}{\beta}\right)}{\Gamma(\alpha)}$
Cumulative distribution function	No closed form
Parameter restriction	$\alpha > 0, \beta > 0$

Domain	$x \geq 0$
Mean	$\alpha\beta$
Mode	$\begin{array}{ll} \beta(\alpha - 1) & \text{if } \alpha \geq 1 \\ 0 & \text{if } \alpha < 1 \end{array}$
Variance	$\alpha\beta^2$
Skewness	$\dfrac{2}{\sqrt{\alpha}}$
Kurtosis	$3 + \dfrac{6}{\alpha}$

# Geometric
VoseGeometric(p)

Graphs

Geometric(p) models the number of *failures* that will occur before the first success in a set of binomial trials, given that p is the probability of a trial succeeding.

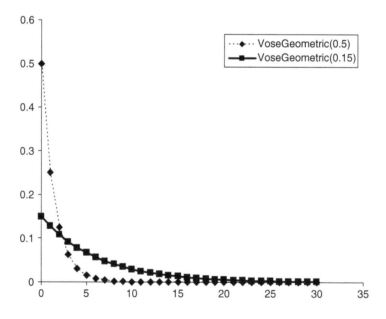

Uses

1. *Dry oil wells.* The geometric distribution is sometimes quoted as useful to estimate the number of dry wells an oil company will drill in a particular section before getting a producing well. That would, however, be assuming that (a) the company doesn't learn from its mistakes and (b) it has the money and obstinacy to keep drilling new wells in spite of the cost.

2. *More sensible example.* You need to purchase some item, conduct a test or operation on that item and, if you fail, go and buy another. For example, you need to find a cow with disease X, but a definitive test involves an expensive procedure, so you randomly select a cow, test it, etc. The number of cows you'll need to buy is $1 + \text{Geomet}(p)$, where p is the prevalence of disease X among the cows.

Note that this would not work if you bought cows in batches. For example, if you bought batches of five cows. Then the number you'd have to buy to get an infected cow would be $= (1 + \text{Geometric}(P)) * 5$, where $P = 1 - (1 - p)^5$, i.e. the probability that a batch of five cows contains at least one infected cow.

Comments

The geometric distribution is a special case of the negative binomial for $s = 1$, i.e. $\text{Geometric}(p) = \text{NegBin}(1, p)$, which means that the sum of s independent $\text{Geometric}(p)$ distributions $= \text{NegBin}(s, p)$. The geometric distribution is the discrete analogue of the exponential distribution and gets its name because its probability mass function is a geometric progression. The geometric distribution is occasionally called a *furry distribution*.

Equations

Probability mass function	$f(x) = p(1 - p)^x$
Cumulative distribution function	$F(x) = 1 - (1 - p)^{\lfloor x \rfloor + 1}$
Parameter restriction	$0 < p \leq 1$
Domain	$x = \{0, 1, 2, \ldots\}$
Mean	$\dfrac{1 - p}{p}$
Mode	0
Variance	$\dfrac{1 - p}{p^2}$
Skewness	$\dfrac{2 - p}{\sqrt{1 - p}}$
Kurtosis	$9 + \dfrac{p^2}{1 - p}$

Generalised Logistic

VoseGLogistic(α, β, γ)

Graphs

The generalised logistic distribution can be either left or right skewed (when parameter γ is less than 1 or greater than 1 respectively) or symmetric ($\gamma = 1$). When $\gamma = 1$ the distribution is logistic.

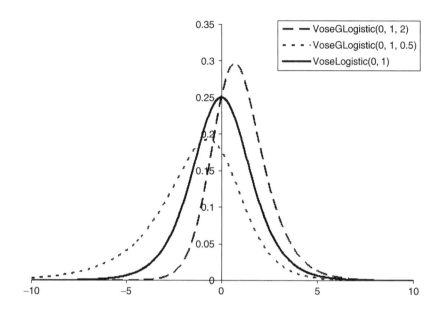

Uses

The generalised logistic distribution has been used to fit values of extremes; for example, extremes of share return fluctuations (Gettinby *et al.*, 2000) and sea levels (van Gelder *et al.*, 2000). It has been used extensively for maximum rainfall modelling, and in the UK and elsewhere it is used in hydrological risk analysis as the standard model for flood frequency estimation (Institute of Hydrology, 1999).

Equations

Probability density function	$f(x) = \dfrac{\gamma}{\beta} \left(\exp\left(\dfrac{x-\alpha}{\beta} \right) \right) \left(1 + \exp\left(\dfrac{x-\alpha}{\beta} \right) \right)^{-\gamma-1}$
Cumulative distribution function	$F(x) = \dfrac{1}{\left(1 + \exp\left(\frac{x-\alpha}{\beta} \right) \right)^{\gamma}}$
Parameter restriction	$\beta > 0, \gamma > 0$
Domain	$-\infty < x < +\infty$
Mean	$\alpha + \beta(EM + \Psi(\gamma))$ where $EM \cong 0.57721$ and Ψ is the digamma function
Mode	$\alpha + \beta \ln[\gamma]$
Variance	$\beta^2 \left(\dfrac{\pi^2}{6} + \Psi'(\gamma) \right) \equiv V$
Skewness	$\dfrac{\Psi''(1) - \Psi''(\gamma)}{V^{3/2}}$
Kurtosis	$\dfrac{\Psi'''(1) - \Psi'''(\gamma)}{V^2}$

# Histogram
VoseHistogram(min, max, $\{p_i\}$)

Graphs

The histogram distribution takes three parameters: a minimum, a maximum and a list of frequencies (or relative frequencies) for a number of equally spaced bands between the minimum and maximum.

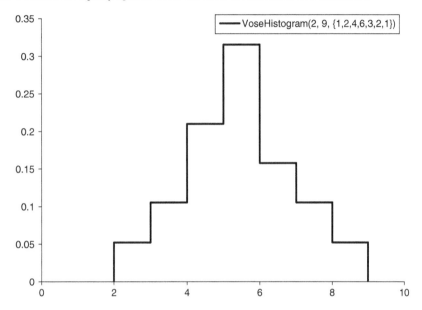

Uses

The distribution is useful in a non–parametric technique for replicating the distribution shape of a large set of data. The technique is simply to collate the data into a number of equal bands between a minimum and maximum you determine, calculate the number of data values that fall into each band and then use this information to define the distribution. It has the disadvantage of "squaring off" into the histogram shape, but with a lot of data and small bands the technique is a transparent and practical way of fitting a distribution to data.

Equations

Probability density function	Assuming the p_i are normalised so that $\dfrac{n \sum p_i}{\text{max} - \text{min}} = 1$ $f(x) = p_i \qquad \text{if } x_i \leq x < x_{i+1}$ $\text{where } x_i = i \dfrac{\text{max} - \text{min}}{n} + \text{min}$
Cumulative distribution function	$F(x) = F(x_i) + p_i \dfrac{x - x_i}{x_{i+1} - x_i} \qquad \text{if } x_i \leq x < x_{i+1}$
Parameter restriction	$p_i \geq 0, \sum p_i > 0, \text{min} \leq \text{max}$
Domain	$\text{min} \leq x \leq \text{max}$

Mean	$\sum\limits_{i=0}^{n} \dfrac{1}{2}(x_{i+1} + x_1)p_i$
Mode	No unique mode
Variance	$\sum\limits_{i=0}^{n-1} \left[\dfrac{1}{2}(x_{i+1} + x_i) - \mu \right]^2 p_i \equiv V$
Skewness	$\dfrac{1}{V^{3/2}} \sum\limits_{i=0}^{n-1} \left[\dfrac{1}{2}(x_{i+1} + x_i) - \mu \right]^3 p_i$
Kurtosis	$\dfrac{1}{V^2} \sum\limits_{i=0}^{n-1} \left[\dfrac{1}{2}(x_{i+1} + x_i) - \mu \right]^4 p_i$

Hyperbolic-Secant

VoseHS(μ, σ)

Graphs

The hyperbolic-secant distribution is a symmetric distribution similar to the normal distribution and defined by its mean and standard deviation, but with a kurtosis of 5, so it is more peaked than the normal. Examples of the hyperbolic-secant distribution are given below.

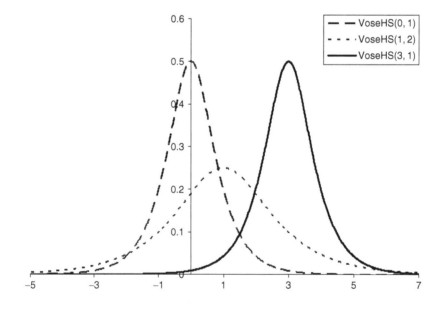

Uses

The hyperbolic-secant distribution can be used to fit data that seem to be approximately normal in distribution but show narrower shoulders, just as the generalised error and Student distributions are an option for data with wider shoulders than a normal.

Comments

The hyperbolic-secant distribution gets its (rather awful) name from the sech function in its probability density function.

Equations

Probability density function	$f(x) = \dfrac{\text{sech }(y)}{2\sigma}$ where $y = \dfrac{\pi}{2\sigma}(x - \mu)$
Cumulative distribution function	$F(x) = \dfrac{2}{\pi}\tan^{-1}[\exp(y)]$
Parameter restriction	$\sigma > 0$
Domain	$-\infty < x < +\infty$
Mean	μ
Mode	μ
Variance	σ^2
Skewness	0
Kurtosis	5

# Hypergeometric
VoseHypergeo(n, D, M)

Graphs

The Hypergeo(n, D, M) distribution models the number of items of a particular type that there are in a sample of size n where that sample is drawn from a population of size M of which D are also of that particular type. Examples of the hypergeometric distribution are shown below.

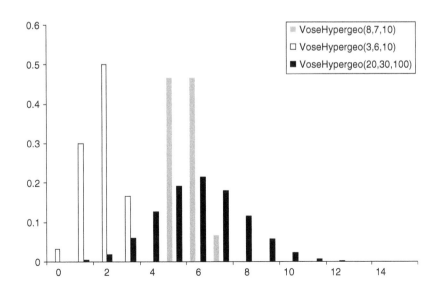

Examples

- *Tiles.* A company has a stock of 2000 tiles that is known to contain 70 tiles that were not fired properly and will probably crack when exposed to the weather. The tiles are all mixed together and the inferior ones unfortunately cannot be visually identified. A customer orders 800 tiles. The number of faulty tiles he will receive can be estimated by Hypergeo(800, 70, 2000).

- *Capture–release–recapture experiment to estimate population size.* An example of using the hypergeometric distribution and Bayes' theorem to estimate the size of a population is given in Section 8.4.4. Several animals (D) are captured and tagged, then released back to the wild. Some time later, another set of animals is captured (n). The number (s) that have tags provides a means, via Bayes' theorem, to estimate the total population, assuming complete diffusion of the tagged sample into the population.

Equations

Probability mass function	$$f(x) = \frac{\binom{D}{x}\binom{M-D}{n-x}}{\binom{M}{n}}$$
Cumulative distribution function	$$F(x) = \sum_{i=0}^{\lfloor x \rfloor} \frac{\binom{D}{i}\binom{M-D}{n-i}}{\binom{M}{n}}$$
Parameter restriction	$0 < n \leq M$, $0 < D \leq M$, $M > 0$ $\;n$, M and D are integers
Domain	$\max(0, n + D - M) \leq x \leq \min(n, D)$
Mean	$$\frac{n\,D}{M}$$
Mode	x_m, x_{m-1} if x_m is an integer $\lfloor x_m \rfloor$ otherwise where $x_m = \dfrac{(n+1)(D+1)}{M+2}$
Variance	$$\frac{n\,D}{M^2}\left[\frac{(M-D)(M-n)}{(M-1)}\right] \qquad \text{for } M > 1$$
Skewness	$$\frac{(M-2D)(M-2n)}{M-2}\sqrt{\frac{M-1}{n\,D\,(M-D)(M-n)}} \quad \text{for } M > 2$$
Kurtosis	$$\left[\frac{M^2(M-1)}{n(M-2)(M-3)(M-n)}\right]\left[\frac{M(M+1)-6M(M-n)}{D(M-D)}\right.$$ $$\left. + \frac{3n(M-n)(M+6)}{M^2} - 6\right]$$ $$\text{for } M > 3$$

# Inverse Gaussian
VoseInvGauss(μ, λ)

Graphs

Right-skewed distribution bounded at zero. Sometimes given the notation IG(μ, λ). Examples of the inverse gaussian distribution are given below.

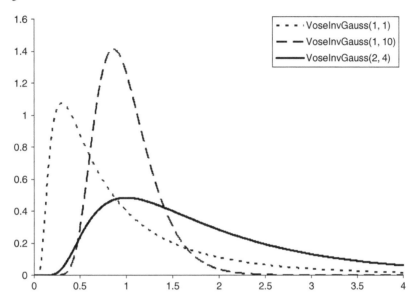

Uses

The inverse gaussian is a distribution seldom used in risk analysis. Its primary uses are:

- as a population distribution where a lognormal distribution has too heavy a right tail;
- to model stock returns and interest rate processes (e.g. Madan, 1998).

Most uses are rather obscure: it has been used, for example, in physics to model the time until a particle, moving with Brownian motion with a drift, will exceed a certain distance from its original position for the first time.

Equations

Probability density function	$f(x) = \sqrt{\dfrac{\lambda}{2\pi x^3}} \exp\left(-\dfrac{\lambda(x-\mu)^2}{2\mu^2 x}\right)$
Cumulative distribution function	No closed form
Parameter restriction	$\mu > 0, \lambda > 0$
Domain	$x > 0$
Mean	μ
Mode	$\mu\left(\sqrt{1+\dfrac{9\mu^2}{4\lambda^2}} - \dfrac{3\mu}{2\lambda}\right)$

Variance	$\dfrac{\mu^3}{\lambda}$
Skewness	$3\sqrt{\dfrac{\mu}{\lambda}}$
Kurtosis	$3 + 15\dfrac{\mu}{\lambda}$

# Inverse Hypergeometric
VoseInvHypergeo(s, D, M)

Graphs

The inverse hypergeometric distribution InvHypergeo(s, D, M) models the number of failures one would have before achieving the sth success in a hypergeometric sampling where there are D individuals of interest (their selection is a "success") in a population of size M. Four examples of the inverse hypergeometric distribution are shown below.

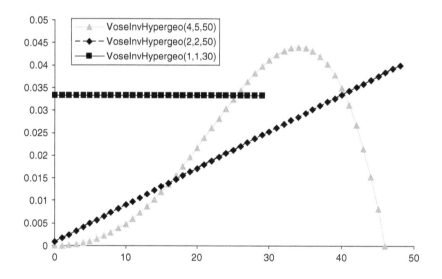

Uses

It should be used in any situation where there is hypergeometric sampling and one is asking the question: "How many failures will I observe before I get s successes?", or alternatively, "How many samples do I need to get s successes?".

Example

The number of cards one needs to turn over to see three hearts will be inverse hypergeometric distributed. If the total number of cards is 54, of which 13 are hearts, the number of cards one needs to turn over is $3 +$ InvHypergeo(3, 13, 54).

Equations

Probability mass function	$f(x) = \dfrac{\dbinom{D}{s-1}\dbinom{M-D}{x-s}(D-s+1)}{\dbinom{M}{x-1}(M-x+1)}$
Cumulative distribution function	$F(x) = \displaystyle\sum_{i=s}^{x} \dfrac{\dbinom{D}{s-1}\dbinom{M-D}{i-s}(D-s+1)}{\dbinom{M}{i-1}(M-i+1)}$
Parameter restriction	$s \le D, D \le M$
Domain	$s \le x \le M - D + s$
Mean	$\dfrac{s(M-D)}{D+1}$
Mode	$x_m, x_{m-1} \quad$ if x_m is an integer $\lfloor x_m \rfloor \qquad$ otherwise where $x_m = \dfrac{(s-1)(M-D-1)}{(D-1)}$
Variance	$\dfrac{s(M-D)(M+1)(D-s+1)}{(D+1)^2(D+2)} \equiv V$
Skewness	$\dfrac{V(D-2M-1)(2s-D-1)}{(D+1)(D+3)\,V^{3/2}}$
Kurtosis	$\dfrac{c(D+1)(D-6s)+3(M-D)(M+1)(s+2)+6s^2-3(M-D)(M+1)s(6+s)/(D+1) \\ +18(M-D)(M+1)s^2/(D+1)^2}{(D+3)(D+4)\,V}$

Johnson Bounded

VoseJohnsonB(α_1, α_2, min, max)

Graphs

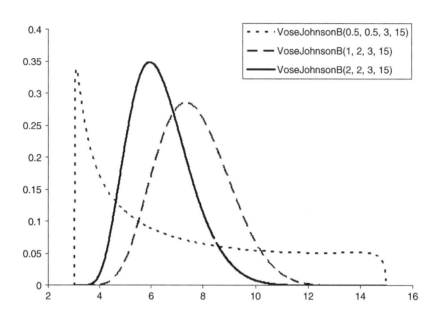

VoseJohnsonB(0.5, 0.5, 3, 15)
VoseJohnsonB(1, 2, 3, 15)
VoseJohnsonB(2, 2, 3, 15)

Uses

The Johnson bounded distribution has a range defined by the min and max parameters. Combined with its flexibility in shape, this makes it a viable alternative to the PERT, triangular and uniform distributions for modelling expert opinion. A public domain software product called VISIFIT allows the user to define the bounds and pretty much any two statistics for the distribution (mode, mean, standard deviation) and will return the corresponding distribution parameters.

Setting min to 0 and max to 1 gives a random variable that is sometimes used to model ratios, probabilities, etc., instead of a beta distribution.

The distribution name comes from Johnson (1949) who proposed a system for categorising distributions, in much the same spirit that Pearson did. Johnson's idea was to translate distributions to be a function of a unit normal distribution, one of the few distributions for which there were good tools available at the time to handle.

Equations

Probability density function	$f(x) = \dfrac{\alpha_2(\max - \min)}{(x - \min)(\max - x)\sqrt{2\pi}} \exp\left[-\dfrac{1}{2}\left(\alpha_1 + \alpha_2 \ln\left[\dfrac{x - \min}{\max - x}\right]\right)^2\right]$
Cumulative distribution function	$F(x) = \Phi\left[\alpha_1 + \alpha_2 \ln\left[\dfrac{x - \min}{\max - x}\right]\right]$ where $F(x) = \Phi[\cdot]$ is the distribution function for a Normal(0, 1).
Parameter restriction	$\alpha_2 > 0$, $\max > \min$
Domain	$\min < x < \max$
Mean	Complicated
Mode	Complicated

Variance	Complicated
Skewness	Complicated
Kurtosis	Complicated

Johnson Unbounded

$$\text{VoseJohnsonU}(\alpha_1, \alpha_2, \beta, \gamma)$$

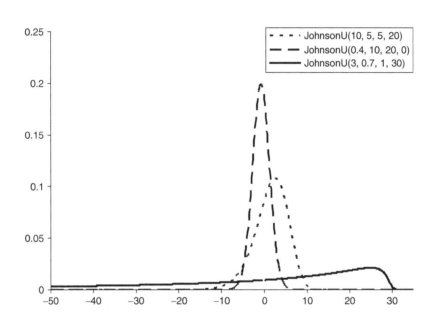

Uses

The main use of the Johnson unbounded distribution is that it can be made to have any combination of skewness and kurtosis. Thus, it provides a flexible distribution to fit to data by matching these moments. That said, it is an infrequently used distribution in risk analysis.

The distribution name comes from Johnson (1949) who proposed a system for categorising distributions, in much the same spirit that Pearson did. Johnson's idea was to translate distributions to be a function of a unit normal distribution, one of the few distributions for which there were good tools available at the time to handle.

Equations

Probability density function	$f(x) = \dfrac{\alpha_2}{\sqrt{2\pi\left((x-\gamma)^2 + \beta^2\right)}} \times$ $\exp\left[-\frac{1}{2}\left(\alpha_1 + \alpha_2 \ln\left[\frac{x-\gamma}{\beta} + \sqrt{\left(\frac{x-\gamma}{\beta}\right)^2 + 1}\right]\right)^2\right]$
Cumulative distribution function	$F(x) = \Phi\left[\alpha_1 + \alpha_2 \ln\left[\dfrac{x-\gamma}{\beta} + \sqrt{\left(\dfrac{x-\gamma}{\beta}\right)^2 + 1}\right]\right]$
Parameter restriction	$\beta > 0,\ \alpha_2 > 0$

Domain	$-\infty < x < +\infty$
Mean	$\gamma - \beta \exp\left[\dfrac{1}{2\alpha_2^2}\right] \sinh\left(\dfrac{\alpha_1}{\alpha_2}\right)$
Mode	Complicated
Variance	Complicated
Skewness	Complicated
Kurtosis	Complicated

Kumaraswamy

VoseKumaraswamy(α, β)

Graphs

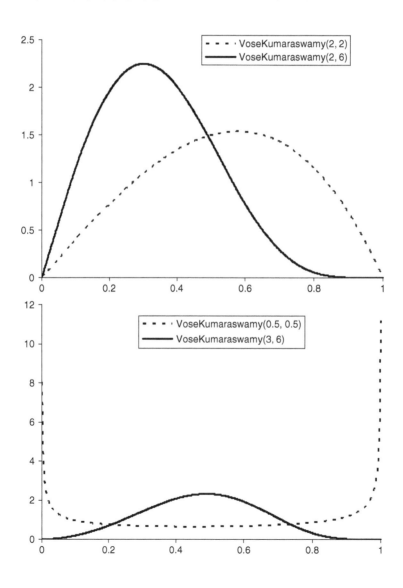

Uses

The Kumaraswamy distribution is not widely used, but, for example, it has been applied to model the storage volume of a reservoir (Fletcher and Ponnambalam, 1996) and system design. It has a simple form for its density and cumulative distributions and is very flexible, like the beta distribution (which does not have simple forms for these functions). It will probably have a lot more applications as it becomes better known.

Equations

Probability density function	$f(x) = \alpha\beta x^{\alpha-1}(1 - x^\alpha)^{\beta-1}$
Cumulative distribution function	$F(x) = 1 - (1 - x^\alpha)^\beta$
Parameter restriction	$\alpha > 0 , \ \beta > 0$
Domain	$0 \leq x \leq 1$
Mean	$\beta \dfrac{\Gamma\left(1 + \dfrac{1}{\alpha}\right)\Gamma(\beta)}{\Gamma\left(1 + \beta + \dfrac{1}{\alpha}\right)} \equiv \mu$
Mode	$\left(\dfrac{\alpha - 1}{\alpha\beta - 1}\right)^{\frac{1}{\alpha}}$ if $\alpha > 1$ and $\beta > 1$ 0 if $\alpha < 1$ 1 if $\beta < 1$
Variance	$\beta \dfrac{\Gamma\left(1 + \dfrac{2}{\alpha}\right)\Gamma(\beta)}{\Gamma\left(1 + \beta + \dfrac{2}{\alpha}\right)} - \mu^2 \equiv V$
Skewness	$\dfrac{1}{V^{3/2}}\left(\beta\dfrac{\Gamma\left(1 + \dfrac{3}{\alpha}\right)\Gamma(\beta)}{\Gamma\left(1 + \beta + \dfrac{3}{\alpha}\right)} - 3\beta\dfrac{\Gamma\left(1 + \dfrac{2}{\alpha}\right)\Gamma(\beta)}{\Gamma\left(1 + \beta + \dfrac{2}{\alpha}\right)}\mu + 2\mu^3\right)$
Kurtosis	$\dfrac{1}{V^2}\left(\beta\dfrac{\Gamma\left(1 + \dfrac{4}{\alpha}\right)\Gamma(\beta)}{\Gamma\left(1 + \beta + \dfrac{4}{\alpha}\right)} - 4\beta\dfrac{\Gamma\left(1 + \dfrac{3}{\alpha}\right)\Gamma(\beta)}{\Gamma\left(1 + \beta + \dfrac{3}{\alpha}\right)}\right.$ $\left.\times\mu + 6\beta\dfrac{\Gamma\left(1 + \dfrac{2}{\alpha}\right)\Gamma(\beta)}{\Gamma\left(1 + \beta + \dfrac{2}{\alpha}\right)}\mu^2 = 3\mu^4\right)$

Kumaraswamy4

VoseKumaraswamy(α, β, min, max)

Graphs

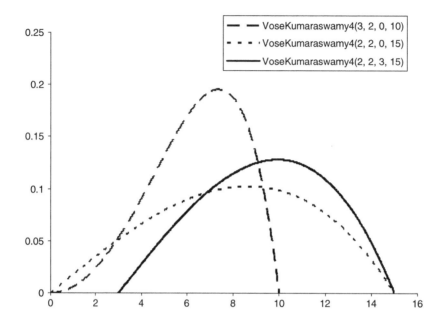

Uses

A Kumaraswamy distribution stretched and shifted to have a specified minimum and maximum, in the same fashion that a beta4 is a stretch and shifted beta distribution.

Equations

Probability density function	$f(x) = \dfrac{\alpha\beta \, z^{\alpha-1}(1-z^\alpha)^{\beta-1}}{(\text{max} - \text{min})}$	where $z = \dfrac{x - \text{min}}{\text{max} - \text{min}}$
Cumulative distribution function	$F(x) = 1 - (1 - z^\alpha)^\beta$	
Parameter restriction	$\alpha > 0$, $\beta > 0$, min $<$ max	
Domain	min $\le x \le$ max	
Mean	$\left(\beta \dfrac{\Gamma\left(1 + \dfrac{1}{\alpha}\right)\Gamma(\beta)}{\Gamma\left(1 + \beta + \dfrac{1}{\alpha}\right)}(\text{max} - \text{min}) \right) + \text{min} \equiv \mu$	
Mode	$\left(\dfrac{\alpha - 1}{\alpha\beta - 1}\right)^{\frac{1}{\alpha}}$ if $\alpha > 1$ and $\beta > 1$ $\quad\quad 0 \quad\quad$ if $\alpha < 1$ $\quad\quad 1 \quad\quad$ if $\beta < 1$	

Variance	$$\left(\beta \frac{\Gamma\left(1+\dfrac{2}{\alpha}\right)\Gamma(\beta)}{\Gamma\left(1+\beta+\dfrac{2}{\alpha}\right)} - (\mu_K)^2\right)(\max-\min)^2 \equiv V$$ where $\mu_K = \mu_{\text{Kumaraswamy}(\alpha,\beta)}$
Skewness	$$\frac{1}{V_K^{3/2}}\left(\beta\frac{\Gamma\left(1+\dfrac{3}{\alpha}\right)\Gamma(\beta)}{\Gamma\left(1+\beta+\dfrac{3}{\alpha}\right)} - 3\beta\frac{\Gamma\left(1+\dfrac{2}{\alpha}\right)\Gamma(\beta)}{\Gamma\left(1+\beta+\dfrac{2}{\alpha}\right)}\mu_K + 2\mu_K^3\right)$$
Kurtosis	$$\frac{1}{V_K^2}\left(\beta\frac{\Gamma\left(1+\dfrac{4}{\alpha}\right)\Gamma(\beta)}{\Gamma\left(1+\beta+\dfrac{4}{\alpha}\right)} - 4\beta\frac{\Gamma\left(1+\dfrac{3}{\alpha}\right)\Gamma(\beta)}{\Gamma\left(1+\beta+\dfrac{3}{\alpha}\right)}\mu_K\right.$$ $$\left. + 6\beta\frac{\Gamma\left(1+\dfrac{2}{\alpha}\right)\Gamma(\beta)}{\Gamma\left(1+\beta+\dfrac{2}{\alpha}\right)}\mu_K^2 - 3\mu_K^4\right)$$

Laplace

VoseLaplace(μ, σ)

Graphs

If X and Y are two identical independent Exponential($1/\sigma$) distributions, and if X is shifted μ to the right of Y, then $(X - Y)$ is a Laplace(μ, σ) distribution. The Laplace distribution has a strange shape with a sharp peak and tails that are longer than tails of a normal distribution. The figure below plots a Laplace(0, 1) against a Normal(0, 1) distribution.

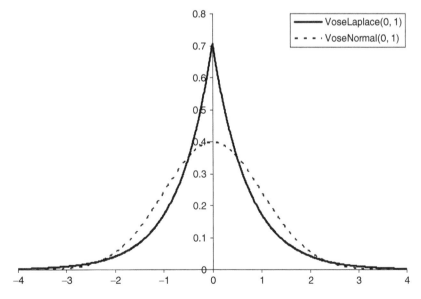

Uses

The Laplace has found a variety of very specific uses, but they nearly all relate to the fact that it has long tails.

Comments

When $\mu = 0$ and $\sigma = 1$ we have the standard form of the Laplace distribution, which is also occasionally called "Poisson's first law of error". The Laplace distribution is also known as the double-exponential distribution (although the Gumbel extreme-value distribution also takes this name), the "two-tailed exponential" and the "bilateral exponential distribution".

Equations

Probability density function	$f(x) = \dfrac{1}{\sqrt{2}\,\sigma} \exp\left[-\dfrac{\sqrt{2}|x-\mu|}{\sigma}\right]$	
Cumulative distribution function	$F(x) = \dfrac{1}{2} \exp\left[-\dfrac{\sqrt{2}|x-\mu|}{\sigma}\right]$	if $x < \mu$
	$F(x) = 1 - \dfrac{1}{2} \exp\left[-\dfrac{\sqrt{2}|x-\mu|}{\sigma}\right]$	if $x \geq \mu$
Parameter restriction	$-\infty < \mu < +\infty$, $\sigma > 0$	
Domain	$-\infty < x < +\infty$	
Mean	μ	
Mode	μ	
Variance	σ^2	
Skewness	0	
Kurtosis	6	

# Lévy
VoseLevy(c, a)

Graphs

The Lévy distribution, named after Paul Pierre Lévy, is one of the few distributions that are stable[1] and that have probability density functions that are analytically expressible. The others are the normal distribution and the Cauchy distribution.

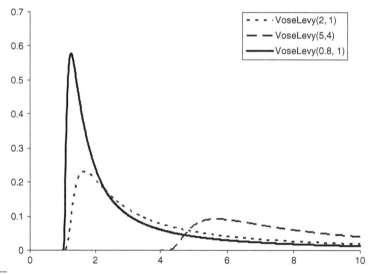

---

[1] A distribution is said to be stable if summing independent random variables from that distribution results in a random variable from that same distribution type.

Uses

The Lévy distribution is sometimes used in financial engineering to model price changes. This distribution takes into account the leptokurtosis ("fat" tails) one sometimes empirically observes in price changes on financial markets.

Equations

Probability density function	$f(x) = \sqrt{\dfrac{c}{2\pi}} \dfrac{e^{-c/2(x-a)}}{(x-a)^{3/2}}$
Cumulative distribution function	No closed form
Parameter restriction	$c > 0$
Domain	$x \geq a$
Mean	Infinite
Mode	$a + \dfrac{c}{3}$
Variance	Infinite
Skewness	Undefined
Kurtosis	Undefined

# Logarithmic
VoseLogarithmic(θ)

Graphs

The logarithmic distribution (sometimes known as the logarithmic series distribution) is a discrete, positive distribution, peaking at $x = 1$, with one parameter and a long right tail. The figures below show two examples of the logarithmic distribution.

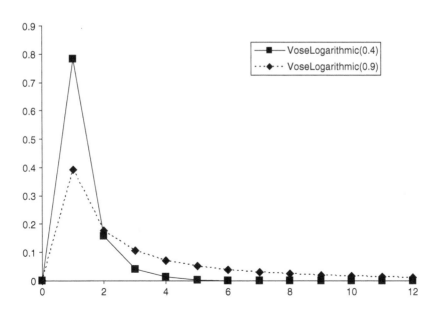

Uses

The logarithmic distribution is not very commonly used in risk analysis. However, it has been used to describe, for example: the number of items purchased by a consumer in a particular period; the number of bird and plant species in an area; and the number of parasites per host. There is some theory that relates the latter two to an observation by Newcomb (1881) that the frequency of use of different digits in natural numbers followed a logarithmic distribution.

Equations

Probability mass function	$f(x) = \dfrac{-\theta^x}{x \ln(1-\theta)}$
Cumulative distribution function	$F(x) = \displaystyle\sum_{i=1}^{\lfloor x \rfloor} \dfrac{-\theta^i}{i \ln(1-\theta)}$
Parameter restriction	$0 < \theta < 1$
Domain	$x = \{1, 2, 3, \ldots\}$
Mean	$\dfrac{\theta}{(\theta - 1) \ln(1 - \theta)}$
Mode	1
Variance	$\mu((1-\theta)^{-1} - \mu) \equiv V$ where μ is the mean
Skewness	$\dfrac{-\theta}{(1-\theta)^3 V^{3/2} \ln(1-\theta)} \left(1 + \theta + \dfrac{3\theta}{\ln(1-\theta)} + \dfrac{2\theta^2}{\ln^2(1-\theta)}\right)$
Kurtosis	$\dfrac{-\theta}{(1-\theta)^4 V^2 \ln(1-\theta)} \left(1 + 4\theta + \theta^2 + \dfrac{4\theta(1+\theta)}{\ln(1-\theta)}\right.$ $\left. + \dfrac{6\theta^2}{\ln^2(1-\theta)} + \dfrac{3\theta^3}{\ln^3(1+\theta)}\right)$

LogGamma

VoseLogGamma(α, β, γ)

Graphs

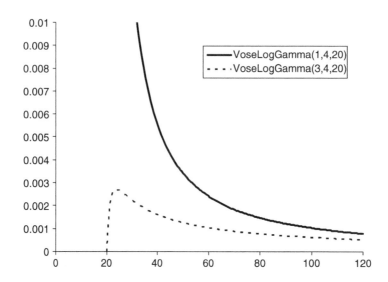

Uses

A variable X is loggamma distributed if its natural log is gamma distributed. In ModelRisk we include an extra shift parameter γ because a standard loggamma distribution has a minimum value of 1 when the gamma variable $= 0$. Thus

$$\text{LogGamma}(\alpha, \beta, \gamma) = \text{EXP}[\text{Gamma}(\alpha, \beta)] + (\gamma - 1)$$

The loggamma distribution is sometimes used to model the distribution of claim size in insurance. Set $\gamma = 1$ to get the standard LogGamma(α, β) distribution.

Equations

Probability density function	$f(x) = \dfrac{(\ln[x - \gamma + 1])^{\alpha-1}(x - \gamma + 1)^{-\left(\frac{1+\beta}{\beta}\right)}}{\beta^\alpha \Gamma(\alpha)}$	
Cumulative distribution function	No closed form	
Parameter restriction	$\alpha > 0, \quad \beta > 0$	
Domain	$x \geq \gamma$	
Mean	$(1 - \beta)^{-\alpha} + \gamma - 1$	if $\beta < 1$
Mode	$\exp\left[\dfrac{\beta(\alpha - 1)}{\beta + 1}\right] + \gamma - 1$ 0	if $\alpha > 1$ else
Variance	$(1 - 2\beta)^{-\alpha} - (1 - \beta)^{-2\alpha} \equiv V$	if $\beta < 1/2$
Skewness	$\dfrac{(1 - 3\beta)^{-\alpha} - 3(1 - 3\beta + 2\beta^2)^{-\alpha} + 2(1 - \beta)^{-3\alpha}}{V^{3/2}}$	if $\beta < 1/3$
Kurtosis	$\dfrac{(1 - 4\beta)^{-\alpha} - 4(1 - 4\beta + 3\beta^2)^{-\alpha} + 6(1 - 2\beta)^{-\alpha}(1 - \beta)^{-2\alpha} - 3(1 - \beta)^{-4\alpha}}{V^2}$ if $\beta < 1/4$	

Logistic

VoseLogistic(α, β)

Graphs

The logistic distribution looks similar to the normal distribution but has a kurtosis of 4.2 compared with the normal kurtosis of 3. Examples of the logistic distribution are given below.

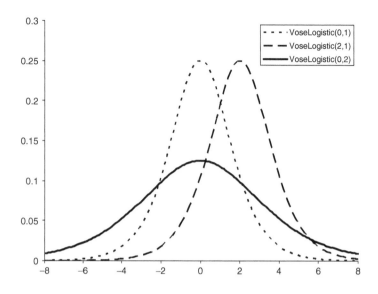

Uses

The logistic distribution is popular in demographic and economic modelling because it is similar to the normal distribution but somewhat more peaked. It does not appear often in risk analysis modelling.

Comments

The cumulative function has also been used as a model for a "growth curve". Sometimes called the sech-squared distribution because its distribution function can be written in a form that includes a sech. Its mathematical derivation is the limiting distribution as n approaches infinity of the standardised mid-range (average of the highest and lowest values) of a random sample of size n from an exponential-type distribution.

Equations

Probability density function	$f(x) = \dfrac{z}{\beta(1+z)^2}$ where $z = \exp\left(-\dfrac{x-\alpha}{\beta}\right)$
Cumulative distribution function	$F(x) = \dfrac{1}{1+z}$
Parameter restriction	$\beta > 0$
Domain	$-\infty < x < +\infty$
Mean	α
Mode	α
Variance	$\dfrac{\beta^2 \pi^2}{3}$
Skewness	0
Kurtosis	4.2

# LogLaplace
VoseLogLaplace(α, β, δ)

Graphs

Examples of the logLaplace distribution are given below. δ is just a scaling factor, giving the location of the point of inflection of the density function. The logLaplace distribution takes a variety of shapes, depending on the value of β. For example, when $\beta = 1$, the logLaplace distribution is uniform for $x < \delta$.

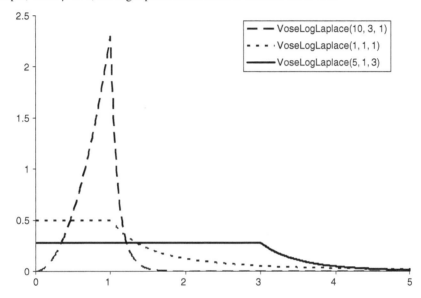

Uses

Kozubowski and Podgórski (no date) review many uses of the logLaplace distribution. The most commonly quoted use (for the symmetric logLaplace) has been for modelling "moral fortune", a state of well-being that is the logarithm of income, based on a formula by Daniel Bernoulli.

The asymmetric logLaplace distribution has been fitted to pharmacokinetic and particle size data (particle size studies often show the log size to follow a tent-shaped distribution like the Laplace). It has been used to model growth rates, stock prices, annual gross domestic production, interest and forex rates. Some explanation for the goodness of fit of the logLaplace has been suggested because of its relationship to Brownian motion stopped at a random exponential time.

Equations

Probability density function	$f(x) = \dfrac{\alpha\beta}{\delta(\alpha + \beta)} \left(\dfrac{x}{\delta}\right)^{\beta-1}$	for $0 \leq x < \delta$
	$f(x) = \dfrac{\alpha\beta}{\delta(\alpha + \beta)} \left(\dfrac{\delta}{x}\right)^{\alpha+1}$	for $x \geq \delta$
Cumulative distribution function	$F(x) = \dfrac{\alpha}{(\alpha + \beta)} \left(\dfrac{x}{\delta}\right)^{\beta}$	for $0 \leq x < \delta$
	$F(x) = 1 - \dfrac{\beta}{(\alpha + \beta)} \left(\dfrac{\delta}{x}\right)^{\alpha}$	for $x \geq \delta$

Parameter restriction	$\alpha > 0$, $\beta > 0$, $\delta > 0$	
Domain	$0 < x < +\infty$	
Mean	$\delta \dfrac{\alpha\beta}{(\alpha - 1)(\beta + 1)} \equiv \mu$	for $\alpha > 1$
Mode	0	for $0 < \beta < 1$
	No unique mode for $\beta = 1$	
	δ	for $\beta > 1$
Variance	$\delta^2 \left(\dfrac{\alpha\beta}{(\alpha - 2)(\beta + 2)} - \left[\dfrac{\alpha\beta}{(\alpha - 1)(\beta + 1)} \right]^2 \right) \equiv V$	for $\alpha > 2$
Skewness	$\dfrac{1}{V^{3/2}} \left(\dfrac{\delta^3 \alpha\beta}{(\alpha - 3)(\beta + 3)} - 3(V + \mu^2)\mu + 2\mu^3 \right)$	for $\alpha > 3$
Kurtosis	$\dfrac{1}{V^2} \left(\dfrac{\delta^4 \alpha\beta}{(\alpha - 4)(\beta + 4)} - 4\dfrac{\delta^3 \alpha\beta}{(\alpha - 3)(\beta + 3)}\mu + 6(V + \mu^2)\mu^2 - 3\mu^4 \right)$	for $\alpha > 4$

# LogLogistic
VoseLogLogistic(α, β)

Graphs

When $\log(X)$ takes a logistic distribution, then X takes a loglogistic distribution. Their parameters are related as follows:

$$\text{EXP[Logistic}(\alpha, \beta)] = \text{LogLogistic}(1/\beta, \text{EXP}[\alpha])$$

LogLogistic(α, 1) is the standard loglogistic distribution.

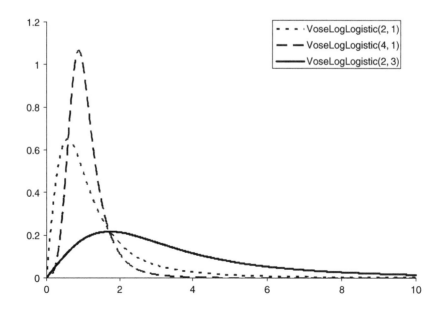

Uses

The loglogistic distribution has the same relationship to the logistic distribution as the lognormal distribution has to the normal distribution. If you feel that a variable is driven by some process that is the product of a number of variables, then a natural distribution to use is the lognormal because of the central limit theorem. However, if one or two of these factors could be dominant, or correlated, so that the distribution is less spread than a lognormal, then the loglogistic may be an appropriate distribution to try.

Equations

Probability density function	$$f(x) = \dfrac{\alpha\, x^{\alpha-1}}{\beta^{\alpha}\left[1+\left(\dfrac{x}{\beta}\right)\right]^{2}}$$
Cumulative distribution function	$$F() = \dfrac{1}{1+\left(\dfrac{\beta}{x}\right)^{\alpha}}$$
Parameter restriction	$\alpha > 0,\ \beta > 0$
Domain	$0 \le x < +\infty$
Mean	$\beta\,\theta\,\csc(\theta) \qquad \text{where } \theta = \dfrac{\pi}{\alpha}$
Mode	$\beta\left[\dfrac{\alpha-1}{\alpha+1}\right]^{\frac{1}{\alpha}}$ for $\alpha > 1$ 0 for $\alpha \le 1$
Variance	$\beta^{2}\,\theta[2\csc(2\theta) - \theta\csc^{2}(\theta)]$ for $\alpha > 2$
Skewness	$\dfrac{3\csc(3\theta) - 6\theta\csc(2\theta)\csc(\theta) + 2\theta^{2}\csc^{3}(\theta)}{\sqrt{\theta}[2\csc(2\theta) - \theta\csc^{2}(\theta)]^{\frac{3}{2}}}$ for $\alpha > 3$
Kurtosis	$\dfrac{6\theta^{2}\csc^{3}(\theta)\sec(\theta) + 4\csc(4\theta) - 3\theta^{3}\csc^{4}(\theta) - 12\theta\csc(\theta)\csc(3\theta)}{\theta\,[2\csc(2\theta) - \theta\csc^{2}(\theta)]^{2}}$ for $\alpha > 4$

Lognormal

VoseLognormal(μ, σ)

Graphs

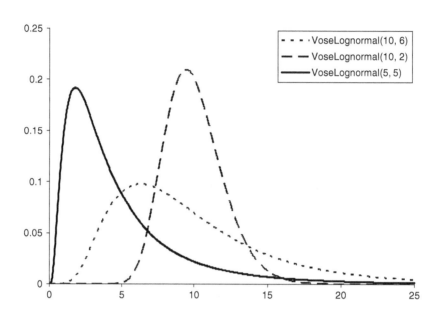

Uses

The lognormal distribution is useful for modelling naturally occurring variables that are the *product* of a number of other naturally occurring variables. The central limit theorem shows that the product of a large number of independent random variables is lognormally distributed. For example, the volume of gas in a petroleum reserve is often lognormally distributed because it is the product of the area of the formation, its thickness, the formation pressure, porosity and the gas:liquid ratio.

Lognormal distributions often provide a good representation for a physical quantity that extend from zero to +infinity and is positively skewed, perhaps because some central limit theorem type of process is determining the variable's size. Lognormal distributions are also very useful for representing quantities that are thought of in orders of magnitude. For example, if a variable can be estimated to within a factor of 2 or to within an order of magnitude, the lognormal distribution is often a reasonable model.

Lognormal distributions have also been used to model lengths of words and sentences in a document, particle sizes in aggregates, critical doses in pharmacy and incubation periods of infectious diseases, but one reason the lognormal distribution appears so frequently is because it is easy to fit and test (one simply transforms the data to logs and manipulates as a normal distribution), and so observing its use in your field does not necessarily mean it is a good model: it may just have been a convenient one. Modern software and statistical techniques have removed much of the need for assumptions of normality, so be cautious about using the lognormal because it has always been that way.

Equations

Probability density function	$f(x) = \dfrac{1}{x\sqrt{2\pi\sigma_1^2}} \exp\left[-\dfrac{(\ln[x] - \mu_1)^2}{2\sigma_1^2}\right]$
	where $\mu_1 = \ln\left[\dfrac{\mu^2}{\sqrt{\sigma^2 + \mu^2}}\right]$ and $\sigma_1 = \sqrt{\ln\left[\dfrac{\sigma^2 + \mu^2}{\mu^2}\right]}$

Cumulative distribution function	No closed form
Parameter restriction	$\sigma > 0, \mu > 0$
Domain	$x \geq 0$
Mean	μ
Mode	$\exp(\mu_1 - \sigma_1^2)$
Variance	σ^2
Skewness	$\left(\dfrac{\sigma}{\mu}\right)^3 + 3\left(\dfrac{\sigma}{\mu}\right)$
Kurtosis	$z^4 + 2z^3 + 3z^2 - 3$ where $z = 1 + \dfrac{\sigma}{\mu}$

LognormalB

VoseLognormalB(μ, σ, B)

Graphs

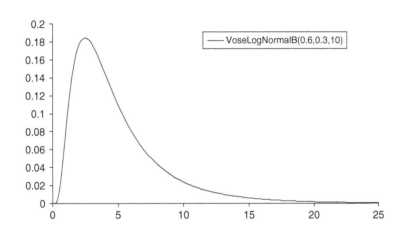

Uses

Scientists often describe data in log form, usually log base 10. This distribution allows the user to specify the base B so, for example:

$$X = \text{VoseLognormalB}(2,3,10) = 10^\wedge \text{Normal}(2, 3)$$

Equations

Probability density function	$f(x) = \dfrac{\exp\left[-\dfrac{(\ln x - m)^2}{2V}\right]}{x\sqrt{V2\pi}}$	where $V = (\sigma \ln B)^2$ and $m = \mu \ln B$
Cumulative distribution function	No closed form	
Parameter restriction	$\sigma > 0, \mu > 0, B > 0$	
Domain	$x \geq 0$	

Mean	$\exp\left(m + \frac{V}{2}\right)$
Mode	$\exp(m - V)$
Variance	$\exp(2m + V)(\exp(V) - 1)$
Skewness	$(\exp(V) + 2)\sqrt{\exp(V) - 1}$
Kurtosis	$\exp(4V) + 2\exp(3V) + 3\exp(2V) - 3$

LognormalE

VoseLognormalE(μ, σ)

Graphs

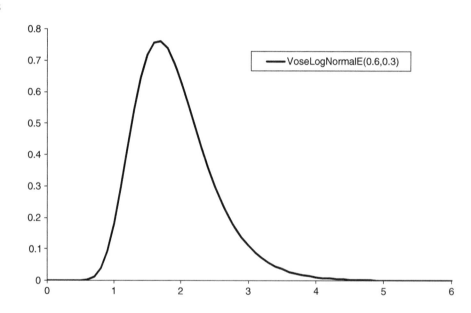

Uses

If a random variable X is such that ln[X] follows a normal distribution, then X follows a lognormal distribution. We can specify X with the mean and standard deviation of the lognormal distribution (see the VoseLognormal distribution above) or by the mean and standard deviation of the corresponding normal distribution, used here. So:

$$X = \text{VoseLognormalE}(2,3) = \exp[\text{Normal}(2,3)]$$

Equations

Probability density function	$f(x) = \dfrac{\exp\left[-\dfrac{(\ln x - \mu)^2}{2\sigma^2}\right]}{x\sigma\sqrt{2\pi}}$
Cumulative distribution function	No closed form
Parameter restriction	$\sigma > 0, \mu > 0$
Domain	$x \geq 0$

Mean	$\exp\left(\mu + \dfrac{\sigma^2}{2}\right)$
Mode	$\exp(\mu - \sigma^2)$
Variance	$\exp(2\mu + \sigma^2)(\exp(\sigma^2) - 1)$
Skewness	$(\exp(\sigma^2) + 2)\sqrt{\exp(\sigma^2) - 1}$
Kurtosis	$\exp(4\sigma^2) + 2\exp(3\sigma^2) + 3\exp(2\sigma^2) - 3$

# Modified PERT
VoseModPERT(min, mode, max, γ)

Graphs

David Vose developed a modification of the PERT distribution with minimum min, most likely mode and maximum max to produce shapes with varying degrees of uncertainty for the min, mode, max values by changing the assumption about the mean:

$$\frac{\text{min} + \gamma\,\text{mode} + \text{max}}{\gamma + 2} \equiv \mu$$

In the standard PERT, $\gamma = 4$, which is the PERT network assumption that the best estimate of the duration of a task = (min + 4mode + max)/6. However, if we increase the value of γ, the distribution becomes progressively more peaked and concentrated around mode (and therefore less uncertain). Conversely, if we decrease γ the distribution becomes flatter and more uncertain. The figure below illustrates the effect of three different values of γ for a modified PERT(5, 7, 10) distribution.

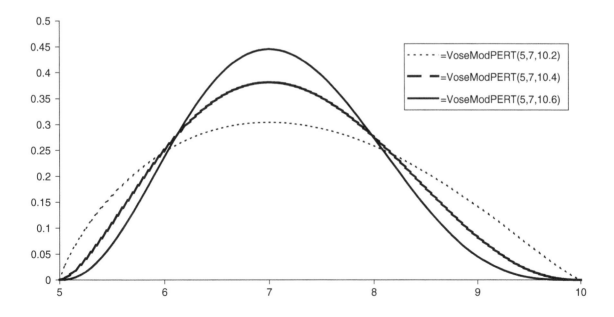

Uses

This modified PERT distribution can be very useful in modelling expert opinion. The expert is asked to estimate three values (minimum, most likely and maximum). Then a set of modified PERT distributions are plotted, and the expert is asked to select the shape that fits his/her opinion most accurately.

Equations

Probability density function	$f(x) = \dfrac{(x - \min)^{\alpha_1 - 1}(\max - x)^{\alpha_2 - 1}}{B(\alpha_1, \alpha_2)(\max - \min)^{\alpha_1 + \alpha_2 - 1}}$ where $\alpha_1 = 1 + \gamma\left(\dfrac{\text{mode} - \min}{\max - \min}\right), \alpha_2 = 1 + \gamma\left(\dfrac{\max - \text{mode}}{\max - \min}\right)$ and $B(\alpha_1, \alpha_2)$ is a beta function
Cumulative distribution function	$F(x) = \dfrac{B_z(\alpha_1, \alpha_2)}{B(\alpha_1, \alpha_2)} \equiv I_z(\alpha_1, \alpha_2)$ where $z = \dfrac{x - \min}{\max - \min}$ and $B_z(\alpha_1, \alpha_2)$ is an incomplete beta function
Parameter restriction	$\min < \text{mode} < \max, \quad \gamma > 0$
Domain	$\min \le x \le \max$
Mean	$\dfrac{\min + \gamma\,\text{mode} + \max}{\gamma + 2} \equiv \mu$
Mode	mode
Variance	$\dfrac{(\mu - \min)(\max - \mu)}{\gamma + 3}$
Skewness	$\dfrac{\min + \max - 2\mu}{4}\sqrt{\dfrac{7}{(\mu - \min)(\max - \mu)}}$
Kurtosis	$3\dfrac{(\alpha_1 + \alpha_2 + 1)(2(\alpha_1 + \alpha_2)^2 + \alpha_1\alpha_2(\alpha_1 + \alpha_2 - 6))}{\alpha_1\alpha_2(\alpha_1 + \alpha_2 + 2)(\alpha_1 + \alpha_2 + 3)}$

# Negative Binomial
VoseNegBin(s, p)

Graphs

The negative binomial distribution estimates the number of failures there will be before s successes are achieved where there is a probability p of success with each trial. Examples of the negative binomial distribution are shown below

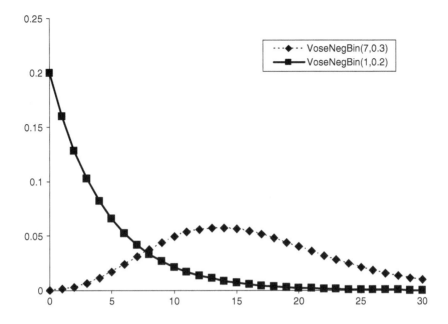

Uses

Binomial examples

The NegBin distribution has two applications for a binomial process:

- the number of failures in order to achieve s successes = NegBin(s, p);
- the number of failures there might have been when we have observed s successes = NegBin ($s + 1, p$).

The first use is when we know that we will stop at the sth success. The second is when we only know that there have been a certain number of successes.

For example, a hospital has received a total of 17 people with a rare disease in the last month. The disease has a long incubation period. There have been no new admissions for this disease for a fair number of days. The hospital knows that people infected with this problem have a 65 % chance of showing symptoms and thus turning up at the hospital. They are worried about how many people there are infected in the outbreak who have not turned up in hospital and may therefore infect others. The answer is NegBin(17 + 1, 65 %). IF we knew (we don't) that the last person to be infected was ill, the answer would be NegBin(17, 65 %). The total number infected would be 17 + NegBin(17 + 1, 65 %).

Poisson example

The negative binomial distribution is frequently used in accident statistics and other Poisson processes because the negative binomial distribution can be derived as a Poisson random variable whose rate parameter lambda is itself random and gamma distributed, i.e.

$$\text{Poisson}(\text{Gamma}(\alpha, \beta)) = \text{NegBin}(\alpha, 1(\beta + 1)) \quad \text{for } \alpha = 1, 2, 3\ldots$$

The negative binomial distribution therefore also has applications in the insurance industry, where, for example, the rate at which people have accidents is affected by a random variable like the weather, or in marketing. This has a number of implications: it means that the negative binomial distribution must have a greater spread than a Poisson distribution with the same mean; and it means that, if one attempts to fit frequencies of random events to a Poisson distribution but finds the Poisson distribution too narrow, then a negative binomial can be tried, and, if that fits well, this suggests that the Poisson rate is not constant but random and can be approximated by the corresponding gamma distribution.

Equations

Probability mass function	$f(x) = \binom{s + x - 1}{x} p^s (1 - p)^x$
Cumulative distribution function	$F(x) = \sum_{i=0}^{\lfloor x \rfloor} \binom{s + i - 1}{i} p^s (1 - p)^i$
Parameter restriction	$0 < p \le 1$ $s > 0$ where s is an integer
Domain	$x = \{0, 1, 2, \ldots\}$
Mean	$\dfrac{s(1 - p)}{p}$
Mode	$z, z + 1$ if z is an integer $\lfloor z \rfloor + 1$ otherwise where $z = \dfrac{s(1 - p) - 1}{p}$
Variance	$\dfrac{s(1 - p)}{p^2}$
Skewness	$\dfrac{2 - p}{\sqrt{s(1 - p)}}$
Kurtosis	$3 + \dfrac{6}{s} + \dfrac{p^2}{s(1 - p)}$

# Normal
VoseNormal(μ, σ)

Graphs

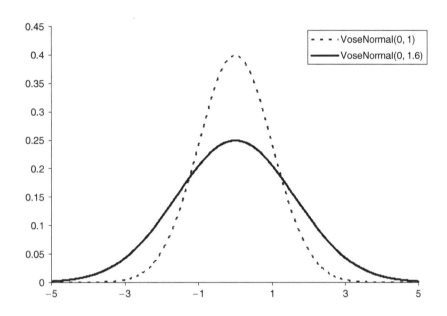

Uses

1. *Modelling a naturally occurring variable.* The normal, or *gaussian*, distribution occurs in a wide variety of applications owing, in part, to the *central limit theorem* which makes it a good approximation to many other distributions.

    It is frequently observed that variations in a naturally occurring variable are approximately normally distributed; for example: the height of adult European males, arm span, etc.

    Population data tend *approximately* to fit to a normal curve, but the data usually have a little more density in the tails.

2. *Distribution of errors.* A normal distribution is frequently used in statistical theory for the distribution of errors (for example, in least-squares regression analysis).

3. *Approximation of uncertainty distribution.* A basic rule of thumb in statistics is that, the more data you have, the more the uncertainty distribution of the estimated parameter approaches a normal. There are various ways of looking at it: from a Bayesian perspective, a Taylor series expansion of the posterior density is helpful; from a frequentist perspective, a central limit theorem argument is often appropriate: binomial example, Poisson example.

4. *Convenience distribution.* The most common use of a normal distribution is simply for its convenience. For example, to add normally distributed (uncorrelated and correlated) random variables, one combines the means and variances in simple ways to obtain another normal distribution.

Classical statistics has grown up concentrating on the normal distribution, including trying to transform data so that they look normal. The Student *t*-distribution and the chi-square distribution are based on a normal assumption. It's the distribution we learn at college. But take care that, when you select a normal distribution, it is not simply through lack of imagination, that you have a good reason for its selection, because there are many other distributions that may be far more appropriate.

Equations

Probability density function	$f(x) = \dfrac{1}{\sqrt{2\pi\sigma^2}} \exp\left(-\dfrac{(x-\mu)^2}{2\sigma^2}\right)$
Cumulative distribution function	No closed form
Parameter restriction	$\sigma > 0$
Domain	$-\infty < x < +\infty$
Mean	μ
Mode	μ
Variance	σ^2
Skewness	0
Kurtosis	3

Ogive

VoseOgive(min, max, {data})

Graphs

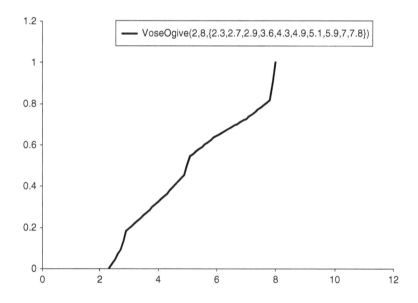

Cumulative graph of the Ogive distribution.

Uses

The Ogive distribution is used to convert a set of data values into an empirical distribution (see Section 10.2.1).

Equations

Probability density function	$f(x) = \dfrac{1}{n+1} \cdot \dfrac{1}{x_{i+1} - x_i}$ for $\begin{array}{c} x_i \leq x < x_{i+1} \\ i \in \{0, 1, \ldots, n+1\} \end{array}$ where $x_0 = \min$, $x_{n+1} = \max$, $P_0 = 0$, $P_{n+1} = 1$
Cumulative distribution function	$F(x_i) = \dfrac{i}{n+1}$
Parameter restriction	$x_i < x_{i+1}, n \geq 0$
Domain	$\min < x < \max$
Mean	$\dfrac{1}{n+1} \displaystyle\sum_{i=0}^{n} \dfrac{x_{i+1} + x_i}{2}$
Mode	No unique mode
Variance	Complicated
Skewness	Complicated
Kurtosis	Complicated

# Pareto
VosePareto(θ, a)

Graphs

The Pareto distribution has an exponential type of shape: right skewed where mode and minimum are equal. It starts at a, and has a rate of decrease determined by θ: the larger the θ, the quicker its tail falls away. Examples of the Pareto distribution are given below

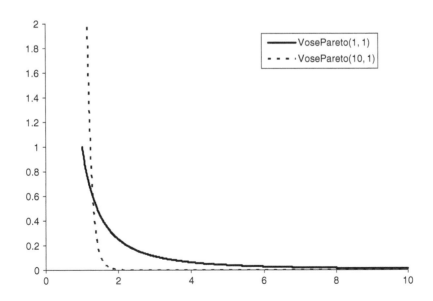

Uses

1. *Demographics.* The Pareto distribution was originally used to model the number of people with an income of at least x, but it is now used to model any variable that has a minimum, but also most likely, value and for which the probability density decreases geometrically towards zero.

    The Pareto distribution has also been used for city population sizes, occurrences of natural resources, stock price fluctuations, size of companies, personal income and error clustering in communication circuits.

    An obvious use of the Pareto is for insurance claims. Insurance policies are written so that it is not worth claiming below a certain value a, and the probability of a claim greater than a is assumed to decrease as a power function of the claim size. It turns out, however, that the Pareto distribution is generally a poor fit.

2. *Long-tailed variable.* The Pareto distribution has the longest tail of all probability distributions. Thus, while it is not a good fit for the bulk of a variable like a claim size distribution, it *is* frequently used to model the tails by splicing with another distribution like a lognormal. That way an insurance company is reasonably guaranteed to have a fairly conservative interpretation of what the (obviously rarely seen, but potentially catastrophic) very high claim values might be. It can also be used to model a longer-tailed discrete variable than any other distribution.

Equations

Probability density function	$f(x) = \dfrac{\theta a^{\theta}}{x^{\theta+1}}$
Cumulative distribution function	$F(x) = 1 - \left(\dfrac{a}{x}\right)^{\theta}$
Parameter restriction	$\theta > 0, a > 0$
Domain	$a \leq x$
Mean	$\dfrac{\theta a}{\theta - 1}$ for $\theta > 1$
Mode	a
Variance	$\dfrac{\theta a^2}{(\theta - 1)^2(\theta - 2)}$ for $\theta > 2$
Skewness	$2\dfrac{\theta + 1}{\theta - 3}\sqrt{\dfrac{\theta - 2}{\theta}}$ for $\theta > 3$
Kurtosis	$\dfrac{3(\theta - 2)(3\theta^2 + \theta + 2)}{\theta(\theta - 3)(\theta - 4)}$ for $\theta > 4$

# Pareto2
VosePareto2(b, q)

Graphs

This distribution is simply a standard Pareto distribution but shifted along the x axis so that it starts at $x = 0$. This is most readily apparent by studying the cumulative distribution functions for the two distributions:
   Pareto

$$F(x) = 1 - \left(\frac{a}{x}\right)^{\theta}$$

Pareto2

$$F(x) = 1 - \left(\frac{b}{x + b}\right)^{q}$$

The only difference between the two equations is that x for the Pareto has been replaced by $(x + b)$ for the Pareto2. In other words, using the notation above:

$$\text{Pareto2}(b, q) = \text{Pareto}(\theta, a) - a$$

where $a = b$ and $q = \theta$

Thus, both distributions have the same variance and shape when $a = b$ and $q = \theta$, but different means.

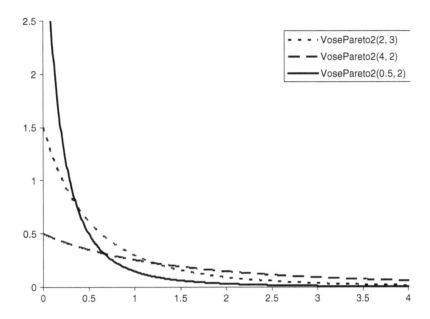

Uses

See the Pareto distribution.

Equations

Probability density function	$f(x) = \dfrac{qb^q}{(x + b)^{q+1}}$	
Cumulative distribution function	$F(x) = 1 - \dfrac{b^q}{(x + b)^q}$	
Parameter restriction	$b > 0, q > 0$	
Domain	$0 \le x \le +\infty$	
Mean	$\dfrac{b}{q - 1}$	for $q > 1$
Mode	0	
Variance	$\dfrac{b^2 q}{(q - 1)^2(q - 2)}$	for $q > 2$
Skewness	$2\dfrac{q + 1}{q - 3}\sqrt{\dfrac{q - 2}{q}}$	for $q > 3$
Kurtosis	$\dfrac{3(q - 2)(3q^2 + q + 2)}{q(q - 3)(q - 4)}$	for $q > 4$

# Pearson5
VosePearson5(α, β)

Graphs

The Pearson family of distributions was designed by Pearson between 1890 and 1895. It represents a system whereby for every member the probability density function $f(x)$ satisfies a differential equation:

$$\frac{1}{p}\frac{dp}{dx} = -\frac{a+x}{c_0 + c_1 x + c_2 x^2}$$ (1)

where the shape of the distribution depends on the values of the parameters a, c_0, c_1 and c_2. The Pearson type 5 corresponds to the case where $c_0 + c_1 x + c_2 x^2$ is a perfect square ($c^2 = 4c_0 c_2$). Thus, equation (1) can be rewritten as

$$\frac{d\log f(x)}{dx} = -\frac{a+x}{c_2(x+c_1)^2}$$

Examples of the Pearson type 5 distribution are given below.

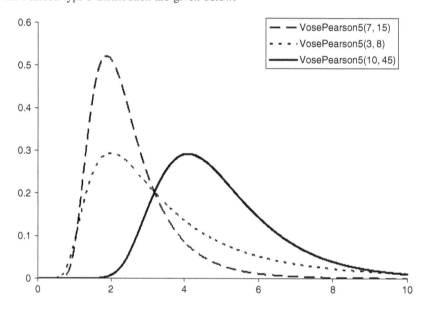

Uses

This distribution is very rarely used correctly in risk analysis.

Equations

Probability density function	$f(x) = \dfrac{1}{\beta\Gamma(\alpha)}\dfrac{e^{-\beta/x}}{(x/\beta)^{\alpha+1}}$
Cumulative distribution function	No closed form
Parameter restriction	$\alpha > 0, \beta > 0$
Domain	$0 \le x < +\infty$

Mean	$\dfrac{\beta}{\alpha - 1}$	for $\alpha > 1$
Mode	$\dfrac{\beta}{\alpha + 1}$	
Variance	$\dfrac{\beta^2}{(\alpha - 1)^2(\alpha - 2)}$	for $\alpha > 2$
Skewness	$\dfrac{4\sqrt{\alpha - 2}}{\alpha - 3}$	for $\alpha > 3$
Kurtosis	$\dfrac{3(\alpha + 5)(\alpha - 2)}{(\alpha - 3)(\alpha - 4)}$	for $\alpha > 4$

# Pearson6
VosePearson6(α_1, α_2, β)

Graphs

The Pearson type 6 distribution corresponds in the Pearson system to the case when the roots of $c_0 + c_1 x + c_2 x^2 = 0$ are real and of the same sign. If they are both negative, then

$$f(x) = K(x - a_1)^{m_1}(x - a_2)^{m_2}$$

Since the expected value is greater than a_2, it is clear that the range of variation of x must be $x > a_2$. Examples of the Pearson type 6 distribution are given below.

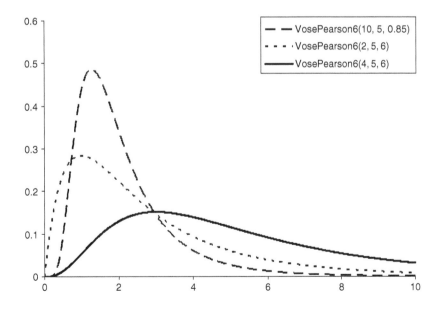

Uses

At Vose Consulting we don't find much use for this distribution (other than to generate an F distribution). The distribution is very unlikely to reflect any of the processes that the analyst may come across, but its three parameters (giving it flexibility), sharp peak and long tail make it a possible candidate to be fitted to a very large (so you know the pattern is real) dataset to which other distributions won't fit well.

Like the Pearson type 5 distribution, the Pearson type 6 distribution hasn't proven to be very useful in risk analysis.

Equations

Probability density function	$f(x) = \dfrac{1}{\beta B(\alpha_1, \alpha_2)} \dfrac{(x/\beta)^{\alpha_1 - 1}}{\left(1 + \dfrac{x}{\beta}\right)^{\alpha_1 + \alpha_2}}$ where $B(\alpha_1, \alpha_2)$ is a beta function	
Cumulative distribution function	No closed form	
Parameter restriction	$\alpha_1 > 0, \alpha_2 > 0, \beta > 0$	
Domain	$0 \le x < +\infty$	
Mean	$\dfrac{\beta \alpha_1}{\alpha_2 - 1}$	for $\alpha_2 > 1$
Mode	$\dfrac{\beta(\alpha_1 - 1)}{\alpha_2 + 1}$ 0	for $\alpha_1 > 1$ otherwise
Variance	$\dfrac{\beta^2 \alpha_1 (\alpha_1 + \alpha_2 - 1)}{(\alpha_2 - 1)^2 (\alpha_2 - 2)}$	for $\alpha_2 > 2$
Skewness	$2 \sqrt{\dfrac{\alpha_2 - 2}{\alpha_1 (\alpha_1 + \alpha_2 - 1)}} \left[\dfrac{2\alpha_1 + \alpha_2 - 1}{\alpha_2 - 3} \right]$	for $\alpha_2 > 3$
Kurtosis	$\dfrac{3(\alpha_2 - 2)}{(\alpha_2 - 3)(\alpha_2 - 4)} \left[\dfrac{2(\alpha_2 - 1)^2}{\alpha_1 (\alpha_1 + \alpha_2 - 1)} + (\alpha_2 + 5) \right]$	for $\alpha_2 > 4$

# PERT
VosePERT(min, mode, max)

Graphs

The PERT (aka betaPERT) distribution gets its name because it uses the same assumption about the mean (see below) as PERT networks (used in the past for project planning). It is a version of the beta distribution and requires the same three parameters as the triangular distribution, namely minimum (a), most likely (b) and maximum (c). The figure below shows three PERT distributions whose shape can be compared with the triangular distributions.

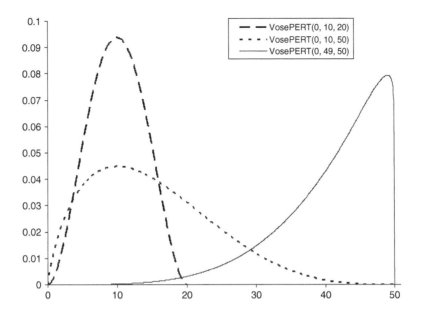

Uses

The **PERT** distribution is used exclusively for modelling expert estimates, where one is given the expert's minimum, most likely and maximum guesses. It is a direct alternative to a triangular distribution.

Equations

Probability density function	$f(x) = \dfrac{(x - \min)^{\alpha_1 - 1}(\max - x)^{\alpha_2 - 1}}{B(\alpha_1, \alpha_2)(\max - \min)^{\alpha_1 + \alpha_2 - 1}}$ where $\alpha_1 = 6\left[\dfrac{\mu - \min}{\max - \min}\right]$, $\alpha_2 = 6\left[\dfrac{\max - \mu}{\max - \min}\right]$ with $\mu(= \text{mean}) = \dfrac{\min + 4\text{mode} + \max}{6}$ and $B(\alpha_1, \alpha_2)$ is a beta function
Cumulative distribution function :	$f(x) = \dfrac{B_z(\alpha_1, \alpha_2)}{B(\alpha_1, \alpha_2)} \equiv I_z(\alpha_1, \alpha_2)$ where $z = \dfrac{x - \min}{\max - \min}$ and $B_z(\alpha_1, \alpha_2)$ is an incomplete beta function
Parameter restriction :	$\min < \text{mode} < \max$
Domain :	$\min \leq x \leq \max$
Mean :	$\dfrac{\min + 4\text{mode} + \max}{6} \equiv \mu$
Mode :	mode
Variance :	$\dfrac{(\mu - \min)(\max - \mu)}{7}$

Skewness :	$\dfrac{\min + \max - 2\mu}{4}\sqrt{\dfrac{7}{(\mu - \min)(\max - \mu)}}$
Kurtosis :	$3\dfrac{(\alpha_1 + \alpha_2 + 1)(2(\alpha_1 + \alpha_2)^2 + \alpha_1\alpha_2(\alpha_1 + \alpha_2 - 6))}{\alpha_1\alpha_2(\alpha_1 + \alpha_2 + 2)(\alpha_1 + \alpha_2 + 3)}$

# Poisson
VosePoisson(λt)

Graphs

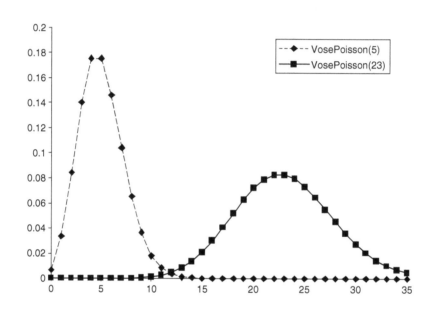

Uses

The Poisson(λt) distribution models the number of occurrences of an event in a time t with an expected rate of λ events per period t when the time between successive events follows a Poisson process.

Example

If β is the mean time between events, as used by the exponential distribution, then $\lambda = 1/\beta$. For example, imagine that records show that a computer crashes on average once every 250 hours of operation ($\beta = 250$ hours), then the rate of crashing λ is 1/250 crashes per hour. Thus, a Poisson(1000/250) = Poisson(4) distribution models the number of crashes that could occur in the next 1000 hours of operation.

Equations

Probability mass function	$f(x) = \dfrac{e^{-\lambda t}(\lambda t)^x}{x!}$
Cumulative distribution function	$F(x) = e^{-\lambda t}\displaystyle\sum_{i=0}^{\lfloor x \rfloor}\dfrac{(\lambda t)^i}{i!}$

Parameter restriction	$\lambda t > 0$
Domain	$x = \{0, 1, 2, \ldots\}$
Mean	λt
Mode	$\lambda t, \lambda t - 1$ if λt is an integer $\lfloor \lambda t \rfloor$ otherwise
Variance	λt
Skewness	$\dfrac{1}{\sqrt{\lambda t}}$
Kurtosis	$3 + \dfrac{1}{\lambda t}$

# Pólya
VosePolya(α, β)

Graphs

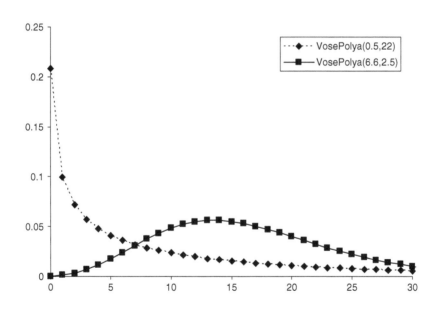

Uses

There are several types of distribution in the literature that have been given the Pólya name. We employ the name for a distribution that is very common in the insurance field. A standard initial assumption of the frequency distribution of the number of claims is Poisson:

$$\text{Claims} = \text{Poisson}(\lambda)$$

where λ is the expected number of claims during the period of interest. The Poisson distribution has a mean and variance equal to λ, and one often sees historic claim frequencies with a variance greater than the mean so that the Poisson model underestimates the level of randomness of claim numbers. A standard method to incorporate greater variance is to assume that λ is itself a random variable (and the claim frequency distribution is called a mixed Poisson model). A Gamma(α, β) distribution is most commonly used to describe the random variation in λ between periods, so

$$\text{Claims} = \text{Poisson}(\text{Gamma}(\alpha, \beta)) \tag{1}$$

This is the Pólya(α, β) distribution.

Comments

Relationship to the negative binomial

If α is an integer, we have

$$\text{Claims} = \text{Poisson}(\text{Gamma}(\alpha, \beta)) = \text{NegBin}(\alpha, 1/(1+\beta)) \tag{2}$$

so one can say that the negative binomial distribution is a special case of the Pólya.

Equations

Probability mass function	$f(x) = \dfrac{\Gamma(\alpha+x)\beta^x}{\Gamma(x+1)\Gamma(\alpha)(1+\beta)^{\alpha+x}}$
Cumulative distribution function	$F(x) = \displaystyle\sum_{i=0}^{x} \dfrac{\Gamma(\alpha+i)\beta^i}{\Gamma(i+1)\Gamma(\alpha)(1+\beta)^{\alpha+i}}$
Parameter restriction	$\alpha > 0, \beta > 0$
Domain	$x = \{0, 1, 2, \ldots\}$
Mean	$\alpha\beta$
Mode	$\begin{array}{ll} 0 & \text{if } \alpha \leq 1 \\ z, z+1 & \text{if } z \text{ is an integer} \\ \lceil z \rceil & \text{if } z \text{ is not an integer} \\ \multicolumn{2}{l}{\text{where } z = \beta(\alpha-1) - 1} \end{array}$
Variance	$\alpha\beta(1+\beta)$
Skewness	$\dfrac{1+2\beta}{\sqrt{(1+\beta)\alpha\beta}}$
Kurtosis	$3 + \dfrac{6}{\alpha} + \dfrac{1}{\alpha\beta(1+\beta)}$

# Rayleigh
VoseRayleigh(b)

Graphs

Originally derived by Lord Rayleigh (or by his less glamorous name J. W. Strutt) in the field of acoustics.

The graph below shows various Rayleigh distributions. The distribution in solid line is a Rayleigh(1), sometimes referred to as the standard Rayleigh distribution.

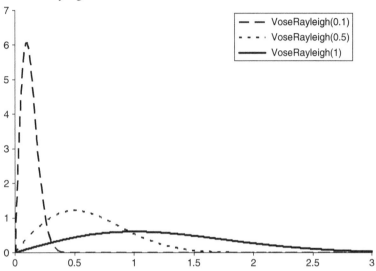

Uses

The Rayleigh distribution is frequently used to model wave heights in oceanography, and in communication theory to describe hourly median and instantaneous peak power of received radio signals.

The distance from one individual to its nearest neighbour when the spatial pattern is generated by a Poisson distribution follows a Rayleigh distribution.

The Rayleigh distribution is a special case of the Weibull distribution since Rayleigh(b) = Weibull($2, b\sqrt{2}$), and as such is a suitable distribution for modelling the lifetime of a device that has a linearly increasing instantaneous failure rate: $z(x) = x/b^2$.

Equations

Probability density function	$f(x) = \dfrac{x}{b^2} \exp\left[-\dfrac{1}{2}\left(\dfrac{x}{b}\right)^2\right]$
Cumulative distribution function	$F(x) = 1 - \exp\left[-\dfrac{1}{2}\left(\dfrac{x}{b}\right)^2\right]$
Parameter restriction	$b > 0$
Domain	$0 \leq x < +\infty$
Mean	$b\sqrt{\dfrac{\pi}{2}}$
Mode	b

Variance	$b^2\left(2 - \dfrac{\pi}{2}\right)$
Skewness	$\dfrac{2(\pi - 3)\sqrt{\pi}}{(4 - \pi)^{3/2}} \approx 0.6311$
Kurtosis	$\dfrac{32 - 3\pi^2}{(4 - \pi)^2} \approx 3.2451$

Reciprocal

VoseReciprocal(min, max)

Graphs

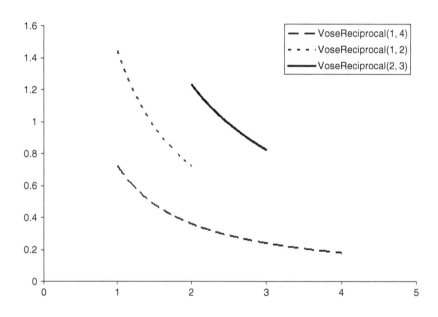

Uses

The reciprocal distribution is widely used as an uninformed prior distribution in Bayesian inference for scale parameters.

It is also used to describe "$1/f$ noise". One way to characterise different noise sources is to consider the spectral density, i.e. the mean squared fluctuation at any particular frequency f and how that varies with frequency. A common approach is to model spectral densities that vary as powers of inverse frequency: the power spectrum $P(f)$ is proportional to f for $\beta \geq 0$. $\beta = 0$ equates to white noise (i.e. no relationship between $P(f)$ and f), $\beta = 2$ is called Brownian noise and $\beta = 1$ takes the name "$1/f$ noise" which occurs very often in nature.

Equations

Probability density function	$f(x) = \dfrac{1}{xq}$ where $q = \log(\max) - \log(\min)$
Cumulative distribution function	$F(x) = \dfrac{\log(x) - \log(\min)}{q}$
Parameter restriction	$0 < \min < \max$

Domain	$\min \leq x \leq \max$
Mean	$\dfrac{\max - \min}{q}$
Mode	$\min$
Variance	$\dfrac{(\max - \min)[\max(q - 2) + \min(q + 2)]}{2q^2}$
Skewness	$\dfrac{\sqrt{2}\left[\begin{array}{c}12q(\max-\min)^2 + \\ q^2(\max^2(2q-9) + 2\min\max q + \min^2(2q+9))\end{array}\right]}{3q\sqrt{\max - \min}(\max(q - 2) + \min(q + 2))^{3/2}}$
Kurtosis	$\dfrac{\begin{array}{c}36q(\max-\min)^2(\max+\min)-36(\max-\min)^3-16q^2(\max^3-\min^3)+ \\ 3q^3(\max^2+\min^2)(\max+\min)\end{array}}{3(\max - \min)(\max(q - 2) + \min(q + 2))^2}$

Relative

VoseRelative(min, max, $\{x_i\}$, $\{p_i\}$)

Graphs

The relative distribution is a non-parametric distribution (i.e. there is no underlying probability model) where $\{x_i\}$ is an array of x values with probability densities $\{p_i\}$ and where the distribution falls between the minimum and maximum. An example of the relative distribution is given below.

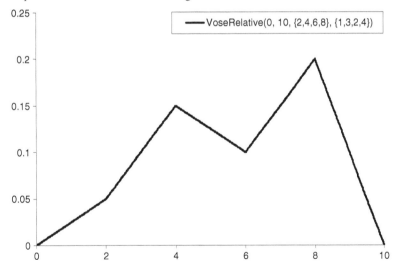

Uses

1. *Modelling expert opinion.* The relative distribution is very useful for producing a fairly detailed distribution that reflects an expert's opinion. The relative distribution is the most flexible of all of the continuous distribution functions. It enables the analyst and expert to tailor the shape of the distribution to reflect, as closely as possible, the opinion of the expert.

2. *Modelling posterior distribution in Bayesian inference.* If you use the construction method of obtaining a Bayesian posterior distribution, you will have two arrays: a set of possible values in ascending order, and

a set of posterior weights for each of those values. This exactly matches the input parameters for a relative distribution which can then be used to generate values from the posterior distribution. Examples: turbine blades; fitting a Weibull distribution.

Equations

Probability density function	$f(x) = \dfrac{x - x_i}{x_{i+1} - x_i}(p_{i+1} - p_i) + p_i$	if $x_i \le x < x_{i+1}$
Cumulative distribution function	$F(x) = F(x_i) + \dfrac{x - x_i}{x_{i+1} - x_i} \cdot \dfrac{p_i + p_{i+1}}{2(x_{i+1} - x_i)}$	if $x_i \le x < x_{i+1}$
Parameter restriction	$p_i \ge 0,\, x_i < x_{i+1},\, n > 0,\, \displaystyle\sum_{i=1}^{n} p_i > 0$	
Domain	$\min \le x \le \max$	
Mean	No closed form	
Mode	No closed form	
Variance	No closed form	
Skewness	No closed form	
Kurtosis	No closed form	

# Slash
VoseSlash(q)

Graphs

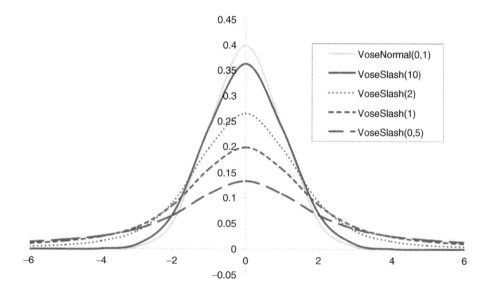

Uses

The (standard) slash distribution is defined as the ratio of a standard normal and an exponentiated uniform(0,1) distribution:

$$\text{Slash}(q) = \text{Normal}(0, 1)/\text{Uniform}(0, 1)^{1/q}$$

The slash distribution may be used for perturbations on a time series in place of a more standard normal distribution assumption, because it has longer tails. The q parameter controls the extent of the tails. As q approaches infinity, the distribution looks more and more like a normal.

Equations

Probability density function	$f(x) = q \displaystyle\int_0^1 u^q \phi(ux)\mathrm{d}u$	
	where $\phi(x)$ is the standard normal pdf	
Cumulative distribution function	$F(x) = q \displaystyle\int_0^1 u^{q-1} \Phi(xu)\mathrm{d}u$	
	where $\Phi(x)$ is the standard normal cdf	
Parameter restriction	$q > 0$	
Domain	$-\infty < x < +\infty$	
Mean	0	for $q > 1$
Mode	0	
Variance	$\dfrac{q}{q-2}$	for $q > 2$
Skewness	Complicated	
Kurtosis	Complicated	

SplitTriangle

VoseSplitTriangle(low, medium, high, low$P$, medium$P$, high$P$)

Graphs

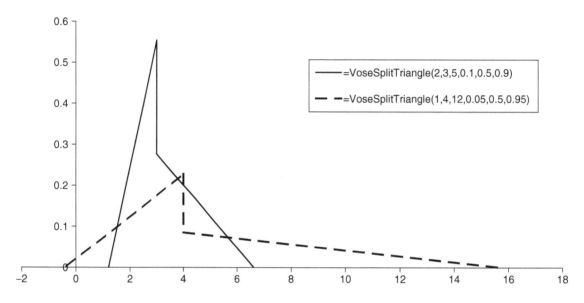

Legend:
- ──── =VoseSplitTriangle(2,3,5,0.1,0.5,0.9)
- ── ── =VoseSplitTriangle(1,4,12,0.05,0.5,0.95)

Uses

The split triangle is used to model expert opinion (see Chapter 14) where the subject matter expert (SME) is asked for three points on the distribution: for each point the SME provides a value of the variable and his or her view of the probability of it being less than that value. The split triangle then extrapolates from these values to create a distribution composed of two triangles as in the figure above.

Equations

Probability density function:	$f(x) = \dfrac{\text{Height1} \, (x - \min)}{(\text{mode} - \min)}$ if $\min \le x \le \text{mode}$ $f(x) = \dfrac{\text{Height2} \, (\max - x)}{(\max - \text{mode})}$ if $\text{mode} < x \le \max$ where $\text{Height1} = \dfrac{2 * \text{mediumP}}{\text{mode} - \min}$ $\text{Height2} = \dfrac{2 * (1 - \text{mediumP})}{\max - \text{mode}}$ and $\min = \dfrac{(\text{low} - \text{mode}*\sqrt{\text{lowP}/\text{mediumP}})}{(1 - \sqrt{\text{lowP}/\text{mediumP}})}$ $\text{mode} = \text{medium}$ $\max = \dfrac{(\text{mode} - \text{high}*\sqrt{1 - \text{mediumP}/1 - \text{highP}})}{(1 - \sqrt{1 - \text{mediumP}/1 - \text{highP}})}$

Cumulative distribution function:	$F(x) = 0$ if $x < \min$ $F(x) = \dfrac{\text{Height1}(x - \min)^2}{2(\text{mode} - \min)}$ if $\min \leq x \leq \text{mode}$ $F(x) = 1 - \dfrac{\text{Height2}(\max - x)^2}{2(\max - \text{mode})}$ if $\text{mode} < x \leq \max$ $F(x) = 1$ if $\max < x$
Parameter restriction:	$\min \leq \text{mode} \leq \max, \min < \max$
Domain:	$\min < x < \max$
Mean:	$\dfrac{\text{mediumP} + (1 - \text{mediumP})\max + 2 * \text{mode}}{3}$
Mode:	mode
Variance:	$\dfrac{\text{mode}^2 - 2*\text{mode}*\text{mediumP}*\min + 2*\text{mode}*\text{mediumP}*\max - 2*\text{mode}*\max - 2*\text{medium}P^2*\min^2 + \max^2}{18}$ $+ \dfrac{-2*\text{mediumP}^2*\max^2 + 4*\text{mediumP}^2*\max*\min + 3*\text{mediumP}*\min^2 + \text{mediumP}*\max^2 - 4*\min*\text{mediumP}*\max}{18}$
Skewness:	Complicated
Kurtosis:	Complicated

Step Uniform

VoseStepUniform(min, max, step)

Graph

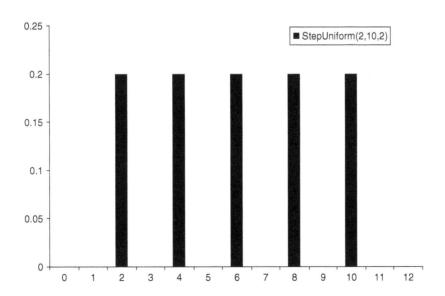

Uses

The step uniform distribution returns values between the min and max at the defined step increments. If the step value is omitted, the function assumes a default value of 1.

The step uniform function is generally used as a tool to sample in a controlled way along some dimension (e.g. time, distance, x) and can be used to perform simple one-dimensional numerical integrations. By setting the step value to give a specific number of allowed values n

$$\text{Step} = \frac{\text{max} - \text{min}}{n - 1}$$

and using Latin hypercube sampling with n iterations, we can ensure that each allowed value is sampled just once to get a more accurate integral.

StepUniform(A, B), where A and B are integers, will generate a random integer variable that can be used as an index variable as an efficient way to select paired data randomly from a database.

Equations

Probability mass function	$f(x) = \dfrac{\text{step}}{\text{max} - \text{min} + \text{step}}$	for $x = \text{min} + i \cdot \text{step}$, $i = 0$ to $\dfrac{\text{max} - \text{min}}{\text{step}}$
	0	otherwise
Cumulative distribution function	$F(x) = 0$	for $x < \text{min}$
	$\left(\left\lfloor \dfrac{x - \text{min}}{\text{step}} \right\rfloor + 1\right) * \dfrac{\text{step}}{\text{max} - \text{min} + \text{step}}$	for $\text{min} \leq x < \text{max}$
		for $\text{max} \leq x$
Parameter restriction	$\dfrac{\text{max} - \text{min}}{\text{step}}$ must be an integer	
Domain	$\text{min} \leq x \leq \text{max}$	
Mean	$\dfrac{\text{min} + \text{max}}{2}$	
Mode	Not uniquely defined	
Variance	$\dfrac{(\text{max} - \text{min})(\text{max} - \text{min} + 2\text{step})}{12}$	
Skewness	0	
Kurtosis	$\dfrac{3}{5}\left[\dfrac{3(\text{max} - \text{min})^2 + 2\text{step}(3\text{max} - 3\text{min} - 2\text{step})}{(\text{max} - \text{min})(\text{max} - \text{min} + 2\text{step})}\right]$	

# Student
VoseStudent(ν)

Graphs

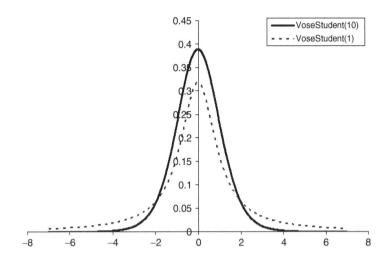

Uses

The most common use of the Student distribution is for the estimation of the mean of a (n assumed normally distributed) population where random samples from that population have been observed, and its standard deviation is unknown. The relationship

$$\text{Student}(\nu) = \text{Normal}(0, \text{SQRT}(\nu/\text{ChiSq}(\nu)))$$

is at the centre of the method. This is equivalent to a t-test in classical statistics.

Other sample statistics can be approximated to a Student distribution, and thus a Student distribution can be used to describe one's uncertainty about the parameter's true value, in regression analysis, for example.

Comments

First discovered by the English statistician William Sealy Gossett (1876–1937), whose employer (the brewery company Guinness) forbade employees from publishing their work, so he wrote a paper under the pseudonym "Student". As ν increases, the Student t-distribution tends to a Normal(0, 1) distribution.

Equations

Probability density function	$f(x) = \dfrac{\Gamma\left(\frac{\nu+1}{2}\right)}{\sqrt{\pi\nu}\,\Gamma\left(\frac{\nu}{2}\right)\left[1+\left(\frac{x^2}{\nu}\right)\right]^{\frac{\nu+1}{2}}}$	
Cumulative distribution function	$F(x) = \dfrac{1}{2} + \dfrac{1}{\pi}\left[\tan^{-1}\left(\dfrac{x}{\sqrt{\nu}}\right) + \dfrac{x\sqrt{\nu}}{\nu+x^2}\displaystyle\sum_{j=0}^{\frac{\nu-3}{2}}\dfrac{a_j}{\left(1+\frac{x^2}{\nu}\right)^j}\right]$	if ν is odd
	$F(x) = \dfrac{1}{2} + \dfrac{x}{2\sqrt{\nu+x^2}}\displaystyle\sum_{j=0}^{\frac{\nu-2}{2}}\dfrac{b_j}{\left(1+\frac{x^2}{\nu}\right)^j}$	if ν is even
	where $a_j = \left(\dfrac{2j}{2j+1}\right)a_{j-1}, a_0 = 1$ and $b_j = \left(\dfrac{2j-1}{2j}\right)b_{j-1}, b_0 = 1$	

Parameter restriction	v is a positive integer	
Domain	$-\infty < x < +\infty$	
Mean	0	for $v > 1$
Mode	0	
Variance	$\dfrac{v}{v-2}$	for $v > 2$
Skewness	0	for $v > 3$
Kurtosis	$3\left(\dfrac{v-2}{v-4}\right)$	for $v > 4$

Triangle

VoseTriangle(min, mode, max)

Graphs

The triangular distribution constructs a triangular shape from the three input parameters. Examples of the triangular distribution are given below.

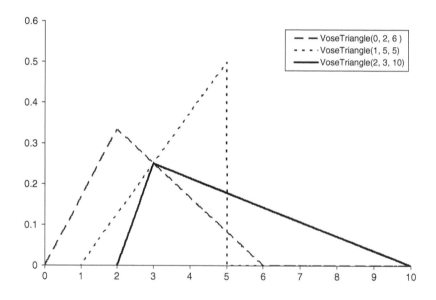

Uses

The triangular distribution is used as a rough modelling tool where the range (min to max) and the most likely value within the range (mode) can be estimated. It has no theoretical basis but derives its statistical properties from its geometry.

The triangular distribution offers considerable flexibility in its shape, coupled with the intuitive nature of its defining parameters and speed of use. It has therefore achieved a great deal of popularity among risk analysts. However, min and max are the absolute minimum and maximum estimated values for the variable, and it is generally a difficult task to make estimates of these values.

Equations

Probability density function	$f(x) = \dfrac{2(x - \min)}{(\text{mode} - \min)(\max - \min)}$	if $\min \le x \le \text{mode}$
	$f(x) = \dfrac{2(\max - x)}{(\max - \min)(\max - \text{mode})}$	if $\text{mode} < x \le \max$
Cumulative distribution function	$F(x) = 0$	if $x < \min$
	$F(x) = \dfrac{(x - \min)^2}{(\text{mode} - \min)(\max - \min)}$	if $\min \le x \le \text{mode}$
	$F(x) = 1 - \dfrac{(\max - x)^2}{(\max - \min)(\max - \text{mode})}$	if $\text{mode} < x \le \max$
	$F(x) = 1$	if $\max < x$
Parameter restriction	$\min \le \text{mode} \le \max, \min < \max$	
Domain	$\min < x < \max$	
Mean	$\dfrac{\min + \text{mode} + \max}{3}$	
Mode	mode	
Variance	$\dfrac{\min^2 + \text{mode}^2 + \max^2 - \min\,\text{mode} - \min\,\max - \text{mode}\,\max}{18}$	
Skewness	$\dfrac{2\sqrt{2}}{5} \dfrac{z(z^2 - 9)}{(z^2 + 3)^{3/2}}$	where $z = \dfrac{2(\text{mode} - \min)}{\max - \min} - 1$
Kurtosis	2.4	

# Uniform
VoseUniform(min, max)

Graphs

A uniform distribution assigns equal probability to all values between its minimum and maximum. Examples of the uniform distribution are given below.

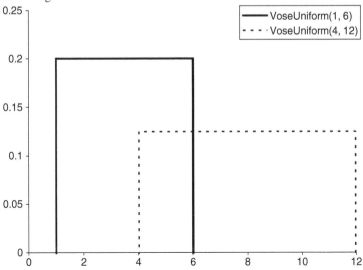

Uses

1. *Rough estimate.* The uniform distribution is used as a very approximate model where there are very little or no available data. It is rarely a good reflection of the perceived uncertainty of a parameter since all values within the allowed range have the same constant probability density, but that density abruptly changes to zero at the minimum and maximum. However, it is sometimes useful for bringing attention to the fact that a parameter is very poorly known.

2. *Crude sensitivity analysis.* Sometimes we want to get a rough feel for whether it is important to assign uncertainty to a parameter. You could give the parameter a uniform distribution with reasonably wide bounds, run a crude sensitivity analysis and see whether the parameter registered as having influence on the output uncertainty: if not, it may as well be left crudely estimated. The uniform distribution assigns the most (reasonable) uncertainty to the parameter, so, if the output is insensitive to the parameter with a uniform, it will be even more insensitive for another distribution.

3. *Rare uniform variable.* There are some special circumstances where a uniform distribution may be appropriate, for example a Uniform(0, 360) distribution for the angular resting position of a camshaft after spinning, or a Uniform(0, L/2) for the distance from a random leak in a pipeline of segments of length L to its nearest segment end (where you'd break the pipeline to get access inside).

4. *Plotting a function.* Sometimes you might have a complicated function you wish to plot for different values of an input parameter, or parameters. For a one-parameter function (like $y = $ GAMMALN(ABS(SIN(x)/ (($x - 1$)^0.2 + COS(LN(3 * x)))), for example), you can make two arrays: the first with the x values (say between 1 and 1000), and the second with the correspondingly calculated y values. Alternatively, you could write one cell for x ($=$ Uniform(1, 1000)) and another for y using the generated x value, name both as outputs, run a simulation and export the generated values into a spreadsheet. Perhaps not worth the effort for one parameter, but when you have two or three parameters it is. Graphic software like S-PLUS will draw surface contours for $\{x, y, z\}$ data arrays.

5. *Uninformed prior.* A uniform distribution is often used as an uninformed prior in Bayesian inference.

Equations

Probability density function	$f(x) = \dfrac{1}{\text{max} - \text{min}}$
Cumulative distribution function	$F(x) = \dfrac{x - \text{min}}{\text{max - min}}$
Parameter restriction	min ¡ max
Domain	min $< x <$ max
Mean	$\dfrac{\text{min} + \text{max}}{2}$
Mode	No unique mode
Variance	$\dfrac{(\text{max} - \text{min})^2}{12}$
Skewness	0
Kurtosis	1.8

# Weibull
VoseWeibull(α, β)

Graphs

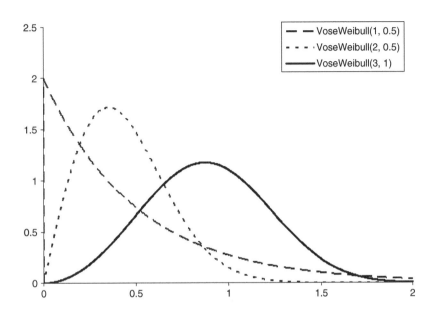

Uses

The Weibull distribution is often used to model the time until occurrence of an event where the probability of occurrence changes with time (the process has "memory"), as opposed to the exponential distribution where the probability of occurrence remains constant ("memoryless"). It has also been used to model variation in wind speed at a specific site.

Comments

The Weibull distribution becomes an exponential distribution when $\alpha = 1$, i.e. Weibull(1, β) = Exponential(β). The Weibull distribution is very close to the normal distribution when $\beta = 3.25$. The Weibull distribution is named after the Swedish physicist Dr E. H. Wallodi Weibull (1887–1979) who used it to model the distribution of the breaking strengths of materials.

Equations

Probability density function	$f(x) = \alpha\beta^{-\alpha}x^{\alpha-1}\exp\left[-\left(\dfrac{x}{\beta}\right)^{\alpha}\right]$
Cumulative distribution function	$F(x) = 1 - \exp\left[-\left(\dfrac{x}{\beta}\right)^{\alpha}\right]$
Parameter restriction	$\alpha > 0, \beta > 0$
Domain	$-\infty < x < +\infty$
Mean	$\dfrac{\beta}{\alpha}\Gamma\left(\dfrac{1}{\alpha}\right)$

Mode	$\beta \left(\dfrac{\alpha - 1}{\alpha} \right)^{\frac{1}{\alpha}}$ if $\alpha \geq 1$ 0 if $\alpha < 1$
Variance	$\dfrac{\beta^2}{\alpha} \left[2\Gamma \left(\dfrac{2}{\alpha} \right) - \dfrac{1}{\alpha} \Gamma \left(\dfrac{1}{\alpha} \right)^2 \right]$
Skewness	$\dfrac{3\Gamma \left(\dfrac{3}{\alpha} \right) + \dfrac{6}{\alpha} \Gamma \left(\dfrac{2}{\alpha} \right) \Gamma \left(\dfrac{1}{\alpha} \right) + \dfrac{2}{\alpha^2} \Gamma^3 \left(\dfrac{1}{\alpha} \right)}{\sqrt{\dfrac{1}{\alpha} \left[2\Gamma \left(\dfrac{2}{\alpha} \right) - \dfrac{1}{\alpha} \Gamma^2 \left(\dfrac{1}{\alpha} \right) \right]^{\frac{3}{2}}}}$
Kurtosis	$\dfrac{\left(\begin{array}{c} 4\Gamma \left(\dfrac{4}{\alpha} \right) - \dfrac{12}{\alpha} \Gamma \left(\dfrac{1}{\alpha} \right) \Gamma \left(\dfrac{3}{\alpha} \right) - \dfrac{12}{\alpha} \Gamma^2 \left(\dfrac{2}{\alpha} \right) \\ + \dfrac{24}{\alpha^2} \Gamma^2 \left(\dfrac{1}{\alpha} \right) \Gamma \left(\dfrac{2}{\alpha} \right) - \dfrac{6}{\alpha^3} \Gamma^4 \left(\dfrac{1}{\alpha} \right) \end{array} \right)}{\dfrac{1}{\alpha} \left[2\Gamma \left(\dfrac{2}{\alpha} \right) - \dfrac{1}{\alpha} \Gamma^2 \left(\dfrac{1}{\alpha} \right) \right]}$

III.7.2 Multivariate Distributions

# Dirichlet
VoseDirichlet({α})

Uses

The Dirichlet distribution is the multivariate generalisation of the beta distribution. {VoseDirichlet} is input in Excel as an array function.

It is used in modelling probabilities, prevalence or fractions where there are multiple states to consider. It is the multinomial extension to the beta distribution for a binomial process.

Example 1

You have the results of a survey conducted in the premises of a retail outlet. The age and sex of 500 randomly selected shoppers were recorded:

<25 years, male: 38 people
25 to <40 years, male: 72 people
>40 years, male: 134 people
<25 years, female: 57 people
25 to <40 years, female: 126 people
>40 years, female: 73 people

In a manner analogous to the beta distribution, by adding 1 to each number of observations we can estimate the fraction of all shoppers to this store that are in each category as follows:

$$= \text{VoseDirichlet}(\{38 + 1, 72 + 1, 134 + 1, 57 + 1, 126 + 1, 73 + 1\})$$

The Dirichlet then returns the uncertainty about the fraction of all shoppers that are in each group.

Example 2

A review of 1000 companies that were S&P AAA rated last year in your sector shows their rating 1 year later:

AAA:	908
AA:	83
A:	7
BBB or below:	2

If we assume that the market has similar volatilities to last year, we can estimate the probability that a company rated AAA now will be in each state next year as

$$= \text{VoseDirichlet}(\{908 + 1, 83 + 1, 7 + 1, 2 + 1\})$$

The Dirichlet then returns the uncertainty about these probabilities.

Comments

The Dirichlet distribution is named after Johann Peter Gustav Lejeune Dirichlet. It is the conjugate to the multinomial distribution. The first value of a $\{\text{Dirichlet}(\alpha_1, \alpha_2)\} = \text{Beta}(\alpha_1, \alpha_2)$.

Equations

The probability density function of the Dirichlet distribution of order K is

$$f(x) = \frac{1}{B(\alpha)} \prod_{i=1}^{K} x_i^{\alpha_i - 1}$$

where x is a K-dimensional vector $x = (x_1, x_2, \ldots, x_K)$, $\alpha = (\alpha_1, \ldots, \alpha_K)$ is a parameter vector and $B(\alpha)$ is the multinomial beta function

$$B(\alpha) = \frac{\prod_{i=1}^{K} \Gamma(\alpha_i)}{\Gamma\left(\sum_{i=1}^{K} \alpha_i\right)}$$

Parameter restrictions: $\alpha_i > 0$. Domain: $0 \le x_i \le 1; \sum_{i=1}^{k} x_i = 1$.

Inverse Multivariate Hypergeometric

VoseInvMultiHypereo($\{s\}, \{d\}$)

The inverse multivariate hypergeometric distribution answers the question: How many extra (wasted) random multivariate hypergeometric samples will occur before the required numbers of successes $\{s\}$ are selected from each subpopulation $\{D\}$?

For example, imagine that our population is split up into four subgroups {A, B, C, D} of sizes {20, 30, 50, 10} and that we are going randomly to sample from this population until we have {4, 5, 2, 1} of each subgroup respectively. The number of extra samples we will have to make is modelled as

$$= \text{VoseInvMultiHypergeo}(\{4, 5, 2, 1\}, \{20, 30, 50, 10\})$$

The total number of trials that need to be performed is

$$= \text{SUM}(\{4, 5, 2, 1\}) + \text{VoseInvMultiHypergeo}(\{4, 5, 2, 1\}, \{20, 30, 50, 10\})$$

The inverse multivariate hypergeometric 2 is a multivariate distribution that responds to the same question but breaks down the number of extra samples into their subgroups. This is a univariate distribution, though belonging to a multivariate process. I have placed it in the multivariate section for easier comparison with the following distribution.

Inverse Multivariate Hypergeometric 2
VoseInvMultiHypergeo2($\{s\}$, $\{D\}$)

The second inverse multivariate hypergeometric distribution answers the question: How many extra (wasted) random multivariate hypergeometric samples will be drawn from each subpopulation before the required numbers of successes $\{s\}$ are selected from each subpopulation $\{D\}$.

For example, imagine that our population is split up into four subgroups {A, B, C, D} of sizes {20, 30, 50, 10} and that we are going randomly to sample from this population until we have {4, 5, 2, 1} of each subgroup respectively. The number of extra samples we will have to make for each subpopulation A to D is modelled as the array function:

$$\{= \text{VoseInvMultiHypergeo}(\{4, 5, 2, 1\}, \{20, 30, 50, 10\})\}$$

Note that at least one category must be zero, since once the last category to be filled has the required number of samples the sampling stops, so for that category at least there will be no extra samples.

The inverse multivariate hypergeometric 2 responds to the same question as the multivariate hypergeometric distribution but breaks down the number of extra samples into their subgroups, whereas the inverse multivariate hypergeometric simply returns the total number of extra samples.

Multivariate Hypergeometric
VoseMultiHypergeo(N, $\{D_j\}$)

The multivariate hypergeometric distribution is an extension of the hypergeometric distribution where more than two different states of individuals in a group exist.

Example

In a group of 50 people, of whom 20 were male, a VoseHypergeo(10, 20, 50) would describe how many from 10 randomly chosen people would be male (and by deduction how many would therefore be female). However, let's say we have a group of 10 people as follows:

German	English	French	Canadian
3	2	1	4

Now, let's take a sample of four people at random from this group. We could have various numbers of each nationality in our sample:

German	English	French	Canadian
3	1	0	0
3	0	1	0
3	0	0	1
2	2	0	0
2	1	1	0
2	1	0	1
2	0	2	0
2	0	1	1
2	0	0	2
...	...	...	...
Etc.			

and each combination has a certain probability. The multivariate hypergeometric distribution is an *array distribution*, in this case generating simultaneously four numbers, that returns how many individuals in the random sample came from each subgroup (e.g. German, English, French and Canadian).

Generation

The multivariate hypergeometric distribution is created by extending the mathematics of the hypergeometric distribution. The hypergeometric distribution models the number of individuals s in a sample of size n (that are randomly sampled from a population of size M) that come from a subgroup of size D (and therefore $(n - s)$ will have come from the remaining number subgroup $(M - D)$) as shown in the following figure:

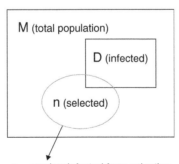

s = number infected from selection

resulting in the probability for s:

$$f(x) = \frac{\dbinom{D}{x} \dbinom{M - D}{n - x}}{\dbinom{M}{n}}$$

The numerator is the number of different sampling combinations (each of which has the same probability because each individual has the same probability of being sampled) where one would have exactly s from the subgroup D (and by implication $(n - s)$ from the subgroup $(M - D)$. The denominator is the total number of different combinations one could have in selecting n individuals from a group of size M. Thus, the equation is just the proportion of different possible scenarios, each of which has the same probability, that would give us s from D.

The multivariate hypergeometric probability equation is just an extension of this idea. The figure below is a graphical representation of the multivariate hypergeometric process, where D_1, D_2, D_3 and so on are the number of individuals of different types in a population, and $x_1, x_2, x_3, \ldots$ are the number of successes (the number of individuals in our random sample (circled) belonging to each category).

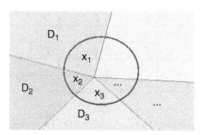

and results in the probability distribution for $\{x\}$:

$$f(\{x\}) = \frac{\binom{D_1}{x_1} \binom{D_2}{x_2} \cdots \binom{D_{k1}}{x_k}}{\binom{M}{n}}$$

where

$$\sum_{i=1}^{k} D_i = M \text{ and } \sum_{i=1}^{k} x_i = n$$

Equations

Probability mass function	$f(\{x_1, x_2, \ldots, x_j\}) = \dfrac{\binom{D_1}{x_1} \binom{D_2}{x_2} \cdots \binom{D_{k1}}{x_k}}{\binom{M}{n}}$ where $M = \sum_{i=1}^{j} D_i$
Parameter restriction	$0 < n \leq M, n, M$ and D_i are integers
Domain	$\max(0, n + D_i - M) \leq x_i \leq \min(n, D_i)$

# Multinomial
VoseMultinomial(N, $\{p\}$)

The multinomial distribution is an array distribution and is used to describe how many independent trials will fall into each of several categories where the probability of falling into any one category is constant for all trials. As such, it is an extension of the binomial distribution where there are only two possible outcomes ("successes" and, by implication, "failures").

Uses

For example, consider the action people might take on entering a shop:

Code	Action	Probability
A1	Enter and leave without purchase or sample merchandise	32%
A2	Enter and leave with a purchase	41%
A3	Enter and leave with sample merchandise	21%
A4	Enter to return a product and leave without purchase	5%
A5	Enter to return a product and leave with a purchase	1%

If 1000 people enter a shop, how many will match each of the above actions?

The answer is {Multinomial(1000, {32 %, 41 %, 21 %, 5 %, 1 %})} which is an array function that generates five separate values. The sum of those five values must, of course, always add up to the number of trials (1000 in this example).

Equations

Probability mass function	$f(\{x_1, x_2, \ldots, x_j\}) = \dfrac{n!}{x_1! \ldots x_j!} p_1^{x_1} \ldots p_j^{x_j}$
Parameter restrictions	$p_i \geq 0, n \in \{1, 2, 3, \ldots\}, \sum\limits_{i=1}^{n} p_i = 1$
Domain	$x_i = \{0, 1, 2, \ldots, n\}$

# Multivariate Normal
VoseMultiNormal($\{\mu_i\}$, $\{\text{cov}_{\text{matrix}}\}$)

Uses

A multinormal distribution, also sometimes called a multivariate normal distribution, is a specific probability distribution that can be thought of as a generalisation to higher dimensions of the one-dimensional normal distribution.

Equations

The probability density function of the multinormal distribution is the following function of an N-dimensional vector $x = (x_1, \ldots, x_N)$:

$$f(x) = \frac{1}{(2\pi)^{N/2} |C|^{1/2}} \exp\left[-\frac{1}{2}(x - \mu)^T C^{-1}(x - \mu)\right]$$

where $\mu = (\mu_1, \ldots, \mu_N)$, C is the covariance matrix ($N \times N$) and $|C|$ is the determinant of C.

Parameter restrictions: C must be a symmetric, positive, semi-definite matrix.

# Negative Multinomial
VoseNegMultinomial($\{s\}$, $\{p\}$)

The negative multinomial distribution is a generalisation of the negative binomial distribution. The NegBin(s, p) distribution estimates the total number of binomial trials that are failures before s successes are achieved where there is a probability p of success with each trial.

For the negative multinomial distribution, instead of having a single value for s, we now have a set of success values {s} representing different "states" of successes (s_i) one can have, with each "state" i having a probability p_i of success. This is a univariate distribution, though belonging to a multivariate process. I have placed it in the multivariate section for easier comparison with the following distribution.

Now, the negative multinomial distribution tells us how many failures we will have before we have achieved the total number of successes

$$\sum_{i=1}^{k} s_i$$

Example

Suppose you want to do a telephone survey about a certain product you made by calling people you pick randomly out of the phone book.

You want to make sure that at the end of the week you have called 50 people who have never heard of your product, 50 people who don't have the Internet at home and 200 people who use the Internet almost daily.

If you know the probabilities of success p_i, the NegMultinomial({50, 50, 200}, {p_1, p_2, p_3}) will tell you how many failures you'll have before you've called all the people you wanted and so you also know the total number of phone calls you'll have to make to reach the people you wanted.

The total number of phone calls = the total number of successes (300) + the total number of failures (NegMultinomial ({50, 50, 200}, {p_1, p_2, p_3})).

Negative Multinomial 2
VoseNegMultinomial2({s}, {p})

The negative multinomial 2 is the same distribution as the negative multinomial, but, instead of giving you the global number of failures before reaching a certain number of successes, the negative multinomial 2 gives you the number of failures in each "group" or "state".

So, in the example of the telephone survey (see the negative multinomial) where the total number of phone calls was equal to the total number of successes plus the total number of failures, the total number of failures would now be a sum of the number of failures in each group (three groups in the example).

III.8 Introduction to Creating Your Own Distributions

Risk analysis software offer a wide variety of probability distributions that cover most common risk analysis problems. However, one might occasionally wish to generate one's own probability distribution. There are several reasons why one would prefer to make one's own distributions, and four main ways to do this. The choice of which method to use will be determined by the following criteria:

- Do you know the cdf or the pdf of the continuous distribution, or the pmf of the discrete distribution? If "yes", try method 1.

- Do you know a relationship to another distribution provided by your software? If "yes", try method 2.

- Do you have data from which you wish to construct an empirical distribution? If "yes", try method 3.

- Do you have points on a curve you want to convert to a distribution? If "yes", try method 4.

In addition to creating your own distributions, sometimes it is very useful to approximate a distribution with another one, which is discussed in the following section.

III.8.1 Method 1: Generating Your Own Distribution When You Know the cdf, pdf or pmf

Situation

You wish to use a parametric probability distribution that is not provided by your software, and you know:

- the cumulative distribution function (continuous variable);
- the probability density function (continuous variable); or
- the probability mass function (discrete variable).

This section describes the technique for each situation.

Known cumulative distribution function (cdf)

This method applies when you know the cdf of a continuous probability distribution. The algebraic equation of the cdf can often be inverted to make x the subject of the equation. For example, the cdf of the exponential probability distribution is

$$F(x) = 1 - e^{-x/\beta} \tag{III.4}$$

where β is the mean of the exponential distribution. Inverting equation (III.4) to make x its subject gives

$$x = -\beta \ln(1 - F(x)) \tag{III.5}$$

A random sample from any continuous probability distribution has equal probability of lying in any equally sized range of $F(x)$ between 0 and 1. For example, the variable X has a 10 % probability of producing a value between x_1 and x_2 ($x_2 > x_1$), where $F(x_2) - F(x_1) = 0.1$. Looking at it the other way round, $F(x)$ can be thought of as being a Uniform(0, 1) random variable. Thus, we can write Equation (III.5) as an Excel formula to generate values from an exponential distribution with a mean of 23 as follows:

$$= -23 * \text{LN}(1 - \text{VoseUniform}(0, 1)) \tag{III.6}$$

This is exactly equivalent to writing

$$= \text{VoseExpon}(23)$$

in a cell. If we use Latin hypercube sampling (LHS) to draw from the Uniform(0, 1) distribution, we will get Latin hypercube samples from the constructed exponential distribution too. Similarly, if we force the uniform distribution to sample from its lower end – a technique necessary for advanced sensitivity analysis and stress analysis, for example, Equation (III.6) will generate values from the lower end of the exponential distribution.

There is a disadvantage: the method hinges on being able to perform the algebra that inverts the cdf. If that proves too difficult, it may be easier to construct the cdf with a cumulative distribution.

Known probability density function (pdf)

We may sometimes start with the pdf for a variable, determine the cdf by integration and then use the first method, although this generally requires good maths skills. Another reason one might like to determine the cdf could be an interest in the probability of the variable being below, between or above certain values. Integration of the pdf will give the cdf that can give you these probabilities. The example below shows you how to determine a cdf, starting with a pdf, in this case of a sine curve distribution.

Imagine that you want to design a distribution that follows the shape of a sine curve from 0 to a, where a is an input to the distribution. This distribution shape is shown in Figure III.3.

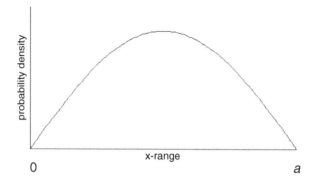

Figure III.3 The sine curve distribution we wish to create in our example.

The probability density function $f(x)$ is given by

$$f(x) = b \sin\left(\frac{\pi x}{a}\right)$$

where b is a constant to be determined, so that the area under the curve equals 1, as required for a probability distribution.

The cdf $F(x)$ is then $(0 < x < a)$

$$F(x) = b \int_0^x \sin(\pi x/a)\, dx$$

$$= \left[(ab/\pi)\left\{-\cos(\pi x/a)\right\}\right]_0^x \qquad (III.7)$$

$$= (ab/\pi)(1 - \cos(\pi x/a))$$

For the area under the curve to equal 1, b must be determined such that $F(a) = 1$, i.e.

$$F(a) = (ab/\pi)(1 - \cos(\pi)) = 2ab/\pi = 1$$

Therefore,

$$b = \pi/2a$$

and, from Equation (III.7), $F(x)$ becomes

$$F(x) = \frac{1}{2}(1 - \cos(\pi x)/a)$$

We now need to find the inverse function to $F(x)$. So, rearranging the equation above for x

$$x = (a/\pi)\cos^{-1}(1 - 2.F(x))$$

To generate this distribution, we put a Uniform(0, 1) distribution in cell A1 (say), the value for a in cell B1 (say) and, in the cell that generates values of x, we write

$$= B1/PI() * ACOS(1 - 2 * A1)(\text{The Excel function ACOS(y) returns } \cos^{-1}(y))$$

If we use Latin hypercube sampling to generate the values from the Uniform(0, 1) distribution, we will generate a smoothly distributed set of x values that will replicate the desired distribution.

Known probability mass function (pmf)

If you know the pmf of a distribution, it is a simple matter (in principle) to create the distribution. The techniques above are not applicable because a cdf for a discrete variable is just the sum of the discrete probabilities, and it is thus not possible to construct an inverse transformation.

The method requires that you construct two arrays in Excel:

- The first array is a set of values that the variable might take, e.g. $\{0, 1, \ldots, 99, 100\}$.
- The second array is a set of probabilities using the pmf calculated for each of these values $\{p(0), p(1), \ldots, p(99), p(100)\}$.

These two arrays are then used to construct the required distribution. For example, using ModelRisk's discrete distribution

$$= \text{VoseDiscrete}(\{x\}, \{p(x)\})$$

Of course, this method can become cumbersome if the $\{x\}$ array is very large. In which case:

- Make the $\{x\}$ list with a spacing larger than 1, e.g. $\{0, 5, 10, \ldots, 495, 500\}$.
- Calculate the associated probabilities $\{p(0), p(5), \ldots, p(495), p(500)\}$.
- Construct a VoseRelative(min, max, $\{x\}$, $\{p(x)\}$) distribution, e.g. VoseRelative(-0.5, 500.5, $\{5, 10, \ldots, 490, 495\}$, $\{p(5), p(10), \ldots, p(490), p(495)\}$).
- Wrap a ROUND function around the relative: $= \text{ROUND}(\text{VoseRelative}(\ldots), 0)$ to return a discrete value.
- Note that using a minimum $= -0.5$ (min $= -0.5$) and a maximum 500.5 (max $= 500.5$) will allocate a more accurate probability to the end values.

III.8.2 Method 2: Using a known relationship with another distribution

Sometimes you will know a direct relationship between the distribution you wish to simulate and another provided by your Monte Carlo simulation software. For example, one parameterization of the LogWeibull distribution gives the following simple relationship:

$$\text{LogWeibull}(\alpha, \beta) = \text{EXP}(\text{Weibull}(\alpha, \beta))$$

If you tend to use sensitivity analysis tools (Sections 5.3.7 and 5.3.8), be careful that the two distributions increase or decrease together.

There are plenty of examples where a distribution is a mixture of two other distributions. For example:

$$\text{Poisson-Lognormal}(\mu, \sigma) = \text{Poisson}(\text{Lognormal}(\mu, \sigma))$$

$$\text{Delaporte}(\alpha, \beta, \lambda) = \text{Poisson}(Gamma(\alpha, \beta) + \lambda)$$

$$\text{Beta-Binomial}(n, \alpha, \beta) = \text{Binomial}(n, \text{Beta}(\alpha, \beta))$$

Many of these relationships are described earlier in this Appendix. Again, be aware that by employing sensitivity analysis with a mixture distribution you can get misleading results: so, for example, the Lognormal, Gamma and Beta distributions in the relationships above will generate values that the Monte Carlo software will think of as belonging to a separate variable.

III.8.3 Method 3: Constructing an Empirical Distribution from Data

Situation

You have a set of random and representative observations of a single model variable, for example the number of children in American families (we'll look at a joint distribution for two or more variables at the end of this section), and you have enough observations to feel that the range and approximate random pattern have been captured. You want to use the data to construct a distribution directly.

Technique

It is unnecessary to fit a distribution to the data: instead one can simply use the empirical distribution of the data (if there are no physical or biological reasons a certain distribution should be used, we generally prefer an empirical distribution). Below, we outline three options you have to use these data to construct an empirical distribution:

1. A discrete uniform distribution – uses only the list of observed values.
2. A cumulative distribution – allows values between those observed and values beyond the observed range.
3. A histogram distribution – when you have huge amounts of data.

Option 1: A discrete uniform distribution

A discrete uniform distribution takes one parameter: a list of values. It then randomly picks any one of those values with equal probability (sampling with replacement). Thus, for example, = VoseDUniform({1, 4, 5, 7, 10}) will generate, with each iteration, one of the five values 1, 4, 5, 7 or 10 (each value has during each iteration a probably of being picked of 20 %). Figure III.4 shows what the probability distribution looks like.

  Let's imagine that we have our data in an array of cells called "observations". By simply writing = VoseDUniform (Observations) we will generate a distribution that replicates the pattern of the observed data. You can use the discrete uniform distribution for both discrete and continuous data providing you have sufficient observations.

Option 2: A cumulative distribution

If your data are continuous you also have the option of using a cumulative ascending distribution that takes four parameters: a minimum, a maximum, a list of values and a list of cumulative probabilities associated with those values. From these parameters it then constructs an empirical cumulative distribution by straight-line interpolation

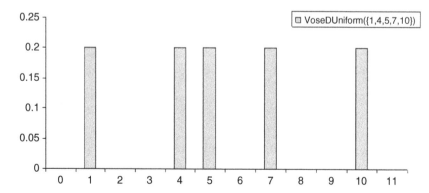

Figure III.4   Example of a discrete uniform distribution.

between the points defined on the curve. In ModelRisk there are two forms of the cumulative distribution: the cumulative ascending distribution and the cumulative descending distribution.

Our best guess of the cumulative probability of a data point in a set of observations turns out to be $r/(n + 1)$, where r is the rank of the data point within the dataset and n is the number of observations. Thus, when choosing this option, one needs to:

- rank the observations in ascending or descending order (Excel has an icon that makes this simple);
- in a neighbouring column, calculate the rank of the data: write a column of values 1, 2, …, n;
- in the next column, calculate the cumulative probability $F(x) = \text{rank}/(n + 1)$;
- use the data and $F(x)$ columns as inputs to the VoseCumulA or VoseCumulD distribution, together with subjective estimates of what the minimum and maximum values might be.

Note that the minimum and maximum values only have any effect on the very first and last interpolating lines to create the cumulative distribution, and so the distribution is less and less sensitive to the values chosen as more data are used in its construction.

Option 3: A Histogram Distribution

Sometimes (admittedly, not as often as we'd like) we have enormous amounts of random observations from which we would like to construct a distribution (for example, the generated values from another simulation). The discrete uniform and cumulative options above start to get a bit slow at that point, and model the variable in unnecessarily fine details. A more practical approach now is to create a histogram of the data and use that instead. The array function FREQUENCY() in Excel will analyse a dataset and say how many lie with any number of contiguous bin ranges. The ModelRisk distribution VoseHistogram has three parameters: the minimum possible value, the maximum possible value and an array of bin frequencies (or probabilities), which is just the FREQUENCY() array.

Option 4: Creating an empirical joint distribution for two or more variables

For data that are collected in sets (pairs, triplets, etc.) there may be correlation patterns inherent in the observations that we would like to maintain while fitting empirical distributions to data. An example is data of people's weight and height, where there is clearly some relationship between them. A combination of using a step uniform distribution (with min = 1 and max = number of rows) with an Excel VLOOKUP() (slower) or OFFSET() (faster) function allows us to do this easily, as shown in the model in Figure III.5.

III.8.4 Method 4: Create a Distribution from a Set of Points on a Curve

Situation

We have a set of coordinates that we wish to use to construct a distribution:

- $\{x, f(x)\}$ for a continuous distribution, where $f(x)$ is (or is proportional to) the probability density at value x;
- $\{x, F(x)\}$ for a continuous distribution, where $F(x)$ is the cumulative probability ($P(X <= x)$) at value x; or
- $\{x, p(x)\}$ for a discrete distribution, where $p(x)$ is (or is proportional to) the probability of value x.

Uses

There are many uses of this technique. For example:

- converting the results of a constructed Bayesian inference calculation into a distribution;

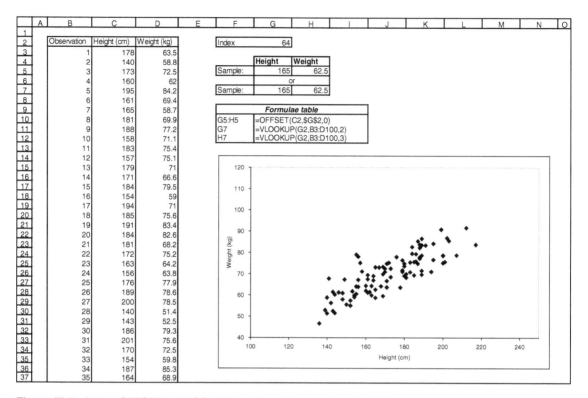

Figure III.5 Using OFFSET or VLOOKUP functions to sample paired data.

- constructing a spliced or mixed distribution by averaging or manipulating probability density functions for the component distributions;
- knowing the pdf or pmf of a specific distribution not offered by your risk analysis software.

Application

We can use the same techniques as explained in method 2 to create distributions from a set of points:

- If the dataset is of the form $\{x, f(x)\}$, we can use the VoseRelative function in ModelRisk.
- If the dataset is of the form $\{x, F(x)\}$, we can use the VoseCumulA (or VoseCumulD) function in ModelRisk.
- If the dataset is of the form $\{x, p(x)\}$, we can use the VoseDiscrete function in ModelRisk.

The three functions have similar formats:

$$= \text{VoseRelative}(\min, \max, \{x\}, \{f(x)\})$$

$$= \text{VoseCumulA}(\min, \max, \{x\}, \{F(x)\})$$

$$= \text{VoseDiscrete}(\{x\}, \{p(x)\})$$

The $\{x\}$ values must be in ascending order for the VoseRelative and VoseCumulA functions because they construct a distribution shape. For the VoseDiscrete function this is unnecessary because it is simply a list of values.

III.9 Approximation of One Distribution with Another

There are many situations where it is convenient, or just plain necessary, to approximate one distribution with another. For example, if I toss a coin 1 million times, how many heads will there be? The appropriate distribution is Binomial(1 000 000, 0.5), but such a distribution is utterly impractical to calculate. For a start, you would need to calculate every factorial for integers between 0 and a million. However, under certain conditions, the Binomial(n, p) distribution is very well approximated by a Normal(np, $(npq)^{1/2}$) distribution (where $q = 1 - p$). In our example, that would mean using a Normal(500 000, 500), and we could readily calculate, for example, the probability of having exactly 501 000 heads:

$$f(501\,000) = \frac{1}{\sqrt{2\pi}(500)^2} \exp\left(\frac{(501\,000 - 500\,000)^2}{2(500)^2}\right) = 0.0108\,\%$$

This section looks at a number of approximations, why they work and how to use them. It also provides an interesting way to gain a better understanding of the interrelationships between a number of the most common distributions.

Before proceeding, it is worthwhile reminding ourselves of one of the most important theorems in probability theory, the central limit theorem. In one of its forms it states that the sum of n random variables, each of which is identically distributed, is normally distributed for large n. Moreover, if each of the random variables comes from a distribution with mean μ and standard deviation σ, the sum of these n random variables has a Normal($n\mu$, $\sqrt{n}\sigma$) distribution. The theorem works for large n, but how large is "large"? The answer depends in part on the shape of the distribution of the individual random variables: if they are normally distributed, then n is 1 or more; if they are symmetric, then $n > 10$ or so; if they are moderately asymmetric, then $n < 20$–30 or so; and if they are very skewed indeed (for example, more skewed than an exponential distribution with skewness = 2.0), then $n > 50$ will be reasonably accurate. The answer, of course, also depends on how good a fit one is happy with. For some problems a rough fit may be perfectly adequate, and for other problems it may prove totally unacceptable. The central limit theorem is particularly useful in this section to explain why several distributions gravitate to the shape of a normal distribution under certain circumstances.

III.9.1 Approximations to the binomial distribution

The binomial distribution is a good starting point as it is the most fundamental distribution in probability theory. It models the number of successes s in n trials, where each trial has the same probability of success p. The probability of failure $(1 - p)$ is often written as q to make the equations a bit neater.

Normal approximation to the binomial

When n is large, and p is neither very small nor very large, the following approximation works very well:

$$\text{Binomial}(n, p) \approx \text{Normal}(np, (npq)^{1/2})$$

The mean and standard deviation of a binomial distribution are np and $(npq)^{1/2}$ respectively, so this approximation is quite easy to accept. It also fits nicely with the central limit theorem, because the Binomial(n, p) distribution can be thought of as the sum of n independent Binomial(1, p) distributions, each with mean p and standard deviation $(pq)^{1/2}$.

The difficulty lies in knowing whether, for a specific problem, the values for n and p fall within the bounds for which the normal distribution is a good approximation. A Binomial(1, 0.5) is symmetric, so we can intuitively guess that one needs a fairly low value for n for the normal approximation to be reasonable when $p = 0.5$. On the other hand, a Binomial(1, 0.95) is very highly skewed and we would reasonably expect that n would need to be large for the normal approximation to work for such an extreme value of p. An easy way to judge this is to think

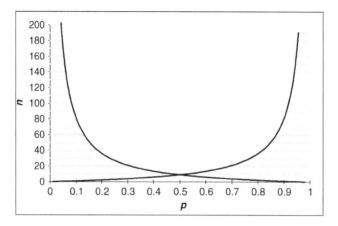

Figure III.6 Conditions for the normal approximation to the binomial.

about the range that a normal distribution takes: almost all of its probability is contained within a range ± three standard deviations from the mean. Now, we know that the binomial distribution is contained within the range [0, n]. It would therefore be reasonable to say that the normal distribution is a good approximation if its tails stay reasonably within these limits (Figure III.6), i.e.

$$np - 3\sqrt{np(1-p)} > 0 \quad \text{and} \quad np + 3\sqrt{np(1-p)} < n$$

which simplify to

$$n > \frac{9p}{1-p} \quad \text{and} \quad n > \frac{9(1-p)}{p}$$

A more stringent condition (using four instead of three standard deviations for the normal) would be to use 4 and 16 instead of 3 and 9 in the above equations. Figure III.6 shows how these two conditions work together symmetrically to show the $\{p, n\}$ combinations that will work well. Decker and Fitzgibbon (1991) advise using the normal approximation when $n^{0.31} p > 0.47$, which is discussed more below. At larger values of n, which is when one might wish to use an approximation, their rule of thumb is somewhat more conservative than that presented here, even using a range ± three standard deviations from the mean.

The normal distribution is continuous while the binomial distribution is discrete, and this approximation leads to an additional error that can be avoided. Rather than use $f(x)$ from the normal distribution to give the binomial distribution probability $p(x)$, it is more accurate to use $F(x + 0.5) - F(x - 0.5)$, where $F(x)$ is the cumulative distribution function for the normal distribution. If one is simulating the distribution, the equivalent is to use a ROUND(..., 0) function around the normal distribution.

Poisson approximation to the binomial

The probability density function for the Poisson distribution can be derived from the binomial probability density function by making n extremely large while p becomes very small, but within the constraint that np remains finite, as shown in Section 8.3.1. Thus, the following approximation can be made to the binomial:

$$\text{Binomial}(n, p) \approx \text{Poisson}(np) \quad \text{when } n \to \infty, p \to 0, np \text{ remains finite}$$

The Poisson approximation tends to overestimate the tail probabilities at both ends of the distribution. Decker and Fitzgibbon (1991) advise using this approximation when $n^{0.31} p < 0.47$ and the normal approximation otherwise.

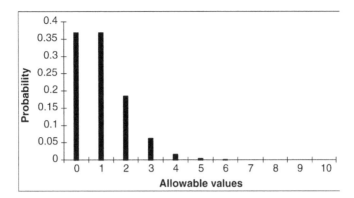

Figure III.7   The Poisson(1) distribution.

We can use a Poisson approximation to the binomial when p is close to 1, i.e. as $(1 - p) \to 0$, by simply reflecting the formula. In this case, Binomial$(n, p) \approx n - Poisson(np)$, and the Decker–Fitzgibbon condition is then $n^{0.31}(1 - p) < 0.47$.

III.9.2 Normal approximation to the poisson distribution

The Poisson(λt) distribution describes the possible number of events that may occur in an exposure of t units, where the average number of events per unit of exposure is λ. A Poisson(λt) distribution is thus the sum of t independent Poisson(λ) distributions. We might intuitively guess then that, if λt is sufficiently large, a Poisson(λt) distribution will start to look like a normal distribution, because of the central limit theorem, as is indeed the case. A Poisson(1) distribution (see Figure III.7) is quite skewed, so we would expect to need to add together some 20 or so before the sum would look approximately normal.

The mean and variance of a Poisson(λt) distribution are both equal to λt. Thus, the normal approximation to the Poisson is given by

$$\text{Poisson}(\lambda t) \approx \text{Normal}(\lambda t, (\lambda t)^{1/2}), \lambda t > 20$$

A much more generally useful normal approximation to the Poisson distribution is given by the formula

$$\text{Poisson}(\lambda) \approx [\text{Normal}(2\,\lambda^{1/2}, 1)/2]^2$$

This formula works for values of λ as low as 10.

The discrete property of the variable is lost with this approximation. The comments presented above for the normal approximation to the binomial also apply here for retrieving the discreteness and at the same time reducing error.

III.9.3 Approximations to the hypergeometric distribution

The Hypergeometric(n, D, M) distribution describes the possible number of successes one may have in n trials, where a trial is a sample without replacement from a population of size M, and where a success is defined as picking one of the D items in the population of size M that have some particular characteristic. So, for example, the number of infected animals in a sample of size n, taken from a population M, where D of that population are known to be infected, is described by a Hypergeometric(n, D, M) distribution. The probability mass function for the hypergeometric distribution is a mass of factorial calculations, which is quite laborious to calculate and leads us to look for suitable approximations.

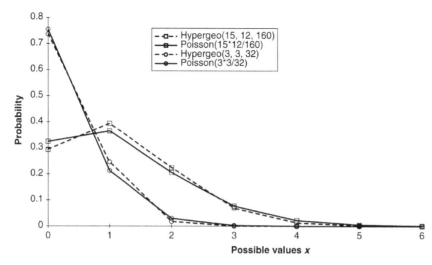

Figure III.8 Examples of the Poisson approximation to the hypergeometric.

Binomial approximation to the hypergeometric

The hypergeometric distribution recognises the fact that we are sampling from a finite population without replacement, so that the result of a sample is dependent on the samples that have gone before it. Now imagine that the population is very large, so that removing a sample of size n has no discernible effect on the population. Then the probability that an individual sample will have the characteristic of interest is essentially constant and has the value D/M, because the probability of resampling an item in the population, were one to replace items after sampling, would be very small. In such cases, the hypergeometric distribution can be approximated by a binomial as follows:

$$\text{Hypergeometric}(n, D, M) \approx \text{Binomial}(n, D/M)$$

The rule most often quoted is that this approximation works well when $n < 0.1M$.

Poisson approximation to the hypergeometric

We have just seen how the hypergeometric distribution can be approximated by the binomial, providing $n < 0.1M$. We have also seen in the previous section that the binomial can be approximated by the Poisson distribution, providing n is large and p is small. It therefore follows that, where $n < 0.1M$ and where D/M is small, we can use the following approximation:

$$\text{Hypergeometric}(n, D, M) \approx \text{Poisson}(nD/M)$$

Figure III.8 illustrates two examples.

Normal approximation to the hypergeometric

When $n < 0.1M$, so that the binomial approximation to the hypergeometric is valid, and when that binomial distribution looks similar to a normal, we can use the normal approximation to the hypergeometric. This amounts to three conditions:

$$n > 9\left(\frac{M-D}{D}\right), \quad n > 9\left(\frac{D}{M-D}\right), n < \frac{M}{10}$$

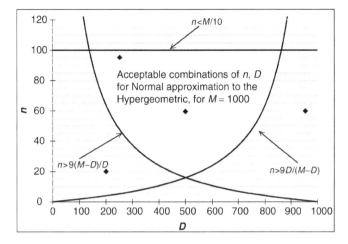

Figure III.9   Conditions for the normal approximation to the hypergeometric.

in which case we can use the approximation

$$\text{Hypergeometric}(n, D, M) \approx \text{Normal}\left(\frac{nD}{M}, \sqrt{n\frac{D}{M}\frac{(M-D)}{M}}\right)$$

$$= \text{Normal}\left(\frac{nD}{M}, \sqrt{\frac{nD(M-D)}{M^2}}\right)$$

Figure III.9 illustrates how the three conditions on n, D and M combine to determine the region in which this approximation is valid. Figure III.10 shows some examples of hypergeometric distributions, taking the parameter values indicated by the diamonds in Figure III.9, which fall inside and outside the allowed region for the normal approximation. For the normal approximation to the binomial, we originally chose the condition that the mean np should be at least three standard deviations $(npq)^{1/2}$ away from both 0 and n. However, we could be more stringent in our conditions and make it four standard deviations instead of three. For the conditions above, that would mean replacing each 9 with 16. Again, the discrete property of the variable is lost with this approximation, and the comments on correcting this that were presented above for the normal approximation to the binomial also apply.

III.9.4 Approximations to the negative binomial distribution

The negative binomial distribution has a probability mass function that includes a binomial coefficient, and therefore factorials that, like the binomial distribution, make it laborious or impossible to calculate directly. Approximations to the negative binomial are thus very useful.

Normal approximation to the negative binomial

The negative binomial distribution NegBin(s, p) returns the number of failures one will have in a binomial process before observing the sth success, where each trial has a probability p of success. A NegBin(1, p) is therefore the number of failures before observing the first success. If one wanted to observe two successes, one would wait until the first success with attendant NegBin(1, p) failures, then wait for the second success, with another attendant NegBin(1, p) failure. Extending this, it is easy to see how a NegBin(s, p) is simply the sum of s independent NegBin(1, p) distributions. This is another ideal candidate for the central limit theorem. The mean and standard deviation for a NegBin(1, p) distribution are $(1 - p)/p$ and $(1 - p)^{1/2}/p$ respectively. The NegBin(1,

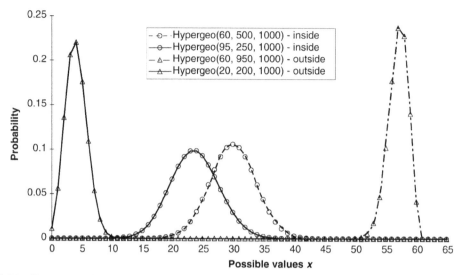

Figure III.10 Examples of the normal approximation to the hypergeometric inside and outside the conditions suggested in Figure III.9.

p) has a skewness of *at least* 2.0 (for very low p), so we would expect to need to add 50 or so of these NegBin(1, p) distributions to reach something that looks fairly normally distributed. So, when $s > 50$, we can use the approximation

$$\text{NegBin}(s, p) \approx \text{Normal} \left(\frac{s(1 - p)}{p}, \frac{\sqrt{s(1 - p)}}{p} \right)$$

The NegBin(s, p) distribution has the same mean and standard deviation of $s(1 - p)/p$ and $\{s(1 - p)\}^{1/2}/p$ respectively, which gives a useful check to this approximation. Again, the discrete property of the variable is lost with this approximation, and the comments on correcting this that were presented above for the normal approximation to the binomial also apply.

Exponential and gamma approximations to the negative binomial

As the probability of success of a trial p tends to zero, the binomial process becomes a Poisson process, as described in Section 8.3.1. Now, since p is so small, we will need a very large number of trials before observing a success. The Poisson process provides the exponential distribution Expon(β) as the "time" we will have to wait until our first observation, and the gamma distribution Gamma(x, β) as the "time" we will have to wait to observe x events. Here, β is the average time we will wait before observing an event, which, for the binomial process, equates to the average number of trials before the first success, i.e. the mean of the NegBin(1, p) distribution, which is $(1 - p)/p$ and tends to $1/p$ as p gets small. So, by comparison, we can see that the following approximation will work for small p:

$$\text{NegBin}(1, p) \approx \text{Expon} \left(\frac{1}{p} \right)$$

$$\text{NegBin}(s, p) \approx \text{Gamma} \left(s, \frac{1}{p} \right)$$

In fact, the first of these two approximations is redundant since Gamma(1, β) = Expon(β) anyway.

III.9.5 Normal approximation to the gamma distribution

The Gamma(α, β) distribution returns the "time" we will have to wait before observing α independent Poisson events, where one has to wait on average β units of "time" between each event. The "time" to wait before a single event occurs is a Gamma($1, \beta$) = Expon(β) distribution, with mean β and standard deviation β too. The Gamma(α, β) is thus the sum of α independent Expon(β) distributions, so the central limit theorem tells us for sufficiently large α (>30, for example, from the discussion of the central limit theorem at the beginning of this section) we can make the approximation

$$\text{Gamma}(\alpha, \beta) \approx \text{Normal}(\alpha\beta, \sqrt{\alpha}\beta)$$

The Gamma(α, β) distribution has mean and standard deviation equal to $\alpha\beta$ and $\alpha^{1/2}\beta$ respectively, which provides a nice check to our approximation.

III.9.6 Normal approximation to the lognormal distribution

When the Lognormal(μ, σ) distribution has an arithmetic mean μ that is much larger than its arithmetic standard deviation σ, the distribution tends to look like a Normal(μ, σ), i.e.

$$\text{Lognormal}(\mu, \sigma) \approx \text{Normal}(\mu, \sigma)$$

A general rule of thumb for this approximation is $\mu > 6\sigma$. This approximation is not really useful from the point of view of simplifying the mathematics, but it is helpful in being able quickly to think of the range of the distribution and its peak in such circumstances. For example, I know that 99.7 % of a normal distribution is contained within a range $\pm 3\sigma$ from the mean μ. So, for a Lognormal($15, 2$), I would estimate it would be almost completely contained within a range $[9, 21]$ and that it would peak at a little below 15 (remember that the mode, median and mean appear in that order from left to right for a right-skewed distribution).

III.9.7 Normal approximation to the beta distribution

The beta distribution is difficult to calculate, involving a beta function in its denominator, so an approximation is often welcome. A Taylor series expansion of the beta distribution probability density function, described in Example 9.5 of Section 9.2.5, shows that the Beta(α_1, α_2) distribution can be approximated by the normal distribution when α_1 and α_2 are sufficiently large. More specifically, the conditions are

$$\frac{\alpha_1 + 1}{\alpha_1 - 1} \approx 1 \text{ and } \frac{\alpha_2 + 1}{\alpha_2 - 1} \approx 1$$

A pretty good rule of thumb is that α_1 and α_2 should both equal 10 or more, but they can be as low as 6 if $\alpha_1 \approx \alpha_2$. In such cases, an approximation using the normal distribution works well where we use the mean and standard deviations from the exact beta distribution:

$$\text{Beta}(\alpha_1, \alpha_2) \approx \text{Normal}\left(\frac{\alpha_1}{\alpha_1 + \alpha_2}, \sqrt{\frac{\alpha_1\alpha_2}{(\alpha_1 + \alpha_2)^2(\alpha_1 + \alpha_2 + 1)}}\right)$$

III.9.8 Normal approximation to the chi-square distribution

The chi-square distribution ChiSq(ν) is quite easy to calculate, but for large n it can be approximated by a normal distribution. The ChiSq(ν) distribution is the sum of ν independent (Normal($0, 1$))^2 distributions, so ChiSq(α) + ChiSq(β) = ChiSq($\alpha + \beta$). A (Normal($0, 1$))^2 = ChiSq(1) distribution is highly skewed (skewness =

2.83). The central limit theorem says that ChiSq(v) will look approximately normal when v is rather large. A good rule of thumb is that $v > 50$ or so to get a pretty good fit. In such cases, we can make the following approximation by matching moments (i.e. using the mean and standard deviation of a ChiSq(v) distribution in a normal distribution):

$$\text{ChiSq}(v) \approx \text{Normal}(v, \sqrt{2v})$$

The ChiSq(v) distribution peaks at $x = v - 2$, whereas the normal approximation peaks at v, so acceptance of this approximation depends on being able to allow such a shift in the mode.

III.9.9 Normal approximation to the student t-distribution

The Student t-distribution Student(v) is quite difficult to calculate, but when v is large it is well approximated by a normal distribution, as follows:

$$\text{Student}(v) \approx \text{Normal}(0, 1)$$

A general rule for this approximation is that $v > 30$. The relationship between the Student t and normal distributions is not intuitively obvious but is readily made apparent by doing a Taylor series expansion about $x = 0$ of the probability density function for the Student distribution.

III.10 Recursive Formulae for Discrete Distributions

The Binomial(10^6, 10^{-6}) distribution is shown in Figure III.11. Although in theory it extends from 0 to 10^6, in practice it is very much constrained to the lowest values. Calculating the probabilities for each possible value of this distribution is a problem, since one needs to evaluate $10^6!$, which is beyond the capacity of most computers (Excel will calculate factorials up to 170, for example). The Stirling formula (see Section 6.3.4) can be used to obtain a very good approximation of high factorials, but we still end up with the problem of having to deal with manipulating very high numbers. An easier approach is to use recursive formulae. These formulae relate the equation for the probability of the $(i + 1)$th value to the probability of the ith value. Then one simply has to calculate the probability of any one value explicitly (a value chosen to give the simplest calculation) and thereafter use the recursive formula to determine all other probabilities.

The binomial probability mass function gives

$$p(i) = \frac{n!}{i!(n-i)!} p^i (1-p)^{n-i} \quad \text{and} \quad p(i+1) = \frac{n!}{(i+1)!(n-i-1)!} p^{i+1} (1-p)^{n-i-1}$$

Thus,

$$\frac{p(i+1)}{p(i)} = \frac{\dfrac{n!}{(i+1)!(n-i-1)!} p^{i+1} (1-p)^{n-i-1}}{\dfrac{n!}{i!(n-i)!} p^i (1-p)^{n-i}} = \frac{(n-i)p}{(i+1)(1-p)}$$

i.e.

$$p(i+1) = \frac{(n-i)p}{(i+1)(1-p)} p(i)$$

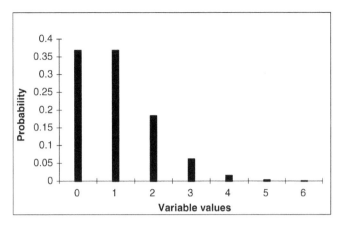

Figure III.11 The Binomial(10^6, 10^{-6}) distribution.

The binomial probability of zero successes is easily calculated:

$$p(0) = (1 - p)^n$$

so $p(1)$, $p(2)$, etc., can be readily determined using the recursive formula

$$p(1) = (1 - p)^n \frac{(n - 0)p}{(0 + 1)(1 - p)} = np(1 - p)^{n-1}$$

$$p(2) = np(1 - p)^{n-1} \frac{(n - 1)p}{(1 + 1)(1 - p)} = \frac{n(n - 1)p^2(1 - p)^{n-2}}{2}$$

If this binomial distribution is needed for a simulation, it is a simple enough task to use the x values and calculated probabilities as inputs into a discrete distribution, as shown in Figure III.12. The discrete distribution then acts as if it were the required binomial distribution.

If the binomial probability in this example had been extremely high, say 0.999 99, instead of 0.000 01, we would use the same technique but calculate backwards from $p(1\ 000\ 000)$, i.e.

$$p(n) = p^n$$

and work backwards using

$$p(i) = \frac{(i + 1)(1 - p)}{(n - i)p} p(i + 1)$$

Here are other useful recursive formulae for some of the most common discrete probability distributions:
Poisson

$$p(i + 1) = \frac{\lambda}{i + 1} p(i), \, p(0) = e^{-\lambda}$$

Negative binomial

$$p(i + 1) = \frac{(s + i)(1 - p)}{i + 1} p(i), \, p(0) = p^s$$

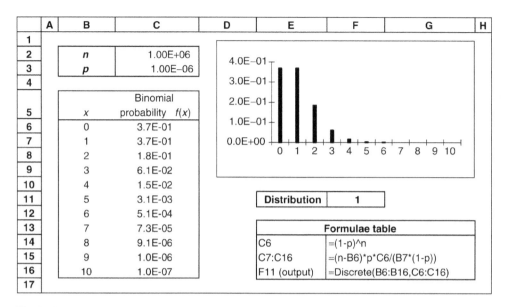

Figure III.12 Model example of using a recursive formula to generate a binomial distribution.

Geometric

$$p(i + 1) = (1 - p)p(i), \; p(0) = p$$

Hypergeometric

$$p(i + 1) = \frac{(D - i)(n - i)}{(1 + i)(1 - D + M - n + i)} p(i),$$

$$p(0) = \frac{\binom{M - D}{n}}{\binom{M}{n}}$$

The formula for $p(0)$ for the hypergeometric distribution is unwieldy but can still be very accurately approximated without resorting to factorial calculations by using the Stirling formula (see Section 6.3.4) to give

$$p(0) \approx \sqrt{\frac{(M - D)(M - n)}{M(M - D - n)}} \frac{(M - D)^{(M-D)}(M - n)^{(M-n)}}{(M - D - n)^{(M-D-n)} M^M}$$

This last formula will usually have to be calculated in log space first, then converted to real space at the end in order to avoid intermediary calculations of very large numbers. Another formula for $p(0)$ that is only *very* slightly less accurate for larger M and generally more accurate for small n is provided by Cannon and Roe (1982):

$$p(0) = \left(\frac{2M - 2n - D + 1}{2M - D + 1} \right)^D \tag{III.8}$$

This formula is produced by expanding the factorials for the equation for $p(0)$ and cancelling common factors top and bottom to give

$$p(0) = \frac{\binom{M-D}{n}}{\binom{M}{n}} = \frac{(M-n)!(M-D)!}{M!(M-D-n)!}$$

$$= \frac{(M-n-D+D)(M-n-D+(D+1))\cdots(M-n-D+2)(M-n-D+1)}{(M-D+D)(M-D+(D+1))\cdots(M-D+2)(M-D+1)} \qquad \text{(III.9)}$$

We then take the first and last terms in each of the numerator and denominator, average the two terms and raise to the power of the number of terms (D) top and bottom:

$$p(0) \approx \left(\frac{(M-n-D+D)+(M-n-D+1)}{(M-D+D)+(M-D+1)}\right)^D = \left(\frac{2M-2n-D+1}{2M-D+1}\right)^D$$

An alternative formulation is obtained by swapping around n and D to give

$$p(0) \approx \left(\frac{2M-2D-n+1}{2M-n+1}\right)^n \qquad \text{(III.10)}$$

This works since Equation (III.9) is symmetric in n and D, i.e. if n and D swap places the equation remains the same. Equation (III.8) is a better approximation when $n > D$, and Equation (III.10) is better when $n < D$.

III.11 A Visual Observation On The Behaviour Of Distributions

During the courses I run on risk analysis modelling, I often get up in front of the class and ask them to imagine that I am some generic distribution: my head is the peak and my arms, extended to the sides, form the tails of the distribution. I stand in the middle of the room and proclaim myself to be "normal". My outstretched arms do not perceive any restrictions as they do not touch the walls of the room. I then walk towards one side of the room until an outstretched hand touches a wall. I start to contort, losing my symmetry since I am constrained not to pass through the wall, my unfettered arm remaining outstretched. At this point, I proclaim that I am starting to look "lognormal". I continue to approach the wall until my head (the distribution's peak) touches it. I suddenly shoot up my greatly restricted arm above myself and declare that I now look "exponential" – actually, I look more like the white-suited John Travolta in his famous cinematic pose.

The exercise may make me look like a particularly eccentric Englishman, but it is memorable and gets the point across (after all, probability theory can be rather a dry subject). The idea is that one can quite easily picture the behaviour of a lot of distributions that can change shape. If the distribution is centred far from its boundaries, with a small enough spread that it does not "see" those boundaries, it very often looks normal. On the other hand, if the distribution "sees" one of its boundaries, it will often be skewed away from that limit and takes on a shape we usually think of as being "lognormal". Finally, if the distribution has its mode at, or very close to, an extreme, it will often look similar to an exponential distribution.

Appendix IV

Further reading

I always appreciate it when someone personally recommends a good book, and "good" for me, in the context of risk analysis, is one that goes light on the theory, unless you need it, and focuses on practical applications. Here is a list of books from our library that I particularly like, organised by topical area. The number of stars represents how intellectually challenging they are:

- 1 star = somewhat simpler than this book;
- 2 stars = about the same as this book;
- 3 stars = suitable for researchers and masochists.

Some books carry one star because they are very accessible, but they may nonetheless represent the highest level in their field. For the very latest in modelling techniques, particularly the development of financial models and numerical techniques, we mostly rely on the web and journal articles. If you have some book suggestions for me, please send me an email (David@voseconsulting.com), or a copy if it's your own book (you can find our office addresses at our website www.voseconsulting.com), and if we like it we'll put it up on the website.

Simulation

Banks, J., Carson, J. S., Nelson, B. L. and Nicol, D. M. (2005). *Discrete-event System Simulation*, 4th edition. Upper Saddle River, NJ: Prentice-Hall.**

Evans, J. R. and Olson, L. (1998). *Introduction to Simulation and Risk Analysis*. Upper Saddle River, NJ: Prentice-Hall. [*Simple, and with lots of illustrations.*]*

Law, A. M. and Kelton, W. D. (2000). *Simulation Modeling and Analysis*, 3rd edition. New York, NY: McGraw-Hill.**

Morgan, M. G. and Henrion, M. (1990). *Uncertainty*. Cambridge, UK: Cambridge University Press. [*Old now, but has aged well.*]**

Business risk and decision analysis

Clemen, R. T. and Reilly, T. (2001). *Making Hard Decisions*. Pacific Grove, CA: Duxbury Press.*

Goodwin, P. and Wright, G. (1998). *Decision Analysis for Management Judgment*. New York, NY: John Wiley & Sons Inc.*

Raiffa, H. and Schlaiffer, R. (2000). *Applied Statistical Decision Theory*. New York, NY: John Wiley & Sons Inc.***

Schuyler, J. (2001). *Risk and Decision Analysis in Projects*. Pennsylvania, USA: Project Management Institute.**

Extreme value theory

Gumbel, E. J. (1958). *Statistics of Extremes*. New York, NY: Columbia University Press.**

Embrechts, P., Klupperberg, C. and Mikosch, T. (1999). *Modelling Extreme Events for Insurance and Finance*. New York, NY: Springer-Verlag.**

Insurance

Daykin, C. D., Pentikainen, T. and Pesonen, M. (1994). *Practical Risk Theory for Actuaries*. New York, NY: Chapman and Hall.**

Dickson, D. C. M. (2005). *Insurance: Risk and Ruin*. Cambridge, UK: Cambridge University Press.***

Embrechts, P., Klupperberg, C. and Mikosch, T. (1999). *Modelling Extreme Events for Insurance and Finance*. New York, NY: Springer.**

Kleiber, C. and Kotz, S. (2003). *Statistical Size Distributions in Economics and Actuarial Sciences*. New York, NY: John Wiley & Sons Inc.**

Klugman, S. A., Panjer, H. H. and Willmot, G. E. (1998). *Loss Models: from Data to Decisions*. New York, NY: John Wiley & Sons Inc. [*Very theoretical, but thorough.*]***

Financial risk

Brealey, R. M. and Myers, S. C. (2000). *Principles of Corporate Finance*, 6th edition. New York, NY: McGraw-Hill.**

Cherubini, U., Luciano, O. and Vecchiato, W. (2004). *Copula Methods in Finance*. New York, NY: John Wiley & Sons Inc. [*A really great book.*]**

Clewlow, L and Strickland, C (1998). Implementing Derivatives Models. New York, NY: John Wiley & Sons Inc.**

Cox, J. C., Ross, S. and Rubenstein, M. (1979). Option pricing: a simplified approach. *J. Financial Economics* **7**, 229–263.***

Cox, J. C. and Rubinstein, M. (1985). *Options Markets*. Englewood Cliffs, NJ: Prentice-Hall.***

De Servigny, A. and Renault, O. (2004). *Measuring and Managing Credit Risk*. New York, NY: Standard & Poor's, a division of McGraw-Hill. [*A really good practical perspective.*]**

Dunis, C. (1996). *Forecasting Financial Markets*. New York, NY: John Wiley & Sons Inc.**

Dunis, C. and Zhou, B. (1998). *Nonlinear Modelling of High Frequency Financial Time Series*. New York, NY: John Wiley & Sons Inc.***

Glasserman, P. (2004). *Monte Carlo Methods in Financial Engineering*. New York, NY: Springer-Verlag.***

Hull, J. C. (2006). *Options, Futures, and other Derivative Securities, 6th edition*. Englewood Cliffs, NJ: Prentice-Hall. [*A classic.*]**

Jackson, M. and Staunton, M. (2001). *Advanced Modelling in Finance Using Excel and VBA*. New York, NY: John Wiley & Sons Inc.***

James, J. and Webber, N. (2000). *Interest Rate Modelling*. New York, NY: John Wiley & Sons Inc.***

London, J. (2006). *Modeling Derivatives Applications in Matlab, C++, and Excel*. Upper Saddle River, NJ: FT Press.***

McNeil, A. J., Rüdiger, F. and Embrechts, P. (2005). *Quantitative Risk Management*. Princeton, NJ: Princeton University Press. [*Pretty theoretical but very thorough.*]***

Schönbucher, P. J. (2003). Credit Derivatives Pricing Models. New York, NY: John Wiley & Sons Inc.***

Wilmott, P. (1998). *The Theory and Practice of Financial Engineering*. New York, NY: John Wiley & Sons Inc.***

Wilmott, P (1998). *Derivatives*. Chichester, UK: John Wiley & Sons Ltd.***

Wilmott, P. (2001). *Paul Wilmott Introduces Quantitative Finance*, New York, NY: John Wiley & Sons Inc. [*In fact, anything that Paul produces has been great so far.*]***

The bootstrap

Chernick, M. R. (1999). *Bootstrap Methods – a Practitioner's Guide*. New York, NY: John Wiley & Sons Inc.**

Davison, A. C. and Hinkley, D. V. (1997). *Bootstrap Methods and their Applications*. Cambridge, UK: Cambridge University Press.**

Efron, B. and Tibshirani, R. J. (1993). *An Introduction to the Bootstrap*. New York, NY: Chapman and Hall.***

General statistics and probability theory

Barnett, V. (1999). *Comparative Statistical Inference*, 3rd edition. New York, NY: John Wiley & Sons Inc.**

Good, P. H. and Hardin, J. W. (2003). *Common Errors In Statistics (and How to Avoid Them)*. New York, NY: John Wiley & Sons Inc.*

Evans, M., Hastings, N. and Peacock, B. (1993). *Statistical Distributions*. New York, NY: John Wiley & Sons Inc.*

Feller, W. (1966). *An Introduction to Probability Theory and its Applications*, 2nd edition. New York, NY: John Wiley & Sons Inc.***

Gilks, W. R., Richardson, R. and Spiegelhalter, D. J. (1996). *Markov Chain Monte Carlo in Practice*. New York, NY: Chapman and Hall.***

Groebner, D. E. and Shannon, P. F. (1993). *Business Statistics: a Decision-making Approach*. New York, NY: Macmillan.*

Jensen, F. V. (2001). *Bayesian Networks and Decision Graphs*. New York, NY: Springer-Verlag.***

Johnson, N. L., Kotz, S. and Balakrishnan, N. (1994). *Continuous Univariate Distributions*. New York, NY: John Wiley & Sons Inc.**

Johnson, N. L., Kotz, S. and Balakrishnan, N. (1997). *Discrete Multivariate Distributions*. New York, NY: John Wiley & Sons Inc.**

Johnson, N. L., Kotz, S. and Kemp, A. W. (1993). *Univariate Discrete Distributions*. New York, NY: John Wiley & Sons Inc.**

Kleiber, C. and Kotz, S. (2003). *Statistical Size Distributions in Economics and Actuarial Sciences*. New York, NY: John Wiley & Sons Inc.**

Kloeden, P. E., Platen, E. and Schurz, H. (1994). *Numerical Solution of SDE Through Computer Experiments*. New York, NY: Springer-Verlag.***

Kotz, S., Balakrishnan, N. and Johnson, N. L. (2000). *Continuous Multivariate Distributions*, 2nd edition. New York, NY: John Wiley & Sons Inc.**

Kreyszig, E. (1993). *Advanced Engineering Mathematics*, 7th edition. New York, NY: John Wiley & Sons Inc. [*Not specifically about probability, but an excellent maths refresher.*]***

Levin, R. I. and Rubin, D. S. (1994). *Statistics for Management*. Englewood Cliffs, NJ: Prentice-Hall.*

Lipschutz, S. (1974). *Probability, Schaum's Outline Series*. New York, NY: McGraw-Hill.*

McClave, J. T., Dietrich, F. H. and Sincich, T. (1997). *Statistics*, 7th edition. Upper Saddle River, NJ: Prentice-Hall.*

Norman, G. R. and Streiner, D. (2000). Biostatistics: the bare essentials. Toronto, ON: BC Decker. [*A statistics book with jokes!*]*

Ross, S. M. (1976). *A First Course in Probability*. New York, NY: Macmillan.*

Ross, S. M. (1997). *Introduction to Probability Models*, 6th edition. Boston, NY: Academic Press.**

Taylor, H. M. and Karlin, S. (1998). *An Introduction to Stochastic Modeling*, 3rd edition. London, UK: Academic Press.**

Project risk analysis

Chapman, C. and Ward, S. (1997). *Project Risk Management*. Chichester, UK: John Wiley & Sons Ltd.*

Grey, S. (1995). *Practical Risk Assessment for Project Management*. New York, NY: John Wiley & Sons Inc.*

Kerzner, P. (2001). *Project Management: a Systems Approach to Planning, Scheduling and Controlling*, 7th edition. New York, NY: John Wiley & Sons Inc. [*Not really risk analysis, but good planning leads to less risk.*]*

Simon, P. (ed.) (1997). *Project Risk Analysis and Management*. Norwich, UK: APM.*

Reliability theory

Bentley, J. P. (1999). *Reliability and Quality Engineering*. Harlow, UK: Addison-Wesley. [*Short, good, simple explanations.*]*

Kottegoda, N. T. and Rosso, R. (1998). *Statistics, Probability and Reliability for Civil and Environmental Engineers*. New York, NY: McGraw-Hill.**

Kuo, W., Prasad, V. R., Tillman, F. A. and Hwang, C. (2001). *Optimal Reliability Design*. Cambridge, UK: Cambridge University Press.***

O'Connor, P. D. T. (1994). *Practical Reliability Engineering*, 3rd edition. New York, NY: John Wiley & Sons Inc.*

Queueing theory

Bunday, B. D. (1996). *An Introduction to Queueing Theory*. London, UK: Arnold.*

Bayesian statistics

Berry, D. A. and Stamgl, D. K. (1996). *Bayesian Biostatistics*. New York, NY: Dekker.**

Carlin, B. P. and Louis, T. A. (1996). *Bayes and Empirical Bayes methods for Data Analysis*. New York, NY: Chapman and Hall.**

Congdon, P. (2003). *Applied Bayesian Modelling*. New York, NY: John Wiley & Sons Inc. [*Has excellent models included.*]**

Gelman, A., Carlin, J. B., Stern, H. S. and Rubin, D. B. (1995). *Bayesian Data Analysis*. New York, NY: Chapman and Hall.***

Jensen, F. V. (2001). *Bayesian Networks and Decision Graphs*. New York, NY: Springer-Verlag.***

Neapolitan, R. E. (2004). *Learning Bayesian Networks*. Upper Saddle River, NJ: Prentice-Hall.***

Pole, A., West, M. and Harrison, J. (1999). *Applied Bayesian Forecasting and Time Series Analysis*. New York, NY: Chapman and Hall, CRC Press.***

Press, S. J. (1989). *Bayesian Statistics: Principles, Models and Applications*. New York, NY: John Wiley & Sons Inc.**

Tanner, M. A. (1996). *Tools for Statistical Inference*, 3th edition. New York, NY: Springer-Verlag.***

Forecasting

Dunis, C. (1996). *Forecasting Financial Markets*. New York, NY: John Wiley & Sons Inc.**

Newbold, P. and Bos, T. (1994). *Introductory Business and Economic Forecasting*, 2nd edition. Cincinnati, OH: South Western Publishing.**

Pole, A., West, M. and Harrison, J. (1999). *Applied Bayesian Forecasting and Time Series Analysis*. New York, NY: Chapman and Hall, CRC Press.***

General risk analysis

Bedford, T. and Cooke, R. (2001). *Probabilistic Risk Analysis: Foundations and Methods*. Cambridge, UK: Cambridge University Press.**

Newendorp, P. (1975). *Decision Analysis for Petroleum Exploration*. Tulsa, OK: Penwell.**

Risk communication

Granger Morgan, M., Fischhoff, B., Bostrom, A. and Atman, C. J. (2002). *Risk Communication: a Mental Models Approach*. Cambridge, UK: Cambridge University Press.*

Kahneman, D. and Tversky, A. (2000). *Choices, Values and Frames.* Cambridge, UK: Cambridge University Press.*

National Research Council (1989). *Improving Risk Communication.* Washington, DC: National Academy Press.*

Slovic, P. (2000). *The Perception of Risk.* London, UK: Earthscan Publications. [*Read his articles too.*]*

Epidemiology

Clayton, D. and Hills, M. (1998). *Statistical Models in Epidemiology.* Oxford, UK: Oxford University Press.**

Dijkhuizen, A. A. and Morris, R. S. (1997). *Animal Health Economics: Principles and Applications.* Sydney, Australia: University of Sydney.**

Dohoo, I., Martin, W. and Stryhn, H. (2003). *Veterinary Epidemiological Research.* Prince Edward Island, Canada: AVC Inc.**

Fleiss, J. L., Levin, B. and Cho Paik, M. (2003). *Statistical Methods for Rates and Proportions.* New York, NY: John Wiley & Sons Inc.**

Groenendaal, H. (2005). *Epidemiologic and Economic Risk Analysis on Johne's Disease Control.* Wageningen, The Netherlands: Wageningen University.**

McKellar, R. C. and Lu, X. (2004). *Modeling Microbial Responses in Food.* New York, NY: Chapman and Hall, CRC Press.**

McMeekin, T. A., Olley, J. N., Ross, T. and Ratkowsky, D. A. (1993). *Predictive Microbiology: Theory and Application.* Taunton, UK: Research Studies Press.**

Pearl, J. (2000). *Causality: Models, Reasoning and Inference.* Cambridge, UK: Cambridge University Press. [*Beautiful turn of phrase.*]***

Shipley, W. (2000). *Cause and Correlation in Biology.* Cambridge, UK: Cambridge University Press.**

Torrence, M. E. and Isaacson, R. E. (2003). *Microbial Food Safety in Animal Agriculture.* Iowa, IO: Iowa State University Press.**

Software

Aberth, O. (1998). *Precise Numerical Methods Using C++.* San Diego, CA: Academic Press.***

Hauge, J. W. and Paige, K. N. (2004). *Learning Simul8: the Complete Guide.* Bellingham, WA: Plain Vu Publishers.*

Kloeden, P. E., Platen, E. and Schurz, H. (1994). *Numerical Solution of SDE Through Computer Experiments.* New York, NY: Springer-Verlag.***

London, J. (2006). *Modeling Derivatives Applications in Matlab, C++, and Excel.* Upper Saddle River, NJ: FT Press.***

Shepherd, R. (2004). *Excel VBA Macro Programming.* New York, NY: McGraw-Hill.**

Walkenbach, J. (2002). *Excel 2002 Formulas.* New York, NY: M&T Books.*

Fun

Aczel, A. (1998). *Probability 1: Why There Must Be Intelligent Life in the Universe.* New York, NY: Harcourt Brace.*

Bennett, D. J. (1998). *Randomness.* Cambridge, MA: Harvard University Press.*

Bernstein, P. L. (1996). *Against the Gods.* New York, NY: John Wiley & Sons Inc. [*I particularly enjoyed the first, non-financial half.*]*

Laplace, Marquis de (1951). *A Philosophical Essay on Probabilities.* New York, NY: Dover.**

Peterson, I. (1998). *The Jungles of Randomness: a Mathematical Safari.* New York, NY: John Wiley & Sons Inc.*

by Dr Huybert Groenendaal
Partner, Consulting

Our mission

We are risk analysis specialists and our goal is to help our clients make better risk-based decisions by making use of, and teaching, the most up-to-date and effective risk analysis methodologies and techniques.

A little history

Founded in 1989 by David Vose, Vose Consulting has an interesting history. In the 1990s, risk analysis certainly was not as well known and accepted as it is now. In those early years, Vose Consulting played a pioneering role in defining and further developing the field of risk analysis. David wrote the first edition of his book *Risk Analysis – a Quantitative Guide* and taught hundreds of courses in risk analysis worldwide. In addition, Vose Consulting was involved in, and often led, the development of national and international guidelines in risk analysis, in areas such as project, animal import and food safety risk analyses.

Vose Consulting has the privilege of being involved in many varied, intriguing and challenging risk analysis consulting projects, in fields as diverse as exchange rate forecasting, shipping movement, inventory optimisation, animal health and food safety risk assessments, copper mining, financial modelling of investments, such as FPSO vessels, theme parks and film companies, and insurance and banking risk. We even once performed a project on the fairness of a cheerleader selection process!

The growing interest in risk analysis and the availability of a range of user-friendly Monte Carlo simulation software packages meant that there was an increasing need for good-quality training in risk analysis. We have found that our clients can interact with us to solve their problems far more effectively if we have a common understanding of basic terminology and techniques. In 2005 we therefore released two versions of *ModelAssist* (one for Crystal Ball and one for @RISK). ModelAssist is comprehensive risk analysis training software that helps users perform accurate and defensible risk analyses – "a Vose risk analysis expert 24/7 on your computer". It contains some 300 topics on risk analysis and a large number of illustrative models that you can load, run and modify. ModelAssist is now available for download free of charge from our website.

We have this year released "ModelRisk for Insurance and Finance", a quantitative risk modelling software tool designed specifically for the insurance and finance fields that features widely in this book. And last but not least, this third edition of *Risk Analysis – a Quantitative Guide* provides you with a much expanded and improved version of an already popular book.

We are very excited about the future!

Services and products

While our company name may suggest we are purely consultants, we actually offer our clients three primary services and products:

1. Risk analysis consulting.
2. Risk analysis software.
3. Risk analysis training.

We very often provide our clients with a mix of these services to make sure that they not only get the best solution or analysis but also will understand and can, if necessary, repeat that analysis (e.g. we typically provide our clients with a detailed explanation and manual of each model we develop).

Risk analysis consulting

We think of consulting and teaching as inseparable. We may be quite different from the "typical" consulting firm you may have worked with before – our goal is not to provide you with "bodies" or "hours" so we can squeeze the most money from a client, but to provide you with high-quality risk analysis expertise to help you make better decisions *and* to teach you to do it yourself in the future. We like to think that, if we did a good job, you'd use us again when something tricky comes along, and when risk analysis pops up in a conversation you might mention our name.

Our focus on risk analysis, as opposed to adding risk analysis as an extra service to a consultancy for a specific field, means that we are able to provide consulting services in a wide variety of industries and applications working alongside industry-specific experts (the client!). The benefit to the client is that we can make use of techniques and methods that are typically used in one field but with some imagination have plenty of applications in others. For example, we have successfully used a risk analysis technique we developed in banking operational risk to help a diamond mining firm determine the optimal ore milling size, and we've introduced a sophisticated insurance modelling technique to microbial food safety.

In a typical consultancy engagement, one of the partners will review the potential client's problem and figure out if and how we can help. Then we'll decide on who might be best to lead the project: it could be any one of our consultants. Then that consultant will speak to the client together with a partner, but from the beginning the selected consultant heads the project: they agree to the scope and deadline with the client and take responsibility for its successful completion and interact with the client. The interesting part is that, once a person is project leader, that person has the authority to call on anyone in the company from a partner to a programmer to another consultant with a different specialisation to ensure that the solution is delivered. We believe that a client should know who is doing the work for them, so we publish the profiles of everyone in the company on our website. This has allowed us continually to provide our team with interesting and varied work, build up a great team spirit and spread knowledge within the company.

We also have quite a lot experience in providing expert witness services: David has certainly acquired something of a reputation in this area – he hasn't been on the losing side yet, probably because we won't take on an assignment unless he thinks the client has a pretty good argument.

Risk analysis software

There are some really great software tools on the market that have a role to play in risk analysis, from statistical analysis to mathematical modelling, from Monte Carlo simulation to expert elicitation. But there are still some important gaps, and sometimes we just can't do what is required with a tool like Crystal Ball or @RISK, WinBUGS or Mathematica and their add-ons, so for quite some time now we have also developed customised software applications for our clients as part of a consulting project. The modelling tools are usually written in C++ for speed and accuracy or VBA for its transparency. We also have developed some considerable know-how in writing html, etc., so we could attach help files to models with videos and interactive content. In its turn that led to the development of the two commercial risk analysis software packages already mentioned:

- ModelAssist, the most comprehensive training and reference software available. It can be used as a "personal risk analysis expert".
- ModelRisk for Insurance and Finance, a quantitative risk modelling tool specially developed for the insurance and finance fields that features in this book.

All of our software are "developed by risk analysts, for risk analysts" and come from really figuring out what problems people need to solve. We have a number of other tools in the pipeline, and we expect to release versions of ModelRisk for other disciplines too, so please take a look at www.vosesoftware.com to see what we're up to.

Risk analysis training

We teach a variety of risk analysis courses worldwide in four general areas:

1. Banking and insurance risk analysis modelling.
2. General risk analysis – from introductory to advanced courses.
3. Business risk analysis, including project and financial risk analysis.
4. Risk analysis in animal and human health, epidemiology and food safety.

The courses are sometimes offered publicly but most are commissioned by a client and tailored to their particular needs – which keeps it interesting for us too. What makes our courses unique is that:

• We teach risk analysis techniques and methods, not software. Yes, we do use software during our classes and explain how to use the techniques, but our emphasis is on how to perform useful risk analysis and solve real-world problems.

• Our risk analysis training courses are taught by our consultants, not by specialised trainers – therefore, our course material is based on applications and problems we have faced in consulting projects, not on textbook problems. The people teaching have modified the material with their own examples and language (have you ever tried giving a lecture with someone else's slides?) and have real experience, so you can ask those tricky questions and expect a useful answer.

• Our consultants are friendly and really can teach.

• Most people just need to learn the basics, but they want to be taught by people who aren't at their limit of understanding. Our consultants understand that, set the level appropriate to your needs and will modify the tempo accordingly.

• We make links to ModelAssist topics so the participants have an excellent way of reviewing the material and delving more deeply into a particular topic.

• If the consultant/instructor doesn't know the answer to a question, he or she will say so and seek help from someone else in Vose Consulting.

• Last but not least, our courses build continually on the subject matter that has already been presented as a course unfolds. This emphasises the interrelationships between different aspects of risk analysis modelling and helps the participants recall past material and build experience. It also encourages creative problem solving which is critically important in risk assessment.

Recruitment

We would love to have more people in our consulting team, but we are rather choosy. Our consultants must have a masters or doctorate degree in a relevant field and some meaningful industry experience, but we are perhaps even more focused on a person's ability to listen, to think creatively, to gain a client's confidence and to communicate what are sometimes quite complicated analyses to our clients. We also like to have people working with us from different cultures and language skills because we work in some thirty countries around the world.

If you've understood (most of) this book, found it really interesting, love to travel, can handle deadlines, can take responsibility (people actually use what we do to make big decisions), would enjoy working with a dynamic team and want to make a difference, then send us an email with your CV. We get a lot of CVs, so put in a little effort to help us see how you might fit in and pique our interest. We like people who do things outside work: within Vose Consulting we have ironman triathlon, squash, karate, tennis and horse riding competitors, lots of skiers, trekkers and cyclists and maybe a well-read couch potato or two. If you think you'd be a great consultant, then approach our US office. If you're the sort of person who loves to tinker with equations and do research, then the Belgian office is the place to go, and our Russian office is always looking for fine programmers and designers.

Our locations, and how to contact us

USA:
2891 20th Street,
Boulder,
CO 80304,
USA
+1 303 440 8524
usa@voseconsulting.com

Europe:
Iepenstraat 98,
Gent 9000,
Belgium
+32 932 406 23
europe@voseconsulting.com

Russia:
Ardonskaya 209,
362003 Vladikavkaz,
Russia
+7 8672 753 112
russia@voseconsulting.com

References

Akaike, H. (1974). A new look at the statistical model identification. *IEEE Transactions on Automatic Control* **AC19**, 716–723.

Akaike, H. (1976). Canonical correlation analysis of time series and the use of an information criterion, in *System Identification: Advances and Case Studies*, ed. by Mehra, R. K. and Lainotis, D. G. New York, NY: Academic Press; 52–107.

Anderson, T. W. and Darling, D. A. (1952). Asymptotic theory of certain "goodness of fit" criteria based on stochastic processes. *Ann. Math. Stat.* **23**, 193–212.

Artzner, P., Delbaen, F., Eber, J.-M. and Heath, D. (1997). Thinking coherently. *Risk* **10**(11).

Bartholomew, M. J., Vose, D. J., Tollefson, L. R., Curtis, C. and Travis, C. C. (2005). A linear model for managing the risk of antimicrobial resistance originating in food animals. *Risk Analysis* **25**(1).

Bayes, T. (1763). An essay towards solving a problem in the doctrine of chances. *Philos. Trans. R. Soc. London* **53**, 370–418. Reprinted in *Biometrica* **45**, 293–315 (1958).

Bazaraa, M. S., Jarvis, J. J. and Sherali, H. D. (2004). *Linear Programming and Network Flows*, 3rd edition. New York, NY: John Wiley and Sons Inc.

Bazaraa, M. S., Sherali, H. D. and Shetty, C. M. (2006). *Nonlinear Programming: Theory and Algorithms*, 3rd edition. New York, NY: John Wiley and Sons Inc.

Bernoulli, J. (1713). *Ars Conjectandi*. Basilea: Thurnisius.

Birnbaum, Z. W. and Saunders, S. C. (1969). A new family of life distributions. *J. Appl. Prob.* **6**, 637–652.

Bollerslev, T. (1986). Generalized autoregressive conditional heteroskedasticity. *Journal of Econometrics* **31**, 307–327.

Boone, I., Van der Stede, Y., Bollaerts, K., Vose, D., Daube, G., Aerts, M. and Mintiens, K. (2007). Belgian "farm-to-consumption" risk assessment-model for *Salmonella* in pigs: methodology for assessing the quality of data and information sources. Research paper available from: ides.boone@var.fgov.be.

Bühlmann, H. (1980). An economic premium principle. *ASTIM Bulletin* **11**, 52–60.

Cannon, R. M. and Roe, R. T. (1982). *Livestock Disease Surveys. A Field Manual for Veterinarians*. Bureau of Resource Science, Department of Primary Industry. Australian Government Publishing Service, Canberra.

Chandra, M., Singpurwalla, N. D. and Stephens, M. A. (1981). Kolmogorov statistics for tests of fit for the extreme value and Weibull distribution. *J. Am. Stat. Assoc.* **76**(375), 729–731.

Cherubini, U., Luciano, O. and Vecchiato, W. (2004). *Copula Methods in Finance*. New York, NY: John Wiley & Sons Inc.

Clark, C. E. (1961). Importance sampling in Monte Carlo analysis. *Operational Research* **9**, 603–620.

Clemen, R. T. and Reilly, T. (2001). *Making Hard Decisions*. Belmont, CA: Duxbury Press.

Cox, J. C., Ingersoll, J. E. and Ross, S. A. (1985). A theory of the term structure of interest rates. *Econometrica* **53**, 385–407.

Dantzig, G. B. and Thapa, M. N. (1997). *Linear Programming: 1: Introduction*. New York, NY: Springer-Verlag.

Dantzig, G. B. and Thapa, M. N. (2003). *Linear Programming 2: Theory and Extensions*. New York, NY: Springer-Verlag.

Davison, A. C. and Hinkley, D. V. (1997). *Bootstrap Methods and their Applications*. Cambridge, UK: Cambridge University Press.

Decker, R. D. and Fitzgibbon, D. J. (1991). The normal and Poisson approximations to the binomial: a closer look. *Department of Mathematics Technical Report No. 82.3*. Hartford, CT: University of Hartford.

De Pril, N. (1986). On the exact computation of the aggregate claims distribution in the individual life model. *ASTIN Bulletin* **16**, 109–112.

De Pril, N. (1989). The aggregate claims distribution in the individual model with arbitrary positive claims. *ASTIN Bulletin* **19**, 9–24.

Dickson, D. C. M. (2005). *Insurance Risk and Ruin.* Cambridge, UK: Cambridge University Press.

Ding, Z., Granger, C. W. J. and Engle, R. F. (1993). A long memory property of stock market returns and a new model. *Journal of Empirical Finance* **1**, 83–106.

Efron, B. (1979). Bootstrap methods: another look at the Jackknife. *Ann. Statis.* **7**, 1–26.

Efron, B. and Tibshirani, R. J. (1993). *An Introduction to the Bootstrap*. New York, NY: Chapman and Hall.

Embrechts, P. (2000). Extreme value theory: potential and limitations as an integrated risk management tool. *Derivatives Use, Trading and Regulation* **6**, 449–456.

Engle, R. (1982). Autoregressive conditional heteroscedasticity with estimates of the variance of United Kingdom inflation. *Econometrica* **50**, 987–1007.

EU (2005). PMWS case definition (Herd level). Sixth Framework Programme Prority SSP/5.4.6. Available at: www.pcvd.org/documents/Belfast_Presentations_PCVD/Final_pmws_case_definition_EU_October_2005.doc [4 April 2006].

Evans, E., Hastings, N. and Peacock, B. (1993). *Statistical Distributions*, 2nd edition. New York, NY: John Wiley & Sons Inc.

FAO/WHO (2000). Risk assessment: *Salmonella* spp. in broilers and eggs: hazard identification and hazard characterization of *Salmonella* in broilers and eggs. Preliminary report.

FAO/WHO (2003). Hazard characterization for pathogens in food and water: guidelines. Microbiological Risk Assessment Series No. 3, ISBN 92 4 156 237 4 (WHO). ISBN 92 5 104 940 8 (FAO). ISSN 1726–5274.

Fletcher, S. G. and Ponnambalam, K. (1996). Estimation of reservoir yield and storage distribution using moments analysis. *Journal of Hydrology* **182**, 259–275.

Fu, M. (2002). Optimization for simulation: theory vs. practice. *INFORMS Journal on Computing* **14**(3), 192–215.

Funtowicz, S. O. and Ravetz, J. R. (1990). *Uncertainty and Quality in Science for Policy*. Dordrecht, The Netherlands: Kluwer.

Furumoto, W. A. and Mickey, R. (1967). A mathematical model for the infectivity–dilution curve of tobacco mosaic virus: theoretical considerations. *Virology* **32**, 216–223.

Gelman, A., Carlin, J. B., Stern, H. S. and Rubin, D. B. (1995). *Bayesian Data Analysis*. London, UK: Chapman and Hall.

Gettinby, G. D., Sinclair, C. D., Power, D. M. and Brown, R. A. (2004). An analysis of the distribution of extreme share returns in the UK from 1975 to 2000. *J. Business Finance and Accounting* **31**(5), 607–646.

Gilks, W. R., Richardson, R. and Spiegelhalter, D. J. (1996). *Markov Chain Monte Carlo in Practice. London, UK:* Chapman and Hall.

Glover, F., Laguna, M. and Martí, R. (2000). Fundamentals of scatter search and path relinking. *Control and Cybernetics* **39**(3), 653–684.

Goldberg, D. E. (1989). *Genetic Algorithms in Search, Optimization, and Machine Learning*. Reading, MA: Addison-Wesley.

Gzyl, H. (1995). *The Method of Maximum Entropy*. London, UK: World Scientific.

Hald, T., Vose, D., Wegener, H. C. and Koupeev, T. (2004). A Bayesian approach to quantify the contribution of animal-food sources to human salmonellosis. *Risk Analysis* **24**(1); *J. Food Protection*, **67**(5), 980–992.

Haldane, J. B. S. (1948). The precision of observed values of small frequencies. *Biometrika* **35**, 297–303.

Hannan, E. J. and Quinn, B. G. (1979). The determination of the order of an autoregression. *Journal of the Royal Statistical Society, B* **41**, 190–195.

Hertz, D. B. and Thomas, H. (1983). *Risk Analysis and its Applications*. New York, NY: John Wiley & Sons Inc. (reprinted 1984).

Iman, R. L. and Conover, W. J. (1982). A distribution-free approach to inducing rank order correlation among input variables. *Commun. Statist.-Simula. Computa.* **11**(3), 311–334.

Iman, R. L., Davenport, J. M. and Zeigler, D. K. (1980). Latin hypercube sampling (a program user's guide). Technical Report SAND79-1473, Sandia Laboratories, Albuquerque, NM.

Institute of Hydrology (1999). *Flood Estimation Handbook*. Crowmarsh Gifford, UK: Institute of Hydrology.

Jeffreys, H. (1961). *Theory of Probability*, 3rd edition. Oxford, UK: Oxford University Press.

Johnson, N. L. (1949). Systems of frequency curves generated by methods of translation. *Biometrika* **36**, 149–176.

Kaplan, S. and Garrick, B. J. (1981). On the quantitative definition of risk. *Risk Analysis* **1**, 11–27.

Klugman, S., Panjer, H. and Willmot G. (1998). *Loss Models: From Data to Decisions*. New York, NY: John Wiley and Sons Inc.

Kozubowski, T. J. and Podgórski, K. (no date). *Log-Laplace Distributions*. Document found at http://unr.edu/homepage/0_log1.pdf.

Kreyszig, E. (1993). *Advanced Engineering Mathematics*, 7th edition. New York, NY: John Wiley & Sons Inc.

Laplace, P. S. (1774). Memoir on the probability of the causes of events. *Mémoires de Mathematique et de Physique, Presentés á l'Academie Royale des Sciences, par divers savants et lûs dans ses Assemblés*, **6**, 621–656. Translated by S. M. Stigler and reprinted in translation in *Statistical Science* **1**(3), 359–378 (1986).

Laplace, P. S. (1812). *Théorie analytique des probabilités*. Paris: Courcier. Reprinted in *Oeuvres Completes de Laplace*, Vol. 7. Paris, France: Gauthiers-Villars (1847).

Madan, D. B., Carr, P. P. and Chang, E. C. (1998). The variance gamma process and option pricing. *European Finance Review* **2**, 79–105.

McClave, J. T., Dietrich, F. H. and Sincich, T. (1997). *Statistics*, 7th edition. Englewood Cliffs, NJ: Prentice-Hall.

Morgan, M. G. and Henrion, M. (1990). *Uncertainty: a Guide to Dealing with Uncertainty in Quantitative Risk and Policy Analysis*. Cambridge, UK: Cambridge University Press.

Morris, C. N. (1983). Natural exponential families with quadratic variance functions: statistical theory. *Ann. Statis.* **11**, 515–529.

Neapolitan, R. E. (2004). *Learning Bayesian Networks*. Upper Saddle River, NJ: Pearson Prentice-Hall.

Newcomb, S. (1881). Note on the frequency of use of different digits in natural numbers. *Amer. J. Math.* **4**, 39–40.

OIE (2004). *Handbook on Import Risk Analysis for Animals and Animal Products – Volume 2: Quantitative Risk Assessment*. ISBN: 92-9044-629-3.

Panjer, H. H. (1981). Recursive evaluation of a family of compound distributions. ASTIN Bulletin 12, 22–26

Panjer, H. H., and Wilmot, G. E. Insurance Risk Models, 1992. Society of Actuaries, Schaumburg, IL.

Paradine, C. G. and Rivett, B. H. P. (1964). *Statistical Methods for Technologists*. London, UK: English Universities Press.

Pardalos, P. M. and Resende, M. G. C. (eds) (2002). *Handbook of Applied Optimization*. New York, NY: Oxford Academic Press.

Pearl, J. (2000). *Causality: Models, Reasoning and Inference*. Cambridge, UK: Cambridge University Press.

Popper, K. R. (1988). *The Open Universe: An Argument for Indeterminism*. Cambridge, UK: Cambridge University Press.

Press, S. J. (1989). *Bayesian Statistics: Principles, Models, and Applications*. Wiley series in probability and mathematical statistics. John Wiley & Sons Inc., New York.

Press, W. H., Flannery, B. P., Tenkolsky, S. A. and Vetterling, W. T. (1986). *Numerical Recipes: The Art of Scientific Computing*. Cambridge, UK: Cambridge University Press.

Randin, R. L. (1997). *Optimization in Operations Research*. Upper Saddle River, NJ: Prentice-Hall.

Robertson, J. P. (1992). *The Computation of Aggregate Loss Distributions*. Proceedings of the Casualty Actuarial Society, Arlington, VA, 57–133.

Rubinstein, R. (1981). *Simulation and Monte Carlo Methods*. New York, NY: John Wiley & Sons Inc.

Savage, L. J. *et al.* (1962). *The Foundations of Statistical Inference*. New York, NY: John Wiley & Sons Inc. (Methuen & Company, London).

Schwarz, G. (1978). Estimating the Dimension of a Model. *The Annuals of Statistics* **6**, No.2 (Mar., 1978), 461–464.

Shipley, W. (2000). *Cause and Correlation in Biology*. Cambridge, UK: Cambridge University Press.

Sivia, D. S. (1996). *Data Analysis: a Bayesian Tutorial*. Oxford, UK: Oxford University Press.

Stephens, M. A. (1974). EDF statistics for goodness of fit and some comparisons. *J. Am. Stat. Assoc.* **69**(347), 730–733.

Stephens, M. A. (1977). Goodness of fit for the extreme value distribution. *Biometrica* **64**(3), 583–588.

Stern, N. J., Clavero, M. R. S., Bailey, J. S., Cox, N. A. and Robach, M. C. (1995). *Campylobacter* spp. in broilers on the farm and after transport. *Pltry Sci.* **74**, 937–941.

Stern, N. J. and Robach, M. C. (2003). Enumeration of *Campylobacter* spp. in broiler feces and in corresponding processed carcasses. *J. Food Protection* **66**, 1557–1563.

Stumbo, C. R. (1973). Thermobacteriology in food processing. New York, NY: Academic Press.

Taylor, H. M. and Karlin, S. (1998). *An Introduction To Stochastic Modelling*, 3rd edition. New York, NY: Academic Press.

Teunis, P. F. M. and Havelaar, A. H. (2000). The beta–Poisson dose–response model is not a single-hit model. *Risk Analysis* **20**(4), 513–520.

Van der Sluijs, J. P., Risbey, J. S. and Ravetz, J. (2005). Uncertainty assessment of VOC emissions from paint in the Netherlands using the Nusap system. *Environmental Monitoring and Assessment* (105), 229–259.

Van Boekel, M. A. J. S. (2002). On the use of the Weibull model to describe thermal inactivation of microbial vegetative cells. *Intl J. Food Microbiology* **74**, 139–159.

Van Gelder, P., de Ronde, P., Neykov, N. M. and Neytchev, P. (2000). Regional frequency analysis of extreme wave heights: trading space for time. *Proceedings of the 27th ICCE Coastal Engineering 2000*, Sydney, Australia, **2**, 1099–1112.

Wang, S. S. (1996). Premium calculation by transforming the layer premium density. *ASTIN Bulletin* **26**(1), 71–92.

Wang, S. S. (2003). Equilibrium pricing transforms: new results using Buhlmann's 1980 economic model. *ASTIN Bulletin* **33**(1), 57–73.

Williams, P. R. D. (1999). A comparison of food safety risks: science, perceptions, and values. Unpublished doctoral dissertation, Harvard School of Public Health.

Index

@RISK   109–110
Accident insurance   509
Accuracy
  Of mean   156
  Of percentile   158
Aggregate distributions   305, 466
  Compound Poisson approximation   312, 508
  De Pril method   311, 507
  Fast Fourier transform method   310, 317, 495, 497, 510
  Implementing in ModelRisk   578
  Moments   305
  Panjer's recursive method   308
AIC
  See Akaike Information Criterion
Akaike Information Criterion   295
Anderson-Darling statistic   284–286, 292–294
Approximating one distribution with another   703
Archimedean copulas   368–371
Arrhenius–Davey attenuation model, bacteria   524
Assumptions   22, 69
Attenuation models, bacteria   519
Autoregressive time series models   335–339
  APARCH   338
  AR   335
  ARCH/GARCH   337
  ARMA   337
  EGARCH   339

Bayes' theorem   126, 215
Bayesian belief networks   427
Bayesian bootstrap   254
Bayesian inference   215
  By simulation   225
Bělehrádek growth model, bacteria   522
Bernoulli distribution   599
Bernoulli, Jakob   599
Beta distribution   158, 171, 232–4, 249, 254, 272, **600**
  Approximation   238, 709

Beta4 distribution   601
Beta-Binomial distribution   173, 193, 233, **602**
Beta-binomial dose-response model   530
Beta-Geometric distribution   604
Beta-Negative Binomial distribution   173, **605**
Beta-Poisson dose-response model   529
BetaPERT distribution
  See PERT distribution
BIC
  See Schwarz Information Criterion
Bilateral Exponential distribution
  See Laplace distribution
Binned data   283–284
Binomial coefficient   124
Binomial distribution   226, 249, 344, **606**, 710
  Approximations   703
  Derivation   168
Binomial process   **167**, 212, 234
Binomial theorem   124
Bootstrap   246–254
  Non-parametric   247–249
  Parametric   249–254, 298
Bradford distribution   607
Bradford law of scattering   607
Bradford, Samuel Clement   607
Brainstorming sessions   414
Bounded and unbounded distributions   586, 588
Bühlmann credibility factor   494
Burr distribution   609
Burr, Type III
  See Burr distribution

Calibrating experts   412
Cauchy distribution   610
Causality   423–434
Cdf
  See Cumulative distribution function
Censored data   283–284
Central limit theorem   122, 188

Chi distribution   612
Chi-Squared distribution   210, **613**, 630
  Approximation   709
Chi-Squared goodness-of-fit   287–290
Chi-Squared test   210
Claim size distribution   509
Classical statistics   208, 297
Classification trees   426
Clayton copula   313, 368–371
Compound Poisson approximation for aggregate
      distribution   312, 518
Confidence intervals   285
Contingency allocation in projects   476–477
Continuous distributions   586
Copulas   362, **367–380**
  Archimedean   313, 368–371
  Clayton   313, **369**
  Direction   378
  Elliptical   371–376
  Empirical   379
  Frank   317, **370**
  Gumbel   370
  Implementing in ModelRisk   576
  Modelling with   377–380
  Normal   372
  Student   373
Correlation   354
  Copulas   367–380
  Envelope method   380–391
  In insurance portfolios   511
  Lookup method   391–392
  Rank order   356–367
  Of aggregate distributions   312
  Of risks in a project portfolio   487–491
Counterfactual world   423
Covariance   354
Creating your own distributions   696
Credit rating, transition   499–503
Credit risk   494
Critical index   483
Critical path analysis in schedule risk   483–486
Critical values   285
Crystal Ball   109–110
Cumulative Ascending distribution   270, **614**
Cumulative Descending distribution   615
Cumulative distribution function (cdf)   **115**, 596
Cumulative distribution plots   73
  Overlaying   77
  Relationship to density plots   78
  Second order   76
Cyclicity, in a time series   323

DAG
  See Bayesian belief networks
Dagum distribution   616
Data
  Errors   266
  Overdispersion   267
  Truncated, censored or binned   283–284
DCF
  See Discounted cashflow
de Finetti's theorem   226
De Pril method   311, 507
Death model
  See Pure death model
Decision trees   40
Deductible (in insurance)   509
Default probability   494, 499
Delaporte distribution   183, **618**
Dependency   265
Directed acyclic graphs
  See Bayesian belief networks
Dirichlet distribution   175, **690**
Disaggregation, in subjective estimates   401
Discounted cashflow models   461–472
Discrete distribution   619
Discrete distributions   408, **585**
Discrete event simulation   40
Discrete Uniform distribution   226, 248, 621
Dose-response model   527–532
Double-Exponential distribution   650
Distributions
  Approximations   703
  Bernoulli   599
  Beta   158, 171, 232–4, 238, 249, 254, 272, **600**
  Beta4   601
  Beta-Binomial   173, 193, 233, **602**
  Beta-Geometric   604
  Beta-Negative Binomial   173, **605**
  Binomial   168, 226, 249, 344, **606**, 710
  Bradford   607
  Bounded and unbounded   586
  Burr   609
  Cauchy   610
  Chi   612
  Chi-squared   210, **613**, 630
  Continuous   264, 586
  Creating your own   696
  Cumulative Ascending   270, **614**
  Cumulative Descending   615
  Dagum   616
  Delaporte   183, **618**
  Dirichlet   175, **690**

Discrete   264, 408, 585, **619**
Discrete Uniform   226, 248, **621**
Empirical   700
Erlang   623
Error Function   622
Expert estimates   593
Exponential   179, 235, **626**
Exponential family   627
Extreme Value Max   627
Extreme Value Min   629
F   630
Fatigue Life   631
Fitting   263–300
Four-parameter beta
   See Beta4 distribution
Four-parameter Kumaraswamy distribution
   See Kumaraswamy4 distribution
Frequency   590
Gamma   180, 189, 298, **632**
Geometric   **634**, 712
Generalised Logistic   635
Histogram   275, **637**
Hyperbolic-Secant   638
Hypergeometric   **639**, 712
Inverse Gaussian   641
Inverse Hypergeometric   642
Inverse Multivariate Hypergeometric   691
Inverse Multivariate Hypergeometric2   692
Johnson Bounded   644
Johnson Unbounded   645
Kumaraswamy   646
Kumaraswamy4   648
Laplace   649
Lévy   650
Logarithmic   651
LogGamma   652
Logistic   653
LogLaplace   655
LogLogistic   656
LogNormal   123, **658**
LogNormalB   659
LogNormalE   660
LogWeibull   699
Modified PERT   406, **661**
Multinomial   174, 340, **694**
Multivariate   589, 690
Multivariate Hypergeometric   692
Multivariate Normal   695
Negative Binomial   169, 171, 343, **662**, 711
Negative Multinomial   174, **695**
Negative Multinomial2   696

Normal   122, 189, 209, 235, 252, 301, **665**
Ogive   270, **666**
Parametric and non-parametric   587
Pareto   512, **667**
Pareto2   668
Pearson5   670
Pearson6   671
PERT   405, **672**
Poisson   178, 235, 252, 618, **674**, 711
Poisson-Lognormal   699
Pólya   183, 618, 675
Rayleigh   116, **677**
Reciprocal   678
Relative   407, **679**
Risk impact   590
Slash   680
Split Triangle   682
Step Uniform   379, **683**
Student   210, 269, 685
Time or trials until   590
Triangle   163, 403, **686**
Uniform   163, 229–231, 404, **687**
Variations in a financial market   591
Weibull   689

Elliptical copulas   371–376
Empirical copula   379
Envelope method of correlation   380–391
Erlang, A.K.   624
Erlang B distribution   624
Erlang C distribution   624
Erlang distribution   623
Error distribution   624
Error function distribution   622
Errors, in data   266
Errors, in subjective estimates   394–401
Errors, most common modelling   159
Esscher principle, in insurance premiums   514
Event trees   39
Excel   109
   Running faster   147
   Solver   152, 283, 439–444
Expected shortfall   497, 505–506
Expected value principle, in insurance premiums   514
Exponential distribution   179, 235, **626**
Exponential dose-response model   527
Exponential family of distributions   627
Exponential growth model, bacteria   521
Exponential Power distribution
   See Error distribution
Extreme Value Max distribution   627

Extreme Value Min distribution 629
Extreme values, modelling 512–513

F distribution 630
Fast Fourier transform 310, 317, 495, 497, 510
Fatigue Life distribution 631
Fault trees 40
Fisher information 232
Fisher–Snedecor distribution
    See F distribution
Forecasting
    See Time series
Four-parameter beta distribution
    See Beta4 distribution
Four-parameter Kumaraswamy distribution
    See Kumaraswamy4 distribution
Frank copula 317, **370**
Frequency distributions 590
Furry distribution
    See Geometric distribution

Gamma distribution 180, 189, 298, **632**
    Approximation 709
Generalized Logistic 635
Generalized Error distribution
    See Error distribution
Geometric Brownian motion 328–332
    With mean reversion 332–334
    With jump diffusion 334–335
    With mean reversion and jump diffusion 335
Geometric distribution **634**, 712
Gibbs sampling 246
GOF
    See Goodness-of-fit statistics
Goodness-of-fit plots 285–297
Goodness-of-fit statistics 284–295
Gossett. William Sealy 685
Growth models, bacteria 519
Gumbel copula 370
Gumbel–Hougard copula
    See Gumbel copula

Hannan-Quinn information criterion 295
Histogram distribution 275, **637**
Histogram plots 70
HQIC
    See Hannan-Quinn information criterion
Hyperbolic secant distribution 638
Hypergeometric distribution 183, **639**, 712
    Approximations 184, 705

Hypergeometric process 183
    Multivariate 184
Hyperparameters 225, 233
Hyperpriors 233

Importance sampling 62
Individual life model 507
Influence diagrams 38
Information criteria 294–295, 351
Insurance
    Accident 509
    Correlated portfolio 511
    Permanent life 508
    Term life 506
Internal rate of return 470
Interpercentile range 97
Inverse Burr distribution
    See Dagum distribution
Inverse Gaussian distribution 641
Inverse Hypergeometric distribution 185, 642
Inverse Multivariate Hypergeometric distribution 691
Inverse Multivariate Hypergeometric2 distribution 692
Inverse Paralogistic distribution 617
IRR
    See Internal rate of return

Jacknife 247
Jacobian transformation 230
Johnson Bounded distribution 644
Johnson Unbounded distribution 645

Kappa distribution
    See Dagum distribution
Kolmogorov-Smirnoff statistic 284–286, 291–292
Kumaraswamy distribution 646
Kumaraswamy4 distribution 648
Kurtosis 97, 141, 596

Laplace distribution 624, **649**
Latin hypercube sampling **59**, 267, 684, 697
Leading indicators, in forecasting 348–351
Least squares regression 131, 256, 355
Lecturers, guide for 567
Lévy distribution 650
LHS
    See Latin hypercube sampling
Likelihood function 216, 235, 236–242
Likelihood principle 236
Liquidity risk 503

Location parameters   231, **594**
Logarithmic distribution   651
LogGamma distribution   652
Logistic distribution   653
Logistic model, bacterial growth and attenuation   525
LogLaplace distribution   655
LogLogistic distribution   656
LogNormal distribution   123, **658**
  Approximation   709
LogNormalB distribution   659
LogNormalE distribution   660
Long-term forecasts   352
Lookup table method of correlation   391–392
Loss given default   494, 497

m-Erlang distribution
  See Erlang distribution
Macros   152, 203, 444, 581
Market risk   503
Markov chain Monte Carlo   246
Markov chain time series   339–343, 499–503
Markov inequality   129
Martingales   194
MaxEnt
  See Maximum entropy principle
Maximum entropy principle   254
Maximum likelihood estimators   237, 250, 281
Mean   93, 137, 156, 209, 596
Mean deviation   96
Median   92, 138
Megaformulae   456
Mersenne twister   570
Metropolis algorithm   245
Mid-point Latin hypercube sampling   62
Mixture distributions   193
MLE
  See Maximum likelihood estimators
Mode   92, 138, 696
ModelRisk   111–112, 569
  and Excel   570
  distribution functions   570
  object functions   572
  risk event   576
Modified PERT distribution   406, **661**
Moments, raw and central   141
Monte Carlo simulation   45, 57
Monte Hall problem   228
Multinomial distribution   174, 340, **694**
Multivariate distributions   589
Multivariate Hypergeometric distribution   692

Multivariate Normal distribution   695
Multivariate Poisson process   181
Munchausen, Baron   247

Negative Binomial distribution   171, 343, **662**, 711
  Approximations   707
  Derivation   169
Negative Multinomial distribution   174, **695**
Negative Multinomial2 distribution   696
Net present value   469
Neural nets   426
Non-parametric
  Bootstrap   247–249
  Copula (empirical)   379
  Distribution fitting   269–280
Normal copula   372
Normal distribution   122, 139, 189, 209, 235, 242–245, 252, 301, **665**
Notation used in this book   112
NPV
  See Net present value

Ogive distribution   270, **666**
Operational risk   493
Optimisation   435–449
OptQuest   445–449

Panjer's recursive method   308
PAR
  See Population attributable risk
Parametric
  Bootstrap   249–254, 298
  Distribution fitting   281–300
Parametric and non-parametric distributions   587
Pareto distribution   512, **667**
Pareto2 distribution   668
Pascal's triangle   125
Pdf
  See probability density function
Pearson family of distributions   670
Pearson5 distribution   670
Pearson6 distribution   671
Percentiles   100, 158
Permanent life insurance   508
PERT distribution   406, **672**
PH principle, in insurance premiums
  See Risk-adjusted principle
P-I tables
  See Probability-impact tables
Pivotal method   209

Pmf
  See probability mass function
Poisson distribution   182, 235, 252, 282, 618, **674**,
    711,
  Approximation   242, 705
  Derivation   178
  Mixture   182
Poisson process   **176**, 213, 229, 240
  Compound Poisson approximation   312
  Multivariate   181
  Regression   345–347
Pólya distribution   183, 618, 675
Pólya regression   346–347
Population attributable risk   424
Posterior distribution   216, 236
P-P plots   296–297
Premium calculations   513–515
Prior distribution   215, **228**
  Conjugate   233
  Improper   232
  Jeffreys   231
  Multivariate   236
  Subjective   234
  Uninformed   229
Probability, definition of   118
Probability density function   **116**, 594
Probability equations, how to read   593
Probability mass function   **115**, 594
Probability-impact tables   14
Project risk analysis   473–491
  Cascading risks   487–491
  Contingency allocation   476–477
  Cost risk analysis   474–478
  Critical index   483
  Critical path analysis   483–486
  Risk portfolio   486
  Schedule risk analysis   478–483
Prompt lists   6
Pure death model   **344**, 523

Q-Q plots   296–297

Random number generator seed
    63
Randomness, in a time series   323
Rank order correlation   356–367
  Coefficient   136
Raspe, Rudolph Erich   247
Rayleigh distribution   116, **677**
Reciprocal distribution   678
Recursive formulae   710

Relative distribution   407, **679**
Renewal process   190
Report writing   67
Risk-adjusted principle, in insurance premiums   515
Risk analyst, qualities   24
Risk event   159, 490, 576
Risk factor   424
Risk management
  Evaluation   10
  Possible options   7
Risk ranking   16
Risk registers   13
Risk-return plots   90
Risk transfer   11
Risks, identifying   5

Sample size, in data   267
Scale parameters   231, **594**
Scatter plots
  For sensitivity analysis   87
  Of data in correlation analysis   355–359
  Of simulation results   154–156
  Of time series   321, 350
Schwarz Information Criterion   295
Seasonality, in a time series   343
Semi-standard deviation   96
Semi-variance   96
Sensitivity analysis   80–88
Severity scores   17
Shape parameters   594
SIC
  See Schwarz Information Criterion
Slash distribution   680
Skewness   97, 140, 596
Solver, Excel's   152, 283, 439–444
Spearman's rank order correlation coefficient   136
Spider plots   85
Split Triangle distribution   682
Stable distributions   650
Standard deviation   95, 96, 97, 139
Standard deviation principle, in insurance premiums
    514
Step Uniform distribution   379, **683**
Stirlings' formula   126
Stochastic dominance tests   100
Stochastic optimization   438
Strong law of large numbers   121
Student copula   373
Student distribution   210, 269, 685
  Approximation   710

Subadditivity 504
Subjective estimation 393–422
   Brainstorming sessions 414
   Calibrating experts 412
   Conducting an interview 416
   Cumulative distribution 407
   Disaggregation 402
   Discrete distribution 408
   Errors in 394–401
   Managing differing opinions 410
   PERT distribution 405, 406
   Relative 407
   Triangle distribution 403
   Uniform distribution 404
Sufficient statistic 209

T copula
   See Student copula
T distribution
   See Student distribution
T-test 211
Taylor series 128, 236
Tchebysheff's rule 129
Term life insurance 506
Time series
   Autoregressive models 335–339
   APARCH 338
   AR 335
   ARCH/GARCH 337
   ARMA 337
   EGARCH 339
   Geometric Brownian motion (GBM)
      328–332
   GBM with jump diffusion 334–335
   GBM with mean reversion 332–334
   GBM with mean reversion and jump diffusion 335
   Implementing in ModelRisk 579
   Intervention, effect of 463
   Leading indicators 348–351
   Long-term 352
   Market share 464
   Markov Chains 339–343
   Poisson regression 345–347
   Pólya regression 346–347
   Pure death model 344
   Sales volumes 465–466
   Yule growth model **343**
Tornado charts 80, 489
Trend, in a time series 323
Trend plots 88
Triangle distribution 163, 403, **686**
Truncated data 283–284
Two-tailed Exponential distribution
   See Laplace distribution

U-parameter 570
Uncertainty 48
Uniform distribution 163, 229–231, 404, **687**
Utility theory 11–13

Validation, of model 451–560
Value at risk 503–505
Value of information 102
   Value of imperfect information (VOII) 104
   Value of perfect information (VOPI) 103
Van Boekel attenuation model, bacteria 526
Vandermonde's theorem 126
VaR
   See Value at risk
Variability 47
Variance 94, 96, 138, 210, 596
Velhulst, Pierre 525
Venn diagrams 119
VISIFIT software 644
VOII
   See Value of information
VOPI
   See Value of information
Vose Consulting 721

Weibull distribution 689
Weibull-gamma dose-response model 531
What-if scenarios 3
WinBUGS 246, 298, 547–550

Yule growth model 343, 522

Z-test 209

Complimentary 90-day license for ModelRisk

As a purchaser of the text '*Risk Analysis: a quantitative guide*', Vose Software (www.vosesoftware.com) would like to offer you a FREE 90-day license for *ModelRisk for Insurance and Finance*.

You can download the software from www.vosesoftware.com/book3rdedition.htm and activate it using the license ID number and password on the reverse of this card.

To help you gain the most from this book the Web page also provides fully working versions of all of the models featured in the text.

We hope ModelRisk will help you explore the world of risk analysis modelling.

90-day ModelRisk license

To receive your free 90-day license of ModelRisk please follow the following process:

1. Go to www.vosesoftware.com/book3rdedition.htm
2. Provide your contact information, including a valid email address, and the following data:

   License ID: 919181
   Password: dvra3rd3F7Byf23

3. This license ID and password can only be used on one computer and for one installation.
4. An email will then be sent you with a link to download the installation file.
5. Download and run the installation file. It will require the License ID and password again to activate.

If you have any difficulties during installation, please contact us using the information provided in the email. The software will automatically deactivate after 90 days. You can remove the program at any time using the uninstall routine in Windows Control Panel/ Add or Remove Programs.